CASES IN
MARKETING STRATEGY

Richard T. Hise
Stephen W. McDaniel

Texas A&M University

Charles E. Merrill Publishing Company
A Bell & Howell Company
Columbus Toronto London Sydney

To Carol, Rich, Amy, and Emily, and Nancy and Brian

Published by Charles E. Merrill Publishing Co.
A Bell & Howell Company
Columbus, Ohio 43216

This book was set in Univers.
Production Editor: Jeffrey Putnam
Cover Design Coordination: Tony Faiola
Text Designer: Ben Shriver
Cover painting by Marko Spalatin

Library of Congress Catalog Card Number: 83-43117
International Standard Book Number: 0–675–20103–9
Printed in the United States of America
1 2 3 4 5 6 7 8 9 10—88 87 86 85 84

Preface

*C*ases in Marketing Strategy is designed for use in both undergraduate and graduate marketing management courses. Along with the thirty-five cases, the book presents textual material that is an important part of its total offering.

In planning this text we carefully assessed the existing marketing management casebooks and evaluated the needs of the student and instructor. This exercise aided us enormously in writing the text, writing and selecting cases, and developing a relevant framework for the study of the cases. It is our belief that the most effective and useful text must have certain qualities and characteristics. These qualities and characteristics are:

1. Cases should be about well known companies.
2. Cases should be as current as possible.
3. Cases should be of varying length and complexity.
4. Cases should emphasize strategic aspects of market.
5. Cases should concern a variety of industries and businesses.
6. A framework should be provided for studying the cases.

Approximately two-thirds of the cases concern companies the students know something about and will be interested in studying: Levi Strauss, Exxon, Eastern Air Lines, Hershey, Ford, and Xerox. (The other cases deal with smaller companies, but involve situations that students should find interesting and relevant.) The majority of our cases cover the time period of the mid-1970s to the early 1980s. All deal with real-life, ongoing organizations, and will, we hope, involve students in the realism of the situations.

This text has a good blend of short and long cases. We probably have, however, more longer cases than most marketing casebooks. We feel these longer cases are desirable so that students will have sufficient material with which to carefully analyze the companies involved. These cases, to a greater extent than those in competing texts, tend to emphasize the strategic aspects of marketing management and the comprehensive, long-run outlook which must accompany this orientation. The companies in this text are drawn from a wide variety of industries, including retailing, wholesaling, banking, airlines, food processing, high technology, health care, and manufacturing.

A structural framework, managerial in nature, ties the material together, provides section headings for the cases, and gives students a taxonomy for understanding the decision-making process in marketing. The sections include Opportunity Assessment, Setting Objectives, Developing Marketing Strategies, and Marketing Control. A complete, step-by-step methodology for analysis of the cases has also been provided.

A book is never the result of only the author's efforts. We would like to acknowledge the contributions of a number of individuals. At Texas A & M, outstanding assistance was provided by graduate students Elise Dupont, Charles Martin, and Terry Clark. Likewise, much appreciated typing support was supplied by Lisa Sorensen and Margaret Young. A special thanks is due to the reviewers of the material, including Richard F. Beltramini of Arizona State University, M. Bixby Cooper of Michigan State University, Charles van Nederpelt of Oklahoma State University, and Fred Kraft of Wichita State University.

Although most of the cases in this book were written by the authors, several were written by others. We wish to express our gratitude to these individuals for their labor with the cases and their kindness in granting us permission to use them: Richard F. Beltramini, Nancy J. Stephens, Earl R. Sage, Adrian B. Ryans, Robert T. Davis, Terrell F. Pike, Leon C. Megginson, Ben Kedia, D.E. Ezell, Kenneth W. Olm, C.P. Rao, G.E. Kiser, Linda E. Swayne, James Harbin, Robert P. Crowner, and Charles Cross. We give special thanks to Elaine Hubbard and the Graduate School of Business at Stanford University, for permission to use several of its cases.

Various editors with Charles E. Merrill gave unstintingly of their time and energies on this project. These include Gary Bauer, Steve Smith, Jennie Owen, Jeff Putnam and Mark Garrett. We would like to express thanks to those executives who provided important data and material about their companies and, as a result, facilitated our efforts to capture the essence of a marketing situation at a particular time. And, because we were able to test a number of these cases in both undergraduate and graduate classes, we would like to thank our students for their feedback.

Most importantly, we wish to thank our lovely wives, Carol and Nancy, for their sweet and understanding natures.

We wish you well in using this book. We hope you find it informative, challenging, and thought-provoking.

Richard T. Hise
Stephen W. McDaniel

Contents

INTRODUCTION TO CASE ANALYSIS

This textbook contains thirty-five cases about marketing management. Because all cases are recent and are built around existing companies or organizations, you will have the opportunity to analyze actual situations that have occurred recently. Most of the facts and figures presented in the cases are authentic; in a few instances, names, locations, or other information have been disguised. The types of decisions required and the process for making these decisions are unchanged, however, from what they were in the original situation.

Business cases were first used in an educational setting at the Harvard Business School in the early 1900s. Since that time, the use of cases in marketing and other business courses has become common. There are several reasons for this increased popularity and numerous benefits to you from a thorough analysis of the cases in this book.

First, a case enables you to bridge the gap between academia and the "real business world." This may require reviewing material you covered in earlier courses. By studying and discussing these cases, you will gain a working knowledge of what you learned in your college classes.

Another benefit from case analysis is the further development of necessary marketing management skills. Case analysis requires you to examine a critical point in the life of a business. Typically, the business will be at the fork in the road, where a key decision must be made on what course to chart for the future. You are put in the position of the decision-maker. In a real business situation, the key decision will have to be made logically, objectively, and in a timely manner. In a case analysis, you will have to apply your analytical skills to identify and solve whatever problems appear in the case. Studying cases will help you develop the experience to make these decisions.

A third benefit should occur as you become involved in the operation of the interesting and different kinds of organizations presented in this book.

Cases range from small retail stores to hospitals to the world's largest corporations; they will expose you to many different situations requiring many different types of decisions. You will become familiar with different organizational structures, different philosophies of business, and alternative techniques of marketing products, all of which should broaden your knowledge of business and marketing in particular. Since over half of the cases in the book deal with some of the largest and most successful corporations in the world, you will get a close-up look at the inner workings of these proven companies.

The whole process involved in preparing a case analysis will benefit you in other ways. You will develop your communication skills as you write and present your final report. The cases will give you an opportunity to use your initiative, decide on a course of action, and follow it through. If you work in groups, you will develop your ability to work with other people—a crucial skill in today's business world.

Approach the task of analyzing these cases with a feeling of anticipation and excitement. In each situation, you will have the opportunity to place yourself in the center of the company, to look at events from the viewpoint of the retail store manager, the sales manager, the vice president of marketing, the president, or a marketing consultant. All the relevant information necessary to make critical decisions is there; you may have to go out on a limb to make these decisions. You will learn by doing.

FORMAT FOR CASE ANALYSIS

Nearly everything needs a formalized plan of action: studying for an exam, taking a trip, playing a football game. Analyzing a business situation is no exception. Although there are probably as many different formats as there are business consultants/analysts, most case analysis methods are based on the scientific method. Here is one definition:

> "principles and procedures for the systematic pursuit of knowledge involving the recognition and formulation of a problem, the collection of data through observation and experiment, and the formulation and testing of hypotheses."[1]

Some key parts of this definition should be noted. The definition indicates that the goal of the process is the *pursuit of knowledge.* This is very much so in a marketing case analysis. The case analyst tries to understand all elements in a particular business situation so that he can recommend action to improve that situation. The scientific method requires that *principles and procedures* be present for gaining this knowledge, and that the entire process be *systematic.* In a marketing case analysis ,there should be a systematic set of principles and procedures followed in examining a situation and making appropriate recommendations.

---

[1] *Webster's New Collegiate Dictionary* (1981), G. C. Merriam and Co., Springfield, Massachusetts.

Finally, the definition specifies the steps that make up this systematic process:

1. Recognition and formulation of a problem
2. Collection of data through observation and experiment
3. Formulation and testing of hypotheses

Each of these critical elements should also be addressed in a case analysis. With this understanding of the scientific method as a base, let us propose a logical format for analyzing any business situation.

Case Overview

Suppose for a moment that you are a marketing consultant who has just been hired to analyze a company and advise it on its marketing strategy. Also suppose that you know little about the company. Where would you begin? First, you would acquaint yourself with the entire organization, including its products, processes, situation, and any other relevant general factors. You would try to get a broad picture in your mind of the whole organization. With this overview, you would then be able to deal with specific elements of the situation.

Analyzing a marketing management case involves the same process. Your first objective should be to get an overall feel for the case, an overview of what is going on. Do this by skimming over the case quickly, perusing its highlights. During this initial reading, don't underline or mark, skim exhibits, and read only parts of each paragraph. Try to answer these general types of questions: What kind of organization is it? What are some of the general factors at work in the case? What kind of problems is the organization having?

After you have this overview of the case, go over it again, reading it carefully, underlining or identifying key statements in the case, and jotting down a few notes. After this read it over a third time. During this in-depth reading of the case, you should not only try to understand the case situation, but also identify at least on a preliminary basis, some of the problem areas. These problems will be formally delineated later. In writing up the first section of your case analysis, present a brief two or three sentence overview of the situation; this will set the stage for your analysis.

Situation Analysis

Now that you understand the case, and have identified some problem areas, you should break the case down into parts so you can critically evaluate all aspects of the organization. Look closely at all details of the case, then try to pull this information together into a more manageable form. The situation analysis involves analyzing four general areas: the company, the customer, the competition, and the environment. Although all four are important, the most extensive analysis will be of the internal operations of the company. Here is an outline to help you organize your situation analyses:

A. Company Analysis
   1. Financial Situation
      a. Balance Sheet/Income Statement Analysis
         You should analyze the financial statements both vertically and horizontally. *Vertical analysis* involves the calculation of meaningful figures from the financial statements of one year. For the balance sheet, each item may be expressed as a percentage of total assets. For the income statement, each item may be expressed as a percentage of sales. These figures can then be compared with industry figures, competitors, or other divisions of the same company.
         Horizontal analysis consists of comparing items on the financial statements, or calculations derived from the vertical analysis, with the same items in other time periods. A comparison of key items over a five-year period can be especially enlightening. For example, you might analyze sales trends over the past five years, calculating the percentage change from one year to the next. You might do the same for other key items such as cost of goods sold or net income. Not only can these figures be compared between years, but they may also be compared with industry trends, those of competitors, or other divisions of the same company.

      b. Ratio Analysis
         To obtain an accurate measure of a firm's financial position, it is best to calculate several financial ratios. Some of the more frequently used financial ratios are shown in Exhibit 1. We recommend that you calculate at least one or two ratios from each of the four categories. These ratios might be calculated for two or more years to uncover any significant trend in the company's financial performance. You can also compare those calculated ratios with other companies in the industry, or with industry averages. To gather financial information on the industry or specific companies in the industry, several sources are available. Three of the most helpful are

         Dun's Review, Dun and Bradstreet Inc., New York (annual, Sept. to Dec. issues)
         Annual Statement Studies, Robert Morris Associates, New York (annual)
         Industrial Surveys, Standard and Poor's Corporation, New York (quarterly)

c. Other Quantitative Analyses

Depending on the information provided in the case, you may be able to carry out other quantitative analyses. For example, *break-even analysis* is a helpful technique for analyzing the relationship among fixed costs, variable costs, and revenue. *Sales variance analysis* examines the differences between actual sales and standard or budgeted results to uncover problem areas. *Marketing profitability analysis* examines the profitability of various segments of the company or of various market segments served by the company. You should carefully evaluate all of the quantitative information you are given in a case and ask yourself, "What can I do with these data to make them more meaningful?"

d. Overall Financial Assessment

After you have scrutinized all of the financial information in the case, you should be able to make some general statements regarding the financial position of the firm. For example, you may have determined from your ratio analysis that the firm is in a precarious position relative to its liquidity. You should draw attention to this, since it limits what the company is able to do in the short run and, thus, what you are able to recommend. It is imperative that you concisely state the firm's financial position since it directly impacts on future marketing strategy.

2. Organization Structure

Examine all aspects of the organization structure: the various components, the formal lines of authority and responsibility, the communication flow, as well as the management style and capabilities.

3. Marketing System

Critically evaluate all elements of the marketing system: product(s); marketing channel(s); physical distribution; pricing strategy; and promotion strategy.

4. Examine other relevant aspects of the company: corporate philosophy; mission or purpose; attitudes in the company; key individuals, etc.

B. Customer (Market) Analysis

Since the customer should be the focal point of the business, take a careful look at the market for the company's products: Who are the customers? Why do they buy the product? When or how frequently do they buy? Has the organization segmented the market properly and clearly defined its target market?

Ask yourself questions like these to get some feel for the type of people who are likely customers for the company. You can then evaluate whether the company is reaching this market. Also carefully analyze what changes are taking place in the market and how the market of the future will be different from today's.

C. Competitive Analysis

It is important to understand the competitive structure of the industry. Where does the company stand relative to the competition? Is the company a leader, a follower, or a "nicher" (i.e. after a special market segment)? What are the organization's strengths and weaknesses relative to the competition? What changes are occurring in the industry?

D. Environmental Analysis

In addition to the company, customers, and competition, evaluate the external environment. Are there any changes taking place, or expected to take place, in the political, legal, technological, or economic environment that may affect the organization? Look for environmental *threats* as well as environmental *opportunities;* realize, however, that what at first may appear to be a threat may actually be a great opportunity for the firm.

EXHIBIT 1   Selected Financial Ratios

Ratio	*How calculated*	*What it measures*
I. *Liquidity ratios*		
A. Current ratio	$\dfrac{\text{Current assets}}{\text{Current liabilities}}$	Measures the ability of the firm to meet short-term debt. The rule-of-thumb for this ratio is 2
B. Quick (Acid test) ratio	$\dfrac{\text{Current assets-Inventory}}{\text{Current liabilities}}$	A more accurate measure of a firm's ability to immediately pay off its short-term debt
C. Inventory to Working Capital	$\dfrac{\text{Inventory}}{\text{Current assets-Current liabilities}}$	Measures the extent to which the firm's working capital is tied up in inventory
II. *Profitability ratios*		
A. Return on Net Worth (Return on equity)	$\dfrac{\text{Profit after taxes}}{\text{Net worth}}$	Measures the rate of return on stockholders' equity

EXHIBIT 1 (continued)

B. Return on Assets (Return on investment)	$\dfrac{\text{Profit after taxes}}{\text{Total assets}}$	Measures the return on total investment in the firm
C. Net Profit Margin (Return on sales)	$\dfrac{\text{Profit after taxes}}{\text{Sales}}$	Indicates return on sales

III. *Leverage Ratios*

A. Debt to Assets ratio	$\dfrac{\text{Total liabilities}}{\text{Total assets}}$	Measures the extent to which borrowed funds have been used to finance the operation of the business
B. Debt to Equity ratio	$\dfrac{\text{Total liabilities}}{\text{Stockholders' equity}}$	Provides a comparison of the equity of the owners with the funds provided by the creditors
C. Times Interest Earned	$\dfrac{\text{Profit before taxes} + \text{Interest charges}}{\text{Interest charges}}$	Measures the risk that a firm might not be able to meet its interest payments

IV. *Activity Ratios*

A. Inventory Turnover	$\dfrac{\text{Sales}}{\text{Inventory}}$	Measures the number of times the average inventory is turned over in the year
B. Fixed Assets Turnover	$\dfrac{\text{Sales}}{\text{Fixed assets}}$	Measures the sales productivity and utilization of plant and equipment
C. Total Assets Turnover	$\dfrac{\text{Sales}}{\text{Total assets}}$	Measures the sales productivity and utilization of all the firm's assets
D. Average Collection Period	$\dfrac{\text{Accounts receivable}}{\text{Total sales} \div 365}$	Measures the average collection period for accounts receivable

Formal Problem Identification

Now that you understand the case and have critically evaluated all of its key elements, you are ready to formalize the problems existing in the organization. Not only is this normally the most difficult part of the case analysis, it is also the most crucial. Since the remainder of the case analysis centers around solving the problems defined in this step, it is important to consider the problems very carefully. A case analysis that tries to solve an unimportant problem is practically useless.

Perhaps a good place to start is to jot down all of the problem areas you see in the case. Then go over each of these, and try to sort out the *symptoms* of problems from the actual problems themselves. You may have to search to find the problem behind the symptoms. One problem can be manifested in several different ways. For example, a sick person may have a high fever, an upset stomach, and a headache—these are all symptoms of a problem. A business may be having problems with increasing inventory costs, declining profitability, and declining customer services quality. After examining all aspects of the situation, you may conclude that the company's major problem is poor product management, particularly the lack of a formal product elimination strategy.

As you carry out this process, you may find that there is more than one problem in the case, just as the physician may find that the patient has not only the flu but also an ingrown toenail. In this situation you need to prioritize the problems into major and minor. Center your case analysis around what you define as the one major problem. On occasion, you may identify two major problems. If so, treat them separately; solve one completely, then solve the other. In most situations, try to pick out the one problem that is more immediate than any other and focus your analysis on it. However, you should not disregard the minor problems; deal with them fully at the end of the case analysis.

In writing up this section of your case analysis, concisely define the major problem (or, occasionally, problems). Also list the appropriate symptoms. Following this statement of the major problem, list all of the minor problems, along with the corresponding symptoms.

Statement and Evaluation of Alternatives

Now that you have identified the major problem, you are ready to solve it. Develop as many possible solutions as you can, and then weed out those ideas that are illogical until you have a set of realistic alternatives. You can then examine the advantages and disadvantages of these remaining alternatives to reach a solution.

The initial process of alternative generation is similar to idea generation in the creative process. The goal is to generate as many alternative courses of action as possible, jotting each of these down on a piece of paper. The next step involves mentally making a pass over each of these to eliminate any that are not feasible. This process should leave you with anywhere from two to eight realistic alternatives to be evaluated more critically.

In writing up your case analysis, list these realistic alternatives, making sure that each relates to the major problem you defined. Each alternative should be a potential solution to the major problem; the alternatives should be completely different ways of solving the problem, *independent* of one another and *mutually exclusive.* Then, list the specific advantages and disadvantages of carrying out each alternative. You may even wish to construct a "T-account" for each alternative, listing the pros on one side and the cons on the other. If you stated more than one major problem, you should follow this same process for each.

Recommended Solution and Justification

After following this logical approach to identifying potential solutions to the major problem and evaluating the alternatives, you should be in a position to recommend a course of action. In this section of your case analysis, state the alternative you selected and explain why. In cases where you defined more than one major problem and set of realistic alternatives, choose and justify an alternative for each problem. Remember that, ideally, no more than one alternative should be selected. If you *could* select more than one, it is probably because (1) the alternatives in that set were not really independent and mutually exclusive, or (2) your major problem statement is too general and should be more specific.

Implementation

You may feel that after you have recommended a solution the case analysis is finished. However, in many respects the important decisions have yet to be made. All you have accomplished so far is to decide on a specific course of action for the future. Now you must answer such questions as

- ☐ How will it be accomplished?
- ☐ When will it be accomplished (i.e., short term, long term)?
- ☐ Who will do it?
- ☐ Where will it be done?
- ☐ How much will it cost?
- ☐ How much is the projected revenue?

Perhaps one-third of your written analysis will be devoted to your plans for implementation. In addition, you may have a technical appendix at the end of your paper in which you specify each part of your plan, along with the corresponding cost and revenue projections. In your recommendations for the company, also consider how these plans will impact on the minor problems you identified earlier in the case analysis. Address each of these minor problems and make appropriate recommendations for their solution as well.

The final paragraph should attempt to tie a bow around your analysis. Briefly summarize how your recommendations will solve the major and minor problems faced by the company. Set forth what the company should do in the future and how it will be better off because of it.

FINAL SUGGESTIONS

As you embark on your analyses of the cases in this book, keep the following points in mind:

1. Place yourself in the role of a marketing consultant or a particular decision maker in the company, and address your comments to the appropriate company executive.

2. As with any report sent to an executive, you should keep it as short and concise as possible. Do not rehash all the information contained in the case. A company executive knows all about the company's history, etc.; stick with a critical evaluation of the facts.

3. Remember to operate *within the time frame of the case.* Do not spend your time trying to find out what the company actually did and then recommend that as your solution. This destroys the whole purpose of the case analysis. And just because the company did something does not mean it was right. A solution you come up with may be better than what the company actually did.

4. Do not use the cop-out expression, "I need more information." The information provided for you in each case is sufficient for making a decision. Marketing managers would always like to have more data, but cost and time limitations prevent this. Assume you have all the information possible and make a decision based on it.

5. In your recommendations and implementation, be aware of constraints on the company. Some important constraints include deadlines, strength of competition, company resources, production and warehouse capacities, budgets, and philosophies and capabilities of top management.

6. Remember to take a logical approach to identifying and solving problems. Exhibit 2, a flow chart of the recommended case analysis process, will aid your efforts.

EXHIBIT 2 Flowchart of Case Analysis

I. Case Overview	II. Situation Analysis	III. Formal Problem Identification	IV. Statement and Evaluation of Alternatives	V. Recommended Solution and Justification	VI. Implementation

A. General observations
B. Preliminary problem identification
	A. Company analysis
	  1. Financial situation
	  2. Organization structure
	  3. Marketing system
	  4. Other
	B. Customer (Market) analysis
	C. Competitive analysis
	D. Environmental analysis
	  1. Threats
	  2. Opportunities
		A. Major problem(s)
		B. Minor problem(s)
			Alternative 1
			Pros Cons
			
			Alternative 2
			Pros Cons
					A. How, when, who, where, how much?
					B. Solution to minor problems
					C. Conclusion

OPPORTUNITY ASSESSMENT

I

Opportunity Assessment 1

L ooking at the top companies in various industries today, it is clear that the key to corporate success is the ability to seize the right opportunity at the right time. It is Sears anticipating the population shift and opening stores in the suburbs. It is General Motors realizing that many people did not want just a black car and providing an assortment of colors for those people. It is Xerox taking another company's discarded idea and developing the process of xerography. It is McDonald's not only revolutionizing the fast food industry with the "Big Mac Attack," but then further outdistancing the competition by adding a fast food breakfast. No other task of marketing management is more important than identifying marketing opportunities, evaluating them, and selecting the ones the company should pursue. Nothing else the company does has more impact on its long-term success than how well it anticipates the future and then seizes the appropriate marketing opportunities.

SOURCES OF OPPORTUNITIES

Where does the marketing manager look for such opportunities? Everywhere. All a marketing manager needs to do is actively search out such opportunities and they will be there. There is a story of two shoe salesmen who were sent to Africa by their company. The first had no sooner gotten off the plane than he telegrammed back to the home office: "Please send a return plane ticket. Nobody here wears shoes. Nobody needs shoes." The second salesman, however, after surveying the situation, promptly sent a different telegram: "Please send more shoes. Nobody here wears shoes. Everybody needs shoes!"

The second salesman typifies the viewpoint marketing managers should take in investigating opportunities for new products or services. To a large extent, identifying an opportunity is just a function of the viewpoint of the marketing manager. After all, problems are simply opportunities in disguise. When one is able to look past these problems and search for better ways of doing things, one sees innumerable opportunities for new products and services, or new ways of marketing them. There are three general sources of opportunities: the marketplace, the company itself, and other elements in the business environment.

CORPORATE PURPOSE AND OBJECTIVES

A firm's search for opportunities should be limited to those that are congruent with the corporate purpose (mission) and in line with the corporate objectives. The *corporate statement of purpose* is essentially the firm's definition of its business domain or the business in which it operates. In it the firm defines either the product it is producing or the market it wishes to serve. For example,

> Shaklee Corporation manufactures and distributes nutritional, household and personal care products.[1]
>
> Data General Corporation designs, manufactures, and sells general purpose computer systems and related products and services, including peripheral equipment, software services, training and maintenance.[2]

Any prospective marketing opportunity will conform to this corporate statement of purpose. Shaklee would probably not consider opportunities that may exist for a new computer software program, nor would Data General Corporation consider a new vitamin supplement. Additionally, top executives of a company tend to have carefully defined long-term and short-term *objectives* for the firm. These objectives, which essentially set forth where the company wants to go in the future, determine to some extent the type of marketing opportunities that might be considered. For example, Shaklee sets a five-year objective of increasing nutritional product sales from 70 percent to 80 percent of total corporate sales, while reducing personal care product sales from 20 percent to 10 percent. Given these objectives, a marketing opportunity for a nutritional soft drink will be looked at more favorably than one for a new eye shadow.

TYPES OF OPPORTUNITIES

In assessing marketing opportunities, the marketing manager must realize that not all possible opportunities are necessarily realistic opportunities for the firm. In effect, there are *environmental opportunities* and *company mar-*

---

[1]*Shaklee Corporation 1981 Annual Report.*
[2]*Data General 1980 Annual Report.*

keting opportunities. Environmental opportunities consist of all opportunities for which there is a latent demand in society. This includes the myriad products, services, new marketing methods, etc. that people would like to see, but, for whatever reason, are not available.

From that set of environmental opportunities, only a subset are actually realistic opportunities for one firm. These are company marketing opportunities, and include those that meet the specific requirements set forth by the firm for consideration as marketing opportunities. In some cases, an opportunity might be very attractive, but the firm may not feel it should enter that area. The opportunity assessment process should involve careful evaluation of all environmental opportunities to separate and further investigate the most promising company marketing opportunities.

EVALUATING OPPORTUNITIES

The firm should have a systematic method of assessing opportunity that enables the marketing manager to decide whether an opportunity is an environmental opportunity or an actual company marketing opportunity, and whether that opportunity is desirable for the firm. An example from Procter & Gamble, one of the best marketing companies in the world, illustrates the opportunity assessment process.

In the early 1960s, a Procter & Gamble engineer came up with the idea for a disposable diaper. The company thought the idea had merit but had to more fully assess the situation before embarking on the multi-million dollar project. Three basic questions were answered before the final decision was made to produce and market the product.

1. Was there a consumer need for the disposable diaper?
2. Did the company have the scientific and technological ability to develop the product?
3. Was the potential market for such a product large enough to offer some promise of making a profit?

Procter & Gamble investigated the market potential for such a product. Extensive market research on consumer satisfaction with traditional diapering methods indicated a real need for a better way of diapering babies. The company decided its considerable experience inventing, manufacturing, and marketing absorbent paper products like paper towels and facial tissue qualified it to develop the disposable diaper. Finally, the company calculated that there were more than fifteen billion diaper changes a year in the United States. Since Procter & Gamble determined it could mass produce enough of the product to realize large economies of scale and lower per unit costs, it decided the new product was a promising investment.

In 1961, the revolutionary disposable diaper, Pampers, was introduced to the market. Within twenty years, almost half the babies in the United States were wearing Pampers—because Procter & Gamble realized a marketing opportunity and capitalized on it.[3]

ASSESSMENT FACTORS

What factors should influence the firm's decision of whether a particular environmental opportunity is necessarily a company marketing opportunity and whether the company should pursue it? What considerations are important in assessing opportunities as they arise? There are three broad categories of factors marketing managers should take into account in assessing each opportunity: market factors, company factors, and environmental factors.

Market Factors

The primary concern is whether there is a demand (potential customers) for the proposed product or service, and whether those potential customers are numerous and accessible enough to constitute a viable market. Experienced marketers know that many great sounding ideas lose their luster after the results of market research studies are in. Here are some questions that should be answered at this stage of the opportunity assessment:

1. What is the composition of the market for this product/service?
   a. demographic (sex, age, income, education, occupation, stage of family life cycle, etc.)
   b. psychograhic (attitudes, interests, opinions)
2. How large is this market?
3. What is the likelihood of these people buying/using the product/service?
4. How accessible is this market? (i.e. Where is it? Would it be a problem to reach it?)
5. What is the present or potential competitive structure? How strong are the present or potential competitors? What are the financial, technical, and marketing strengths of these firms? What market share can be expected of each of these firms?

Company Factors

Even though an identifiable and sizeable demand may exist for a product or service, the opportunity may not fit well with the company. The company

---

[3]*Consumer Choice* (Cincinnati, Ohio: Procter & Gamble 1977).

may find that it may not be in its best interest to introduce a particular product or service. To determine this, the following company factors should be considered:

1. Is the opportunity consistent with the firm's purpose (or mission) and business domain, as defined by top management?
2. Would the opportunity help the company achieve its corporate objectives and goals?
3. Does the company have the financial, technological, raw material, personnel, and other resources necessary to meet the requirements of the opportunity?
4. Does the firm have the marketing system required to successfully market the product or service?

Environmental Factors

Finally, the marketing manager should evaluate each opportunity in light of the known and expected environmental factors. There may be a significant demand for the product or service, and the firm may feel that the opportunity is appropriate for it, but there may be some other factor that clouds its probability of success. The following questions should be addressed:

1. What economic conditions might impact on the opportunity (e.g., interest rates, availability of capital, inflation, unemployment)?
2. What technological factors might be significant (e.g., expected technological advances in the future)?
3. How might political and legal factors affect the opportunity (e.g., current or expected political issues and legislation)?
4. What social and cultural factors are significant (e.g., changing values, morals, lifestyles)?
5. What changes in the natural environment might affect the opportunity (e.g., changes in the supply or physical composition of such natural resources as water, air, land, oil, or minerals)?

SELECTION OF OPPORTUNITIES

After the marketing manager gathers the relevant information about the impact of various environmental factors on each opportunity, a go-no go decision must be made for each product or service under consideration. At this point, it should be possible to make both short-term and long-term sales projections, based on the market, company, and environmental analysis. The marketing manager then evaluates these projections.

Predetermined criteria are typically used to make these evaluations. In most cases, quantitative criteria should be set (e.g., ''sales increase of 20 percent per year," "a minimum R.O.I. of 25 percent before taxes"). But some qualitative criteria may also be appropriate (e.g., "a growing market," "present and expected competition weak," "a synergistic fit with present products"). In any event, the company must make a final decision on each opportunity. This decision should be the result of a systematic effort to assess the probable outcome of pursuing an opportunity and to compare that outcome with a predetermined criteria for success.

SUMMARY

This chapter details the need for carefully assessing possible marketing opportunities. The company needs to systematically evaluate each opportunity on the basis of market, company, and environmental factors. No other task of marketing management is more important than identifying, evaluating, and selecting appropriate marketing opportunities. After these are chosen, the marketing manager sets both short- and long-term goals for the new opportunities, as well as for existing programs. This process of setting goals is discussed in Chapter 2.

QUESTIONS

1. In what way is the corporate statement of purpose a significant factor in opportunity assessment?
2. What are the two types of opportunities? How do they differ?
3. What considerations are important in the assessment of opportunities?
4. How might market research be used to determine market factors that affect opportunity?
5. What environmental factors affect opportunity assessment?

SUGGESTED READINGS

Abell, D.F., "Strategic Windows," *Journal of Marketing,* July 1978, 21–26.

Abell, D.F. and J.S. Hammond, *Strategic Market Planning,* Englewood Cliffs, N.J.: Prentice-Hall, Inc., 1979, 47–64.

"Americans Change," *Business Week,* February 20, 1978, 64.

Cravens, D.W. and G.E. Hills, *Marketing Decision Making: Concepts and Strategy,* Homewood, Ill.: Richard D. Irwin, Inc. 1976.

Day, G.S., A.D. Shocker, and R.K. Srivastava, "Customer-Oriented Approaches to Identifying Product-Markets," *Journal of Marketing,* 43, Fall 1979, 8–19.

King, W.R. and D.I. Cleland, "Environmental Information Systems for Strategic Marketing Planning," *Journal of Marketing,* 38, October 1974, 35–40.

Kotler, P., *Marketing Management, Analysis, Planning, and Control,* Fourth edition, Englewood Cliffs, N.J.: Prentice-Hall, Inc., 1980, 63–127.

Levitt T., "Marketing Myopia," *Harvard Business Review,* July-August 1960, 45–56.

Levitt, T., "Marketing When Things Change," *Harvard Business Review,* November-December 1977.

"Lucrative Marketing Opportunities Will Abound in the 'Upbeat' 1980s," *Marketing News,* July 11, 1980, 1, 14.

Rothschild, W.E., "Competitor Analysis: The Missing Link in Strategy," *Management Review,* July 1979, 22–39.

Steiner, G., *Strategic Planning,* New York: Free Press, 1979.

"The Graying of the Soft-Drink Industry," *Business Week,* May 23, 1977.

Thomas, P.S., "Environmental Analysis for Corporate Planning," *Business Horizons,* October 1977, 27–38.

Woodruff, R.B., "A Systematic Approach to Market Opportunity Analysis," *Business Horizons,* August 1976, 55–65.

Seven-Up Company

In June 1978 Philip Morris, Inc. bought out Seven-Up Company for $520 million. The purchase sent shock waves throughout the soft drink industry. Philip Morris, the multi-billion dollar giant in the tobacco industry (Marlboro, Virginia Slims, Benson & Hedges, Merit, Parliament), as well as the beer industry (Miller, Miller Lite, Lowenbrau), immediately served notice that it was

---

This case was prepared by Stephen W. McDaniel and Valarie Zeithaml, Assistant Professors of Marketing, Texas A&M University, as a basis for class discussion rather than to illustrate either effective or ineffective marketing management.

going to put its marketing expertise to work in the soft drink industry. Coke and Pepsi had better stand back!

As 1981 drew to a close, however, and company executives looked over the progress of the past three years, it was clear that Seven-Up had not been turned overnight into the darling of the soft drink industry. In fact, during that period, it lost its claim to be the third largest-selling soft drink, slipping to fourth behind Dr. Pepper. The 7-UP brand went from a 5.9 percent share of the market to 5.4 percent, and Diet 7-UP held constant at 1.1 percent. In 1980 Seven-Up Company had an operating loss of $7.1 million, prompting one beverage industry analyst to conclude, "Philip Morris made a mistake in purchasing Seven-Up."

Philip Morris executives insist that the Seven-Up acquisition was not a mistake. They feel that if the Seven-Up Company can come up with an effective long-range marketing strategy, it can become not only profitable but also a dominant force in the soft drink industry.

THE SOFT DRINK INDUSTRY

There are over sixty brands of soft drinks on the market. Two firms, the Coca-Cola Company and PepsiCo, Inc., dominate the soft drink industry with a combined market share of almost sixty percent. In addition, the top ten brands, representing the five largest soft drink manufacturers, account for almost seventy percent of the soft drink market. (See Exhibit 1 for a complete breakdown of sales and market shares for the soft drink manufacturers.)

The soft drink industry can be characterized in several different ways:

1. *By product type*:
   A. Regular   (82.8% of the market)
   B. Diet   (17.2% of the market)

2. *By package type:*
   A. Cans   (28.5% of the market)
   B. Returnable, 13-17 oz.   (21.5% of the market)
   C. Returnable, 18-36 oz.   (13.6% of the market)
   D. 2 Liter Plastic   (15.8% of the market)
   E. Other   (20.6% of the market)

3. *By flavor:*
   A. Cola (62.4% of the market; includes Coke, Pepsi, RC)
   B. Lemon-Lime (11.8% of the market; includes "green bottle" drinks: 7-UP, Sprite, Mountain Dew, Mellow Yellow, Fresca)
   C. Peppers (8.0% of the market; includes Dr. Pepper, Mr. Pibb)
   D. Orange (7.4% of the market; includes Crush, Sun Crest Orange)
   E. Root Beer (5.5% of the market; includes Frostie, A&W, Dad's)
   F. Other flavors (4.9% of the market)

4. *By intermediaries:*

A. Grocery stores: By far the largest business segment through which soft drinks are sold. It is estimated that 61% of all soft drinks are purchased in grocery stores. This includes all supermarkets as well as the other grocery stores (except convenience stores).

B. Convenience stores: A growing business segment in recent years. The number of convenience stores in the U.S. has increased 76% in the past seven years, while the number of grocery stores has decreased, and sales have almost tripled during this period, while grocery store sales have only doubled. Soft drink sales are a significant part of convenience store sales, accounting for approximately 10% of convenience store sales (as opposed to 2.6% of grocery store sales). Convenience stores presently account for approximately 4% of all soft drink sales.

C. Vending machines: There are approximately 2 million vending machines in the U.S., accounting for around 8% of soft drink sales. Approximately 52% of vending machine sales are canned drinks, 29% are bottles, and 19% are cups.

D. Fountains: The oldest means of selling soft drinks. Initially, soft drinks were sold exclusively in drug stores, but as packaging and distribution technology grew, fountain sales diminished. In recent years the rise in fast food outlets has added impetus to this side of the business again. In fact, fountain sales are growing at a larger percentage than the industry as a whole (3.1% growth in the soft drink industry compared to 8% growth in fountain sales last year). Today, 20% of soft drink sales are from fountains, with nearly half of this coming from the fast food outlets. Another recent event that has added to the attractiveness of the fountain business is the addition of fountain drinks by the largest convenience store-chain, Southland Corporation's 7-Elevens. Convenience stores now account for approximately 25% of total fountain sales.

The undisputed leader in fountain sales is Coca-Cola. According to statistics from Coca-Cola, 93 of the top 100 food service chains serve Coca-Cola. Pepsi Cola is a distant second in the number of outlets in which it is served, but has recently launched a strong effort to appropriate some of Coke's dominant fountain market share. Pepsi's efforts included a strong promotion program with glass giveaways, featuring Looney Tunes and Walt Disney cartoon characters.

E. Others: Soft drinks are sold through other intermediaries, as well, such as drug stores, discount stores, the airlines, and others. None of these account for more than 2% of soft drink sales.

Considerable regional variations appear in sales by product type and package type (Exhibit 2), and also in consumer flavor preference (Exhibit 3).

EXHIBIT 1 Soft drink sales by company

	1976 Mil. Cases	1976 Pct. Market	1977 Mil. Cases	1977 Pct. Market	1978 Mil. Cases	1978 Pct. Market	1979 Mil. Cases	1979 Pct. Market	1980 Mil. Cases	1980 Pct. Market
Coca-Cola Company										
Coca-Cola	1,190.0	24.3%	1,290.0	24.5%	1,335.0	24.3%	1,365.0	23.9%	1,425.0	24.3%
Sprite	130.0	2.7	150.0	2.8	158.0	2.9	165.0	2.9	171.0	2.9
Tab	125.0	2.6	137.0	2.6	149.0	2.7	170.0	3.0	188.0	3.2
Fanta	112.0	2.3	119.0	2.3	112.0	2.0	107.0	1.9	98.0	1.7
Mr. Pibb	37.0	0.7	45.0	0.9	46.0	0.8	43.0	0.8	39.0	0.7
Fresca	31.0	0.6	28.0	0.5	27.0	0.5	25.0	0.4	26.0	0.4
Mellow Yello	—	—	—	—	—	—	38.0	0.7	50.0	0.8
Others	10.0	0.2	15.0	0.3	19.0	0.4	23.0	0.4	25.0	0.4
Total	1,635.0	33.4	1,784.0	33.9	1,846.0	33.6	1,936.0	34.0	2,022.0	34.4
PepsiCo, Inc.										
Pepsi-Cola	803.0	17.0	903.0	17.2	969.0	17.6	1,022.0	17.9	1,056.0	17.9
Mountain Dew	73.0	1.5	100.0	1.9	130.0	2.4	156.0	2.8	169.0	2.9
Diet Pepsi	90.0	1.9	109.0	2.1	127.0	2.3	142.0	2.5	154.0	2.6
Pepsi Light	25.0	0.5	27.0	0.5	22.0	0.4	24.0	0.4	24.0	0.4
Teem	12.1	0.2	12.6	0.2	14.0	0.3	15.0	0.3	15.0	0.3
Others	15.3	0.3	20.0	0.4	19.0	0.3	18.0	0.3	17.0	0.3
Total	045.4	21.4	1,171.9	22.3	1,281.0	23.3	1,377.0	24.2	1,435.0	24.4
Dr Pepper Company										
Dr. Pepper	243.0	5.0	278.0	5.3	299.5	5.4	311.5	5.5	323.0	5.5
Sugar Free Dr. Pepper	39.0	0.8	52.0	1.0	60.5	1.1	62.9	1.1	69.1	1.2
Total	282.0	5.8	330.0	6.3	360.0	6.5	374.4	6.6	392.1	6.7
Seven-Up Company										
7-Up	305.8	6.3	315.0	6.0	322.0	5.9	320.0	5.6	317.0	5.4
Diet 7-Up	60.0	1.2	62.3	1.2	63.0	1.1	63.6	1.1	64.0	1.1
Dixie Cola	10.0	0.2	10.5	0.2	10.2	0.2	10.0	0.2	9.0	0.2
Howdy Flavors	1.3	—	1.2	—	1.0	—	1.0	—	1.0	—
Total	377.1	7.7	389.0	7.4	396.2	7.2	394.6	6.9	391.0	6.7
Royal Crown Companies										
Royal Crown	162.2	3.3	168.0	3.2	164.0	3.0	159.0	2.8	163.0	2.8
Diet Rite Cola & RC 100	40.6	0.8	40.6	0.8	40.2	0.7	38.0	0.7	40.5	0.7
Nehi and Others	55.6	1.2	53.0	1.0	53.5	1.0	53.0	0.9	50.0	0.8
Total	258.4	5.3	261.6	5.0	257.7	4.7	250.0	4.4	253.5	4.3

	1		2		3		4		5	
Crush International										
Hires, Crush, etc.	136.4	2.8	150.7	2.9	169.6	3.1	180.0	3.4	186.3	3.2
Sun Drop	19.5	0.4	23.0	0.4	24.0	0.4	25.0	0.5	25.9	0.4
Total	155.9	3.2	173.7	3.3	193.6	3.5	205.0	3.6	212.2	3.6
Canada Dry Corp.										
Ginger Ale	52.4	1.1	52.7	1.0	55.0	1.0	56.7	0.9	60.2	1.0
Tonic, Bitter Lemon	25.2	0.5	25.2	0.5	25.0	0.5	26.5	0.5	26.8	0.4
Club Soda	19.0	0.4	19.0	0.4	18.0	0.3	20.7	0.4	27.0	0.5
Barrelhead		—	15.0	0.3	15.0	0.3	15.5	0.3	15.3	0.3
Wink	5.5	0.1	5.5	0.1	5.5	0.1	5.0	0.1	4.0	0.1
Others	45.0	0.9	42.5	0.8	40.0	0.7	38.0	0.7	31.0	0.5
Total	147.1	3.0	159.9	3.1	158.5	2.9	162.4	2.9	164.3	2.8
Moxie Incorporated Monarch Company										
Nesbitts	21.8	0.4	21.9	0.4	23.2	0.4	19.0	0.3	18.0	0.3
Frostie Root Beer	NA-		NA-		NA-		15.0	0.3	16.0	0.3
NuGrape	12.8	0.3	13.8	0.3	15.1	0.3	14.3	0.2	14.4	0.2
Sun Crest Orange	7.2	0.2	8.3	0.2	9.3	0.2	8.9	0.2	8.5	0.2
Moxie	1.8	—	2.0	—	2.2	—	2.2	—	2.2	—
Kickapoo Joy Juice	NA-	—	0.6	—	1.0	—	0.7	—	NA-	
Mason's Root Beer	4.0	0.1	4.2	0.1	4.3	0.1	3.9	0.1	3.5	0.1
Flavette	2.0	—	2.2	—	2.5	—	2.1	—	1.9	—
Dr. Wells	0.7	—	0.8	—	2.4	—	2.0	—	1.8	—
Other	22.6	0.5	24.6	0.5	26.9	0.5	31.9	0.6	33.0	0.6
Total	72.9	1.5	78.4	1.5	86.9	1.5	100.0	1.7	99.3	1.7
Consolidated Chocolate Co.										
Chocolate Soldier	—		2.1		2.4		2.6	0.1	2.7	0.1
Brownie	—		1.0		1.3		1.4		1.4	
Choc-ola	—		1.3		1.8		1.9		2.0	
Other	—	0.1	4.0	0.1	4.5	0.1	4.7	0.1	4.9	0.1
Total	6.7	0.1	8.4	0.1	10.0	0.2	10.6	0.2	11.0	0.2
Grand Total	79.6	1.6	86.8	1.6	96.9	1.7	110.6	1.9	110.3	1.9
Shasta Beverages	95.0	1.9	103.1	2.0	106.5	1.9	100.0	1.7	105.0	1.8
Cadbury Schweppes USA, Inc.	28.4	0.6	35.5	0.7	43.0	0.8	55.8	1.0	64.8	1.1
A & W Beverages	29.5	0.6	40.0	0.8	46.2	0.8	54.0	0.9	58.0	1.0
Dad's Root Beer Company										
Dad's Root Beer	32.0	0.6	33.0	0.6	34.0	0.6	33.5	0.6	34.1	0.6
Bubble Up	15.0	0.3	15.0	0.3	17.0	0.3	16.0	0.3	15.6	0.3
Diet Dad's	7.2	0.2	7.2	0.1	7.0	0.1	6.5	0.1	6.7	0.1
Total	54.2	1.1	55.2	1.0	58.0	1.0	55.5	1.0	58.4	1.0

EXHIBIT 1 (continued)

	1976		1977		1978		1979		1980	
	Mil. Cases	Pct. Market	Mil. Cases	Pct. Market	Mil. Cases	Pct. Market	Mil. Cases	Pct. Market	Mil. Cases	Pct. Market
Cott Corporation	67.0	1.4	65.0	1.2	60.0	1.1	57.0	1.0	54.5	0.9
Squirt Company	36.4	0.7	37.0	0.7	40.0	0.7	47.6	0.8	53.8	0.9
Double Cola Co.	31.3	0.6	33.5	0.6	35.8	0.7	39.1	0.7	39.9	0.7
Welch's (Welch Foods)	9.0	0.2	18.0	0.3	31.0	0.6	31.0	0.5	30.0	0.5
Frank's Beverages	27.9	0.6	28.4	0.5	29.0	0.6	29.0	0.5	29.5	0.5
Faygo	22.3	0.4	27.3	0.5	26.1	0.5	23.9	0.4	22.1	0.4
No-Cal	23.8	0.5	22.4	0.4	22.4	0.4	22.4	0.4	21.0	0.4
Big K (Kroger)	13.5	0.3	14.4	0.3	16.0	0.3	17.0	0.3	17.5	0.3
Barq's	NA-		NA-		7.9	0.1	11.6	0.2	13.9	0.2
Cragmont (Safeway)	12.8	0.3	12.5	0.2	12.5	0.2	12.5	0.2	12.8	0.2
Chek (Winn-Dixie)	12.8	0.2	13.3	0.2	12.0	0.2	11.0	0.2	10.5	0.2
Yoo Hoo	10.0	0.2	10.0	0.2	11.0	0.2	11.0	0.2	10.4	0.2
Cotton Club	7.2	0.1	8.2	0.2	8.5	0.2	8.0	0.1	8.0	0.1
King Cola	NA-	—	NA-		NA-				7.0	0.1
Yukon (A&P)	NA-	—	NA-	—	NA-	—	2.6	0.1	2.9	—
Total	4,448.8	91.1	4,880.7	92.8	5,155.8	93.7	5,399.0	94.7	5,598.4	95.3
Others	441.2	8.9	378.3	7.2	344.2	6.3	301.0	5.3	276.6	4.7
Grand Total	4,890.0	100.0%	5,289.0	100.0%	5,500.0	100.0%	5,700.0	100.0%	5,875.0	100.0%

*Case: 24 pack, 8 oz. containers

SOURCE: John C. Maxwell, *Beverage Industry,* April 24, 1981

ESTIMATED MARKET SHARE BY TYPE

	1976	1977	1978	1979	1980
Cola	62.2%	62.4%	62.3%	62.3%	62.4%
Lemon-Lime	12.7	12.4	12.3	12.1	11.8
Pepper Type	6.7	7.3	7.7	7.9	8.0
Orange	7.8	7.4	7.4	7.3	7.4
Root Beer	5.2	5.3	5.4	5.5	5.5
All Others	5.4	5.2	4.9	4.9	4.9
Total	100.0%	100.0%	100.0%	100.0%	100.0%

SOURCE: John C. Maxwell, *Beverage Industry,* April 24, 1981

EXHIBIT 2 Soft drink share of the market - 1980 by product and package types

Region	Product Type		Package Type				
	Diet	Regular	Cans	Returnable Bottles 13-17 oz.	Returnable Bottles 18-36 oz.	2 Liter Plastic	All other
New England	24.7	75.3	21.0	—	—	20.3	58.7*
New York Metro	23.4	76.6	24.7	—	—	23.6	52.7*
Middle Atlantic	18.8	81.2	18.0	—	—	18.6	63.4*
East Central	15.2	84.8	19.0	49.2	9.6	13.5	8.7
Southeast	11.9	88.1	22.4	18.0	17.9	22.3	21.4
Chicago Metro	22.1	77.9	22.9	49.3	12.8	11.9	3.1
West Central	18.9	81.1	38.5	31.0	12.5	8.4	9.6
Southwest	13.8	86.2	30.7	8.4	29.6	15.0	16.3
Los Angeles Metro	22.7	77.3	54.8	9.5	9.6	16.8	9.3
Remaining Pacific	24.0	76.0	48.9	18.8	14.8	8.9	9.6
TOTAL U.S.A.	17.2	82.8	28.5	21.5	13.6	15.8	20.6

*Primarily nonreturnable bottles

SOURCE: "Consumer Preference Study — Soft Drink Flavors," Seven-Up Co., 1980.

EXHIBIT 3 Summary of findings from national study on consumer flavor preference of soft drinks — 1980 (%)

Region	Cola	Lemon-lime	Peppers	Root Beer	Orange	Ginger-ale	Grape	All others
New England	55.4	8.8	1.1	6.7	4.9	11.6	1.7	9.8
New York Metro	55.1	12.3	1.8	4.9	5.0	8.5	1.5	10.9
Middle Atlantic	57.0	9.2	1.9	6.4	4.8	7.6	1.6	11.5
East Central	63.3	9.8	2.6	5.7	2.9	2.7	1.2	11.8
Southeast	69.0	7.0	4.2	2.9	2.6	2.5	2.1	9.7
Chicago Metro	60.8	15.9	2.3	7.2	2.5	2.7	1.3	7.3
West Central	55.4	13.5	4.9	7.5	3.5	0.7	1.7	12.8
Southwest	56.5	8.7	18.9	4.0	2.3	0.5	1.6	7.5
Los Angeles Metro	52.1	17.8	4.7	6.1	5.1	1.6	1.7	10.9
Remaining Pacific	55.1	15.1	5.8	7.7	4.0	1.2	1.2	9.9
TOTAL U.S.A.	59.9	10.7	5.5	5.4	3.4	3.1	1.7	10.3

SOURCE: "Consumer Preference Study — Soft Drink Flavors," Seven-Up Co., 1980.

HISTORY OF SEVEN-UP

The Company

In the early 1920s, C. L. Grigg ran a general store in a small town in Missouri. His interest in developing new and improved merchandising techniques soon took him to St. Louis, where he eventually went into the soft drink business. In 1920, Mr. Grigg developed an orange-flavored beverage called the Howdy Orange Drink and started the Howdy Orange Company to market his new product. Before long, he decided that lemon was a more popular flavor than orange, and began working on a lemon-lime formula that would be "unmatched in quality, taste and refreshment." Finally in 1929, after trying 11 different drinks, he came up with a satisfactory product and named it "Bib-Label Lithiated Lemon Lime Soda."

Despite the product's unwieldy name, a price higher than its competition, and the stock market crash two weeks after introduction, the product sold. Soon the new drink was renamed "7-UP" (the "7" stood for its seven-ounce bottle and the "Up" for "bottoms up" or for the bubbles rising from its heavy carbonation), and in 1936 the company was renamed The Seven-Up Company. By the late 1940s, 7-UP was the third largest selling soft drink in the world. Seven-Up remained a private company, continuously managed by its founding family, until 1967, when the decision was made to go public. Then in June, 1978, Philip Morris, Inc., acquired the Company.

Reorganization

With Philip Morris' takeover, there was a complete reorganization of Seven-Up. The first change involved separating the international operations from the domestic operations. Presently they are treated as two separate companies—Seven-Up International, with Andreas Gembler as President, and the Seven-Up Company, headed by Edward W. Frantel, President and Chief Executive Officer. Both report to John Murphy, Group Executive Vice President of Philip Morris, Inc. It was under John Murphy's leadership that Miller Brewing Company, with new product introductions, massive advertising, and upgraded distribution, jumped from seventh place, with 4 percent of the beer market, to second place, with 19 percent of the market in just eight years (1971–1979).

The 7-UP Brand

7-UP, with its clear, bubbling waterlike appearance, was initially promoted for its health properties; helping to soothe upset stomachs is one example. Since the first "soft drinks" of many centuries ago were simply effervescent waters from natural springs, 7-UP tried to build on images people had of these refreshing and therapeutic sparkling waters. Early 7-UP advertis-

EXHIBIT 4

ing used slogans like "Tunes Tiny Tummies" and "Takes the Ouch out of Grouch." 7-UP also got an early reputation as a mixer to use with alcoholic beverages; "Glorifies Gin" was another early slogan used by the company.

By 1939, 7-UP was nationally known as a high quality, special purpose beverage. This positioning as a health and mixer beverage worked very efficiently, but in the 1940s and '50s 7-UP broadened its appeal. With such slogans as "You like it, it likes you" and "Fresh up with 7-UP," the company tried to promote the product for general rather than specialized use. It particularly tried to get away from its reputation as a hangover cure. Network television was used to stress that 7-UP was not a remedy, but an enjoyable, refreshing soft drink. This appeal was carried over into the 1960s, with such slogans as "Nothing does it like 7-UP."

In 1966, 7-UP kept the same "refreshing" type appeal, but zeroed in on a target market. With a swinging new ad campaign using the dual themes "Wet and Wild" and "First Against Thirst," the company tried to present itself as the soft drink of the different, active, younger set. However, 7-UP was still searching for the message that would change its specialized image to that of an all-purpose soft drink, one to be enjoyed frequently, especially by young people. This dramatic shift in promotional emphasis came in 1968 when "The Uncola" campaign was born. This unique approach at product positioning had a tremendous effect on sales; one month after the new campaign began, sales of 7-UP had increased 20 percent. Over the next five years, total cash sales went up 50 percent, as 7-UP enjoyed much success in capturing the attention of the younger consumer. By presenting 7-UP as different from the colas, and matching the tastes of the younger consumer, Seven-Up achieved a major repositioning for the soft drink. The campaign became one of the classic success stories in advertising and marketing history.

In late 1978, the company, now under a new management team, decided to change ad agencies and campaign theme. Feeling that it had established itself as a major alternative to the colas, Seven-Up chose to move into the soft drink mainstream and try to position itself as America's first choice soft drink. With the new campaign theme, "America's Turning 7-UP," the company tried to position 7-UP as the lighter, cleaner, more refreshing soft drink that "fits the way Americans are today."

Diet 7-UP

During the early 1960s, calorie-conscious Americans began flocking to low calorie soft drinks. Seven-Up marketing research determined that there was a demand for a high quality, lemon-lime diet beverage. The company responded in 1963 with the artificially-sweetened Like. The diet lemon-lime soft drink achieved national distribution in 1966 and sales continued to increase until 1969, when the soft drink industry was hit with a government ban on cyclamate sweeteners. The product was soon discontinued.

In April 1970, the company introduced Sugar Free 7-UP, with a different formulation of sweeteners. Product development research continued and in 1974, the company introduced a new, completely sugar-free Diet 7-UP with non-caloric saccharin as the sole sweetening agent. The new sugar-free Diet 7-UP, offering only one-third of a calorie per fluid ounce, achieved a 1.2 percent market share in 1976. Presently the product has 1.1 percent of the market.

Currently, domestic sales account for 84 percent of 7-UP and Diet 7-UP sales. In comparison, 81 percent of Pepsi Cola's sales are in the U.S., while 54 percent of Coca Cola's sales are domestic.

PROMOTION

As shown in Exhibit 5, 7-UP doubled its advertising expenditures between 1977 and 1980 in an effort to compete more effectively with Coke and Pepsi. The company increased Diet 7-UP's advertising almost tenfold during that period. Most of 7-UP's advertising budget is spent on television advertising.

The latest 7-UP advertising campaign, begun in late 1978, pictures 7-UP as a soft drink for active, healthy, outdoor people who enjoy hiking, biking, running, swimming, sailing, and camping. In trying to get this message across to the audience, the company initially shot several commercials with people doing these activities. But the company decided the commercials were too similar to Coke's and Pepsi's. Following the lead of its sister company, Miller, which successfully used former sports stars to promote its Lite beer, Seven-Up turned to present day sports stars. The company hired superstars such as football players Tony Dorsett, Pat Haden and Earl Campbell, and baseball players Jim Rice and Dave Kingman to be spokesmen to promote 7-UP as the drink for active people with modern, active lifestyles. The same campaign continued into the '80s, with the help of John McEnroe and Tracy Austin (tennis), Earvin "Magic" Johnson and Larry Bird (basketball), Mike Schmidt and Dave Parker (baseball), and Sugar Ray Leonard (boxing). One of

EXHIBIT 5   Leading soft drink brands, advertising expenditures 1976-1980

Brand	1980	1979	1978	1977	1976
Regular					
Coca-Cola	$38,043,000	$41,906,800	$35,050,000	$29,914,200	$24,653,000
Pepsi-Cola	42,266,800	36,129,700	25,739,600	24,547,500	20,665,600
Dr Pepper	11,750,600	9,623,800	10,185,000	7,026,400	5,265,000
7-UP	26,404,800	26,120,399	15,722,300	13,222,200	12,848,900
Sprite	11,113,400	9,725,600	7,914,200	4,217,400	2,264,650
Mountain Dew	10,802,200	8,375,200	6,822,800	4,457,500	2,677,700
Royal Crown	6,939,800	7,811,200	7,348,000	7,575,600	8,723,300
Diet					
Tab	13,686,100	13,644,500	8,660,500	4,140,800	7,054,400
Diet Pepsi	11,950,400	8,659,400	6,381,900	6,387,500	4,964,300
Fresca	8,168,800	6,347,500	6,101,800	1,273,000	4,182,400
Diet 7-UP	7,935,500	5,703,700	3,964,600*	1,489,100*	1,130,600
Pepsi Light	5,646,600	6,287,100	3,715,600	6,565,000	6,168,200
Shasta Diet	4,203,000	641,900	2,260,900	608,400	2,450,200
Diet Rite	3,594,500	3,074,600	3,117,200	2,378,000	5,192,400
Sugar Free Dr. Pepper	3,065,300	2,818,200	1,942,400	1,771,500	2,446,000
A&W Sugar Free	1,276,300	1,579,100	598,600	481,500	381,000

*7UP Sugar Free

SOURCE: "AD $ Summary," Leading National Advertisers, Inc., 1976-1980

the most popular television advertisements in 1981 featured Sugar Ray Leonard and his son in a boxing workout. Set to a bouncy "feelin' good . . . 7-UP" tune, the advertisement was designed to create a happy feeling and depict 7-UP as the way to quench thirst and feel refreshed after invigorating exercise.

Diet 7-UP is advertised primarily on television, by spokespersons such as Don Rickles, Linda Carter, Tommy Smothers, and Margaux Hemingway. The advertising theme presently being used for Diet 7-UP is, "The only thing you give up is calories."

PRICING

There is no retail price difference between brands of soft drinks in vending machine sales or fountain sales. It is a completely different story, however, with grocery stores, convenience stores, and other types of retailers. For the past few years, Coca-Cola and Pepsi-Cola have been fighting an increasingly hot price war. Both companies have been offering generous discounts on all of their brands of soft drinks to retailers, and they encourage retailers to pass these discounts on to consumers in the form of lower prices. Seven-Up has not responded to these price cuts; it believes that discounting cheapens product image and weakens brand loyalty. As a result, the average price of a unit of 7-UP is slightly higher than a unit of Coke or Pepsi.

DISTRIBUTION

Like other soft drink companies, Seven-Up distributes its products through bottling companies, most of which are privately (independently) owned. The few parent company bottlers owned by Seven-Up account for only 5 percent of sales, compared with 20 percent for Pepsi and 12 percent for Coke. The other 95 percent of the company's sales come from local bottling companies with whom Seven-Up signs a franchise agreement. This agreement gives the private franchise the right to sell and distribute 7-UP in a particular geographic area. Since the private franchise is independently owned, it differs from the parent company bottler because it usually handles other brands of soft drinks, often Pepsi, Coke, or Royal Crown, in addition to 7-UP. Presently, 337 of Seven-Up's 464 bottlers also distribute a cola. The normal franchise agreement in the soft drink industry prohibits a franchise from carrying two "competing products," such as two colas.

Sizes of bottlers vary, from family operations selling as few as 100,000 cases annually in relatively small population areas to large operations in urban centers that may sell more than 15 million cases a year. These bottlers purchase 7-UP extract from the company and convert it into bottled, canned, or fountain 7-UP. Bottling plants carry out many different functions. Plant facilities include not only conveyors, fillers, sealers and packaging machinery, but also warehouse areas for container supplies and the finished products. In addition, these bottlers distribute, warehouse, advertise, merchandise and sell the brand to local customers. Each bottler maintains a trucking fleet to distribute the product. These bottling companies coordinate all local marketing activities with the national 7-UP marketing programs developed by the company.

Some Seven-Up Company executives have been privately questioning whether the present distribution network is necessarily the best for the company in the long run. Because most bottlers produce and distribute various brands of soft drinks, a problem might exist if Seven-Up ever wanted to expand its product mix. These private franchise bottlers would probably object to handling an additional high sales brand since it would, in many cases, involve deleting another brand to make room for the new one. Company officials have discussed whether it might be desirable to start phasing out the independent bottlers and emphasizing parent company bottlers. The company has recently completed a large parent company bottling plant in Houston, which is one of the fastest growing soft drink markets in the U.S. (although presently a weak one for 7-UP). With a capacity of 20 million cases, this plant could support bottling operations all over southern Texas. This type of distribution network is being considered by the company.

FUTURE MARKETING STRATEGIES

As Seven-Up considers its marketing strategies for the next few years, one of the key decisions will be whether to pursue a particular consumer market segment, and, if so, which one. Coca-Cola uses predominantly a mass marketing approach, as indicated recently by a spokesperson for the industry leader:

> (Coke tries) to appeal to everyone who might be thirsty, who wants a refreshing beverage. We give a youthful flavor to our advertising simply because everybody likes to feel youthful. We don't feel that age has a whole lot to do with the way we market our product. We're not going to ignore the large demographic segment, but it happens that that segment fits in with our general advertising theme, which is youth and fun and refreshment and the standards of our business.[1]

Pepsi-Cola also uses a widespread marketing approach with its "Pepsi Generation" slogan. A spokesperson for Pepsi comments on the company's means of identifying the product with an active, youthful lifestyle:

> The Pepsi Generation is rather broadly based and is more a lively, energetic state of mind than an actual age group. But, most people would probably identify it as between twenty-five and thirty-four. Our public relations programs are quite sophisticated and very often are tailored to that age group. Of course none

---

[1] *1980 Beverage Industry Annual Manual,* pp. 17–18

EXHIBIT 6   Consumer expenditures for beverages, by age groups of household heads

	Under 25	25-34	35-44	45-54	55-64	Over 65
Percent of all household heads	9.0%	22.5%	15.5%	17.0%	15.5%	20.5%
Cola drinks, nondiet	9.5	29.0	23.0	20.0	11.0	7.5
Fruit carbonated drinks, nondiet	7.5	22.5	20.5	21.5	14.0	14.0
Other carbonated drinks, nondiet	6.0	22.0	20.5	21.5	14.0	16.0
Diet carbonated drinks	5.0	24.0	23.0	23.5	15.0	9.5
Carbonated water	3.5	20.0	23.0	25.0	16.5	12.0
Beer, ale, at home	10.5	27.0	21.0	20.5	13.5	7.5
Wine, at home	7.0	28.0	19.5	18.0	15.5	12.0
Beer, ale, away from home	15.0	35.0	17.0	17.5	11.5	4.0
Other alcoholic beverages, away from home	12.0	29.5	20.5	20.0	11.5	6.5
Instant coffee	2.5	16.0	19.5	24.0	18.5	19.5
Tea	4.5	22.5	25.0	21.0	15.0	11.5
Coffee, tea, between meals	8.0	29.5	22.0	23.5	13.0	4.0
Fresh whole milk	6.0	24.5	24.0	21.0	12.0	12.5
Fresh fruit juices	5.0	22.0	21.0	20.5	16.5	15.0
Frozen orange juice	6.0	23.0	22.0	21.5	13.5	14.0
Noncarbonated fruit drinks	6.5	29.5	25.0	21.0	10.0	8.0
Powdered fruit drinks	7.5	31.5	28.5	16.5	8.5	7.5

	18-24	25-34	35-44	45-54	55-64	65 and over	Total
1985 (Projected)							
Population	27,976	39,917	31,388	22,688	21,665	26,782	170,416
% of total	16.4	23.4	18.4	13.3	12.7	15.7	100%

SOURCE: 1980 Beverage Industry Annual Manual

EXHIBIT 7

of this overlooks the real young kids, nine-nineteen. We do things for them, as well, and they are still a part of the Pepsi Generation. But you don't see them in action as much in the advertising.[2]

Seven-Up has recently gathered some data on beverage expenditures by age group as well as population projections for 1985. These figures appear in Exhibit 6.

Changes in beverage preference and consumption reflect demographic changes. For example, one study has shown that the typical 13-24-year-old consumes an average of 2⅓ cans of soft drink per day, while the average for all other age groups is 1½ cans per day. The popularity of diet drinks can also be attributed to a population that is growing older. Americans born during the post-World War Two baby boom, now in their middle- and late-thirties, are less apt to drink a sugared product. As a result, sales of diet drinks have been on a slight upswing.

Another marketing decision will be whether the company should be satisfied with its current product mix. Can the Seven-Up Company be profitable featuring a lemon-lime drink, or should it introduce other flavors, even its own cola? If it does decide to market a cola, will there be any distribution problems since most Seven-Up bottlers are major bottlers for Coke, Pepsi, or Royal Crown and would not be able to distribute another cola?

[2]Ibid.

Hurcu-Link

Dr. Bill Bassichis, an associate professor of physics at Texas A&M University, has just received the results of a market research study on a product he invented and has been trying to market. The product, Hurcu-Link, is attached to the inside of large windows and glass doors to protect them from wind damage, particularly hurricanes. The 44-year-old professor has thoroughly tested the product, both in the laboratory and in an actual hurricane, and Hurcu-Link has passed all tests with flying colors. In spite of its proven effectiveness, Dr. Bassichis has had little success selling his invention. He lamented, "I can't understand it. The device works. Everyone I've talked to thinks it's a good idea. But people won't buy it. I've run out of ideas on how to sell it."

After five years of trying everything he could think of, Dr. Bassichis contacted a group of marketing experts. Because they felt that what was needed most was some market research information, in the summer of 1981 this group performed an extensive market research study of potential purchasers of this type of product. With the results of this study, the professor is now trying to make a decision on whether to pursue his idea further and, if so, what marketing strategies to use to make Hurcu-Link a success.

BACKGROUND

Dr. Bassichis received his Ph.D. in physics from Case Western Reserve University in Cleveland in 1963. Since that time he has been actively involved in both college teaching and scientific research. In 1975, he began a series of laboratory studies on methods to increase the resistance of glass to breakage when under a strong force, such as a hurricane. He theorized that a window could be made stronger by reducing the size of its unsupported surface area, thus reducing the stress placed on the glass by high winds. He could accom-

---

This case was prepared by Stephen W. McDaniel and Valarie Zeithaml, Assistant Professors of Marketing, Texas A&M University, as a basis for class discussion rather than to illustrate either effective or ineffective marketing management.

plish this by placing a supported object against the center of a window, halving the unsupported surface area of the window. This would increase the structural strength of the entire window. The professor received engineering assistance on the project from a mechanical engineer friend who had an interest in the project; his daughter had been injured by flying glass in an office tower during Hurricane Celia in 1970.

Dr. Bassichis worked on several different methods of placing a supported object in the center of a window and finally came up with the Hurcu-Link. While developing the product he talked with several engineers in large companies and asked their feelings about such a product. All agreed that the idea was sound, and each stressed the importance of using the best quality materials. The professor set out to make "the best quality product possible."

THE PRODUCT

Soon Dr. Bassichis purchased about $1,000 worth of equipment, bought enough raw materials to make several of the devices, and set up shop in his garage. Hurcu-Link consists of a ten-inch sandcast-aluminum plate that presses firmly against the inside of the glass. On the flat surface of the plate are six adhesive strips of two-sided tape that bind the glass and prevent it from being pulled away from the plate. The plate is held in place by an aluminum bar that must be cut to fit the size of each window. The plate is held onto the bar with a nine-inch stainless steel stud, one end of which is screwed into the plate; the other end is fastened by a wing nut to the bar. Aluminum brackets are attached to each end of the bar to permit fastening the entire device to the window facing. The wing nut of the stud is then used to adjust the device so that it fits tightly against the glass. The device shifts the mode of the bending of the glass pane, greatly reducing stress on the glass when it is subjected to intense wind pressure.

A customer buying Hurcu-Link can install the device in less than thirty minutes with a drill, screwdriver, and wrench. A drill is needed to make screw holes in the window facing so that the aluminum brackets can be positioned to hold the bar. Hurcu-Link need only be put up when a hurricane is imminent. It can be taken down when no longer needed, leaving the aluminum brackets in the window facing. Reinstallation takes five to ten minutes, since all that is involved is attaching it to the brackets, and then tightening the wing nut to firm the plate against the glass.

The six adhesive strips of two-sided tape are essential because the high winds of a hurricane not only exert a strong force against the outside of the glass, but the imbalance of inside and outside pressure tends to push the glass outward as well. It is a slight problem to remove the tape-held plate from the window after a hurricane threat. However, some alcohol around that area will easily remove the tape from the window.

COST

Dr. Bassichis does the assembly work himself, but contracts out the sandcasting and machining of the plate, as well as the cutting of the aluminum bar. He pays a man thirty dollars an hour to cut the bars. The approximate costs of the Hurcu-Link components for a typical large window (four feet by four feet) are:

Aluminum bar ($1 per foot)	$ 4.00
Cutting of aluminum bar (@ 30 per hour)	$ 1.00
Casting of plate	$ 5.00
Machining of plate	$ 3.00
9" stainless steel stud	$ 1.50
Wing nut	$ .50
2 regular nuts	$ .75
2 aluminum brackets	$ 2.00
2 rivets	$ .75
TOTAL COST	$18.50

Some economies of scale could be realized with quantity buying and increased production, but so far the level of sales has not permitted the per-unit costs to be much lower than this. Dr. Bassichis estimates the maximum number he could produce a month is approximately 800. At this rate, the per-unit costs could be reduced to approximately $15.50. He is presently selling the device for $50.

THE MARKET

Dr. Bassichis was excited about the product's potential. Since he knew of no competitor, he reasoned he would have what he felt was a tremendous market to himself, at least initially. The major geographic market, as he saw it, was the Gulf Coast, particularly Texas and Florida. These areas had the most frequent and serious hurricanes. The hurricane season is from June to October, and a year rarely passes when at least one hurricane does not hit somewhere along the Gulf Coast. Millions of dollars in property damage results, as well as loss of life.

Although Dr. Bassichis considered high hurricane-frequency areas to be the major markets, he also thought there may be a market in high tornado-frequency areas. Even areas that have occasional high winds might be a market for the product, he reasoned. For example, in early 1982, Denver had winds of over fifty miles per hour, which caused extensive damage to windows. The market was out there.

MARKETING EFFORT

Since he had never done anything like this before, Dr. Bassichis was unsure of how to tap this huge market. He wound up trying several different methods of promoting Hurcu-Link. "Our marketing efforts could be termed haphazard," he explained. "We didn't have any real marketing program. Somebody would say 'Why don't you try this?' and we'd do it."

The first thing he did was try to obtain the insurance industry's support. He hoped that insurance companies might be willing to provide some kind of insurance rate reduction for people who bought Hurcu-Link. He expected the companies to be open to the idea, since Hurcu-Link would cut down on damage claims. Because much hurricane damage is caused by water coming into the house or office after a window is broken, the product could cut down on interior property damage, as well as glass breakage. Dr. Bassichis met with the Commissioner of Insurance for the State of Texas, but his request for insurance rate reductions fell on deaf ears: "The insurance industry didn't seem at all interested in the product. It was almost as if insurance companies would rather pay for the damage and collect higher premiums than reduce the overall premium rates."

In spite of this setback, Dr. Bassichis knew people would buy his product; he just had to decide how to sell it. Feeling that the most lucrative and least time-consuming method would be to simply supply Hurcu-Link to a large retail chain and let it sell it for him, he made up some promotional literature and sent it to a corporate buyer for Montgomery Ward. The buyer was initially very interested and flew to Texas to see and discuss the device. The buyer agreed that it was a good idea but wanted to see some market research information. Since no marketing research data had been obtained and he was not sure the product would sell, the buyer decided against carrying the product. He told Dr. Bassichis, however, that he would consider Hurcu-Link after the product had sold 100,000 units. The buyer estimated that Ward's would retail the product for approximately seventy dollars. Dr. Bassichis was at least encouraged by this, since he was selling Hurcu-Link for twenty dollars at that time.

Next, the inventor talked with manager of hardware stores to see if they would stock Hurcu-Link. A couple of stores were interested in the device, but hesitant to carry it in stock. The major objection the managers raised was the necessity of cutting the bar to the specifications of each window. Because each Hurcu-Link sold would have to be customized, the managers had reservations about either having to do it themselves or special order each one from Dr. Bassichis. They felt that any product they carried should be ready to use.

From 1977 to 1980, Dr. Bassichis tried many other methods of selling his product. He telephoned various executives, including the Chairman of the Board of Holiday Inn, to set up appointments to show how the device could protect windows in their motels or businesses. None were interested. He contacted the corporate headquarters of several companies that specialized in repairing broken glass or installing new windows; again, none were interested.

By 1980 he had sold only seventy-four units. A condominium owner in Miami heard about the device and placed an order, and some offices at the Galveston Branch of Texas A&M University purchased the rest. After more than five years of research, development, manufacturing, and attempts to sell Hurcu-Link, Dr. Bassichis was discouraged.

HURRICANE ALLEN

In August 1980, the fortunes of Hurcu-Link took a turn for the better. Dr. Bassichis had contacted the major hotels in hurricane-prone Corpus Christi, Texas. One large hotel, the Sheraton Marina Inn, bought 130 of the devices at twenty dollars each.

Before long, Hurcu-Link got its first major test—Hurricane Allen, with winds of over 100 miles per hour. Before the hurricane, Dr. Bassichis assisted in installing the devices on the windows for the hotel's restaurant and club at the top of the eleven-story hotel. When the hurricane hit, Dr. Bassichis and the Sheraton's general manager, Bob MacLean, stayed on the top floor and checked the windows every few minutes, tightening some of the plates when necessary. The result was almost complete success. The only glass breakage occurred when a sliding glass door, to which a Hurcu-Link device was attached, jumped off its track and broke. All 126 windows, however, survived the hurricane. The successful test received some publicity in the local newspaper. In a favorable article, the reporter told about Dr. Bassichis, Hurcu-Link, and interviewed Mr. MacLean, who had praised the device warmly. The article appears in Exhibit 1.

Rejuvenated by the successful real-world test of Hurcu-Link and the resulting favorable publicity, Dr. Bassichis began a new marketing push. He made up some single-page advertisements which contained a brief sales message, a reprint of the newspaper article, and several postcards. The unstamped postcards were addressed to "Hurricane Protection Devices." The message side read, "Yes, I am interested in protecting my windows with a hurricane protection device," and left blanks for the person's name, address, phone number, and number, width, and height of windows. The postcards were slipped into two cuts made in each sheet of the ad. Although the postcards covered up a large part of the newspaper article, the headline was visible, and Dr. Bassichis felt that prospects could always take out the postcards to read the entire article (see Exhibit 2).

The advertisements were distributed in Corpus Christi and a few other Texas coastal areas. Dr. Bassichis used bulletin boards in laundromats, apartment complexes, restaurants, and any other place he could find. He put out 50 advertisements in Corpus Christi and around 200 in the coastal area, but received only 5 inquiries. Following up even these few produced no sales.

Corpus Christi Caller Times

SUNDAY, AUGUST 17, 1980

Windows withstand winds

Glass protector passes major test

By GRADY PHELPS
Business Writer

A Texas A&M University physics professor says a stress-reducing glass support device passed its first major test to protect against hurricane-force winds here last weekend.

Of the 126 windows atop the Sheraton Marina Inn on Shoreline Drive here which were equipped with the metal window braces, only one broke in Hurricane Allen's winds.

And that was on a sliding glass door. Hotel officials think it jumped off its track and broke rather than its glass protector failing.

The 11-story Sheraton fared much better than other local office towers, which suffered considerable glass breakage in the high wind gusts that peaked around 100 mph.

Dr. William Bassichis, 43, of Texas A&M, helped design the three-pound metal frame with the help of a former Corpus Christi mechanical engineer whose daughter was injured by flying glass in a local downtown office tower during Hurricane Celia in 1970.

Bassichis now markets the glass protection devices as a private business venture. They sell for $50 a window under the brand name Hurcu-Link.

"There's no doubt whatsoever they work beautifully," Bob MacLean, the Sheraton's general manager, said. "The glass supports saved our whole top floor.

"I didn't leave this property, and we checked them (the windows) every 30 minutes for two days. Sometimes we had to tighten some of the metal bars, but I swear some of the wind gusts coming off the water at the top floor were really stronger than what they recorded out at the airport."

Saving the upper floor glass windows, which are 10 feet by 4 feet in size, meant a cost replacement bill of at least $35,000 and probably more, MacLean said.

"Each glass costs $277. Then we'd probably have to hire a crane to lift them up from the ground. It's no telling what installation would have cost us."

But it also meant the hotel's restaurant and club could resume business as soon as the winds quit, at a tidy savings in revenue.

"Our restaurant was in full operation at the lunch hour Monday, and we packed in the customers," MacLean said. "If we'd lost those windows, we would have had to close down and lost a month of business at the minimum."

MacLean said he only used the metal brace on the top floor windows. The bottom-floor bayfront windows were boarded up with plywood. Two of those broke.

Bassichis said his Hurcu-Link brace when installed "quite simply support the center of the window. It actually cuts a big window into four small windows. The smaller the window, the more pressure it can take before it breaks."

The thin metal mechanism contains a center disc which is connected to a metal bar that is fastened to each side of the wall encasing the glass. The support works to shift the mode of the bending of the pane, causing a large stress reduction when the glass is subjected to intense wind loads.

Bassichis estimates the Sheraton windows possibly could have withstood wind gusts of 200 mph with the supports but there is no guarantee.

Bassichis said large windows, at least 4 by 6 feet in size, are best suited for the support. It generally wouldn't pay average homeowners to invest that much in small windows, except perhaps a plate glass picture window.

"Glass is an imperfect substance and just cannot be manufactured so that it is guaranteed to withstand a large stress," he said.

"I am very pleased with the results. This is the Hurcu-Link's first real hurricane test."

Up to now he's had trouble selling the device, because of its cost. He's sold only 200 of them. In addition to the 126 at the Sheraton, a condominium owner in Miami bought some and Texas A&M offices in Galveston purchased other units.

"It's like trying to sell insurance or cemetery lots," Bassichis said. "People aren't too interested in making such an investment until a hurricane comes and then it's too late."

But he may find an increased market for his product here, using the Sheraton results as a selling card.

EXHIBIT 1

The most recent marketing attempt by Dr. Bassichis was contracting with a selling agent in Florida. He gave the agent several of the devices and copies of sales literature and advertisements. The selling agent was to sell Hurcu-Link for fifty dollars each and would receive a 20 percent commission on each sale. Dr. Bassichis felt confident that the selling agent would do an exceptional job of bringing in orders and that he could fill the orders. Unfortunately, Dr. Bassichis has not heard from the man for a year and a half.

THE MARKET RESEARCH STUDY

In the summary of 1981 he employed a marketing research group to conduct a study of the potential market for the hurricane protection device. A major part of the study involved analyzing the consumer market for the product. Based on the frequency of hurricanes in particular areas and the population density of those areas, cities were selected for the study sample. These cities, with demographic information are given in Exhibit 3.

A questionnaire was mailed to a random sample of homeowners in each sample city. The two-page questionnaire had been carefully constructed

EXHIBIT 2

TAKE ONE

YOU SHOULD PROTECT
YOUR WINDOWS TODAY ...
Before the next Hurricane!

Effective New Device installs from the
inside when a hurricane is eminent!

Protect Your Family and Your Property From
the High Winds of the Next Destructive Hurricane

Write: *Hurricane Protection Devices*
P.O. Box 9027
College Station, Tx. 77840

DON'T BE THE NEXT HURRICANE'S VICTIM

Corpus Christi Caller Times   SUNDAY, AUGUST 17, 1980

Windows withstand winds

test

B'
8u

fe

protect against hurricane
here last weekend.

Of the 126 windows atop
Marina Inn on Shoreline
which were equipped wit
window braces, only one br
cane Allen's winds.

And that was on a slidin
Hotel officials think it ju
track and broke rather th
protector failing.

The 11-story Sheraton far
ter than other local office t∈
suffered considerable glass
the high wind gusts that pe
100 mph.

Dr. William Bassichis,
A&M, helped design the
metal frame with the help
Corpus Christi mechanic
whose daughter was injur
glass in a local downtown
during Hurricane Celia in 1

Bassichis now markets tl
tection devices as a private business
venture. They sell for $50 a window un-
der the brand name Hurcu-Link.

"There's no doubt whatsoever they
work beautifully," Bob MacLean, the
Sheraton's general manager, said. "The
glass supports saved our whole top floor.

"I didn't leave this property, and we

**Yes, I am interested in protecting my windows
with a hurricane protection device.**

Name _____

Address _____

_____

Telephone No. _____

Number of Windows _____

Approximate width and height _____

_____

Bassichis said his Hurcu-Link brace
when installed "quite simply support the
center of the window. It actually cuts a
big window into four small windows. The
smaller the window, the more pressure
it can take before it breaks."

The thin metal mechanism contains a
center disc which is connected to a metal

each side of the
ss. The support
of the bending of
ge stress reduc-
glass is subjected to in-
ads.

stimates the Sheraton win-
could have withstood wind
mph with the supports but
iarantee.

aid large windows, at least
size, are best suited for the
nerally wouldn't pay aver-
ners to invest that much in
vs, except perhaps a plate
window.

n imperfect substance and
e manufactured so that it is
o withstand a large stress,"

y pleased with the results.
ircu-Link's first real hurri-

he's had trouble selling the
ise of its cost. He's sold only
In addition to the 126 at the
 condominium owner in Mi-
ome and Texas A&M offices
purchased other units.

"It's like trying to sell insurance or
cemetery lots," Bassichis said. "People
aren't too interested in making such an
investment until a hurricane comes and
then it's too late."

But he may find an increased market
for his product here, using the Sheraton
results as a selling card.

EXHIBIT 3   Demographic information on target cities

City	Population	Number of Residences	Number of Hotels & Motels	Number of Businesses
Mobile	200,452	75,577	31	1,601
Daytona Beach	65,108*	31,639*	177	851
Fort Lauderdale	155,882*	82,351*	222*	N/A
Hollywood	117,188	54,813	225	N/A
Miami and Miami Beach	561,672*	271,988*	401	6,945
West Palm Beach	25,368*	16,326*	36	1,010
New Orleans	557,482	226,452	104	4,647
Beaumont	118,102	47,065	28	N/A
Corpus Christi	231,999	81,587	80	1,869
Galveston	61,902	27,850	42	508

*Indicates the city and the beach areas

so that on the first page respondents answered questions about their fear of and experience with hurricanes, insurance coverage, need for glass protection, protective action presently taken, and willingness to purchase *this type of hurricane protection device.* On the second page were specific questions about their willingness to purchase Hurcu-Link. At the top of the second page were pictures and a 120-word description of the device. A total of 370 questionnaires was returned.

RESULTS

A copy of the questionnaire and a summary of the overall results are shown in Exhibit 4. The data was analyzed to determine how specific segments of the sample felt about the product type (i.e., a generic product designed to protect windows), as well as the specific product, Hurcu-Link. The marketing group hoped this analysis might provide some information on possible target markets.

The first question had four parts and investigated consumer attitudes toward hurricanes. Each part required the respondent to place a check mark along a five-point scale indicating level of agreement or disagreement to a statement. Answers to question I-5 (which asked their probability of buying this product type) and question II-1 (which asked their probability of buying Hurcu-Link) were then analyzed. Statistical correlation analysis on the data indicated a very significant relationship between consumer willingness to purchase both the product type and Hurcu-Link and (1) perceived chance of a hurricane hitting the house; (2) consumer fear of hurricanes; (3) consumer concern about a hurricane hitting the house; and (4) consumer concern about window breakage from a hurricane. Other findings are shown in Exhibits 5–13.

EXHIBIT 4

HURRICANE PROTECTION QUESTIONNAIRE

I.

1. For each of the following, please place a checkmark in the appropriate location on the scale that represents your level of agreement/disagreement: **n**

The chances of hurricane-strength winds hitting my house are great

5.2%	7.4%	21.3%	21.5%	44.7%	367
strongly disagree				strongly agree	

I am afraid of hurricanes

16.0%	16.0%	24.7%	15.5%	17.7%	368
strongly disagree				strongly agree	

I am concerned about hurricane-strength winds hitting my house

4.3%	9.0%	19.8%	23.1%	43.8%	368
strongly disagree				strongly agree	

I am concerned about window breakage that might be caused by the high winds of a hurricane

9.1%	11.8%	20.6%	19.8%	38.7%	364
strongly disagree				strongly agree	

2. Have you ever been in a hurricane or had property damage to your residence as a result of a hurricane?

22.9% No   77.1% Yes   371

If yes, did the damage include any breakage of windows or glass doors in your house?

79.2% No   20.8% Yes   283

If yes, what was the approximate amount of damage?

$2,653 (mean)   66

3. Does your insurance policy cover window or glass door breakage?

17.2% No   82.8% Yes   332

If yes, what is the deductable on this policy? $ 150 (mean)   192

(or what % of damage is covered?)   (92 (mean))   27

4A. How many large, solid glass windows are in your house (i.e. at least 4'X 4')?   3.1 (mean)   355

Estimated replacement cost per window? $ 203 (mean)   124

B. How many large solid glass doors are in your house? (i.e. sliding door)?   1.2 (mean)   360

Estimated replacement cost per door? $ 250 (mean)   133

C. What kind of protective action have you taken in the past to guard these large windows/glass doors from possible breakage during a forthcoming hurricane?

Tape 56.6%   337
Plywood 46.6%
Other (please specify) 21%

Approximately how many times have you taken that action in the past 5 years?   1.4   314

How effective were these protective measures?

0.7%	7.8%	91.5%	282
Not Effective	Partially Effective	Effective	

5. If a product were available that would allow you to attach it to each large window or glass door prior to a hurricane, and which was guaranteed to protect the glass from wind breakage during the hurricane, would you buy this product?

8.0%	35.2%	47.3%	9.5%	349
Definitely not	Probably not	Probably would	Definitely would	

32

11. To the right are pictures of one such device
designed to protect large windows and glass
doors from hurricane-speed winds. The 10"
sandcast-aluminum center presses firmly
against the inside of the glass and is held
in place by an aluminum bar. Aluminum brackets are then fastened to the window facing
to hold the device in place. You can install
the device initially in 20-30 minutes with a
drill, screwdriver and wrench. It can then
be taken down when the need is no longer present, leaving the small aluminum brackets in
the window facing. Reinstallation can then
be accomplished in 5-10 minutes when high
winds are again imminent. The non-corrosive
device can be most effectively used for large
(at least 4' x 4') windows and glass doors.
The hurricane device has been extensively
tested in laboratory situations as well as
in actual hurricanes, and is unconditionally
guaranteed to prevent glass breakage caused
by the high winds of a hurricane.

Viewed from inside

Viewed from outside

1. Would you buy this product?

17.2%	43.5%	36.7%	2.7%	338
Definitely not	Probably not	Probably would	Definitely would	

2. What is the likelihood that you would buy this product at each of the following
   price levels? (Check one for each price)

	Definitely not	Probably not	Probably would	Definitely would	
$100	81.2%	15.1%	3.3%	0.4%	271
$ 75	74.8%	22.9%	2.3%	0	262
$ 50	56.1%	33.5%	9.3%	1.0%	269
$ 25	28.6%	31.9%	34.4%	5.0%	276
$ 10	16.9%	17.0%	37.4%	28.9%	273
$ 5	15.7%	12.7%	28.5%	43.0%	267

3. Where would you be most likely to purchase such a product?

42.2% Department store (i.e. Sears)   61.3% Hardware store

30.7% Lumber yard   5.3% Order it through the mail   303

3.0% Grocery store   5.0% Other (please name) _____

4. What do you see as the major disadvantage of a product like this?

No protection from debris 33.1%	Doubt effectiveness 9.7%	248
Installation/Put up-take down 20.2%	No need 9.7%	
Storage/find when needed 12.1%		

III. For classification purposes, please answer the following questions about yourself:

1. Age: ☐ Under 20 ☐ 20-29 ☐ 30-39 ☐ 40-49 ☐ 50-59 ☐ 60-70 ☐ Over 70 368
   15%   15.2%   22.3%   19.0%   20.1%   14.9%   7.9%

2. Education:

1.9% ☐ Grade school   17.1% ☐ High school graduate   23.% ☐ College graduate   363

5.0% ☐ Some high school   31.0% ☐ Some college   21.5% ☐ Post-graduate study

3. Total Family Annual Income:

3.2% ☐ Under $8,000   19.7% ☐ $15,000-$24,999   6.9% ☐ $50,000-$64,999   346

11.9% ☐ $8,000-$14,999   25.4% ☐ $25,000-$34,999   9.8% ☐ $65,000+

23.1% ☐ $35,000-$49,999

4. Your occupation: Prof.-20.2%, other white c...8%, blue collar - 15.6%   357
   Your spouse's occupation: _____

5. Approximate present value of your house:

9.2% ☐ Under $40,000   20.6% ☐ $60,000-$79,999   14.2% ☐ $100,000-$124,999   360

23.9% ☐ 40,000-$59,999   18.1% ☐ $80,000-$99,000   6.4% ☐ $125,000-$150,000

7.8% ☐ Over $150,000

EXHIBIT 5 Primary demand by market area

Market area	N	% Indicating they probably or definitely would purchase product type	% Indicating they definitely would purchase product type
Corpus Christi, TX	60	68.3%	8.3%
Galveston, TX	12	75.0%	25.0%
Beaumont, TX	28	53.6%	7.1%
New Orleans, LA	49	55.1%	8.2%
Mobile, AL	44	43.2%	2.3%
Miami, FL	72	56.9%	11.1%
Hollywood, FL	23	65.2%	21.7%
Ft. Lauderdale, FL	35	42.9%	11.4%
W. Palm Beach, FL	17	70.6%	0%
Daytona Beach, FL	8	50.0%	12.5%
	348	56.8%	9.5%

EXHIBIT 6 Primary demand by previous hurricane experience

Previously been in or had property damage from a hurricane	N	% Indicating they probably or definitely would purchase product type	% Indicating they definitely would purchase product type
No	79	64.6%	13.9%
Yes	270	54.4%	8.1%
Previously had glass breakage from a hurricane			
No	215	51.6%	5.6%
Yes	53	66.0%	18.9%

EXHIBIT 7 Primary demand by house characteristics

Value of home	N	% Indicating they probably or definitely would purchase product type	% Indicating they definitely would purchase product type
Under $40,000	29	51.7%	6.9%
$40,000–60,000	81	54.3%	8.6%
$60,000–80,000	73	67.1%	13.7%
$80,000–100,000	63	49.2%	6.3%
$100,000–125,000	45	60.0%	11.1%
Over $125,000	48	50.0%	10.4%
Number of large windows			
0	164	50.6%	4.3%
1–2	71	59.2%	7.0%
3–6	53	67.9%	18.9%
7+	45	62.2%	17.8%
Number of solid glass doors			
0	159	52.8%	5.7%
1–2	129	62.0%	12.4%
3+	50	58.0%	14.0%
Insurance coverage on glass breakage			
No	53	56.6%	13.2%
Yes	260	56.9%	8.5%

EXHIBIT 8   Primary demand by demographic characteristics

	N	% Indicating they probably or definitely would purchase product type	% Indicating they definitely would purchase product type
Education			
Non-college graduate	187	60.0%	13.4%
College graduate	155	54.2%	5.2%
Age			
Under 30	56	55.4%	10.7%
30–39	76	55.3%	7.9%
40–49	68	64.7%	10.3%
50–59	71	54.9%	8.5%
60–70	51	56.9%	9.8%
Over 70	25	52.0%	12.0%
Total family income			
Under $15,000	46	58.7%	10.8%
$15,000–$25,000	67	53.4%	9.0%
$25,000–$35,000	84	59.5%	9.5%
$35,000–$50,000	73	57.5%	11.0%
Over $50,000	55	58.2%	9.1%
Professional	72	62.5%	6.9%
Other white collar	122	50.8%	7.4%
Blue collar	55	56.4%	14.5%
Others	87	62.1%	12.6%

EXHIBIT 9   Selective demand for Hurcu-Link by market area

Market area	N	% Indicating they probably or definitely would purchase Hurcu-Link	% Indicating they definitely would purchase Hurcu-Link
Corpus Christi, TX	60	54.6%	3.6%
Galveston, TX	12	38.5%	7.7%
Beaumont, TX	28	34.5%	0.0%
New Orleans, LA	49	33.4%	4.2%
Mobile, AL	44	33.3%	0.0%
Miami, FL	72	39.7%	2.9%
Hollywood, FL	23	43.5%	4.4%
Ft. Lauderdale, FL	35	25.7%	0.0%
W. Palm Beach, FL	17	52.9%	5.9%
Daytona Beach, FL	8	42.9%	0.0%
	338	39.4%	2.7%

EXHIBIT 10   Selective demand for Hurcu-Link by previous hurricane experience

Previously been in or had property damage from a hurricane	N	% Indicating they probably or definitely would purchase Hurcu-Link	% Indicating they definitely would purchase Hurcu-Link
No	81	43.2%	1.2%
Yes	257	38.1%	3.1%
Previously had glass breakage from a hurricane			
No	205	38.0%	2.9%
Yes	50	38.0%	4.0%

EXHIBIT 11 Selective demand for Hurcu-Link by house characteristics

Value of home	N	% Indicating they probably or definitely would purchase Hurcu-Link	% Indicating they definitely would purchase Hurcu-Link
Under $40,000	26	50.0%	2.0%
$40,000–60,000	77	41.6%	2.6%
$60,000–80,000	71	43.7%	2.8%
$80,000–100,000	63	28.6%	0%
$100,000–125,000	46	41.3%	2.2%
Over $125,000	46	41.3%	6.5%
Number of large windows			
0	158	38.0%	0.6%
1–2	69	40.6%	2.9%
3–6	51	49.0%	5.9%
7+	45	35.6%	6.7%
Number of solid glass doors			
0	159	39.0%	2.5%
1–2	121	37.2%	2.5%
3+	50	50.0%	4.0%
Insurance coverage on glass breakage			
No	52	38.5%	3.8%
Yes	255	39.2%	2.4%

EXHIBIT 12 Selective demand for Hurcu-Link by demographic characteristics

	N	% Indicating they probably or definitely would purchase Hurcu-Link	% Indicating they definitely would purchase Hurcu-Link
Education			
Non-college graduate	182	39.0%	3.3%
College graduate	150	40.0%	2.0%
Age			
Under 30	55	45.5%	.3%
30–39	76	40.8%	5.3%
40–49	66	39.4%	3.0%
50–59	70	34.3%	0%
60–70	47	40.4%	4.3%
Over 70	22	36.4%	0%
Total family income			
Under $15,000	44	43.2%	2.3%
$15,000–$25,000	65	40.0%	1.5%
$25,000–$35,000	78	43.6%	2.6%
$35,000–$50,000	78	35.9%	2.6%
Over $50,000	51	39.2%	5.9%
Occupation			
Professional	71	46.5%	1.4%
Other white collar	121	35.5%	3.3%
Blue collar	54	37.0%	5.6%
Others	82	42.6%	1.3%

EXHIBIT 13   Demand for Hurcu-Link at various price levels

Price	N	*Likelihood of purchase*			
		Definitely Not	*Probably Not*	*Probably Would*	*Definitely Would*
$100	271	81.2%	15.1%	3.3%	.4%
$75	262	74.8%	23.0%	2.3%	0%
$50	269	56.1%	33.5%	9.3%	1%
$25	276	28.6%	31.9%	34.4%	5%
$10	273	16.9%	17.0%	37.4%	28.9%
$5	267	15.7%	12.7%	28.5%	43.0%

General Telephone Company of the Southwest

R. Rex Bailey, Vice President of Marketing and Customer Service for General Telephone Company of the Southwest (GTSW), is making some key decisions that will have long-range consequences for his company. As he reflects on the dramatic changes that have occurred in the telecommunications industry over the past few years and ponders the impact of deregulation and continued improvement in technology on the industry, he is giving much thought to the direction GTSW should take in the future. Of immediate concern to him is whether GTSW should continue to lease telephones to its customers or, instead, emphasize direct sales. He will also need to formulate some general marketing strategies for whatever approach he chooses.

This case was prepared by Stephen W. McDaniel, Assistant Professor of Marketing at Texas A&M University, with the assistance of Michael J. May as a basis for class discussion rather than to illustrate either effective or ineffective marketing management.

THE TELECOMMUNICATIONS INDUSTRY

In late 1981 one of the most widely recognized business analysts predicted that the next five years would be the most dynamic and profitable period in the history of the telecommunications industry. However, he also predicted that the only telephone companies to survive would be those that were truly marketing-oriented.

> You can't do anything in a company run by an "engineering" or "operations" mentality. Too many telephone companies still do things because it suits *them*— *not* because it suits their customers. Too many engineers and operations personnel are afraid of successful marketing. They feel that if the sales types actually do succeed in getting the customer to buy more phones, more custom calling features, more terminal equipment, all this extra demand will create an intolerable burden on the engineers and their comfortable life style.[1]

A combination of factors will make the 1980s a very lucrative but very competitive marketplace for telephone companies in the United States: (1) Practical applications of the microprocessor and other innovative devices will lead to a tremendous proliferation of technology; (2) As the government continues to ease regulatory restraints of the telephone industry, more companies will enter the field; (3) Many changes will occur in the marketplace. For example, the telephone is predicted to become the major marketing tool of American business. As these changes take place, and as competition heats up, the companies to survive will be those with the best marketing strategies.

In the past there has been very little competition in the telecommunications industry. The Public Utilities Commission (PUC) has regulated all telephone company activities, including rate increases and equipment. In return, the telephone companies have had a monopoly on telephone service in their geographic areas. As deregulation occurs, however, and more companies are allowed to compete for equipment and services, the industry will naturally become less monopolistic and more competitive. The primary competition facing GTSW is Southwestern Bell Telephone Company (a subsidiary of giant AT&T) and Central Telephone Company.

Southwestern Bell Telephone Company

Southwestern Bell offers lease arrangements and decorator phones similar to GTSW. However, Southwestern Bell's monthly lease prices are somewhat more expensive, as shown in Exhibit 1.

Southwestern Bell has recently begun selling decorator phones directly through its Phone Center Stores and encouraging customers to buy their telephones. The monthly access-to-line charge is lower if customers provide their own telephone, and the company offers brochures explaining how to connect a telephone.

---

[1]Newton, Harry, "To Sink or to Swim—Your Choice As a Telephone Company," *Telephone Engineer and Management,* July 15, 1981, pp. 84–88.

EXHIBIT 1   Comparison of similar models

Southwestern Bell		GTSW	
Model	*Lease price/month*	*Model*	*Lease price/month*
Trimline	$3.60	Styleline	$2.60
Princess	$3.40	Compact	$2.57
Standard	$1.80	Fashion Plate	$1.50

These figures are based on monthly costs for touch call (GTSW) and push button (Southwestern Bell) models. The costs may vary by area and choice of rotary dial. These costs do not include wall mount outlet plates or hookup.

Central Telephone Company

Central Telephone & Utilities (Centel) has competed aggressively in the residential direct sales market since February, 1979. Centel makes phones available through its Pick-a-Phone Centers, opened in 1977 as service and repair centers and later evolving into telephone sales outlets. In 1980 Centel sold an estimated 114,000 instruments.

Comparative financial data for some of the telecommunications companies are given in Exhibit 2.

EXHIBIT 2   Comparative company financial analysis

Gross revenues (million 1967$)

Company	1977	1978	1979	1980
Bell System				
American Telephone & Telegraph	281	315	349	390
Cincinnati Bell	281	320	348	370
Pacific Tel. & Tel.	262	291	322	374
Southern New England Tel.	265	312	340	381
	1089	1238	1359	1515
Independent Telephone Companies				
Central Telephone & Utilities (Centel)	328	440	508	605
Continental	377	457	568	634
General Telephone	291	330	378	377

Net Income (million 1967$)

Company	1977	1978	1979	1980
Bell System				
American Telephone & Telegraph	222	257	277	297
Cincinnati Bell	267	328	332	289
Pacific Tel. & Tel.	248	208	217	231
Southern New England Tel.	208	278	254	280
	945	1071	1080	1097

EXHIBIT 2 (continued)

Gross revenues (million 1967$)

Company	1977	1978	1979	1980
Independent Telephone Companies				
Central Telephone & Utilities (Centel)	333	393	450	492
Continental	336	430	533	542
General Telephone	255	286	317	380

Net Income (As a % of Revenues)

Company	1977	1978	1979	1980
Bell System				
American Telephone & Telegraph	12.5	12.9	12.5	12.0
Cincinnati Bell	13.9	15.0	14.0	11.4
Pacific Tel. & Tel.	9.9	7.6	7.1	6.5
Southern New England Tel.	10.1	11.4	9.6	9.4
Independent Telephone Companies				
Central Telephone & Utilities (Centel)	13.0	11.4	11.3	10.3
Continental	10.1	10.1	10.7	9.7
General Telephone	11.1	11.9	7.0	6.1

Return on equity (%)

Company	1977	1978	1979
Bell System			
American Telephone & Telegraph	12.3	13.1	13.0
Cincinnati Bell	15.4	17.0	15.2
Pacific Tel. & Tel.	11.0	8.8	8.6
Southern New England Tel.	10.3	13.1	10.8
Independent Telephone Companies			
Central Telephone & Utilities (Centel)	16.6	17.0	
Continental	13.0	14.4	14.6
General Telephone	14.7	15.3	15.1

Debt/equity ratio (%)

Company	1977	1978	1979
Bell System			
American Telephone & Telegraph	38.3	37.7	37.1
Cincinnati Bell	34.6	31.7	29.0
Pacific Tel. & Tel.	39.3	47.2	49.7
Southern New England Tel.	38.8	34.3	31.1
Independent Telephone Companies			
Central Telephone & Utilities (Centel)	47.6	45.8	43.9
Continental	51.3	48.8	49.0
General Telephone	47.0	46.3	45.8

GTSW OPERATIONS

The Company

GTSW is a subsidiary of General Telephone & Electronics Corporation (GTE). GTSW was incorporated in 1926 as State Telephone Company of Texas. In 1931 the name was changed to Southwestern Associated Telephone Company, and the present name was adopted in April, 1952. From its original base in Texas, the company has since expanded into Oklahoma, Arkansas, and New Mexico. As indicated in Exhibit 3, GTSW has 399 exchanges and 1,693,404 telephones in this four-state area. GTSW provides both local and long distance telephone service to an estimated two and one-half million people. The long distance service is provided by toll lines owned and operated by GTSW and through interconnections with the lines of the Bell Telephone Companies. (See Exhibit 4 for GTSW Balance Sheets and Income Statements).

Organization

The company's organizational chart is shown in Exhibit 5. R. Rex Bailey, Vice President of Marketing and Customer Service, reports directly to E. L. Langley, President. Reporting to Mr. Bailey are the five regional general managers, as well as the V.P.-Service, V.P.-Marketing, and Supply & Transportation Director. The Oklahoma regional general manager has three district managers reporting to him. The other four regional general managers each have an area operations manager who then supervises either five or six division managers.

Product Line and Pricing

In accordance with prices regulated by the Public Utility Commission, GTSW leases all residential instruments. The exceptions to this are the decorator type telephones, which are not leased but for sale only by Phone Marts, or telephones purchased from retail outlets (e.g., K-Mart, Radio Shack). Telephones are leased for a monthly charge and are available in several different styles, as shown in Exhibit 6.

The lease product line consists of (1) the regular desk phone (Fashion Plate) in five different colors, (2) the Compact phone in six wall model colors and five desk model colors, and (3) the Styleline or dial-in-hand set available in fifteen different colors. The prices currently being considered for these instruments are shown with the current monthly lease rates in Exhibit 7.

The prices currently being considered for decorator direct sale telephones are also shown in Exhibit 7. These include Snoopy and Woodstock, Mickey Mouse, the Candlestick Phone, Flip Phone II, Solitare I & II, Empress Deluxe, Circlephone, Cradle Phone, Coin Phone, and Chest Phone.

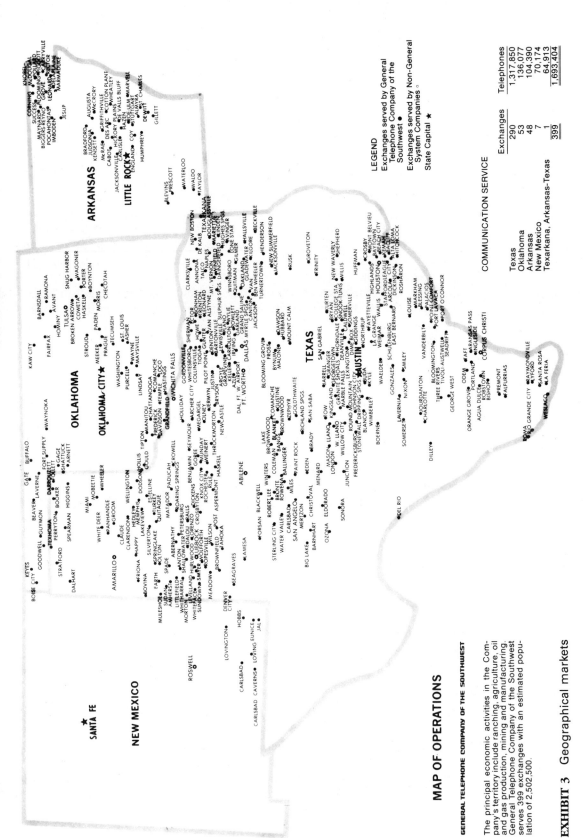

MAP OF OPERATIONS

GENERAL TELEPHONE COMPANY OF THE SOUTHWEST

The principal economic activities in the Company's territory include ranching, agriculture, oil and gas production, mining and manufacturing. General Telephone Company of the Southwest serves 399 exchanges with an estimated population of 2,502,500.

EXHIBIT 3 Geographical markets

LEGEND

Exchanges served by General Telephone Company of the Southwest ●

Exchanges served by Non-General System Companies ○

State Capital ★

COMMUNICATION SERVICE

	Exchanges	Telephones
Texas	290	1,317,850
Oklahoma	53	136,077
Arkansas	48	104,390
New Mexico	7	70,174
Texarkana, Arkansas-Texas	1	64,913
	399	1,693,404

EXHIBIT 4 General Telephone Company of the Southwest, balance sheets

		December 31,	
Assets	1980	1979	1978
		(Thousands of dollars)	
TELEPHONE PLANT			
Original Cost	$1,728,280.	$1,509,636.	$1,304,714.
Accumulated depreciation	(362,252.)	(308,026.)	(271.225.)
	$1,366,028.	$1,201,610.	$1,033,489.
INVESTMENTS AND OTHER ASSETS, AT COST	$ 773.	$ 2,295.	$ 2,280.
CURRENT ASSETS,			
Cash	$ 2,357.	$ 3,474.	$ 3,330.
Receivables	59,968.	42,141.	39,778.
Materials & supplies, at average cost	18,205.	17,614.	10,701.
Prepayments and other	10,529.	1,704.	2,013.
Total Current Assets	$ 91,059.	$ 64,933.	$ 55,822.
OTHER ASSETS	$ 5,284.	$ 5,142.	$ 3,605.
TOTAL ASSETS	$1,463,144.	$1,273,980.	$1,095,196.

		December 31,	
Shareholders' Equity and Liabilities	1980	1979	1978
		(Thousands of dollars)	
SHAREHOLDERS' EQUITY			
Common Stock	$ 330,000.	$ 280,000.	$ 250,000.
Preferred Stock	7,600.	7,600.	7,600.
Reinvested earnings	130,171.	112,049.	99,264.
Other capital	296.	247.	307.
Total Shareholders' equity	$ 468,067.	$ 399,896.	$ 357,171.
PREFERRED STOCK — SUBJECT TO MANDATORY REDEMPTION	$ 70,650.	$ 72,618.	$ 48,938.
LONG TERM DEBT	$ 583,924.	$ 493,086.	$ 428,140.
CURRENT LIABILITIES			
Loans for construction	$ 17,800.	$ 47,885.	$ 53,494.
Current maturities	2,605.	8,699.	2,584.
Accounts payable	23,152.	11,314.	11,211.
Due to affiliated companies	18,690.	20,305.	20,121.
Advanced billings	13,888.	12,038.	10,251.
Accrued taxes	20,090.	9,205.	10,070.
Accrued interest	11,412.	8,731.	6,216.
Accrued dividends	12,249.	10,114.	7,203.

EXHIBIT 4   (continued)

	1980	1979	1978
Accrued vacation	9,134.	7,047.	5,018.
Other	6,988.	4,536.	3,231.
Total current liabilities	$ 136,008.	$ 139,874.	$ 129,399.
DEFERRED CREDITS			
Deferred income taxes	$ 126,145.	$ 103,523.	$ 82,063.
Deferred investment tax	77,301.	64,298.	48,608.
Other	1,049.	685.	877.
	$ 204,495.	$ 168,506.	$ 131,548.

COMMITMENTS

	1980	1979	1978
TOTAL SHAREHOLDERS' EQUITY AND LIABILITIES	$1,463,144.	$1,273,980.	$1,095,196.

Income statement

	Year Ended December 31,		
	1980	1979	1978
	(Thousands of dollars)		
OPERATING REVENUES			
Toll Service	$ 308,110.	$ 221,557.	$ 180,777.
Local Service	210,176.	185,136.	168,258.
Miscellaneous	12,348.	11,085.	10,030.
Provision for uncollectible accts:	(7,251.)	(4,380.)	(3,415.)
Total Operating Revenues:	$ 523,383.	$ 413,398.	$ 355,650.
OPERATING EXPENSES AND TAXES			
Maintenance	$ 113,593.	$ 86,681.	$ 73,384.
Depreciation and amortization	98,362.	75,207.	65,235.
Traffic	26,279.	22,752.	18,348.
Commercial	33,223.	27,327.	22,590.
General office salaries & expenses	35,175.	26,918.	23,652.
Other operating expenses	29,917.	25,304.	20,372.
General taxes	32,991.	29,262.	25,787.
Income taxes	38,756.	26,458.	27,688.
Total Operating Expenses and Taxes:	$ 408,796.	$ 319,909.	$ 277,056.
NET OPERATING INCOME:	$ 114,587.	$ 93,489.	$ 78,597.
MISCELLANEOUS INCOME — Net			
Allowance for funds used during construction	$ 1,381.	$ 2,460.	$ 3,307.
Other income (expense) — Net	1,096.	120.	(279.)
Total Miscellaneous Income — Net	$ 2,477.	$ 2,580.	$ 3,028.
Income Available For Interest Charges:	$ 117,064.	$ 96,069.	$ 81,625.

EXHIBIT 4 (continued)

INTEREST CHARGES			
Interest on long term debt	$ 43,766.	$ 34,356.	$ 32,015.
Other interest charges	9,343.	9,522.	3,766.
Amortization of debt expenses	258.	223.	216.
Total Interest Charges:	$ 53,367.	$ 44,101.	$ 35,997.
NET INCOME:	$ 63,697.	$ 51,968.	$ 45,628.

Advertising

GTSW uses primarily print advertising; these advertisements appear regularly in the *Wall Street Journal* and in local newspapers. Some television advertising is used to enable customers to see product lines and to show trends in the telecommunications industry. The primary objective of GTSW advertising is to make the customer aware of local services and products. These include custom calling features like call waiting, call forwarding, and speed calling. The advertising also informs customers of the complete product line of telephones and accessories available to them at their local Phone Mart. With the proposed direct sale plan, GTSW will still emphasize print media advertising promotion. Advertising will focus primarily on consumer awareness of the concept of direct sale.

Channels of Distribution

GTSW contracts for its telephones from GTE Automatic Electric (AE); they are shipped directly from AE to each division's supply warehouse. Phone Marts in each division call the divisional supply director regularly, except during heavy periods, to request the telephones needed to complete their inventory. The telephones are transported by truck from the supply warehouse to the Phone Marts, a method of distribution which will not change under the direct sale proposal.

Customer Service

Under the current system of customer service, all lease telephones are repaired at no charge to the customer. If the lease instrument cannot be repaired by the repairman, installer, or Phone Mart personnel, it is replaced at no charge. Decorator telephones are repaired at no charge for thirty days following the purchase date. However, after the thirty-day warranty period expires, the decorator instrument must be sent to Automatic Electric (which gives a one-year warranty on the instrument). The Phone Mart furnishes a shipping container, packing material and the address where the package should be mailed. After the one-year free repair warranty from Automatic Electric expires, there is a charge for repairing the instrument.

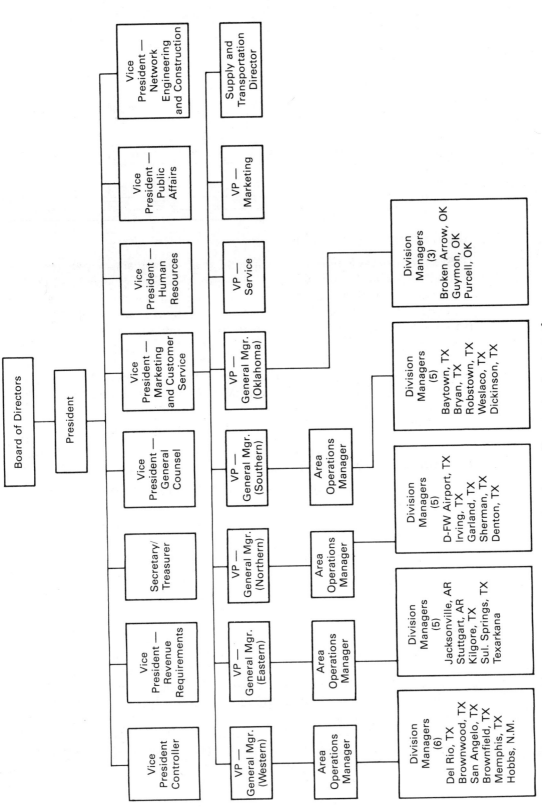

EXHIBIT 5 General Telephone Company of the Southwest (Corporate structure effective August, 1981)

**COMPACT
DESK**
TELEPHONE
Price $59.95
Lease 2.75/mo.

STYLELINE
TELEPHONE

Price $74.95
Lease 2.60/mo.

**FASHION
PLATE**
TELEPHONE
Price $34.95
Lease 1.10/mo.

EXHIBIT 6   Product line — standard models

Under the proposed direct sale plan, GTSW will offer a ninety-day warranty and repair the telephones free during this period. Also, if the instrument fails in the first thirty days, the Phone Mart will replace it free. Automatic Electric will continue its one-year warranty even though the ninety day warranty may have expired from GTSW. The Phone Mart will again furnish a shipping container, packing material and the address to ship the instrument to Automatic Electric.

Market Research

In the first half of 1981, Mr. Bailey decided to conduct two different market research studies to get some idea of the market's acceptance of direct sale of telephones. The first study was an Ownership/Lease study of customer awareness, attitudes, and potential actions towards purchase and/or lease of telephones. It sought information pertinent to GTSW's marketing effort and attempted to prepare the company for changes brought about by competi-

**THE
SNOOPY &
WOODSTOCK**
TELEPHONE

Price $129.95

**MICKEY
MOUSE**
TELEPHONE

Price $129.95

America's Sweetheart
**The
Candlestick
Phone**

Price $89.95

FLIP PHONE II

Price $54.95

SOLITARE I
TELEPHONE

Price $17.95

SOLITARE II
TELEPHONE

Price $34.95

**EMPRESS
DELUXE**

Price $129.95

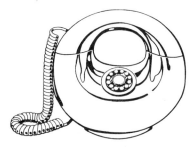

CIRCLPHONE

Price $99.95

EXHIBIT 7   Product line — decorator models

tive activity. Findings showed that 43.6 percent of respondents in non-metro areas would prefer to lease telephones, 36.7 percent would rather own their telephone, and 15.6 percent would like to do both. For the metro areas, the data revealed that 55.9 percent would rather own their telephones, 28.1 percent would rather lease, and 12.2 percent would like both.

The second study was a Past Performance study that involved a telephone survey of a random sample of GTSW customers. The purpose was to measure customer preference for lease or purchase, based on actual customer experience. Of the total non-metro area respondents, 27.5 percent had purchased telephones, 17.7 percent had purchased more than one instrument, and an average of 12 percent had gone outside the telephone company to purchase telephones. However, for the metro area sample, 38.8 percent had purchased their telephones and 23.6 percent of these had purchased more than one instrument. Of those individuals who had purchased a telephone, 67.5 percent bought it from a phone store, not a general retail outlet.

Rex Bailey must now make some critical marketing decisions based on these data. Should GTSW continue leasing telephones to its customers or begin emphasizing direct sale? What are some general marketing strategies for the approach he chooses?

Bank of America

In early 1975, the Marketing Research Department at Bank of America was requested by the California Division to do an exploratory focus group research project on the "women's market." The California Division was responsible for serving consumers and commercial customers through a 1000-branch network spanning the state. It was in the process of developing a new advertising campaign to communicate that Bank of America provides "equal credit to all." The focus group project was designed to provide information helpful in the development of the advertising campaign.

The specific objectives of the focus group research project were defined as:

1. To explore women's expectations with respect to banks and their satisfaction with the types of services offered.

2. To investigate women's perceptions of the banks' attitudes toward female patrons—both general and specific to Bank of America—as perceived through personal contacts and media communications.

3. To explore the degree to which different groups of women feel that they have/have not been given equal and fair treatments by banking institutions.

4. To determine whether any real or assumed inequalities in the treatment of women customers are perceived as justified or resented as unfair.

5. To study specific responses to a series of advertising messages, including three story boards for Bank of America, two of which were specifically addressed to women (shown in Exhibits 2 and 3).

Prepared by Ranie Bangalore and Professor Adrian B. Ryans, Stanford University Graduate School of Business. Reprinted from *Stanford Business Cases 1980* with permission of the publishers, Stanford University Graduate School of Business, © 1980 by the Board of Trustees of the Leland Stanford Junior University.

A decision was made to use ten focus groups each with about ten participants. Nine of the groups were all-female and one was all-male. A profile of the *total* sample used is presented in Exhibit 1. Half of the group meetings were conducted in the Los Angeles area and the other half were conducted in San Francisco. One of the San Francisco groups was composed of business and professional women aged between 25 and 39. Excerpts transcribed from a recording of this group's discussion start on page 52.

Assignment

1. *Before* reading the focus group discussion, put yourself in the place of the moderator. How would you plan to structure the discussion to obtain the required information?

2. Read the transcript. What did you learn that was relevant to Bank of America's objectives?

3. On the basis of the excerpts from this one tape, do you feel this exploratory research will be useful to Bank of America?

EXHIBIT 1 Profile of the ten focus groups

Sex of participants		*Households with children under 18 years**	
Female	86	Yes	42%
Male	10	No	58%
Total	96		
		*Education of participant**	
*Marital status of women**		High School	27%
Married	53%	Some College	45%
Single	47%	College Graduates	10%
		N.A.	3%
*Ages of women**			
21 - 24	4%	*Household income**	
25 - 34	29%	Less than $10,000	12%
35 - 44	29%	$10,000 - $14,000	23%
45 - 54	21%	$15,000 - $19,000	35%
55 - 64	11%	$20,000 and over	29%
65 and over	6%	N.A.	1%
*Holders of bank charge cards**		*Patronage of Bank of America*	
Bank Americard	23%	Checking Accounts	31%
Master Charge	39%	Savings Accounts	16%
Both	13%	Checking and Savings	14%
None	25%	Installment Credit (no other acct.)	6%
		Not a patron	33%

*Based on sample of 86 women only.

TRANSCRIPT

Moderator: I think the first thing I'd like to do before we do anything is a relaxation exercise. Unwind a little bit. I like to do some deep breathing. You don't have to do that, but I'd like you to close your eyes for a minute and get in touch with how you feel, whether you are tired, hurried, or whatever it is . . . all unwind. Would you believe my eyes stay shut. (Laughter) Anybody here who would like a sandwich?

Unidentified woman: No, not right now, thank you.

Moderator: Anyway, you can leave your eyes closed a little longer. I need to. What I would like to do is go around and try to get in touch with how we feel after work especially. You know you are in another world and you forget that you are a person and you have a body. I'll start. I'm a little tired tonight and very excited about a number of things. I just bought a new raincoat—I haven't gotten over the excitement yet, because I've been looking for one. I live in L.A. and I couldn't find one there. I'm looking forward to this group tonight. I've been doing these groups with different types of women and this intrigues me because you're all women in responsible positions.

(Women spend about 3 minutes introducing themselves and saying a few things about how they feel.)

Moderator: Now the subject tonight is "Women and Money Management" and their contacts with banks—just the place of women in relation to money. The money you make. I don't know if any of you are married. I'm sure some are, some aren't, or were married—but that kind of relationship comes into it. Just women in relation to money and their place in their society. And we might start with someting very mundane—your relationship to your bank, just because it's a starting point. What kind of contacts do you have with your bank? How satisfactory are they to you?

Sandy I: As often as possible by mail only. A stamp does a lot for me. I really resent standing in line when I get into a bank and having to wait to do any sort of business. I just heard that Wells Fargo was going to be opening banking hours from 8:30 to 4:30 starting March 10 which is an incentive for me to switch over because those hours are certainly more agreeable than 10 to 3, which is very limited.

Moderator: How do you feel about the change of hours?

Unidentified woman: I think it'll be good.

Crystal: What I would like to see is evening hours. I was in Oklahoma or someplace like that. I think it was Tulsa—no, Oklahoma City—and they had an all-night bank.

Unidentified woman: Twenty-four hours?

Crystal: Yes, I thought that was just terrific.

Kathy: Does the Bank of America at Market open all night?

Crystal: I think there is one on Market, near Woolworth's, and I think they are open later, but they have limited services after 7 o'clock.

Unidentified woman: The one that's getting robbed all the time? (Laughter)

Kathy: I'm happy with the bank I bank with. The Bank of America. The reason is that I always go there, so I've gotten to know everyone there. . . .

Moderator: Anybody else have that kind of personal relationship with their bank?

Sandy I: Yes, I go twice a week and that helps me personally. Anything I need personally, I'm halfway there already.

Unidentified woman: Are we talking of relationship to business or to our own personal needs?

Moderator: Both. You know, whatever contacts you have are your contacts, of course—your personal needs. You work for your company, but that in a way facilitates . . . whatever.

Sandy II: I have the same kind of situation. I supervise payroll for a university and we do our computerizing with Wells Fargo. We changed over from Bank of America. So being in the capacity that I am, I can just walk in and I know many officers and I get very good service.

Moderator: Yes, Nancy.

Nancy: Well I had a hassle with Wells Fargo and switched over to a new bank in my building.

Moderator: Tell me about your hassle and about this new bank that just opened.

Nancy: Okay, well . . . Wells Fargo—I had the Gold Account—free checking . . . Mastercharge. . . . A $250 charge was made to me with no receipt except for this little pink slip saying that they'd give me the receipt once they found it. When they finally found it, it had had my number penciled in and I called them in December and I finally got a letter a week ago . . . they weren't very helpful. It really made me feel very bad. . . . There is a service charge every month for the Gold Account and I had to pay that every month . . . so I chopped up the card into little pieces and gave it back to them. (Laughter)

Moderator: Do you feel they were dealing with you like you had made a mistake rather than they?

Nancy: Yeah. I felt, you know, I was naturally rather worried about the money, because $250 is a lot of money to just throw out of the window and they were defensive like it was my mistake and they knew that I had done the charging. I felt very, very nervous about it until I actually had the letter in my hands . . . that it was taken care of. When Lloyd's opened up there was some sort of a rumor going around saying that they had free accounts. So I went down there and they said we have to approve your credit and I found out that three other people in the department didn't have to have their credit approved and I asked the manager, "Why me?"

Unidentified woman: What did he say?

Nancy: Well, he said that they hadn't really established their policies yet and they had a lot of new employees and they didn't know exactly why or who had said this but he would look into it and, you know, I kept going from one person to another, up higher, and I finally got the top manager. I talked to him so now I know all the people over there. (Laughter)

Sandy II: Were the other people men or women who had not had their credit approved?

Nancy: Men.

Sandy II: Well that's the answer right there!

Nancy: Except that there was one woman that had been working for the company for seven years and was married and her husband. . . . She got credit because he had an account there. (Laughter) I notice that particular discrepancy there. They kept trying to tell me—well, I had been employed there for a little over a year, but one of the people who had gotten a free account had only worked there six months!

Another woman: It's not a discrepancy—it is discrimination.

Kathy: You know, I found the reverse though. When I first moved here and I wasn't married and I wanted to get an automobile and I had only been at my job just a few months, and I went to Hibernia, Sunset Branch, and I talked to Mr. Smith. Do you know, I bought my automobile and I paid what amounted to $4,000 and I was divorced and had three minor children. I thought he was wonderful when he said that he would take a chance. He thought that I was sincere. Now, see, there's the reverse. This was before anyone ever spoke about being unfair to women.

Moderator: Do you think that was a unique experience because of this man?

Kathy: Yes, because I went back again and he did the same thing; but then I was so happy that I opened up a savings account there. I have sent other women there and he did the same thing. So I just think that maybe he had a little more faith in people in general. A lot of them don't.

Sandy II: Had you filled out the papers before he was so nice to you? Or was he nice to you before he got you to fill them out.

Kathy: He was nice. He talked to me for a while; we talked about the family and such, and he had said to me that he felt that he was a good judge of character. You know, I don't know what he meant by that, but then I thought it wasn't a very extensive . . . and I didn't even have a relative in the city—no one. I knew no one here. Everyone was back East and he didn't say, ''Well, I'll have to write.'' He had the check ready for me in a half-hour.

All: Oh wow! (Laughter) Where is that?

Kathy: And he was an older gentleman. It was not that, you know, that I wondered what he means by that. Nothing at all. I have spoken to other people about him. . . .

Sandy II: There is a sixth sense which the credit people get, because they can feel vibrations.

Kathy: Yes, I think so.

Crystal: I think a great deal depends upon the bank, too. I've been into a lot of banks and have had many, many different experiences. I find some of the banks, that are not as well-known as Bank of America, are much better to deal with—like the Security Pacific and the Chartered Bank of London. I've had very good experience with the two. The most traumatic experience is in attempting to get loans because of this SBA hangup, being a minority, more so than being a woman. Regardless of what your credit standing is, what it is you want or how much, they have this hang-up that all you really need is two bank refusals and then you can get a direct SBA loan. That's what it's there for and they've got a lot of money. "All you have to do is get our nice little refusal and we'll give you a pretty letter and you can trot yourself right on over to the SBA."

Unidentified woman: What is the SBA?

Crystal: Small Business Administration.

Woman: Oh.

Crystal: Now, we know that there is a limit for direct loans from the SBA of $25,000. Any amount over that, you must find your own financing and then seek the ninety percent guarantee. . . . Actually, this is the kind of a discriminatory thing from the standpoint that the banks get a hundred and ten percent guarantee on any money that they loan to minorities—if they lend it in the first place. And so I find that that is probably the most traumatic experience in dealing with the banks, from the standpoint of loans. They have two or three different standards for lending. But again, I have found my most satisfactory experiences have been with the banks that I mentioned, and those experiences have come about from real hassles with them. That's where you get to know your banker. (Laughter) Otherwise, you can have very large, pleasant bank accounts or checking accounts and so forth—no one ever knows you. And frequently, if you are out of town and you want to cash a personal check or do some bank transfers and so forth, they say, who is your banker? So I have found that it is very important to negotiate with them on some basis where you get to know somebody in the bank who you can deal directly with since he knows you.

(Discusses experiences with Crocker Bank and perceptions of Bank of America.)

Crystal: That wasn't the only problem I've had with Crocker Bank.

Moderator: You've never actually banked with Bank of America?

Crystal: Oh yes, I have been right up there on the 40th floor hassling with those people. Oh yes, I've had a lot of dealings with the Bank of America. You name it.

Judy: I've found them to be very helpful except for the time that I first moved out here and being a female and under 25, I had a lot of problems with them; they didn't want to give me a BankAmericard and I had no credit established and I really needed to borrow some money right away and I wanted to get a car. But since then they've been very helpful to me.

Moderator: What did you do at the time? Did you go somewhere else?

Judy: I had to borrow money from two friends that I have here who I barely knew. I didn't feel comfortable doing that, but I had to.

Moderator: But you've had an account with that particular bank?

Judy: Uh huh.

Sandy I: Again, I'm very happy with the Bank of America, or the particular branch that I go to. I see the same person everytime. It's a brand new branch and it has nice soft chairs. (Laughter) 'Cause I do go alot and I'm usually there for awhile. But again, I had the same time with credit when I first came into the country.

Moderator: Yeah, and you could not provide good credit references?

Sandy I: No, no. You couldn't buy just anywhere—not even at a store if you didn't have it. If you didn't have money, you couldn't borrow it. Uh huh. You'd find one tiny little shop. And when you'd got credit there then you could go back to all the others. You know, it's ridiculous.

Kathy: The reason why I was a little luckier was because my first job here was running a credit department in a small company collecting their delinquent accounts. (Laughter) I just loved it because I used a whole new approach with people and I was real successful. So, when I went out for charge accounts and I was turned down by one, then I went to Montgomery Wards. I talked to the woman in their credit department, got friendly, and they were the first people—I'd only been here two months—to give me a charge account. And from then its simple. All you do is mention one. Maybe it was the line of work I was in—I don't know.

Moderator: Were you working Sandy when you were. . .?

Sandy I: Yes, I was fine.

Moderator: Yeah, you had a job but you couldn't get any bank credit?

Sandy I: No.

Moderator: Did you try? Did you talk to anybody?

Sandy I: No, I really didn't need a bank loan as much as I wanted the store's credit.

Kathy: I found out the best thing was to go in person and, if it didn't work out, tell them to put you on trial for a couple of months and to allow—I think at first that I could only charge up to $50 for the first six months. I went down personally because they refused over the telephone. I thought that maybe a personal approach . . . And it worked!

Unidentified woman: If you've got an account at a bank—at least a few years ago—every bank would send you a MasterCharge or a BankAmericard.

They didn't even care if you wanted one. So all you had to do. . . . You could have an account at five different banks, you could get five different cards, and you could go to town. I mean, in the mail—unsolicited—you got them.

Unidentified woman: Not consistent.

Nancy: Another thing that bothered me about Wells Fargo credit cards. They started sending me instant money checks. For taxes and things, they would sit in a mail box just out in the street . . . you could open it up and take them out. Somebody else could have used them. It's like having five credit cards just sitting there in your mail box saying, "Here take me and sign me." I kept getting these things in the mail.

Sandy I: You could have used these to pay your $250, you know? (Laughter)

Nancy: They never explained to me how that happened. They just said, "Oh, mistakes will happen."

Unidentified woman: Did you ever put anything in writing, just out of curiosity, when that first happened? I mean, in your first phone call to the bank did you find out who you talked to and did you put it in writing?

Nancy: No, I didn't. I should have. I thought it would just be taken care of right away, and finally they sent me the original. They didn't send me a copy. They sent me the original and I Xeroxed it and sent it to this office, because that's what they said, after about the fifth call, I would have to do.

Moderator: Jean, how about you?

Jean: Well, I had my first account at Crocker and I couldn't get anything from them other than opening an account because I was single and they couldn't write anything down on a piece of paper. So they wouldn't give me anything at all. I had a lot of trouble with them because my statements were always wrong. They were always screwing up somehow. I was very unhappy with them, so I closed out my account right away and I went to Wells Fargo and *they* gave me trouble. But then when my business switched our account over to Wells Fargo, they couldn't be nicer to me—they couldn't do more for me—free checking, free everything, "Take anything you want to take." That was only about two months ago. So now I'm not having any problems at all and that's fine if that's the way it has to be, but I've been to different banks where, because I'm single and I'm only twenty-five, they don't want to touch you, they don't want to give you loans, they don't want to give you anything —especially because you're a woman. I think they discriminate a lot.

Kathy: You were lucky. I mean, I don't really. . . .

Moderator: Carol, what has been your experience with just banks, in general.

Carol: Well, I've had contacts with only two and that's Wells Fargo and Hibernia. I'm dismayed with the former but pleased with the latter, and I'll have nothing, whatsoever, to do with Bank of America and that's because of that period of mass proliferation of credit cards. I'm rather old fashioned I think. I grew up with very old-world values and some of it took—much to my distress—but it did, and I just foresaw disaster with this broadcasting of "Credit, credit, credit." Of course, my soul would just cringe. (Laughter) I was not raised to live that way. No, no, you got money in your pocket, you may spend that money. When that money is gone, you do not spend anymore. So when I see banks behave that way, and when I see other people behave that way, I get very nervous. I mean, an institution that large cannot be personal. So I didn't—I was never interested in loans. My Wells Fargo experience was strictly a family account. The initial one out on Irving was very pleasant, but when we moved to the Mill Valley area the Wells Fargo branch there was so appalling in just plain personal rudeness. You know I'm not talking about getting loans there or any kind of financial transactions. The fact that you could bank there for four years and you couldn't even go in there and write a check for cash without them ever looking at your face, going to check the files, never remembering your name. Such an aura of hostility and hatred. (Laughter)

Unidentified woman: You are taking money out of my bank!

Carol: That's right. You have made it so difficult that I found it personally repulsive so that when it came time for me to start my own account, I found myself another bank—Hibernia.

Moderator: Is this a business account that you opened that you call your own?

Carol: Well, yeah, my own account. And I've been very pleased. If anything, they tend to the "mother-hennish" approach. So I'm almost afraid to bring a problem. (Laughter) They tell me a lot more than I really care to know. But I feel good about them, and I am recognized and treated pretty well.

Kathy: Hibernia creates kind of an "old world" sort of feeling. In fact I was in there a few minutes after it was robbed. (Laughter) I just pulled in as they pulled out.

All: Oh, no kidding!

Kathy: . . . utter confusion, but they remained calm through that, too. Only one teller had to be sent home.

Mary: Well, two of the services, I've had small hassles—some of which are my own because I'm not a fantastic bookkeeper. My feeling about banks is not as much about services, it's just more political. I think that they represent a lot of financial ripoffs that are going on in this country and I think that, like on the minority issue, they are just beginning to hire minorities. Like the one down on Golden Gate—I asked a guy who had fairly long hair (apparently a relatively new policy) and he said that the manager said that he could grow his hair down to his ass as long as he did good work. (Laughter) I see this as a change that's going along with some other social changes where banks have been very resistive and unresponsive. I think that the less money you have, the more money you pay for letting them deal with your money. And that I resent a great deal.

Moderator: Do you single out any particular bank as being good or better?

Mary: Well, I think the smaller ones have to hustle harder, and B of A is notorious.

Moderator: What do you mean by that.

Mary: I mean that its publicity is bad in alot of areas and as you mentioned, if they put their credit cards all over the world, you know, they're just making money on it. But I must admit that when my credit cards were stolen, I got very good service.

(Mary describes how credit cards were stolen and her difficulties in establishing credit.)

Moderator: Now, I think this whole group here is highly intelligent and highly confident as to how to deal with these matters, and you all do quite well. I wonder how you feel about women, in general, and what banks can do to provide services to women who are not at your level. And what's going to happen? Not everybody's going to make $20,000 a year and be in this position. But what's coming ahead and what will be the situation with the new generation?

Unidentified woman: A comment. I just put some money in a savings and loan bank on a one-year basis at 6½ percent because it was more than I could get anywhere else and I saw no reason to leave it at 4¾ percent. The lady in charge of the bank is Chinese and very pleasant, very aggressive, came right over, sat down, talked with me. . . . As I waited at a desk, a young girl came right over saying, "Yes, you want to open an account." I thought she was very poised and she was in charge of the offices of the savings and loan. Again, it's small, personal service and, I mean, I didn't care if it was a male or a female, but she certainly had her eyes wide open.

Kathy: Don't you think, though, that you've got to appear confident; regardless of being a woman or not, give the impression that you will succeed. It has to be kind of a personal thing. I think women can do it.

Crystal: I don't think we need any super standards. Just like in this matter about minorities, everybody should be considered as an individual. Now, there are many women, in fact a high percentage of women, who are sole providers just as men are, and this should be recognized. Now, whether you're a part of the feminist movement or a part of any kind of movement—I'm not part of any movement—I mean, all of them have something very good about them. I feel that the move toward dealing with people as individuals, rather than as women or men, (is good) . . . and I think one of the critical moves in this direction toward treating (people equally) is for women to be in these positions that you are talking about, like this Chinese woman who has a greater understanding of the needs of women. . . . I don't always like to look at it from the standpoint of "the needs of women" or "the needs of any special group," but here you have an individual, she might only make $400 a month, but her needs for credit are just as great as a man who makes $400 a month and has a family to support. I think that it is very critical for maybe those who are in the better positions in banks, or in businesses, or what-have-you, to be a little bit more aggressive, as Sandy says, using it in a different context.

Moderator: Now, this has to be communicated to the great majority of women who have not, at this point, achieved the security and position that this group here has. You have learned how to battle for yourselves.

Crystal: But I have found some of these women are very aggressive. (Laughter) But the people who are in the position of management or decision making, have a tendency to regard them with less favor than they do the more intelligent. . . . Sometimes, even when dealing with employees, you will find that you have aggressive, lower-scale employees who know what's happening to them but they're not particularly articulate; and so those of us who hold a better position sometimes have to articulate for them.

Moderator: But let's assume now that you are in a position at a large institution of some kind, whether it's savings and loan, a bank, or an insurance company, where you decide, "All right there is this large segment of the population . . . not fully aware of their rights." How would you communicate it to them? By saying, "Okay we will be more open to women and we will treat you all alike." That you might call, "Reverse discrimination."

Sandy II: I have one suggestion. I think that one of the problems here, basically, with managing money and things, is that in our society kids are very much treated as children until they're all the way through high school. Then all of a sudden, one fine day, they are eighteen and it's the magic age—"Here we go kids," and they don't know money. If I were in a bank what I would do is send out training programs to talk to schools, to give kids the idea that there is such a thing as budget, and you manage money, and you should start thinking about savings—explaining what credit is. There's alot of people who don't know what credit is, and they get this first bank card and they go "hog-wild." I have a friend who went just berserk. She ran up something like $3,000 on charge accounts and MasterCharge. She only made, at the time, about $600 a month. She took home, may not even $500, and that's a hell of a load to be carrying. It's just due to ignorance, and banks have always been so ferocious and frightening—I think to younger people—and it's very difficult to go in and break the ice for them. And if the banks are interested in starting to get to different groups, the one way to break the ice is, like I say, to have a speaker go to schools, explain what a bank is, what it does, what its services are and that there are differences in bank services, because some people have free checking while others get charged for it and, you know, to let people be aware. I think the (uneducated) lower-income groups, like this lady pointed out, do get ripped off because of the fact that they're not aware of different things.

(Discussion continues for 15 more minutes)

Moderator: Now let's talk a little about communication. I have a series of ads; they are all roughs, and they come from all kinds of banks. The whole idea is they are examples of types of communication. They're very rough and I don't want you to be super-critical of the format because not all of them are good, but each one has a somewhat different type of message. In viewing these ads, I want you to react to them pretty much on a gut level rather than an intellectual level. How you feel in reading it and what reactions you get. One may be of utter boredom—"It tells me absolutely nothing. . .," you know, but whatever your reaction is, I'd like you to jot it down on a piece of paper there and then we will have an opportunity for discussion. . . . Probably communication is one way of getting across certain ideas. Now, this is the first rough ad that I'm going to show you. It has a headline that says, "Depend on Us. More Californians Do."[1] Then this man says, "I Got My BankAmericard (could be any charge really) Right Along with My Checking Plan—Talk about Convenience." And then there is a lady saying, "I Never Knew Getting a Car Loan Could be so Quick and Simple," and a man saying, "The Payments We Agreed on For My Home-Improvement Loan Fit into My Budget." Whatever your reaction is, just write down one or two words. I'll have fun reading them later. . . . By the way, would anybody like some more coffee. There is more coffee in the pot.

Unidentified woman: Oh I'd love some.

Moderator: And you would like a sandwich, I'm sure, at this point, wouldn't you?

Unidentified woman: No, I'm trying to diet.

Another woman: Oh, well, um. . . .

Someone else: Does a house loan constitute an installment?

Moderator: Anyone else want coffee?

Unidentified woman: Yes.

Carol: You make me appreciate my mother more and more.

Moderator: Why?

Carol: Small business woman drummed in the value of money, the work ethic, the evil of credit. . .

Moderator: Okay, you all saw the first one? Okay, I'm going to wait for Nancy to sit down so she can. . . . This ad had a headline saying, "Depend on us. More California women do."[2] And there are three ladies, the first one says, "My BankAmericard sure comes in handy in emergencies (Laughter) The second one says, "I get all the checking service I need for just $2 a month." The third one says, "They gave me more service when I needed a

---

[1]See Exhibit 2.
[2]See Exhibit 3.

loan." Again, whatever your reaction is, put a number 2 next to it. Is there anything you relate to, you know, is there anything that irks you, or bothers you, or irritates you, or bores you? All done? Now we go to the third one. It's the same headline with the same ladies, but the message is different. This one says, "Depend on us. More California women do." But this one says, "I got my BankAmericard based on my own income, not my husband's."

Unidentified woman: Hear, hear!

Moderator: The second one says, "They gave me a loan when I was pregnant, even though I could not go back to work for two months." The third one says, "When I applied for car financing, they let me list alimony as part of my income." Now, before we discuss these different approaches, uh, this was number 3, middle is 2, and to my right is number 1. Jot down on your piece of paper which one of the three you relate to the most, like the most, and like the least. I mean, pick the one that you think is the best of the three. Whatever personal context you want to use.

Unidentified woman: One, two or three.

Moderator: Right. The one that you prefer although it is a relative matter, I realize.

Unidentified woman: This is question number 4 then.

Moderator: Yeah, you don't need to put that down. Just put a number and circle it, or whatever. Everybody done? Now I'll pick up all your sheets. Now, we'll go back to number 1. Now, we'll go into a discussion. I'd like to hear your comments and we'll go over them when we're all done. Okay, where was it? Here is the first ad. What was your reaction?

Sandy II: Dull—I wouldn't have read it if you hadn't put it there.

Another woman: Yeah, right!

Sandy I: I mean, I wouldn't even have seen it if you hadn't made me read it.

Kathy: Nothing new.

Sandy II: Nothing new. Nothing eye-catching.

Unidentified woman: I can't think about, . ., it's male oriented.

Sandy II: The first thing you see is, no doubt, two males and one female. She gets a car loan because it's "quick and simple."

Mary: Yeah . . . She doesn't have to strain her little brain—dumb!

Kathy: Don't you think it's too wordy. Sometimes wordy ads just lose you somewhere in midstream.

Moderator: Crystal, what did you say about "depend on us"?

Crystal: Yeah, it's so paternalistic like uh, "depend on us." "You should do what others do." You know, it's not directed toward what this particular bank has to offer. I don't like that kind of form, and I don't think anyone else does.

Moderator: Was anybody else bothered by that phrase, "depend on us"?

Sandy II: No, it's just by some other things, "so quick and simple." . . . identified with no brain in her head. Well, everyone's supposed to think about banks as being a dependable organization, you know. You relate to trust, in theory, that they're the "rock of Gibralter" type and, you know, it's a cliché, I guess.

Crystal: Was the ad left over from the big bank failure of '29? (Laughter)

Moderator: Was there any other reaction to it? (Pause) Let's see if there's anything in these notes that we might want to discuss.

Nancy: Do you think colors would have any effect?

Moderator: Well, it's a rough. . ., you know. They all are. It's just really a concept we're trying to get through. Okay, now we come to number 2, "Depend on us. More California women do." How does that strike you?

Mary: I dislike the women thing.

Unidentified woman: Yeah, it's unusual. I have never seen that, "praise you, for being a woman."

Moderator: Don't you like the "women" phrase?

Sandy I: I didn't notice it 'til you pointed it out.

Sandy II: I noticed it, but then when you put that against what they're saying,. . . California women, I mean, what they're saying isn't all that, you know . . .

Crystal: And even so, I like the message better, for a simple reason, it is more general like, "This is what the bank does. I needed some money and I got it. I needed a loan and I got it. It came in handy for emergencies." Whereas that third one . . . when we get to it . . .

Nancy: It doesn't say they gave me the loan, it just says they gave me service when I needed a loan. They were very nice and explained why I didn't get a loan. (Laughter) And anywhere you can get all the checking services you need for less than two dollars. Like, you can go . . .

Sandy I: But it sounds good to people who don't know that. That sounds good to people who can't—ignorant—no—uneducated people—who don't know that. "Gee! that sounds good."

Sandy II: Yes, but still too general.

Kathy: Too general. Yeah.

Moderator: Did you relate to this one better than the first one, personally.

All: Yes.

Moderator: And what do you think caused that?

Crystal: What they offered is more specific. Well one reason, too, is they didn't make the women look like they were stupid. It's still very paternalistic . . .

Moderator: How do you react to the mention of women in the headline and the use of three women in the picture?

One woman: I like it.

Another woman: Oh, I don't.

Sandy I: It doesn't bother me either way.

Kathy: I would rather have "people" than "women." Everybody should be equal. This should be directed to people.

Sandy II: My question is, "Why are there more women, why aren't there men banking there." Gee . . . it makes you think, "What's wrong here—only women bank here." (Laughter)

Kathy: I don't want to compete with them. I just want to be equal.

Mary: I think it's good to put social pressure on. I think that an ad like that makes people conscious of women's problems and growing strength.

Kathy: You know, a lot of women resent that.

(Everyone speaks together)

Moderator: Now wait a minute! One at a time, or I won't get anything. Now, you feel its exploitive?

Unidentified woman: Yeah—exploitive without being offensive, you know, like it wouldn't grab your average Orange County housewife who's not on the Women's Lib thing and make her not want to go there. Cause they're very careful about how they're doing it, it's a very careful exploitive ad.

Moderator: Well don't you think it does anything positive, such as bringing attention to a segment of the population that has been neglected?

Mary: Yeah, but you have Blacks also.

Unidentified woman: Yeah.

Crystal: I don't think I would appreciate it if it said, "Depend upon us. More blacks do." (Laughter) I'm afraid we are being super-critical.

Unidentified woman: They seem very young. I mean, I don't know if you want to criticize them on that but I think that all the girls are about twenty.

One woman: At least they say "women."

Another: Right.

Sandy II: But when you read the verbiage, you know, why are all these women depending on this bank. It doesn't really seem like they're doing too much.

Moderator: Well, let's eliminate the word "depend." That seems to bother everybody. Supposing that's not in the headline—some other headline—but it addresses itself to women, nonetheless. It says, "Women bank with us," or whatever they might want to say.

Sandy II: I think we should integrate everyone, regardless of their sex, their age, their color, their race. You know, we're all people and everybody has different needs and a lot of females are very Anti-Women's Lib . . . They feel that we're all pushing, to achieve our rights or whatever it is to their detriment. And many women want to stay in their medieval status.

Kathy: They're completely happy.

Sandy II: Uh huh, and they get very offended when you would like them to push Women's Lib.

Moderator: Do you find it pushy. . .?

Sandy II: I don't find it pushy. To me it really doesn't excite me in any way. But it's offensive to very many people. They don't like this "persons" bit. They really get uptight about that. You're going to chase all the men in town away. The men might like to go to the bank where women are. (Laughter)

Unidentified woman: I think the point is, you really have to point out and offer something specific to make it appealing. You want someone to read your ad, but what are you saying that's really going to get them to read it? It's going to have to be specific facts. And the third one at least throws out some specific facts—"I was divorced and I was able . . . " or "I was pregnant. . . ." It says something that someone can relate to.

Sandy II: Maybe if you show a man getting a car loan and a woman getting a house-repair loan? That's a little out-of-the-ordinary. Men get car loans all the time—women get car loans all the time—but you don't see too many women getting a house loan, like in that first ad you had the man getting a house improvement loan.

Sandy I: It depends on who you're trying to get in. Where is your business? Is it your married women who don't care about a house loan? What you are after is what we want.

Moderator: Well, who do you think they seem to be trying to get in this type of advertising? Who would you get?

Sandy II: Dumb women!

Others: Yeah!

Anther woman: Why do they say "more California women do"? All these are just general services. I mean, why women? If they're not going to be specific about "what can we do for women in particular?"

Another woman: If you could point out some negatives like, "Did you have a problem getting. . .? We can. . .," you know, that type of thing.

Carol: If you kind of appeal to a segment of the population that you're talking about. . . .

Kathy: Men have problems, too. We all have problems.

Carol: Yeah. In dealing with the twenty to thirty-year-old or the eighteen to twenty-five-year old, I don't know. Is it a personal checking account you're seeking?

Moderator: Am I right in interpreting your reaction in saying that it seems to promise something special to women, but it's not delivering it. Is that how you feel?

Sandy II: Yeah. It looks like you're trying to pull a fast one by just using the sex thing only.

Another woman: All they did was put the word "women."

All: Yeah—nothing else, nothing offered.

Crystal: What does a woman need, if you are trying to attract California women? What are you offering specifically, to fulfill California women's needs?

Moderator: Now, what is your reaction to the third ad.

Mary: The first one is "anti-man" kind of.

Unidentified woman: Oh I don't think that's anti-man. It's just pointing that it's possible.

Moderator: Right! Well that's all we're after really. Was that your first instinct that it was anti-man? And you felt the same way?

Sandy II: Yes, but for example, if you have a couple there and each of them have the card in their own name, but they're both recognized as individuals, they're both people, they are not favoring the wife—in other words, you're not trying to pull something over on the husband. She's got this card over here in her own name and he doesn't know anything about it. It's like we got our personal card . . . each based upon our own income, treating us each as individuals. This is the way the new thing is coming now with this new law. And you have to recognize men.

Unidentified woman: And show male and female up there together, hand-holding, saying this together.

Kathy: Yeah. We have twin BankAmericards. (Laughter)

Sandy II: Now the idea is, if each person has their own individual, based upon their individual earnings and credit, that would, I think, go over a lot better and the men wouldn't be so pushed off by this bank that's letting its women run around loose with their own credit. Well, men think this way. They're very, very scared about their identities, you know. Women's Lib has got them all sitting on the edge of their seats. (Laughter)

Carol: I responded almost as like leafing through a magazine. The first one I would not see, it would be a piece of gray paper filling in. The second one I would look at, note the word "women," scan it, say "Ho-hum" and turn the page. This one I would read and I would think Wow! That's a gutsy ad!

Moderator: Whether you like it or not.

Carol: Oh yeah. I'm not saying I'm not going to respond to it, but this one I would read totally—find what these people are doing. For instance, because that's a gutsy thing to do, and highly novel, very specifically for a woman. The first one would please me because I can really relate to that. It has what Crystal was saying; it's got something that's very specifically related to my own experience. Now, I do not have the bottom two, so I cannot identify. I'd glance at those and be surprised, as they talk about alimony and pregnancy in a bank ad.

Sandy II: But the problem about the pregnancy is that, basically, it's got to be based on the husband's earnings.

Another woman: Oh for sure, for sure.

Judy: Why? Does she have to be married?

Sandy II: Well, there's no way any un-wed mother (can get) a nickel—nothing. She's going to have to be married.

Kathy: I wouldn't either if I were a bank or lending institution, to someone who is unmarried and pregnant and didn't have a job. Let's face it. You've got to be realistic.

Another woman: Let's say she has a job—in the end she has a job.

Kathy: Yes, she has a job.

Unidentified woman: That's still unbelievable to me because, for instance, when I first came out to California I was married and, like Sandy said, my husband wasn't working; he was a student and I was the only one working—in the school where I'm working right now. And because I was working there, he went to school there and got tuition and admission completely; and because we were married, he got the GI bill on top of it. So the only income was my salary and the GI bill—which he got because he was married to me in the first place, going to school, getting the whole tuition bit. And when we went to the bank for a loan, they said, "No, you may get pregnant. We can't get you a loan." And then my husband turned around and got a part-time job and then he got that loan.

Unidentified woman: Yeah—That's highly discriminating.

Mary: Yeah, that one if you wanted to back it up somehow . . .

Sandy II: Most of us that have been pregnant . . . I've always been able to get credit even when pregnant, but I know a lot of people who have not been able to.

Other woman: Uh huh, yeah.

Kathy: But I really think it's because you were aggressive. You have to speak right up. I really believe in telling them.

Sandy II: Yes, you do. You have to say, "I pay my bills. Look at my credit rating. I've got four kids and I've made my payments every month."

Kathy: That's what I said when I took care of my children ever since they were little, never had any support for them, made my own way, and I think that does it.

Moderator: Okay, now, is there anything else besides that? Let's look at the third statement . . .

Sandy II: The alimony! That's going to upset men. That is going to really upset men! Although child support is not too bad. But I think, also, you should make that person at the bottom white—put the black someplace else because that is also going to incite some people. It really will. Because they're going to think that . . . Alimony is upsetting, as it is, but I think if you make that person white and made it child-support, instead of alimony, you wouldn't get as much . . .

Nancy: I'm in the group that speaks for all the women that are insulted at the mere mention of the word "alimony." I wouldn't want alimony if I got a divorce.

Sandy II: That's right. It's very out-of-fashion, very out-of-fashion. I didn't take alimony.

Crystal: Child-support is getting to be out-of-fashion. Uh huh, uh, huh.

Kathy: And the banks don't recognize child-support as being income today.

Sandy II: Mine does

Unidentified woman: Not Crocker.

Sandy II: Sumitomo Bank does. I can put it down. It's right on there. I have a court order.

Crystal: It's a tax break for a male to give child-support and not alimony, so that if he was going to give $100 to child-support and $200 alimony, he might make it $300 child-support and take a tax breakout. So you've got to look at it that way too.

Sandy II: Yeah, but as far as the income of the wife . . .

Crystal: Uh huh, yeah.

Unidentified woman: In a lot of cases alimony is not going to be applicable. But it's really getting out-of-hand.

Moderator: What I get now is that you're objecting to some of the specifics that they have selected here, because you feel it would get a lot of people upset.

Sandy II: Right.

Moderator: But how do you feel about the approach? . . . speaking about some kind of a thing that might relate to women?

Sandy II: There's one other thing that I think we should point out at this point. To a lot of women, the most important thing in their life is their man. And the total absence of men does bother some women—the fact that you think that well, we're going to go off and start our own little bank here and ignore the men.

Moderator: I think that's a very good point. How do the rest of you feel about that?

Judy: I have a hard time relating to that and that's why I starred the second one. To me, that's geared to an older age bracket. Like, I don't have a husband, I'm not pregnant, and I don't have to worry about alimony. So that's me. That's the one that I might go by except for the fact, like you said, it's so dynamic it would catch my eye and I would read it, but it doesn't apply to me in any one of those areas.

Carol: I feel kind of funny about this. I don't know if I can articulate it well, though, but it's still quite sexist. And the reason that they're out there in this financial problem is all in relationship to a man. My income, not my husband's; She, pregnant. Alimony—she used to have a man and she doesn't anymore. Still, the man is lurking around in different kinds of relationships. . . . Can you imagine an ad that was positive, with no reference to a man, about women?

Kathy: Yeah, "I'm too young/too old."

Carol: "As you start your small business, we can give you a loan."

Kathy: Being a woman—that's it—just too young and too old . . .

Unidentified woman: Race too.

Kathy: Okay and race, and just being a woman, that would be the best bet.

Unidentified woman: What Judy brought up—she was new in town, with a new job. It has nothing to do with a man.

Unidentified woman: That's right.

Nancy: But that wouldn't catch your eye.

Unidentified woman: It would have caught hers at the time.

Unidentified woman: Right.

Sandy II: Alone in a strange place. There you are, all by yourself . . . Where do I go? To my friendly neighborhood banker, get a loan, set up my credit and my business and everything I have to do.

Unidentified woman: But these extreme cases show a definite trend of thought, too, though. If they are thinking this way on these specifics, then you would think, "Well, maybe these specifics don't apply to me but my problems will probably get a lot more attention there also." Because I can relate to the fact that these are really basic problems of women, not me specifically, but women in general.

Sandy II: A middle-aged woman, who is still the product of the male-dominated society, will not think that. She'll be turned off by that thing. The men will have a hissy when they see that. And then the blacks are going to

EXHIBIT 2

get upset because she's the only one who's getting the alimony and not this poor little man, you know.

Crystal: One other thing. We know how conservative banks are generally. And they have always been in favor of the older, staid property owners (the gray flannel suit type). But hey! Look—here's a bank who is really recognizing the fact that there is another segment of the population that exists. Now you can't satisfy everybody; I don't care what kind of ad you have. Somebody's going to be mad, somebody's going to be turned off, and somebody's going to be happy. But this says one thing, that this one bank is aware of a segment of the population that has been ignored—whether they like it or not.

Kathy: But still, that middle woman, with the way it's stated, would never get a loan. She needs a husband! (Laughter)

Sandy II: It's false. It rings false somewhere in there.

Kathy: And the first one—she's married. She doesn't have a problem, really. She can get credit. And the one at the bottom, if she is making enough in alimony and stuff, she'll do it on her own.

EXHIBIT 3

Sandy II: That's right.

Kathy: They're either new in town, they're young, are single, or are too old, or they don't have very much money.

Sandy I: I think the attitude of the bank changes instantly as to what potential or what money you have.

Sandy II: Well obviously, because they're not going to make as much money loaning you $100 at a $10-a-month payment as they are lending to someone, for example, to finance a $200,000 home.

Sandy I: It leaves other people out. They should, you now, be getting it, too.

Nancy: Also, I think people should get credit for never having had credit.

Sandy II: No, our system does not work that way.

Another woman: I've lived in San Francisco for three years, I've always had a really, really steady job, and this time last year—I'd been here three years—I tried to buy a car. And, you know, I'd always paid cash for everything. I bought a car before, but I bought it cash and I had done these other things cash. And boom! Right!

Sandy II: 'Cause you're some sort of weirdo in our society when you pay cash.

Another woman: Right!

Sandy II: Try to pay for a big item in cash; they don't know how to handle it. They don't know how to handle it! You know, when you come in and lay the green-backs down, they don't know what to do.

(Discussion then moves to three ads being used by other banks in the United States—discussion lasts 15 more minutes.)

Gerber Products Company

"Perhaps the single most important new fact of recent statistical vintage is that, in America, the Population Explosion has ended. . . . And there is every indication that having ended, it will stay ended. The Baby Boom has been replaced by a Birth Dearth. Although the Dearth will not cure all the ills that were wrongly attributed to the Explosion, its effect will be quite salutary. In the years to come, it may well prove to be the single greatest agent of an ever-increasing, ever-wealthier middle class in America."[1]

The Gerber Products Company, the largest producer of baby foods in the world, found nothing salutary in Wattenberg's "birth dearth." To the contrary, starting in 1973 the reduction in the baby population translated directly into lower sales and reduced profits for the company. In response to this adversity Gerber accelerated its diversification efforts. By 1980 the company's products included 140 varieties of baby food, various allied products such as baby clothing and baby furniture, insurance, child care centers, and a trucking operation.

In 1976 the long downward trend in birth statistics came to a halt, and a slightly upward drift emerged. As a consequence of this circumstance and mixed results from the company's diversification efforts, an intensive review by top management of the company's strategic direction is in order.

The case describes the strategic situation facing Gerber as it enters the century's ninth decade. It focuses on recent environmental and competitive trends in the baby food industry and the company's response to them. It poses the question, "whither goest thou?" An appendix describing an attempted takeover of Gerber in 1977 by a larger firm is included.

BRIEF HISTORY

Gerber was founded in 1901 as the Fremont Canning Company in Fremont, Michigan. The fledgling company operated a canned food business that

---

This case was prepared by B. L. Kedia, Edmund R. Gray, and D. E. Ezell with the assistance of, but not necessarily endorsement of Gerber Products Company. The statements made and the conclusions drawn are not necessarily those of the company except where direct quotations are indicated.

[1]Ben S. Wattenberg, *The Real America,* New York: Doubleday & Co., 1974.

73

served the midwestern states. In 1928 it entered the commercial food business. Its name was changed to Gerber Products Company in 1941.

The corporate headquarters is still situated in Fremont, Michigan and its food plants are located in Fremont; Oakland, California; Rochester, New York; Ashville, North Carolina; and Fort Smith, Arkansas. The company operates worldwide through exports, licensees, and subsidiaries.

THE BABY FOOD INDUSTRY

In 1979, the baby food market was estimated to be a $524 million industry in the U.S. In recent years, Gerber's share of the market has fluctuated between 60 and 70 percent of the total, the remainder being divided between Beech-Nut and Heinz. The East Coast is regarded as the strongest market for Beech-Nut, while Heinz has its strength in the Midwest area. Gerber, on the other hand, has fairly uniform strength throughout the country and its foods are distributed in 95 percent of the major supermarkets in the United States. In recent years, the consumption of baby food per baby has been relatively steady. However, the recent increase in the number of births has tended to offset this levelling effect. Furthermore, medical opinion appears to be shifting in favor of earlier introduction of solid foods depending upon the baby's weight, appetite, and growth rate, rather than upon age alone (four to six months old rather than six months or older).

A very significant characteristic of the industry is the nature of its market. It loses its current customers after a year (babies outgrow baby food), and then must rely on the future population of babies for continued prosperity. Two other important characteristics of the industry involve competitive factors and demographic changes.

Competitive Factors

The third of the market which Gerber does not control is divided between Heinz and Beech-Nut. In the year 1976-77, Beech-Nut made significant gains in the market primarily through an advertising campaign which stressed that its baby foods contain "no added salt, preservatives, artificial flavors or colors." This "all natural" campaign propelled Beech-Nut into the number two position in the industry. Gerber and Heinz, interestingly, had also significantly reduced the salt and sugar content of their baby foods but did not emphasize this fact in their promotions. Hence, it appears Beech-Nut capitalized on something that had become common practice in the industry.

Even before Beech-Nut's "all natural" blitz, a movement was emerging where more and more mothers were forsaking the "little glass jars" for fresh foods they cook and strain themselves. This trend was in response to charges made by Ralph Nader, *Consumer Reports,* and others that the nutritional values in prepared baby foods were not all they should be. Although this "anti-processed" attitude gained acceptance across the country, it was especially prevalent on the Pacific Coast. Statistics show an increase in the anti-processed attitude from 8 percent in the early seventies to 15 percent in the mid-seventies. It has also been suggested that some increased consumer resistance may have been due to the high prices as well. After the lifting of federal price controls in 1974, Gerber raised its prices 8 percent in May and boosted them another 10 percent in October.

Product price clearly is an important competitive factor in the industry. The first price war, was initiated by Gerber's competitors in 1959. Although it was limited to California and Florida, it was a cause for concern because during this period Gerber's production costs were increasing and its profitability was declining. Fortunately for Gerber and the industry, the price war was short-lived and none of the producers of commercially prepared baby foods suffered great financial damage.

The next price war did not come for another ten years, but this time it lasted for three years. Again it was started by Gerber's competitors in reaction to the prediction of a continuing drop in both the birth rate and the total number of births in the United States. They felt they needed to get a larger share of the total dollars spent on babies. Gerber's Vice President of Marketing, Floyd N. Head, explained the action of his competitors as "a simple thing of economics." According to Head, a company needs so much volume and distribution in this business, and neither Heinz nor Beech-Nut commanded a large market share; they decided to cut prices in order to gain new customers. So long as the price differential was 1 cent per jar, Gerber was still able to compete effectively and hold its market share. However, when the spread opened up to 1½ to 2½ cents per jar, Gerber's market share started eroding, and when the spread hit 3 cents or 4 cents a jar, Gerber had to retaliate. For example, in Detroit, Gerber's local market share tumbled from 65 percent to 30 percent. In retaliation, Gerber lowered its prices and narrowed the margin to 1 cent to 1½ cents a jar. At this point in 1971, price controls were imposed and all three companies were trapped at their "bargain-basement" prices. To make matters worse the industry's costs increased significantly during the price war—meat costs alone nearly doubled during one twelve-month period.

Gerber was hurt by the price war, but its competitors were crippled. When the price controls were lifted in 1974, the price war was over and the wounded producers retreated to rebuild. At this time Swift and Company, which had held 3 percent to 4 percent of the market, withdrew from the industry. Heinz Baby Food profits suffered and Beech-Nut, a subsidiary of the Squibb Corporation, was sold to Baker Laboratories. Surprisingly enough, Gerber showed a profit during the period.

Birth Trends

Perhaps the most important environmental factors affecting the baby food industry are the rate of birth and the number of births per country. It can be said that the birth rate has a ripple effect on almost all industries, but when babies are your principle market, any change in this rate is critical. It is generally accepted that the baby boom of the fifties and sixties in the United States has slowed down. This is the result of such factors as improved birth control methods, abortions, and changing lifestyles. The fact that a large number of couples no longer feel the need to formalize their marriage has a depressing effect on the birth rate. Moreover, even among married couples, there is a trend toward the wife working and smaller family units.

According to *Current Population Reports,* almost one-half (45 percent) of the women in the age group of 20 to 24 were unmarried in 1979. This level of marriage postponement was in sharp contrast to 28 percent in 1960. Furthermore, the number of unmarried women in the 25 to 29 category approximately doubled between 1970 (10.5 percent) and 1979 (19.6 percent) after showing no change during the 1960s. The divorce rate approximately doubled during the 1970–79 period, rising from 47 divorced persons per 1,000 married persons in 1970 to 92 in 1979. The number of divorces in 1979 (1,170,000) was approximately one-half the number of marriages (2,317,000); the corresponding numbers in 1970 were 708,000 and 2,159,000 respectively. The number of unmarried couples of opposite sex living together increased more than twice in 1979 as compared to 1970 (1,346,000 versus 523,000).

The number of babies born in the U.S. in 1973 dropped to 3.1 million, the lowest level since World War II. The highest level of births occurred through 1956–62 averaging 4.2–4.3 million births per year, and was 3.7 million as recently as 1970. The number of babies born in the U.S. during the four-year period 1973–1976 remained fairly constant averaging 3.15 million births per year. The rate of birth per 1,000 population during this period was also fairly constant, averaging 14.8 births per 1,000 population. The birth rate increased in 1977 and 1978 when it was 15.3 and was still higher in 1979 when it reached 15.8 per 1,000 population. Exhibit 1 shows population change for the United States during a ten-year period, from 1970 to 1980.

The fertility rate in 1979 was estimated to be 1,840 children per 1,000 women. The fertility rate has steadily declined from the 1955–59 period, when it was 3,690. It is believed that the declining rates of childbearing reflect changing attitudes about early marriage and childbearing, as well as the pursuit of educational and career goals. There was, however, a slight increase in the fertility rate during the period 1977–1979. Exhibit 2 shows the total fertility rate during the period 1920–1979. Exhibit 3 illustrates the total fertility rate as well as changes in numbers of live births in the 1970s.

The increase in births for the years 1977–79 in a proportion greater than the increase in the fertility rate is the result of a large number of women entering the main childbearing ages of 20 to 29. By 1985 there will be 21 million women in that age group, compared with 11 million in 1957. Even at the present low birth rate of 1.8 children per woman, the actual number of births should rise by 500,000 to 3.6 million in 1984. The normal childbearing ages are regarded to be between 15 and 44 years. Exhibit 4 provides a perspective on the present and future age structures of the population. In 1978, the

EXHIBIT 1   Estimates of the components of population change for the United States: January 1, 1970, to January 1, 1980 (Numbers in thousands. Includes Armed Forces overseas)

Calendar year	Popula-tion at beginning of period	Components of change during year				
		Total increase[1]	Natural increase	Births	Deaths	Net civilian immigration
Number						
1980	221,719	—	—	—	—	—
1979	219,699	2,019	1,560	3,468	1,908	460
1978	217,874	1,825	1,403	3,328	1,925	427
1977	216,058	1,816	1,426	3,327	1,900	394
1976	214,446	1,611	1,258	3,168	1,910	353
1975	212,748	1,698	1,251	3,144	1,894	449
1974	211,207	1,541	1,225	3,160	1,935	316
1973	209,711	1,496	1,163	3,137	1,974	331
1972	208,088	1,623	1,293	3,258	1,965	325
1971	206,076	2,012	1,626	3,556	1,930	387
1970	203,849	2,227	1,812	3,739	1,927	438
Rate per 1,000 Midyear population						
1979	(X)	9.2	7.1	15.7	8.7	2.1
1978	(X)	8.3	6.4	15.3	8.8	2.0
1977	(X)	8.4	6.6	15.3	8.8	1.8
1976	(X)	7.5	5.8	14.7	8.9	1.6
1975	(X)	8.0	5.9	14.7	8.9	2.1
1974	(X)	7.3	5.8	14.9	9.1	1.5
1973	(X)	7.1	5.5	14.9	9.4	1.6
1972	(X)	7.8	6.2	15.6	9.4	1.6
1971	(X)	9.7	7.9	17.2	9.3	1.9
1970	(X)	10.9	8.8	18.2	9.4	2.1

[1] Includes estimates of overseas admissions into and discharges from the Armed Forces and for 1970, includes error of closure between censuses.

SOURCE: Data consistent with U.S. Bureau of Census, *Current Population,* Series P-25, No. 878. Estimates of births and deaths (with an allowance for deaths of Armed Forces overseas) are from the National Center for Health Statistics. Estimates of net civilian immigration are based partly on data from the Immigration and Naturalization Service.

largest aggregation of females were those aged 15 to 24. This group and the category 25 to 29 years were the only age groups in which there were more females in 1978 than are projected for the year 2000. The size of these groups reflects the higher fertility rates of the post-World War II "baby boom" generation, the effects of which can be seen carried through to the year 2000 when these groups reach ages 35 to 54.

EXHIBIT 2   Total fertility rate: 1920 to 1979

Year or period	Rate	Year or period	Rate	Year or period	Rate
1979[1]	1,840	1971	2,275	1955–59	3,690
1978	1,800	1970	2,480	1950–54	3,337
1977	1,826	1969	2,465	1945–49	2,985
1976	1,768	1968	2,477	1940–44	2,523
1975	1,799	1967	2,573	1935–39	2,235
1974	1,857	1966	2,736	1930–34	2,376
1973	1,896	1965	2,928	1925–29	2,840
1972	2,022	1960–64	3,459	1920–24	3,248

[1]Provisional estimate.

SOURCE: The rate for 1979 is estimated by the Bureau of Census; for 1940 to 1978, National Center for Health Statistics, Vital Statistics of the United States and Monthly Vital Statistics Report (various issues); for 1920–24 to 1935-39, U.S. Bureau of the Census, *Current Population Reports*, Series P–23, No. 36.

The total fertility rate for a given year shows how many births a group of 1,000 women would have by the end of their childbearing period, if during their entire reproductive period they were to experience the age-specific birth rates for that given year. A fertility rate of 2,000 is necessary for long run replacement of the population in the absence of net migration.

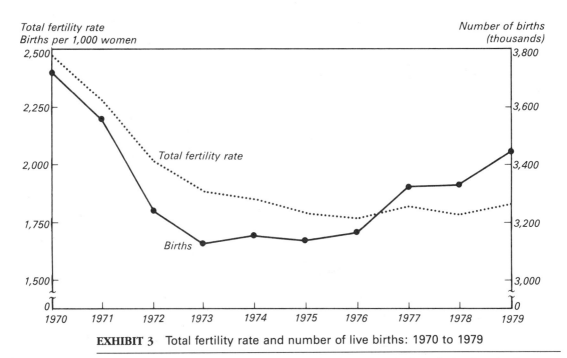

EXHIBIT 3   Total fertility rate and number of live births: 1970 to 1979

SOURCE: U.S. National Center for Health Statistics, *Monthly Vital Statistics Report* (various issues) and unpublished Census Bureau estimates.

EXHIBIT 4 Estimates and projections of the population of the United States, by age and sex: 1970 to 2000 (table truncated)

(Numbers in thousands. As of July 1. Total population including Armed Forces overseas.)

Sex, year, and series	All ages	Under 5 years	5–14 years	15–24 years	25–44 years	45–64 years	65 years and over	Median age
Women:								
1970	104,609	8,406	19,980	18,048	24,599	21,896	11,681	29.3
1975	109,346	7,765	18,497	19,898	27,238	22,711	13,236	30.0
1978	112,046	7,507	17,373	20,511	29,549	22,831	14,276	31.0
1985								
[1]Series I	122,437	11,161	16,965					31.9
[2]Series II	119,514	9,171	16,032	19,049	36,036	22,932	16,293	32.7
[3]Series III	117,564	7,919	15,333					33.2
2000								
[1]Series I	144,746	11,517	24,270	20,972				34.1
[2]Series II	133,790	8,699	19,087	18,018	38,409	30,473	19,105	36.8
[3]Series III	126,714	6,899	15,786	16,042				38.5
PERCENT DISTRIBUTION								
Women:								
1970	100.0	8.0	19.1	17.3	23.5	20.9	11.2	(X)
1975	100.0	7.1	16.9	18.2	24.9	20.8	12.1	(X)
1978	100.0	6.7	15.5	18.3	26.4	20.4	12.7	(X)
1985								
[1]Series I	100.0	9.1	13.9	15.6	29.4	18.7	13.3	(X)
[2]Series II	100.0	7.7	13.4	15.9	30.2	19.2	13.6	(X)
[3]Series III	100.0	6.7	13.0	16.2	30.7	19.5	13.9	(X)
2000								
[1]Series I	100.0	8.0	16.8	14.5	26.5	21.1	13.2	(X)
[2]Series II	100.0	6.5	14.3	13.5	28.7	22.8	14.3	(X)
[3]Series III	100.0	5.4	12.5	12.7	30.3	24.0	15.1	(X)

[1]Based on women who enter childbearing age and will average 2.7 births/woman.
[2]Based on women who enter childbearing age and will average 2.1 births/woman.
[3]Based on women who enter childbearing age and will average 1.7 births/woman.

SOURCE: U.S. Department of Commerce, Bureau of the Census, Current Population Reports, Series P-25, Nos. 800, 721, and 704.

DIVERSIFICATION EFFORTS

With the declining birth rate, it was felt that Gerber needed to diversify if it was to continue to grow and prosper. In keeping with the slogan "Babies are our business," the company focused its diversification strategy on the concept of selling more items of merchandise per baby. To facilitate the diversification process, a Gerber venture group was established early in 1974. The group met every Monday morning for the purpose of screening new ideas and forwarding promising proposals to the company's planning committee. The concept of venture group was abandoned within a year.

Categories below represent the major areas of Gerber's diversification.

Special Products

In keeping with company philosophy, Gerber has sought to grow through the sale of additional baby products and services (non-food items), primarily to families with infants and small children. There were approximately 400 different items in the special product line in 1979, which were sold through approximately 50,000 retail outlets (including a small number of company-owned outlet stores) in the United States. The success of special products is attributed to the confidence which parents have in products bearing the Gerber name. During the decade of the eighties, the company plans to become an increasing factor in the total baby needs market by adding new items to, and additional distribution of, special products.

Gerber first entered the infant clothing market in 1960 by acquiring a vinyl pants and bib company. During the year 1979–80, the company was the leader in the submarket of vinyl pants; however, a much larger market exists in disposable diapers. Disposable diapers eliminate the need for rubber pants. In addition to vinyl pants and bibs, the Babywear division produces shirts, training pants, and socks. Gerber has also expanded its clothing line to include children through their preschool years. During 1978–79, new sneakers were introduced in six different patterns in sizes 2 to 8. The sneakers were a part of the Gerber "footwear line" which includes shoes, socks, booties, and "funzie" slippers. A special line of screen-printed shirts in six different patterns was also added during the year.

In 1970, Gerber Products purchased an infant toiletries and accessories company operating under the name of Hankscraft. In 1979–80, Hankscraft was the leader in the sale of humidifiers and vaporizers. During this year, its line of carry-all bags, which serve as multi-purpose bags as well as the familiar diaper bag, was expanded. In addition, four new safety items were introduced: outlet covers, a cabinet lock, door knob covers, and outlet plugs. Hankscraft Division also produced nursers and nurser accessories and a number of infant care products.

The Spartan Printing and Graphic Arts Company was acquired in 1971. This division now offers internal and external photographic, design, printing, and advertising services. Additionally, Gerber Metal Products division was organized in the late seventies. This division consists of two units, a container manufacturing plant (acquired in 1971) and a metal lithographic operation (built in 1977), at which flat metal sheets are printed for later use in the manufacturing of containers. This division also serves both internal needs and outside customers.

In 1974–75, Gerber acquired the Walter W. Moyer Company, Inc., a manufacturer of children's underwear and knit apparel. At the time of the takeover, the Moyer Company, with plants in Pennsylvania and Arizona, had annual sales between $16 and $17 million. It currently produces a broad line of knitwear garments for sale under the Gerber name, as well as for private label distribution. The Health Care Division, formed in 1978, distributes and sells an incontinent pant system and a variety of other products designed for use in medical and extended care facilities. In 1979, Gerber opened a subsidiary, G & M Finishing, for the purpose of bleaching and dyeing knit fabrics. In addition to supplying the needs of the Moyer plant, G & M Finishing has the capacity to provide bleaching and dyeing services to other knit users.

A line of plush stuffed toys are produced by the Atlanta Novelty division, acquired in 1973. The popular Gerber baby doll is also produced and sold by this division. In 1980, Gerber purchased the Reliance Products Corporation of Woonsocket, Rhode Island. Reliance produces a broad line of products for infants including the widely accepted NUK line of nurser bottle nipples and orthodontic exercisers for infants.

Life and Health Care Insurance

Gerber organized a life insurance subsidiary in 1968 to sell low-priced policies to young parents by mail. In 1970 a "child care" policy, providing hospitalization insurance for children under legal age, was introduced. The unique characteristic of this policy is that the child's parents need not be insured. Gerber considered this to be a natural extension of its business of helping young parents provide for their children. The company is licensed by most states to write and sell life and other types of personal insurance. While the company has used some licensed agents in its insurance business, direct response, including extensive newspaper and television advertising, remains the principle avenue of marketing insurance policies.

The life insurance division was a disappointment through 1975, having lost $858,000 in 1973 and $945,000 in 1974. However, Gerber tightened administrative control over the unit, and profits from the insurance operation amounted to $109,000 in 1976–1977, an increase of $49,000 from the previous period, 1975–1976. The life insurance has since continued to make contributions to the overall performance of the company and experienced the best year in 1980, at which time the company had about one-half billion dollars of insurance in force.

Day Care Centers

Gerber announced the formation of a Children's Centers Division in early 1971. The initial nursery schools were established in Villa Park, Illinois; Cleveland, Ohio; and Costa Mesa, California. In 1980, there were thirty-two such nursery school and day care centers in seven metropolitan areas of the United States. These centers have encountered some problems, mostly at the local administrative level. The company regards them as a test marketing of the day care centers concept that will provide experience for determining whether or not to expand. Their performance, to date, has been only marginally profitable. In addition to expecting a major extension of child care activity in the decade of the eighties, the company is planning to operate a Gerber children's center for a private employer.

The Adult Market

Gerber faces a tough challenge in trying to crack the adult market. In hopes of appealing to this market, Gerber developed a "Rediscover Gerber" ad campaign, that promoted specialty fruits and desserts, waffle toppings, and "the 60-second parfait." One ad puts it, "Next time you're looking for something to eat, baby yourself with the unexpected snack." A Gerber executive acknowledged the challenge of the adult market this way, "Let's face it, people think of baby food as pretty bland stuff." Currently, the firm is planning to reintroduce its "dessert line" and promote it as snack food for young people (particularly teenage girls).

Another attempt to penetrate the adult market was through single-serving adult foods under the "Singles" label introduced in 1974. At that time, about 11.2 million households, out of a total of 63.2 million households, were single-person households. In addition, the number of two-person households accounted for another 18.9 million. Thus, the primary and secondary target markets for these products included nearly half of all households in the United States. This contrasts markedly with the 10 percent of U.S. households which have babies.

A number of problems have been encountered with the Singles line. In an interview reported in *Advertising Age,* John C. Suerth, then Chairman of Gerber, conceded that in spite of a different jar design and label, the Singles line still gave the appearance of baby food. He also conceded that the word "Singles" was misleading. When the company used the word "Singles" it was thinking in terms of single-serving and not in terms of food for singles. Because of these problems, the Singles line did not gain consumer acceptance and was dropped, which resulted in a writedown of about $450,000.

Gerber also test marketed three other adult products—a peanut spread, a catsup, and a spaghetti sauce—during the 1974–77 period. These products would put Gerber in competition with such companies as Best Foods, makers of Skippy; Swift Derby Foods, makers of Peter Pan; Procter and Gamble, makers of Jif peanut spread; and Kraft Foods and Borden, which also recently entered the peanut butter market. In the catsup and spaghetti sauce market, Gerber would have to compete against companies such as Heinz, Hunt-Wesson, and Del Monte. The test market results led to the abandonment of these products.

C.W. Transport Acquisition

Gerber acquired C.W. Transport, Inc. in August 1979 through a stock transfer. The Wisconsin-based common carrier trucking firm, serving eleven states in the Midwest and Southeast, represents Gerber's largest acquisition to date. Company officials plan to integrate the new unit into internal shipping operations and also maintain it as a profit center in its own right.

MARKETING POLICIES

Distribution System

Traditionally, Gerber has marketed its baby food products through grocery stores and supermarkets across the U.S., as well as in sixty-eight foreign countries. As noted earlier, however, grocery outlets are now being asked to sell special products such as vinyl pants, baby and preschool children's clothing, infant toiletries, vaporizers, and other infant accessories—the concept being to build a sort of baby center in the stores. The company has met some resistance in this effort, however. For example, Thriftmart, Inc., a southern California food chain, stocks many Gerber baby food items, but only one nonfood product: plastic pants. According to Thriftmart, the traffic just did not warrant carrying other Gerber products.

In recent years, in an attempt to increase market penetration, Gerber expanded its channels to include discount houses, drug chains, department stores, and specialty shops for the growing line of nonfood baby products. Moreover, in 1979 two divisions, grocery products and special products, were created. A principal reason for the reorganization was the divergent marketing channels utilized by the two product lines. The grocery products division concentrates on food stores, while the special products division focuses on mass merchandising, drug outlets, and other segments of Gerber distribution.

A major strength of Gerber's distribution system is a new computerized market information system, covering 50,000 food stores that account for about 85 percent to 90 percent of the country's total retail food sales. The system, called MARS (market auditing report service), provides instant information relative to various Gerber products in terms of store inventory, shelf space, mix, movement, and turnover compared with competition. The system enables the company to isolate almost any facet of its distribution.

Promotion

Gerber's promotional efforts have been largely directed toward two groups: mothers and pediatricians. The company tries to reach mothers through advertising in baby publications and by direct mail promotions. It also relies on the word of mouth advertising by mothers who have used Gerber products.

The direct mail campaign is perhaps Gerber's key promotional tool. The lists used in the campaign are derived from birth records. Three to six weeks after a birth, the new mother receives literature and coupons for Gerber baby foods that are redeemable at the local grocery stores. Afterwards, follow-up coupons are sent. The redemption rate of these coupons is around 20 percent.

Promotion to pediatricians takes other forms. Gerber sponsors *Pediatric Basics,* a respected journal for pediatricians. The company also maintains a professional relations department, whose staff calls upon hospitals and doctors to promote Gerber products. Information about new Gerber products and latest findings in infant nutrition are shared with the health professionals who serve new parents throughout the country.

In keeping with its attempts to diversify, in 1972 Gerber shortened its slogan from "Babies are our business . . . our *only* business" to "Babies are our business." The slogan, "Gerber prepares foods for the most important person in the world . . . your baby," is also used in various advertisements. The company considers its name a valuable asset. Former Chairman Suerth explained it this way,"Everything we're doing is really based on our success in the baby food area. So you better keep the lead dog pretty healthy."

FOREIGN OPERATIONS

Gerber was a late entrant in the overseas market. In 1965, it derived only 7 percent of its total sales from overseas operations. However, since 1974, international sales have ranged between 16 to 20 percent of the consolidated sales. In 1980, Gerber maintained subsidiaries in Canada, Mexico, Venezuela, and Costa Rica. It operated a joint venture in Brazil and had licensees in Australia, France, Italy, Japan, the Phillipines, and South Africa. In addition, export shipments were made to about eighty countries around the world. Food items constituted most of the overseas sales, although some special products, particularly vinyl waterproof pants, nursers and nurser accessories, and vaporizers, were also exported.

Sales and pre-tax earnings attributable to international operations (foreign subsidiaries, foreign licensees, and exports) as an approximate percentage of consolidated sales, and consolidated pre-tax earnings for the years 1975-1980 were as follows:

	1975	1976	1977	1978	1979	1980
Sales	17.2%	19.6%	18.2%	16.2%	17.1%	16.9%
Pre-tax earnings	22.2%	16.9%	2.7%	2.8%	6.9%	7.2%

Increase sales were attained primarily in major Latin American markets, despite political uncertainties in much of that part of the world. Subsidiaries in Mexico, Costa Rica, and Venezuela experienced growth in sales volume. However, contribution of international sales to earnings was severely limited due to increasing costs and stringent price controls in foreign markets. In Venezuela, for example, baby food selling prices have been frozen since limited price increases were permitted in the later part of the fiscal 1978.

In 1980, Gerber sold its 82 percent interest in its Venezuelan subsidiary. The Venezuelan company now produces and markets a broad line of Gerber baby foods under a licensing agreement.

Sales and pre-tax earnings of the Venezuelan company and the rest of the international operations for the years 1978 through 1980 were as follows:

	1978	1979	1980
International sales:	*Thousands of dollars*		
Venezuela	33,182	42,847	45,687
Other	38,628	42,717	56,305
International pre-tax earnings			
Venezuela	951	2,990	1,100
Other	482	829	3,241

In spite of the pressures of rising costs, inflation, and price controls, Gerber expects continued growth in the international markets. Improvement in the economic and educational standards, along with the knowledge of nutrition, are regarded as the primary reasons for increasing demand of Gerber products.

FINANCE

After a steady growth in sales and profit, Gerber was faced with eroding sales and earnings during 1973, 1974 and 1975. (See Exhibits 5 and 6). "We got hit with so many things at one time: reduced births, price controls, rising costs, and severe price competition," said Suerth. The company has, however, recovered from the setback. With a minor exception in the year 1977, profits have steadily increased since 1976. In the years 1979 and 1980, the profits were at an all-time high. In 1980, Gerber had an equity of nearly $228 million and a long term debt of only $20 million.

Until the acquisition of CW Transport, Inc. in August 1979, the company's operations were divided into two industry segments: (1) sales of food, and (2) sales of special products and services. In the year 1980, a third segment, sales from transportation services was added. The relative contribution of each segment to the consolidated sales for the last six years was as follows (000's omitted):

Year	Food	Special products and services	Transportation	Total
1975	283,512	44,627	—	328,139
1976	314,693	57,725	—	327,418
1977	335,412	69,186	—	404,498
1978	364,210	78,868	—	443,078
1979	404,203	94,812	—	499,016
1980	435,838	108,084	58,064	601,986

Net earnings from the new transportation services segment in 1980 were $2,328,000.

In Gerber's *Annual Report to Stockholders* for the years 1979 and 1980, it was noted that the increases in sales of domestic food in the two preceding years of the report were primarily due to higher selling prices, rather than the increases in the sales volume. Furthermore, net earnings for special products and services declined in the last two fiscal years. This was especially true in the petroleum-based products.

EXHIBIT 5   Consolidated Income Account, years ended March 31

$000's	1969	1970	1971	1972	1973
March 31					
Net Sales	202,179	217,170	261,851	282,600	278,473
Other Income	1,127	1,365	1,087	1,138	823
Equity Earnings					
Transport Revenue					
Total Income	203,307	218,536	262,938	283,739	279,296
Cost of Sales	116,381	126,306	156,466	170,793	176,742
Transport Expense					
Selling Expense	55,672	59,667	69,305	73,572	71,371
Interest Expense	53		287	291	584
Eq. Affil. Earn.				cr 30	dr 964
Income Tax	16,620	16,880	18,170	18,699	13,980
Minority Interest	80	179	214	159	234
Foreign Exch. Losses					
Net Profit	14,498	15,502	18,494	20,253	15,419
Prev. Retained Earn.	74,292	79,603	83,450	91,895	101,265
Com. Divs.	9,187	9,337	10,082	10,883	11,353
Pool Int. Adjustment			cr 32		
Retained Earning	79,603	85,768	91,895	101,265	105,331
Earn. Com. Share	$1.74	$1.87	$2.19	$2.40	$1.84
No. of Com. Shrs.	8,304,629	8,295,230	8,447,214	8,440,130	8,250,800

SOURCE: *Moody's Industrial Manual* (1968-78), *Standard and Poors Industrial Manual* (1978), *Gerber Annual Reports* (1970-80).

RESEARCH AND DEVELOPMENT

Gerber research activities are located at the corporate headquarters in Fremont, Michigan. Research efforts primarily concentrate on the development of new foods, product formulations, new processing methods, and improved material usage. In light of ever-increasing knowledge of infant nutrition and frequent feedback provided by practicing pediatricians, product formulas are continuously evaluated and retested. For example, the use of salt was completely discontinued in 1978 and sugar usage was significantly reduced. Studies in packaging and agricultural research are also carried out on a regular basis. Cornucopia Farms, headquartered at Barker, New York, which supplies the firm with fresh produce and apple juice, also serves as a natural laboratory for the company's agricultural research projects. Charles F. Whitten, Professor of Pediatrics, Wayne State University School of Medicine and Dena C. Cederquist, Professor Emeritus, Department of Food Science and Human Nutrition, Michigan State University, are on the Gerber Board of Directors.

1974	*1975*	*1976*	*1977*	*1978*	*1979*	*1980*
285,437	328,139	372,418	404,598	443,078	499,016	543,922
1,401	1,290	1,651	1,974	2,077	2,217	2,209
			291	267	208	312
						58,064
286,838	329,430	374,069	406,863	445,422	501,441	604,507
189,818	214,164	236,409	263,569	291,870	336,457	368,790
						49,558
73,556	79,661	90,358	95,543	104,895	110,740	126,130
1,661	2,321	1,672	1,961	2,636	3,661	6,175
dr 1,258	dr 645	dr 135				
9,100	16,070	22,281	22,611	22,033	22,798	24,254
323	228	325	cr 251	cr 11	321	cr 116
			1,060			
11,122	16,338	22,889	22,334	23,999	27,464	29,716
105,331	106,083	114,248	128,191	140,155	152,478	167,944
10,371	8,173	8,946	10,370	11,406	12,268	13,852
106,083	114,248	128,191	140,155	152,748	167,944	183,808
$1.35	$2.00	$2.81	$2.75	$2.95	$3.36	$3.45
8,214,680	8,132,803	8,133,201	8,134,014	8,164,278	8,192,264	8,901,151

EXHIBIT 6   Consolidated Balance Sheet as of March 31

$000's	1969	1970	1971	1972	1973
Assets:					
Cash	3,591	3,579	3,877	1,408	2,861
Commercial Paper	12,079	8,190			
Market Security Cost	—	—	13,794	3,286	4,557
Receivables	14,761	16,672	21,686	23,244	25,128
Finish Products	34,931	39,878	39,638	47,973	44,946
Raw Mat. & Supplies	7,071	9,605	10,977	12,392	14,395
Total Current	72,435	77,926	89,974	88,305	91,827
Net Properties	35,800	37,890	43,184	53,250	58,844
Inv. Uncons. Sub.	5,089	5,509	5,527	8,772	9,311
Goodwill	1	1			
Misc. Receivables	1,596	1,989	3,440	2,374	1,918
Intangibles	701	854			
(Patents)			1,083	867	767
Total	115,622	124,170	143,210	153,521	162,670
Liabilities:					
Accounts Payable	5,492	7,575	18,421	18,837	17,423
Notes Payable	257	82	1,419	1,701	10,984
Accruals	5,905	6,536			
Income Tax	3,395	3,849	4,383	3,934	2,360
Debt Due	414	—			
Total Current	15,465	18,043	24,224	24,472	30,769
Long Term Debt	75	—	1,904	1,808	2,835
Deferred Credit	550	825	1,816	1,963	3,250
Minority Interest	450	480	695	1,671	2,556
Pension Costs	680	583			
Common Stock (2.50)	21,234	21,234	21,234	21,234	21,234
Paid in Surplus	3,045	3,045	2,983	2,946	2,946
Retained Earnings	79,603	85,768	91,895	101,265	105,331
Stockhold Equity	103,884	110,048	116,114	124,446	129,512
Reacquired Stock	5,483	5,810	1,542	1,841	6,252
Net Stockholder Eq.	98,400	104,237	114,571	123,605	123,259
Total	115,622	124,170	143,210	153,521	162,670

SOURCE: *Moody's Industrial Manual* (1968-78), *Standard and Poors Industrial Manual* (1978), *Gerber Annual Reports* (1970-80).

1974	1975	1976	1977	1978	1979	1980
2,722	4,357	3,045	1,558	2,366	3,254	7,105
1,925	1,766	15,522	11,987	9,873	3,475	4,484
28,939	28,192	30,233	35,815	42,914	53,662	65,733
46,542	47,569	43,984	49,320	49,713	59,475	62,949
17,076	21,366	24,844	30,779	30,390	42,571	40,096
96,204	103,252	117,628	129,459	135,256	162,437	180,367
62,834	68,523	70,823	80,700	89,820	100,978	129,060
9,462	10,000	10,572	11,778	12,813	13,455	24,912
3,644	3,635	4,729	4,759	6,555	7,376	10,308
1,413	1,171	406	431	324	238	8,149
173,558	186,582	204,158	227,127	244,768	284,484	352,796
20,348	19,936	26,996	34,168	33,193	40,132	55,380
18,562	14,014	1,802	8,317	12,321	24,173	50,262
2,388	2,566	6,875	4,860	3,368	4,139	5,492
41,298	36,517	35,673	47,345	48,882	68,444	101,134
3,420	13,244	17,360	15,728	18,112	21,994	19,990
4,239	4,654	4,666	5,836	6,535	6,855	8,505
1,337	1,564	1,890	1,675	1,664	1,985	1,906
21,235	21,234	21,235	21,235	21,235	21,235	22,980
2,946	2,946	2,942	2,935	2,720	2,549	20,759
106,083	114,248	128,191	140,155	152,748	167,944	183,808
130,263	138,428	152,368	164,325	176,703	191,728	227,547
6,999	7,807	7,799	7,782	7,128	6,522	6,286
123,264	130,621	144,569	156,543	169,575	185,206	221,261
173,558	186,582	204,158	227,127	244,768	284,484	352,796

REFERENCES

"Anderson Clayton Withdraws Gerber Bid," *Financial Times* (September 20, 1977), p. 28.

"Baby Talk," *Forbes* (August 1, 1975), pp. 40–41.

"But It's Cold Out There," *Forbes* (September 15, 1973), p. 40.

"Conversation with Gerber's John Suerth," *Advertising Age* (February 3, 1975).

"Does Father Know Best?" *Forbes* (March 6, 1978).

Fifty Years of Caring, Gerber Products Co., internal brochure.

Gerber's Annual Report to Stockholders, Gerber Products Co. (1970–1980).

"Gerber Back on the Ad Track," *Advertising Age* (March 6, 1978).

"Gerber Finds There is Still Plenty of Profits in Moppets," *Barrons* (March 3, 1975).

"Gerber Jumps on No-Salt Bandwagon," *Advertising Age* (June 6, 1977), p. 4.

"Gerber Products Says Bid to Settle Walkout at Plant is Rejected," *The Wall Street Journal* (April 4, 1977), p. 20.

"Gerber: Selling More to the Same Mothers is Our Objective Now," *Business Week* (October 16, 1978), pp. 192–195.

"Gerber: Where Have All the Babies Gone?" *Commercial and Financial Chronicle* (March 22, 1976).

"Growing Pains in the Baby Market," *Forbes* (December 15, 1959), p. 19.

"Lower Birthrate Crimps the Baby Food Market," *Business Week* (July 13, 1974), pp. 44–48.

Moody's Industrial Manual, Gerber Products Inc. (1968–1978).

"Outlook on the Baby-Food Market," *Business Week* (July 13, 1974), p. 45.

Standard and Poors Industrial Manual, Gerber Products Inc. (1978).

Standard and Poors Stock Report, Gerber Products Inc. (1978).

"The Bad News in Babyland," *Dun's* (December, 1972), p. 104.

"The Lost Generation Wasn't," *Forbes* (October 1, 1965), pp. 51–52.

U.S. Bureau of Census, *Current Population Reports,* Series P-20, No. 350, May 1980.

"What Population Explosion?" *Forbes* (March 1, 1967), pp. 60–61.

Appendix A

Anderson, Clayton and Company, a Houston-based foods and oil-seeds group, offered on April 18, 1977 to buy all 8.1 million shares of Gerber at $40 a share. In 1976 Anderson, Clayton's return was 11.5 percent on $759 million sales, while Gerber's was 16.6 percent on $372 million sales. According to President Guinee of Anderson, Clayton, the acquisition would boost his company's return on equity and increase its stake in the grocery products business. Gerber's stock has sold as low as 8½ in 1974, at 21 in November 1976, and was selling at the mid-30s at the time of the offer. The purchase of 90,000 shares in the open market by Anderson, Clayton was instrumental in boosting the stock price.

Gerber executives defiantly resisted the takeover attempt and filed suits in state and federal courts charging: (1) Anderson, Clayton manipulated Gerber's stock price before making the offer; (2) the proposed offer would be in violation of antitrust laws because it would give Anderson, Clayton monopoly power in the baby food industry and reduce competition in the salad dressing market, which Gerber had been thinking about entering (Anderson, Clayton held 12 percent of the market with its Seven Seas brand); and (3) Anderson, Clayton had failed to disclose $2.1 million in illegal payments the company had made abroad during the preceding several years.

The situation resulted in legal entanglements and consequent delays. On September 19, Anderson, Clayton withdrew its offer, saying that because of the legal problems any takeover could not be completed until late 1978 or early 1979. "These delays aren't acceptable," said Mr. Barlow, the Anderson, Clayton Chairman.

During the takeover struggle, Gerber stock rose to a high of 39½. On September 19, the day Anderson, Clayton withdrew its offer, the price of the Gerber stock dropped from 34⅜ to 28¼. Those who bought a large number of shares anticipating a successful takeover lost heavily. In August and September 1977, four class action suits were filed by stockholders against Gerber alleging violation of the Securities and Exchange Act of 1934 because the company's opposition to tender offer was not in the best interest of the shareholders, but rather in the self-interest of the directors. All four suits were dismissed by the court.

REFERENCES

"Bid by Anderson, Clayton to Buy Gerber Dropped," *The Wall Street Journal* (September 20, 1977), p. 38.

Koshetz, Herbert. "Gerber Charged With Damaging Its Shareholders," *New York Times* (August 10, 1977), p. dl.

"Nothing Is Too Good For Our Stockholders," *Forbes* (May 15, 1977).

Serrin, William. "How Gerber Foiled a Takeover," New York Times (September 2, 1977), p. F1–2.

ROLM Corporation

In October 1973, Kenneth Oshman, President of the ROLM Corporation, and other members of ROLM's top management team were finalizing a business plan to market a private branch exchange system (PBX), thereby entering the telecommunications industry. The plan was to be presented to ROLM's Board of Directors at its November meeting in order to obtain approval for market entry. The initial product was to be a computer-controlled electronic PBX with capacity to handle from 100 to 800 telephone extensions. This market entry would bring ROLM into direct competition with AT&T, ITT, Northern Electric, Philips, Nippon Electric, and many others.

THE COMPANY

ROLM Corporation had been founded in 1969 by four electrical engineers: Mr. Richeson, Mr. Oshman, Mr. Loewenstern and Mr. Maxfield. In fact, the name of the corporation was an acronym based on the first letters of their names. All were in their late-twenties to early-thirties at the time of the founding and all were, or had been, employed by electronic or computer firms in the San Francisco Bay area. As Bob Maxfield recalled, "The company was the result of four guys deciding they wanted to go into business for themselves and having a couple of ideas about the kinds of products they might offer." Their original ideas were basically commercial applications of systems developed originally for the military and included a system for police departments to keep track automatically of the location of every police vehicle. Another idea was a system that would allow toll bridges to monitor regular users of the bridge automatically by means of a transponder attached to each vehicle, thus permitting bills to be issued to each regular user at the end of the

This case was prepared by Professor Adrian B. Ryans as a basis for class discussion rather than to illustrate either effective or ineffective handling of an administrative situation. The cooperation of Mr. Mike Korek and SRI International in allowing certain data from a report on the telephone interconnect industry to be included here is gratefully acknowledged. Reprinted from *Stanford Business Cases 1979* with permission of the publishers, Stanford University Graduate School of Business, © 1979 by the Board of Trustees of the Leland Stanford Junior University.

month. A business plan was developed around these ideas and was presented to venture capitalists, but it did not arouse much enthusiasm among potential suppliers of capital.

In the fall of 1968, Bob Maxfield and Gene Richeson attended the Fall Joint Computer Conference. This particular show in many respects heralded the coming minicomputer boom. Data General, subsequently to become a major factor in the minicomputer industry, and a dozen other new manufacturers, announced their first products at this show. A few months later, while the four of them were sitting around "blue-skying" about potential businesses, Gene Richeson suggested that what the world really needed was a low-cost, off-the-shelf military minicomputer.

No standard computer could withstand the severe environmental conditions encountered in military missions. At that time, the major manufacturer of militarized computers (*mil-spec*) were IBM and Sperry Univac, who manufactured the computers on a custom basis resulting in long lead times and high cost—often $150,000 for a system. The Data General commercial NOVA minicomputer, on the other hand, cost about $10,000 and Gene Richeson, based on his knowledge of the requirements of the various military applications, felt that such a computer would have sufficient power for most of these applications. Bob Maxfield, who had the most experience with computers, felt that a militarized version of the Data General computer could be manufactured to sell for less than $30,000. As they discussed the possibilities further, they decided that it would be ideal from the customer's viewpoint if a militarized computer could be made software-compatible and input/output-compatible with an existing commercial minicomputer. This would allow the user to do the development work and system testing on the lower cost commercial machine in a laboratory environment, only using the mil-spec computer when the system was actually deployed in the military equipment.

The next question they addressed was which commercial minicomputer they should choose. They selected the Data General NOVA computer for two reasons. First, Data General was a start-up company and thus might be interested in licensing the design and software to ROLM and, given its small size, the decision would probably be made quickly. The second reason was the Data General machine used the latest technology, which required a smaller number of components than competitive minicomputers. This was an important factor in designing a reliable machine for military applications. They phoned Edson de Castro, President of Data General, and told him they were thinking of starting up a company to manufacture mil-spec computers and asked him if he would be interested in licensing hardware and software designs to them. Mr. de Castro was interested, so they flew to Data General's home office in Boston and negotiated an agreement with him.

On the basis of their idea, they developed a business plan and were successful in getting sufficient money to start the business. ROLM began operation on June 1, 1969, and a working model was displayed at the Fall Joint Computer Conference in 1969. The first production unit was shipped in March 1970. In the first quarter of fiscal year 1971, which began in July 1970,

ROLM showed a profit and remained profitable thereafter. Subsequent computers were based on ROLM's own designs.

The ROLM mil-spec computers typically were purchased by contractors of the U.S. Department of Defense, the Defense Department itself, and certain industrial customers who required computers that could operate in severe environments. The computers were generally used in research, development and testing applications. Individual purchase orders were usually for small quantities. The company generally provided a central processing unit (CPU), a main memory, a chassis, a power supply and a variety of input/output equipment, peripheral equipment (terminals, printers, magnetic discs and tapes), and software. The customer could thus configure a system to meet his own needs. The company employed a direct sales organization which totalled about eight people in 1973. Kenneth Oshman, besides being President of ROLM, also acted as head of the marketing organization.

The Decision to Diversify

By fiscal 1973, sales had reached $3.6 million. An income statement and balance sheet for ROLM are included in Exhibit 1. Early in 1973, top management of ROLM became concerned about the potential size of the segment of the military computer market in which ROLM competed. There was a strong feeling among ROLM's top management that their market segment would be saturated by the time their annual sales reached $10 to $20 million. Given that they had an objective to build a major company, they began to look for areas of diversification that would allow ROLM to continue its growth. They felt that any diversification should build on their main technological expertise in computers, so they investigated other computer-related businesses that they might enter. The PBX market was an obvious candidate. As Oshman pointed out, "The computer-based PBX is very much a computer system, and we already had 80 percent of the technology; we figured we could get the other 20 percent easier than the telephone companies could get the computer technology." The idea was initially abandoned when they realized that the cost of setting up a national sales and service organization would be beyond ROLM's resources. Nevertheless, the proposal kept resurfacing during the following months. As Bob Maxfield recalled, "We all felt it would be fun to develop a computer-controlled telephone system, so we decided to look at it more carefully in March 1973." Once the decision had been made to look at the PBX business more closely, it was decided to set up a separate organization to do the product development and market analysis. They felt either the mil-spec computer business or the proposed PBX business would receive second-class treatment if personnel attempted to work in both areas simultaneously.

To head the product development side of the project, Maxfield was successful in recruiting Jim Kasson from Hewlett-Packard. Kasson, whom Maxfield had known socially for a number of years, had a background in data acquisition and control systems and was very knowledgeable about comput-

EXHIBIT 1 ROLM Corporation financial data

Income Statement for fiscal year ending June 29, 1973

Net sales	$3,637,000
Costs and expenses	
Cost of goods sold	1,572,000
Product development	455,000
Marketing, administrative & general	964,000
Interest	14,000
Total costs and expenses	3,005,000
Income before taxes	632,000
Provision for income taxes	311,000
Net income	$ 321,000

Balance Sheet for quarter ending September 28, 1973

Current assets:		*Current liabilities:*	
Cash	$ 202,000	Accounts payable & accrued payroll	$ 306,700
Receivables	442,000	Income tax payable	139,400
Inventories	994,600	Other current liabilities	31,900
Other current assets	43,100	Notes payable	24,400
Total current assets	$1,681,700	Total current liabilities	$ 502,400
Other assets:		Lease contracts payable — Long term	$ 97,500
Capital equipment	$ 440,700		
Accumulated depreciation	228,300	*Stockholders' equity:*	
		Capital stock	$ 170,800
Net capital equipment	212,400	Paid in surplus, net	610,800
Other assets	24,100	Retained earnings	536,700
Total other assets	$ 236,500	Total equity	$1,318,300
Total assets	$1,918,200	*Total liabilities and equity*	$1,918,200

SOURCE: Company records.

ers. He also brought with him from Hewlett-Packard another very good engineer. Together with ROLM's top computer software specialist they became, in June 1973, the three-person ROLM PBX technical feasibility team. In August 1973, Dick Moley, a marketing manager in Hewlett-Packard's computer division, joined ROLM to do the market analysis for the PBX.

TELECOMMUNICATIONS INDUSTRY IN THE UNITED STATES

The telecommunications system in the United States was operated by American Telephone and Telegraph (AT&T) and some 1760 independent telephone companies. AT&T was split into five major operations:

1. The General Department, which provided staff assistance in advertising, finance, engineering, legal and marketing to the rest of the corporation.

2. Western Electric, which manufactured telephone equipment for the Bell System operating companies. Under the terms of a 1956 consent decree with the Justice Department, Western Electric sold its products exclusively to the Bell System operating companies and to the U.S. Government. In 1972, Western Electric's total sales were greater than $7 billion.

3. The Bell Telephone Laboratories, which conducted basic research and designs equipment for manufacture by Western Electric.

4. The Long Lines Department, which installed and operated the interstate long distance network and handled all international calls. It received revenues from both the Bell System operating companies and the independent telephone companies for providing these services.

5. The twenty-four Bell System operating companies which provided and operated the telephone system at a local level. They covered about 85 percent of the telephones in the United States. Sixteen of the operating companies were wholly owned by AT&T, and it owned a majority interest in six of the others.

In 1972, AT&T had telephone operating revenues of $21.4 billion and had 109 million phones in service of which some 14 million were business phones connected to PBX, or functionally similar, systems.

The 1760 independent telephone companies provided local telephone service in areas not served by AT&T. These companies, as well as the Bell System operating companies, were regulated by state public utility commissions. They varied greatly in size from very small rural telephone companies to major corporations such as General Telephone which had operating revenues in the United States of almost $2 billion. The ten largest independent telephone companies are shown in Exhibit 2.

The Emergence of the Telephone Interconnect Industry

Prior to 1968, all telephone company tariffs in the United States had contained a blanket prohibition against the attachment of customer-provided terminal equipment (such as telephones, answering machines and PBXs) to the telecommunications network. The historic 1968 Carterfone decision of the Federal Communications Commission (FCC) held that these blanket prohibitions were unreasonable, discriminatory and unlawful, and the FCC required that the telephone companies file new tariffs that did not contain such blanket prohibitions. This decision opened up the vast market for terminal equipment to a variety of new competitors.

The Carterfone decision did allow the telephone companies to take reasonable steps to protect the telephone system from any harmful effects of interconnected equipment. New tariffs filed in early 1969 by the telephone companies required that protective connecting arrangements be installed on each line to protect and insulate the public network. In the next few years

EXHIBIT 2 Ten largest independent telephone companies

Names and addresses	Telephones	% of total independent telephone industry	Total operating revenues
1. General Telephone & Electrics Corp. (U.S. only), New York, N.Y.	10,622,000	45.81	$1,881,000,000
2. United Telecommunications, Inc., Kansas City, Missouri	2,642,300	11.40	448,684,000
3. Continental Telephone Corporation (U.S. Only), Chantilly, Virginia	1,774,200	7.65	299,536,000
4. Central Telephone & Utilities Corporation, Lincoln, Nebraska	1,059,600	4.57	194,055,000
5. Mid-Continent Telephone Corporation, Hudson, Ohio	593,500	2.56	82,842,000
6. Rochester Telephone Corporation, Rochester, New York	535,100	2.31	89,502,000
7. Puerto Rico Telephone Company, San Juan, Puerto Rico	357,400	1.54	64,277,000
8. Lincoln Telephone & Telegraph Company, Lincoln, Nebraska	239,800	1.03	37,176,000
9. Commonwealth Telephone Company, Dallas, Pennsylvania	154,900	.67	18,857,000
10. Florida Telephone Corporation, Ocala, Florida	143,600	.62	29,068,000

these connecting arrangements became a major bone of contention between the suppliers of customer interconnect equipment and the telephone companies. Interconnect equipment suppliers charged that the connection arrangements sometimes caused technical problems, that the telephone companies used delaying tactics in installing them, and that they unnecessarily raised costs (an average charge by the telephone companies of $7-10 per line per month) for the users of the interconnect equipment. The telephone companies responded to these charges by pointing out that they had rapidly developed a large number of protective connecting arrangements for different types of terminal equipment and had installed several hundred thousand of them by 1974.

PBXs and Key Systems

Interconnect equipment was any equipment attached to where incoming telephone company lines terminated on a customer's premises. Although such equipment took a wide variety of forms, including answering and recording devices, in the business market most of the sales volume was in two product classes: private branch exchanges (PBX) and key telephone systems.

A PBX is a local telephone switching system within a company which handles incoming, outgoing, and intra-office calls.[1] As shown schematically in Exhibit 3, a PBX consists of four major parts:

1. *Switching equipment and control system.* The switching system is the electromechanical or electronic equipment that connects the various internal (telephone extensions) and external lines in the system and provides ringing, busy signals, dial tone and intercom services. The control system is the system that actuates the switching functions.

2. *Trunk circuits.* These are lines connecting the PBX to the public switched network.

3. *Attendant console.* This is the equipment used by an inside operator to complete or transfer calls, to determine which lines are busy and to handle a variety of other tasks such as taking messages and paging.

4. *Telephone station equipment.* These are the individual telephones and key systems (a telephone that allows a person access to several lines with a single illuminated pushbutton set) located throughout the building or organization.

While key systems were commonly part of the PBX telephone system in large companies, stand-alone key systems were commonly used in smaller organizations (typically those with 40 or fewer telephones) as the sole system. Here they connected the outside lines directly to the user's extension telephone. Usually one pushbutton on each telephone was connected to a common line providing an intercom capability.

The technology involved in automatic PBX's had evolved in recent years —from electromechanical step-by-step systems, to electromechanical crossbar systems, to electronic systems.[2]

Step-by-step systems were first offered at the beginning of the century and were the primary PBX product of the telephone companies for many years. These electromechanical systems could be expanded indefinitely as long as the customer had space for the very bulky equipment. If maintained well, they provided economical and reliable service, but offered only very limited features. They were also expensive in terms of installation labor and maintenance and generated a large amount of "noise," making them unsuitable for data communications.

Crossbar systems were the next step in PBX evolution. These were again electromechanical switches, and variations of them had been available

---

[1]Some companies distinguished between PBX, a manually switched private branch exchange, and PABX, an automatic PBX, where all switching was done without operator intervention. Here PBX will be used to cover both types of equipment.

[2]A brief description of the switching and control systems technology can be found in Appendix A.

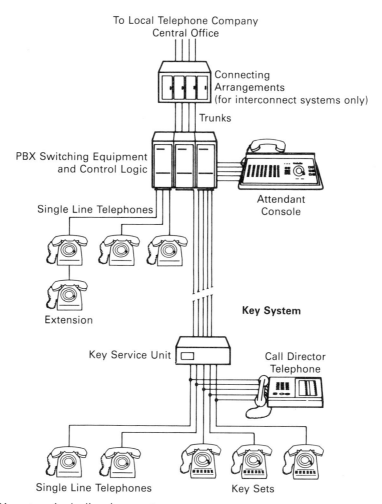

To Local Telephone Company
Central Office

Connecting
Arrangements
(for interconnect systems only)

Trunks

PBX Switching Equipment
and Control Logic

Attendant
Console

Single Line Telephones

Extension

Key System

Key Service Unit

Call Director
Telephone

Single Line Telephones   Key Sets

EXHIBIT 3 PBX system including key system
SOURCE: SRI Long Range Planning Service

for years. These systems were much more compact than the step-by-step systems, being housed in cabinets, and had lower labor and maintenance costs. Once they were set up and adjusted, they provided very reliable service but were costly to expand beyond the capacity of the original installation. Modern crossbar systems offered the user a number of features, such as:

1. *Selective toll restriction.* The system could be set up so that only certain individuals could dial long distance calls.

2. *Station transfer.* The user could transfer an incoming call from outside the company to another extension within the system without going to the switchboard operator.

3. *Consultation hold.* An incoming call could be held while the person dialed another number to secure information for the caller. This pro-

cedure did not require the telephone to be a key telephone equipped with a hold button.

4. *Add-on conference.* A third person could be dialed so that a three-way conference could be held. Again, a key telephone was not required.

Electronic telephone switching systems were the most recent technological development. The original work on electronic switching systems had been done at Bell Laboratories in the mid-1950s and the first commercial electronic central office (i.e., a switching system with the Bell system) was opened in 1965. Electronic switching technology only began to be used in the PBX market in the early 1970s and by 1974 there were about 20 electronic PBX models on the market. Most of these electronic systems used space division multiplexing (SDM).[3] Electronic systems with time division multiplexing (TDM), which allowed several signals and calls to go over one pair of wires, promised to significantly simplify and reduce the costs of cabling a building for the PBX system. Electronic systems contained both memory and logic capabilities. The control logic—that is, how the appropriate circuits were interconnected during use—was implemented in two basic ways. The method greatly affected the flexibility of the equipment. The two ways were:

1. *Wire logic.* Here the logic was stored on printed circuit cards and control actions were predetermined by the wiring connections on the cards. This limited the flexibility of the system and the ease with which it could be modified.

2. *Stored program logic (computer controlled).* Here all logic was stored either in exchangeable memory or by programming. Changes in the control logic could be readily made by changing the program.

Stored program logic gave a PBX great flexibility and the potential to meet future demands that wired logic systems could not match. Besides providing the normal control (connection) functions and a range of features to aid the telephone user, a computer-controlled electronic PBX could be used to record details of all toll calls (call detail recording), could monitor usage of the system, and could even perform self-diagnostic functions if there were problems with the equipment. In addition, if a company placed Tie Lines and WATS (Wide Area Telephone Service) lines on direct access (i.e., no operator was needed) the electronic switch could be programmed to seek the least cost route for a long distance call. With additional memory a wide range of features could be made available on an electronic PBX, including all of those available on a crossbar system. Thus, in an electronic PBX, the systems features were in the central switching unit rather than the particular telephone or key unit. The user could make use of a particular feature either by dialing a

---

[3]Again see Appendix A for explanation of technology.

code or pressing a couple of buttons on the telephone. Some of the features that could be offered on electronic systems included:

1. *Classes of service.* Each telephone station could be given access to only those services necessary for the person to perform his or her job. For example, some telephones could only be allowed to call certain long distance area codes.

2. *Automatic dialing and speed calling.* Each user could store frequently called numbers in the system. The switch dialed the number when the user dialed a code. The stored numbers could easily be changed by the user.

3. *Call forwarding.* A code instructed the switch to forward any incoming call to a specified number.

4. *Station number changes.* When the user was relocated and wished to retain his or her current number, this change could easily be entered into the system. No telephone moving charges would be incurred as long as a telephone existed at the user's new location.

5. *Automatic call distribution.* A number could be set up for a particular department and any incoming calls to that number were distributed by the switch to any free department telephone.

Electronic systems could therefore provide a range of useful features to the user. While basic electronic systems were more costly than similar electromechanical systems, the marginal cost of adding features after installation was much lower. They promised to be more reliable than electromechanical systems, although experience with electronic systems was not yet large enough to provide a convincing maintenance and reliability record. Electronic systems, particularly those based on the TDM technology, were also more suitable for tying into data communication terminals. This was expected to become an increasingly important consideration by the late 1970s, when many more users were expected to be using their telecommunications system for both voice and data transmission.

COMPETITION IN THE PBX AND KEY SYSTEMS MARKET

After 1968 a customer could purchase a PBX or key system from one of two basic types of suppliers: (1) the telephone company providing service in his area, or (2) an interconnect company. As Exhibit 4 suggests, the structure of the interconnect market was quite complex. In some cases companies manufactured the equipment and distributed it through one or more suppliers who installed and serviced the equipment. In other cases, the manufacturer might be a manufacturer-supplier selling directly to the end user or through a separate supplier subsidiary. These subsidiaries often would distribute the products of other manufacturers also.

Telephone Companies

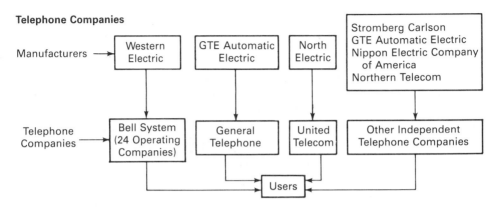

*Also occasionally sell to Bell, GTE, and United Telecom

Interconnect Industry

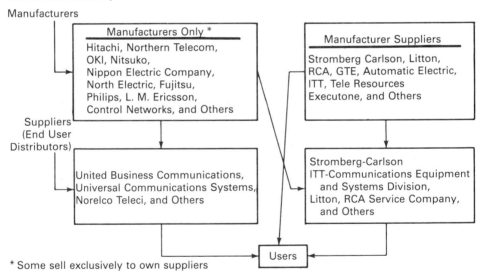

* Some sell exclusively to own suppliers

EXHIBIT 4   Structure of the market for PBXs and key systems
SOURCE: SRI Long Range Planning Service

Manufacturers of PBX and Key Systems

The manufacturers of PBX equipment were a pretty diverse group. Western Electric, the supplier of the Bell System, Northern Telecom, the U.S. subsidiary of Northern Electric, the Bell Canada manufacturing arm, and the major suppliers to the independent telephone companies, such as GTE-Automatic Electric, North Electric and Stromberg Carlson, were all well-established in the North American market—having supplied equipment to the various telephone companies since prior to the 1968 Carterfone decision. The PBX equipment manufactured by these suppliers for the independent telephone companies was, in 1968, generally similar to Western Electric's and offered only traditional features. The Carterfone decision provided an opportunity for another group of manufacturers to enter the U.S. market. These were largely European and Japanese manufacturers who had extensive experience with PBXs and key systems in other markets. With the encouragement of the interconnect suppliers (i.e., the companies selling to the end users), they modified their equipment and were able to offer end users features previously unavailable in the U.S. By the early 1970s the Japanese and European companies had captured about 75 percent of the U.S. PBX and key system interconnect market.[4] The major companies in this group were OKI, Nippon Electric, Hitachi and Nitsuko (all Japanese) and L.M. Ericsson (Swedish). International Telephone and Telegraph (ITT) also entered the U.S. market after the Carterfone decision and by 1973, some industry observers felt it had the best line of PBX equipment available in the U.S. A list of the major manufacturers ranked in terms of their estimated 1973 sales to U.S. interconnect suppliers is shown in Exhibit 5. As Exhibit 4 also suggests, some of these companies had also been quite successful in selling their products to some of the telephone operating companies. This resulted, in some cases, in end users being able to obtain identical equipment from either the telephone operating company or an interconnect supplier. The opening of the interconnect market had also brought a number of new U.S. manufacturers into the market. Wescom, Tele/Resources and Philco Ford had all developed electronic PBXs and were supplying them to the independent telephone companies or to interconnect suppliers. Litton and RCA, which had entered the market as national interconnect companies, were buying PBXs from others and were both rumored to be developing electronic PBXs. Other large manufacturers, active in foreign markets, were also believed to be ready to enter the market. IBM was also viewed as a possible entrant, since it had developed a very strong position in the European PBX market with two expensive electronic PBXs. The major manufacturers of electronic PBXs and a brief description of their equipment and market position is contained in Exhibit 6.

Notable in their absence from the list of manufacturers in Exhibit 6 were the Japanese and European manufacturers. The major Japanese manufacturers (Nippon, Hitachi, Fujitsu and Oki) and the leading European manufacturer, L.M. Ericsson, produced high-quality electromechanical PBX equipment. Until the devaluation of the dollar in 1973, the Japanese PBX equipment had been very competitively priced. Ericsson had always sold its equipment at premium prices in the U.S. Both the major Japanese manufacturers and Ericsson were rumored to be developing electronic PBXs.

Interconnect Companies

The number of interconnect companies had grown rapidly since 1968 and by 1973, there were thought to be about 300 of them in the U.S. These interconnect companies analyzed customer needs for PBXs and key systems, designed and recommended a system, installed it and serviced it. Interconnect

---

[4]That is, 75 percent of PBX and key system market which was not serviced by the AT&T operating companies or the independent telephone companies.

EXHIBIT 5   Major manufacturers of interconnect equipment ranked in order of estimated 1973 sales to U.S. interconnect companies

Company	Manufacturing Locations
OKI Electronics of America/OKI Electric of Japan	Japan and U.S.
Nippon Electric Company	Japan and U.S.
Hitachi	Japan and U.S.
Nitsuko*	Japan
International Telephone and Telegraph (ITT)	U.S. and Spain
L. M. Ericsson	Sweden
Northern Telecom (subsidiary of Northern Electric of Canada)	Canada and U.S.
Stromberg Carlson	U.S.
North Electric (subsidiary of United Telecommunications)	U.S.
Fujitsu	Japan
General Telephone and Electronics (GTE) — Automatic Electric	U.S.
North American Philips-Norelco	Netherlands and U.S.
CIT/TELIC	France and U.S.
Iwatsu*	Japan
Meisei	Japan
Siemens	Germany
Lynch	U.S.
Toshiba*	Japan

*Key systems only

SOURCE: SRI Long Range Planning Service.

companies could be subdivided into two basic groups, national suppliers and small regional or local suppliers. Estimated sales for the major interconnect suppliers in 1973 are shown in Exhibit 7.

The four largest national companies—Litton, Stromberg-Carlson, ITT and United Business Communications—had offices throughout the U.S. and were divisions of much larger corporations. In 1973, ITT was the only one of the four that had a wholly-owned manufacturing subsidiary. Stromberg-Carlson Communications was the result of the acquisition by General Dynamics, in June 1973, of Arcata Communications, Inc. and Arcata Leasing from Arcata National. The two Arcata National units had offices in twenty major metropolitan areas across the United States, and had generated losses of close to $4 million after taxes on sales of $25 million in the final year before General Dynamics acquired them. Eventually, as the acquired interconnect supplier was integrated with the Stromberg-Carlson manufacturing unit, Stromberg-Carlson would, like ITT, have an integrated manufacturing and distribution organization.

EXHIBIT 6 Electronic PBX manufacturers and their product offerings in 1973

Manufacturer	Model	Technologies Used[1]		Number of lines PBX can handle	Comments
		Control	Switching		
Western Electric	8D1A	Electronic-wired logic	Space division (SDM)-reed relay[2]	46-270	Western Electric produced a very broad line of PBXs, most of which were still electromechanical. The 801A and 812A were both semi-electronic. In the 101 systems all switching was actually done in a Bell System central office, not on the customer's premises. An electronic central office was needed for the ESS. Only a small proportion of Bell central offices was electronic.
	812A	Electronic-wired logic	SDM-crossbar	400-2000	
	101 ESS (3A)	Electronic-computer	Time division (TDM)-electronic (PCM)[3]	400-800	
	101 ESS (4A)	Electronic-computer	TDM-electronic (PCM)	2000-4000	
ITT	TD-100	Electronic-wired logic	TDM-electronic (PAM)[4]	40-100	ITT's fully electronic PBXs covered all line sizes. Many observers felt it had the best line of PBXs on the market in 1973. Shipment of the TD-100 PBX was expected to begin in early 1974.
	TE-400A	Electronic-wired logic	SDM-electronic	100-400	
	TE-400G	Electronic-wired logic	SDM-electronic	400-800	
	TCS-2	Elecronic-computer	SDM-electronic	600-6000	
Stromberg-Carlson	400A	Electronic-wired logic	SDM-reed relay	100-400	Both were semi-electronic PBXs.
	800A	Electronic-wired logic	SDM-reed relay	400-800	
Wescom	501	Electronic-wired logic	SDM-electronic	40-120	This PBX was being sold to independent telephone companies. Shipments were expected to begin in early 1974.

EXHIBIT 6 (continued)

Manufacturer	Model	Technologies Used[1]		Number of lines PBX can handle	Comments
		Control	Switching		
Tele/Resources	TR-32	Electronic-wired logic	TDM-electronic (PAM)	40-164	This PBX required unique and expensive phones and was sold only to interconnect suppliers. There were large order backlogs in late 1973.
Philco Ford	PC-192 PC-512	Electronic-computer Electronic-computer	SDM-electronic SDM-electronic	64-192 128-512	The PC-512 was introduced in 1972 and was marketed to independent telephone companies. It was very expensive relative to competitive offerings and was not believed to be selling well.
IBM	2750 3750	Electronic-computer Electronic-computer	SDM-electronic SDM-electronic	256-756 256-2264	IBM had been successfully selling these very expensive PBXs in Europe. They were really only feasible for installations requiring more than 500 telephones.
Northern Telecom	SG-1 SG-2	Electronic-wired logic Electronic-wired logic	TDM-electronic (PAM) TDM-electronic (PAM)	40-80 80-120	The SG-1 was introduced in 1972 and had been selling very well in the U.S. and Canada. The SG-2 was not yet in production.
ROLM	Proposed	Electronic-computer	TDM-electronic (PCM)	100-800	

[1] See Appendix A for a brief discussion of the technological issues.
[2] Reed really was an evolutionary switching approach that bridged the gap between electromechanical crossbar and fully electronic switching.
[3] PCM—pulse code modulation. Here all signals that are transmitted are digital signals.
[4] PAM—pulse amplitude modulation. Here all signals that are transmitted are analogue signals.

There were also three other companies that were national in scope. Universal Communications Systems, a subsidiary of American Motor Inns, and Teleci, a subsidiary of Holiday Inn, both specialized in the hotel/motel segment of the market, and RCA Service Company specialized in hospitals and universities. Industry observers believed these companies were profitable. The hotel/motel segment of the market had some unique characteristics that made it a good candidate for specialization. It required only a voice communications system, phones were not moved, key sets were rarely used, most calls were ingoing or outgoing, and a record of all outgoing calls had to be made for billing purposes. Universal Communications Systems and Teleci chose to meet the needs of this segment by importing Japanese electromechanical PBXs that could meet these requirements at low costs.

The regional interconnect suppliers were generally small companies which typically served a geographical area within a 50- or 100-mile radius of their home office. Many had originally been in the sound and/or communications equipment business and had simply diversified into the interconnect market. Some of the major regional interconnect suppliers were Tele/Resources (New York), The Other Telephone Company (Minnesota), Fisk Electric (Texas) and Scott-Buttner Communications (California). Most of the interconnect companies were very small with telecommunications sales generally being less than $2 million—Tele/Resources, believed to be the largest of these companies, had sales of about $4 million. Industry observers believed that these companies, unlike many of the national suppliers, were profitable. This was probably the result of lower overheads, knowledge of local requirements and the flexibility of small companies. Many of these companies were seriously undercapitalized.

Some industry observers felt that the interconnect suppliers had been unable to fully exploit what they believed to be the major weakness of the telephone companies, namely, their fairly obsolete product line and their inability to respond quickly to the changing market and technology. Much of the Japanese and other PBX equipment the interconnect suppliers were handling was only marginally superior in terms of features to the equipment manufactured by Western Electric. Thus they were forced to compete largely on the basis of lower price, more flexible pricing arrangements and greater installation flexibility. Even the Tele/Resources PBX, while fully electronic and easy to install, was not a great deal more flexible than conventional PBX equipment and, in addition, required expensive special phones. Also, it was said to be difficult to maintain. Nevertheless the first two years of production of this PBX was sold out within a few months of it being introduced.

Interconnect companies, both regional and national, stocked spare parts for their customers' PBXs so that they could rapidly get a customer's malfunctioning telephone system operating again. The faulty parts were then returned to the manufacturer for repair. Since this could take weeks—even months—the interconnect companies generally carried substantial inventories of spare parts.

The Response of the Telephone Companies

The AT&T operating companies and the independent telephone companies were vigorously resisting the encroachment of the interconnect suppliers into the PBX and key systems market. In 1970, AT&T had established a huge task force with people from Bell Labs, Western Electric and AT&T marketing and engineering at a new facility in Denver, Colorado, to develop a new, more competitive PBX product line. This resulted in four new competitively priced electronic or semi-electronic PBXs (shown in Exhibit 7) being introduced between 1971 and 1973. But even this progress was not rapid enough for some of the AT&T operating companies and they began to buy PBXs from outside suppliers. General Telephone had also taken similar steps to remain competitive.

The telephone operating companies also modified their pricing structures to improve their competitive position. Traditionally, telephone companies only leased equipment to users; thus the user paid an installation charge and a monthly rental/service fee (which could, of course, be increased from time to time) that continued as long as the customer had the equipment. By 1973, some of the telephone companies were giving their customers the option of paying for the use of the equipment with a "two-tier" pricing arrangement. With a "two-tier" pricing scheme, the customer signed a lease for the equipment for a specified number of years (usually between 5 years and 10 years). Then the cost of the equipment was split into two portions—the "capi-

EXHIBIT 7   Estimated sales by interconnect companies in 1973

Company	Sales (millions of dollars)
Litton Business Telephone Systems	25
Stromberg-Carlson Communications[1] (subsidiary of General Dynamics)	25
ITT-Communications Equipment and Systems Division	18
United Business Communications (subsidiary of United Telecommunications)	14
Universal Communications Systems (subsidiary of American Motor Inns)	9
RCA Service Company	8
Norelco Communications[1] (subsidiary of North American Philips)	5
GTE-Automatic Electric[1]	7
Teleci (subsidiary of Holiday Inns)	3
Tele/Resources	4
ITT-Terryphone[2]	4
Others (about 300, mostly local)	60
TOTAL	$182

[1]Excluding sales to local suppliers, figures for which are included under "Others."
[2]Key system sales only.

SOURCE: SRI Long Range Planning Service.

tal" cost of the equipment, which could be paid off immediately, and the maintenance/administrative charge, which was paid over the life of the lease and which could be increased during this period.

Current Status of the Interconnect Market and Future Prospects

In a proprietary report published by the Long Range Planning Service (now the Business Intelligence Program) of SRI International, it was estimated that sales by interconnect suppliers had grown from virtually zero in 1968 to $182 million (at end-user prices) in 1973. Manufacturers' selling prices were approximately 50 percent of end-user prices, and given that there was a substantial amount of inventory at the supplier level, manufacturers' shipments were expected to total $120 million in 1973.

The $182 million sales estimate was broken into three categories:

1. $130 million in PBX sales. This included 3300 PBXs with 248,000 telephones. This was estimated to be 12.4 percent of the dollar value of all new and replacement PBX installations in 1973.

2. $47 million in key systems sales. This included 6000 key systems with 72,000 telephones. This was estimated to be 6.7 percent of the dollar value of all new and replacement key system installations in 1973.

3. $5 million in service and maintenance revenues which included charges for telephones added to the original system, moving telephones within an office, etc.

SRI also attempted to project the market growth through 1985. Given the uncertainties surrounding the interconnect market, both conservative and optimistic projections were made. These projections took into account probable shakeouts in the industry, stronger competition from the telephone companies, regulatory factors and a shortening life cycle (hence more frequent replacement) for this type of equipment.

On the basis of SRI's assumptions, total interconnect supplier sales were expected to be in the range of $1.1 to $1.7 billion by 1985; this was expected to give interconnect suppliers an installed base penetration of 21 percent to 30 percent for PBXs and 15 percent to 21 percent for key systems. During this period SRI expected rapid technological development to continue with computer-controlled or stored-logic electronic switching systems being standard in PBX and key systems by 1980.

PBX AND KEY SYSTEMS CUSTOMERS

One of the first things Dick Moley had done after joining ROLM in August 1973 was to talk to several large companies about their communication problems. Commenting on these interviews Moley said: "What they came up with was very interesting, because what they said their problems were, were problems that were not being addressed by the interconnect equipment or the Bell System equipment at the time, and that is where we saw our opportunity. What they said was that the largest portion of their bill, frequently 70-80 percent, is toll expenses. If you are a large electronics company, for example, you have Foreign Exchange lines, Tie lines and WATS lines. Trying to get people to use these, to get them to go to the proper tables and look up how to call a number in a particular city, say Los Angeles—to dial 76 for Los Angeles, then dial 9 for an outside line, then dial the telephone number, is very difficult. Even if a person does all this the line frequently will be busy. Similarly, to gain access to a WATS line the caller may have to call a special operator and wait for a line to become available. So what happens in many companies, of course, is that many people make many long distance calls without bothering to use these expensive facilities. Furthermore, many companies wish to keep track of who was calling which numbers, both to control abuse and to bill departments for their real use of facilities, rather than simply making an arbitrary allocation. Many people also felt restrictions on toll calling on a telephone-by-telephone basis and automated queuing for WATS lines seemed to be needed features. The equipment available in 1973 simply did not address these needs and the Bell System obviously didn't have a great incentive to optimize the use of toll calling facilities, since it would negatively impact its revenues."

A second major area of concern that surfaced in these interviews was the cost of making, and the time required to make, changes in the telephone system when people were relocated. This was particularly true in firms that used a project type of organization or in organizations that were experiencing rapid growth, where the average times between moves of a phone could be as short as six months. Every time personnel changes were made and people were relocated, the telephone company had to be called in to change wires and relocate the phones and sometimes the companies had to wait quite a long time for these changes to be made. Furthermore, the Bell System and independent telephone company tariffs to make these changes varied across the country. In some areas it cost about $15 to move a phone, whereas in other areas, such as New York, it might cost $75 for the same service. ROLM estimated on average the real cost of performing this service was about $50. Many large companies operating in several parts of the country were aware of these differences and realized that, under pressure from the Public Utility Commissions for the telephone companies to stop "subsidizing business," these charges would probably rise in areas where they were low. One very large firm of consultants operating in San Francisco, where the cost of moving a phone was only about $20, was already spending over $400,000 per year on these moves and changes.

"Another area that was an absolute nightmare was key phone systems," commented Dick Moley. "We saw that in our own offices that year when Ken Oshman's office had to be relocated. Two men spent a whole day recabling 125-pair cables to the new location for the key phone system. The cost was nominal, but it clearly cost the telephone company a lot of money to make these changes. We then asked ourselves, why are key systems so difficult to move? The reason is that each light on the call director's pushbutton set takes six wires to activate, so you may need a very thick (one inch in diameter) 125-pair cable from the switching equipment to the call director telephone with twenty or so lines and you clearly can't afford to run such a cable all over the building. So, essentially, the wiring is customized for the key system. That seemed to us to be totally insane with the available electronics. So we said we can do it differently. What we can do is use a key phone with a three-pair cable—one pair for voice, one pair to power the electronics and the third pair to digitally signal which button is depressed and to indicate which button to light. Thus, if we standardize the building wiring completely on three-pair cables which connect to wall sockets much like electrical wiring, the user will not have to rewire the building if some phone is moved. They might have to plug in a special box and make an arrangement back in the switching equipment to make sure it was connected to a switch to drive a key phone rather than a single line phone, but no rewiring will be necessary."

Large customers would be critical to ROLM's success in the marketplace, since the computer-controlled PBX system that they were developing was designed to handle 100 to 800 lines. This line range had been chosen because cost-effective computer controlled models that would provide the kind of benefits customers desired could not yet be cost competitive for installations of less than 100-line capacity. In 1973 only a very small number of Fortune 500 companies were buying from interconnect suppliers. Most of the sales by the interconnect companies had been made to smaller organizations, in fact about 75 percent of the interconnect equipment was sold to hotels and motels, wholesalers and retailers, stockbrokers, insurance agencies, hospitals and clinics, attorneys, banks, manufacturers and service industries. Few of the installations made by the interconnect companies had more than 100 lines. For these reasons, a final issue Dick Moley raised in his interviews with the large companies was why they had not bought equipment from interconnect suppliers. A major reason the companies cited was that they saw few economic benefits from buying from interconnect suppliers. The main benefit was that they could purchase the equipment and hence freeze their equipment cost (since they would be unaffected by telephone company rental rate increases). But since equipment was usually only 20 to 30 percent of their costs, and when a discounted cash flow analysis of the purchase-versus-rental choice was made, the savings often turned out to be minor. Meanwhile if the equipment was purchased, the company was locked into equipment that might soon become obsolete. It seemed that smaller companies were much less likely to do a discounted cash flow analysis and seemed to be largely attracted to the interconnect PBXs by their marginally better features and the belief they would get better service from these companies than they would from the telephone operating companies. An additional factor that might help explain the failure of the interconnect companies to penetrate larger companies was that few of the interconnect suppliers appeared to have sales organizations that were capable of conducting a multilevel sales campaign at several levels of decision making in prospective large companies.

From his discussions with the large companies Mr. Moley also gained a better appreciation of the decision-making process for PBXs and key systems. Voice communication decision makers were generally low level office managers or communication managers. These decisions had historically been made at a low level because the decisions to be made with respect to telecommunications equipment were generally of a minor nature. Until 1968, the Bell System operating company or the independent telephone company was a monopoly supplier and hence there was no choice of vendor. The office of communications manager often relied greatly on the recommendations of the telephone company salesperson and, in fact, frequently the manager was a former Bell System employee. The main responsibilities of the manager were largely those of placing orders with the telephone company and coordinating installation and service activities. When alternative suppliers to the telephone companies became available, they were very cautious about recommending them, since the risks of poor service and the possibility of the interconnect supplier going out of business were not inconsequential. Furthermore, since switching to an interconnect supplier typically required that the equipment be purchased rather than leased, they usually lacked the authority to make the decision themselves, and the capital expenditure had often to be approved at very high levels in the organization, sometimes even at the Board of Directors level. The communication manager was not usually accustomed to preparing these types of proposals and doing the necessary internal selling to get the proposals approved.

The results of the customer interviews made ROLM management very enthusiastic about their potential entry into the telecommunications market. As Mr. Moley remarked, "Out of our discussions I and the others in ROLM management became really enthusiastic, because clearly here is a vast market where we potentially have the capability to solve meaningful customer problems and save companies large amounts of money. Computer technology was the key to solving these problems; we could optimize call routings, handle toll restrictions, etc. If there are telephones in place, handling moves and changes becomes simply a matter of remotely reprogramming the switching equipment. Nobody needs to visit physically the customer's office or plant.

THE ROLM PBX

By October 1973, Jim Kasson and his two associates had made considerable progress on the technical aspects of the ROLM product. The conventional wisdom in the telephone industry trade magazines at the time was that time division multiplexing (TDM) with pulse code modulation (PCM) switching technology and stored logic (computer control) control technology would not be viable, cost-effective technologies until the late 1970s or early 1980s. Jim Kasson was now convinced it was a viable technology in 1973. As a result of some clever circuit work and ROLM's knowledge of minicomputers, software and PCM technology, they were convinced their approach would work and would be cost-effective. They had already "bread-boarded" (i.e., laid out the electronic circuitry in a crude way) key technology elements that were new to ROLM and they even had a couple of telephones in the laboratory working with their switching circuitry. In effect, the technological advances they were taking advantage of promised to change the nature of PBX manufacture from a labor- and capital-intensive operation to a technology-intensive electronic assembly operation which would require the manufacturer to have minicomputer, software and solid-state switching expertise. These were all technologies in which ROLM management felt their company had significant strengths.

The management of ROLM was convinced that the flexibility of a computer-controlled PBX built on a TDM technology would change the economics of a business communication system's installation, maintenance and operation, besides providing excellent user convenience. For example, with their PBX it would be possible to prewire a building with standard 3-pair cable connected to wall outlets. Then all that was necessary to install a complete system was to connect the cables to the PBX, plug the standard telephone sets into the sockets, and enter into the computer the locations and extension numbers of the telephones. In the case of a multiline key set, the information entered into the PBX would include information on all the extensions which are to be routed to the set. Moves and changes of extensions would be a straightforward matter of entering the new configuration information into the computer. No longer would it be necessary to have the wiring tailored to the specific configuration and have ancillary keyset switching equipment located remote from the PBX. The features, both standard and optional, that they proposed to offer on the ROLM PBX are listed in Exhibit 8.

Thus their proposed product was a minicomputer-controlled TDM system which could handle both voice and data communications. In essence it had all the capabilities of the successful IBM computer-controlled PBXs, plus the additional capability of handling key telephones without requiring large cables and key service units. Furthermore, unlike the IBM PBXs, which cost from two to three times as much as conventional systems, the ROLM PBX was expected to be price competitive in the range of 100 to 500 extensions, a range which, they estimated, accounted for 60 percent of the dollar value of all PBX systems.

DECISIONS FACING ROLM IN OCTOBER 1973

Although many of the technical uncertainties with respect to the product had been resolved, there were several dark clouds on the horizon. The Bell System was aggressively attempting to stop the competitive erosion by moves

EXHIBIT 8   Features and services to be offered on the proposed ROLM PBX

A. *Station Features - Standard*
   Direct Outward Dialing
   Station-to-Station Dialing
   Non-consecutive Station Hunting
   Programmable Class of Service
   Consultation Hold - All Calls
   Call Forwarding, Unlimited
   Flexible Station Controlled Conference
   Group Call
   Indication of Camp-On to Station
   Individual Transfer - All Calls
   Lockout with Secrecy
   One-Way Splitting
   Outgoing Trunk Camp-On
   Processor-Controlled Changes - Type A
   Trunk Answer from Any Station
   Tie Trunks
   Toll Restriction
   Trunk-to-Trunk Connections-Station-Type B
   Trunk-to-Trunk Consultation

   Station Features - Optional
   Alternate Routing (toll call optimization)
   Automatic Redial
   CCSA Access
   Dictation Access and Control
   Direct Inward Dialing
   Direct Inward System Access
   Discriminating Ringing
   Plug-in Station (with Keyset Adapter)
   Secretarial Intercept
   Station DTMF to Rotary Dial Conversion
   Tenant Service
   Automatic Identification of Outward Dialing
   Redundancy
   Off Premises Extension
   Private Lines
   Music on Hold - Attendant
   Music on Hold - System
   Music on Camp-On
   Reserve Power - Inverter
   Speed Calling
   Area Code Restriction
   Traffic Measurement
   Paging Interface

B. *Attendant Features - Standard*
   Attendant Camp-On
   Attendant Conference
   Attendant Console
   Attendant Transfer of Incoming Call
   Attendant Transfer - Outgoing
   Attendant Trunk Busy Lamp Field
   Switched Loop Trunk Selection
   Switched Loop Station Selection
   Flexible Intercept
   System Alarm Indications
   Multiple Trunk Groups - Unlimited
   Attendant Key Sending - Touch Tone

   Attendant Features - Optional
   Busy Lamp Field
   Busy Verification of Stations

on both the regulatory front and by improving their equipment, developing new pricing schemes, etc. In June 1973, at the urging of the telephone companies, the North Carolina Utility Commission had proposed banning all interconnect equipment from the state. Although in January the Federal Communications Commission ruled that its own ruling preempted state regulation of interconnect equipment, the issue was still in the courts. ROLM management was also concerned about other regulatory actions the Bell System might take. On the pricing front, the Bell System and the independent telephone companies had made their pricing structures more competitive and had the potential to make further moves in that direction. Furthermore, the Bell System's intensified product development efforts were likely to result in products that were technically much more competitive with the proposed ROLM offering than was the current prdouct line, although ROLM would probably have a year or so lead time. Other interconnect manufacturers would probably be into the market with more competitive offerings even earlier than the Bell System.

ROLM's Board of Directors, in preliminary discussions of the proposed entry, were not totally convinced of the wisdom of ROLM, a $4 million company, moving against such formidable competitors and openly questioned whether this was the best area in which to invest the company's limited resources. Investment bankers also raised similar concerns. Even within the top ranks of ROLM management there were executives who were quite unsure about whether a move into the telecommunications market was in ROLM's best interest. The Treasurer and the Director of Manufacturing had both formerly worked for Arcata Communications and had seen at first hand the problems in the interconnect business. They were among those expressing concern.

From a manufacturing cost viewpoint, ROLM management was not concerned about the disparity in size between ROLM and its competitors, whose manufacturing experience base for the most part was built on electromechanical equipment (which was labor- and capital-intensive), whereas ROLM's equipment was largely electronic. In their view, this made it feasible for ROLM to compete with the likes of Western Electric.

Pricing the PBX

Kasson and his team had concluded that with a further investment of $500,000 in engineering and manufacturing they could get the product into production. If given the go-ahead, they expected to have a prototype working in the laboratory by mid-1974 and to begin shipping systems in early 1975.

Detailed estimates of manufacturing costs had been developed by Kasson and others on the PBX team. With a sales price based on two and one-half times manufacturing cost (direct materials, direct labor and overhead based on direct labor cost) the ROLM PBX promised to be cost competitive with the most closely competitive models available in the United States. They anticipated that volume discounts would be given to customers ordering multiple PBXs, if they decided to market the product through telephone companies or interconnect companies. Since the ROLM PBX made heavy use of electronic components (e.g., the minicomputer, the computer memory and integrated circuits), the cost of the PBX was expected to decline over time as the cost of electronic components continued their decline. Electromechanical PBXs, and even electronic PBXs based on analogue technologies, were expected to experience a much more static cost future.

Channels of Distribution for the PBX

In many respects ROLM's management felt the most crucial decision facing them in 1973 was the choice of channels of distribution for their PBX system. Dick Moley felt they had several alternatives open to them:

1. *Sell to the Bell System.* The operating companies of the Bell System had traditionally relied exclusively on Western Electric for all their equipment. However, the competitive pressures from the interconnect companies had resulted in several of the operating companies, including the largest one, Pacific Telephone, buying equipment from other suppliers. Pacific Telephone had bought electromechanical PBX systems from Japanese suppliers and more recently it had bought Northern Telecom's fully electronic PBX which handled up to 120 lines. The former move was not a very radical one, since the Japanese designs were similar to Western Electric designs and could be installed and maintained by their field service force without any extensive retraining. The Northern Telecom purchase was more significant since this did require retraining the field service force. Since the Bell operating companies were still believed to control some 80 percent of the installed PBX base, even a small share of this market would represent a huge sales volume to ROLM.

2. *Sell to the independent telephone companies,* such as General Telephone. While the independent telephone companies covered about 15 percent of the phones in the U.S., they were more concentrated in rural areas and were growing about 50 percent more rapidly than AT&T. This reflected the movement of industry and population away from major metropolitan areas. Since larger companies still tended to concentrate in major metropolitan areas, the independent telephone companies' share of the large PBX (greater than 100 lines) market was much less than 15 percent. Their captive manufacturing subsidiaries were not as strong as Western Electric and the independent telephone companies had never relied on them as much. But even taking into account that the independent telephone companies were a much smaller factor in the market than the Bell System they still represented, a large, burgeoning market, with companies like Stromberg-Carlson and several Japanese and European manufacturers very active in it.

3. *Sell to the interconnect companies.* These were concentrated in the larger metropolitan areas. Here ROLM had two alternatives: (1) The national companies such as Litton Business Systems, ITT, RCA Service Company, United Business Communications and Stromberg-Carlson Communications; or (2) The regional companies such as Tele/Resources, Fisk Telephone Systems and Scott-Buttner Communications. Many of the national suppliers were in trouble due to the lack of experienced managers, higher than anticipated investments, heavier than anticipated installation and maintenance expenses, too rapid geographic expansion resulting in loss of control, and the difficulty of providing quick and adequate service capability on a nationwide basis. These problems were exacerbated by the fiercely competitive nature of the markets, the heavy legal expenses, and the drain on management time necessary to challenge some of the telephone companies' new pricing schemes before the regulatory commissions. These chaotic market conditions had resulted in some companies getting into difficulties and being forced to merge with others. Some of the regional interconnect companies were doing quite well in their local markets. They bought their equipment from a variety of manufacturers including Nippon, Stromberg-Carlson and Tele/Resources. Generally the manufacturers required them to handle the equipment on a non-exclusive basis, so that two or more interconnect companies in the same market area might carry the same PBX line. The regional companies typically were undercapitalized and sold small systems. It was very seldom that one handled a PBX with a capacity larger than 100 lines. Most of the equipment they were handling was still electromechanical. While marketing through regional interconnect companies had some advantages, particularly from a servicing perspective, there was a real question of whether large companies with multiple locations would want to deal with multiple interconnect companies. Some of the other manufacturers, including Northern Telecom, handled large sales directly, and simply subcontracted with the regional interconnect companies for installation and maintenance services.

4. *Sell direct.* ROLM had given little thought to this alternative, since they felt they were simply too small. But from a sales viewpoint it had some obvious advantages, especially when it came to dealing with large accounts with multiple locations around the country.

Dick Moley's Task

Dick Moley had to make decisions with respect to channels of distribution and pricing and also with respect to such closely related issues as the amount and nature of advertising and sales promotion to be directed at end users. By the November 1973 Board meeting, he hoped to have selected and laid out in some detail the marketing plan for the ROLM PBX. He hoped he would be able to present a convincing case for ROLM's entry into the PBX market.

Appendix A: PBX and Key Systems Technology

Much of the technological change in PBX systems was occurring in the switching and control systems. The technological alternatives in both the switching and control systems are shown in Exhibit A1. With respect to the switching system, two major alternatives were possible: space division multiplexing (SDM) and time division multiplexing (TDM). An SDM system was one in which separate individual transmission paths were set up for the duration of the call. A TDM system was one in which the speech on each active line was sampled at a very high rate, so that no information was lost, and the samples were assigned to unique time slots on a common transmission line. The original signal could be reconstructed from these samples when needed. The ability to handle many calls on one line promised to lower costs. In a TDM system the samples could be transmitted as either an analogue (pulse amplitude modulation [PAM]) signal or a ditigal (pulse code modulation [PCM]) signal. If pulse code modulation was used, then all signals were digital, making such a system ideal for transmitting data as well as voice. This was expected to be an increasingly valuable feature by the late 1970s, as more and more companies wished to transmit both data and voice over the same telecommunications system. Furthermore, if a digital signal was sent over a reliable transmission line there was no cross-talk or distortion, which one could get if an analogue system were used. ROLM engineers believed that a PBX with a TDM analogue system could not (with the technology then available) be designed to handle more than 120 lines without excessive cross-talk. Partly for this reason, TDM with pulse code modulation was carrying an increasing share of the Bell System's long distance traffic. Nevertheless many observers in the early 1970s did not expect that the pulse code modulation technology would be cost-effective in PBXs until the late 1970s.

The control system could be either distributed control or common control. A distributed control system was one in which the control logic was distributed throughout the PBX system (e.g., if key phones were used some of the control logic was in the key phone unit), whereas a common control system was one in which all the control functions were centralized in one set of logic. With a common control system the control equipment was only tied up during the time the connection was made and not during the conversation. A wired logic common control system basically did with electronic components what was otherwise done by electromechanical relays. On the other hand, a computer-controlled common control system added a new dimension to the PBX. New circuits had to be added to a wired logic system in order to alter its properties and capabilities, but a computer-controlled system's functions could be altered by changing its program. This gave a computer-controlled system great flexibility and the potential to meet future demands that wired logic systems could not match.

EXHIBIT A1 PBX technological alternatives

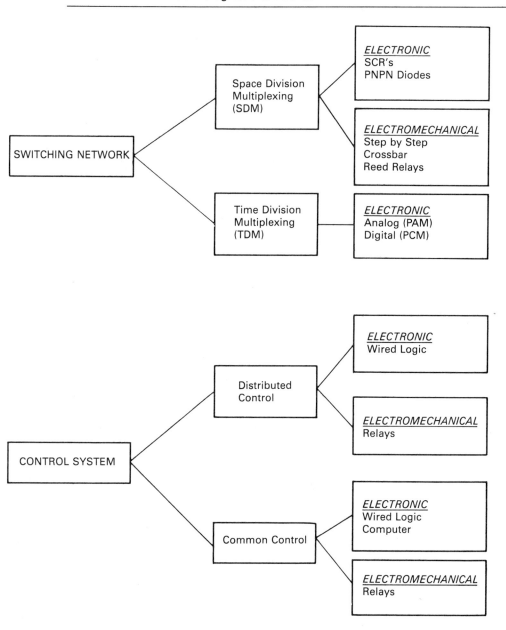

SETTING
OBJECTIVES

II

Establishing Goals

2

A fter the company's marketing executives have assessed the opportunities existing for their firm's products, they are in a position to establish goals or objectives for their various products and to assist top management in developing goals for the company as a whole. (We will use the terms *goals* and *objectives* synonymously.)

It is helpful to consider two broad categories of goals: *Strategic* goals and *tactical* goals. Strategic goals

1. are usually established for the *entire* firm.
2. are a company's *major* goals.
3. are generally established for a period of time *exceeding one year.*
4. are essentially achieved by various *combinations of products and markets* which a company employs.

Tactical goals

1. are usually established for a *sub-unit* of a firm, such as the marketing department.
2. are considered *ancillary* goals in that they are established to help achieve the company's strategic goals.
3. are generally established for a time period of *one year or less.*
4. when established for the marketing department, are usually achieved through the *deployment of the marketing mix.*

An example will help to clarify the relationships between strategic and tactical goals. Assume that the top management of a consumer products company establishes a goal of an average return on investment of 15 percent over the next five years. This strategic goal is to be in part achieved by the development of a new type of toothpaste directed to a new market segment: teenagers who wear braces. A new product-new market combination is used to achieve the 15 percent return on investment strategic goal. To help achieve this strategic goal, marketing's top executives assign this tactical objective, among others, to the marketing department: decrease the cost of a salesman's call from $85 to $75. Marketing's sales management executives decide that the way to achieve this tactical objective is to devise a new routing plan for sales personnel.

Strategic Objectives

Five major strategic objectives are profit, market share, sales volume, growth, and product insulation.

Profit. While some companies may specify their profit objectives in absolute terms, such as $20 million, most prefer to stipulate them in percentage form. It is most common to express absolute profit as return on assets, return on equity, or return on sales.

Return on assets (R.O.A.) is found by dividing the absolute profit figure by the value of total assets. If a firm had generated a $10 million profit on a total asset base of $100 million, its return on assets would be 10 percent ($10 million/$100 million). Return on assets is an important profit measure because it tells top management how good a return its company is achieving on the total amount of resources available. For 1981, the 500 largest manufacturing firms in the United States had an average return on assets of 6.5 percent.

Return on equity (R.O.E.) is calculated by dividing a company's net profit by the value of its equity. In the example above, let's assume that the company's equity is $80 million. Thus, its return on equity is 12.5 percent (a $10 million profit divided by an $80 million equity figure). You recall that equity essentially represents the value of a company's assets which are provided by its owners; R.O.E. indicates the return a company's owners are achieving on their investment. In 1981, the 500 largest manufacturing firms in the United States had a 13.8 percent return on equity.

Return on sales, also called *profit margin,* is found by dividing a company's net profit by its sales figures. In the hypothetical company, if we assume that its sales were $200 million, its return on sales would be 5 percent (a $10 million profit divided by a $200 million sales figure). In 1981, the nation's 500 largest manufacturers had a 4.6 percent profit margin.

The *Du Pont model,* named after the giant chemical manufacturer which pioneered its use, is helpful in showing a company's top management how these three profitability measures are related to each other. It also indicates what is necessary to achieve better profit results. The top half of Exhibit 1 shows the various components of the Du Pont model. Notice that the other four components in the model interact to obtain return on equity. The bottom half of Exhibit 1 shows how each component in the top half is calculated.

Using the data provided for the company in the examples above, Exhibit 2 shows how the Du Pont model works. A profit margin of 5 percent times an asset turnover ratio of 2.0 yields a return on assets figure of 10 percent. When the 10 percent R.O.A. figure is multiplied by the 1.25 leverage ratio, the 12.5 percent return on equity figure is obtained.

Suppose the executives of the company wanted to increase the return on equity figure. The Du Pont model indicates that the return on equity figure could be increased by improving the values for the other four components. Profit margin could be increased, for example, by decreasing costs so that the absolute profit figures of $10 million would be increased. If the level of sales was increased, the asset turnover figure would increase. Improving either the profit margin or the asset turnover figure would improve the return on assets figure. Since the leverage ratio is found by dividing total assets by owners' equity, one way to improve it is to obtain more debt financing; this

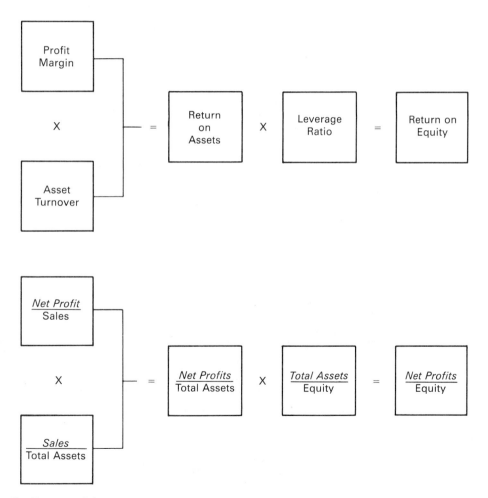

EXHIBIT 1 The Du Pont model

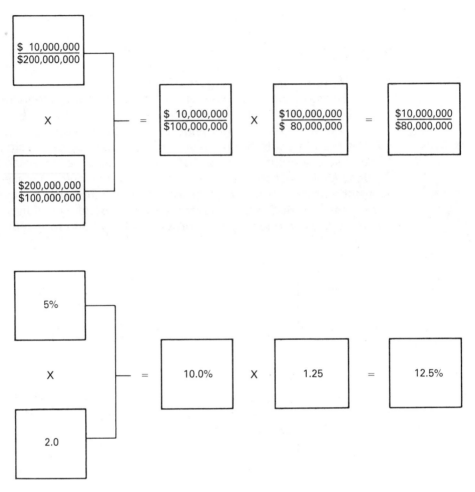

EXHIBIT 2   How the Du Pont model works

would increase total assets while leaving the owners' equity figure unchanged.

Market Share. Much of the drive to obtain the highest possible market share has been fueled by a major study which shows that high profitabilities were associated with high market shares.[1] The study found that market share was one of the most important factors explaining profitability of the companies analyzed. Specifically, firms with market shares over 40 percent had an average return on assets of 30 percent, while those with market shares of less than 10 percent had an average return on assets of only 9 percent. Much of the high profitability associated with high market shares was attributed to these companies' higher levels of production, resulting in lower costs and lower prices.

There is some empirical evidence that high market shares may not necessarily be associated with high profitability. A study of ninety-seven large manufacturers found that, although the highest levels of profitability (return on assets, sales, and equity) were found with firms that had a market share of 60 percent or better, the lowest profitabilities were demonstrated by companies whose market shares were between 40 percent and 49 percent. Some companies that experienced long run increases in market share did not obtain improved return on assets, sales, and equity. Large increases in market share from one year to the next were not necessarily likely to result in improved rates of return. The most important findings of this study were those dealing with companies with market share difficulties. Companies having long run declines (six or more consecutive years) in market share were likely to suffer correspondingly lower rates of return, and those that had large market share decreases (2 percent or higher) from one year to the next were likely to undergo a decrease in rates of return.[2]

A number of factors explain why profitability may decline as market share increases. The customers who have to be attracted to increase market share may be loyal to competitors; getting them to switch may not justify the cost incurred. If the customers the firm is trying to attract are a new market segment, their needs may be unique and not worth meeting.

Sears, Roebuck is a good example of a company whose efforts to increase market share backfired. In 1977, Sears used promotional increases and longer sales to increase market share. The advertising allocation was increased to $518 million in 1977, a $100 million increase over the 1976 figure. Sales lasted three to four weeks in 1977, compared to three to nine days the previous year. Although Sears' sales increased 15 percent to $17.2 billion in 1977 and its market share increased, profits dropped to $421 million in 1977 from the $466 million figure the previous year. Sears' profit margin dropped to 2.4 percent in 1977, compared to the 3.0 percent figure obtained in 1976.

A number of firms have found that having the dominant market share in their industry can have undesirable consequences. Such firms can become targets of competitors, especially if they are vulnerable and perceived as such by competitors. Procter & Gamble, for example, successfully eroded Scott Paper's dominant market share for paper products in the 1970s. Scott assumed its market position was unassailable and ignored its most important line, diversifying into other fields. Firms with high market share can also become the target of governmental agencies because of their dominance. IBM, for example, has been brought into court by the Justice Department because of its high market share and some of the practices it used to obtain that position.

Sales Volume. Sales volume is a commonly pursued strategic objective. Sales volume figures may be expressed in units or dollars. They may be expressed in absolute terms (150,000 units or $5.2 million) or as percentage increases (15 percent increase in units, 10 percent increase in dollars).

Growth. The objective of growth can pertain to a number of different aspects of a company's operations, including profit, sales, assets, and number of employees. It generally means *increases* in these figures. During the 1970s, Dr.

Pepper expressed its growth objectives like this: double profits and sales every four years. Canadian Tire Corp. is striving for an annual growth rate of 10 percent in sales volume during the 1980s. In the 1970s, C. Peter McColough, the chairman and CEO of Xerox, specified a long-term objective of an annual growth in earnings (profits) of 15 percent.

Product Insulation. Product insulation is a strategic objective which is rarely articulated in management circles as such, but it is a goal which is highly desirable and actively pursued, particularly by the marketing department, for a firm's various products. Product insulation means that a product has secured such a protected niche in the marketplace that it is relatively immune to the marketing tactics of competitive firms.

Obtaining product insulation is desirable for a number of reasons:

1. The company achieving product insulation can devote important resources to other products.

2. Relatively small commitments of resources to insulated products may result in sizable sales volume and profit increases.

3. Competition will waste valuable resources as it attempts to erode the protected position of an insulated product.

4. The absence of strong competitive products may result in an inelastic demand curve for an insulated product.

An insulated position for a product can be achieved in a number of different ways, but the major (and probably best) strategy is by gaining differential advantage through a distinct and observable product attribute that satisfies consumer needs more effectively than competitive offerings. Although an insulated position can be obtained through other means, such as advertising, channels of distribution, or pricing, these are probably not as effective or long lasting. Patents tend to be less effective in obtaining product insulation than is generally believed. Competitive firms frequently ignore the patent and bring out a similar product, preferring to battle it out eventually in the courts. In the meantime, they enjoy the profits.

Product insulation is measured primarily by calculating the coefficient of the cross elasticity of demand. Assume the following conditions:

1. When a competitive product P_2 has a price of $2.00, product P_1 ordinally sells 1,000 units a week.

2. The price of product P_2 is reduced to $1.50. Product P_1's weekly sales drop to 900 units.

The coefficient of cross elasticity of demand is expressed by the formula;

$$E_c = \frac{\% \ \Delta \ Q \ P_1}{\% \ \Delta \ p \ P_2}$$

The coefficient of cross elasticity of demand is found by dividing the percentage change in the quantity of product P_1 sold by the percentage change in the price of product P_2. We have:

$$E_c = \frac{-10\%}{-25\%} = .40$$

This example shows a product which is relatively well insulated. A 25 percent slash in the price of a competitive product results in only a 10 percent reduction in the sales of product P_1.

The coefficient of cross elasticity of demand can employ other marketing mix modifications than price to determine how well protected a particular product is. Consider these data:

1. When a competitive product P_2 has an annual advertising budget of $50,000, product P_1 ordinarily sells 10,000 units.
2. The annual advertising budget for product P_2 is increased to $55,000. Product P_1's sales fall to 6,000 units a year.

In this example, the cross elasticity of demand would be expressed by:

$$E_c = \frac{\% \ \Delta \ Q \ P_1}{\% \ \Delta \ A \ P_2}$$

The percentage change in the quantity sold of product P_1 is divided by the percentage change in the advertising budget of product P_2. In this case, we have:

$$E_c = \frac{-40\%}{+10\%} = -4.0$$

This product is not very well insulated because a slight (10 percent) increase in the annual advertising budget for a competitive product lowers the sales of product P_1 by 40 percent.

Tactical Objectives

We stated earlier that tactical objectives are established for a company's subunits, are used to help achieve strategic goals, embrace a time period of one year or less, and are obtained through a company's marketing mix. With these notions in mind, here are some examples of tactical objectives:

1. achieve an average cost per sales call for the sales force of $80
2. reduce the sales force's annual expenses by $150,000

3. reduce the average percentage of time the sales force spends on paper work to 15 percent

4. achieve an average delivery time to customers of 3.0 days

5. reduce inventory levels by 15 percent

6. have 20 percent of the readers of a magazine recall seeing our ad

7. have 10 percent of adults between the ages of 20 and 45 remember our product slogan.

For each tactical objective, a plan must be developed for obtaining it. For example, the plan to achieve the first objective in the list, "to achieve an average cost per sales call for the sales force of $80," might be:

1. eliminating entertainment of all customers who provide less than $500 of business a year

2. limiting to $12.50 the price of any evening meal for sales personnel

3. designing a routing plan to reduce travel distances and times for the sales force

4. requiring the purchase of gasoline from only those stations which provide the company with a 10 percent discount

Factors to Remember in Establishing Goals

There are a number of factors which marketing executives need to consider as they establish their own tactical objectives or assist top management in setting company-wide objectives. The most important of these are:

1. *Goals must be reasonable.* They should have a good chance of being achieved. They should be neither so easy to achieve that personnel don't need to work hard to achieve them, nor so difficult to obtain that personnel become easily discouraged and give up.

2. *Goals must recognize the company's resource constraints.* Budgets, warehousing capacities, and size of sales force are examples of important resource constraints, but many others should be considered.

3. *Goals must be explicitly stated* so that individuals responsible for achieving them know what is expected of them. "Being a leader in the field," "producing and marketing quality products," "obtaining an acceptable rate of growth," and "securing a dominant market position" are examples of fuzzy goals which are too common. "Obtaining a market share of 15 percent" is a more appropriate way to express the goal of securing a dominant market position.

4. *Goals should be expressed quantitatively.* When they are expressed numerically, there is less chance they will be misunderstood.

5. *Goals should recognize developments in the marketplace, technology, the economy, and with competition.* These developments are very important in setting various goals.

6. *Goals should be few in number.* Having few goals allows the company to deploy scarce resources more effectively, with less ambiguity. Furthermore, there is less chance goals will conflict, and the company will be able to focus its energy on worthwhile projects.

7. *If multiple goals do exist, they should be prioritized.* This policy will provide direction to executives. One of the most common ways used to prioritize goals is by assigning weights; a goal with a weight of four is twice as important as one with a weight of two.

8. *Goals should contain a time dimension.* They should have a deadline by which they are to be achieved.

9. *Goals should have a plan for achieving them.* The plan should indicate the precise means by which the goal will be met (review the example of how an average cost per sales call of $80 was to be achieved).

10. *Goals should stipulate who is responsible for achieving them.*

11. *Goals should be mutually exclusive* or independent of each other. If multiple goals are stated, they should all be achievable together. It may be impossible, for example, for a company to obtain an abnormally high level of profitability in the same time period that it hopes to secure a dramatic improvement in market share.

SUMMARY

We have discussed two types of goals in this chapter, strategic and tactical. Strategic goals are those major goals for the entire firm which take more than one year to achieve. Tactical goals assist in achieving strategic goals and take one year or less to implement. We indicated that strategic goals are accomplished primarily through the deployment of various combinations of products and markets (marketing strategies). In the next chapter, we will discuss developing marketing strategies.

QUESTIONS

1. What are the major differences between strategic and tactical goals?
2. Why should a firm be cautious in pursuing high market share objectives?
3. What is the major way in which the level of product insulation can be measured?
4. Indicate how the three major measures of profit are determined.
5. Describe how the DuPont model works.

6. What appears to be the most important measure of profit as contained in the DuPont model?

REFERENCES

1. R.D. Buzzell, B.T. Gale and R.G.M. Sultan. "Market Share—A Key to Profitability." *Harvard Business Review,* January-February, 1975, pp. 97–107.

2. Richard T. Hise and Robert H. Strawser. "The Validity of Market Share as a Marketing Objective: Some Disconcerting Evidence." *Southern Journal of Business,* August, 1972, pp. 8–21.

SUGGESTED READINGS

Boyd, H.W. Jr., and S.J. Levy. "What Kind of Corporate Objectives?" *Journal of Marketing,* October, 1966, pp. 53–58.

Edmonds, C.P. III, and J.H. Hand. "What are the Real Long-Run Objectives of Business?" *Business Horizons,* December 1976, pp. 75–81.

Etzel, M.J., and J.M. Ivancevich. "Management By Objectives in Marketing: Philosophy, Process and Problems." *Journal of Marketing,* October, 1974, pp. 47–55.

Fogg, C.D. "Planning Gains In Market Share." *Journal of Marketing,* July, 1974, pp. 30–38.

Granger, C.H. "The Hierarchy of Objectives." *Harvard Business Review,* May-June, 1964, pp. 63–74.

Hise, R.T., and R.H. Strawser. "Application of Capital Budgeting Techniques to Marketing Operations." *Business Topics,* Summer 1970, pp. 69-76.

Schoeffler, S., et al. "The Impact of Strategic Planning on Profit Performance." *Harvard Business Review,* March-April, 1974, pp. 137–145.

Hershey Foods

Milton S. Hershey, the founder of the giant chocolate manufacturing firm bearing his name, did not find the road to success an easy one. He tried a number of business ventures before eventually succeeding in the chocolate business. In his early teens, he found that he was not cut out to be an apprentice typesetter, but did enjoy his four-year stint as an apprentice candy maker for Joseph H. Royer, a Lancaster, Pennsylvania confectioner.

At the age of nineteen, Hershey decided to go into the candy business for himself. His venture in Philadelphia failed, as did efforts with his father in Denver and Chicago. Another solo attempt in New York also failed.

Back in his native Lancaster, Hershey began to manufacture caramels, an operation with which he was experienced, and the caramel business expanded rapidly. In 1900, he sold his company for $1 million, an unheard of price in those days, and used the proceeds to begin construction of a chocolate processing plant in Derry Township, about fifteen miles east of Harrisburg.

Within 10 years, the company prospered so much that Hershey and his wife were accumulating so much money they could not possibly spend it all. In 1909, Mrs. Hershey suggested they build a home for unfortunate boys. Hershey eagerly agreed, feeling that, although his own childhood had not been all he had wished it to be, he could try to provide security and love for others. Thus, 486 of the initial 1,000 acre construction tract were set aside for the Hershey Industrial School.

In subsequent years, other community projects were built by the Hershey Company. The Community Building, containing two theaters, a dining room and cafeteria, a gymnasium, swimming pool, bowling alley, fencing and boxing room, and photographic room was finished in 1933. The Hershey Hotel was also completed in 1933. The 7,200 seat Hershey Sports Arena was constructed in 1936, and the Hershey Stadium was finished in 1939. Later, Hershey's Chocolate World, which contains a free ride through a simulated chocolate manufacturing operation, Hershey Park, a theme park, the Hershey

This case was prepared by Richard T. Hise, Professor of Marketing at Texas A&M University, as a basis for class discussion rather than to illustrate either effective or ineffective marketing management.

Museum of American Life, and the Hershey Gardens were constructed by Hershey.

In the 1920s, Milton Hershey decided to reorganize the company. The Hershey Chocolate Company was dissolved, and three separate companies organized. The Hershey Chocolate Corporation controlled all of the chocolate properties; the Hershey Corporation was responsible for the Cuban sugar interests; the Hershey Estates was established to conduct the various businesses and municipal services in the town of Hershey.

The Hershey Trust Company administers the funds of the Milton Hershey School. As trustee for this school, it owns or controls the other three companies because Milton Hershey provided the trust with a sizable block of shares of common stock. In 1981, the Hershey Trust Company owned about 51 percent of the company's common stock.

The Hershey Chocolate Corporation continued to prosper. During World War II, the army commissioned Hershey to develop a chocolate bar for troops in the field; the result was the "Field Ration D," and the company was soon producing 500,000 bars a day.

Milton S. Hershey died on October 13, 1945. For fifteen years after his death, the Hershey Chocolate Corporation continued to emphasize its chocolate products. Since 1960, however, the company has pursued a strategy of becoming a multi-product corporation. The name of the Hershey Chocolate Corporation was changed to the Hershey Foods Corporation, its current name. In 1961, the company's sales were $185 million, compared to over $1.4 billion in 1981.

MAJOR PRODUCT GROUPS

In 1982, Hershey had three major product groups. These included the chocolate and confectionery group, restaurant operations (Friendly Ice Cream Corporation), and the other food products and services group: San Giorgia-Skinner (pasta) and Cory Food Services, Inc. The chocolate and confectionery group has grown through both internal means and acquisitions, while the other two groups have grown primarily through acquisitions. Exhibits 1 and 2 show overall company performance between 1971 and 1981. Exhibit 3 shows performance figures for the various product groups between 1979 and 1981.

Chocolate and Confectionery Group

The company produces a broad line of chocolate and confectionery products. The major product lines in the chocolate and confectionery group are bar goods, bagged items, baking ingredients, chocolate drink mixes, and desert toppings. Hershey uses a variety of packages, such as boxes, trays, and bags for bar products. Sizes include standard, large, and giant bars, and about thirty brand names are used. The most important of these are Hershey's Almond Bars, Hershey's Chips, Hershey's Cocoa, Hershey's Kisses, Hershey's

(All dollar and share figures in thousands—except market price and per share statistics)

Summary of Earnings	1975	1974	1973	1972	1971
Continuing Operations					
Net Sales	$556,328	491,995	415,944	392,004	379,229
Cost of Goods Sold	$368,992	357,830	294,174	255,162	247,784
Operating Expenses	$105,102	81,792	88,318	91,595	86,439
Interest Expense (Net)	$ 1,259	2,190	4,848	3,246	2,610
Income Taxes	$ 41,682	25,812	13,929	20,679	21,947
Income from Continuing Operations	$ 39,293	24,371	14,675	21,322	20,449
Losses from Discontinued Operations	$ (1,433)	(2,277)	(369)	(680)	44
Loss Related to Disposal of					
Discontinued Operations	$ (4,898)	—	—	—	—
Net Income	$ 32,962	22,094	14,306	20,642	20,493
Net Income—Per Share of Common Stock					
Continuing Operations	$3.02	1.87	1.13	1.63	1.55
Discontinued Operations					
Losses from Operations	$(.11)	(.17)	(.03)	(.05)	—
Loss related to Disposal	$(.38)	—	—	—	—
Net Income	$2.53	1.70	1.10	1.58	1.55
Dividends per—Common Share	$ .85	.80	1.10	1.10	1.10
Preferred Share	$ .60	.60	.60	.60	.60
Average number of Common Shares and					
Equivalents Outstanding during the year	13,024	13,024	13,024	13,064	13,212
Per Cent of Net Income to Sales*	7.1%	5.0%	3.5%	5.4%	5.4%
Financial Statistics					
Capital Expenditures	$ 10,203	10,887	17,564	25,137	22,602
Depreciation*	$ 7,541	7,912	7,010	5,622	5,597
Advertising*	$ 9,325	1,744	9,565	13,954	10,506
Current Assets	$151,217	124,172	97,106	108,667	102,965
Current Liabilities	$ 52,494	57,579	23,456	29,789	44,486
Working Capital	$ 98,723	66,593	73,650	78,878	58,479
Current Ratio	2.9:1	2.2:1	4.1:1	3.6:1	2.3:1
Long-Term Debt	$ 29,856	31,730	51,470	51,364	26,533
Debt-to-Equity Per Cent	15%	18%	32%	32%	17%
Stockholders' Equity	$195,847	173,173	160,777	159,714	156,280
Stockholders' Data					
Outstanding Common Shares at Year-End	13,024	11,824	11,824	11,824	11,977
Market Price of Common Stock—					
At Year-End	$ 18⅝	9¾	12⅝	23⅞	28
Range During Year	$10⅛-20⅞	8½-15	12½-24¾	21⅛-28¾	26-31⅜
Number of Common Stockholders	19,279	19,362	19,095	17,980	18,346
Employees' Data					
Payrolls	$ 74,329	72,936	74,464	67,700	62,189
Number of Employees—Year-End	7,150	7,200	8,500	8,530	9,140

*Restated to reflect continuing operations only.

EXHIBIT 1   Five-year financial summary, 1971-1975

(all dollar and share amounts in thousands except market price and per share statistics)

	1981	1980	1979	1978	1977	1976
Summary of Earnings						
Continuing Operations						
Net Sales	$1,451,151	1,335,289	1,161,295	767,880	671,227	601,960
Cost of Sales	$1,015,767	971,714	855,252	560,137	489,802	417,673
Operating Expenses	$ 267,930	224,615	184,186	128,520	110,554	94,683
Interest Expense	$ 15,291	16,197	19,424	2,620	2,422	2,240
Interest (Income)	$ (2,779)	(2,097)	(1,660)	(5,303)	(2,931)	(1,883)
Income Taxes	$ 74,580	62,805	50,589	40,450	35,349	45,562
Income from Continuing Operations	$ 80,362	62,055	53,504	41,456	36,031	43,685
Income from Discontinued Operations	$ —	—	—	—	—	1,112
Gain Related to Disposal of Discontinued Operations	$ —	—	—	—	5,300	—
Net Income	$ 80,362	62,055	53,504	41,456	41,331	44,797
Income Per Common Share						
Continuing Operations	$ 5.61	4.38	3.78	3.02	2.62	3.18
Discontinued Operations	—	—	—	—	—	.08
Gain Related to Disposal	—	—	—	—	.39	—
Net Income	$ 5.61	4.38	3.78	3.02	3.01	3.26
Cash Dividends Per Common Share	$ 1.75	1.50	1.35	1.225	1.14	1.03
Average Number of Common Shares and Equivalents Outstanding During the Year	14,322	14,160	14,153	13,742	13,722	13,720
Percent of Income from Continuing Operations to Sales	5.5%	4.6%	4.6%	5.4%	5.4%	7.3%
Financial Statistics						
Capital Additions	$ 91,673	59,029	56,437	37,425	27,535	20,722
Depreciation	$ 27,565	24,896	20,515	8,850	7,995	7,539
Advertising	$ 56,516	42,684	32,063	21,847	17,637	13,330
Current Assets	$ 287,030	221,367	170,250	216,659	221,202	169,872
Current Liabilities	$ 117,255	111,660	103,826	74,415	83,149	47,309
Working Capital	$ 169,775	109,707	66,424	142,244	138,053	122,563
Current Ratio	2.4:1	2.0:1	1.6:1	2.9:1	2.7:1	3.6:1
Long-Term Debt and Lease Obligations	$ 158,182	158,758	143,700	35,540	29,440	29,440
Debt-to-Equity Percent	34%	44%	45%	13%	11%	13%
Stockholders' Equity	$ 469,664	361,550	320,730	284,389	259,668	233,529
Total Assets	$ 806,800	684,472	607,199	422,004	396,153	331,870
Return on Average Stockholders' Equity	19.3%	18.2%	17.7%	15.2%	16.8%	20.5%
After-Tax Return on Average Invested Capital	13.9%	12.8%	14.3%	13.0%	14.2%	17.1%
Stockholders' Data						
Outstanding Common Shares at Year-End	15,669	14,160	14,159	13,745	13,730	13,720
Market Price of Common Stock						
At Year-End	$ 36	23½	24⅝	20⅝	19⅞	22⅜
Range During Year	$ 41–23⅛	26–20	26½–17⅜	23½–18½	22⅜–16⅝	27½–18½
Number of Common Stockholders at Year-End	16,817	17,774	18,417	18,735	19,694	20,421
Employees' Data						
Payrolls	$ 273,097	253,297	227,987	112,135	99,322	88,848
Number of Full-Time Employees at Year-End	12,450	12,430	11,700	8,100	7,660	7,670

EXHIBIT 2 Six-year financial summary, 1976-1981

For the Years Ended December 31 (in thousands of dollars)	1981	1980	1979
Net sales:			
Chocolate and Confectionery	$1,015,106	$ 929,885	$ 822,813
Restaurant Operations	302,908	274,297	224,072
Other Food Products and Services	133,137	131,107	114,410
Total net sales	$1,451,151	$1,335,289	$1,161,295
Operating income:			
Chocolate and Confectionery	$ 142,658	$ 118,435	$ 99,880
Restaurant Operations	29,309	25,567	23,322
Other Food Products and Services	7,250	5,148[a]	6,397
Total operating income	179,217	149,150	129,599
General corporate expenses	(11,763)	(10,190)	(7,742)
Interest expense (net)	(12,512)	(14,100)	(17,764)
Income before taxes	154,942	124,860	104,093
Less: Income taxes	74,580	62,805	50,589
Net income	$ 80,362	$ 62,055	$ 53,504
Identifiable assets:			
Chocolate and Confectionery	$ 445,815	$ 333,232	$ 297,296
Restaurant Operations	223,265	219,196	207,125
Other Food Products and Services	63,446	62,553	63,886
Corporate	74,274	69,491	38,892
Total identifiable assets	$ 806,800	$ 684,472	$ 607,199
Depreciation:			
Chocolate and Confectionery	$ 9,554	$ 8,469	$ 7,389
Restaurant Operations	14,379	13,015	10,283
Other Food Products and Services	2,675	2,671	2,185
Corporate	957	741	658
Total depreciation	$ 27,565	$ 24,896	$ 20,515
Capital additions:			
Chocolate and Confectionery	$ 57,504[b]	$ 27,061[b]	$ 29,472
Restaurant Operations	22,098	24,468	20,965
Other Food Products and Services	5,525	6,141	2,233
Corporate	6,546	1,359	3,767
Total capital additions	$ 91,673	$ 59,029	$ 56,437

[a] After a writeoff of deferred location costs of Cory Food Services in the amount of $1.4 million.
[b] Includes $37.8 million in 1981 and $6.5 million in 1980 for a new manufacturing facility currently being constructed.

EXHIBIT 3   Product group information

Milk Chocolate Bar, Hershey's Miniatures, Hershey's Syrup, Kit Kat, Mr. Goodbar, Reese's Peanut Butter Cup, Reese's Pieces, Rolo, and Whatchamacallit.

While most of the company's chocolate and confectionery items have been developed internally, some were acquired or made available through licensing agreements. The Reese's products were added to Hershey's product lines through acquisition of the H.B. Reese Candy Company of Hershey, Pennsylvania, in 1963. H.B. Reese, a former Hershey employee, began operations in 1923. Since one of the major ingredients in the Reese's line is peanut butter, Hershey executives believe that these items reduce to some extent the firm's dependency on the cacao bean, the chief raw ingredient in chocolate. Y & S Candies, Inc., a licorice manufacturer with facilities in Lancaster, Pennsylvania, Moline, Illinois, Farmington, New Mexico, and Montreal, Canada, was acquired in 1977 to serve the same purpose.

A licensing agreement with Rountree Mackintosh Limited of England gives Hershey the right to manufacture and market the Kit Kat and Rolo brands. The agreement with the English firm also allows Hershey to import, manufacture and market After Eight, a thin dinner mint. This product was being test marketed in 1981.

Hershey has three other licensing arrangements. One is with AB Marabou of Sundbyberg, Sweden, the leading Scandinavian chocolate and confectionery company. Several AB Marabou products have been imported and marketed since 1978. Hershey owns 50 percent of Nacional de Dulces, S.A. de C.V., a manufacturer and marketer of chocolate and confectionery products in Mexico. The other licensing arrangement gives Hershey the right to import and sell various high quality licorice products of the Geo. Bassett & Co. of England. In 1981, Hershey executives did not consider any of these agreements to be large moneymakers.

Exhibit 4 delineates the company's most important chocolate and confectionery products, and when they were developed. While Hershey has had a number of successful new products, there have also been several disappointments. Chocolate-covered raisins were introduced in 1975 and withdrawn the same year. The Rally Bar, a chocolate, caramel, and peanut candy bar, was removed from the market; one of its problems was that, in the initial formula, the peanuts became soggy on the retailers' shelves. The original formula was modified, but the product did not measure up to sales expectations. Exhibit 5 shows the importance of new and current products for the Chocolate and Confectionery Division from 1963 to 1977.

Restaurant Operations

This division was acquired in January, 1979. The Friendly Ice Cream Corporation consists of about 626 restaurants (1982) in 16 states, primarily in the Northeast and Midwest. Exhibit 6 shows the number of restaurants in each state. The division's headquarters and major plant are in Wilbraham, Mass.; another plant is in Troy, Ohio. Both plants manufacture the ice cream, syrups, and toppings used by the restaurants, and their capacities are considered sufficient for the current number of restaurants, as well as for some future expansion. The Wilbraham plant processes the meat required by the restaurants; it is shipped frozen to the individual restaurant units. Some items (milk, cream, baked goods, eggs, and produce) are purchased by the restaurants from local sources which are designated by Friendly's central purchasing department.

EXHIBIT 4   Development of
Hershey Products

1894	The Hershey Bar and Almond Bar
	Hershey's Cocoa, Hershey's Baking Chocolate
1907	Hershey's Kisses
1923	Reese's Peanut Butter Cups
	Y&S Nibs
1925	Mr. Goodbar
1926	Hershey's Syrup
1928	Y&S Twizzlers
1938	Krackel
1939	Hershey's Miniatures
1940	Hershey's Hot Chocolate (now Hot Cocoa Mix)
1941	Dainties (now Semi-Sweet Chocolate Chips)
1952	Chocolate Fudge Topping
1956	Instant Cocoa Mix (Hershey's Instant)
1970	Kit Kat
1971	Special Dark
1976	Reese's Crunchy
1977	Reese's Peanut Butter Flavored Chips
	Golden Almond
1978	Reese's Pieces, Giant Kiss
1979	Whatchamacallit

SOURCE: Company document.

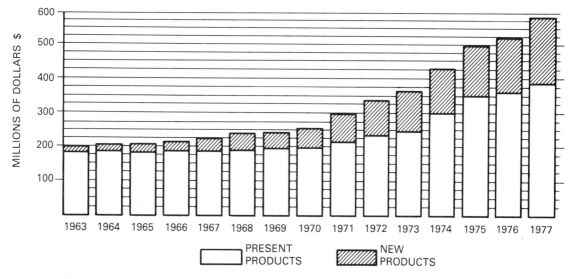

EXHIBIT 5   Sales of new and present chocolate and confectionery products, 1963-1977

SOURCE: *The Wall Street Transcript,* November 13, 1978, by permission.

Friendly Restaurants serve high quality food at moderate prices, specializing in sandwiches, platters, and ice cream products. All units are owned outright by Friendly; there are no franchise agreements.

There are three major types of Friendly Restaurants. The *traditional* Friendly ice cream and sandwich shop offers a limited menu, featuring ice cream, hamburgers, breakfast items, platters, salad, french fries, beverages, and soup and sandwiches. Customers are served in booths or counters, or by take-out service. (The average seating capacity is sixty.) There were 213 traditional operations in 1981. The 351 *modified* shop units offer most of the items available in the traditional shop, but serve a wider variety of full meals and platters. Unlike in the traditional shop, food is prepared out of the customer's sight. The modified units offer take-out service, but have a greater proportion of booth seats than the traditional restaurants. (Seating capacity averages

EXHIBIT 6   Location of Friendly restaurants

seventy seats.) They also have more personalized service and a more pleasant dining atmosphere. The 50 *family* restaurants have the broadest menu, serving seafood, chicken, and other dinners, along with more varied breakfasts and platter meals. Desserts other than ice cream are available, and some units serve beer and wine. Seating is primarily booths and tables, and the floors are usually carpeted. (Seating capacity is from 90 to 120.)

Menus and portions in each type of restaurant are standardized, but prices may vary, generally according to geographical location. Most of the units sell prepackaged ice cream for home consumption. Friendly restaurants feature a colonial decor, and free parking is available.

The Friendly Corporation has followed a policy of refurbishing its restaurants and opening newer ones. The remodeling policy involves converting traditional units into modified units; as of January 1, 1981, 351 units had been modified. Other units have been modernized. In 1980, twenty additional units, fourteen of which are Family restaurants, were opened; eleven units were closed in 1980. All units use modern construction methods. Almost 400 Friendly units have opened since 1970.

As of January 1, 1981, 419 of the Friendly units were free-standing, while the rest were located in shopping centers. Seventy percent of the free-standing sites are owned by Friendly, the other 30 percent are leased, as are all the shopping center sites. Friendly's executives believe that the great majority of its customers are residents of the immediate area surrounding the restaurant. Virtually all units are in suburban areas.

Other Food Products and Services

Pasta. Four acquisitions comprise Hershey's pasta group. San Giorgio Macaroni, Inc. was acquired in 1966, with major markets in Philadelphia, Washington, D.C., Pittsburgh, and New York. Its primary plant is in Lebanon, Pennsylvania, about twenty miles from Hershey. San Giorgio produces 65 varieties of pasta and noodle products. Delmonico Foods, Inc. of Louisville, Kentucky was also acquired in 1966, and was merged with San Giorgio in 1975. Its manufacturing facility is in Louisville, and the company's products are distributed chiefly in Kentucky, Ohio, and parts of West Virginia. The Procino-Rossi Corporation was acquired in 1978. Its brands (P & R brands) are distributed chiefly in upstate New York. The largest pasta acquisition is the Skinner Macaroni Co. of Omaha, Nebraska. Purchased in 1979, it distributes its products to twenty states in the West, Southwest, and South. In 1980, Hershey merged all four pasta companies into one organization, called San Giorgio-Skinner Company.

San Giorgio-Skinner Company produces and sells a great variety of pasta items, including small shells, jumbo shells, large shells, manicotti, lasagna, rippled edge lasagna, macaroni, large elbow macaroni, shell macaroni, spaghetti, long spaghetti, thin spaghetti, curly spaghetti, mastaccioli, egg noodles, extra wide egg noodles, rigatoni, alphabets, linguine, perciatelli, fettucini, soupettes, cut ziti, and spaghetti sauce.

Cory Food Services. Cory Food Services, Inc., founded by Harvey Cory in 1933, was acquired in 1967. Cory developed a vacuum glass brewer with a glass filter that brewed a delicious coffee. In 1964, Cory introduced its coffee service to the business community in the United States and Canada. Cory's corporate headquarters is in Chicago, and the company has fifty-one branch offices in the U.S. These branch offices are grouped into five regional offices: Arlington Heights, Illinois, Long Island, New York, Rockville, Maryland, Glendale, California, and Dallas, Texas. Six branch offices in Canada are serviced by the regional office in Toronto.

As a complement to its coffee business, Cory introduced leased water treatment units, compact refrigerator units, and microwave ovens suitable for offices. The latter two were expanded into more areas in 1981. Growth in these new ventures was good in 1981 and further expansion was anticipated in 1982.

STRATEGIC PLANNING

Hershey began to emphasize strategic planning in the late 1970s. William E.C. Dearden, Hershey's Chief Executive Officer, stated that strategic planning was his number one priority. In 1978, Mr. Dearden established the position of Vice President of Corporate Development, which reports directly to him.

Hershey's strategic plan for accomplishing its basic corporate objectives has centered on its efforts to diversify. In the company's 1980 annual report, Chairman of the Board Harold S. Mohler, Chief Executive Officer William E.C. Dearden, and the company's President and Chief Operating Officer, Richard A. Zimmerman, stated, "In keeping with our strategic plan, we shall continue our drive to become a major, diversified, international food and food-related company." This strategic plan is also reflected in the Statement of Corporate Philosophy developed by the same executives (see Exhibit 7). The statement also includes the company's basic objectives: "We are in business to make a reasonable profit, and to enhance the value of our shareholders' investment."

The company, however, faces strong competition. In the early 1970s, Hershey lost its lead in market share for candy bars to Mars, the privately owned, Hackettstown, New Jersey company which markets such well known brands as Milky Way, Snickers, Three Musketeers, and m&m's. At one time, Mars had a 40 percent share of the candy bar market, compared to Hershey's 23 percent. By 1979, Mars had slipped to 36 percent of candy bar sales, while Hershey increased to 27 percent. Hershey executives maintained that in 1979 it was ahead of Mars in total candy sales.[1]

Another impediment is the slide in candy consumption. In 1978, Americans consumed an annual average of about fifteen pounds of candy. A decade earlier, the figure was about twenty pounds. The highest per capita annual candy consumption was in the 1940s, and the 1978 figure was the lowest since 1935.[2] Competition is also stiff in the pasta division. In 1979, its San Giorgio, Delmonico, Procino-Rossi, and Skinner brands had a 10.2 per-

Hershey Foods Corporation

Hershey, Pennsylvania 17033

STATEMENT OF CORPORATE PHILOSOPHY

We are in business to make a reasonable profit and to enhance the value of our shareholders' investment. We recognize that, to achieve this objective, we must use our resources efficiently, and we must provide for the proper balance between the fundamental obligations that we have to our shareholders, employees, customers, consumers, suppliers and society in general.

We will continue to pursue a policy of profitable growth by maintaining the excellence of our current businesses while concurrently utilizing our financial resources and the expertise and ingenuity of our people to further diversify into other food and food-related businesses, and/or such other businesses which offer significant opportunity for growth.

In seeking to balance our desire for profitable growth with the obligations which we have to the other various interests, we recognize that:

— All employees should be treated fairly and with dignity. They should be provided with good working conditions and competitive wages, and should be rewarded according to performance. To the fullest extent possible, in line with good business practices, promotions should be made from within the Corporation.

— Our Affirmative Action Program is a sincere commitment. Each of us has an obligation to follow it both in the spirit and letter of the law.

— We should be results oriented, and all employees should be given the opportunity to express individual initiative and judgment. Responsibility and authority, however, must be appropriately delegated.

— To successfully conduct the business of the Corporation, it is necessary that each employee strive to improve the communications relating to his or her area of responsibility.

— Our individual and company relationships should be conducted on the basis of the highest standards of conduct and ethics, and it is important that we recognize that the success of our business depends upon the character and integrity of people working in a spirit of constructive cooperation.

— We need to provide to our customers and consumers products of consistent excellent quality at competitive prices that will insure an adequate return on investment.

— We have an inherent responsibility to be a good neighbor and to support community projects, and all employees are encouraged to take an active part in improving the quality of community life.

— We have a responsibility to conduct our operations within the regulatory guidelines and in a manner that does not adversely affect our environment.

It is imperative that we create a climate throughout our entire organization which causes these philosophies to become a way of life.

Adopted: July 26, 1976
Affirmed: April 11, 1980

Chairman of the Board

Vice Chairman and
Chief Executive Officer

President and
Chief Operating Officer

EXHIBIT 7

SOURCE: Company Document.

cent market share. This was well under the 18 percent share of the industry leader, C.F. Mueller Co., a subsidiary of Foremost-McKesson, Inc.[3]

To implement its strategic plan, Hershey has developed the corporate organization presented in Exhibit 8. Gary W. McQuaid is the vice president of marketing for the chocolate and confectionery group, John D. Burke is Friendly's vice president of marketing, and Clifford K. Larsen serves in this capacity for San Giorgio-Skinner.[4]

RESEARCH AND DEVELOPMENT

In 1979, Hershey's 114,000 square foot technical center was completed at a cost of $7.4 million. Management believes this facility and its staff will give it one of the best research and development capabilities in the industry. Included in the facility are offices, laboratories, a library, test kitchen, auditorium, animal testing facilities, and a pilot plant. A year before completion of the technical center, a major reorganization of the company's R&D effort was announced, and a new Vice President of Science and Technology was

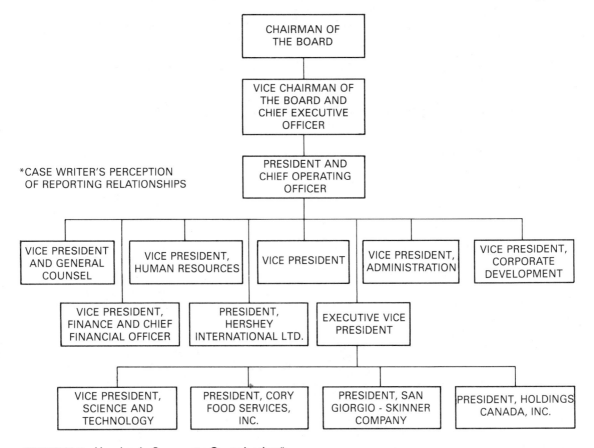

EXHIBIT 8   Hershey's Corporate Organization*

named. This office, consisting of four groups, is responsible for heading up the company's entire R&D effort.

The *Research Group's* efforts have focused on three areas: vegetable fat chemistry, chocolate flavor research, and raw materials, such as peanuts and almonds. There are three subgroups in the Research Group. The Analytical Research Group emphasizes chocolate analysis, and has received international acclaim for its efforts; it has compiled one of the world's largest data banks on the nutritional content of chocolate and cocoa. Microbiological Research focuses on cocoa bean microbiology. This group's importance has increased as the company has purchased more chocolate liquor and less raw cocoa. The Nutrition Group engages in basic nutrition research projects, on subjects like tooth decay, acne, chocolate allergies, and nutrition, and it works closely with the Technical Committee of the Chocolate Manufacturers Association.

The *Product and Process Development Group* continually monitors consumer trends and behavioral patterns to define product opportunities. San Giorgio's Light 'n Fluffy Noodles and the Whatchamacallit candy bar were developed in response to consumers' demand for "lightness."

The *Engineering Group* is mainly responsible for assisting capital programs, and it also provides some engineering skills for moving new products into production.

The *Equipment Design and Development Group* provides support for producing new products and improving existing manufacturing systems. This group designs special equipment not generally available and integrates purchased equipment into the production line. In addition, it is responsible for designing special methods and devices unique to Hershey's products and conditions.

One of the major reasons for Hershey's purchase of Marabou in Sweden was to exchange technological information, with special emphasis on new confectionery products. An interest in Chadler Industrial de Bahia of Brazil was purchased for the same reason. Hershey was interested in Chadler's conversion processes which make chocolate liquor, cocoa butter, and cocoa powder from cacao beans. Hershey has also acquired interests in several cocoa growing ventures in Costa Rica, the Dominican Republic, and Belize, to try to increase yields from cacao bean production. Hershey is committed to continued support of the American Cocoa Research Institute, which works to improve the volume and quality of cacao bean production in the western hemisphere.

The company's R&D efforts have paid important dividends. Whatchamacallit and Reese's Pieces are two successful products which were developed by the company, and their success has encouraged further research. A significant technological breakthrough was the development of a peanut butter-flavored ingredient which reduces dependence on high-priced cacao beans.

Future corporate research and development is expected to continue to work toward creating new ingredients that are readily available domestically and will reduce the dependency on imported commodities. Two major emphases have been testing alternate fat products for cocoa butter and experimenting with new high-fructose corn syrup, which could be used as a sucrose alternate in certain kinds of products.

INTERNATIONAL OPERATIONS

In recent years, Hershey has increased its overseas marketing efforts. As of 1981, the company believes that "overall sales and earnings from international operations remain modest in comparison with the corporation's total performance." However, the company is pleased with its expansion in international sales.

Hershey's major foreign market is Canada. Although some sales growth occurred in Canada in 1980, company executives considered these results well below expectations. As in the United States, higher operating costs forced the company to raise prices to 35¢ for the standard size candy bar.

During 1979 and 1980, several new products were successfully introduced in Canada. Brown Cow proved to be an immediate success, and became one of the company's leading brands in Canada. Brown Cow is a chocolate syrup milk modifier in a plastic dispenser bottle. Top Scotch, a butterscotch sundae topping, was introduced in 1979. Three other products entered the Canadian market in 1979: Special Crisp, the Canadian version of Whatchamacallit; Reese's Crunchy Peanut Butter Cups; and a boxed version of Y&S All Sorts (licorice). 1980 saw the introduction of Reese's Pieces and two clear plastic bag packages of Y&S All Sorts.

Hershey has a number of supply points for cacao beans. The major ones are La Guaria, Venezuela; Guayaquil, Ecuador; Ilheus, Brazil; Abidjan, Ivory Coast; Accra, Ghana; Lagos, Nigeria; and Douala, Cameroon.

Hershey has a policy of joint ventures in entering foreign markets. This strategy allows the company to work with well-established partners with considerable knowledge of local market conditions. Hershey entered a joint venture in 1979 with the Fujiya Confectioning Company, Ltd. of Tokyo. This Japanese firm has been in existence since 1910, and is a leader in chocolate and confectionery products, snack foods, beverages, ice cream, and bakery products in that country; it also has important restaurant operations. The joint venture agreement enables Hershey's products to be imported, manufactured, and sold in Japan, and company executives believe that this arrangement has already resulted in increased Japanese sales. Another joint venture arrangement in Mexico with Nacional de Dulces, S.A. has resulted in increased sales and earnings in that country. The company expects demand for its products to increase, and a new Mexican manufacturing facility is under construction. Two joint ventures exist in Brazil: one with Chadler Industrial de Bahia S.A. involves sales of chocolate and confectionery products. A new joint venture with S.A. Industrias Reunidas F. Matarazzo is concerned with pasta sales. Early indications were that the pasta joint venture was successful. However, the continued devaluation of the cruzeiro has adversely affected the firm's Brazilian operations.

In Sweden, AB Marabou acquired Göteborgs Kex, that country's leading cookie and cracker manufacturer. These additional sales contributed to Hershey's revenues; Hershey has a 20 percent interest in AB Marabou. In the Philippines, Hershey began in 1980 to furnish technical manufacturing assistance and cocoa growing advice to the Philippine Cocoa Corporation.

In 1981, Hershey formed a new subsidiary company, Hershey International Ltd. This company is responsible for Hershey's international operations outside Canada, especially those in Mexico, Brazil, the Philippines, Sweden, and Japan. Company executives believed this "consolidation will further strengthen the overall monitoring, control, and reporting of international operations." Richard M. Marcks, Vice President, International, was named President of the new subsidiary company and his old position was abolished.

DISTRIBUTION

The company believes that its distribution system is critical in maintaining sales growth and providing service to its distributors. Hershey attempts to anticipate distributors' optimum stock levels and provide them with reasonable delivery times. To achieve these objectives, Hershey uses thirty-five field warehouses throughout the United States, Puerto Rico, and Canada. Hershey uses public carriers, contract carriers, and some private trucks to move its products from manufacturing plants to field warehouses, and then to customers. For example, a fleet of company-owned refrigerated trucks transports food and supplies from the two Friendly production sites to the individual restaurants. Some shipments go directly from manufacturing plants to customers. Hershey's executives believe that the distribution system has been very helpful in successfully introducing new products nationally.

Hershey has five major manufacturing plants in the United States and Canada for chocolate and confectionery products, with an additional manufacturing site under construction. Four of the present plants (two in Hershey, one in Oakdale, California and one in Smith Falls, Ontario) produce primarily chocolate products. The Lancaster, Pennsylvania plant produces licorice products. A future manufacturing plant in Stuart's Draft, Virginia will produce chocolate items.

Hershey's chocolate and confectionery products are sold mainly to wholesale, chain, and independent grocers, candy and tobacco stores, syndicated and department stores, vending and concessions, drug stores, and convenience stores. Exhibit 9 shows the percentage of sales of each of these distribution outlets. Exhibit 10 shows the geographical sales pattern for chocolate and confectionery products. Over 375 sales representatives throughout the United States and Canada service over 20,000 direct sales customers. Company executives estimate that over 1 million retail outlets are served in 20,000 cities and towns, and that no single customer accounts for more than 4 percent of the total sales of chocolate and confectionery items. The company's sales representatives are specialized according to the product sold. One type is responsible for candy bars, packaged items, and grocery products. The other handles specialty products, food service, and industrial products. Hershey's pasta products are sold to supermarket chains, cooperatives, independent wholesalers, and wholesaler-sponsored volunteers. Four brand names are marketed (San Giorgio, Skinner, Delmonico, and P&R), but some private label merchandise is also marketed.

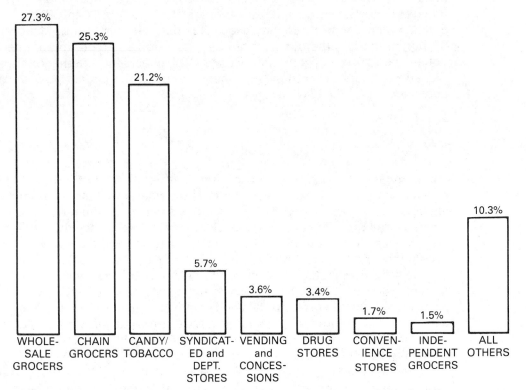

EXHIBIT 9 Percentage of chocolate and confectionery sales by type of distribution outlet
SOURCE: *The Wall Street Transcript*, November 13, 1978, by permission.

EXHIBIT 10 Geographical sales pattern

Region	Percentage of Sales	Percentage of U.S. population
North	31.9%	27.6%
South	24.2%	27.4%
Midwest	25.9%	27.9%
West	18.0%	17.1%
TOTAL U.S.	100.0%	100.0%

SOURCE: *The Wall Street Transcript*, November 13, 1978, by permission.

ADVERTISING

For its first sixty-six years, Hershey did not advertise. The company relied on the quality of its products and its extensive channels of distribution system to gain acceptance in the marketplace. Milton Hershey said, "Give them quality. That's the best kind of advertising in the world." However, Hershey did use various forms of sales promotion, such as the plant tour, to promote sales. The plant tour, seen by almost 10 million people, was replaced by Hershey's Chocolate World in 1973.

In 1968, over twenty years after the death of its founder, Hershey announced plans to initiate a consumer advertising program for its confectionery and grocery products. On July 19, 1970, the program was launched with a full page ad for Hershey's Syrup, which appeared in 114 newspaper supplements. National radio and television advertising appeared in September.

Hershey decided to advertise for several reasons. There was increased competition in the confectionery industry—increased competition which often involved heavy advertising. There was the need to better acquaint people under twenty-five with Hershey products. In 1970, these people accounted for half of the U.S. population. As Hershey developed new products, executives believed that advertising would promote mass distribution, which would, in turn, spur mass production.

Exhibit 11 shows advertising expenditures from 1971 through 1981. Hershey's $43 million of advertising in 1980 moved it into the top 100 of U.S. advertisers, and its 1981 expenditures ranked it 86th. Mars, Inc. spent $78.4 million on advertising in 1981, good for the 69th spot. Figure 12 shows 1981 advertising expenditures for Hershey's major brands. Sales promotion efforts are directed to consumers by such point-of-purchase materials as shelf-takers and case cards, and by coupon and premium offers.

EXHIBIT 11 Annual advertising expenditures, 1971–1981

Year	Amount
1971	$10,506,000
1972	13,954,000
1973	9,565,000
1974	1,744,000
1975	9,499,000
1976	13,330,000
1977	17,637,000
1978	21,847,000
1979	32,063,000
1980	42,684,000
1981	56,516,000

SOURCE: Company Annual Reports.

EXHIBIT 12   Most heavily advertised products in 1981

Product	Advertising expenditure
Hershey's Candy Bars	$7.0 million
Reese's Candies	4.6 million
Hershey's Chocolate Kisses	3.7 million
Whatchamacallit	3.7 million
Hershey's Chocolate Syrup	3.1 million
Reese's Pieces	2.9 million
Chocolate Chips	2.3 million
Rolo Candy	1.6 million
Hershey's Candies	1.4 million

SOURCE: Reprinted with permission from the September 9, 1982 issue of *Advertising Age.* Copyright 1982 by Crain Communications, Inc.

The company has had to defend its advertising from attacks on two fronts: some of the advertising is directed toward children, and some of its products may promote tooth decay. Hershey estimates that about 30 percent of its advertising is directed to children. The Federal Trade Commission on May 28, 1980 began considering a trade regulation which would adversely affect the advertising of many of the company's products. At that time, however, Congress narrowed the FTC's authority to adopt such a trade rule. As of January 1, 1981, company executives were not sure whether the FTC would continue its efforts to regulate advertising to children. In most cases, it would take several years to adopt such a trade rule. Hershey executives announced they were opposed to "any attempt to limit its rights to advertise truthfully its products to any audience." Hershey has developed material about the controversy surrounding tooth decay and nutrition. An example of these materials is presented in Exhibit 13.

PRICING

Pricing is a particularly important element of the marketing mix for Hershey, and it is difficult for a number of reasons. Hershey's chocolate and confectionery products depend on raw materials. The suppliers of these raw materials are usually in foreign countries and their supplies are frequently curtailed because of bad weather or other factors.

Cacao beans are the major raw materials for the Chocolate and Confectionery Division; two-thirds of the world's supply is grown in West Africa, chiefly in Ghana. Prices fluctuated widely in the 1970s because of weather conditions, consuming countries' demands, sales policies of the producing countries, speculative influences, worldwide inflation, and currency movements. Hershey attempts to minimize the effects of bean price fluctuations through forward purchasing of large quantities of cacao beans, cocoa butter, and chocolate liquor. Cocoa future contracts are purchased and sold, and the company holds memberships in the London Cocoa Terminal Market Associa-

Good Nutrition Makes Good Sense

Everyone agrees that good nutrition makes good sense. But what is good nutrition? Nowadays many people are readily willing to answer this question, but many of their answers are contradictory.

While we do not advertise our chocolate products as especially nutritious foods, they do have nutritional value and do contribute to the overall diet since they are composed of such food ingredients as milk, various nuts, chocolate and sugar.

Nearly all Hershey's Chocolate and Confectionery Division products have nutrition information printed on their labels. This practice was begun voluntarily in 1973, and to date we are the only manufacturer in the chocolate and confectionery industry to provide this consumer service. Our effort to convey this information is one clear indication of Hershey's concern for good nutrition and our respect for the consumer's right to know.

Good nutrition comes from a balanced diet; one that provides the right amounts and the right kinds of proteins, vitamins, minerals, fats and carbohydrates. The chart on the next page provides an interesting basis of comparison between Hershey Foods' products and other snack items commonly cited as "more nutritious."

Chocolate and confectionery products and other sugar containing snacks have been coming under attack recently. They are accused of being "empty calorie" or so-called "junk" foods.

We all have substantial caloric needs. At Hershey Foods we believe obtaining the right amount of calories is especially important for active, growing children. Calories come from nutrients; namely carbohydrates, fats and proteins. Our products supply these nutrients and do contribute to good nutrition.

Throughout the world, carbohydrates are the largest single component of the diet. In the United States, about half of all calories (i.e., energy) are provided by carbohydrates commonly referred to as sugars and starches. As far as the body is concerned, all carbohydrates must be reduced to simple sugars before they can be used. Once sugars and starches reach the stomach, their dietary origin is lost. It makes no difference whether they come from fruits, vegetables, milk, honey, or Hershey Bars—before entering the blood stream, they are all alike.

Sugar is currently bearing the brunt of the attack from a variety of sources. Since sugar is a significant component of many Hershey Foods' chocolate and confectionery products, we are naturally concerned about these attacks and the types of evidence used to support them.

At present sugar is not linked in substantive research to the variety of health problems usually mentioned in this context. As for dental caries, a complex issue, there is evidence that sugar, both naturally occurring and added, plays a role. On the other hand, a number of studies in dental literature show that chocolate, especially milk chocolate, does not cause an increase in dental caries.

Researchers report that milk chocolate has a high content of protein, calcium, phosphate and other minerals, all of which have exhibited positive effects on tooth enamel. In addition due to its natural fat (cocoa butter) content, milk chocolate clears the mouth quickly in comparison to some other foods. These factors are thought to be responsible for making milk chocolate less likely to cause dental caries than certain other foods.

The American public is being inundated with numerous attacks on sugar and the role it plays in the diet. Many assertions are made on a partial understanding of the facts or without substantiating research.

Unfortunately the crusade against sugar containing products is well underway despite a lack of adequate, factual support. Federal, state, and local governmental bodies have entered the fray, and considerable media interest has been generated. We fear that great misunderstanding will be created before the issue is resolved, although as a company and an industry, we are trying to raise the information level on all fronts.

One aspect of this very complex situation is the role the Federal Trade Commission has been asked to play regarding the advertisement of products containing sugar. At the present time, the FTC is considering various means of limiting our industry's ability to advertise its products.

Hershey Foods has and will continue to oppose any attempt to limit its right to advertise. We believe we have the right to advertise to all of our audiences and we do not think our advertising has been out of balance. In 1978, less than one-third of all our advertising impressions will be received by children.

Hershey Foods has always been concerned about the content of its advertising as well as the type of programs it supports. We have helped in the development of voluntary codes through the Children's Review Unit of the National Advertising Board, and our ads are constantly reviewed by child psychologists and public affairs specialists to make sure they are not misleading and cannot be misunderstood.

Our standard bar line, which accounts for the majority of advertising expenditures, represents an inexpensive group of products. We feel that children can be appropriately informed about them, especially in light of their nutritional value and the parental approval they have received for generations in the United States. We believe we have the right to remind consumers of our products and to inform new consumers about products their parents have used, enjoyed, and approved.

Perhaps the most paradoxical aspect of this issue is the fact that chocolate and confectionery consumption in the United States is not excessive, representing only about one percent of total food intake. What's more, consumption of these foods has not increased in the last 40 years. Since mass media advertising did not really come into being until the 1950's, it is evident that television advertising has not contributed to increased consumption of chocolate and confectionery products. As far as our industry is concerned, however, advertising has simply fostered competition.

The so-called "junk" food issue in all its complexity will continue to be an important challenge to Hershey Foods Corporation. We shall stand firmly in our position that Hershey's products are mixtures of ingredients which inherently have nutritional value. Hershey has manufactured chocolate and confectionery products of the highest quality for over 80 years. We are very proud of these products and the role they play in the lives of people throughout the world.

EXHIBIT 13 Example of a Hershey's advertisement

EXHIBIT 14   Nutritional value per serving of various foods[2,3]

	A Milk Chocolate	B Mr. Goodbar	C Reese Cup	D Ice Cream	E Saltine Crackers	F Graham Crackers	G Cheese/Peanut Butter Crackers	H Apple	I Dried Dates
Serving size	1.05 oz	1.3 oz	1.2 oz	8 fl oz (1 cup)	1 oz	1 oz	1.5 oz	3¼ in. diam.	1.4 oz
Calories	160	210	190	260	120	110	210	120	120
Protein (grams)	2	5	4	6	2	2	6	0	1
Carbohydrate (grams)	17	18	18	28	20	20	24	30	29
Fat (grams)	10	13	11	14	3	2	10	1	0
Vitamin A[1]	*	*	*	*	*	*	*	2	*
Vitamin C[1]	*	*	*	*	*	*	*	10	*
Thiamine[1]	4	2	2	2	*	4	2	2	2
Riboflavin[1]	*	4	2	15	*	2	8	2	2
Niacin[1]	*	8	8	*	*	*	2	*	4
Calcium[1]	6	4	2	20	*	*	2	*	2
Iron[1]	2	2	2	*	2	2	2	2	6

*Contained less than 2 percent of the U.S. RDA of these nutrients

[1]Vitamin and mineral levels are expressed as a percentage of the U.S. RDA

[2]Information for foods other than Hershey products derived from U.S.D.A. Handbook No. 456 *Nutritive Value of American Foods*

[3]Items A, B, & C, according to at least one state's legislators' list, would be included in a "low-nutritious" category

[4]Items D through I are identified on that list as nutritious food

SOURCE: Company Document.

tion and the Coffee, Sugar, and Cocoa Exchange, Inc. in New York. Crop forecasts, chiefly in West Africa and Brazil, are also made.

Despite these efforts, the prices of cacao beans skyrocketed in the 1970s. Below is the average price of cacao beans for October 1 through September 30, the normal crop year:

Year	Cents per pound
1969-1970	32.5
1970-1971	26.3
1971-1972	26.3
1972-1973	44.5
1973-1974	62.7
1974-1975	57.3
1975-1976	72.1
1976-1977	150.1
1977-1978	141.1
1978-1979	156.4
1979-1980	138.8

SOURCE: Company document.

The other major ingredient is sugar. Like cacao beans, many factors affect the price of sugar, including quantities available, demand by consumers, speculation, currency movements, and the International Sugar Agreement. Another price determinant is the price support provided domestic sugar by the Agriculture Adjustment Act of 1978. The average price per pound of refined sugar, as reported by the U.S. Department of Agriculture, FOB Northeast, has been steadily increasing:

1977	17.3¢
1978	20.8¢
1979	23.2¢
1980	41.0¢
1981	36.1¢

Three other raw materials are important. The company is the largest domestic user of almonds, using only almonds grown in California. The price of almonds doubled in 1979 due to a poor California crop in 1978, and have remained high despite a good 1979 California crop. Marginal crops in the rest of the world kept prices high. In 1980, the peanut crop in the United States was poor, causing significant price increases. The supply of peanuts is expected to be low in 1981, but Hershey did not expect any problem obtaining enough for production. The price of milk has also increased greatly in recent years; both milk and peanut prices are affected by various Federal Marketing Orders and by U.S. Department of Agriculture subsidy programs.

More expensive cacao beans, sugar, almonds, peanuts, and milk have forced Hershey to raise prices. The sizes of various products have also been modified. Below are the price/size adjustments for Hershey's Standard Milk Chocolate Bar since 1949:

Common Retail Price: 5¢

1949	1 oz.
Mar. 1954	⅞ oz.
June 1955	1 oz.
Jan. 1958	⅞ oz.
Aug. 1960	1 oz.
Sept. 1963	⅞ oz.
Sept. 1965	1 oz.
Sept. 1966	⅞ oz.
May 1968	¾ oz.
Discontinued	11-24-69

Common Retail Price: 10¢

Nov. 1969	1½ ozs.
Mar. 1970	1⅜ ozs.
Jan. 1973	1.26 ozs.
Discontinued	1-1-74

Common Retail Price: 15¢

Jan. 1974	1.4 ozs.
May 1974	1.2 ozs.
Sept. 1974	1.05 ozs.
Jan. 1976	1.2 ozs.
Discontinued	12-31-76

Common Retail Price: 20¢

Dec. 1976	1.35 ozs.
Apr. 1977	1.2 ozs.
July 1977	1.05 ozs.
Discontinued	12-1-78

Common Retail Price: 25¢

Dec 1978	1.2 ozs.
Mar. 1980	1.05 ozs.

SOURCE: Company Documents.

Friendly Restaurants use many raw materials. Rising prices of items such as beef, cream, condensed milk, whole milk, and sugar and corn syrup in the late '70s forced Friendly to raise menu prices. Pasta is made from durum wheat flour grown almost exclusively in North Dakota. Poor weather conditions in 1980 sharply reduced the quality of the durum wheat crop, resulting in a 60 percent increase in price. Hershey was forced to raise prices twice in 1980. Coffee prices declined in 1980 from 1979 levels, down from historic highs earlier in the decade, and the Cory Division was able to reduce its prices during 1980.

Hershey uses price concessions to induce its distributors to carry its products. The company hopes that the distributor will feature the item because the price reductions provide them with a higher-than-normal profit.

TOWARD THE FUTURE

As Hershey Foods Corporation moved into 1982, company executives decided to thoroughly review past performance and strategy, and use these assessments to chart the future direction of the firm. Several aspects of the company's operations were chosen for appraisal:

1. Have the company's diversification efforts been effective in accomplishing its objectives? What should Hershey's future diversification strategy be?

2. How effective has Hershey's advertising been? How much emphasis should the company place on advertising in the future?

3. How effective has the company's distribution strategy been? What changes would be appropriate in the future?

4. Has Hershey been able to reduce the risks which appear to be inherent in the kinds of products it sells? What can be done to reduce these risks?

5. How viable is the company's corporate organization? What are its strengths and weaknesses? What modifications are needed?

REFERENCES

1. "Hershey Steps Out," *Forbes,* March 17, 1980, p. 64.
2. "Indulge, Indulge! Enjoy, Enjoy!," *Forbes,* October 15, 1979, p. 45.
3. "Hershey Steps Out," *op. cit.*
4. *Advertising Age,* September 9, 1982, p. 106.

The Sunshine Shop

The Sunshine Shop is a personalized gift shop located in a large metropolitan area on the West Coast. Specializing in hand-painted items and original creations, Sunshine carries everything from hair barrettes for $2.50 to lucite trays for $200. The store attempts to carry as broad a product mix as possible for all ages and occasions.

HISTORY

Diane Evans started Sunshine Shop in 1976 with $10,000 capital. The first store was located in a shopping center at a main intersection in the city. With only 300 square feet of retail space, first year sales totaled $80,000. In 1978, Diane added a partner, Beverly Michaels, and in addition, expanded the retail space to 1100 square feet. With this extra space, they decided to also begin mail-order sales and developed small mail-order pamphlets and catalogues to send to prospective customers. As a result of the combined retail store/mail-order business, the Sunshine Shop experienced sales increases of 50-100 percent each year.

In 1979 the Sunshine Shop incorporated as Sunshine Enterprises, with a board of directors consisting of Diane, Beverly, their husbands, and Gloria and Bob Threadgill—Diane's parents. As business increased, the board of directors realized that more storage space was needed. In 1980, a warehouse was leased six miles from the retail location to provide storage, as well as facilities to house the mail-order business. The new warehouse was not entirely successful because of the distance involved from the store to the warehouse. In May 1981, a new retail space was leased in the same shopping center. The Sunshine Shop now has 1100 square feet of retail space and 300 square feet of storage space in one location. The warehouse also provides extra storage space and a workshop for some of the artists.

This case was prepared by Stephen W. McDaniel, Assistant Professor of Marketing, Texas A&M University, with the assistance of Janet Anderson, as a basis for class discussion rather than to illustrate either effective or ineffective marketing management.

ORGANIZATION

Sunshine's organization chart is depicted in Exhibit 1. Diane, Gloria, and Beverly run the operation, usually working in the store every day except Saturdays. Gloria, Diane's mother, is in charge of all of the books, including invoices, bills, and paychecks. Gloria has no college education and is learning the business as the job requires. Cathy Blevins is manager of the store and its operations. Laura Edwards works full-time and three high school girls work part-time as sales help in the store. Tina Kohutek runs the mail-order business and is in charge of the warehouse operations. Penny Fry is Tina's assistant and two high school girls do the mail-order packaging. Linda Hackburn is in charge of the art department and Jodie Benson paints full-time in the store. Jodie is the only artist in the store during the week; she can correct orders and paint some items while people wait. Linda has a varying number of part-time artists working for her, depending on the season; last Christmas, as many as twenty-nine artists were hired to paint.

ART DEPARTMENT

In 1978, when Sunshine Shop expanded, Susie Putman was hired as art director. Susie had many responsibilities, one of which was to create catalogues and flyers. Other responsibilities included dividing the orders to be

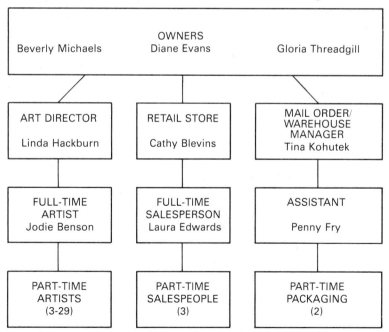

EXHIBIT 1   The Sunshine Shop organization chart

painted between the artists, checking and maintaining the quality of the artists' work, creating new designs, and getting orders done by the due date. Susie did an excellent job, but became very frustrated with the busy Christmas season. The number of Christmas orders taken was so great that Susie and her artists spent day and night painting to get orders completed. She became so frustrated that she finally quit. Three months later, Susie started her own mail-order business, and is now in competition with the Sunshine Shop.

In 1981, Linda Hackburn was hired to take over Susie's position. Diane and Beverly worked closely with Linda to prevent the previous situation from recurring. Linda works at the warehouse with her part-time artists, the number of which has increased with the increase in the number of orders. Since the artists are paid by the hour, a problem has developed in getting them to paint an adequate number of items each day. The Sunshine Shop needs quality work done as rapidly as possible. Part of the reason this does not always happen is that all of the painting is done freehand and, although there are patterns to follow, work varies from artist to artist. Also, since most of the artists paint at the warehouse, Diane feels that they tend to lose touch with the store atmosphere.

MAIL ORDER

The decision in 1978 to go into the mail-order business was made not only to increase sales but also to help finance the inventory, since payment was required at the time the order was placed. Linda Hackburn was in charge of designing the catalogues and flyers. She did an excellent job but it took her away from painting.

The Sunshine Shop sends out a large twenty-two-page catalogue at Christmas, and two-page flyers are mailed for Valentine's Day and Easter. Both a catalogue and flyers are used for Mother's Day, Father's Day, graduation, and Back-to-School. At first, there was a problem keeping track of orders; if the original was lost there was no record of the order. The store's computer system solved this problem by printing a list of orders and shipping dates, but Diane and Beverly felt the $1 per order computer cost was too expensive. They found that making three copies of the order on three-by-five index cards was a viable alternative to using the computer.

Christmas, 1981 was a nightmare for the store's mail-order business. Sunshine had problems receiving shipments from orders they had placed and, consequently, many items in the Christmas catalogue were out of stock. This left many orders unfilled for Christmas, and many customers were unhappy. A note explaining the problem was sent to those customers whose orders would be delayed. But some of the orders had been made in August, with a promised due date of December 1. By December, many of the items were out of stock, or, if in stock, the artist had not painted the order. It was difficult to explain to customers who had placed orders in August that four months later, the order had not been completed.

MARKETING

Since none of the owners have previous experience running a retail store, they have had to learn marketing techniques by trial and error. For example, they initially had trouble deciding how to price their products. They soon decided to keep prices low to encourage more customers. The typical markup is 45 percent of cost (e.g., if an item cost $5, it will retail for $7.25). When art work is also done on the item, an additional markup is added. The owners are very pleased by the many favorable comments they receive from customers on their prices. Many customers express surprise over the excellent quality for such a reasonable price.

Quality and originality are two factors emphasized with all products sold. Many products are original ideas created by Diane and Linda. Two pages from the Christmas catalogue illustrate a few of these products (see Exhibits 2 and 3).

Products are promoted primarily through the mail-order catalogues and flyers. In the past, Sunshine has used no local advertising in newspapers or magazines, but has gotten publicity in the local newspaper. The shopping center in which they are tenants does not do any advertising. For several months, Sunshine did not even have a sign identifying the store. The sign was blown down during a storm, and Diane was unable to agree with the landlord about a replacement sign. It has recently been replaced.

COMPETITION

The Sunshine Shop has many competitors, other local retailers that also sell personalized items. Diane tries to give Sunshine a differential advantage over the competition by always creating new product designs. Another competitor, Ginger's Gift Corner, sells nonpersonalized items at lower price, but also sells the supplies for customers to personalize the items themselves.

Competition also comes from other mail-order gift businesses all over the country. Sunshine mails catalogues to many states. The mail-order business owned by former employee Susie Putman uses some of the same designs as the Sunshine Shop. Since Sunshine does not copyright any of its designs, she is able to use all of the designs she created for Sunshine. Another problem caused by a lack of copyrights was a gift store in a nearby city that used the copy from Sunshine's mail flyers in its advertisements.

INVENTORY

When Sunshine began, it was mainly a special order business, with only a few regularly stocked items. Customers were required to pay at the time of purchase for these special order items. This was advantageous for the store,

Name _____
address _____
city _____
state _____ ZIP ____
phone _____

*Please add packing, insurance, & shipping charges as shown in parenthesis (following item price. There's no additional shipping charge for multiples of the same item shipped to the same address.

*Gift wrap: add 75¢ for each item to be wrapped.

*Please use a separate sheet for additional items or any special instructions concerning personalizing, colors, etc.

☐ Check or money order for $ ___ .   (sorry, no C.O.D.s)
☐ Mastercharge ☐ visa   expir. date _____
account # ☐☐☐☐☐☐☐☐☐☐☐☐
interbank # ☐☐☐☐   for mastercharge only

item #	how many	name	item, size, price, color, etc.	if personalized give name & instructions	item $	*postage	*gift wrap	total charge
								TOTAL

In a hurry or need special help? Please call

Dear Santa, please bring me a letter licker for xmas. I'm tired OF LICKING STAMPS - my tongue is glued to my teeth - thanks, Joyce. My dear husband, if you'll get me

MESSAGETS   a t-shirt message center - a really different way to leave messages to yourself or the whole family. comes complete with stretch cord, clips, acetate reusable shirts & a special white pen. #122...$12.00 (1.50)

LETTER LICKER licks letters & stamps like never before. pour 1/3 cup water into its mouth. simply turn the knob on the side & out rolls the bright red tongue to lick the letter. then return the tongue back inside where it rests in water. letter licker's breath always stays fresh. a mouthful of functional fun! #123...$5.00 (1.50)

PERSONALIZED DESKS to take with you! The "shuffle desk" has a 15¾"x 11¾" hard desk top & cushy pillow bottom. #124...$12.00 (3.00)
The "lap caddie" has a 12½"x 10 desk top, cushy pillow bottom, & opens to pockets & compartments for all your stationery needs. #125...$12.00 (3.00) both desk & caddie come in a variety of prints. give your color preference.

message-T's this year. I won't forget to leave word about where I'm playing bridge anymore - love, Pearl. Dear mom, please get me a lap desk so I can do my homework. your son.

EXHIBIT 2

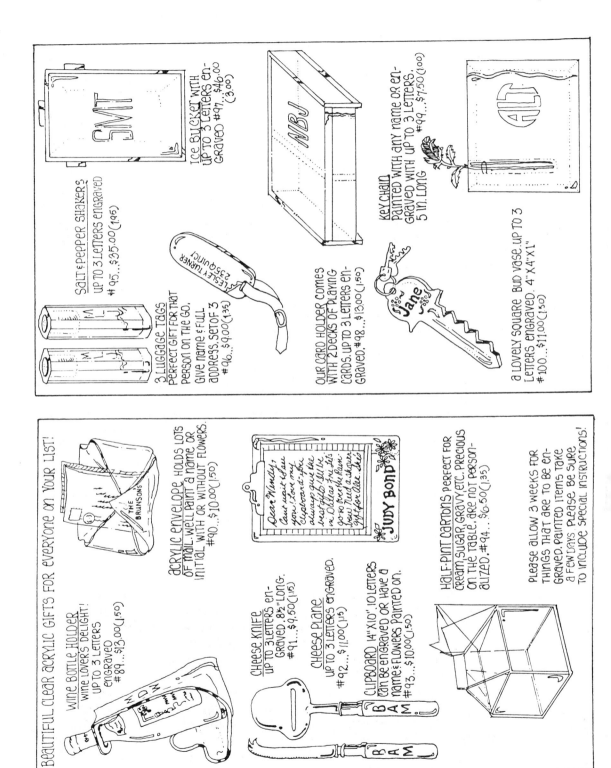

Salt & Pepper Shakers up to 3 Letters engraved #95...$35.00 (1.95)

Ice Bucket with up to 3 Letters engraved #97...$46.00 (3.00)

3 Luggage Tags perfect gift for that person on the go. Give name & full address. Set of 3 #96...$9.00 (1.35)

Our card holder comes with 2 decks of playing cards. up to 3 Letters engraved. #98...$13.00 (1.50)

Key Chain painted with any name or engraved with up to 3 Letters. 5 in. Long #99...$7.50 (1.00)

a lovely square bud vase. up to 3 Letters engraved. 4"x4"x1" #100...$11.00 (1.50)

Beautiful clear acrylic gifts for everyone on your list!

Acrylic envelope holds lots of mail. we'll paint a name or initial with or without flowers. #90...$10.00 (1.50)

Wine Bottle Holder wine lover's delight! up to 3 Letters engraved #89...$13.00 (1.50)

Cheese Knife up to 3 Letters engraved. 8½" Long. #91...$9.50 (1.15)

Cheese plane up to 3 Letters engraved. #92...$11.00 (1.15)

Clipboard 14"x10" 10 Letters can be engraved or have a name & flowers painted on. #93...$10.00 (1.50)

Half-pint cartons perfect for cream, sugar, gravy, etc. Precious on the table. are not personalized. #94...$6.50 (1.35)

Please allow 3 weeks for things that are to be engraved. painted items take a few days. Please be sure to include special instructions!

since Sunshine did not have much inventory cost. The store had the money in hand before the merchandise was ordered.

Diane found, however, that many people wanted items that they could have personalized quickly. This presented a real problem with the special order items, since some items took as long as six weeks for delivery. To help alleviate this problem, Diane began purchasing inventory that could be personalized in-house by Sunshine. A high school girl was hired to hand paint personalized items. As the demand for the painted items grew, more stocked inventory was needed. Soon the available storage space in the store and warehouse became inadequate, and Diane's garage became a major storage room for Sunshine. This presented two problems. Her home was five miles from the store, so a logistics problem existed. Also, it became difficult to keep track of inventory since there were no records kept on whether the inventory was stocked in the store, the garage, or the warehouse.

Diane and Beverly had expanded into the mail-order business in hopes of cutting the inventory-carrying-cost problem. The mail orders were pre-paid, covering some of the high inventory cost. As time passed and the business grew, the number of hand-painted orders became so great that it was soon difficult to keep records of what had been painted and what inventory was on hand. To assist with inventory control, a computer system was leased. This provided Sunshine with the capability of much greater accuracy in dealing with inventory. Now after an order was written up, the item purchased was recorded on a computer sheet. Once a week these sheets were read into the computer and Sunshine received a printout of inventory. Even this, however, did not solve all of the inventory problems. It seemed that the inventory kept growing, particularly the personalized items. Diane, who did all of the buying at market, had a tendency to buy what she liked, and soon she was buying more products to be personalized by Sunshine. It became very difficult to have good quality products painted fast enough to keep up with the orders.

SPECIAL ORDERS

The Sunshine Shop has two kinds of special orders. The first are for items Sunshine buys or has personalized by another source. If this source is in the city, the item can be delivered within a week. However, if a source from out-of-state is used, it can take as long as six weeks. The second type of special order items are those personalized in-house by Sunshine. All special orders are written up on three-by-five cards and contain all necessary information on how the item is to be engraved or otherwise personalized. Mail orders are written the same way on different colored cards. Sunshine has a minor quality control problem with the special order items done in-house. A customer places an order and expects the item to look exactly like the display. Since Sunshine has many artists, and all work is done freehand, final products differ. A few customers are less than satisfied with their purchase.

As Diane, Beverly, and Gloria look over the Sunshine Shop's financial statements for 1981, they are very concerned that, even though sales were a record $322,196.55, the store also had a record loss of $24,463.59. To try to improve the situation for 1982, Bob Threadgill, Gloria's husband, drew up a pro forma Income Statement for the store (Exhibit 4). Everyone at Sunshine hopes these guidelines, as well as the planned promotional expenditures, will lead to a profitable 1982.

EXHIBIT 4   The Sunshine Shop, Inc., Unaudited balance sheet, June 30, 1981

ASSETS

CURRENT ASSETS:

Cash in Preston State Bank—checking	$ 1,030.22	
Cash in Preston State Bank—savings	501.65	
Cash on hand	100.00	
Inventory	28,510.88	
Total current assets		$30,142.75

PROPERTY AND EQUIPMENT

Equipment	6,762.42	
Household improvements	15,858.29	
	22,620.71	
Less: accumulated depreciation and amortization	12,478.03	
Total property and equipment		10,142.68

OTHER ASSETS:

Prepaid rent	1,587.50	
Utility	280.00	
Total other assets		1,867.50
Total assets		$ 42,152.93

LIABILITIES AND SHAREHOLDERS' DEFICIT

CURRENT LIABILITIES:

Note payable — Preston State Bank	$20,000.00	
Accounts payable	3,060.35	
Sales tax payable	831.95	
Payroll taxes payable	2,031.55	
Due to shareholders	21,738.99	
Total current liabilities		$52,662.84

EXHIBIT 4 (continued)

SHAREHOLDERS' DEFICIT:
  COMMON STOCK
    $1.00 par value
    Authorized — 10,000 shares
    Issued and outstanding — 1,000 shares   1,000.00

  ADDITIONAL PAID-IN CAPITAL   11,928.17

  RETAINED DEFICIT   23,438.08

    Total shareholders' deficit   (10,509.91)

      Total liabilities and shareholders' deficit $42,152.93

EXHIBIT 5 The Sunshine Shop, Inc., Unaudited statement of loss and retained deficit for the year ended June 30, 1981

			% of Sales
SALES		$322,196.55	100.0
COST OF SALES:			
Inventory - beginning	$ 23,210.99		
Purchases	145,480.36		43.5
Freight-in	3,289.99		1.0
Personalizing charges	1,654.55		.5
Salaries - personalizing	40,746.42		12.7
	214,382.31		
Less: inventory - ending	28,510.88		
Cost of sales		185,871.43	57.7
Gross profit		136,325.12	42.3
OPERATING EXPENSES:			
Advertising	3,902.23		1.2
Bank charges	10.99		—
Cash short (over)	987.82		.3
Catalogue, printing and mailing	13,575.61		4.2
Computer service	4,806.98		1.5
Contributions	1,935.90		.6
Credit card fees	4,370.72		1.4
Depreciation and amortization	6,567.03		2.0
Equipment rental	1,613.86		.5
Insurance	2,459.57		.8
Mailing catalogues	4,355.47		1.4
Medical reimbursement	2,582.43		.8
Miscellaneous	2,644.60		.8
Postage and UPS	1,072.52		.8
Professional fees	2,363.30		.7
Promotion and gifts	310.68		.1

EXHIBIT 5   (continued)

Rent	26,277.73	8.2
Repairs	212.29	.1
Salaries - officers	12,600.00	3.9
Salaries - sales	38,024.75	11.8
Store expense	7,179.23	2.3
Supplies - art	1,099.81	.3
Taxes	6,519.09	2.0
Telephone	2,950.16	.9
Travel	4,138.42	1.3
Utilities	1,328.95	.4
Warehouse supplies and expense	5,912.81	1.8
Total operating expenses	159,802.95	49.6
Operating loss	(23,477.83)	(7.3)

OTHER INCOME AND (EXPENSE)

Interest income	$693.17		
Miscellaneous income	175.31	869.17	
Interest expense		(1,854.93)	
Total other income and (expense)		(985.76)	(.3)
Loss before provision for federal income taxes		(24,463.59)	(7.6)
PROVISION FOR FEDERAL INCOME TAXES		—	—
Net loss		(24,463.59)	(7.6)
RETAINED EARNINGS - BEGINNING OF YEAR		1,025.51	
RETAINED DEFICIT - END OF YEAR		($23,438.08)	

EXHIBIT 6   The Sunshine Shop, Inc., pro forma income statement—1982

SALES (net)	$450,000
COST OF SALES (assumed at 55%)	247,500
GROSS PROFIT	$202,500
OPERATING EXPENSES	
Advertising and catalogue @6%	24,000*
Computer service	6,000
Contributions	1,000
Credit card fees	5,000
Depreciation and amortization	7,000
Equipment rental	1,600
Insurance	2,500
Miscellaneous	2,500
Postage & UPS	—
Professional fees	2,400
Rent	30,000
Salary - officers	none
Salary - sales	65,000
Store expense	9,200
Supplies - art	1,300
Taxes	6,600

EXHIBIT 6   (continued)

Telephone	3,500
Travel	5,200
Utilities	1,700
Warehouse expense	6,500

TOTAL OPERATING EXPENSES	$181,000
NET PROFIT	$ 21,500

*The $24,000 advertising and catalogue expense is broken down as follows:

A. Christmas catalogue

Printing (18,000)	$5,000
Labels (14,000)	420
Postage	1,400
Mailing service	400
	7,220

B. Spring catalogue
(same as Christmas
catalogue)   7,220

C. Brochures
1. Valentines
2. Easter
3. Back-to-school
(Each is the same as Christmas
except printing will only
be $1,000 for each) $6,600

D. Newspaper or other advertising   2,960

                                             $24,000

Xerox Corporation

Entering the 1980s, the Xerox Corporation was experiencing some significant problems, contrary to its two decades of unqualified success. The firm's market share of copying machines had dropped significantly, profit margins had slipped, and a host of tough, new Japanese and American competitors had arrived on the scene. At the same time, Xerox's leadership was changing. C. Peter McColough, Xerox's chief executive officer since 1968, who had been with the company since its early years, announced on September 29, 1981 that he was stepping down in favor of David T. Kearns, Xerox's president.

HISTORY

Xerography, the technology which started the office copying industry, was developed by Chester Carlson, who worked alone and part-time to develop xerography. He graduated from California Institute of Technology with a degree in physics. Finding a job in the depression was not easy, but he was hired as a research engineer at Bell Telephone Laboratories for $35 a week. Eventually, he was laid off at Bell Labs and went to work with P.K. Mallory & Co., an electronics firm, where he became the head of the patent department. Carlson studied law at night while at Mallory, and earned his degree from New York Law School.

While heading up the patent department at Mallory, Carlson noticed that there never seemed to be enough copies of patent specifications. He believed that the solution to the problem would be a device to make copies of the documents. The alternatives, photographic copies and retyping, were expensive and troublesome.

Carlson spent months in the New York Public Library researching imaging processes. Because many large companies at that time were experimenting with photographic processes, he decided to explore other approaches, chiefly photoconductivity. Starting first in the kitchen of his home

This case was prepared by Richard T. Hise, Professor of Marketing at Texas A&M University, as a basis for class discussion rather than to illustrate either effective or ineffective marketing management.

and later in a lab over a bar, Carlson developed the fundamentals of Xerography; he filed a patent application in 1937. On October 22, 1938, Carlson and German physicist Otto Kornei developed the specific process which became the foundation of the copying industry.

For over five years, Carlson tried to interest a company in his invention, but over twenty turned him down. Finally, in 1944, Battelle Memorial Institute, a nonprofit research organization in Columbus, Ohio, signed a royalty-sharing agreement with Carlson. In 1947, Battelle entered into an agreement with Haloid, a small photo paper company later called Xerox, to develop a Xerographic machine. But it was not until 1959 that the first convenient office copier using Xerography was introduced.

The 914 copier proved to be a phenomenal success. By the end of 1962, over 10,000 of the 914 copiers had been sold, and by 1963, the company's net profit hit $23 million, compared to only $2 million in 1959.

In 1963, the 813 desktop copier was introduced. This was followed by the 2400, so named because it could produce 2400 copies in an hour, in 1964.

EXHIBIT 1   Consolidated statements of income, 1977–1980, Xerox Corporation and subsidiaries

(In millions, except per share data) Year Ended December 31	1980	1979	1978	1977
Operating revenues				
Rentals and services	$5,151.6	$4,606.3	$4,130.5	$3,713.8
Sales	3,044.9	2,390.1	1,887.5	1,368.2
Total operating revenues	8,196.5	6,996.4	6,018.0	5,082.0
Costs and expenses				
Cost of rentals and services	2,117.9	1,862.3	1,691.6	1,477.1
Cost of sales	1,425.3	1,065.8	770.6	579.8
Research and development expenses	434.1	376.4	311.0	269.0
Selling, administrative and general expenses	2,866.7	2,419.6	2,089.0	1,760.9
Total costs and expenses	6,844.0	5,724.1	4,862.2	4,086.8
Operating income	1,352.5	1,272.3	1,155.8	995.2
Other income (deductions), net (includes interest expense: 1980—$115.2; 1979—$102.8; 1978—$125.4)	(1.4)	11.0	(64.6)	82.4
Income before income taxes	1,351.1	1,283.3	1,091.2	912.8
Income taxes	604.5	592.0	528.0	440.5
Income before outside shareholders' interests	746.6	691.3	563.2	472.3
Outside shareholders' interests	127.4	128.2	86.7	68.3
Income before extraordinary item	619.2	563.1	476.5	404.0
Extraordinary income (net of income taxes)	—	—	12.0	—
Net income	$ 619.2	$ 563.1	$ 488.5	$ 404.0
Average common shares outstanding	84.4	84.1	84.1	80.3
Income per common share				
Income before extraordinary item	$7.33	$6.69	$5.67	$5.03
Extraordinary income	—	—	.14	—
Net income per common share	$7.33	$6.69	$5.81	$5.03

MAJOR BUSINESS SEGMENTS

Exhibit 1 shows Xerox's consolidated statements of income, 1977-1980. Exhibit 2 contains a five year review of its performance, 1976-1980. Exhibit 3 shows the company's major business segments in 1981. Exhibits 4 and 5 indicate the results for its major business segments, 1977-1980. (Xerox's profits in 1981 were $598 million on sales of $8.69 billion. Its assets were $7.67 billion and its stockholders' equity was $3.73 billion.)

EXHIBIT 2 Five years in review, 1976–1980

	1980	1979	1978	1977	1976
Yardsticks of progress					
Income per common share					
Income before extraordinary item	$ 7.33	$ 6.69	$ 5.67	$ 4.95	$ 4.35
Extraordinary income	—	—	.14	—	—
Net income per common share	7.33	6.69	5.81	4.95	4.35
Dividends declared per common share	2.80	2.40	2.00	1.50	1.10
Operations (dollars in millions)					
Total operating revenues	$8,197	$6,996	$6,018	$5,190	$4,515
Rentals and services	5,152	4,606	4,131	3,821	3,592
Sales	3,045	2,390	1,887	1,369	923
Cost of rentals, services and sales	3,543	2,928	2,462	2,110	1,852
Depreciation of rental equipment	602	562	512	486	504
Depreciation and amortization of buildings and equipment	201	191	163	156	150
Research and development expenses	434	376	311	269	226
Operating income	1,353	1,272	1,156	1,013	896
Interest expense	115	103	125	114	137
Income before income taxes	1,351	1,283	1,091	932	817
Income taxes	605	592	527	449	383
Outside shareholders' interests	127	128	87	68	69
Income before extraordinary item	619	563	477	415	365
Extraordinary income (net of income taxes)	—	—	12	—	—
Net income	619	563	489	415	365
Financial position (dollars in millions)					
Current assets	$3,515	$3,104	$2,639	$2,338	$2,112
Rental equipment and related inventories at cost	4,692	4,414	4,105	3,935	3,822
Accumulated depreciation of rental equipment	2,770	2,678	2,603	2,519	2,392
Land, buildings and equipment at cost	2,403	2,103	1,879	1,769	1,692
Accumulated depreciation and amortization of buildings and equipment	1,033	880	768	660	569
Total assets	7,349	6,554	5,766	5,223	4,959

EXHIBIT 2 (continued)

	1980	1979	1978	1977	1976
Current liabilities	1,984	1,679	1,401	1,205	1,127
Long-term debt	898	913	938	1,052	1,211
Outside shareholders' interests	500	431	349	315	301
Shareholders' equity	3,625	3,221	2,854	2,520	2,224
Additions to rental equipment and rental inventories	993	927	705	558	460
Additions to land, buildings and equipment	335	300	206	182	214

Selected data and ratios					
Average common shares outstanding	84,423,840	84,125,133	84,092,274	83,901,945	83,923,387
Shareholders at year end	106,293	111,877	119,545	127,044	130,379
Employees at year end	120,480	115,705	107,679	106,677	100,458
Income before income taxes to total operating revenues	16.5%	18.3%	18.1%	18.0%	18.1%
Net income to average shareholders' equity	18.1%	18.5%	18.2%	17.5%	17.5%
Long-term debt to total capitalization[1]	17.9%	20.0%	22.7%	27.1%	32.4%

Certain data have been restated for the years 1977 through 1979 to reflect the changes in the classification of interest income related to notes receivable associated with sold equipment from operating revenues to other income.

[1]Total capitalization is defined as the sum of long-term debt, outside shareholders' interests in equity of subsidiaries, and shareholders' equity.

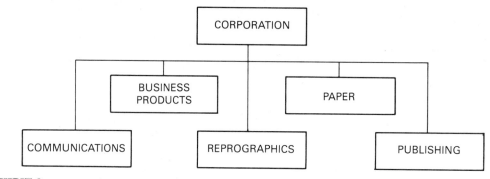

EXHIBIT 3

EXHIBIT 4 Results by major business segments, 1977

(Dollars in millions)	Copiers/ duplicators	Other businesses	Eliminations	Consolidated
1977				
Revenues from unaffiliated customers				
Rentals and services	$3,549.8	$ 184.9	$(20.9)	$3,713.8
Sales	440.7	927.5	—	1,368.2
Transfers between segments	—	14.7	(14.7)	—
Total operating revenues	$3,990.5	$1,127.1	$(35.6)	$5,082.0
Operating profit	$1,003.0	$ 76.3		$1,079.3

EXHIBIT 4 (continued)

(Dollars in millions)	Copiers/duplicators	Other businesses	Eliminations	Consolidated
General corporate expenses				(55.5)
Interest expense				(111.0)
Income before income taxes				$ 912.8
Identifiable assets	$3,546.6	$711.4		$4,258.0
Corporate assets, including investment in Fuji Xerox Co., Ltd.				788.6
Total assets				$5,046.6
Depreciation and amortization	$ 554.1	$ 70.2		
Capital expenditures	$ 618.9	$ 90.7		

EXHIBIT 5 Results by major business segments, 1978–1980

(Dollars in millions)	Repro-graphics	Paper	Other Businesses	Elimi-nations	Consol-idated
1980 Revenues from unaffiliated customers					
Rentals and services	$4,840.9	$ —	$ 409.1	$ (98.4)	$5,151.6
Sales	1,224.1	573.6	1,247.2	—	3,044.9
Transfers between segments	—	—	34.0	(34.0)	—
Total operating revenues	$6,065.0	$ 573.6	$1,690.3	$(132.4)	$8,196.5
Operating profit	$1,397.4	$ 44.6	128.8		$1,570.8
General corporate expenses					(104.5)
Interest expense					(115.2)
Income before income taxes					$1,351.1
Identifiable assets	$5,195.3	$ 215.3	$1,394.6		$6,805.2
Corporate assets					544.0
Total assets					$7,349.2
Depreciation and amortization	$ 682.7	$ 7.6	$ 97.5		
Capital expenditures	$1,103.5	$ 13.1	$ 192.4		
1979 Revenues from unaffiliated customers					
Rentals and services	$4,313.1	$ —	$ 357.1	$ (63.9)	$4,606.3
Sales	990.6	446.4	953.1	—	2,390.1
Transfers between segments	—	—	16.6	(16.6)	—
Total operating revenues	$5,303.7	$ 446.4	$1,326.8	$ (80.5)	$6,996.4
Operating profit	$1,303.0	$ 37.4	110.0		$1,450.4
General corporate expenses					(64.3)
Interest expense					(102.8)
Income before income taxes					$1,283.3

EXHIBIT 5   (continued)

(Dollars in millions)	Repro-graphics	Paper	Other Businesses	Elimi-nations	Consol-idated
Identifiable assets	$4,448.9	$ 175.9	$1,168.4		$5,793.2
Corporate assets					760.4
Total assets					$6,553.6
Depreciation and amortization	$ 639.3	$ 7.2	$ 90.1		
Capital expenditures	$1,017.1	$ 11.3	$ 179.7		

1978 Revenues from unaffiliated customers					
Rentals and services	$3,861.3	$ —	$ 305.1	$ (35.9)	$4,130.5
Sales	795.2	341.9	750.4	—	1,887.5
Transfers between segments	—	—	18.2	(18.2)	—
Total operating revenues	$4,656.5	$ 341.9	$1,073.7	$ (54.1)	$6,018.0
Operating profit	$1,147.6	$ 24.9	110.5		$1,283.0
General corporate expenses					(66.4)
Interest expense					(125.4)
Income before income taxes					$1,091.2
Identifiable assets	$3,920.7	$ 138.2	$ 877.6		$4,936.5
Corporate assets					829.2
Total assets					$5,765.7
Depreciation and amortization	$ 575.1	$ 5.1	$ 80.2		
Capital expenditures	$ 753.5	$ 6.6	$ 123.8		

Reprographic Segment

Xerox's products within this segment include a broad line of Xerographic copiers and duplicators, including desktop and console model copiers, and electronic printers. Their copying speed varies from 600 to 7,200 copies per hour.

Copiers and duplicators may be purchased or rented, and a variety of accessories are available. Maintenance, service, and parts are included in all rental plans in the United States, but toner, developer, paper, and other supplies are sold separately. Different provisions and terms may apply in other countries. Renting Xerographic equipment spreads profit over the period of the rental, while an outright sale results in immediate profit. Financing plans are available in the United States, Canada, and in some foreign countries; these allow customers to finance the purchase of most Xerox equipment over two to five years at competitive rates of interest. Some equipment is sold with trade-in privileges, and the company has considered allowing trade-in of competitive equipment toward the purchase of Xerox machines.

Xerox manufactures various products for use in engineering reproduction departments, particularly printers which reproduce ordinary paper from microfilm, or those which reproduce from engineering drawings.

The 9700 electronic printing system can produce computer-generated text and create business forms at the rate of up to two copies a second, 18,000 lines a minute. Three additional features were announced in 1979 for the 9700 system, including duplexing, microfiche output capability, and communications capability (with the 850 communicating word processing system). In the fall of 1980, Xerox brought out the new 5700 electronic printing system, which combines several office operations: word processor printing, electronic mail, remote computer printing, and direct copying in a single unit. A laser-based system, the 5700 is intended for office use.

A major introduction of the reprographic segment was the 9200, a duplicator which was twice as fast as its competitors and cost $350 million in R&D expenditures. Xerox's executives planned to place a 9200 in each of the 100,000 central reproduction departments located in American corporations by 1980. If this objective were achieved, they estimated that annual revenues for the 9200 would be $1 billion a year, with very little cannibalization of other Xerox machines. By 1978, only 3,000 units had been placed in corporations' central reproduction departments; several factors explained the low level. The 9200 was more expensive than competitive models, and potential customers did not agree with Xerox's contention that the machine's greater automation capability would reduce the number of employees needed. A.B. Dick and Addressograph-Multigraph aggressively pushed their new automated offset machines, which replicated many of the 9200's advantages.

To salvage the 9200, Xerox reduced its price and targeted it to less voluminous, non-central reproduction department users. This resulted in 12,000 installations by 1979, but these placements caused the loss of about 8,000 other middle-of-the-market machines—other machines which were relatively more profitable than the 9200. Unexpectedly heavy usage of the 9200 left company officials optimistic that the predicted $1 billion a year revenues by 1980 may still occur.

A number of new products has been introduced by Xerox since the beginning of 1978:

☐ The Xerox 2600 small office copier is a compact, low-cost model with high quality. Introduced on October 5, 1978, the 2600 offers a low price to customers without high-volume copying requirements. It produces 12 copies a minute, and Xerox has been satisfied with the 2600's number of placements.

☐ Also introduced on October 5, 1978, was the 3109 copier. This machine provides a unique document feeder that positions original documents to save time. Twenty-six copies can be run in a minute, with the first copy available in less than seven seconds. The copier reduces and a microcomputer constantly monitors its performance.

☐ The 2300 copier was introduced in May, 1979. The 2300 is a versatile, desktop model which became Xerox's lowest-priced new copier. Executives believe that the 2300 has sold and rented well.

☐ The 3450 copier, introduced at the same time, can copy large documents or reduce them to letter size. It also features built-in computer diagnostics, document handling, and printing. Placement levels of the 3450 have been acceptable, according to the company.

☐ The Xerox 3300, introduced several months after the 3450, was touted as the company's fastest compact copier. It also featured automatic document positioning, pressure sensitive controls, and alternate-sized paper supply. Many 3300 models did not perform up to Xerox standards, and the company was forced to recall the product and offer customers a choice of other models or their money back.

☐ The 9500 duplicator was announced in October, 1979. This is a high-volume high-quality copier with two-copies-a-second speed, reduction, duplexing, automatic document feeding, and collating. Xerox has been placing the 9500 in company printing units and commercial print shops.

☐ Also introduced in October, 1979 was the 8200 copier/duplicator, a medium-to-high volume machine offering the same copy quality as the 9500, plus a new recirculating document handler that automatically feeds originals and produces collated copies without a collator, optimal online stapling, and three types of reduction.

☐ The 5600, another copier/duplicator, was announced in October, 1979. A medium-volume unit, it features automatic feeding, a recirculating document handler, and optimal stapling. It was the first copier able to automatically make two-sided copies from single-sided or two-sided originals. Xerox has been pleased with the market's acceptance of the 5600, and had to increase production during 1980 to keep up with demand.

Paper Segment

Xerox is one of the world's largest suppliers of standard cut sheet paper used for writing, typing, copying, and other office needs. The company distributes a full range of weights, sizes, and colors made specifically for copiers, duplicators, and other office equipment. Xerox purchases most of its paper from paper manufacturers, but some of the paper requirements of Rank Xerox (a foreign subsidiary) are provided by a French subsidiary of Rank, which packages and distributes bond paper.

Business Products Segment

Xerox entered the word processing field in late 1974. This industry consists of office equipment that ranges from stand-alone office typewriters to communication information processing systems. Xerox product offerings are multi-function word processors and network services, and include the 800 Electronic Typing System; the 850 Display Typing System, with a selection of modular components including a 24-character display typewriter and a full-page screen; and the 860 Information Processing System, available with full page and partial page display screens. The 860 is programmed to handle a variety of text editing applications, process office business records and data, and can be programmed by the user for specialized tasks. Late in 1979, Xerox introduced Ethernet, an intra-office communications network to link free-standing electronic information processing machines. In November, 1980, the company announced the 8000 Network System, which allows anyone at a connected work station to create, process, file, copy, print, and distribute data throughout the Ethernet network electronically. The 860 Information Processing System will also operate on this network.

Xerox's debut into the word processing field in late 1974 was marked by the introduction of its 800 Electronic Typing System. It was originally scheduled for a 1973 introduction, but was delayed because of problems with its high-speed printer. Because of its late introduction, the 800 had lost much of its technological lead and had become almost obsolete. According to one former Xerox sales manager, "Within eighteen months, we had one of the oldest products on the market." Additional problems were design errors which made it incompatible with IBM's typewriters: anyone wanting to switch to Xerox from IBM had high record conversion costs. The machine's complicated editing function frustrated many secretaries.

The problems were so severe with the 800 model that one ex-Xerox word processing manager said, "It's tough when you have to look a customer in the eye and say, 'Yeah, I agree. There's really no reason you should buy this machine.' In my seven years at Xerox, I can think of no product more rejected by major accounts than the 800."[1]

Despite all the problems experienced with the 800, 12,000 units had been placed by the middle of 1978, about 5.5 percent of the $2.6 billion worth of systems then in use, but far behind IBM's 78 percent. However, management had hoped for about 16,000 placements by that time; profits at best were probably only marginal. In addition, so much pressure was put on the sales force to push the 800 that the turnover rate for salespeople increased 50 percent. As turnover increased, the sales force was reorganized and purged, and two of the word processing unit's highest ranking executives were reassigned.

Many of the difficulties experienced by the 800 were expected to be eliminated by the 850 series, brought to the market in late 1978. However, industry analysts believed that this product was introduced too late and was too expensive; similar systems had been available for a year, and some of their prices had already begun to decline. According to one word processing company observer, the 850 was "too late and too expensive. At best, it will be a moderate success; at worst, a failure." This individual was also disturbed by Xerox's failure to integrate the various businesses it already had—

---

[1]Uttal, Bro, "Xerox Is Trying Too Hard," *Fortune,* March 13, 1978 pp. 84–94.

facsimile machines, laser printers, plotters for computer graphics—to develop full-scale office systems. He commented, "A few years ago, everyone thought the office of the future would be a battle of giants between IBM and Xerox. But I doubt it. Xerox has lost too much ground."[2]

In September, 1980, Xerox announced its new 5700 electronic printing system. The 5700 combines laser and electronics with conventional light-lens xerography. As an electronics printer, it is up to 40 times faster than typical word processing printers. It can print an unlimited number of type styles, can receive a page of text in three seconds, and as a copier, it can automatically handle originals, print on one or two sides, collate, and staple. It can accept text directly from one or several word processors, or from tape cassettes, magnetic cards, or floppy disks. It is the first electronic printer to provide automatic distribution and storage of individually addressed electronic mail. Despite its versatility, Xerox claims that the 5700 is easy to use.

In 1982, Xerox was aggressively promoting the Star professional work station. Costing $16,595, it enabled executives to do text and data processing with little training. Xerox believed that the most important objective in office automation systems of the future is to provide help to the professional and managers, not clerical workers. The company claims that little has been done to boost the productivity of professionals and managers, despite their $600 billion a year payroll, double that of clerical personnel.

Xerox manufactures and markets several models of Telecopier transceivers, facsimile devices which transmit or receive images by acoustical coupling with conventional telephones. They are rented or sold to customers. Xerox offers products primarily in the low- and medium-volume manual segments (Telecopier 400 and Telecopier 410) and, until 1979, had only one product (Telecopier 200) in the high-volume automatic segment. These products range in transmission speed from two to six minutes per page. In late 1979, Xerox announced the Telecopier 485 which can receive a typical one-page business letter in about one minute over ordinary telephone lines. The 485 skips over the white space between the lines and transmits only the content of a document when communicating with another 485; this can mean transmission times of less than one minute per document.

Other products include microprinters, master-making equipment, electrostatic printers and plotters, daisy wheel impact printers, computer disk drives, and mail-addressing equipment. Xerox also operates a time-sharing service for small businesses, primarily offering decentralized accounting services, and provides software packages for computerized manufacturing systems. In addition, Xerox markets a reading machine for the blind and a data entry machine.

Communications Segment

Xerox participates in the communications industry through its wholly-owned subsidiary, WUI, Inc., acquired in November, 1979. WUI engages in two lines of business: International Communications (Western Union International,

---

[2]*Ibid.*

WUI's principal subsidiary, is an international carrier, which uses a world-wide network of telecommunications satellites). The Domestic Communications business consists of WUI/TAS, Inc., which owns a number of local telephone answering services, and Airsignal International, Inc., which provides radio paging and mobile radio services.

In addition, Xerox has announced plans to set up the Xerox Telecommunications Network (XTEN). XTEN will be a domestic telecommunications network to serve customers in and between many U.S. cities, and is subject to approval by the Federal Communication Commission.

Publishing Segment

Xerox's first venture into publishing was in 1962, its first departure from reprographics. In 1980, the publishing segment was composed of several companies. R. R. Bowker produces magazines, data bases and reference books. Magazines include *Publisher's Weekly,* and *Library Journal.* Major reference books include *Books in Print, Literary Market Place,* and *American Men & Women in Science.* Ginn and Company, a leading educational publisher, offers textbooks and instructional materials to elementary and high schools.

Xerox Educational Publications (XEP) provides supplemental educational materials to the home and classroom, including newspapers, multimedia instruction kits, and paperback and hard cover book clubs. XEP publishes the widely circulated *Weekly Reader* (ten million copies) and operates the world's largest juvenile book club. XLS (Xerox Learning Systems) provides training programs to improve sales and management skills. Its "Professional Selling Skills" is a standard program which can be fitted to specific customer needs and is generally regarded as the leading program of its type. University Microfilms International (UMI) publishes information from its collection of microfilmed periodicals, rare books, and doctoral dissertations.

Miscellaneous Activities

Through Xerox's Electro-optical Systems, it conducts R&D for advanced military and aerospace technology, and manufactures electro-optical products. Xerox's Medical Systems rents and sells Xeroradiography equipment for medical purposes, particularly for the early detection of breast cancer. The Xerox Credit Corporation is a wholly-owned subsidiary which finances accounts receivable resulting from sales of equipment to customers. Formed in 1980, it also is engaged in the third party equipment financing of transportation, industrial, and commercial equipment through direct financing leases.

INTERNATIONAL OPERATIONS

Xerox's largest interests outside the United States are the Rank Xerox Companies, comprising Rank Xerox Limited of London, and Rank Xerox Holding

B.V. of the Netherlands and their subsidiaries. Approximately 51 percent of the voting power of Rank Xerox Limited and Rank Xerox Holding B.V. is owned directly or indirectly by Xerox; 49 percent is owned directly or indirectly by the Rank Organisation Limited. The earnings of the Rank Xerox Companies are allocated between Xerox and the Rank Organisation, and this allocation varies according to the amount of such earnings. For 1980, the percentage of earnings of the Rank Xerox Companies allocated to Xerox was approximately 66 percent. Under agreements between Xerox and the Rank Organisation and the Articles of Association of Rank Xerox Limited and the Rank Xerox Holding B.V., the proportion allocated to Xerox may not exceed 66⅔ percent.

Rank Xerox Limited manufactures and markets most xerographic copier/duplicator products developed by Xerox. Its manufacturing operations are principally in the United Kingdom, while marketing operations are primarily in Europe, Africa, the Middle East, and Australia. Rank Xerox Limited also has certain rights to manufacture and market other products of Xerox, including computer-related equipment and services, publications and library products and services, medical and diagnostic equipment and services, and other office equipment and services. Rank Xerox Holding B.V., through a subsidiary, manufactures certain Xerox products in Europe.

Fuji Xerox Co., Ltd., of Tokyo, equally owned by Fuji Photo Film Co., Ltd., of Japan and Rank Xerox Limited, manufactures copiers, duplicators, and supplies which are marketed in Japan and other areas of the Far East. Other subsidiaries market and manufacture products in Canada, Latin America, and the Caribbean.

Xerox's management believes that business in foreign countries involves risks that domestic operations do not have. These risks include controls on the repatriation of earnings and capital and currency fluctuations. Exhibits 6 and 7 show the results for Xerox's international and domestic operations between 1977 and 1980.

In 1978, Xerox's international operations benefited from favorable foreign currency exchange rates. About $10 million of Rank Xerox's earnings were contributed by its share in Fuji Xerox. In Latin America, the Caribbean, and Canada, revenues increased 18 percent to $711 million. In 1979, the company's international operations again benefited from favorable exchange rates. Fuji Xerox contributed around $42 million and revenues in Latin America, the Caribbean, and Canada increased 16 percent to $824 million.

During 1980, adverse foreign exchange rates helped drop the increase in net income from international operations to only 7 percent. The 15 percent increase of Rank Xerox Limited and Rank Xerox Holding B.V. and their subsidiaries was attributed to strong growth in service and supplies, increased sales of copier and duplicator equipment, and increased usage of installed equipment. Fuji Xerox generated $14 million in profit for Xerox, while revenues in the Caribbean, Latin America, Canada and the Middle East rose 16 percent to $973 million.

EXHIBIT 6   Domestic/international operations, 1977

(Dollars in millions)	United States	Rank-Xerox Companies	Other	Elimina- tions	Consol- idated
1977					
Revenues from unaffiliated cus- tomers	$2,841.1	$1,656.0	$605.8	$ (20.9)	$5,082.0
Transfers between geographic areas	126.1	3.3	10.1	(139.5)	—
Total operating reve- nues	$2,967.2	$1,659.3	$615.9	$(160.4)	$5,082.0
Income before out- side shareholders' interests	$ 263.2	$ 155.4	$ 51.6	$ 2.1	$ 472.3
Outside sharehold- ers' interests	—	63.3	5.0	—	68.3
Identifiable net in- come	$ 263.2	$ 92.1	$ 46.6	$ 2.1	$ 404.0
Identifiable assets	$2,736.7	$1,769.5	$595.2	$ (54.8)	$5,046.6

In 1980, Xerox matched the high level of machine placements it achieved in 1979, and set a new record in total copy volume. Over twenty five new competing copiers were introduced, raising the total of plain paper copiers available from thirty competitive companies for overseas copier customers to 130. Internationally, Xerox introduced three high-volume machines during the year: the 5600, 8200, and 9500. The 2300 and 2600 were popular in the small-volume market.

The company's operations in South and Central America and the Caribbean met ambitious revenue and profitability goals for the fifth consecutive year in 1980, in spite of a number of negative developments. Among these were a major currency devaluation in Brazil, double digit inflation in many countries, and political unrest in Central America. In November, 1980 Xerox established a new operating company, Xerox Limited, Hong Kong, to conduct business in mainland China. During 1980, Xerox's operations in Egypt were close to being profitable after only three years; the company employs about 100 people there including 15 technical representatives.

Fuji Xerox received in 1980 the Deming Prize, which is annually awarded to a Japanese company judged to excel in productivity and product quality. The prize is named for Dr. W. Edwards Deming, whose series of lectures and seminars after World War II is credited with much of Japan's resurgence in manufacturing quality and efficiency. Other Xerox operating units are studying the total quality control program for which Fuji Xerox received the award.

EXHIBIT 7   Domestic/international operations, 1978–1980. Information about the company's operations in different geographic areas.

Dollars in millions	United States	Rank-Xerox Companies	Other	Elimina- tions	Consol- idated
1980 Revenues from unaffiliated customers	$4,465.5	$2,856.4	$ 973.0	$ (98.4)	$8,196.5
Transfers between geographic areas	222.6	3.5	45.4	(271.5)	—
Total operating revenues	$4,688.1	$2,859.9	$1,018.4	$(369.9)	$8,196.5
Income before outside sharehold- ers' interests	$ 343.1	$ 296.0	$ 111.3	$ (3.8)	$ 746.6
Outside shareholders' interests	—	114.2	13.2	—	127.4
Identifiable net income	$ 343.1	$ 181.8	$ 98.1	$ (3.8)	$ 619.2
Identifiable assets	$3,979.1	$2,591.0	$ 837.2	$ (58.1)	$7,349.2
1979 Revenues from unaffiliated customers	$3,744.5	$2,479.7	$ 836.1	$ (63.9)	$6,996.4
Transfers between geographic areas	197.1	4.2	31.8	(233.1)	—
Total operating revenues	$3,941.6	$2,483.9	$ 867.9	$(297.0)	$6,996.4
Income before outside sharehold- ers' interests	$ 302.4	$ 299.5	$ 91.0	$ (1.6)	$ 691.3
Outside shareholders' interests	—	117.6	10.6	—	128.2
Identifiable net income	$ 302.4	$ 181.9	$ 80.4	$ (1.6)	$ 563.1
Identifiable assets	$3,581.5	$2,265.1	$ 757.5	$ (50.5)	$6,553.6
1978 Revenues from unaffiliated customers	$3,266.6	$2,068.5	$ 718.8	$ (35.9)	$6,018.0
Transfers between geographic areas	151.0	2.0	16.1	(169.1)	—
Total operating revenues	$3,417.6	$2,070.5	$ 734.9	$(205.0)	$6,018.0
Income before outside sharehold- ers' interests	$ 305.3	$ 191.1	$ 67.6	$ (0.8)	$ 563.2
Outside shareholders' interests	—	79.2	7.5	—	86.7
Income before extraordinary item	$ 305.3	$ 111.9	$ 60.1	$ (0.8)	$ 476.5
Extraordinary income	12.0	—	—	—	12.0
Identifiable net income	$ 317.3	$ 111.9	$ 60.1	$ (0.8)	$ 488.5
Identifiable assets	$3,224.8	$1,973.6	$ 623.5	$ (56.2)	$5,765.7

COMPETITION

Competition with Non-Reprographic Products

There is active competition in the paper market. All manufacturers of fine or cut-sheet paper produce paper that can be used in reprographic equipment, and they sell these products directly or through local distributors.

Competition has also been increasing in recent years in the facsimile business and has been characterized by the introduction of faster, more sophisticated systems. The word processing field is also competitive, where IBM is the largest firm. IBM offers a wide range of products, including dictating equipment, electric typewriters, memory typewriters, and magnetic card and tape systems.

Many independent companies sell supplies for copiers and duplicators. Xerox's major competitors have established national manufacturing operations, and hundreds of local distributors, affiliates, resellers, and merchant operations also exist.

Xerox's Western Union International competes in the international communications business with such other record carriers as AT&T and the airmail service. Domestically, the major competitors are ITT World Communications, Inc., FTC Communications (formerly French Telegraph Cable Company), and TRT Telecommunications. The three principal U.S. international carriers are Western Union International, ITT World Communication, Inc., and RCA Global.

The telephone answering service business is geographically limited to the immediate locale of each office, and is highly competitive in each geographic area. Although radio paging and mobile services are local operations, the FCC requires licenses, some states require certification, and radio frequencies are limited. Pricing appears to be a major strategy in the competitive publishing business, more so in book club sales, than in textbooks.

Competition in the Reprographic Market

Xerox believes that competition in the reprographics business is becoming even more intense. The firm estimates that there are several hundred competitors worldwide making, selling, leasing, or renting copying and duplicating products, many of whom have substantial resources. Competitors offer broad ranges of products, with different performance characteristics based on their reproduction methods. Many companies market their product lines through their own sales branches and subsidiaries, or through independent distributors and dealers. Product performance, price, and service are the major fields of competition.

Because of increasing competition during the 1970s, Xerox dramatically lost market shares for copying machines. Exhibit 8 shows that Xerox's market share of domestic copier revenues was 96 percent in 1970, but only 46 percent in 1980. It was still falling in 1981. Xerox still had a dominant position in

1981 for medium- and high-speed machines costing over $40,000, with a market share of 60 percent, but its share of the low end of the market was only about 30 percent in 1981. Worldwide, Xerox was also losing market share. In 1970, it was getting about 98 percent of worldwide copier revenues; by 1981, its market share was less than 60 percent.

Xerox's declining market share in low-priced copiers was mainly caused by Japanese competitors, and Xerox was largely unprepared for their onslaught. Company executives had anticipated competition, led by IBM and Kodak, with their medium- and high-priced machines, but were caught napping when Japanese firms aggressively entered the market for low-priced copiers in 1975.

Led by a three-way partnership of Ricoh and two U.S. firms, Savin Corp. and Nashua Corp., the new competitors offered plain paper models at such low prices that they appealed to many small businesses which had not previously purchased copiers. These machines also lured users who were dissatisfied with the inexpensive coated paper copiers, which proved to be inefficient and difficult to use. By 1980, the sales of plain paper copiers jumped to 34,000 units, from almost none in 1974.

The Japanese used a variety of strategies to chip away at Xerox's market share. Japanese machines use a liquid ink or toner instead of the powder which Xerox uses. Mechanisms in the Japanese machines are much simpler,

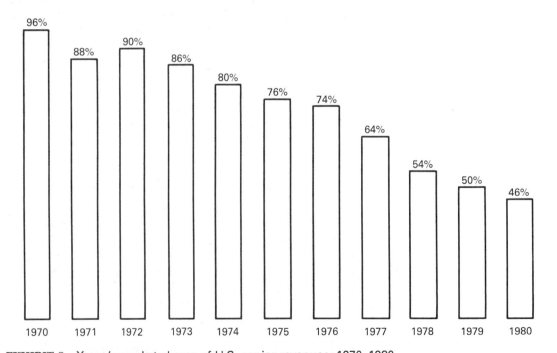

EXHIBIT 8   Xerox's market shares of U.S. copier revenues, 1970–1980

which means lower manufacturing costs (about $60 a machine in 1979) and lower prices. Also, Japanese copiers are more reliable and easier to repair. Savin's Model 770 averages 17,000 copies before breakdown, compared to Xerox's 6,000 to 10,000. The Savin machine takes less than thirty minutes to repair, while Xerox's takes longer. A Savin service technician can support 100 machines, a Xerox technician only about 50. Savin can then pass along substantially lower service charges to customers.

Another strategy employed by the Japanese was to market machines through independent office equipment dealers, which allowed them to quickly and cheaply establish themselves in the market. They were also able to convince customers to purchase machines, rather than lease them. Because this does not tie up capital, Japanese manufacturers were able to quickly line up distributors, instead of having to slowly and expensively build up a sales force and service staff. Attractive prices lured dealers. For example, it has been estimated that in 1980 a Savin dealer could make gross profits of about $300,000 or more annually by selling 200 copiers or less. Such potential returns convinced many Xerox sales managers to take Savin dealerships.

Xerox's officials claim they were not surprised by the advent of Japanese competition. Former CEO C. Peter McColough said, "We've known for years that the Japanese were coming. And the liquid toner technology is no breakthrough; it has been around for twenty years. What really surprised us was that they could make the machines so cheaply." Yet industry analysts claim that Xerox failed to anticipate the large demand for low-priced machines, misjudged the speed at which the Japanese could become established, and reacted much too slowly to the competitive threat.

Xerox may have gotten a reprieve in 1979 in the low-priced copier market, with the dissolution of the partnership between Ricoh, Savin, and Nashua. These companies had established exclusive territorial rights: Ricoh in the Far East, Savin in the U.S., and Nashua in the rest of the world, except Europe, where it shared rights with another company. With the announced breakup, the former partners are each expected to wage aggressive warfare in the U.S. market. However, without the support of the other two, each will have a decided disadvantage. Savin will have to learn how to manufacture copiers, and some analysts question the company's production capabilities. Nashua will have to develop a U.S.-based sales force and manufacturing base, and Ricoh must establish an American distribution system.[3]

Xerox has also had problems in medium-priced copiers during the 1970s. IBM's machines have become increasingly more sophisticated, with higher speeds, document feeding, reduction, collation, and two-sided copying. Around 1975, Eastman Kodak developed a "third generation" model with a microprocessor that diagnoses breakdowns more effectively and produces what is probably the best copy quality available.

It has been estimated that IBM's Copier II displaced 20,000 Xerox machines, but an even greater disaster was avoided by the reliability problems

---

[3]"The New Lean, Mean Xerox," *Business Week,"* October 12, 1981, pp. 126–132.

which plagued the IBM copier. Kodak's sales were slowed down by its desire to slowly build a sales and service force. One industry analyst has said, "Xerox has been lucky. If IBM had Kodak's machine, they would have been handed Xerox's head on a platter."[4]

Despite the vigorous domestic competition faced by Xerox for its medium-priced machines, the company's greatest fear is that the Japanese will enter this market. By the middle of 1981, this had already begun. Canon had brought out a new line of medium-speed copiers, and the major Japanese manufacturers were expected to follow suit because they had been selling such machines in their domestic market for years. In advance of this move, the Japanese were increasing the training of dealer sales forces, providing more service backup, increasing financial support to dealers, experimenting with their own direct sales forces in large metropolitan areas, and distributing copiers through IBM, Pitney Bowes, and Monroe because of their extensive sales and distribution networks.[5]

STRATEGIES

In 1980, Xerox executives defined the businesses their company participated in. Xerox believed that, in a strategic sense, defining its business is the most important question for it to answer. The five definitions the company settled on were that it is in the *information* business; the *reprographics* business; the business of *putting marks on paper* (this assumes both technology and the person using the machine); the *office systems* business; and, combining the first four definitions, the *productivity* business.

Beginning in the middle of the 1970s, C. Peter McColough announced on a number of occasions what he considered to be Xerox's major goal: "To increase earnings annually by 15 percent over the long term."

In spite of mounting skepticism, McColough continued to espouse this objective. "It is," he said, "a reasonable goal." Few analysts of the copier industry and Xerox agreed with him. One respected office equipment industry consultant said, "If you believe that 15 percent, there's a bridge I would like to sell you!" Much of the skepticism centered on various disappointments which occurred from 1974 to 1977, such as an $84 million tax writeoff of the billion dollar Scientific Data Systems acquisition, an FTC consent degree which decimated the company's patent wall, and the departure of three top executives, including its president.

Profits have been sluggish: a 2 percent drop in 1975 (the first decline in 25 years); a 5 percent increase in 1976; and a 12 percent increase in 1977; for a 5 percent annual growth rate in this time span. One copier industry analyst, viewing this three year record, asked "McColough says 15 percent over the long term, but when are we supposed to start measuring?"[6]

---

[4]Uttal, *op.cit.*

[5]"The New Lean, Mean Xerox," *op.cit.*

[6]Uttal, *op.cit.*

McColough pointed to the "office of the future" as the major strategy for achieving this 15 percent objective. Through the early part of the 1980s, Xerox has delineated a number of other important strategies, including:

☐ An aggressive marketing effort must be complemented by increased emphasis on cost control and "more thoughtful deployment of our valuable human and technological resources."

☐ Xerox must remain on the "cutting edge of technological change."

☐ Xerox will likely be successful by consistently meeting customer needs by "balancing product capability, quality, price, and timely market response."

☐ Top management was reorganized in June, 1978 to better recognize Xerox's two major business thrusts at that time: the reprographic and information products segments.

☐ Xerox wanted to maintain its leadership in the reprographic market and "steadily expand this healthy copier/duplicating business—a business that will produce the bulk of our revenues for as long as we can reasonably predict."

☐ To survive and grow in the information products segment, different strategies will be necessary than those employed in the reprographic business and, because of the different requirements of this unit's sub-division (word processing systems, computer services, facsimile machines, computer-related products, and printers), centralized management, as employed for the reprographic segment, will be difficult to implement in the near future.

☐ Reprographic service strategy, technical planning, and the design and manufacture of reprographic products will be done globally; this should result in substantial efficiencies.

☐ Xerox's various products will be designed to work with each other rather than as stand-alones. They must also work with the products of other companies, as part of multifunction office information systems.

☐ Since Xerox will not have the technological edge in the information products sector that it has in the reprographic segment, business planning will drive technological planning and the marketplace will determine its strategy.

☐ The development of planning units to span broad business areas will focus on customer needs, and developmental funds will be put where needs are, not necessarily where technological capabilities exist.

☐ Xerox's twenty-three operating companies were broken down into field business units (FBUs). An FBU is considered the optimal size to serve a given market area. According to management, FBUs are the "building blocks for a more regularized and more efficient structure."

☐ In Xerox Business Systems, the engineering, marketing, service, and manufacturing functions in two divisions (one producing document-creation and facsimile equipment, the other developing data systems capability) were combined to strengthen the Xerox presence in the office system marketplace.

☐ The increased use of electronics will be necessary to improve Xerox's product lines.

☐ The best growth opportunities in copier markets will be in the very high end, at the expense of offset equipment, and at the low end, at the expense of treated-paper units.

☐ Generations of more capable, more productive, and easier to use copiers and duplicators will be introduced.

☐ Innovative marketing strategies will be designed to meet the needs of customers, particularly small businesses needing low-priced units.

☐ Marketing efforts will become increasingly specialized and segmented by type. For example, service to Xerox's 1,000 largest accounts will be coordinated nationally by its national account managers.

☐ Information-products will account for an increasing share of future company profits and revenues.

☐ New businesses will be acquired and new information-handling capabilities developed to keep Xerox at the forefront in all aspects of the office environment.

☐ More integration of various technologies and capabilities will be introduced into Xerox's information products.

☐ Xerox will use its high-volume manufacturing capabilities to produce high-quality information products at competitive prices.

☐ Xerox will continue to develop integrated office systems capable of handling a variety of information management tasks in an increasingly productive and cost-effective manner.

In mid-1980, Xerox launched its *Business Effectiveness Program* to counter an unstable economy, continuing inflation, and intense competition. "It calls for nothing less than a reassessment of every aspect of the company's operation, in a structured process of self-examination by every part and unit of the company everywhere in the world." The objective of BEF is to improve the quality of performance in every way. Cost reduction and increased productivity are important factors, but the major emphasis will be on quality.

"The stress on quality and performance will be maintained and intensified throughout the 1980s and beyond."[7]

PERSONAL SELLING

In 1978, Xerox's marketing executives delineated two distinct buying and selling patterns and used these patterns to restructure its sales force. *Standalone* customers are those who require copiers and other office products to use themselves for specific information processing tasks. *Systems* customers are those who require products designed to work together within a broader office information network.

When dealing with the stand-alone customer, Xerox's salesperson usually works with a single decision maker, and the value of the item is easily determined based on product price, product features and service. Sales personnel dealing with systems customers usually encounter multiple decision makers, must help customers find answers to overall information problems, and are often required to enlist the aid of systems support personnel to make a sale.

In 1978, Xerox established the position of National Accounts Managers (NAMs) to handle larger customers. One NAM is assigned to each large commercial account and government customer. NAMs are responsible for every aspect of Xerox service to that customer. NAMs underwent extensive training at the company's International Center for Training and Management Development at Leesburg, Virginia to learn the latest developments in data processing, electronic communications, and management techniques. In addition, a new equipment service information system was developed so that each NAM would have detailed reports on every machine operated by his or her account.

Xerox also redefined sales jobs and restructured sales territories. Two types of selling positions were defined: One type of salesperson serves all customers or potential customers whose needs can be satisfied by low-volume copiers. Another type, account representatives, cover only those accounts who have large, diversified needs requiring across-the-board sales assistance. The number of sales regions was increased from five to twenty and the number of branches from 86 to 145, with the objective of increasing the effectiveness and responsiveness of the sales force. Xerox also hoped to develop an entrepreneurial spirit among sales personnel.

Concomitant with this restructuring was the belief that Xerox would have to trim the size of its sales force. Because of rapid growth during the previous two decades, sales personnel were added as quickly as they could be hired and trained, and productivity took a back seat. New CEO Kearns announced in fall, 1981, that the size of the sales force would be trimmed; no specific cuts were decided at that time.

---

[7]Company Annual Reports.

A major problem facing the company is how to combine the sales forces of the copier and office product divisions. The merger is necessary because the two markets are expected to coalesce over the next ten years. Timing will be critical. To combine the sales forces without regard to the markets' needs could damage the company. Complete integration of the sales forces is considered years away.

Xerox believes that it will have a distinct competitive advantage when the sales forces are merged because copier sales personnel apparently understand the needs of their customers and could effectively sell various office products. The copier sales force has traditionally been used to provide support for the product lines of the office products division, and have gained an understanding of customers' needs this way. In late 1981, Kearns decided to give the 820 personal computer and the new electronic typewriter to the copier sales force; other products from OPD are likely to be transferred later. However, this will occur only when various OPD products begin selling better. This will help insure that copier sales personnel give sufficient attention to the transferred products, since current copier sales still account for most of Xerox's total sales.

As long as Xerox had two separate sales forces, it was in danger of having more than one sales representative call on large customers. Also, it may be difficult to maintain morale for different sales organizations covering the same territory. Kearns has increased the number of national accounts managers; juggling compensation levels is expected to improve morale.[8]

Several sales innovations are being tried at Rank Xerox. The most important of these is team selling, in which sales personnel are organized by function, not by territory: one group of salespeople concentrates on gaining new business, while another is responsible for existing customers—handling machine installations, making sure operators are properly trained, etc. Xerox believes strongly in training its new sales reps. Basic knowledge about Xerox products, company history, sales philosophy, and ethics is provided at various branch offices around the country. The basic sales course is conducted at Leesburg. Emphasis is on sharpening the various skills needed to sell specific products to specific prospects. Role playing is stressed. Sales reps may return to Leesburg for advanced training, and special assignments may require a third trip. For example, the 9200 high-speed duplicator requires specialized training in selling to the centralized reproduction centers in large organizations.

DISTRIBUTION

Xerox's copiers, duplicators, and other reprographic products are, for the most part, marketed directly to customers by the company's worldwide sales force. Several regional distribution centers around the world maintain product inventories, supplies, and machine parts. During 1980, Xerox began using

---

[8]"The New Lean, Mean Xerox," *op.cit.*

new types of channels, including retail stores, dealers and distributors, and direct mail.

Retail stores

The first Xerox store for office products opened in Dallas on April 9, 1980. Company executives called its entry into retailing "an exciting, experimental initiative to bring modern office equipment to even the smallest of small businesses." The store contained 4,000 square feet and allowed customers to inspect, test, and purchase office products. Some inventory was on display at the first store, including small copiers, word processors, Telecopier units, and mailing devices.

To maintain its intended image as a "supermarket for the office," other companies' products will also be available, including Apple, Hewlett-Packard and Panasonic. Their products include small business computers, calculators, dictating equipment, telephone answering machines, security systems, and on-line data base access services. The store will also sell supplies and other office needs.

Robert F. Reiser, President and General Manager of the recently formed Xerox Retail Markets Division, said that the Xerox store is only one of several efforts to find cost effective ways to reach small businesses. Reiser cited doctors, dentists, lawyers, real estate agents, accountants, and architects as potential markets for Xerox's retail stores. Reiser also indicated that most of the five million businesses in the United States are small businesses, and he mentioned that there were six million offices in homes.

Xerox believes that its stores will supplement, not supplant, its traditional method of marketing through direct sales representatives. The Xerox store will be open six days a week and will be staffed by veteran company employees, as well as experienced retail people. Three more stores were scheduled to open in the Dallas-Fort Worth area within a few months, and three more in Denver by the middle of 1980. The first seven stores were to be test stores; if they obtained a desired return on investment, more stores would be opened. By August 24, 1981, Xerox had opened a total of twenty-six stores; Exhibit 9 shows their locations.

Dealers and Distributors

On September 4, 1980, Xerox announced the signing of two independent office equipment dealers and one distributor to sell and service some of its small copiers, chiefly the 2300 and 2600, and the 3100 family of copiers, all low-volume units. The dealers will also handle Xerox toner and paper and will maintain and repair machines according to Xerox training and service criteria.

Reiser said, "This program is designed to determine whether dealers and distributors can be a cost effective way for Xerox to broaden its market coverage. We plan to use this approach to supplement our current selling activities in an effort to participate more fully in this expanding marketplace."

EXHIBIT 9   Completed retail stores as of August 24, 1981

East Coast (12)	*West Coast (14)*
● Boston/Chestnut Hill	● St. Paul/Wabasha Court
● Boston/Federal Street	● Edina, MN/Hazelton Road
● Hartford/Farmington Ave.	● Minneapolis/Nicollet Mall
● Atlanta/Cumberland Mall	● Denver/University Hills
● Tampa/Fowler	● Denver/Champa Center
● Miami/Dadeland	● Denver/Aurora
● Florida/Ft. Lauderdale	● Houston/Greenspoint
● Mass./Burlington	● Houston/Spectrum
● Tampa/Kennedy	● Houston/1010 Lamar
● Dallas/Prestonwood	● Torrence/Village Del Amo
● Dallas/Caruth Plaza	● L.A./Pasadena
● Dallas/Dallas Center	● L.A./Costa Mesa (temp.)
	● Phoenix/Mesa
	● Phoenix/Metro Park

According to Reiser, using dealers and distributors is compatible with Xerox's stores and traditional sales force method of distribution because each "offers an opportunity to meet the intense competition in the small copier market."[9]

If the initial results from dealers and distributors is favorable, company executives plan to expand their use. They did not indicate how long the evaluation period would be, or how many dealers or distributors might eventually be signed.

Direct Mail

Another marketing approach tested by Xerox to sell to the small office was direct mail. In 1979, the company conducted two mail order tests to answer two questions: Are there potential customers who are not being reached by Xerox in any other way? Will people buy Xerox machines by mail? The company interpreted the results of the tests, a local and national one, positively, and, by the end of 1980, was testing a variety of large, national direct mail variations, satisfied that the concept was viable.

PRICING

Because Xerox both leases and sells copiers, pricing strategies were necessary for each approach. The cost to users of leased machines is generally a function of the number of copies produced over a specific time period. With the entry of the Japanese into the low-priced copier market, Xerox has had to turn increasingly to the pricing element of its marketing mix to stem the ero-

---

[9]Company Press Release, September 4, 1980.

sion of its market share. The price of the 660 was slashed to as low as $1,500, making it the least expensive of all low-priced models. However, various industry analysts believe that this price cut would not make the 660 competitive because of its lack of significant features and unreliability. However, the price slash of the 3100 model, the Cadillac of low-volume copiers, is believed to have been more effective. Its price of $12,000 minimum was reduced over two months to a minimum of $4,400. Between 1977 and 1978, an estimated 70,000 to 80,000 3100s were placed. However, the deep price cut meant that Xerox was getting smaller margins than Japanese firms; the 3100 cost Xerox $1,500 to make, almost twice what it cost Japanese manufacturers to make its competition. Its service charges were about double those for liquid toner machines.

In 1978, Xerox offered two new small copiers at low prices. The 2600 carried a price of $4,295 and the 2300 was offered at $3,795. Xerox executives explained the low prices as necessary because low-volume purchasers (under 3,000 monthly copies) are extremely price conscious.

During 1982, Xerox cut prices on fourteen small and mid-sized copiers. An average price reduction of 27 percent was announced to meet competitors' low prices. Actually, Xerox had little choice. During the first quarter of 1982, copier sales dropped 12 percent, the first quarterly drop in copier sales ever. Nine of the price cuts were on machines no longer in production for which inventory was still available. Industry analysts believe that the Japanese cannot meet the price cuts and make a profit.

On leased machines, Xerox has also had to make some price concessions to meet competition, particularly for its older, more vulnerable copiers. Prices per copy have been reduced and discounts have been offered to customers to encourage them to take out one- or two-year leases.[10]

SERVICE

Xerox copiers, duplicators, and other reprographic products are maintained by a worldwide service force. In 1978, Xerox introduced, on a pilot basis, a Field Work Support System (FWSS), a computer-based system which will gradually replace the manual system of dispatching service personnel to customer calls. Under FWSS, service personnel will be provided instant data on parts availability, distribution of service resources, and detailed service histories of each machine. Management believes that this information will result in better customer service.

At the same time, Xerox began experimenting with separating the service and sales functions. This system was tried on a limited basis in Canada and Washington, D.C., and Xerox decided in 1981 to completely remove the service function from the sales area and establish separate service offices in its various territories. The company knows that it will still need to coordinate

---

[10]Uttal, *op.cit.*

the efforts of the sales and service functions, but believes that each will work better as a separate unit. Service personnel undergo initial and follow-up training at the training facility in Leesburg. Most of this training is conducted in the fifty training machine laboratories, where service personnel receive hands-on training.

Xerox believes that customers acquiring their first copier, particularly at the low end of the market, generally prefer to purchase rather than lease. A customer who buys a machine can also buy a service contract; one who rents receives free service. Xerox executives anticipate that service contracts with outright purchases can become a billion dollar business for the company in the 1980s.

Xerox's Level of Service concept is based on customer service requirements, rather than on an arbitrarily established schedule of service calls. Service representatives visit a customer only in response to a call. When the call is made, the service representative is responsible for making the repair and for checking for Level of Performance and doing whatever is required to bring the machine up to that level. With this system, fewer service calls are required and those that are made are faster and more flexible. Xerox estimates that it made about 6.5 million service calls in the United States in 1980 and about the same number overseas.

RESEARCH AND DEVELOPMENT

Xerox's research and development program focuses primarily on improved copying and duplicating equipment and supplies, facsimile and digital communications equipment, computer peripheral equipment and services, and new products and capabilities in other aspects of information systems. Exhibit 10 shows total company expenditures for R&D annually from 1969–1980 and also expresses these totals as percentages of sales.

One of the company's main R&D objectives has been to improve its overall product development process. Because customers and competitors forced Xerox to define its product options earlier, there has been increased emphasis on developing products more rapidly. Xerox believes it is learning to delay substantial dollar commitments until it is sure a prospective product is feasible. The company's technical researchers explore alternative technologies while the configuration of the emerging product is still flexible.

In the reprographic area, a new management system was developed in the late 1970s to better use the company's technical and scientific talent. Formerly, R&D personnel in a particular field would work on individual product programs. Under the new system, R&D personnel are now part of a "competency center," made up of all experts in a particular product area. Xerox believes that this new system will more efficiently use resources, decrease time, and increase flexibility.

EXHIBIT 10 Xerox expenditures
for research and development

Year	Dollars (Millions)	Percentage of Sales
1969	101	7.4
1970	87	5.3
1971	96	5.1
1972	117	5.0
1973	154	5.3
1974	179	5.1
1975	198	4.9
1976	226	5.1
1977	269	5.3
1978	311	5.3
1979	376	5.4
1980	434	5.3
Totals	2,548	5.3

SOURCE: Company Annual Reports

Sharing technology across product and international boundaries is an important part of Xerox's R&D. Researchers from many Xerox organizations contributed to the 9700 electronic printing system; the 2202 copier, developed by Fuji Xerox for Japanese customers in the low-price market, was successfully introduced into European markets. Xerox believes that products should be designed for international distribution.

ADVERTISING

Xerox spent approximately $67.7 million on advertising in 1980, and the 1981 budget was $84.2 million, a 24.4 percent increase over 1980. During these two years, Xerox continued to emphasize the Brother Dominic campaign, in which a monk introduces new Xerox products in a medieval monastery setting.

A worldwide print and television campaign was introduced in 1982 under the direction of the advertising agency of Needham, Harper, & Steers. Two major themes will dominate Xerox's new campaign. The first will stress various Xerox capabilities, such as its technological expertise, breadth of product line, quality of service, and compatibility of systems. The second theme focuses on specific Xerox products and their features.

For both 1980 and 1981, Xerox's advertising budgets have emphasized expenditures for network TV, magazines, and newspapers. In 1980, 52.3 percent of advertising expenditures were allocated to network TV, 28.8 percent went for magazines, and 14.2 percent was spent on newspapers. The 1981 figures were 36.2 percent, 34.4 percent and 15.8 percent.[11]

[11]*Advertising Age,* September 9, 1982.

EPILOG

For 1981, Xerox's sales reached $8.69 billion. Net profits after taxes in 1981 were $598 million. In May of 1982, Mr. David T. Kearns moved up to replace Mr. C. Peter McColough as the Company's chief executive officer. Mr. McColough was to remain as chairman of the board. During the time of his appointment, Mr. Kearns stated that he "intended to reverse his corporation's market share erosion in reprographics and increase market share in office systems." Mr. Kearns confirmed that, since Xerox had been receiving tough competition from the Japanese in the market for smaller copiers, the most likely areas of future emphasis would be in the company's mid- and upper-range copiers.[12]

Gulf + Western Industries, Inc.

Charles Bluhdorn escaped from Nazi-occupied Austria in the late 1930s. He completed his schooling in England, and came to the United States in 1942, virtually penniless. After fourteen months in the Army Air Corps, Bluhdorn began studying at Columbia while selling cotton, plate glass and coffee.

Bluhdorn did not complete his studies at Columbia. He did, however, raise enough capital in 1958 to acquire Michigan Plating & Stamping Co., a firm with $8.4 million in sales that held a virtually worthless contract to sup-

This case was prepared by Richard T. Hise, Professor of Marketing at Texas A&M University, as a basis for class discussion rather than to illustrate either effective or ineffective marketing management.

[12]*Advertising Age,* September 9, 1982.

ply rear bumpers to Studebaker. Bluhdorn believed that auto parts distribution was a growth industry.

During the 1960s, Gulf + Western, as Bluhdorn had renamed his company, began to branch out. With generous financial backing from Chase Manhattan, Gulf + Western had made almost 100 acquisitions by 1968. While most of these were small distributors, some were large acquisitions, including Paramount Pictures, New Jersey Zinc, South Puerto Rico Sugar, and Brown Co. By 1968, Gulf + Western's sales exceeded $1 billion and Charles Bluhdorn had a fortune of $22 million in Gulf + Western stock alone.

The firm stayed on the acquisition trail in the 1970s, despite the nagging presence of tight money. Some notable companies acquired included Madison Square Garden, Kayser-Roth and the Simmons Co. Bluhdorn tried, but failed, to bring under the G + W umbrella Talcott National, Pan American Airways, Signal Co., Great Atlantic & Pacific Tea Co. (A&P), House of Ronnie, Inc. (maker of intimate apparel), and EMI'S music operations (Capital Records).[1]

Gulf + Western looks for undervalued assets. For example, in 1977 Bluhdorn paid twice the market price for Madison Square Garden; he was after MSG's vastly undervalued real estate holdings, which included a Manhattan office building and land adjacent to New York's Roosevelt Raceway and Chicago's Washington Park. Gulf + Western's acquisition strategy has emphasized diversification. Bluhdorn has stated, "Diversification in a rapidly changing economy afforded the greatest opportunity for growth and prosperity with a built-in safeguard against decline in any one area."

By 1981, Gulf + Western had become one of the giant corporations in America. Sales for 1981 had reached $5.7 billion, making the firm the forty-second largest industrial company in the United States, and total assets stood at $5.9 billion. Net earnings were slightly below $300 million and the company had over 92,000 employees. With $234 million spent on advertising in 1980, G + W was the nation's eleventh largest advertiser.

In 1981, Gulf + Western consisted of seven major operating groups. These operating groups are indicated in Exhibit 1, along with each group's divisions or companies. Until 1980, G + W also included a Paper and Building Products group, but this group was dissolved in 1980 with the sale of the Brown Co., Gulf + Western's paper processor. The building products companies remaining after the sale of the Brown Co. were transferred to the Automotive Group, which was renamed the Automotive and Building Products Group.

In 1981, Charles Bluhdorn and other G + W executives were faced with a number of important strategic decisions. Should the company continue to try to acquire new firms? If so, what direction should these acquisitions take? Should they closely complement those company's operations which Bluhdorn considers most promising, such as leisure time, financial services, apparel, and cement, or should acquisitions move the firm into different areas, such as energy technology, which the company reportedly was favoring? Or should the firm refrain from making new acquisitions and concentrate on

---

[1]*Forbes,* September 3, 1979, pp. 33–36.

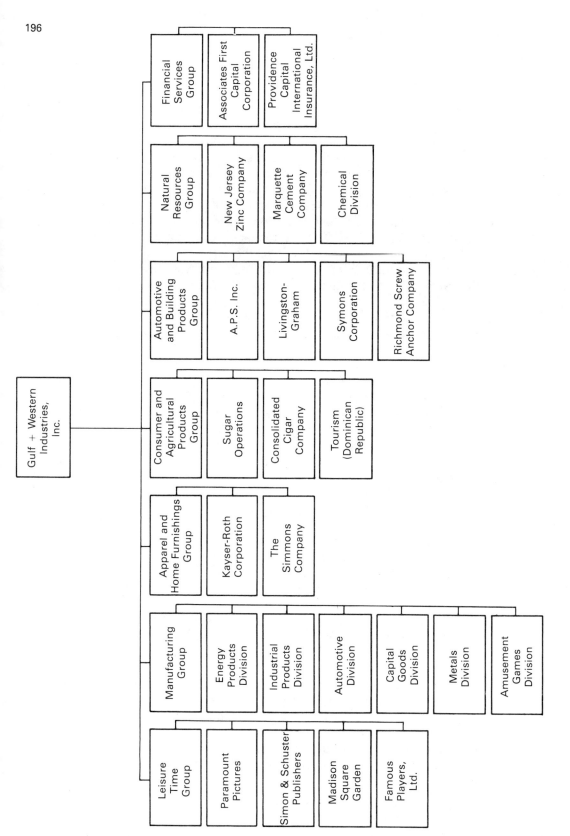

EXHIBIT 1 Operating groups of Gulf+Western Industries, Inc. (1981)

managing more effectively the companies it already has. Should the company continue to divest itself of marginal operations, like the Brown Co., which was sold for $122 million because G + W was reluctant to spend the $300 million needed to modernize the paper producer, and Schrafft Candy? There was speculation in early 1980 that Bluhdorn was considering selling New Jersey Zinc, Schrafft Candy, Consolidated Cigar, and various coal properties.

Exhibit 2 shows the company's consolidated income statement and financial position from 1977 to 1981. Exhibit 3 shows its domestic and international performance in 1979, 1980, and 1981.

THE LEISURE TIME GROUP

Paramount Pictures. Paramount Pictures Corporation derives most of its revenues and profits from the production and distribution of motion pictures, television series, and other programs. The motion pictures developed by Paramount are shown primarily in movie theatres, but are also released for other media, such as broadcast television, pay cable television and video cassettes. Paramount distributes its films throughout the world.

Between 1976 and 1982, Paramount released a number of successful films, including *King Kong, Marathon Man, Black Sunday, Islands in the Stream, The Last Tycoon, Orca, The Bad News Bears in Breaking Training, Looking for Mr. Goodbar, Grease, Saturday Night Fever, Goin' South, Heaven Can Wait, The One and Only, Foul Play, The Bad News Bears Go To Japan, Cheech & Chong's Up In Smoke, Days of Heaven, Death in the Nile, Oliver's Story, King of the Gypsies, Prophecy, Players, Escape from Alcatraz, The Warriors, North Dallas Forty, Star Trek—The Motion Picture, American Gigolo, Nijinsky, Urban Cowboy, Starting Over, Ordinary People, Raiders of the Lost Ark, Airplane, Gallipoli, Paternity, Mommie Dearest, Ragtime, One From the Heart,* and *Reds.*

During the mid-1970s, Paramount debuted with two prime time network shows, "Happy Days" and "Laverne and Shirley," which proved to be two of the most successful shows in television history. Both were still being aired during the 1981–1982 season, "Happy Days" for the ninth year and "Laverne and Shirley" for its seventh. Both had previously gone into syndication, "Happy Days" for the highest fee at that time ever paid for a half-hour show (a fee surpassed when Paramount's "Mork and Mindy" and "Taxi" were syndicated in 1981). These shows were still being shown as regular series as well in 1981, each in its fourth season. The revenues from syndication of "Mork and Mindy" and "Taxi" will not be realized until 1984 and after. Previous television series produced by Paramount that have gone into syndication include "Star Trek," "Mission Impossible," "The Brady Bunch," "The Lucy Show," "The Untouchables," and "Love American Style."

Paramount also has produced a number of miniseries for television. Some of these include "Golda," "The Winds of War," "Shogun," and "Flesh and Blood."

EXHIBIT 2 Income statement and financial position, 1977–1981

Income statement

(000 omitted)

Year Ended July 31	1981	1980	1979	1978	1977
Income					
Net sales and other revenues—Note B	$5,702,476	$5,338,483	$4,842,909	$3,921,597	$3,276,476
Equity in earnings of unconsolidated affiliates—Notes A and D	131,528	107,481	152,245	107,125	62,260
Other income—Notes B and I	112,345	76,038	14,192	30,110	22,491
	$5,946,349	$5,522,002	$5,009,346	$4,058,832	$3,361,227
Expenses					
Cost of goods sold	$4,191,938	$3,925,322	$3,623,109	$2,948,919	$2,420,184
Selling, administrative and general expenses	1,013,534	940,147	785,611	632,367	554,962
Depreciation and depletion—Note A	116,535	103,869	100,470	81,341	64,576
Interest expense (income):					
Interest expense—Note A	$ 232,702	$ 211,480	$ 183,871	$ 153,259	$ 123,964
Interest income	(45,554)	(37,315)	(27,438)	(24,481)	(17,114)
	$ 187,148	$ 174,165	$ 156,433	$ 128,778	$ 106,850
Minority interest	6,307	8,715	9,185	9,511	8,728
Provision for income taxes—Notes A and J	140,000	114,500	107,100	77,400	55,600
	$5,655,462	$5,266,718	$4,781,908	$3,878,316	$3,210,900
Net earnings	$ 290,887	$ 255,284	$ 227,438	$ 180,516	$ 150,327
Dividends on preferred stock	$ 7,865	$ 9,619	$ 10,156	$ 10,411	$ 10,575
Average common and common equivalent shares outstanding—Note A	75,381	56,046	58,829	60,221	60,269
Net earnings per share—Note A:					
Primary:					
Reflecting conversions	$ 3.75	$ 3.47	$ 2.96	$ 2.31	$ 1.91
As reported	3.75	4.38	3.69	2.82	2.32
Fully diluted	3.47	3.12	2.68	2.13	1.77
Cash dividends declared per common share	.75	.638	.58	.536	.504

Financial position

(Dollars in Thousands, Except Per Share)

Year Ended or at July 31	1981	1980	1979	1978	1977
Working capital	$1,470,161	$1,255,251	$1,228,413	$1,098,689	$1,023,136
Total assets	5,893,224	5,416,776	5,160,193	4,507,759	4,159,096
Notes payable and current maturities of debt	312,043	348,353	318,088	202,152	228,068
Long-term debt, net of current maturities	1,750,628	1,801,162	1,872,922	1,706,205	1,656,458
Redeemable preferred stock	28,970	30,361	31,886	33,276	34,456
Convertible preferred and common stockholders' equity	2,179,038	1,666,095	1,469,472	1,341,030	1,197,489
Book value per common share	27.48	27.21	23.73	19.76	17.41
Number of stockholders:					
Common Stock	57,000	54,000	55,000	57,000	55,000
Preferred stock	15,000	17,000	19,000	20,000	20,000
Capital expenditures	$ 216,000	$ 217,308	$ 199,028	$ 248,713	$ 213,082

EXHIBIT 3   Domestic/foreign performance of Gulf + Western, 1979–1981

| | *(Millions of Dollars)* | | | | | |
| Year Ended or at July 31 | *1981* | | *1980* | | *1979* | |
	Domestic	*Foreign*	*Domestic*	*Foreign*	*Domestic*	*Foreign*
Net sales and other revenues:						
Business segments	$ 4,491	$ 1,211	$ 4,208	$ 1,130	$ 3,853	$ 990
Financial services	1,543	164	1,433	140	1,188	91
Total	$ 6,034	$ 1,375	$ 5,641	$ 1,270	$ 5,041	$ 1,081
Operating income:						
Business segments	$ 268.5	$ 206.0	$ 283.2	$ 158.4	$ 285.8	$ 117.2
Financial services	124.3	13.4	122.8	12.0	136.3	5.9
Corporate expenses and other Non-segment items	(103.5)	3.4	(99.6)	(.2)	(83.3)	24.1
Total	$ 289.3	$ 222.8	$ 306.4	$ 170.2	$ 338.8	$ 147.2
Identifiable assets:						
Business segments	$3,290.6	$ 831.2	$3,109.2	$ 913.5	$2,828.2	$ 884.6
Investment in financial services ...	492.2	162.4	493.3	140.6	460.0	109.2
Corporate and other non-segment items	963.1	153.7	656.5	103.7	766.2	112.0
Total	$4,745.9	$1,147.3	$4,259.0	$1,157.8	$4,054.4	$1,105.8

In the late 1970s, Paramount began to diversify into the home entertainment market by becoming involved with pay TV, videocassettes, and videodiscs. Company executives believed that these efforts were making increasing contributions to its revenues and profits by 1981. In that year, Paramount began to market to the international home entertainment market through Cinema International Corporation (CIC). Paramount Pictures allocated $106 million for advertising in 1980, compared to $82 million for 1979.

Simon & Schuster. Gulf + Western acquired Simon & Schuster in June, 1975, and sales doubled in four years. S & S executives attribute this success to a number of factors, including the reputation of their editors and improved marketing.

Editors' reputations are believed to be a major factor in attracting and retaining a number of already well-known authors. Some of these are Graham Greene, Joseph Heller, Mario Puzo, William L. Shirer, John Dean, Sam Levenson, John Ehrlichman, Irving Wallace, and Harold Robbins. S & S editors strongly believe that they must continue to represent their authors after the books have been edited, in such areas as flap and jacket copy and advertising programs.

In the marketing area, S & S has become increasingly sophisticated since it was acquired by G + W. Computer programs have been developed to assist the sales force, run profit-and-loss evaluations on books, and insure that books are not oversold, resulting in returned inventory.

The sales of books has a decided 20/80 phenomenon; of the close to 1000 books S & S may publish each year, only a few will make it big. Each book, however, requires individual attention and promotion. The trade book division produces about 300 to 350 books a year, the Pocket Books division

EXHIBIT 4   Operating statistics and group revenues, leisure time group, 1976–1981

All Dollar Amounts in Millions

Operating Statistics	1981	1980	1979	1978	1977	1976
Revenues	$1,129.1	$1,041.6	$966.7	$802.0	$469.6	$451.4
Operating income	$ 96.3	$ 100.1	$116.4	$ 84.1	$ 36.2	$ 49.6
Operating income to revenues	8.5%	9.6%	12.0%	10.5%	7.7%	11.0%
Capital expenditures	$ 24.4	$ 17.4	$ 23.5	$ 19.1	$ 33.9	$ 38.3
Depreciation	$ 14.6	$ 12.6	$ 12.7	$ 13.2	$ 9.6	$ 7.6
Motion pictures released—U.S.A.	21	15	16	14	15	17
Television series produced	11	12	12	7	6	7

Group Revenues	1981		1980		1979		1978		1977		1976	
	$	%	$	%	$	%	$	%	$	%	$	%
Motion pictures	483	43	392	38	427	44	287	36	150	32	152	34
Series and films for television	178	16	211	20	124	13	97	12	82	17	65	14
Theater operations	126	11	122	12	113	12	103	13	102	22	103	23
Book publishing	158	14	127	12	98	10	86	11	72	15	71	16
Sports, racing and entertainment	201	18	187	18	173	18	157	19	—	—	—	—
Eliminations and other	(17)	(2)	2		32	3	72	9	64	14	60	13

SOURCE: Company Annual Reports.

360 to 370, and the rest are from other company entities. About 40 percent of S & S's yearly titles are reprints, one of the highest percentages in the industry; because of their lower costs, reprints are very profitable. S & S centralized its five warehouses into a new 700,000 square foot facility in Bristol, Pennsylvania to save money. Order processing will be enhanced by a computer system linking the new warehouse with various sales and administrative offices.

In 1979, a new division of Simon & Schuster, Wanderer Books, began to publish quality paperbacks for the juvenile market. In 1981, Silhouette Romances made a successful debut in the rapidly expanding romance novel market. 1982 plans called for two expansions to the Silhouette line: a First Love From Silhouette series for teenagers, and a Silhouette Special Edition of larger novels for adult readers. Simon & Schuster was the second highest advertiser in the leisure time group in 1980 with an outlay of $15 million, up from 1979's outlay of $10.9 million.

Madison Square Garden.   Madison Square Garden includes the ownership of the Madison Square Garden Center for sporting and entertainment events, ownership and operation of the New York Knicks of the National Basketball Association, the New York Rangers of the National Hockey League, and the Washington Diplomats of the North American Soccer League. The company also has an 80 percent interest in International Holiday on Ice, owns and operates Roosevelt Raceway, and manages Arlington Park Racetrack in the Chicago area, a thoroughbred and harness racing operation. Through the Madison Square Garden Network, the company provides sports and entertainment programming for both broadcast and cable television. Madison Square Garden's advertising budget for 1979 was $7.5 million. A slight increase to $7.6 million occurred in 1980.

Famous Players. Famous Players, Ltd. operates 226 theatres with 434 screens in Canada and 30 theatres in France. In 1981, a motion picture production venture was discontinued. Two entertainment centers, one in the United States and the other in Canada, were not profitable during 1981. Famous Players, Ltd. spent $5.6 million, $5.1 million and $5.3 million for advertising, respectively, in 1978, 1979 and 1980.

THE MANUFACTURING GROUP

Energy Products Division. The Energy Products division manufactures forged steel components for the following industries: chemical processing, electrical utilities, oil refineries, natural gas pipelines, and oil and gas drilling operations. Much of this division's increased sales in 1981 was attributed to the continuing oil boom in Mexico. The Custom Forgings division posted a record year due to strong demand by oil field equipment manufacturers.

EXHIBIT 5   Operating statistics and group sales, manufacturing group, 1976–1981

All Dollar Amounts in Millions

Operating Statistics	1981	1980	1979	1978	1977	1976
Net sales	**$1,310.3**	$1,292.4	$1,303.0	$1,097.3	$1,042.8	$1,019.8
Operating income	**$ 106.8**	$ 111.8	$ 91.3	$ 72.6	$ 93.9	$ 114.8
Operating income to net sales	**8.2%**	8.6%	7.0%	6.6%	9.0%	11.3%
Capital expenditures	**$ 38.3**	$ 35.0	$ 63.4	$ 33.3	$ 22.2	$ 28.2
Additions to properties and equipment held for rental or sale	**$ 20.4**	$ 41.3	—	—	—	—
Depreciation (1)	**$ 33.0**	$ 32.3	$ 30.5	$ 25.3	$ 19.1	$ 19.0

Group Sales	1981		1980		1979		1978		1977		1976	
	$	%	$	%	$	%	$	%	$	%	$	%
Industrial products	**218**	**17**	222	17	—	—	—	—	—	—	—	—
Energy products	**248**	**19**	216	17	239	18	211	19	219	21	270	27
Metals	**172**	**13**	165	13	—	—	—	—	—	—	—	—
Capital goods	**132**	**10**	183	14	320	24	287	26	202	19	197	19
Amusement games	**150**	**11**	140	11	101	8	37	3	—	—	—	—
Automotive	**180**	**14**	160	12	—	—	—	—	—	—	—	—
Other	**210**	**16**	206	16	118	9	97	9	40	4	48	5
Automotive and appliance	—	—	—	—	372	29	340	31	352	34	297	29
Electrical equipment	—	—	—	—	153	12	125	12	—	—	—	—
Controls, electronics, and wire and cable	—	—	—	—	—	—	—	—	118	11	113	11
Air conditioning and refrigeration	—	—	—	—	—	—	—	—	82	8	66	6
Aviation and marine	—	—	—	—	—	—	—	—	30	3	29	3

SOURCE: Company Annual Reports.

Industrial Products Division. It produces electrical wire and cable, microprocessor-based control systems and components, industrial cutting tools, and commercial and marine hardware. It also distributes musical equipment.

Collyer Wire, which produces electrical wire and cable for the construction, shipbuilding, utility, transportation, and coal markets, paced the division's upswing in 1981. This company is a market leader in sales to the marine industry. Other strong performances were turned in by North & Judd, a producer of commercial hardware, and Unicord, a distributor of musical equipment. Two other companies, however, had sluggish years in 1981: Eagle Signal, a supplier of traffic and industrial controls, and Morse Cutting Tools, a manufacturer of industrial drills, tapes, dies, and cutters. Demand fell for both companies' products.

Automotive Division. This manufactures bumpers, torque rods, chrome-plated plastic grills, stamping assemblies for hinges, lock and parking brake applications, and electronic components for the auto, truck, farm implement, and off-highway equipment industries. This division's sales of electrical and electronic components increased in 1981, despite the continued slump in the automobile industry. Development of new products like noise suppression devices offset decreases in the demand for ignition timing components.

Capital Goods Division. This division suffered from a downturn in the economy in 1981, which resulted in lower revenues and profits. Major products manufactured and distributed include rolling mill equipment, metalworking presses and coke oven equipment. The division's metalworking machinery manufacturer, E.W. Bliss, experienced improved operations. In 1981, G + W acquired Thomas Ryder, an English producer of machine tool equipment, including high production horizontal spindle lathes and special purpose machinery used in applications like automotive crankshaft manufacturing.

Metals Division. The nation's leading producer of aluminum pistons for gasoline and diesel engines, it also produces iron, steel, and aluminum castings, and aluminum and brass extrusions and forgings. This division has achieved higher income in 1981, due primarily to increased demand for aluminum pistons in trucks, automobiles, and other diesel-powered vehicles. A new facility, reflecting expanded demand for the division's piston design and metallurgical and engineering services, was opened in South Haven, Michigan in 1981. The Metals Division has benefited in recent years from greater penetration of its aluminum tubing in the automotive and residential air conditioning markets.

Amusement Games Division. Sharp increases in domestic demand in the electronic games market helped this division to higher sales in 1981. However, sales in Japan, this division's other major geographical market, dropped from 1980 to 1981. Sega Enterprises, Inc. an 85 percent-owned

G + W subsidiary, announced in 1981 expansion plans for its Pizzazz futuristic family entertainment centers, which feature a full line of advanced electronic games combined with restaurant facilities. Sega also decided to add to its chain of fifteen Sega Centers (family entertainment facilities) located in shopping centers in California. Approximately $5 million was spent on advertising by this group in 1980.

THE APPAREL AND HOME FURNISHING GROUP

Two major companies make up Gulf + Western's apparel and home furnishings group. Kayser-Roth is a diversified manufacturer of apparel, hosiery, and textiles. The Simmons Co. is a worldwide leader in the manufacture of bedding products, institutional furnishings, wall coverings, health care equipment, and burial caskets.

Kayser-Roth. Kayser-Roth produces a wide variety of apparel, which it sells to over 90,000 retail outlets, particularly department stores, chain stores, mail order houses, supermarkets, drug stores, and independent retail stores. Some apparel is sold to wholesalers and jobbers. Women's swimwear and sportswear are distributed under the brand names "Catalina," "Cole of California," "Sandcastle," and "Going Places," as well as for private labels. Men's swimwear and sportswear are sold under the company's "Catalina," "Pacer," "Interwoven," "John Newcombe," and "Cresco" brand names. Other apparel categories are lingerie, children's wear and gloves; men's shirts ("Excello," "John Weitz," and "Oscar de la Renta" brands); and men's wear ("Movest," "Champion," "Cresco," and "Oscar de la Renta").

EXHIBIT 6 Operating statistics and group sales, apparel and home furnishings group, 1976–1981

All Dollar Amounts in Millions

Operating Statistics	1981	1980	1979	1978	1977	1976
Net sales	**$1,531.2**	$1,407.8	$1,134.4	$725.2	$629.6	$601.1
Operating income	**$ 91.7**	$ 85.8	$ 68.4	$ 54.8	$ 45.2	$ 33.2
Operating income to net sales	**6.0**%	6.1%	6.0%	7.6%	7.2%	5.5%
Capital expenditures	**$ 28.1**	$ 36.8	$ 28.4	$ 18.1	$ 9.6	$ 15.9
Depreciation	**$ 17.0**	$ 8.9	$ 12.4	$ 6.9	$ 5.3	$ 4.1

Group Sales	1981		1980		1979		1978		1977		1976	
	$	%	$	%	$	%	$	%	$	%	$	%
Apparel	585	38	517	37	449	40	457	63	375	60	347	58
Hosiery	255	17	232	16	216	19	187	26	176	28	173	29
Bedding products	361	24	341	24	221	19	—	—	—	—	—	—
Furnishings	199	13	199	14	137	12	—	—	—	—	—	—
Other	131	8	119	9	111	10	81	11	78	12	81	13

SOURCE: Company Annual Reports.

Kayser-Roth is one of the two leading producers of hosiery in the United States. Principal women's brands are "No-Nonsense," "Sheer Indulgence," "Mojud," and "Supp-hose;" principal men's brands are "Interwoven," "Supp-hose," "Esquire," and "Fruit of the Loom."

Kayser-Roth also manufactures and imports men's and women's shoes. It operates its own men's retail shoe stores (twenty-three in 1981), primarily under the "Bostonian" name. About 125 men's shoe departments are operated by K-R as leased departments in men's wear specialty stores. About 50 percent of the men's shoes sold in K-R's stores or leased departments are manufactured by K-R.

Kayser-Roth owns the rights to the Miss Universe and Miss USA beauty pageants, and earns money from the sale of broadcasting rights, as well as from the host city, personal appearances by the contest winners, and the "Miss Universe" and "Miss USA" trademarks.

Kayser-Roth markets its products primarily through its own sales force and promotes its branded products by point-of-sale promotions and a variety of advertising media, including national magazines, television, radio, and newspapers. Expenditures on advertising in 1979 were $45 million, with an increase to $50 million in 1980. Approximately 100 sales offices have been opened in major U.S. cities, as well as Canada, Puerto Rico, Australia, New Zealand, and Hong Kong.

Most of K-R's sales are made to retail stores, and the company's performance tends to be strongly affected by the general condition of the nation's retailers, who, in turn, are particularly sensitive to general economic conditions. Close to 25 percent of Kayser-Roth's sales go to four retailers: J. C. Penney Co.; Sears, Roebuck, & Co.; K-Mart; and Montgomery Ward & Co.

K-R's executives believe they are faced with substantial competition in all of their product lines. Price, style, and quality are the major competitive elements, along with the fashion phenomenon, availability of imported merchandise, the large number of apparel manufacturers, and the wide variety of channels of distribution used (especially retailers).

The Simmons Company. The Simmons Company manufactures and markets a wide variety of products which are directed to a number of different markets, including mattresses, box springs, upholstered furniture, and a broad line of home furnishings: wood and metal tables, chairs, fabrics, draperies, decorative pillows, wall coverings, lamps and sculptures, and specialized bedding and furniture. Major markets served are the home (adult, youth, infants), hospitals, nursing homes, hotels, motels, and other commercial institutions. Simmons also manufactures and sells wood and metal burial caskets through three subsidiaries: York-Hoover, Elgin Metal Casket Company, and Wallace Metal Products Division. The company distributes caskets through assemblers, who apply additional finishes and other decorative hardware, and funeral directors.

Simmons was the first national manufacturer of mattresses and box springs. Its "Beautyrest" pocketed-coil mattresses and coordinated box springs have been in existence for over fifty years and Simmons is considered a leader in quality, style, and comfort. Simmons also manufactures open-coil, innerspring mattresses, and box springs. The company's bedding products are sold nationwide through home furnishings stores, retail sleep shops, department stores, and mass merchandisers.

In 1958, Simmons launched the first Beautyrest supersize mattress campaign. So many Americans have switched to queen- and king-sized beds that today nearly half of Simmon's bedding sales are supersized. In October, 1978, Simmons began producing and marketing foam mattresses under the "Beautyfoam" label. In January, 1979, the company started to manufacture and market hybrid waterbeds. Simmons' "Hide-A-Bed" offers the style and seating comfort of a sofa along with the additional features of a concealed Simmons bed. Other contempory sofas and chairs are manufactured and marketed by Simmons' Selig and Debu/Flair subsidiaries. Simmons produces and markets its bedding products in Puerto Rico and eleven foreign countries.

Simmons' competition in the furniture industry comes from 5,000 other manufacturers, almost two-thirds of which have fewer than twenty employees. The fifteen largest domestic furniture manufacturers are Simmons' strongest competition; together, these fifteen companies are believed to represent 15 percent of the industry's sales.

Simmons' bedding products are marketed in the United States by Simmons salesmen, who are compensated on a straight commission, or salary plus commission basis, and who sell directly to retailers. Under Simmons' Authorized Dealer Program, which was adopted in 1977, these retailers are authorized dealers, who, in exchange for Simmons' support of their advertising, floor displays and promotional and sales strategies, have agreed to maintain certain minimum levels of floor sampling, service and promotion.

Although the initial impact of the program was to reduce sales and the number of domestic retailers, Simmons believes that the enhanced customer service, promotion, and display attention is beginning to increase sales. Simmons advertises its products, primarily bedding, through national magazines, television, radio, and newspapers.

Bedding products are manufactured and held in inventory at Simmon's thirty-five shipping points throughout the United States. To increase the efficiency of its distribution system and reduce operating costs, Simmons closed twenty of its domestic shipping locations during 1978 and 1979. Its production cycle is very short and scheduled according to both specific orders and projected sales; order backlog is not significant.

Upholstered furniture and diversified furnishings are sold directly to retailers by the Simmons sales force, except for certain decorator items sold only through licensed designers at Simmons showrooms. The production cycle for these products is also short and scheduled by both specific orders and projected sales, so order backlog here is not significant either.

Simmons markets burial caskets to jobbers and funeral directors. During the past ten years, the mortality rate in the United States has been declining, although the decline appears to have halted in the latter half of 1976. Increased market penetration and sales of caskets have been dependent on the company's ability to price and deliver its caskets better than its competitors.

Simmons owns a number of trademarks, the most significant of which are Beautyrest and Hide-A-Bed. Certain subsidiaries of Simmons sell decorative products and have obtained numerous copyrights for their designs. While Simmons is continually developing and improving its products and manufacturing methods, research and development costs are not material. Simmons' largest customer is Sears, Roebuck, and Co., whose purchases accounted for approximately 14 percent of Simmons' net sales in 1976, 12 percent in 1977, 9 percent in 1978 and 6 percent in 1979.

The company's advertising outlay in 1979 was $12.3 million. A 41 percent boost pushed 1980 expenditures to $17.4 million. In late 1979, Simmons introduced new Beautyrest mattresses with an advertising campaign that compared Beautyrest's features to competitive brands' qualities. The promotion effort for the company's Hide-A-Bed sofas emphasized magazine advertising and is believed to be the largest campaign in the furniture industry in the last ten years; it particularly emphasized the "Speed Service" line. The Hide-A-Bed sofa campaign was handled by Simmon's in-house agency, Springtime Advertising.

THE CONSUMER AND AGRICULTURAL PRODUCTS GROUP

In 1981, the consumer and agricultural products group consisted of three major sections: sugar operations, the Consolidated Cigar Company, and the Dominican Republic tourism operation. Until 1980 Schrafft Candy was part of this group, but G + W sold this operation in 1980.

Schrafft Candy. Schrafft was acquired by G + W in June, 1974. In 1975 and 1976, the company generated a profit, but it had lost money for a number of years. The improvement in profit was achieved by broadening the company's distribution base. Prior to the acquisition, Schrafft's sales were concentrated chiefly in exclusive distributors, primarily candy stores. After the acquisition, super markets, convenience stores, mass merchandise, and other channels of distribution were added. A new product for the mid-morning snack market was developed, *10:30,* and more appealing packages were also introduced.

During 1977, Schrafft eliminated nearly 50 percent of its offerings and continued to develop new package designs. Package changes were believed to be partially responsible for increased sales of such items as *Old Fashioned,* valentine chocolates, and stackable items (boxes of candy which can be stacked on shelves). Expansion of the distribution base continued. Declining profits and sales plagued Schrafft in 1978. In response, the company continued eliminating unprofitable and marginally profitable items and stepped up marketing efforts for new specialty and traditional items.

1979 sales levels approximated those of 1978, in spite of decreasing industry sales. The company continued its product elimination program.

Schrafft's sales are concentrated chiefly in the Eastern United States.

EXHIBIT 7   Operating statistics and group sales, consumer and agricultural products group, 1976–1981

All Dollar Amounts in Millions

Operating Statistics	1981	1980	1979	1978	1977	1976
Net sales	**$669.1**	$540.7	$457.0	$439.7	$398.6	$444.4
Operating income	**$184.9**	$ 87.0	$ 56.6	$ 76.4	$ 52.1	$ 99.1
Operating income to net sales	**27.6%**	16.1%	12.4%	17.4%	13.1%	22.3%
Capital expenditures	**$ 41.3**	$ 28.9	$ 26.5	$ 26.7	$ 38.6	$ 33.0
Depreciation	**$ 15.5**	$ 14.6	$ 13.5	$ 13.1	$ 12.1	$ 11.6
Sugar produced (1,000's of tons)	**626**	601	626	542	546	555
Cigars sold, worldwide (billions)	**1.8**	1.9	1.9	2.0	2.1	2.1
Share of U.S. cigar dollars sales	**28.7%**	30.2%	29.6%	29.6%	29.4	28.8%

Group Sales	1981		1980		1979		1978		1977		1976	
	$	%	$	%	$	%	$	%	$	%	$	%
Raw and refined cane sugar	**337**	**50**	201	37	143	31	—	—	—	—	—	—
Furfural and molasses	**49**	**7**	37	7	40	9	—	—	—	—	—	—
Cigars	**179**	**27**	180	33	175	38	—	—	—	—	—	—
Candy	**—**	**—**	—	—	43	10	43	10	46	11	45	10
Other	**104**	**16**	123	23	56	12	55	12	43	11	52	12

SOURCE: Company Annual Reports.

Sugar Operations. G+W grows sugar cane in the Dominican Republic and processes it into raw sugar, cane juice molasses, and blackstrap molasses. About 70 percent of the cane grown in G+W's mill is grown on land the company owns. Blackstrap molasses is sold for use in animal feed and the production of rum. *Bagasse,* which is a byproduct from the sugar cane production process, is used to make furfural, a basic chemical used in a number of industrial applications, including the purification of lubricating oils, and the production of butadiene, a component of synthetic rubber. In 1979, the company produced 92 million pounds of furfural and 21 million gallons of molasses. G+W also grows sugar cane in Florida, from which it produces raw sugar, blackstrap molasses and refined sugar. About 70 percent of the Company's sugar tonnage is produced in the Dominican Republic, 30 percent in Florida.

The success or failure of Gulf+Western's sugar operations depends largely on the price of sugar on the world market. In 1981, sugar prices reached a high of 43¢ a pound, then fell to 16.6¢ a pound by the end of the year. Despite this decrease, G+W's sugar operations' performance held firm, due chiefly to the negotiation of timely forward sales at favorable prices.

Consolidated Cigar Company. Consolidated Cigar Company manufactures and markets cigars. The company's major production facilities are in the United States, Puerto Rico, the Dominican Republic, and Europe. Cigar sales account for about 90 percent of the company's sales, and the rest comes from smoking tobacco, tobacco pouches, pipe lighters and paper products in England. Among Consolidated's major cigar brands are Dutch Masters, El Producto, Muriel, and La Palina. Dutch Masters, El Producto, and Muriel account for about 50 percent of Consolidated's sales. Although the company's cigar's are sold worldwide, the United States is the primary market. Independent wholesale distributors are the primary means of distribution.

Cigar consumption has declined during the 1970s. Consolidated's president, Alexander Brainard, points to the results of a marketing research study conducted by the company to explain this decline. Smokers, non-smokers, and women were interviewed, 10,000 people in all. Smokers were asked why they liked cigars, non-smokers why they did not smoke them, and women what they thought of cigar smoking. Respondents answered that (1) cigar smoking caused an unpleasant aroma; (2) cigar smoking resulted in a lingering room smell; (3) anti-social comments were made by friends and associates; and (4) cigar smokers were characterized as old, fat, and sedentary. In spite of this consumption decline, Consolidated has been able to keep sales and profits up. Brainard believes that the following reasons explain Consolidated's success:

1. Consistent advertising of the company's traditional brands, particularly Dutch Masters, El Producto, and Muriel. Instead of emphasizing advertising, most other cigar companies stress sales promotion efforts or price reductions; Consolidated spent $8.4 million on advertising in 1979, $9.8 million in 1980. The 1979 expenditures represented almost 50 percent of the cigar industry's total allocation for advertising that year. Consolidated continued its television campaign for Dutch Masters Cigars in 1980 featuring tobacco buyers, growers, and agronomy experts (i.e., masters), who backed up the slogan, *There really are masters at Dutch Masters.* This theme was begun in 1974. El Producto continued to use sports personalities like Maury Wills and Sonny Jurgensen in its promotion. Aggressive advertising, packaging, and point-of-sale merchandising were used to promote Muriel Cigars' improved blend.

    Consolidated's premium cigar division continued in 1980 to use magazines, like *The New Yorker, New York Times Magazine,* and *The Wall Street Journal,* and newspaper advertisements for such brands as Don Diego, H. Upmann, and Primo del Rey. Prominent businessmen, like Chrysler's Lee Iacocca, were featured in the advertising of Don Diego Cigars.

2. Product innovation. Dutch Masters and El Producto brands introduced the dark colored Cameroon wrapper to non-premium feature cigars. Muriel Air Tips and Dutch Treats feature cigars with a pipe aroma. Consolidated entered the premium cigar field with Primo del Rey, H. Upmann, Montecruz, Montecristo, Don Diego, Don Marcos, Don Miguel, and Flamenco. Under development is a mild cigar that does not smell like a cigar; the company hopes that it will allow individuals to smoke confidently in any social setting. A Dutch-type cigar is being developed for American smokers willing to pay a premium

price. Much research has gone into developing a tobacco-sheet wrapper that looks like a tobacco leaf but is not. This wrapper would substantially reduce the cost of manufacturing cigars (regular tobacco wrappers can cost up to 50 percent of the total cigar cost) and would result in price decreases which should expand sales.

3. Expanded distribution. In particular, the company is using more convenience store locations such as Cumberland Farms and 7-Eleven Stores.

4. Trends in age composition of men appear to be in Consolidated's favor. By 1990, it is expected that there will be 79 percent more men in the 35 to 55 age group—the age group which smokes the most cigars.

Tourism. G + W's tourism operations are in the Dominican Republic; 1981 revenues were up, despite a downturn in overall travel in the Caribbean. The company owns four major sites: the Casa de Campo is located in the eastern part of the country; the Hotel Santo Domingo and the neighboring Hotel Hispaniola were merged in 1980; and the Altos de Chavon is an international culture center which provides facilities for concerts, exhibitions, workshops, and cultural exchange programs. A 5,000-seat amphitheater was under construction in 1981.

Other Operations. G + W owns about 264,000 acres in the Dominican Republic; about 118,000 are used to grow sugar cane, 112,000 are used for livestock pasture, 15,000 are related to the tourist business, and 3,000 are used for growing citrus and vegetables. In Florida, about 86,000 acres are owned and 4,500 acres are leased, to grow sugar cane. The firm owns about 133,000 acres in Paraguay, a small portion of which is used for cattle grazing and farming. G + W has entered into a joint venture for the future development of the rest of the Paraguayan acreage.

AUTOMOTIVE AND BUILDING PRODUCTS GROUP

Four major companies comprised the automotive and building group in 1981. A.P.S., Inc. (American Parts System) is a leading distributor of automotive replacement parts. Livingston-Graham is a major supplier of rock, sand, gravel, and transit-mixed concrete in southern California. Symons Corporation and Richmond Screw Anchor Company manufacture and distribute factory-built reusable forms and accessories for construction using concrete.

A.P.S. This company sells automotive replacement parts in the United States through an integrated distribution network consisting of 32 auto parts warehouses, 113 jobber outlets owned by the company, and more than 1,000 independently owned jobber outlets. The jobber outlets are identified by the trade name "Big A Auto Parts." A.P.S. warehouses stock over 100,000 different parts, including both private label and national brands. These parts are sold by the company to the jobber outlets owned and operated by A.P.S., and to the independently owned associate jobbers, who sell the parts to service stations, repair shops, garages, dealers, fleet operations, and retail consumers.

A.P.S. carries six general categories of trademarked products:

1. "Big A Poweride" engine, chassis, and automotive transmission parts, timing gears, chains and water pumps.
2. "Big A Powerlady" ignition parts, carburetor kits, automotive switches, spark plug wire and cable.
3. "Big A Service Line" tire gauges and valves, floor mats, chamois cloths, sponges, tail light lenses, and mirrors.
4. "Big A Rogers" a paint line including a full array of automotive paints and body finishing products.
5. "Powerized" rebuilt parts, such as brake shoes, carburetors, full pumps, crank shafts, and alternators.
6. "Big A" exhaust parts, shock absorbers, batteries, fuel pumps, antifreeze, and filters.

Competition for A.P.S. comes mainly from automobile manufacturers, mass merchandisers, and major oil companies which distribute automobile parts through their service stations. A.P.S.' domestic income was down

EXHIBIT 8   Operating statistics and group sales, automotive and building products group, 1976–1981

All Dollar Amounts in Millions

Operating Statistics	1981	1980	1979	1978	1977	1976
Net sales	$560.4	$569.1	$391.8	$350.1	$306.8	$277.7
Operating income	$ 35.6	$ 47.9	$ 31.9	$ 29.3	$ 26.5	$ 25.2
Operating income to net sales	6.4%	8.4%	8.1%	8.1%	8.6%	9.1%
Capital expenditures	$ 17.2	$ 10.8	$ 3.6	$ 4.5	$ 5.0	$ 5.1
Depreciation and depletion	$ 6.0	$ 5.9	$ 3.5	$ 2.5	$ 2.1	$ 2.0
Rock, sand and gravel produced (1,000's of tons)	5,460	6,390	—	—	—	—	—	—

Group Sales	1981		1980		1979		1978		1977		1976	
	$	%	$	%	$	%	$	%	$	%	$	%
Automotive	363	65	357	63	338	86	297	85	232	76	213	77
Industrial	45	8	50	9	19	10	38	11	—	—	—	—
Other	11	2	16	3	15	4	15	4	75	24	65	23
Building products	141	25	146	25	—	—	—	—	—	—	—	—

SOURCE: Company Annual Reports.

slightly in 1981 from 1980's performance. This downturn was attributed chiefly to a soft economy in which consumers tended to postpone car repairs and maintenance. The overseas performance, however, was strong in 1981. Especially good performances were turned in by the company's operations in Mexico and Venezuela, but the Italian division had lower operating results. In 1981, the company also opened new distribution centers in Houston and Great Bend, Kansas.

Livingston-Graham. Livingston-Graham mines rock, sand, and gravel (aggregate) in five southern California locations and sells it to customers or uses it for manufacturing its transit-mixed concrete. Aggregate is used for asphalt pouring, concrete roads, dams, and construction fills.

Symons Corporation and Richmond Screw Anchor. These manufacture or rent prefabricated concrete forming equipment used by the construction industry for on-site placement of concrete. Symons also manufactures various chemicals used to facilitate the hardening and surface sealing of concrete, and produces mining cars and other equipment used in mining. The principal markets for Symons' and Richmond's products are contractors for heavy or engineering construction, water and sewage treatment plants, electric powerplants, industrial and commercial buildings, highrise apartment houses, highway structures, and institutional buildings.

Both companies had 1981 sales about equal to those of 1980, in spite of decreased construction activity. Symons offset poorer domestic performance with an expanded overseas effort, and Richmond overcame lower demand for its products by introducing two improved items: a new type hardware used in tilt-up construction and an improved threaded insert device used in the installation of piping in nuclear power plants. Advertising expenditures in 1980 were about $4 million for the automotive and building products group.

NATURAL RESOURCES GROUP

The New Jersey Zinc Company is an integrated producer of zinc products, metal powders, anhydrous ammonia, liquid carbon dioxide, lead concentrates, limestone, cadmium, sulphuric acid, and titanium dioxide pigments, and also mines metallurgical coal. The Marquette Cement Company manufactures and markets portland and masonry cements. The Chemical division produces titanium dioxide and titanium tetrachloride.

New Jersey Zinc. Mining operations are carried out at seven sites: Friedensville, Pa., Austinville and Ivanhoe, Va., Sterling, N.J., and Beaver Creek, Elmwood, Idol, Jefferson City, and Lost Creek in Tenn. The ore from these mines is shipped to the company's smelters in Palmerton, Pa. or to the Clarksville, Tenn. refinery. At the Palmerton smelter, zinc concentrates are processed to produce zinc metal for galvanizing steel products, producing brass,

EXHIBIT 9 Operating statistics and group sales, natural resources group,
1976–1981

All Dollar Amounts in Millions

Operating Statistics	1981	1980	1979	1978	1977	1976
Net sales	$ 502.4	$ 486.9	$ 469.8	$ 413.9	$ 349.2	$ 177.5
Operating income	$ 14.2	$ 32.5	$ 22.5	$ 5.3	$ 54.8	$ 46.5
Operating income to net sales	2.8%	6.7%	4.8%	1.3%	15.7%	26.2%
Capital expenditures	$ 62.1	$ 86.0	$ 84.5	$ 141.5	$ 95.9	$ 44.6
Depreciation and depletion	$ 29.1	$ 28.0	$ 25.1	$ 18.2	$ 14.3	$ 7.7
Cement produced (1,000's of tons)	2,777	3,055	3,537	3,626	3,437	—
Ore mined (1,000's of tons)	2,740	2,762	2,619	2,778	2,734	2,246
Pigments produced (1,000's of tons)	160	167	155	167	141	132
Zinc metal produced (1,000's of tons)	114	142	126	81	70	65
Coal mined (1,000's of tons)	309	340	649	607	438	—

Group Sales	1981		1980		1979		1978		1977		1976	
	$	%	$	%	$	%	$	%	$	%	$	%
Cement	139	28	142	29	148	32	140	34	123	35	—	—
Zinc pigments	83	17	76	16	71	15	67	16	63	18	60	34
Zinc metal	92	18	93	19	82	17	58	14	53	15	55	31
Titanium dioxide	77	15	67	14	61	13	52	13	51	15	42	24
Coal	18	4	20	4	36	8	33	8	24	7	—	—
Other metals and minerals	93	18	89	18	72	15	64	15	35	10	21	11

SOURCE: Company Annual Reports.

or using in the diecasting industry. Further processing produces rolled zinc and zinc dust. Zinc oxide pigments are produced at Palmerton for sale to the paint, rubber, and reprographic paper industries. Zinc powders and other zinc-bearing non-ferrous metal powders are produced for sale to the battery industry, metal powder parts fabricators, and other industries. Anhydrous ammonia is sold to industrial users and fertilizer manufacturers. Three by-products—cadmium metal, sulphuric acid and liquid, and carbon dioxide—are sold for industrial use. The Clarksville electrolytic zinc refinery produces slab zinc.

In September, 1981, Gulf+Western announced that it had sold the Palmerton facility, the Depue, Ill. plant, which produced zinc dust, and the Sterling Mine in New Jersey which supplied concentrates to Palmerton. Total sales involved were $125 million.

Marquette Cement Company. Portland cement is used primarily as the principal ingredient in construction concrete. The company owns eleven production plants in Mississippi, Missouri, New York, Tennessee, Maryland, Illinois, Pennsylvania, Georgia, and Ohio. Most of Marquette's cement is distributed within a 200-mile radius of the production plants under the Marquette trade name.

Chemical Division. Titanium tetrachloride is a raw material in the titanium metal used to manufacture aircraft; stronger demand in 1981 for this material paced the Chemical Division's improved performance. Expansion of the company's Ashtabula, Ohio plant in late 1981 increased annual capacity for titanium tetrachloride from 125,000 to 150,000 tons and raised the annual capacity for titanium dioxide from 30,000 to 35,000 tons. In 1980, the Natural Resources Group spent about $2 million for advertising.

THE FINANCIAL SERVICES GROUP

Associates First Capital Corporation. Associates Corporation of America, a subsidiary of Associates First Capital Corporation, is one of the ten largest independent finance companies in the United States; it conducts business in 1,200 offices in the United States, Canada, the United Kingdom, Japan, and Puerto Rico. "Associates" has four major types of financing activities: consumer financing; transportation and industrial equipment financing; commercial loans; and wholesale financing. In addition, the company, through its insurance subsidiaries, writes or reinsures credit life and health insurance and property/casualty insurance, offered primarily to its financing customers.

Consumer financing includes direct installment loans made to individuals and generally secured by liens on personal or real property. Consumer financing also includes retail financing of the purchases from dealers of secured retail obligations arising from the sale of such consumer goods as automobiles, recreational vehicles, household appliances, and other consumer goods. Transportation and industrial equipment financing involves the pur-

EXHIBIT 10 Operating statistics and group revenues, financial services group, 1976–1981

All Dollar Amounts in Millions

Operating Statistics	1981	1980	1979	1978	1977	1976
Revenues	$1,706.9	$1,572.7	$1,219.1	$ 994.4	$ 771.1	$ 641.2
Operating income	$ 137.7	$ 134.8	$ 142.2	$ 93.7	$ 42.1	$ 18.1
Operating income to revenues	8.1%	8.6%	11.7%	9.7%	5.4%	2.8%
Finance receivables	$5,932.1	$5,057.2	$4,204.4	$3,218.6	$2,640.7	$2,161.2
Average interest cost on borrowings	12.3%	10.8%	8.8%	7.3%	6.7%	6.8%
Ordinary life insurance in force	$4,090.0	$3,633.0	$2,949.7	$2,923.9	$2,055.3	$1,701.7
Property/casualty insurance premiums written	$ 133.3	$ 129.4	$ 131.2	$ 145.1	$ 113.2	$ 80.3

Group Revenues	1981		1980		1979		1978		1977		1976	
	$	%	$	%	$	%	$	%	$	%	$	%
Financing	883	52	737	47	559	46	432	43	358	46	319	50
Life insurance	576	34	585	37	419	34	419	42	301	39	208	32
Property/casualty insurance	156	9	144	9	141	12	138	14	112	15	114	18
Real estate and other	61	3	82	5	100	8	11	1	—	—	—	—
Equity in earnings before income taxes of unconsolidated company	31	2	25	2	—	—	—	—	—	—	—	—

SOURCE: Company Annual Reports.

chase of time sale obligations and leases, direct leases, and secured direct loans on heavy duty trucks, communication equipment, construction equipment, transportation equipment, and manufacturing equipment. Commercial loans involve short and medium term loans made mainly to wholesalers, retailers, and manufacturers. The company also factors accounts receivable. Wholesale financing or "floor planning" consists of short advances principally to truck dealers to permit them to carry inventories.

Percentages of finance receivables made or purchased during the year ended July 31, 1978 were: consumer financing, 47.9% and 57.4%; transportation and industrial equipment financing, 21.7% and 36.3%; commercial financing, 18.5% and 3.8%; wholesale financing, 11.9% and 2.5%. Percentages of finance receivables made or purchased during the year ended July 31, 1979 and held on July 31, 1979 were: consumer financing, 46.1% and 56.5%; transportation and industrial equipment financing, 18.7% and 34.9%; commercial financing, 23.3% and 5.3%; and wholesale financing, 11.9% and 3.3%. Credit losses during the years ending July 31, 1978 and 1979, as a percentage of receivables liquidated for the period, were .95% and .77%, respectively. The percentage of total outstanding account balances delinquent 60 days and more was 1.84% at July 31, 1979, and 2.09% at July 31, 1978; 2.55% at July 31, 1977; 3.35% at December 31, 1976; and 5.40% at December 31, 1975.

In 1981, revenues of The Associates were $1.02 billion, a 21 percent increase over 1980's revenues; operating income in 1981 was $89.6 million, compared to $87.1 million in 1980. Associates increased its total financial receivables by 17 percent in 1981 to $5.9 billion. This increase helped to offset, in part, an increase of $116.4 million in interest expense, of which $60.1 million was attributable to higher money costs.

The operating results of Associates in 1981 were a result of:

☐ A 36 percent gain in 1981 in total commercial financing to $4.7 billion.

☐ A 23 percent increase in commercial financing receivables to $2.7 billion.

☐ Expansion of the Associates Business Loan program, which increased its receivables to $296 million in 1981, up from $220.5 million in 1980.

☐ An increase in the proportion of rate-sensitive commercial loans with improved margins.

☐ An increase in the factoring business to a rate of $1.3 billion in 1981. Much of this increase was the result of G + W acquiring the assets of two major factoring firms: Rusch Factors Division of BVA Credit Corporation and the Factoring Group of First National Bank in Dallas.

☐ A shift of its consumer business toward larger, more profitable, real estate-secured loans from unsecured direct loans.

☐ Increased international growth. The number of associates offices in Australia was expanded from 3 to 29 and in the United Kingdom, the number of branch offices was expanded to 62. Including 31 branches in Puerto Rico, 95 in Canada, and 12 in Japan, Associates had a total of 227 overseas offices in 1981, up from 164 in 1980.

☐ Acquisition of Fidelity Bank of Concordia, California, which provides consumer banking services.

☐ Consolidation of its newer kinds of consumer financial services— Execu-charge/VISA credit card, money orders, loan-by-mail program for professionals and executives, and national auto club services— into an integrated operating unit called Diversified Services.

☐ Moderate expansion (6 percent) of credit life and accident and health insurance premiums to $1.03 million.

☐ Arranging $1.6 billion in credit facilities and funded debt, of which $1.4 billion was revolving/term.

Providence Capital International Insurance, Ltd. The insurance business is conducted through various subsidiaries of Providence Capital International Insurance, Ltd. The Capital Life Insurance Company provides a complete line of group and individual life insurance, group health insurance, and annuity products. Providence Washington Insurance Company, an indirect subsidiary, offers a full line of property/casualty insurance coverage.

Revenues for Providence Capital were $686.6 million in 1981, compared to $726.1 million in the previous year; total assets in 1981 were $2.1 billion compared to $2.0 billion in 1980. Operating income for Providence in 1981 was about the same as in 1980. The Capital Life Insurance Company was hurt by higher interest rates in 1981, which increased annuity contract terminations. However, these were offset by higher investment yields and continued profitability of other life insurance operations. The Providence Washington Insurance Group achieved record earnings in 1981 despite only small increases in 1981 premiums; the property/casualty industry in general suffered heavy losses in 1981.

EPILOG

A number of Wall Street analysts have criticized Gulf + Western for its mediocre performance, claiming that the company has not been generating sufficient returns on its assets and sales; such criticisms persisted even when the company obtained record sales and profits in 1981. In 1982, Gulf + Western's sales and profits dropped from these record figures; sales were $5.5 billion and net income was $169 million; as a percentage of assets, 1982's profits were 2.8 percent; as a percentage of sales, they were 2.9 percent.

The continuation of Gulf + Western's lackluster profit picture brought into sharp focus a number of strategic questions for the firm's top management. Should Gulf + Western continue its basic strategy as a conglomerate, or should it restrict its operations to companies with more compatible products and services? If acquisitions are pursued in the future, what criteria should be used? Should the firm continue to divest itself of some of its operations and, if so, what criteria should be used and which companies or groups should be considered for divestiture? Which of G + W's current operations should receive management's greatest attention as it attempts to improve its financial performance?

Domino's Pizza

While waiting in Tom Monaghan's office one becomes aware of the many architecture journals and books lying on the tables. Mr. Monaghan, the president and chairman of the board of directors of Domino's Pizza, Inc., originally intended to become an architect and is still very much interested in the subject. While attending the University of Michigan School of Architecture, he worked to pay his way and at times had to stop school in order to accumulate enough money for tuition. It was during one of these intensive working periods in 1960 that his brother, who was a mailman in Ann Arbor, Michigan, heard of a pizza shop that was for sale by one of the people on his route. Tom and his brother decided to buy the shop known as Dominick's Pizza, which was located in Ypsilanti, Michigan near Eastern Michigan University. After six months of operation Tom's brother knew he was not interested in continuing

The research and written case information were presented at a Case Research Symposium and were evaluated by the Case Research Association's Editorial Board. This case was prepared by Robert P. Crowner of Eastern Michigan University as a basis for class discussion.

the business, so Tom bought him out by giving him a Volkswagen delivery car. Tom Monaghan was successful with the shop through long hours of hard work and liked the business so well that he never returned to the university to finish his architecture degree.

From this small beginning Mr. Monaghan has built Domino's Pizza into the third largest pizza seller in the United States with 292 stores having sales at $68.5 million. Of these stores, 115 are company owned. He is a soft-spoken, unassuming, creative, energetic entrepreneur whose goal for the company is for it to be the largest pizza operation in the world. This he says is not "an obsession but is something to shoot at." The company objective is to be the best pizza seller. Right now, it is a "one horse race" because Pizza Hut, which is owned by Pepsico, is so far ahead of the rest of the pack in volume.

The mission of Domino's Pizza is "to sell a good pizza at a competitive price and fair profit, a pizza that is hot and delivered free within thirty minutes of ordering." In order to accomplish this mission each store has territorial boundaries in which it operates which average about a one and a half mile radius. In general, stores are clustered in a given area so that the area is thoroughly covered.

Domino's basic strategy is to open pizza stores near a college campus and then gradually add stores to fill in the residential area surrounding the campus. The young adult male is the target customer since he eats more than the young female does. This strategy was broadened to include ten military bases in 1978 while seeking the same customer who has more spendable money and, probably, worse food in the mess hall. The pizza stores near the bases proved to be less profitable because they were difficult to supervise in their more remote locations, they were new marketing areas for the company and there was little opportunity to cluster stores since there are fewer residences near military bases, there are delivery problems in the time required to get through the base gates, and there is usually not a company commissary nearby. On the other hand, military bases do not have the seasonal factor experienced at colleges.

HISTORY

In December 1961, a partnership was formed with J. Gilmore and a second store was opened at Central Michigan University in Mt. Pleasant, Michigan. In 1962 the first store was opened in Ann Arbor and in 1963 the Mt. Pleasant store was sold and a second store was opened in Ypsilanti. In 1964 two more stores were opened in Ann Arbor.

In January 1965, the partnership was dissolved, with Mr. Monaghan taking the two Ypsilanti stores and one in Ann Arbor. In February the name was changed to Domino's and the logo was designed. Sales doubled this year, while J. Gilmore's operation was heading toward bankruptcy.

By 1966 J. Gilmore's business failed and Mr. Monaghan bought the Central Michigan store. The first store was opened in Lansing in 1967 to serve

Michigan State University; it had the largest pizza oven in the world. Two more stores were opened in Ann Arbor and the first franchise was sold in Ypsilanti.

A fire in the West Cross Street store in Ypsilanti in 1968 destroyed the corporate records and the commissary. Insurance proved to be inadequate and a $100,000 loss was sustained. However, by September complete recovery was made and sales were at their highest level to that time. Five more stores were opened including the first outside of Michigan, at Burlington, Vermont, to serve the University of Vermont. Domino's was averaging 2000 pizzas a week per store by the end of the year.

By 1969, according to Mr. Monaghan, Domino's was "caught up in the franchise fever, had tremendous charisma" and sold many franchises. Unfortunately almost all failed and Domino's carried them too long.

By 1970 heavy debt had been built up and bankruptcy impended. About 150 law suits from creditors were filed, with the bank being the largest creditor. An expert was brought in by the bank to run the company, and Mr. Monaghan had to give up all of the stock, with the agreement that he could get 49 percent back if the crisis was passed in two years. After ten months, the situation had worsened.

The expert alienated the franchisees by differentially raising commissary prices too high for them. Eight franchisees filed a federal class action antitrust suit. In 1971 Mr. Monaghan regained control of the stock from the bank by making an agreement to let the bank have the Cross Street store and property in Ypsilanti until the debt was paid. Further law suits developed, and the Internal Revenue Service threatened for payment of back taxes. The crisis was passed by borrowing from suppliers, the Vermont franchise, and by selling 50 percent of the Illinois store. The class action suit was slowly settled by buying back franchises, paying off franchisees, and by mutual termination agreements. The first store on a military base was opened in Plattsburg, New York in 1971.

The Cross Street store was regained in 1972 and by 1973 the company was in reasonably good condition, with many of the creditors paid. With more than sixty stores open, recovery was certain. The first television commercial was produced.

Mr. Monaghan's actions could be characterized as very entrepreneurial and he was criticized for this by more conservative people, such as the bankers. He became sensitive to this criticism of himself and hired Mr. Russ Hughes in 1974 as executive vice president. Mr. Hughes had good managerial credentials, having been president of several large companies. He became president of Domino's in October of 1975, a year in which the 100th store was opened, and Amstar Corporation sued Domino's for trademark infringement of the Domino name used on Amstar's sugar.

Under Mr. Hughes leadership problems developed. According to Mr. Monaghan, Hughes was a "cold, very organized individual." Mr. Monaghan did not like what Mr. Hughes did and felt helpless and frustrated. It was painful to have someone else run the company with the opposite philosophy. The commissary and a Lansing store were unionized. Franchise relationships suffered with fifteen stores leaving and fifty more threatening to leave. Mr. Monaghan fired Mr. Hughes in 1976 following a proposal Hughes shared with him to buy him out and run the company without him. Subsequently, the unionized store was sold and the unionized commissary was closed. Mr. Monaghan summed up this whole experience by saying he realized that prior to Hughes management he, Monaghan, had been "doing the little things wrong but the big things right"; therefore, he should actively run Domino's.

The year 1977 saw the first store opened on the West coast in California. Arthur Andersen & Company was hired as the company's auditor. The corporate offices were moved to Ann Arbor, Michigan from Ypsilanti. Finally, a franchise department was created for the development of a franchise program to be offered to the public. It had formerly been the policy to permit franchise sales only to Domino's employees. The year ended with 159 stores located in eighteen states.

In 1978 several additions and changes were made in the management group. The training program was begun with David Grisham as director of personnel development. Richard Mueller was promoted to vice president of operations and became a member of the board of directors. Townsend Beaman and Eugene Power were also added to the board. Douglas Dawson, formerly with Arthur Andersen & Company joined Domino's as the chief financial officer. Don Vlcek was hired as president of the National Commissary Holding Corporation. Finally, David Kilby, a former employee and franchisee returned to Domino's as director of franchise sales.

ORGANIZATION

The organization of the top management of Domino's is shown in Exhibit 1. The president is responsible to the board of directors, who are the following men:

Thomas Monaghan: chairman of board and president of Domino's Pizza, Inc.

Richard Mueller: vice president of operations of Domino's Pizza, Inc.

Robert Cotman: president of Group 243 Design, Inc. who handles the marketing function for Domino's Pizza, Inc.

Townsend Beaman: attorney specializing in trademark and patent law

Eugene Power: founder and former owner of University Microfilms, now a division of Xerox, Inc., and presently a philanthropist

Robert Ulrich: attorney

The finance, marketing, administration, and operations functions are described in detail in the following pages. Other functions shown on the organization chart are described below.

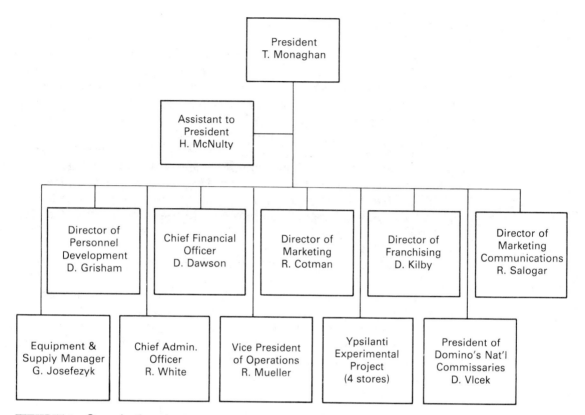

EXHIBIT 1   Organization chart

Mrs. Helen McNulty is assistant to the president and secretary of Domino's Pizza, Inc. Mrs. McNulty received her B.S. degree in Home Economics and Psychology from the University of Illinois. She spent eight years in personnel and training work for a chain of retail stores in Chicago, and was assistant personnel manager for a manufacturing company in Michigan. After raising a family, she worked for three years as an administrative and business manager for a management consulting firm in Ann Arbor. At that point Mr. Monaghan heard of her through a management consultant and asked her to join Domino's and write her own job description.

Mrs. McNulty's job has included doing some personnel work and personal counseling for management employees. She has worked with Mr. Monaghan in thinking of management concepts and, in fact, suggested the concept of a management team to him. She brainstorms and throws out ideas for his consideration. She serves as a communication link and Mr. Monaghan likens her to a "Mother Superior" in some of the roles she fills. She is also an implementer for him.

She serves as a liaison between Domino's and the outside members of the board of directors. The board meets ten times a year, basically on a monthly basis. The board has an executive compensation committee and Mr. McNulty anticipates other committees may be forthcoming. The board is getting more involved in company affairs, now that outside members have been added. For instance, an ad hoc committee was formed to investigate what some of the problems were in absorbing Pizzaco (Boulder) into Domino's.

The equipment and supply manager, Gary Josefczyk, is responsible for purchasing equipment and supplies used in the company and franchised stores. He and his two employees, through volume purchases, are able to obtain these items at a considerable cost savings, compared to the prices normally paid by an individual store. Mr. Josefczyk has a background in accounting based upon his education and is planning to take his CPA examination in 1980.

The personnel development manager, David Grisham, and his three employees are responsible for Domino's training program. This relatively new activity has concentrated on store level training but is now moving into supervisory training. Training materials include a video cassette module that illustrates and describes how to do each job at a store in detail.

The director of franchise sales is David Kilby. Mr. Kilby was one of the early Domino employees but was terminated in 1976, with the loss of nine stores in Florida and Georgia. He was rehired in 1978 and together with two employees handles both external and internal Domino employee franchising.

The Ypsilanti Experimental Project, which includes the four stores in Ypsilanti, reports directly to Mr. Monaghan because he "wanted to get his hands dirty," so that new creativity would be forthcoming. Domino's stores are being operated using the same concepts as were established in 1966, when Mr. Monaghan last had his hands in the store level business. He has been looking for a new infusion of creativity but has not been happy with the results of this arrangement. He attributes this to two factors: (1) he does not have sufficient personal time to devote to the Ypsilanti Project and (2) the stores were pretty well stripped of their management before they were turned over to him. He expects these stores will soon be returned to the operations function.

In late 1979 Robert Salogar was added to the corporate staff as director of marketing communications. He is responsible for public relations work.

OPERATIONS

Richard Mueller is the company's only vice president and is responsible for operations, including all company owned stores as well as franchised stores. He began his career in the pizza business as a driver for Domino's and later went to Columbus, Ohio as a franchisee. He built the Columbus area into a fifty-four store operation, of which twenty were franchised. Domino's owned 51 percent of the Columbus operation and Mr. Mueller owned 49 percent. The Columbus activity was absorbed into Domino's in 1978 by exchanging Domino stock for Mr. Mueller's part of the Columbus company. Mr. Mueller ended up owning 10 percent of Domino's stock and became an officer and director of Domino's.

Mr. Mueller has the reputation of being a workaholic. He is considered to be very creative, in much the same sense as Mr. Monaghan, and is very self-confident. With these characteristics, he can be difficult to work with at times. He sees the executive group needing to work more as a team in the future. Although goals for the company are set by Mr. Monaghan, Mr. Mueller believes that the executive team needs to be convinced the goals are realistic and attainable, that they are worthwhile for the executives individually, and that attaining the goals will be rewarded. In this regard, Mr. Mueller sees the board of directors, which is now composed of half outside directors, as providing a sounding board and restraint on management, particularly in the financial aspects of the business.

When Mr. Mueller came back to the home office, he found Domino's had some big problems—"sales were mediocre and costs were out of line." He set about improving costs and believes he has made significant progress by instituting performance measurements against sales, as well as by improving sales.

The acquisition of the Boulder, Colorado company, Pizzaco, in February 1979 was a severe digestion problem for Domino's and "took a lot of effort to get it under our belt." Mr. Mueller believes a combination of factors caused the problem:

1. Some stores had to be closed because of overlap with franchised stores.

2. The top people were taken out of the operation to go to the corporate office or to become franchisees.

3. Eight department heads were giving individual instruction to "Domino-ize" the operation, and the Boulder people were offended and resisted change.

4. The quality of some of the Boulder people was below standard and, therefore, some turnover was experienced.

These problems have been largely solved by having one man in charge of the operation, Joe Romano, and all changes are funneled through him. He has phased the changes in gradually. The Boulder region turned a profit in August with the return of the college students and hopefully is out of the woods.

Mr. Mueller used to travel 50 percent of his time but has now been able to reduce that to 25 percent. While he believes a "gut-feeling" is a very valid management tool, he has learned to rely more heavily on financial analysis. He tried to see each store twice a year and does this as efficiently as possible by concentrating his visits geographically. Company stores are seen more frequently than franchise stores. He is restructuring how stores are contacted by Domino's. He is considering using regional seminars with less individual contact. He thinks this will be more cost effective and that the cross-fertilization of ideas between managers will get everyone excited.

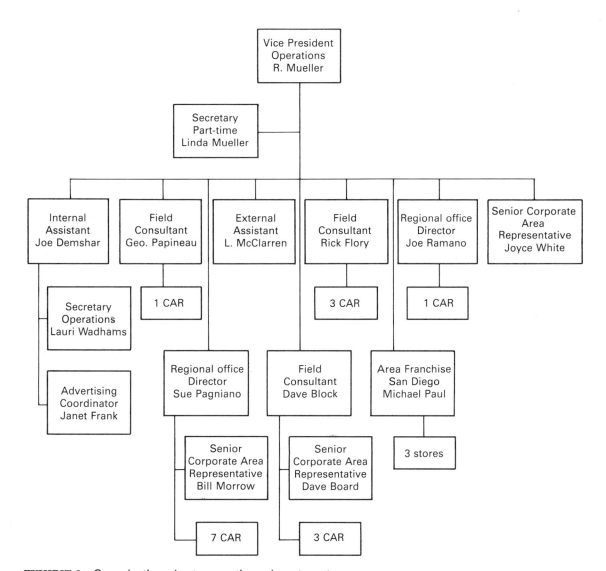

EXHIBIT 2 Organization chart, operations department

Mr. Mueller believes sales volume is the main determinant of profit. Although store location is important, he believes a good manager "attacks sales instead of sales attacking him" and is the key to a profitable store. For instance, he believes the way employees answer the telephone can increase 3 to 4 percent. Drivers are important since a customer can feel "threatened" psychologically by the wrong person. Most drivers are now in uniform, which helps minimize this phenomenon.

More women are being employed in all categories from driver through field consultant. There is presently one female field consultant and a second will be added in January. They have proven to be very competent as managers.

The organization of the operations function is shown in Exhibit 2. The majority of Domino's employees fall within this department's responsibility.

Domino's stores sell two size pizzas, twelve-inch and sixteen-inch, with eleven kinds of toppings, and one size of Coke or Pepsi. All food must be eaten off premises, as no sit-down eating facilities are provided. Orders for 95 percent of the pizzas are called into the store and about 85 percent of the orders are delivered.

Joe Demshar, internal operations assistant, is an example of how store managers progress with Domino's. He is twenty-nine years old and graduated from Ohio State in 1973. He managed a store for two-and-one-half years and was a corporate area representative for one-and-one-half years. He has been in his current position for eleven months. His present duties include assembling data for use within the operations department, writing policy manuals, and organizing incoming data to make it usable.

Through Joe Demshar, three manuals are kept up-to-date. These are the Bookwork & Policy manual, the Operations manual, and the Corporate Area Representative manual.

The Bookwork and Policy manual is kept in each store. At this time it includes a job description (four pages) of the corporate store manager, a policies section (thirty-seven pages) regarding store standards, a policies section (twenty-five pages) regarding personnel and administration and a bookwork and instructions section (thrity-three pages) covering the various forms in use and how to complete them. Additional sections covering record keeping, food specifications, personnel development, franchising, and marketing and advertising are planned to be added in the future.

The Operations manual is provided for each store, both corporate and franchise. It contains the following sections:

The Domino People	3 pages
Domino's Product and Service	7 pages
Domino's System	30 pages
People Management	55 pages
Scheduling & Record Keeping	14 pages
Food Cost Control	5 pages
Delivery Expense and Theft Control	6 pages
Advertising and Promotion	14 pages
Sanitation and Safety	22 pages
Profit and Loss Statement	16 pages
The Domino's Order Taker	15 pages
The Domino's Driver	13 pages

Exhibit 3 contains excerpts from the manual describing the store manager's responsibilities. This manual is used along with audiovisual cassettes provided by the training department to train employees and managers. Each store has a copy of each cassette and required equipment to utilize them.

EXHIBIT 3 Domino's Pizza, Inc. excerpts from *Operations Manual*

THE DOMINO'S MANAGER

The shop manager is the key to Domino's success. He is the vital link between the customer and the company as well as the employee and the company. While his responsibilities are many, we can provide the following general outline.

The Manager's Responsibilities Are:
1) To maintain product and service standards:
   a) a tasty, hot, good-looking pizza
   b) fast, free, friendly delivery (30 minutes)
   c) courtesy to the customer
   d) a wholesome product, clean shop and cars, and well-groomed personnel

2) To supervise all phases of production:
   a) order-taking
   b) pizza-making
   c) oven-tending
   d) routing
   e) delivery

3) To hire quality people and train them for:
   a) better job performance
   b) accepting increased responsibilities

4) To schedule and motivate personnel to achieve maximum efficiency and effectiveness

5) To maintain open, two-way communication with employees, immediate supervisor, and company staff

6) To make all necessary repairs for keeping the facilities in good operating condition

7) To purchase food and supplies

8) To maintan accurate and complete business records and execute the necessary bookkeeping procedures

9) To conduct an effective advertising/promotional program, or work with the agencies; and maintain community public relations

10) To keep operating costs within the budget, especially food and labor costs

11) To make a profit.

The Corporate Area Representative manual contains the job description of a corporate area representative, which is reproduced in Exhibit 4 and two sections of 51 pages and 127 pages concerning policies, procedures and forms. The CAR is considered a key employee in the management structure, since he directly supervises six to ten store managers arranged in geographical areas.

All of the present seventeen corporate area representatives have previously been store managers. The turnover in CARs is very high, with one year being common. The reason for this turnover is that Domino's encourages it by moving them up in the organization or out as franchisees. During the last one-and-one-half years two CARs have franchised and three more would like to franchise. The income of the CAR is lower than the $25,000 to $30,000 a store manager will make including his bonus, which also stimulates the CAR

EXHIBIT 4   Domino's Pizza, Inc. *from Corporate Area Representative Manual*

JOB TITLE: Corporate Area Representative

PLACEMENT: Geographical Area Encompassing Assigned Stores

FUNCTION: Directs, assists, coordinates all activities relating to area store operations in accordance with corporate policies, standards and needs.

PRIMARY GOALS: —To increase volume and profits of assigned stores
—To prepare Managers and/or Franchisees for the next level of responsibility, whether it be administrative, supervisory, franchising, or expansion
—To assist in meeting ongoing company needs for trained personnel by directly and indirectly assuring the recruitment, selection and training of qualified management persons

REPORTS TO: Vice President of Operations or his delegate

SUPERVISES: Store Managers, Management Trainees and Franchisees

DUTIES AND RESPONSIBILITIES:

1. Responsible for sales volume and profit levels of the stores assigned; related duties include, but are not limited to, the training of management in the use of such tools as advertising, operational guidelines, recruitment policies and procedures, training materials, and/or acting as a resource person for other needed assistance.

2. Responsible for maintaining accurate and complete reporting, whether by memo or required form; duties include, but are not limited to, personnel evaluations, weekly inspections, weekly and monthly budgets and cost reviews, daily visitations, review of required management paperwork, etc.

3. Responsible for assisting Operations in preparing volume and profit projections; duties include, but are not limited to, monthly budgets, planned promotions, weekly reporting of results of operations as to projections, results of operations as compared to projections.

4. Responsible for assisting Manager in supervision and training store personnel (hourly and management staff); duties include, but are not limited to, assisting with and training the Manager for effective personnel evaluations, effective scheduling, training and fair pay schedules.

5. Responsible for assisting managers in controlling costs; duties include, but are not limited to, budget review, P & L review, food cost controls implementation, labor cost control implementation, training of manager in day-to-day cost reviews and management within all areas of store operations.

6. Responsible for assisting manager in problem solving; duties include, but are not limited to, being aware of store operations, policies and standards in order to assist the manager in preventing problems, acting as a resource to solve problems, acting as the spokesperson for company policy as relates to specific problems.

7. Responsible, aware and responsive to specific store area concerns; duties include, but are not limited to, assisting the manager in assessing competitors, population concerns, such as income levels affecting store sales fluctuations, delivery problems, such as access roads.

8. Responsible for assuring the staffing of the stores; duties include, but are not limited to, transfer of personnel within the area on an as-need basis, training manager to recruit, hire and train, realistic appraisals as regards promotion, transfer or termination of managers and/or management trainees.

9. Responsible for regularly scheduled management evaluations; duties include, but are not limited to, Job Planning & Reviews for managers, management trainees, as outlined by schedule or need, training of managers to use effective Job Planning & Review within their own staff.

10. Responsible for assuring the store operations meet Federal, State and City regulations and laws regarding sanitation, food handling, safety and personnel; duties include, but are not limited to store inspections as regards health and safety codes, review of personnel records as regards pay schedules and adherence to recruitment and hiring policies.

11. Responsible for maintaining ongoing training of management staff; duties include, but are not limited to, regularly scheduled meetings for purposes of informing and training, in-house training regarding specific job tasks, referral to specific in-house resources for information and/or training.

12. Responsible for monitoring store operations as regards product, service and cost controls; duties include, but are not limited to, regular weekly visitations per operational guidelines, observation of store operations, determination of product, service and costs per company guidelines, monthly budgeting in conjunction with the manager and weekly and daily review of operations as compared to normal budgeting, timely and accurate reporting.

13. Responsible for personnel and store-level adherence to company policies, standards and ethics as regards professional conduct and image; duties include but are not limited to, personal and professional conduct representative of the company standards, ethics and policy.

14. Responsible for community image of company; duties include, but are not limited to, personal and professional conduct as representative of company standards, ethics and policy.

15. Responsible for opening of new stores within assigned area; duties include, but are not limited to, assisting operations in the seeking out of suitable leases, completion of leasehold improvements and coordinating the receipt and installation of equipment.

16. Other job duties as assigned.

JOB RELATIONSHIPS:

The Area Representative works closely with the following personnel in assuring the maximum productivity of his units:

1. Store managers as relates to store operations.

2. Management Trainees as relates to their performance, training needs, evaluations, transfers, promotions or terminations.

3. Training Director in projecting trainee needs, recruiting, hiring and in-store training.

4. Advertising Coordinator as relates to store needs, information as regards effectiveness of specific campaigns.

5. Equipment and Supply as relates to the specific store equipment and/or maintenance needs of the stores; in some instances, through the direction of Operations, the supervisor will work directly with outside purveyors or contractors to meet store needs.

6. Accounting Department as relates to accurate and timely reporting of store activities to asssure the completion of monthly P & L's, timely payment of accounts.

7. Operations to assure the accurate and timely projection of company resources and/or needs.

8. Site Developer or general contractors.

9. Personnel Department to assure adequate, accurate and timely record keeping and policies are being completed.

ACCOUNTABILITY:

The Area Representative is accountable to Operations for:

1. Sales volume

2. Profit volume

3. Daily store operations per company policy and standards including maintenance and cleanliness

EXHIBIT 4   (continued)

4. Ongoing training of management staff to assure the success of the manager or trainee in the next step of his career

5. Management attitude and morale

6. Company image

7. Store record keeping

8. Setting and maintaining store cost standards

PHYSICAL DEMANDS:

The following physical activities are required for the performance of the job duties:

A.   Ability to work under physical and emotional stress.

B.   Ability to work in varying extreme temperatures, both hot and cold, both inside and outside, with sudden temperature changes.

C.   Ability to work with others and around others.

D.   Ability to work with the following hazards prevalent: travel by vehicle, exposure to burns, and cramped quarters.

E.   Ability to work with food products (with odors present) such as flour, sauce, meat products, etc. with no allergies or reactions.

F.   Ability to perform for long periods of time with a wide range of physical demands such as sitting (while driving), standing, carrying, talking, seeing, color vision, handling and a quick working speed.

G.   Ability to remain flexible and responsive as a result of varying store needs.

EDUCATIONAL DEMANDS:

A.   Ability to both read and write concise written reports

B.   Ability to verbalize well, quickly and accurately on an as-need basis

C.   Ability to train, teach, instruct and motivate differing levels of employee responsibility groups

D.   Ability to delegate and follow through

E.   Ability to evaluate, determine and correct judgment errors of both self and others

F.   Ability to implement written and/or verbal policy or directives

---

to move into another job. This has been recognized and as of October 1, 1979 a bonus system for the CAR is being introduced. It should provide him between 10 and 30 percent of his salary depending upon his performance against these factors: sales budget (25 percent), profit budget (25 percent), significant increase in sales (25 percent) and significant increase in profit (25 percent).

Another key employee in the system is the store manager. He is well compensated by receiving a monthly bonus equal to 25 percent of the pretax profit of his store. While the normal store manager may make $25,000 per year, the "sky is the limit" in a well-managed large store. In 1978 one twenty-year old manager made $82,000. These high income figures make it difficult to get an experienced manager to take on the management of a new store that is being opened. All new stores lose money for a few months.

The average manager has been in his job for two to three years. No particular education is required to qualify, and many have worked their way up from store drivers. All of these factors are the reasons one company executive said "the way we treat our people is the reason for our success."

The efficiency of the Operations department is measured and controlled by looking at "key indicators," a program which was first instituted by Mr. Mueller in November, 1978. It was in full swing on a corporate-wide basis by January, 1979. There are four key indicator reports that form the heart of the system: weekly and monthly Corporate Area Representative reports and weekly and monthly Field Consultant reports. Both have approximately the same kind of information shown by corporate and franchise stores as listed below:

	Estimated	*Goal*
Store Numbers or CAR names		
Cash Sales with coupons	X	
Cash Sales without coupons	X	X
Cash Sales last week		X
Cash Sales last year (week)		X
Food with cola	X	X
Food without cola	X	X
Labor	X	X
Coupons	X	X
Number of store visits by CAR	X	X
Comments		

In addition, the monthly reports show:

	Estimated	*Goal*
Mileage	X	X
Delivery Time		
(This month, last month, year to date)	X	
Job planning & review reports		
(This month, last month)	X	
Profit-pretax after bonus		
This month	X	
Last month	X	
Last year	X	
Next month		X
Number of visits	X	X

A master record of these key indicators is maintained by Joe Demshar and he plots much of the data in graph form for management's use.

These costs are considered controllable by the manager: food, labor, advertising, coupons, and mileage. The goals themselves are set by the store managers and corporate area representatives and are based on comparable area data and past performance.

Food costs will vary by the kind of pizza desired by the clientele but are expected to range within plus or minus 1 percent of the individual store's goal. The goals will range from 28 percent to 33 percent of the sales dollar. The food costs plus labor and coupons should not exceed 60 percent. Any store which has been in existence for six months and has sales under $2,600 per week is considered a problem. Actual store costs are determined by a sample of actual orders produced.

The reason for using the costs with and without cola is due to the basic, but not universal, policy the company has for providing a free cola with each pizza. This policy was changed without adequate experimentation recently in order to combat inflation without raising pizza prices. The result was bad for sales, particularly in lower-middle income areas where fewer people bought pizza without the free cola. This dropoff in sales caused Domino's to increase advertising and coupons, which cost more than the free colas did. The company has returned to free colas for the most part. A free cola costs $.089 or about 5 percent of sales.

The corporate area representative makes out an in-store report each time he visits a store, covering various items of quality and cleanliness. He writes up a weekly summary of what he sees in the stores. A weekly inspection sheet is made out and sent to the home office and left with the manager. A monthly rating of less than 70 percent on this inspection report leads to disciplinary action. He also keeps a mileage chart on his travel.

Another check the CAR makes is done on the order slips at each store. Again by picking a random sample, he checks for price versus what was ordered. A numbered order slip is required for each order so adequate checking will verify cash flow and uncover any dishonest practices, once the material usage in the store is compared to the order slips.

The Job Planning and Review Form (JPR) is a three-part form used to evaluate each employee on a sixty to ninety day basis. The employee defines his responsibilities, as well as departmental responsibilities, for which he is accountable. Working conditions, resources, training, etc., for which his supervisor is responsible, are shown. The employee's achievements and needs are listed, particularly in relation to the goals and action plans which were set on the final page of the previous JPR. Finally, the goals and action plans are established for the next period.

The field consultants are responsible for supervising the corporate area representatives. Their salary is quite good and they are eligible for a bonus based upon non-specific criteria.

The part-time secretary, Linda Mueller, is Mr. Mueller's wife. She is particularly skilled at doing in-store layouts and spends most of her time doing this in conjunction with Group 243, as explained later under the marketing section. The advertising coordinator, Janet Franks, also works with Group 243 in coordinating advertising with the operations department.

In late 1979 Joe Demshar decided to become an area franchisee effective January 1, 1980.

MARKETING

The marketing function for Domino's is completely contracted outside the company to Group 243 Design, Inc. of Ann Arbor, Michigan. This rather unusual arrangement goes back to the personal relationship established in the '60s between Robert Cotman, President of Group 243, and Tom Monaghan. Mr. Cotman, along with Dave Kilby and Tom Monaghan, ran Domino's in the early days. Mr. Cotman handled marketing and "whatever anyone else would not mess with." In fact, he was asleep in the building the night fire destroyed the corporate office in 1968 and he narrowly escaped with his life. As a measure of the confidence Mr. Monaghan has in Robert Cotman, he said sometime ago before the present management team was assembled that he would want Cotman to be the president if he, Monaghan, "kicked the bucket."

Mr. Cotman attended the University of Michigan for five years and finished his work on his bachelor's degree in industrial design at Ohio State University. He then did graduate work at Ohio State up to the writing of his thesis. While at Ohio State he kept in touch with Domino's and did troubleshooting work for them during his vacations.

Group 243 was formed in Columbus in 1974 by Mr. Cotman and some other graduate students who wanted to apply their creativity. They became involved with Domino's in establishing a corporate identity as a result of the Amstar law suit. Group 243 standardized the typography of the trademark and developed consistency in relating typography to the mark.

Mr. Monaghan then asked Group 243 to implement the program they had designed. He helped them get a loan to get started and they came to Ann Arbor in September, 1975. Approximately 70 percent of Group 243's total work is for Domino's.

Mr. Cotman serves as the marketing director and consultant to Domino's for a monthly retainer fee. The firm, Group 243, provides marketing communication, store construction management and materials production for the training function at Domino's. Originally, Group 243 did all of the training work, but after David Grisham was hired this activity was transferred to Domino's.

The store construction management, which includes site selection, ordering of equipment and supervision of construction, is handled by three people at Group 243. The standard fee for this work is $3,500 per store. The average store contains 1500 square feet and uses an equipment package including a counter system, phone system, ovens and exhaust system, a walk-in cooler, and an ice machine.

Mr. Cotman states that Group 243 is different than an advertising agency and Domino's needs are different than those of most firms. 3 percent of all monies are delegated to Group 243. The franchise stores have much more input on the use of their funds than the company-owned stores. A separate account record is kept by Group 243 for the receipts and expenditures for each store and a monthly summary is provided for each store.

The initial effort at nationwide advertising was found not to be cost effective. As a result, regional customizing of advertising was done. Once again there is some shift toward national programs, such as the gift certificate. Group 243 needs to "sell the stores on the need" even though the funds come out of the 3 percent charge made by Domino's. The franchise stores tend to follow at a distance what the corporate stores are doing.

Television spot commercials are prepared for national usage, but are customized by region and time is purchased by region. The FCC will not allow national advertising at this time, since not enough states are covered and delivery is stressed in three of the ads. The other three ads stress quality and the general concept of Domino's. So far all ads have been informational in character and not the humorous, "slice of life" type ads used by the other fast food chains.

Mr. Cotman believes Group 243 is particularly economical on spot commercials because use is made of the training material in preparing the spots. However, he believes in the future more will have to be spent in order to meet competition from other chains. He expects new spots will cost about $16,000 to produce. This production work is contracted out by Group 243 because of time constraints, although there are people in-house who have been in TV production and could do the work.

All company stores are on six-month advertising proposals by Group 243 based upon projected sales for each store. Each store is the responsibility of one of Group 243's five team leaders.

Newspaper advertising and promotional flyers are handled directly by the store manager.

Bills are checked thoroughly by the Domino's executive team, which meets biweekly. Mr. Cotman believes "everything is questioned which is good for Domino's and not bad for Group 243." Lately, Group 243 has been breaking even on the Domino's work because of the interest payments on the money borrowed to finance Group 243's account receivable from Domino's. Group 243 is paid last if there is a cash crunch and, in effect, becomes the "243 bank" for Domino's. For instance, the receivable reached $250,000 in the spring of 1979.

Group 243, which has forty-four employees, billed Domino's about $2,000,000 for the fiscal year ending June 30, 1979 and expects to bill $2.5 to $3 million for this fiscal year. About $500,000 of the $2,000,000 is actually net sales to Group 243, the balance being subcontracted work.

DOMINO'S NATIONAL COMMISSARY CORPORATION

Domino's National Commissary Corporation is part of Domino's Pizza, Inc. and is included in the consolidated financial statements. DNC consists of nine wholly owned commissaries and one, Domino's Ohio Commissary, which is 59 percent owned by Domino's. The organization chart for DNC is shown in Exhibit 5. There are 225 employees in the entire organization.

Each commissary carries out two functions: purchasing items for resale and processing purchased items for subsequent resale. The processing consists of grinding cheese, making dough, processing pizza sauce, and slicing onions and green peppers. Purchased items for resale include sliced meat, canned mushrooms, hot peppers and olives, boxes, and other paper items.

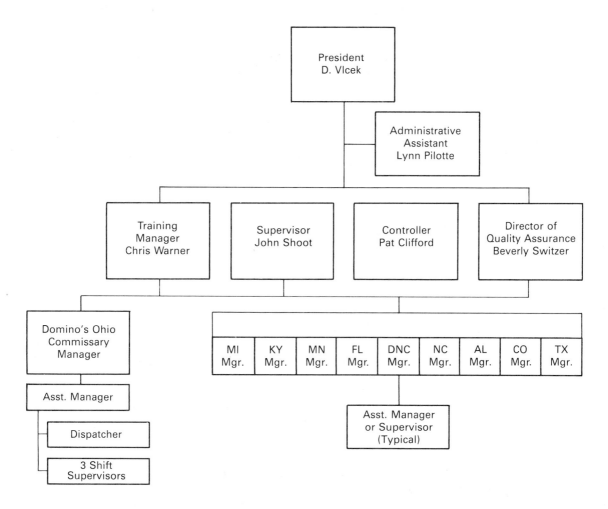

EXHIBIT 5 Organization chart, Domino's National Commissary Corporation

The largest commissary is the Ohio unit, with $440,000 per month in sales from a 4,700 square-foot building. This unit operates on a three-shift basis. The second largest unit is Kentucky, with $225,000 per month in sales from a 8,800 square-foot building. The smallest unit is $12,000 sales per month from a 1600 square-foot building.

Each commissary building contains a heated and air conditioned production or kitchen area, including a cooler for meat and sauce, a cooler for dough, and a freezer for meat; a dry storage area; and a small office. All buildings are rented with a five-year lease and a five-year optional renewal.

The Minnesota facility, which is 2,400 square-feet, was leased for $783 per month, including all leasehold improvements. This facility was located by DNC personnel after Group 243 had submitted three other sites that cost $1,250 per month. This difference has prompted DNC to do its own site work, with the use of local real estate brokers. A recent rental for 1,600 square feet was $275 per month plus $9000 for leasehold improvements, which was paid by DNC initially.

Don Vlcek is the president of DNC. He is twenty-nine years old and graduated from the University of Michigan in 1971 with a bachelor's degree in Business Administration. He has been with Domino's for a year. Prior to joining Domino's, he worked in the meatpacking business as a plant manager.

Since joining Domino's, Mr. Vlcek has made a number of changes to convert a loss operation into one that will earn $500,000 in 1979 without raising prices. One of the first moves was to introduce an incentive into the management pay structure and increase the management salaries. The commissary manager was upgraded to a $15,000 salary from $12,000 and given a bonus of 3 percent of profits. Assistant managers receive a 1 percent bonus. Mr. Vlcek sees "management as being needed to combat Murphy's Law." He believes there is a lack of respect for profits at Domino's with the heavy emphasis on sales growth.

The commissary manager makes all of the decisions for his commissary. Purchasing is, of course, a key activity. By planning ahead and by aggressive buying, purchasing costs have been lowered 25 percent. The cost of food purchased should be 76-78 percent of the DNC sales dollar. Other costs are transportation, 3 to 7 percent; labor, 6 to 10 percent; rent, 1 to 3 percent; and, of course, fixed overhead. DNC is not allowed to exceed a 5 percent after tax profit. Any profit above this percentage is rebated to the stores on a prorata basis.

Prices are set by adding a 22-24 percent markup to the cost a competitive, efficient inside buyer will achieve. There are two pricing categories: *Class I* is for Michigan, Ohio and Kentucky stores, which have much of the corporate volume, and *Class II,* which is all other stores. Lately, the profits have been good enough that price reductions are contemplated, which is unusual in inflationary times.

Presently, 64 percent of the franchise stores and 93 percent of the company stores buy from DNC. Some commissaries are run by franchisees because of remote location or simply because they think they can do a better job. Mr. Vlcek considered selling to competing pizza stores, but the idea was emphatically turned down by Mr. Monaghan.

Another change that has been made is to give the commissary managers the power to collect their receivables. Prior to this change, overdue receivables exceeded $400,000. The basis for receivables is now net, seven days and 1½ percent per month is charged after fourteen days.

The improved collection has allowed DNC to, in turn, pay their payables more promptly. Payables had normally run at forty-five days and as high as ninety days, if the vender did not complain. This kind of payable record made it impossible to take advantage of discounts for larger purchases and for cash.

Prior to Mr. Vlcek's arrival, there was no inventory control system. Now each commissary keeps a written record of purchases and sales. A daily physical inventory of the major processed items is taken so it is possible to reconstruct theoretical usage. It is planned to use a computer in the future to keep track of inventory. The new system has made it possible to discover and prosecute employees for thievery. DNC has about twenty-five items in finished goods and about ten items in raw materials.

DNC delivers to the stores using rental trucks or trucks and vans that are owned by DNC. They do not know the transportation cost per mile yet but they are collecting the needed data. Two kinds of delivery charges are made to the stores: a weekly charge which is determined by dividing the cost of gas, oil and drivers' wages by the number of stores served, and a monthly charge, which is the truck depreciation cost or rental cost divided by the number of stores. These figures are later modified if the charge seems too high. To make this adjustment, the divisor is increased to reflect the number of stores expected to eventually be served by the particular commissary. This practice created an unfavorable variance of $226,000 between the charges and the actual costs in the first eight months of 1978. Since delivery charges are such a point of contention, Mr. Vlcek is considering incorporating part of the delivery cost into a higher markup percentage.

Another interdepartmental problem with Domino's is five small commissaries each serving two or three stores which are presently run by the Operations department. Mr. Mueller does not want to run these, yet they are too small to be attractive to DNC. Mr. Vlcek is adding the training manager for DNC, who is shown on the organization chart, with the idea that he will be responsible for these small commissaries as part of his training activity. It is difficult to justify a commissary manager for such small operations, yet a remote location may make a small commissary necessary.

FINANCIAL

The year 1976 was the first year Domino's had audited financial statements by Arthur Andersen. Douglas Dawson, who is now Domino's treasurer, acquired Domino's as a client that year when he was working for Arthur Andersen as an audit manager in the Small Business division of the Detroit office. He worked for Arthur Andersen for nine years before joining Domino's in May, 1978. He graduated from Michigan State University with an MBA in 1969 and obtained his CPA designation. He is thirty-five years old.

At the time of Mr. Dawson's arrival, financial statements were made on a quarterly basis. He began issuing monthly financial statements in 1979. Financial reporting had been very poor prior to 1976, with balance sheets prepared only once a year. Many adjustments were required on the 1976 statements in order to properly reflect prior years' transactions. Exhibit 6 shows the Income Statements for 1976 through 1979 and Exhibit 7 shows the Balance Sheets for the same period. Financial statements are now issued monthly by the fifteenth of the following month. The minority interest shown on the statements represents a 49 percent interest in the Ohio commissary and the Tallahassee and San Antonio groups of pizza stores.

Mr. Dawson has seen dramatic sales growth since 1976. The Florida chain of pizza stores was acquired in 1976 and the Minnesota chain in 1977.

EXHIBIT 6   Consolidated income statement Domino's Pizza, Inc.

	1976	1977	1978	Unaudited 1979
Revenues				
Retail food sales	$5,767,420	$10,200,416	$18,674,144	$27,138,092
Product sales to franchises	1,708,387	2,638,464	4,590,327	7,603,679
Royalties from franchises	491,341	580,107	861,256	1,372,627
Franchise fees	—	—	—	143,985
Total revenues	7,967,148	13,418,987	24,125,727	36,258,383
Costs & expenses				
Food and supplies	2,865,492	4,860,007	8,644,467	13,156,631
Payroll & related	2,278,964	3,918,436	7,460,803	11,520,745
Advertising	463,665	781,816	1,248,108	1,195,034
Delivery expense	404,675	773,583	1,401,169	1,494,582
Depreciation & amortization	288,328	448,651	629,167	827,020
Rent	143,649	307,298	579,538	1,006,446
Other general & adm. expense	1,041,645	1,697,360	3,294,573	5,481,535
Total costs & expenses	7,486,148	12,787,151	23,257,825	34,681,993
Income from operations	480,730	631,836	867,902	1,576,390
Other (Income) expense				
Interest expense	58,388	137,660	178,071	326,617
Gain from sale of subsidiary	(119,157)	(23,895)	—	—
Loss (gain) on sale of equip.	—	22,789	(44,484)	—
Miscellaneous, net	6,413	(10,680)	—	—
	(54,356)	125,874	133,587	326,617
Income before provision for income taxes & minority interest	545,086	505,962	734,315	1,249,773
Provision for income taxes	252,900	222,000	126,000	360,624
Income before minority interest	282,186	283,962	608,315	889,149
Minority interest in net income	135,787	169,541	246,686	139,616
Net income	$146,399	$114,421	$361,629	$749,533
Earnings per share	$.08	$.065	$.204	$.39

EXHIBIT 7 Consolidated balance sheet Domino's Pizza, Inc. as of December 31

	1976	1977	1978	Unaudited 1979
Current assets				
Cash	$375,691	$636,183	$815,140	$750,187
Accounts receivable	153,521	417,134	554,280	625,741
Note receivable	—	—	—	158,325
Refundable income taxes	74,000	135,337	126,328	—
Inventories	218,787	365,693	645,301	874,487
Prepaid expenses	73,558	135,477	64,180	94,142
Total	895,557	1,689,824	2,205,229	2,502,882
Property, plant & equipment				
Land	50,725	50,725	65,725	65,725
Buildings	142,679	142,679	142,679	142,679
Leasehold improvements	288,657	491,239	776,213	1,117,135
Equipment	765,360	1,327,699	1,991,555	2,850,346
Vehicles	290,270	485,615	483,871	602,260
Aircraft	119,600	—	—	—
Total	1,657,291	2,497,957	3,460,043	4,778,145
Less depreciation	584,359	816,340	1,235,344	1,870,898
Net	1,072,932	1,681,617	2,224,699	2,907,247
Other Assets				
Favorable franchise & leasehold rights & covenants not to compete	258,677	358,738	368,231	690,550
Less amortization	30,028	97,744	177,131	282,792
	228,649	260,994	191,100	407,758
Cost in excess of fair value of acquired assets	71,301	71,501	148,137	381,644
Less amortization	1,695	3,503	5,730	47,813
Net	69,606	67,998	142,407	333,831
Deposits & other	39,653	125,396	235,025	214,069
Note receivable	63,503	—	—	50,140
	417,611	454,388	568,532	1,005,798
Total assets	$2,386,100	$3,825,829	$4,998,460	$6,415,927
Current liabilities				
Current portion of long term debt	$447,432	$450,000	$605,000	$638,459
Demand notes payable	—	75,069	—	—
Accounts payable	401,322	893,092	1,137,968	519,550
Accrued liabilities	158,059	262,289	410,525	840,847
Accrued income taxes	149,219	170,242	98,908	398,411
Total	1,156,032	1,850,692	2,252,401	2,397,267
Long term debt	632,815	1,151,518	1,305,415	1,801,969
Minority interests in subsidiaries	195,702	296,221	489,904	368,484
Stockholders' investment				
Common stock (stated value $.05/share)	98,607	98,607	98,607	98,821
Paid in capital	165,602	165,602	165,763	170,493
	264,209	264,209	264,370	269,314
Less notes receivable from sale of stock	69,868	65,542	—	—
	194,341	198,667	264,370	269,314
Retained earnings	412,640	527,061	888,690	1,638,223
Less treasury stock @ cost	(205,430)	(198,330)	(202,320)	(59,330)
Total	401,551	527,398	950,460	1,848,207
	$2,386,100	$3,825,829	$4,998,460	$6,415,927

The Boulder chain of fifteen stores called Pizzaco was acquired in 1979. All of these acquisitions were made from existing franchisees or former employees, so the operations followed the same strategy as Domino's. Nevertheless, each acquisition has been followed by a traumatic assimilation period. Domino's has not acquired other companies except as described above and does not plan to do so. On the other hand, starting up new stores means an unprofitable period of six months.

The royalties from franchises are placed back into the company to cover projects such as the training program and corporate overhead. Other sources of income used to cover corporate overhead are flat fees charged the company stores for accounting services and corporate supervision of operations. This royalty income is then divided among the corporate departments as shown below:

Executive	12%	Personnel Development programs	11%
Administrative	12%	Franchising	5%
Operations	36%	Marketing	3%
Finance	11%	Debt Service	10%

The percentage figures were originally established by Mr. Monaghan and have been altered little since then.

The organization chart for the Financial department is shown in Exhibit 8. The controller position is presently vacant due to a promotion. The corporate office supervisor is responsible for preparing the financial statements and general ledger for Domino's Pizza, Inc. She is also responsible, through subordinates, for monitoring the weekly royalty and advertising receipts. A corporate accountant in the Columbus regional office also reports to her. The store supervisor monitors store accounting through a bookkeeper in each of the regions shown. The Columbus bookkeeping is done by an outside firm and there are three bookkeepers in the Boulder regional office. Each store has its own bank account.

Domino's has an IBM System 32 computer, which was installed in March, 1979. Presently, seventeen stores are handled on the computer. A System 34 is on order to make the use of remote terminals possible. The company plans to install the first remote terminal in Minnesota and to eventually have all stores on the computer.

Domino's uses a programmer and a systems designer on a part-time basis. The computer work has deliberately gone at an inexpensive pace. The manual systems were in such poor shape that these had to be cleaned up first and the accounting people trained, before any computer system could be started.

Mr. Dawson is very involved personally in managing the cash flow, in developing departmental budgets with the individual department managers, and in doing internal consulting work. The budgets are made up, based upon the allocated income previously described. Budget reports are issued month-

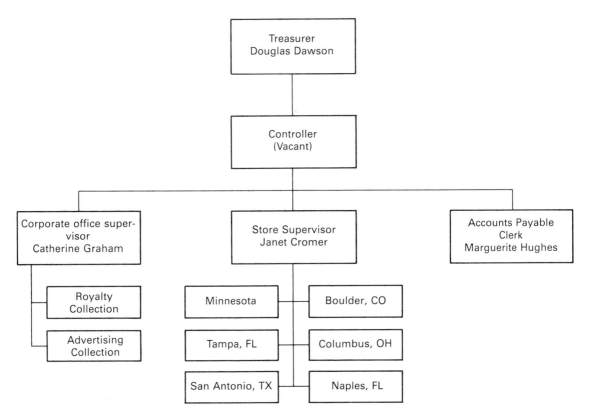

EXHIBIT 8 Organization chart, treasurer department

ly. Mr. Dawson has spent considerable time with individual departments helping them to understand the budget process and how to use it to control their operations.

As an internal consultant, Mr. Dawson worked with Mr. Vlcek for the six-month period after he arrived to help him analyze costs, collect bills, and generally make the commissaries profitable. He also worked with the Equipment and Supply department for several months to accomplish similar things. He has presently been asked by Operations to help them also, beginning with the Columbus regional office.

The executive team of the company, which includes department heads and Mr. Monaghan, meets biweekly. One of these meetings each month includes a written report by each department. Mr. Dawson includes the financial statements in his report, including a balance sheet, income statement, sources and applications of funds statement, statement of stockholders' investment, the profit by region and individual store and commissary, and financial highlights by month for the current year of the current ratio, working capital, debt to equity ratio, and total liabilities to equity ratio. A sample month's statements for the regions and commissaries are shown in Exhibit 9. Quarterly income statements for 1979 are shown in Exhibit 10.

EXHIBIT 9   Individual profit and loss before federal income tax, Domino's Pizza, Inc.
(   ) equals the number of stores

		Month of March, 1979		Month of August, 1979		Month of October, 1979		Month of December, 1979
Corporate stores		$		$		$		$
Region 100	(11)	26,577	(11)	22,075	(12)	6,986	(12)	10,712
Region 150		1,013	(47)	5,712	(49)	80,853	(50)	82,230
Region 200	(9)	16,310	(9)	10,872	(9)	15,930	(9)	15,250
Region 300	(9)	11,791	(10)	1,710	(11)	4,787	(11)	4,105
Region 310	(5)	12,210	(5)	1,673	(5)	9,725	(5)	4,195
Region 320		—	(1)	(3,299)	(1)	(532)	(1)	(4,674)
Region 330		—		—		—	(1)	(874)
Region 340	(3)	9,207	(6)	31,954	(6)	9,036	(5)	30,214
Region 350	(2)	(5,329)	(2)	(1,725)	(2)	(1,064)	(2)	17
Region 360		—	(1)	(3,045)	(1)	(3,791)	(1)	(4,268)
Region 400	(1)	(15,718)	(5)	(18,504)	(5)	(22,459)	(5)	(6,431)
Region 410	(8)	(2,711)	(8)	(4,834)	(8)	2,291	(8)	6,960
Region 420	(1)	(3,852)	(1)	2,920	(1)	177	(1)	4,680
Region 500	(1)	(235)	(1)	(7,672)	(1)	(2,176)	(1)	(2,812)
Region 600	(32)	(52,344)	(14)	775	(14)	18,694	(14)	6,048
Total		(3,081)		38,612		118,457		145,352
Commissaries								
Region 100		10,913		8,598		29,114		6,066
Region 150		35,893		39,510		35,308		(29,392)
Region 160		16,287		10,776		16,834		955
Region 200		2,641		4,491		9,323		6,764
Region 300		2,686		4,671		4,085		477
Region 320		(1,399)		(8,789)		(3,271)		—
Region 330		—		—		—		(975)
Region 340		2,279		1,167		9,777		9,872
Region 400		7,956		7,328		6,987		7,655
Region 600		(2,159)		6,020		2,322		2,820
National		(863)		8,753		12,340		10,098
Total		74,234		82,525		122,819		14,340
Corporate office		(6,991)		(4,997)		(46,361)		(48,851)
Equipment & supply		7,277		11,721		12,088		12,006
Total profit before income tax		$8,519		$127,861		$207,003		$122,847

The only part of the financial activity of Domino's that does not report to Mr. Dawson is the controller for Domino's National Commissaries. While Mr. Dawson is not in favor of this arrangement, he believes it will not be changed.

ADMINISTRATION

Mr. Richard White manages the Administration department of Domino's. His undergraduate and graduate degree, master's in Accounting, were attained at Eastern Michigan University, and he functioned as the financial officer of

EXHIBIT 10 Quarterly income statements for 1979, Domino's Pizza, Inc. (Unaudited)

	3 Months Ending 3/31/79	6 Months Ending 6/30/79	9 Months Ending 9/30/79
Revenues			
Retail food sales	$6,329,811	$12,819,702	$19,441,594
Product sales to franchisees	1,405,908	2,833,481	4,593,041
Royalties from franchisees	370,961	746,271	968,390
Franchise fees			153,985
TOTAL REVENUE	8,106,680	16,399,454	25,157,010
Costs and expenses			
Food and supplies	2,840,146	5,999,141	9,224,311
Payroll and related taxes	2,581,292	5,503,337	8,463,721
Advertising	250,495	525,424	847,112
Delivery expense	334,867	680,781	1,017,184
Depreciation & amortization	184,333	412,185	649,003
Rent	224,162	456,988	740,842
General & admin. expense	1,459,568	2,487,485	3,520,312
TOTAL COSTS & EXPENSES	7,874,863	16,065,341	24,462,485
Income from operations	231,817	334,113	694,525
Provision for income taxes	72,822	56,753	159,100
Income before minority interest	158,995	277,360	535,425
Minority interest in net income	29,879	62,757	99,304
NET INCOME	$129,116	$214,603	$436,121

Domino's from September, 1976 to May, 1978. He is a CPA and spent eight years with public accounting firms prior to joining Domino's.

Most of Mr. White's time is spent on legal matters, including franchises and insurance matters, but, particularly in recent months, on the Amstar suit against Domino's for trademark infringement. Amstar, which uses the trademark *Domino* on its sugar, sued Domino's Pizza in 1975 for trademark infringements. Domino's has been fighting the suit in the courts since then and was surprised to lose the suit in federal court in Atlanta in September, 1979. The company is appealing the decision, of course, but the threat of the consequences of ultimately losing the case is universally recognized by all of the company executives as the major problem the company faces. Mr. White describes it as a lose-lose situation in that legal fees to win will be tremendous and the costs of losing such as changing signs, etc. would exceed $1,000,000, not to mention the identity problems. An alternate name, *Pizza Dispatch* has been selected but, hopefully, will not be needed. This name was picked and is being field tested in nearby stores. After the field testing project was underway, it was discovered that there was a competing store, in Virginia Beach near a Domino's store, with the name Pizza Dispatch. Domino's is in the process of buying out the owner of this store for $50,000 in order to avoid further trademark problems.

The Administration department handles all contracts from franchises for stores and regional area agreements, as well as contracts to purchase or lease stores. Each contract to purchase or lease a store is unique but the franchise agreements are standardized as follows:

- ☐ A 5½ percent of sales fee is paid weekly for the use of name, trademark, and other programs and benefits
- ☐ A 3 percent of sales fee is paid weekly for national and regional advertising
- ☐ Quality standards are outlined in detail
- ☐ No trade secrets are to be revealed
- ☐ The franchisee agrees not to compete for a period of three years
- ☐ The franchisee cannot hold another job other than his pizza operation. (This precludes investors from obtaining a franchise.)

The company encourages its corporate people to franchise stores.

A franchisee can get into business for $55 to 60,000 and could probably finance 70 percent of that cost. Mr. White believes Domino's will always have more franchised stores than corporate-owned stores, because corporate stores cost more to open and operate. Domino's is in twenty-six states now and he sees the growth limited only by the overall population base. Right now competition is not a major factor and is primarily from local individual proprietor stores: Little Caesar, a Michigan and Florida chain; and Dino's, a nationwide, but smaller, chain. Others such as big Pizza Hut are not in the same market, since they offer sit-down eating facilities, rather than delivery and carry-out only. Financial statements for Pizza Inn, the second largest sit-down chain, are shown in Exhibit 11.

Administration handles the insurance program and the fringe benefits program. Salaried employees have life insurance, $50 deductible hospital and medical insurance, including dental and disability insurance. Administration is currently looking into a pension-profit sharing plan. Office wages are believed to be more than competitive, as are hourly wages in the stores. Hourly employees do not have the fringe benefit program because they are part-time employees.

Reporting to Mr. White are an assistant, an insurance coordinator, a legal coordinator, and a coordinator for the delivery and service program described below. Administration is also responsible for the receptionist-telephone service activities, which consist of five employees.

The delivery and service program, or "mystery panel," is a specialized type of quality control program. Each month, one or two pizzas per store are ordered by a member of a sample panel who is unknown to the stores. The pizzas are delivered. The sampler eats the pizza, rates it, and times the delivery service. The panel is selected at random from the telephone book and is changed every six months. The store manager with the best record gets a prize.

EXHIBIT 11   Financial statements Pizza Inn, Inc.

Income Statement (in Thousands $)	1977	1978	1979 9 mos.
Revenues			
Net sales	$71,339	94,169	
Franchise royalties	2,311	2,953	
Other income	838	856	
Total revenues	74,488	97,978	83,980
Costs & expenses			
Cost of sales	59,255	79,876	
Selling & administrative expense	8,399	10,698	
Total costs & expenses	67,654	90,574	
Other expenses			
Interest expense	3,826	4,871	
Income before taxes	3,008	2,533	2,069
Provision for income taxes	875	831	620
Net income	2,133	1,702	1,449
Earnings per share	$.78	$.61	$.48
Balance sheet (in thousand $)			
Current assets			
Cash	1,593	2,250	1,905
Accounts receivable	2,838	4,125	
Refundable income taxes	395	125	
Inventories	3,808	4,358	4,950
Property for resale	424	748	
Prepaid expenses	404	694	
Total	9,463	12,300	13,933
Net property, plant & equipment	16,400	21,010	
Capitalized leased property	20,721	23,939	
Intangibles	3,622	3,797	
Other assets	3,092	1,910	
Total assets	53,298	62,956	65,612
Current liabilities			
Notes payable	996	2,221	
Capitalized lease obligations	1,616	1,443	
Accounts payable	3,437	5,481	
Accruals	2,345	2,541	
Income taxes	164	2	
Total	8,557	11,690	13,081
Long term debt	8,528	10,823	
Deferred income	533	280	
Deferred income taxes	—	47	
Capitalized lease obligations	21,295	24,563	
Equity			
Common stock	2,571	2,847	
Capital stock	9,911	11,286	

EXHIBIT 11   (continued)

Income Statement (in Thousands $)	1977	1978	1979 9 mos.
Retained earnings	1,076	1,000	
Less treasury stock	(174)	(118)	
Total	13,384	15,015	
Total liabilities & equity	53,298	62,956	

Pizza Inn, Inc. develops, operates, or franchises restaurants in thirty-three states, Mexico, Japan, and Africa, offering a limited menu of moderately priced Italian foods. In 1976 the company had 240 company-owned restaurants and 235 franchised restaurants.

Pizza Hut, Inc., a division of Pepsico, develops, operates and franchises restaurants located in all states except Delaware, offering pizza, pasta, salad and sandwiches. Approximately 1,875 company-owned restaurants are operated and 1,670 restaurants are franchised.

TOM MONAGHAN

Tom Monaghan, who is now forty-two years old, experienced the loss of his father when he was four and was raised and educated by Roman Catholic nuns. He attributes his personal value system and the strength of it to this period in his life and is grateful for it.

In his struggle to pursue his education he enlisted in the Marines at age nineteen because he accrued the right to tuition and subsistence pay as one of the fringe benefits of being in the service. Everyone who knew him then knew he was intensely dedicated to succeeding in business in some way and making a lot of money. While in the Marines he spent some time thinking about his personal goals for his life as shown below:

1. Spiritual: "For what does it profit a man, to gain the whole world and suffer the loss of his soul."

2. Social: Apply the Golden Rule, beginning with family life, and proceeding to friendships, business relationships, and everyone you come in contact with.

3. Mental: Development of mind by reading, learning, being inquisitive, and having a clear conscience and lots of enthusiasm.

4. Physical: Physical health is worth more than money. He now jogs three miles per day.

5. Financial: Be successful in business.

Although he wanted to be wealthy, he recognized he could not be happy unless the first four priorities were handled first.

He has tried to apply this priority system to his life since then, and, judging by many of the voluntary statements by his employees, his strong sense of ethics comes through clearly in his business relationships. One mentioned that he thought Mr. Monaghan used the Golden Rule as the basis for his major business decisions. Another said he thought Mr. Monaghan went further than he needed to in being fair in the tough business decisions, so that the other fellow was always treated honestly and fairly. Mr. Monaghan believes it is easy to be honest, for "what a tangled web we weave when first we practice to deceive." He believes honesty is also good for business, although that is not his reason for being honest.

Mr. Monaghan's plan for Domino's is a 50 percent per year growth rate. The plan is well known throughout the Domino organization and derivative plans are based upon it. He sees the recent profit improvement as significant in that it will relax the financial constraints that had placed a damper on this growth plan. He believes stores can be opened as fast as good sites can be found and financing arranged. There are probably 100 possibilities in their current target areas and only the Domino trademark suit is inhibiting moving at this time. The Appeals Court decision is expected in the next few months, and Domino's lawyers are optimistic about winning. Nevertheless, the contingency plan to change to Pizza Dispatch is moving along concurrently.

Mr. Monaghan considers product and service to be the most important factor in Domino's business. He is concerned that delivery times as reported in the *Pepperoni Press,* an in-house newspaper that tells "What's Cooking at Domino's Pizza," are averaging thirty-four minutes, against the goal of an average of twenty-five minutes which was attained a while back. Coincident with this has been a deteriorating volume per store when inflationary effects are removed. Bigness is the enemy, he believes; there is just not the same intensity in handling the rush periods. A lot of emphasis has been placed on controls in the past year, including inventory, pilferage, and costs in general. Supervision has spent a great deal of time with store managers trying to improve their P & L Statements. Does this mean there is an inevitable tradeoff between sales and profitability? Tom thinks not.

Other concerns he sees in the future are the oil crisis and government regulation. Obviously, gasoline shortages or rationing could have a drastic effect on Domino's, with its delivery strategy. He hopes provisions would be made for such businesses to get gasoline.

Mr. Monaghan believes government regulation, with its red tape and endless reporting forms has already killed 80 percent of the new franchise business in the United States. Domino's now makes an initial charge of $9,500 to a new franchise to handle this government paperwork, and even this figure does not cover Domino's costs. This fact is distressing to him as a businessman who started a small business. He notes that people are afraid to start on their own anyway, and often seek a partner for security, as he himself did. Franchising seems to give people courage to go into business and, in that sense, it fulfills part of the role a partner fills. Thus, excessive government regulation as is now being experienced will further jeopardize the formation of small businesses, leading to the stagnation which often accompanies big business.

Free Spirit Toys

In late 1980, Ralph R. Goodman,[1] owner of Free Spirit Toys, was getting a lot of pleasure out of directing the operation of his toy manufacturing business and was enjoying his life style. Ralph wanted the good times to continue. His basic philosophy of business was:

"Business is a game, and I like risk-taking. Business people can be the biggest gamblers in the world. Take me, for instance. Ten years of my life are tied up in something that might never make it. I enjoy gambling, but it is hard to be a gambler when you have responsibilities. The reason I can be one is that I am not into material things, and I have very few responsibilities.

"In my opinion, all a person really needs is a 'six-pack' of beer and two pairs of blue jeans. The reason for having two pairs of jeans is so that you can wear one pair while the other pair is at the laundry. Then, even if you lose all of your material possessions, you are as well off as the next person, as long as you still have your health, family, friends, and clear conscience. So, what I am doing here is just gambling.

"I think the whole human race is in a struggle to keep from being bored. They would prefer to develop marital problems or even become hypochondriac rather than to be bored. People get involved with all kinds of crazy hobbies just to escape boredom. The more imaginative one is, the better off that person will be.

"Every day I come here to this business, and I play my game. It thoroughly entertains me. All of my systems, machines, and projects are really fascinating to me.

"My employees have to do the actual work and endure the monotony of carrying out my projects. These people really work hard. See that stack of toys over there? It takes forty hours to process all that material. If I had to do all that work myself, I am sure I would be a lot less enthusiastic about it . . . but that is the nice thing about being the boss."

The research and written case information were presented at a Case Research Symposium and were evaluated by the Case Research Association's Editorial Board. This case was prepared by Terrell F. Pike and Leon C. Megginson of the University of South Alabama as a basis for class discussion.

Reprinted from *Case Research Journal* (Athens, GA: Case Research Association, 1982), pp. 35–51.

[1]All names are disguised.

BACKGROUND

Free Spirit Toys was a small manufacturing operation which made hand-crafted wooden toys. The organization was developed in 1969 by Ralph R. Goodman upon his graduation from State University with a degree in production management. Ralph said that he knew from the time he was seventeen years old that he wanted to own and manage a light manufacturing business. He worked part-time during high school and college for his father, Robert Goodman, the owner of a small, but profitable, light manufacturing plant. Mr. Goodman's firm produced hand-held nut-gathering equipment for pecans and walnuts. These nut-gathering devices were invented and patented by Mr. Robert Goodman and were distributed throughout the U.S.

Looking for a Product

Upon his graduation from State University, Ralph Goodman came home to Woodville, a small city in the South. He set up an office for himself in his father's plant. During the first three months, he investigated the pallet business and eventually found out that "nobody was making any money in the pallet business." Later, he became interested in kitchen gadgets, what-nots, wooden puzzles, antiques, and "anything that would sell." He bought antiques and reproduced them.

Finally Ralph settled on producing wooden toys. He manufactured a few samples of different items and then went to the big markets in Atlanta and Dallas with the samples. He got $3,000 worth of orders with his promise to deliver within ninety days. Ralph returned to Woodville, rented a building, and began to fill the orders, doing most of the work himself with the help of one employee. It took considerably longer than the ninety days to fill the orders. According to Ralph, "you would be surprised at how little one person can accomplish in a day."

Ralph continued to search for a product that he could profitably produce and sell. By 1974, he was manufacturing twenty different items. At that time, he took some samples to the Chicago Gift Mart, to the editor of *Toy Magazine,* and later to the New York Toy Fair, where he obtained $5,000 worth of orders.

Ralph said that for a while after his return, every time he shipped $5,000 worth of toys, he lost another $5,000 because his production costs were high relative to the wholesale price he could charge. Trying to produce a high-quality toy and sell it for a low price did not permit him to break even. For a toy to retail at six dollars he had to sell it to a wholesaler at a dollar and a half. Yet, the dollar and a half did not cover the cost of direct labor.

Making a Breakthrough in Marketing

During 1974, Ralph made what he felt was an important breakthrough in marketing. He decided to go to an art show held in a nearby city, taking with him all the stock he had left. These toys consisted of "seconds" and were less than perfect, in his opinion, but he was eager to see if they would sell. Much to his delight, the toys sold rapidly, and he actually made money on them.

Ralph returned to Woodville, made up a new batch of toys, put them in a truck, and sold them at craft shows, flea markets, and in shopping malls in small cities relatively close to Woodville. He then began improving his product, widening his lines, and eventually began getting accepted at art shows in major cities.

Getting Spots at Major Shows

The planning for major art shows in large cities took place months in advance, and the competition among exhibitors for spots was highly competitive. Each potential exhibitor submitted photographs or slides of his or her work months in advance to a jury selected by the sponsors of the show. The jury then evaluated the submitted materials in light of their artistic quality, excellence of design, and appropriateness in view of the desired combination of arts and crafts that were to be represented at the show.

By this time, Ralph felt that he had identified his product, targeted his market, and established his production facilities. He was still, in his words, "unorganized, unstaffed, and had no controls," but he believed that he was on his way.

ORGANIZING AND THE ORGANIZATION STRUCTURE

Free Spirit Toys operated as a semi-partnership of Ralph Goodman and James Wilson, with Ralph serving as the chief executive officer. A native of Woodville, Ralph was thirty-three years old. He performed all the managerial functions of the business, was the "idea man," and was the catalyst of the organization. Ralph liked to dream up ideas for products that the other members of the organization could then bring to fruition. His special interests were in the areas of production and financial ratios. He was also heavily involved in on-the-road selling.

James (Jim) Wilson, the engineering executive, was twenty-five years old, unmarried, and a graduate of State University with a B.S. in Electrical Engineering. According to Ralph, Jim was a brilliant, young engineer. Jim was also an executive with lots of initiative and good ideas. He performed all of the engineering functions of the organization and some of the sales functions. Jim had worked with Ralph part-time through his high school and college years. Ralph said that Jim's contributions to the organization were invaluable.

Ralph and Jim had no formal ownership structure. The informal structure was based on the concept of *laissez faire* because of the years of trust and cooperation between the two men. They had agreed in the past to form a corporation at some indefinite time in the future and to issue shares reflecting each owner's contribution of time and money invested. The division of ownership would have to be based upon a complex formula reflecting interest, sacrifice, longevity, and back salaries. Ralph was not in a great hurry to finalize the details of the incorporation and did not have a definite timetable for doing so.

Annabelle Ross, an artist, was employed by Free Spirit Toys. She was twenty-four years old, single, and a graduate of State University with a B.A. in Art. Annabelle executed all of the drawings and art work for the organization. Her most recent responsibility was for the development of the designs and drawings in the Free Spirit Coloring Book that the organization planned to publish (see Exhibit 1).

Cynthia Baker, the office manager, had been with Free Spirit Toys for two years. She was responsible for all record keeping, checkwriting, bill paying, wholesale ordering, and for the mechanics of running the office. She was interested in marketing and had studied marketing in college. Cynthia was married and had two teenage children. Ralph felt that she had a lot of potential in sales, but he did not feel that she was interested in developing a sales territory for herself at the time because of the family responsibilities that she had with her two teenage children. He also said that she was tied down with so many details at the office that she did not have the leisure to implement her ideas about increasing retail sales. Wholesale orders increased from two thousand dollars in 1978 to nine thousand dollars in 1979, mainly as a result of Cynthia's interest and efforts, according to Ralph.

Harold Koch, a master wood technician, had had eighteen years of experience. Ralph had hired him away from a local furniture maker. Harold was a middle-aged man with nine children. At twelve thousand dollars per year, Harold was the highest paid person in the organization.

Free Spirit employed two work supervisors, both female, who had worked in the business since 1975. Ralph considered them to be among the firm's key people. They were responsible for the final assembly and packing of the toys and for training the production employees. At the time of this case, there were three additional production employees, and this number was scheduled to increase as the season progressed.

EMPLOYEE RELATIONS

The employees worked on a team basis, and products were manufactured in small lots with the employees being able to see the product from start to finish. Most employees could make a toy from a piece of wood and carry it through to completion. Ralph felt that one of the reasons that the motivational level among the production employees was so high was that they knew exactly what toy they were making and were "not just drilling holes in pieces of wood."

The employees were free to come to work whenever they wished between the hours of 6:00 a.m. and 6:00 p.m. Mondays through Fridays. Most of the female production workers came in at 6:00 a.m. and got their 40 hours in during a four-day week. The only exceptions to the rule of the employees' scheduling their own working hours, were the days that trucks had to be loaded for shipment. On truck-loading days all employees had to be present during scheduled hours. Ralph and Jim usually came in at 9:00 a.m. and left at 6:00 p.m. Occasionally, they worked over the weekend, either when necessary due to work pressures or when they had taken a day off during the week.

Ralph believed in paying the key people "as much as possible" because they were the employees that he counted on for continuity in the business and for training seasonal sales and production employees. The key people were the engineer, the master wood technician, the two work supervisors, the office manager, and the artist. The average hourly wages paid during 1978 and 1979 were $3.85 and $4.20. Overtime wages amounted to only two percent of direct labor. Ralph and Jim lived on "draws." They each withdrew a minimal amount of money to live on. Neither expressed any interest in pursuing a lifestyle based on material possessions.

MANUFACTURING AND THE PRODUCT LINE

The Free Spirit Toy product line included fifty different wooden toys ranging in price from five to one hundred and fifty dollars each. The products included such items as a $5 turtle, a $10 airplane, a $20 dragon, a $40 rocking horse, and a $150 fire wagon. All of the toys, of high quality craftsmanship, were made of hardwoods and were very smoothly sanded and/or rubbed with steel wool. No paints, varnishes, or other coatings were used in the final finishing operations. The only painting ever done was the hand painting of eyes and other features that appeared on certain animal toys such as the fawn and the turtle.

The woods used in production were black walnut, aromatic cedar, and southern maple. Free Spirit had an inventory of fifteen thousand dollars worth of wood, which was a one-year supply. Being able to purchase a large supply at a time was a big economy, according to Ralph. In the past, buying in small lots every few weeks meant that Ralph had to send drivers and trucks to Tennessee on numerous occasions to purchase wood. As a result, the drivers and trucks had not been available to transport finished toys to art shows and malls.

The toys were crafted by some ten or more production employees in a well-ventilated concrete block building near downtown Woodville. The facility, which was leased, was sufficiently large for the production activities being undertaken. The principal piece of production equipment was an automated computerized routing machine.

Ralph explained the operation of the computerized router as follows:

> This machine is really the ultimate. When I began operations here, we had a table saw and one hand saw. We have progressed from using a collection of secondhand equipment to employing this highly automated computerized

router. It is a cutter with a high-speed tooling bit which is moved by a twelve-horsepower motor. The motor, made in Germany, is a very fine one which turns at eighteen thousand revolutions per minute. Basically, this is a simple overhead router. The only thing that is not simple about the router is that the bit is moved in three planes by a series of stepping motors, and all three of the motors work simultaneously because of the sophisticated computer which is built into the system.

In the past, we would take a board, trace a pattern, and cut the wood with a hand saw. Then we would drill holes in it, scroll sand it, and then perhaps put it in a lathe or another machine. The new computerized router eliminates five to six operations that we had to perform separately using our old methods. We now break down our toy patterns mathematically into computer singles by taped memory. Therefore, we only have to give this machine singles one time.

If the router operated twenty-four hours per day, it would take approximately one hundred people to process and finish the wood that the machine could turn out. As a result of the increased productivity of this machine, we can now compete in markets that we were not able to enter before.

The complex mathematical and engineering work involved in breaking down the patterns of the toys into "singles" for the computer memory storage was done by Jim Wilson. During the four months after the installation of the computer, patterns for five toys were computerized. The amount of time required to break down each toy pattern into singles was approximately forty hours.

The price of the machine was fifty thousand dollars, installed, and the notes on it were twelve thousand dollars per year. Ralph said that it would cost him about sixty-six thousand dollars per year to hire employees to turn out the amount of work using conventional methods that the computerized router could do in just a few hours each day.

After the wood for the toys was cut by the computerized routing machine, the pieces were sanded by machine, and assembled and finished by hand. The emphasis in production was on quality.

MARKETING THE TOYS

Free Spirit Toys was among the top ten sellers of hand-crafted wooden toys in the U.S. in terms of sales volume. According to Ralph, "If you want to make money in this business, you have to be really big, or really small. We are really big."

The sales force consisted of Ralph, Jim, Annabelle, and several seasonal employees who were hired to travel to certain art shows and shopping malls for two and three weeks at a time. Cynthia had also handled the marketing at a few art shows. Local employees were hired to staff the stalls at shopping malls. The total cost of marketing the toys was 17 percent of gross sales.

Although sales were still somewhat seasonal—with the volume of toy sales increasing as December grew nearer—Free Spirit Toys had reduced the seasonality somewhat by traveling to art shows all over the U.S., except for California. Ralph felt that the California area was "over-crafted and over-shown." Part of his philosophy was to avoid over-exposure.

Sales at art shows and shopping malls were made directly to the final purchaser. A customer would walk by the kiosk or stall, select a toy, pay for it, and leave. Ralph said that the toys were so attractive that they sold themselves.

Free Spirit Toys sales could be influenced by the dress and general appearance of the employees. The sales people were asked to dress casually so that they would "look the part." Ralph found that sales volume dropped when he, Jim, and the other employees dressed in conventional business attire.

As a rule, Ralph and Jim covered different art shows. Only when a show was very large was it necessary for Ralph and Jim to drive two trucks to the same show. Free Spirit frequently recruited "volunteer" workers from Woodville to help drive the trucks to cross-country shows. These "volunteer" employees had their expenses paid by Free Spirit Toys and took their remuneration in the form of psychic income. In other words, they went along on the trip just for the fun of it. Free Spirit had three trucks going to different shows and malls. A big art show required two trucks and four employees. The largest truck carried twenty-five thousand dollars worth of merchandise. When additional toys were needed for a big show with a high sales volume, one employee would fly back and forth between Woodville and the show with fresh supplies.

Ralph used a percentage break-down of units of items sold in the past at a given show in estimating the numbers of certain units of a given toy to stock at the same show in the future. The percentages of items that were popular in Michigan, for instance, were different from those that sold best in other parts of the country, such as Fort Lauderdale and Miami. Even the weather at the show, whether rainy or sunny, affected the percentage break-down of items sold.

In addition to retail selling at art shows, Free Spirit Toys also sold toys in leased stalls at several high-traffic shopping malls in the New York City-New Jersey area. The first time that Ralph entered the New Jersey mall market, he took two home-town boys with him because he was reluctant to hire local employees. At the end of the three week selling trip, Ralph found that there was a two thousand dollar discrepancy between the value of the toys sold and the amount of cash on hand from sales. It seemed that neither of the two employees had followed the system set up to keep track of the cash receipts from sales, which was designed for the protection of the employee as well as the organization.

Ralph fired both employees. One was very angry, and the other made no complaints. Within two years the first former employee had "cooled off," and although the young man was not in the business, he and Ralph were again the best of friends. Occasionally, the young fellow stopped by the factory during working hours and voluntarily helped out with production.

After the unfortunate experience with the two home-town employees, Ralph lost his aversion to hiring employees who lived in the areas near the mall locations. He also learned to insist on accounting control systems that protected the company and the employees.

Eventually, Ralph felt he would have to go into the finishing, coating, or painting of the toys, but he was not eager to do so. Finishing was a science in itself, and he felt that the cost of finishing would drive the retail price up too high to maintain sales volume. In terms of producing crafted toys, Ralph believed that production would continue to move from being primarily done by hand toward even more manufacturing by highly automated, computerized equipment. Ralph was also interested in experimenting with some innovative manufacturing processes and designs, especially silk-screening.

Ralph believed that the product line would evolve over a period of time into other areas, such as publishing. A coloring book with simplified drawings of the toys, entitled *Free Spirit Toys Coloring Book,* was well on its way to completion (see Exhibit 1). The toy on the front, "Fred," might eventually become the main character in a series of fantasy stories for children.[2] Ralph thought the product line might easily move toward the publishing business.

The long-run, ten-year marketing plan for Free Spirit included continuous coverage of art shows, developing the mall business through leasing of shops, then moving toward mail order, and finally toward the wholesaling of toys for the retail market.

ACCOUNTING AND THE KEEPING OF FINANCIAL RECORDS

Ralph maintained that he could not afford a thirty-dollar-an-hour accountant. Therefore, he kept his own accounting and financial records. During the early years of the business he employed a bookkeeper in the business. He later determined that she embezzled funds over a period of years. The bookkeeper was fired with no charges pressed against her by Free Spirit.

In 1975 Ralph developed an interest in financial ratios and percentages when he was trying to diagnose the problems that he was having in his business. While in college, and for several years thereafter, he felt that ratio analysis was boring and useless, but be subsequently developed a fascination for the topic and spent considerable effort in working out the various ratios that appear in Exhibits 2, 3, and 4.

Ralph had a theory regarding stress in business. He maintained that one of the reasons that many small entrepreneurs experience great stress is that their asset to liabilities ratio was too low. He made an analogy between his business and the idea of one horse pulling one wagon. Ralph said that the business was a lot better off when two horses pulled one wagon.

Ralph made a conscious decision to control the growth of Free Spirit Toys. In order to minimize stress, he determined to maintain a healthy asset

---

[2]According to Ralph, "What we really do at Free Spirit Toys is creating and selling fantasy."

EXHIBIT 1

to liability ratio. He did not want to grow too rapidly. During the early years his ratio was around one to one. The asset/liability ratio of Free Spirit Toys was 2.56 to one at the time of the case, and Ralph was even able to estimate the asset/liability ratio by months, as shown in Exhibit 5.

By 1980 Ralph was at the point at which he could make very accurate forecasts of his monthly sales, production, labor, material, inventory, merchandising, and overhead costs. The accuracy of these forecasts, along with good credit and good collateral, made it fairly easy to obtain bank financing. The results of operations in 1979 are shown in Exhibits 6, 7, and 8.

EXHIBIT 2 Financial analysis
for selected years

Current assets/current liabilities	=	Present current ratio
46,076.63/25,281.10	=	1 to 1.82
Current assets/current liabilities	=	Present current ratio
(Excluding warehouse lumber factor)		
34,070.63/13,275.00	=	1 to 2.56
Increased net worth	=	$ 5,402.66—1978
		19,179.06—1979
Asset/liability ratio		
119,594.58/63,499.19	=	1.88—1977
116,781.56/55,283.51	=	2.11—1978
147,276.89/66,599.78	=	2.11—1979
Asset/liability ratio (Excluding warehouse lumber factor)		
137,270.89/54,593.78	=	1 to 2.47—1979
Adjusted asset liability ratio for machine purchase		
167,270/86,593.78	=	1.93—1979
167,270.89/74,130.00	=	2.25—1980
Assets/total income	=	Return on investment
59,276.00/20,863.00	=	35%—1979
Assets/total income (Including Ray Griffith Co. equipment)		
79,276.89/20,863.00	=	26%—1979
Sales/investment	=	Return on sales
165,147.00/59,276.00	=	35%—1979
Sales/investment	=	Return on sales
(Including R. Griffith Co. equip.)		
165,147.00/79,276.00	=	48%—1979
Sales/liability ratio (long term)		
106,262.61/63,499.19	=	1 to 1.67—1977
145,549.12/55,283.51	=	1 to 2.63—1978
165,147.75/50,930.68	=	1 to 3.24—1979

1977 Interest per sales dollar—5¢
1978 Interest per sales dollar—4¢
1979 Interest per sales dollar—2¢

EXHIBIT 3 Overhead & profit
analysis for selected years

Overhead/production		
64,564.52/118,228.49	=	54.6%—1977
66,023.45/139,470.86	=	47.3%—1978
59,768.12/167,348.64	=	35.7%—1979
Merchandising cost/sales		
28,340.17/106,262.61	=	26.6%—1977
35,909.88/145,133.92	=	24.7%—1978
28,256.78/165,147.75	=	17.1%—1979
Profit or loss on production	=	(−2%)—1977
		7%—1978
		7.9%—1979

EXHIBIT 3   (continued)

Overhead/sales		
64,564.52/106,262.61	=	60.7%—1977
66,023.45/145,133.92	=	45.4%—1978
59,768.12/165,147.75	=	36.1%—1979
Direct cost/sales		
57,823.08/106,262.61	=	54.4%—1977
65,362.50/145,133.92	=	45.0%—1978
94,267.07/165,147.75	=	57.0%—1979
Profit or loss/sales		
(4,159.11)/106,262.61	=	(3.9%)—1977
8,084.91/145,133.92	=	5.5%—1978
13,313.45/165,147.75	=	8.0%—1979

EXHIBIT 4   Direct cost analysis
for selected years

Direct cost/production		
57,823.08/118,228.49	=	48.9%—1977
65,362.50/139,470.86	=	46.8%—1978
94,267.07/167,348.64	=	56.3%—1979
Material/production		
20,214.05/118,228.49	=	17.0%—1977
17,159.61/139,470.86	=	12.3%—1978
27,714.65/167,348.64	=	16.7%—1979
Labor/production		
37,609.03/118,228.49	=	31.8%—1977
50,202.89/139,470.86	=	35.9%—1978
66,552.42/167,348.64	=	39.7%—1979
Labor/productive hours		
66,552.42/15,894	=	4.18—1979
50,202.89/13,074	=	3.84—1978
Increase/average wage per hour		
.30/4.18	=	7%—1979
Overtime/total labor		
1,282.90/48,202.89	=	2.66%—1978
1,261.65/66,552.42	=	1.89%—1979

EXHIBIT 5 Estimated asset/liability ratios for 1980, by month

	January	February	March	April	May	June
Standard assets	131,780.00	131,780.00	131,780.00	136,780.00	171,780.00	171,780.00
Warehouse lumber	15,071.00	14,471.00	13,871.00	13,271.00	12,371.00	11,471.00
Warehouse inventory	7,958.00	13,540.00	21,540.00	23,540.00	31,540.00	38,540.00
Increase inventory	7,958.00	5,582.00	8,000.00	2,000.00	8,000.00	7,000.00
Equipment additions			5,000.00	35,000.00		
Total assets	154,809.00	159,791.00	172,191.00	208,591.00	215,691.00	228,791.00
Current liabilities						
2,391.55 taxes	2,391.00	2,391.00	2,391.00			
1,271.55 J. Wilson	1,088.00	905.00	722.00	539.00	356.00	173.00
12,006.00 lumber	11,601.00	11,001.00	10,401.00	9,801.00	8,901.00	8,001.00
Budgeted inventory loans (accumulated)		5,000.00	10,000.00	10,000.00	10,000.00	10,000.00
Long-term liabilities						
10 Year (50,930.68)	50,530.00	50,130.00	49.730.00	49,330.00	48,930.00	48,530.00
4 Year (35,000.00)				35,000.00	34.432.00	33,864.00
2 Year (5,000.00)			5,000.00	4,800.00	4,600.00	4,400.00
Total liabilities	65,610.00	69,421.00	78,244.00	109,470.00	107,219.00	104,968.00
Asset/liability ratio	2.35	2.30	2.20	1.90	2.01	2.17

	July	August	September	October	November	December
Standard assets	171,780.00	171,780.00	171,780.00	171,780.00	171,780.00	171,780.00
Warehouse lumber	10,571.00	9,521.00	8,471.00	7,271.00	5,921.00	5,021.00
Warehouse inventory	44,540.00	60,540.00	61,540.00	69,540.00	63,290.00	7,290.00
Increase inventory	6,000.00	16,000.00	1,000.00	8,000.00	(6,250.00)	(56,000.00)
Equipment additions						
Surplus cash					9,530.00	32,820.00
Total assets	226,891.00	241,841.00	241,791.00	248,591.00	250,521.00	216,911.00
Current liabilities						
2,391.55 taxes						
1,271.55 J. Wilson						
12,006.00 lumber	7,101.00	6,051.00	5,000.00	3,800.00	2,450.00	1,550.00
Budgeted inventory loans (accumulated)	15,000.00	20,000.00	26,500.00	26,500.00	20,000.00	
Long term liabilities						
10 Year (50,930.68)	48,130.00	47,730.00	47,330.00	46,930.00	46,530.00	46,130.00
4 Year (35,000.00)	33,296.00	32,728.00	32,160.00	31,592.00	31,024.00	30,456.00
2 Year (5,000.00)	4,200.00	4,000.00	3,800.00	3,600.00	3,400.00	3,200.00
Total liabilities	107,727.00	110,509.00	114,790.00	112,422.00	103,404.00	81,336.00
Asset/liability ratio	2.10	2.18	2.10	2.21	2.42	2.66

EXHIBIT 6   Sale income statement December 31, 1979

Revenue:			
Art show operation	96,434.67		
Free Spirit Toys N.Y., N.Y.	53,333.17		
Wholesale & mail order	16,388.20		
Sales total		166,156.04	
Sales returns & allowances		1,008.29	
Gross sales			165,147.75
Merchandise cost:			
Art show expenses	12,786.36		
Free Spirit Toys N.Y., N.Y.	13,806.48		
General merchandise expense	1,663.94		
Total expense			28,256.78
Net income from sales			136,890.97
Sales/merchandising cost	=	17%	

EXHIBIT 7   Free Spirit Toys
profit & loss statement for year
ending December 31, 1979

Production:		
Sales	166,156.04	
Sales returns		
& allowances	1,008.29	
		165,147.75
Inventory		
Beginning Jan. 1, 1979	12,093.13	
Ending Dec. 31, 1979	14,294.02	
		2,200.89
		167,348.64
Total production		
Cost of goods:		
Direct material	27,714.65	
Direct wages	58,381.68	
Payroll taxes	6,370.50	
Payroll insurance	1,800.24	
		94,267.07
Gross profit		73,081.57
General expenses:		
Rent	2,160.11	
Depreciation	1,400.00	
Amortization of R & D	898.00	
Interest	6,457.31	
Insurance	820.05	
Utilities	2,544.71	
Repairs	860.13	
Operating supplies	3,293.47	
Office supplies	523.34	
Truck & truck		
insurance	2,694.32	
Salaries	7,550.67	
Telephone	2,309.23	
Merchandising	28,256.78	
		59.768.12
Operating gain		13,313.45
Other income		20,115.61
Total operation gain		33,429.06

EXHIBIT 8 Free Spirit Toys financial statement for year ending December 31, 1979

	Assets	
Current assets:		
Cash	208.75	
Bank deposits	5,282.03	
Savings	10,000.00	
Accounts receivable	190.01	
Advanced invoice payment	605.00	
Inventory	14,294.02	
Lumber inventory	15,496.82	
		46,076.63
Fixed & other assets:		
Machinery & equipment	21,856.60	
Leasehold improvement	2,400.00	
Unamortized R & D costs	397.41	
Accumulated depreciation	(11,453.75)	
		13,200.26
Personal assets:		
Land holdings	80,000.00	
Stock	8,000.00	
		88,000.00
Total assets		147,276.89
	Liabilities & net worth	
Current liabilities:		
Taxes payable	2,391.55	
Jim Wilson	1,271.55	
Lumber inventory note	12,006.00	
		15,669.10
Long term liabilities		
Foxworth Bank	50,930.68	50,930.68
Total liabilities		66,599.78
Ralph Goodman		80,677.11
Total liabilities & net worth		147,276.89

DEVELOPING MARKETING STRATEGIES

Developing Marketing Strategies

3

O nce a firm has established its strategic objectives, it must decide on the basic strategy to achieve these objectives. The basic decisions usually involve which products to produce and sell and where to sell them.

PRODUCT/MARKET OPTIONS

Firms generally use the four product/market options shown in Exhibit 1. They can continue to produce and market the same products and direct them to the same market segments, or they can continue to produce and market the same products, but direct them to new markets. Different products can be produced, marketed and sold in the same markets, or these different products can be sold in new markets.

Exhibit 1 also indicates that each of the four product/market options can be achieved through internal or external means. An *internal* approach means that the company will be using its own current resources (such as sales personnel or warehousing capacities), or will be adding to them within the company (employing additional salespeople, constructing a new warehouse). When another company becomes involved, an *external* approach is used; the company is going beyond itself for the required resources. Some external options include acquiring or merging with another company, licensing joint ventures, or using marketing consultants, advertising agencies, new product development companies, etc.

Availability of resources and present management expertise are probably the two major factors which determine whether an internal or external option will be used. If a company has additional resource capacities available and believes that it has the management expertise to produce and market the product, then it is more likely to use an internal option for implementing

EXHIBIT 1   Product/market combinations to achieve strategic objectives

Markets

	Same	Different
Same	Internal or External	Internal or External
Different	Internal or External	Internal or External

Products

EXHIBIT 2   The risk/profitability grid

Level of Risk

	Low	High
High		
Low		

Level of Profitability

SOURCE: Based on H. I. Ansoff, *Corporate Strategy*, McGraw-Hill, New York, 1965.

whatever product/market approach it has selected. On the other hand, if resource capacities are strained and management lacks the necessary skills, it is more likely to pursue an external option.

The same product/same market approach is more likely than the other three combinations to be used with an internal approach. This is because the company's management is operating with the same product and market; it has the required knowledge and expertise and will be using the *same type* of resources, although resource capacity inadequacies may require increasing the *level* of resources used. The different product/different market option is the most likely to be implemented by external means. That new products and new markets are involved strongly suggests that management is unlikely to have the skills and training necessary, that different types of resources will be needed, and that additional levels of resources will probably be required because of the need to develop new products and research new markets.

RISK/PROFITABILITY CONSIDERATION

In addition to the internal/external factor, it is important to assess the risk of various product/market combinations. The least risk appears to exist with the same product/same market option because management is already familiar with the products, markets, and types of resources required. The different product/different market approach is probably the riskiest because:

1. management will probably be unfamiliar with the new product;
2. management will probably be unfamiliar with the new market;

3. new unfamiliar resources may be required;

4. management may not be able to exert as much control as it would like over any outside companies if external means are used.

As management considers which product/market combination to employ, it needs to identify the level of risk involved; at the same time, it must assess expected profits. Exhibit 2 shows a risk/profitability grid. A high profit/low risk situation is the most desirable possibility; a low profit/high risk situation is the least desirable and probably not a viable alternative. The low profit/low risk and high profit/high risk options may be desirable situations.

The risk and profitability dimensions can be considered jointly by using *expected values.* To calculate an expected value, multiply a projected profit by the probability that the profit will be achieved. The higher this probability, the lower the level of assumed risk; the lower this probability, the higher the level of assumed risk. Exhibit 3 shows some calculations of expected values for the four product/market combinations for a hypothetical company. In this example, the same product/different market option would be the best because its expected value of $2.1 million is the highest.

Same Product/Same Market. Encouraging greater use of the product by the existing market is one way to employ this product/market combination. This objective can be accomplished by getting purchasers to increase the average size of their purchase and/or encouraging them to increase the frequency of their usage. Devising new uses for the products is another possibility. For example, Arm & Hammer baking soda is advertised as an odor preventive in refrigerators, a bathwater freshener, and a kitty litter additive, as well as a baking ingredient. Attracting customers from competitors can also be tried through such means as lower prices, increased advertising, etc. Timex attracted competitors' customers by offering low-priced watches in such nontraditional outlets as drug stores and supermarkets.

Same Product/Different Market. The same product/different market strategy has been successfully used by a number of companies seeking to reach new market segments. Some examples include: selling Jello to the weight-conscious market segment; selling electronic calculators to the mass market, not just to students and employees in engineering and scientific occupa-

EXHIBIT 3 Calculation of expected values for the four product/market combinations

Product/Market Combination	Projected Profit	Probability of Achieving Projected Profit	Expected Value
Same product/same market	$2 million	.8	$1.6 million
Same product/different market	$3 million	.7	$2.1 million
Different product/same market	$2 million	.6	$1.2 million
Different product/different market	$4 million	.4	$1.6 million

tions; selling bicycles to adults, not only to children; selling Gerber baby food to adults; marketing Geritol to younger people; and expanding Pepsi and Coke operations to international markets.

Different Product/Same Market. Some products in this strategy for achieving objectives may be radically different from those already produced and marketed; nevertheless, they will be directed to the same market. For example, a food processor may add a line of canned fruits to its present line of canned vegetables, or an insurance company may add disability income protection insurance to its already existing lines of whole life and term insurance.

At the other end of the spectrum, a company may choose to slightly modify an existing product: cereal might be improved by adding fruit to it. A product can be made smaller or larger: refrigerators, washers and dryers have been downsized to fit in apartments. The Bissell Company added colors to its line of sweepers, which helped reverse a downward sales trend.

Different Product/Different Market. As indicated earlier, firms preferring to use the different product/different market strategy are usually obliged, to reduce risk, to use other companies. Companies that do so over an extended period of time tend to acquire a number of companies that produce and market a wide variety of products. Such firms are called *conglomerates.* Textron is a good example of a conglomerate, with various divisions selling automatic nailing machines for shoe repairing, helicopters, staplers, chain saws, watch bands, aerospace electronic systems, and livestock feed.

MAKING MARKETING STRATEGIES MORE EFFECTIVE

Here are several things a company seeking to develop marketing strategies should consider:

- ☐ Assess developments in the market.
- ☐ Assess developments in competitive firms.
- ☐ Assess developments in the economy, society, technology, and government.
- ☐ Take a broad view of the company's mission; ask, "What is our business and what businesses should we be in?" This orientation allows a company to be receptive to a wider range of potentially profitable opportunities and to better understand what present and future competitors may do.
- ☐ To the extent possible, use existing resources to reduce risk. John Deere, for example, uses similar hydraulics, transmissions, and engines in its farm equipment and construction machines.
- ☐ Avoid head-on competition with well-entrenched brands.

☐ Use product positioning to avoid competing directly with entrenched brands. Product positioning involves (1) determining what attributes of products are considered important by the market; (2) measuring the extent to which current products are perceived as having these important attributes; and (3) if current products are not favorably perceived, developing and marketing a product that *is* viewed favorably by the market on these important aspects.

☐ Use brand extension to reduce the probability that a new product will fail; put the brand name of currently successful products on a new product. For example, Irish Spring, the brand name for a successful new bar soap, was placed on a new deodorant.

SUMMARY

Marketing strategies involve decisions about which products will be marketed to which target markets. Important factors you should consider when developing initial marketing strategies include management expertise and skills, types and quantities of resources required, the level of risk involved, and projected profitabilities. No matter which product/market combination you select, the resultant marketing strategy must be implemented. Implementing marketing strategies, and the various elements in the marketing mix, are the focus of the next chapter.

QUESTIONS

1. What are the four product/market options which companies can use as a basic strategy?
2. Indicate the two major factors which determine whether an internal or external approach will be used in selecting a product/market option.
3. Which product/market option is most likely to be implemented through internal means?
4. Which product/market option appears to carry the least amount of risk?
5. Explain how expected values are calculated. How are they used to determine which product/market combination is best?
6. Indicate the various ways in which the same product/same market strategy can be accomplished.

SUGGESTED READINGS

Abell, D.F., and J.S. Hammond. *Strategic Market Planning,* Englewood Cliffs, N.J.: Prentice-Hall, Inc., 1979.

Ansoff, H.I. *Corporate Strategy.* New York: McGraw-Hill, 1965.

Bloom, P.N., and P. Kotler. "Strategies For High Market Share Companies." *Harvard Business Review,* November-December, 1975, pp. 63–72.

Cravens, D.W. *Strategic Marketing.* Homewood, Ill.: Richard D. Irwin, Inc., 1982.

Cohen, K.J., and R.M. Cyert. "Strategy: Formulation, Implementation and Monitoring." *Journal of Business,* July, 1973, pp. 349–367.

Constantin, J.A., Evans, R.E., and M.L. Morris. *Marketing Strategy and Management.* Dallas: Business Publications, Inc., 1976.

Hamermesh, R.G., M.J. Anderson Jr., and J.E. Harris. "Strategies For Low Market Share Businesses." *Harvard Business Review,* May-June, 1978, pp. 98–104.

Jain, S.C. *Marketing Planning and Strategy.* Cincinnati: South-Western Publishing Co., 1981.

Lorange, P., and R.F. Vancil. *Strategic Planning Systems.* Englewood Cliffs, N.J.: Prentice-Hall Inc., 1977.

Neidell, L.A. *Strategic Marketing Management.* Tulsa, Okla.: PennWell Books, 1983.

Steiner, G.A. *Strategic Planning.* New York: The Free Press, 1979.

Vancil, R.F. "Strategy Formulation In Complex Organizations." *Sloan Management Review,* Winter, 1976, pp. 1–6.

Weber, J.A. "Market Structure Profile Analysis and Strategic Growth Opportunities." *California Management Review,* Volume XX, No. 1, pp. 34–46.

Wilson, I.H., W.R. George, and P.J. Solomon. "Strategic Planning for Marketers." *Journal of Marketing,* April, 1977, pp. 12–20.

Southland Corporation: 7-Eleven Stores

"What you want when you want it"
"Slurp your way to happiness"
"Get more milk for your moo-lah"
"Oh, thank heaven for 7-Eleven"

Even though such messages might seem corny to some, they have served their purpose: to create a good feeling in the millions of hurried Americans who find the neighborhood 7-Eleven store to be their answer to convenient shopping. The 7-Eleven store concept is one of the great retailing stories in history. From an icehouse in 1927, this Dallas-based company has blossomed into the world's largest convenience store chain, with over 7,000 7-Eleven stores throughout the U.S., Canada, and five other countries. What makes Southland's success even more amazing is that the yearly sales of nearly $5 billion come from customers who spend only $2.08 a trip.

HISTORY

The Southland Corporation got its start in 1927 when Claude S. Dawley bought eight ice manufacturing plants and twenty-one retail ice stores and incorporated them into The Southland Ice Company. One of the original board members and investors in the new company was twenty-six-year old Joe C. Thompson, Jr., a recent business administration graduate from the University of Texas. "Jodie" had grown up working in some of the Dallas ice plants that were purchased by Mr. Dawley, and had acquired a thorough knowledge of the ice business. The hardworking and innovative Thompson was soon named Secretary-Treasurer, and, in 1931, at only thirty years of age, was promoted to president of the company.

This case was prepared by Stephen W. McDaniel, Assistant Professor of Marketing, Texas A&M University, as a basis for class discussion rather than to illustrate either effective or ineffective marketing management.

EXHIBIT 1   7-Eleven, the sign of convenience

SOURCE: Southland Corporation Annual Report.

Selling other products than ice was the idea of Uncle Johnny Green, one of Southland's dock managers. Mr. Green kept his ice store open in the summer sixteen hours every day, seven days a week, to dispense the block ice that was essential for home refrigeration. Many of his customers hinted or asked that he provide other items besides ice, particularly at night and on Sundays. In the summer of 1927, after a brief but successful trial in his own store, Green persuaded Jodie Thompson to finance an inventory of milk, bread, eggs, cigarettes, and some canned goods to be stocked on the ice dock. The groceries sold and the next spring, the fifty-five-year old dock manager strolled into Thompson's office and plopped down $1,000 in cash, Southland's share of the grocery proceeds. At that moment, the convenience store was born.

After Thompson became president of the company, he stocked all of his ice docks with groceries and renamed the stores "Tote'm Ice Stores," to denote that people toted away their purchases. Thompson acquired genuine Indian totem poles to place in front of each store. Soon totem poles began to spring up at ice docks other than Southland's, giving more impetus to this new concept in retailing, but taking away from Southland's uniqueness. As a result, the company decided to make a change in its name and promotional appeal. In 1946 a Dallas advertising agency suggested that the company keep all of its stores open from 7 A.M. to 11 P.M., seven days a week, and then rename them "7-11" stores.

After Mr. Thompson headed a group of investors and bought out the company, he began grooming his two sons, John and Jere, to take over the business. When they were teenagers he put them to work in the stores and hired them again after they graduated from the University of Texas. As they rose in the company, John and Jere were instrumental in directing the expansion of 7-Eleven stores in Texas, Florida, and other Sun Belt states in the 1950s and 1960s. During this time, a revolution of sorts was taking place in America. Urban dwellers were fleeing to the suburbs and becoming commuters; soon America was in a hurry, and retailing opportunities arose to meet this growing market demand for convenience. This convenience store concept has an advantage over supermarkets in that the supermarket might be several miles from the customer's home and would require him or her to wait in line to buy only a couple of items. It also has an advantage over mom-and-pop grocery stores that do not offer long hours and diverse merchandise.

In the late 1950s, the company decided to try opening stores outside of the Sun Belt. There was some reservation about this move, since the popular 7-Eleven lines like cold beer and ice might not sell in colder northern climates. Jodie Thompson decided to open a string of experimental stores in the Washington, D.C. area in 1957. That winter, a blizzard paralyzed the city, and those who could not drive to supermarkets trudged in droves to the nearby 7-Elevens. In the words of a member of the board:

> After that snowstorm hit the Washington area, we sold the stores out to the walls. The managers were so busy most of them slept in the stores for several days. People in Washington discovered 7-Eleven because we were there when they needed us. This really proved our little convenience store could make it in a cold climate and, in my opinion, it was the making of the company.[1]

Jodie Thompson died in 1961. John and Jere, currently Chairman and President, took over and have led an aggressive expansion program. In what may have been the most rapid build-up of individual retail stores in American history, the number of 7-Elevens soared from 1,519 at the beginning of 1965 to 3,537 at the end of 1969. During the 1970s, the company achieved a net increase of 200-400 stores each year. By 1981, Southland had over 7,000 7-Eleven stores in six countries, including 6,680 in forty-two states of the U.S. Two-thirds of all 7-Eleven stores are located in ten states, as shown in Exhibit 2.

COMPANY OPERATIONS

Southland Corporation's business activities are divided into three operating segments: the Stores Group, the Dairies Group, and the Special Operations Group. All 7-Eleven stores are controlled by *the Stores Group,* which is under the direction of forty-three-year old S.R. Dole. As Senior Vice President, Stores Group, Dole oversees not only the 6,680 U.S. 7-Eleven stores, but also

---

[1]Liles, Allen, *Oh Thank Heaven! The Story of the Southland Corporation,* The Southland Corporation, 1977, p. 114.

EXHIBIT 2   Major locations of 7-Eleven stores

State	# of 7-Elevens
1. California	1,049
2. Texas	922
3. Florida	638
4. Virginia	616
5. Colorado	249
6. Maryland	244
7. Washington (state)	224
8. Illinois	195
9. New Jersey	192
10. Pennsylvania	181

215 7-Eleven stores in Canada, 16 7-Eleven stores in England, 100 Gristede's and Charles & Company food stores and sandwich shops in metropolitan New York, and 389 Southland McColl confectionery, tobacco, and news stores in England and Scotland. Southland also has an equity interest in 10 Super Siete stores in Mexico and 32 Näröppet stores in Sweden, seven of which operate under the 7-Eleven name. An additional 377 7-Eleven stores are operated by area licensees, or their franchisees, in the U.S., 1,015 in Japan, 29 in Australia, 28 in Taiwan, and 13 in Canada.

The Dairies Group is headed by fifty-four-year old Vice President C.O. Beshears. As one of the nation's largest processors of dairy products, the Dairies Group processes and distributes milk, ice cream, and related products through twenty-six processing plants and seventy-eight distribution centers in the U.S.

The Special Operations Group consists of Southland's four regional distribution food centers, as well as four subsidiary businesses. The largest of these is the recently acquired Chief Auto Parts, a chain of 216 retail automobile supply stores in California, Texas, Nevada, and Arizona. Reddy Ice is Southland's oldest division, producing and selling ice in nine states; it has recently added "Reddy Wood," bundles of firewood for sale in some states. Tidel Systems manufactures money handling devices such as the new "Timed Access Cash Controller," a microcomputer-based security and dispensing unit used in 7-Elevens and sold to other cash-oriented retailers. The other facet of the Special Operations Group is the Chemical Division, which produces a variety of chemicals for sale to outside customers, as well as for use in Southland's operations. Such items as food flavorings, preservatives, and emulsifiers are sold to domestic and international customers, while dairy product flavorings, cleansers, "Slurpee" flavor concentrates, and many others are supplied to the 7-Eleven stores.

Appendix A presents the financial summaries of each operating group. Appendix B and C contain the Statement of Earnings and Balance Sheet for Southland Corporation.

EXHIBIT 3   The 7-Eleven store

SOURCE: Southland Corporation Annual Report.

THE 7-ELEVEN STORE

Generally, all 7-Eleven stores are open every day of the year and are in neighborhood areas, on main thoroughfares, in shopping centers, or in other accessible sites with plenty of parking. Approximately 95 percent of the 7-Elevens now stay open longer than the traditional 7 A.M. to 11 P.M., with 87 percent now operating twenty-four hours a day.

In Southland's early days, the 7-Eleven store contained 1,200 to 1,800 square feet. Today there are three different sized 7-Elevens—the smallest has 2000 square feet (50 feet × 40 feet) and the largest has 2450 square feet (70 feet × 35 feet). The most common size is 2400 square feet (60 feet × 40 feet). Southland has developed a standardized layout for all stores. The layout for the 60 feet × 40 feet store is shown in Exhibit 4; the other stores have similar layouts.

The company believes in maintaining a modern, neat appearance of each store, and this involves continual remodeling of each store. While building a new store costs about $300,000, remodels cost anywhere from less than $10,000 to $50,000. The company has three different kinds of remodels: (1) the *mini,* a cosmetic remodel done on two- to five-year old units for less than $10,000; (2) the *midi,* a more comprehensive job done on stores built in the early- to mid-'70s for $10,000 to $25,000; and (3) the *maxi,* consisting of ma-

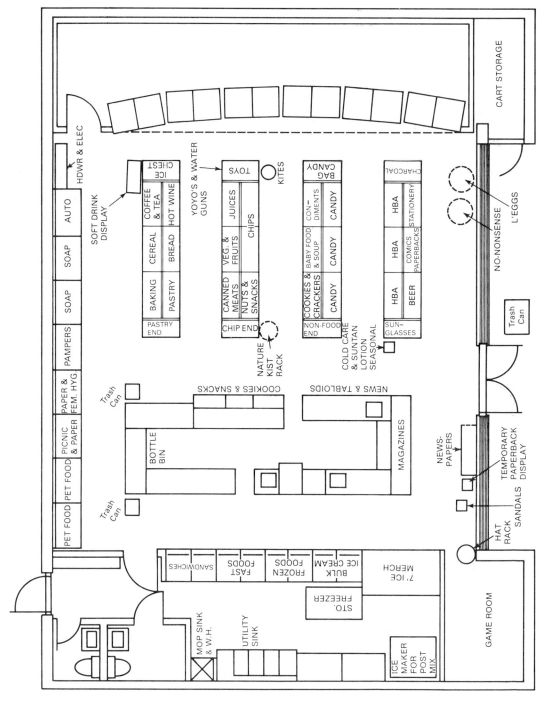

EXHIBIT 4 60' × 40' national store layout—existing stores, January 1981

EXHIBIT 5   7-Eleven's store growth (1976–1980)

	1980	1979	1978	1977	1976
Stores in operation at year-end	6,980	6,805	6,599	6,357	5,939
Stores opened	400	666	550	658	512
Stores closed	225	460	313	254	152
Net openings	175	206	237	404	360
Capital expenditures (Stores and SDC's)	$189,550,000	$223,000,000	$110,500,000	$75,300,000	$80,800,000

SOURCE: Reprinted by permission from Chain Store Age Executive © (November 1980) Copyright Lebhar-Friedman, Inc., 425 Park Ave., New York, NY 10022.

jor work on the oldest stores, such as some in Texas and Florida, that can cost as much as $50,000. The number of necessary remodels has been increasing each year; in 1980, approximately 1,100 were carried out.

Top management also wants to make sure the stores are profitable. New stores are expected to show a profit after six months; a laggard store is given up to a year to straighten things out, or it is closed. As Chairman John Thompson puts it, "We would rather close then and take our licks." All 7-Eleven stores are continually monitored by computer. Southland executives punch the store number into the computer terminal on their desks and the store's current sales and earnings, and how close it is to budget are flashed on a screen. Exhibit 5 provides data on store closings, openings, and capital expenditures on building new stores and modernizing existing stores between 1976 and 1980.

Product Mix

7-Eleven stores have come a long way from the bread, milk, and eggs product mix of the early days. Now, the average 7-Eleven store carries approximately 3,200 items; over 25 percent of those are 7-Eleven's private brands. Although the company does not record sales on the basis of product categories, percentage of store sales based on the total dollar volume of store purchases, is shown in Exhibit 6.

Generally speaking, Southland goes for the high margin, fast turnover product, preferring to carry only one brand of a product, or at least as few brands as possible. As one Southland executive states, "There is no room to store a lot of different brands of the same product. Our customers don't have time to make choices anyway."[2] 7-Elevens try to maintain at least a 25 percent profit margin on each item it sells (compared to a 20-22 percent margin for supermarkets), with many items yielding a much greater margin than that. (Exhibit 7 provides a summary of product category sales and gross margins for the entire convenience store industry.) The only exception to this high-margin rule has been gasoline, which yields the lowest profit margin, but has now become the number one selling item for 7-Eleven, as well as the

[2]Kierman, Michael, "Conveniently, 7-Eleven Sprawls Along with Suburbs," *The Washington Star,* November 26, 1978, p. F–12.

EXHIBIT 6 7-Eleven store sales (by principal product category)

Product categories	Years Ending December 31				
	1976	*1977*	*1978*	*1979*	*1980*
Gasoline	6.8%	9.8%	13.4%	17.2%	23.0%
Groceries	14.6	14.0	13.4	12.6	12.4
Tobacco products	14.7	14.2	12.9	12.9	12.3
Beer/wine	14.4	13.7	12.9	12.4	11.7
Soft drinks	10.7	11.0	10.9	10.3	10.1
Non-foods	10.2	9.9	9.4	8.7	8.0
Dairy products	9.6	9.3	8.9	8.4	6.7
Other food items	4.7	4.7	5.5	6.2	5.6
Candy	5.4	5.0	4.7	4.3	4.0
Baked goods	5.3	5.0	4.6	3.8	3.4
Health/Beauty aids	3.6	3.4	3.4	3.2	2.8
Total	100.0%	100.0%	100.0%	100.0%	100.0%

SOURCE: 10-K Report.

entire convenience store industry. As a result of the increase in the number of customers wanting self-service gasoline and a decrease in gasoline brand loyalty, 7-Eleven began emphasizing this in the mid-1970s. By 1981, 7-Eleven offered self-serve gasoline at 2,246 of its stores. Even though the 5 percent gross margin is well below that of in-store products, sheer volume has made gasoline a profitable product. There are other plusses, too: once the pumps are installed, the customer pumps his own gasoline and pays the cash register attendant as with any other sale, so little extra effort is involved. Also, a 7-Eleven study has shown that 30 percent of the people who buy gasoline also buy something else inside.

The desire to provide what customers want and, at the same time, maintain as high a profit margin per item as possible, has led to continuous changes in the 7-Eleven product mix. A 7-Eleven store may sell many non-food items such as shotgun shells, school supplies, beach and picnic supplies, Christmas trees, television tubes, cancer insurance and even services like TV rentals, floor waxing and polishing machine rentals, and money order sales. Today the biggest non-food sellers are products like cigarettes, disposable diapers, and *Playboy* magazines (of which 7-Elevens sell far more than any other retailer). Recently the big push has been for the "Hot-to-go" fast foods such as pies, hamburgers, hot dogs, sandwiches, burritos and pizzas, all of which can be heated in the store's microwave oven. In 1980, 7-Elevens added "Hot-to-go breakfast" as well, featuring such items as the "Egg Hamlet" and the "Sausage and Egg with Cheese". Over the past two years, new post-mix soda fountains have been installed in all 7-Eleven stores, giving each store the capability of serving a complete fast-food meal. The success of these fast food items has made 7-Eleven the third leading fast food retailer in the U.S.

EXHIBIT 7 Anatomy of industry sales and profits—1980

	Sales			Gross Margin			
Category	(000$)	Rank	% of Total	Average %	(000$)	Rank	% of Total
Bread & pastry	600,000	7	4.8	27.4	164,400	7	4.3
Cookies & crackers	195,000		1.6	30.4	59,280		1.6
Chips & snack foods	395,000	10	3.2	31.9	126,005		3.3
Dairy (incl. cheese & eggs)	1,450,000	2	11.7	23.4	339,300	5	9.0
Ice cream	310,000		2.5	33.6	104,160		2.8
Beer	1,425,000	3	11.5	28.9	411,825	3	10.9
Wine	110,000		0.9	35.1	38,610		1.0
Liquor	15,000		0.1	20.0	3,000		0.1
Soft drinks	1,250,000	5	10.1	32.0	400,000	4	10.6
Chilled juices	60,000		0.5	38.5	23,100		0.6
Frozen, fountain bev.	95,000		0.8	39.9	37,905		1.0
Hot beverages	55,000		0.4	47.4	26,070		0.7
Fresh & frozen meat	60,000		0.5	33.4	20,040		0.5
Deli	395,000	10	3.2	33.3	131,535	9	3.5
Hot sandwiches	300,000		2.4	31.9	95,700		2.5
Other fast foods	175,000		1.4	41.6	72,800		1.9
Produce	80,000		0.6	41.7	33,360		0.9
Grocery	1,375,000	4	11.1	32.1	441,375	2	11.7
Frozen foods (excl. meat)	210,000		1.7	41.7	87,570		2.3
Tobacco	1,790,000	1	14.4	27.2	486,880	1	12.9
Candy & gum	640,000	6	5.2	34.4	220,160	6	5.8
Books, magazines, papers	520,000	8	4.2	22.3	115,960		3.0
Health & beauty aids	455,000	9	3.7	32.3	146,965	8	3.9
Ice	100,000		0.8	54.6	54,600		1.4
General merchandise	300,000		2.4	42.4	127,200	10	3.4
Miscellaneous	40,000		0.3	40.4	16,160		0.4
Total in-store sales	**12,400,000**		**100.0**	**30.5**	**3,783,960**		**100.0**
+ Gasoline	5,900.00			5.0	295,000		
Total sales	**18,300,000**			**22.3**	**4,078,960**		

SOURCE: *Progressive Grocer,* April 1981.

Pricing

7-Eleven stores sell convenience. As a result, prices tend to be higher than prices at the supermarket since people are willing to pay a little more for convenience. Exhibit 8 shows the results of a price comparison study done in a southwestern city over a two-day period during September, 1981. A random sample of products in nine product categories was selected and price comparisons were made between a 7-Eleven store, a Skaggs Alpha Beta store, and a Kroger store; 7-Eleven is higher for virtually every product. In this one study, the only exception was milk, which the company tries to price competitively with supermarkets.

Regarding 7-Eleven's high prices in the recent era of inflation, one Wall Street analyst observes:

> It is perplexing to us why Southland's revenue growth has accelerated when rising prices have stretched the consumer's budget to a considerable extent. Perhaps it is time rather than money which is the precious commodity to most Americans at present.[3]

A New York analyst offers the following:

> The appeal of convenience stores has nothing to do with price. It has to do with people's lifestyles and their constant need for fill-ins. The more tightly the pocketbook is pinched, the less frequently the housewife shops at her supermarket, and the more need she has for last minute fill-ins.[4]

THE 7-ELEVEN CUSTOMER

Southland Corporation does extensive research on the type of people who shop at a 7-Eleven. Here are some of the findings:

- ☐ Over 70 percent of customers are male
- ☐ Over 50 percent are in the 25 to 54 age group
- ☐ Over 80 percent are in the 18 to 49 age group
- ☐ 22 percent shop between 11 P.M. and 7 A.M.
- ☐ Over 80 percent live or work less than one mile from the store
- ☐ Customers average 4.4 trips per week
- ☐ 35 percent of customer visits are on weekends
- ☐ The average purchase is two or three items (including one non-planned)
- ☐ The average purchase amount is $2.08
- ☐ Over half the goods are consumed within 30 minutes of purchase
- ☐ The average customer spends less than four minutes in the store (as compared to 26 minutes in a supermarket)

DISTRIBUTION

As a result of the close relationship between the Dairies Group and the Stores Group, 7-Eleven stores have a definite advantage over most other convenience store chains. Presently, Southland's dairies serve 5,209 of the 7-Eleven stores, supplying 60 percent of the dairy products sold by all the stores.

---

[3]Kierman, Michael, "7-Eleven Creates a Mood of Convenience at a Price," *The Washington Star,* November 27, 1978, p. A–10.

[4]Ibid.

EXHIBIT 8   Price comparisons of a sample of products

	7-Eleven	Skaggs	Kroger
Groceries			
Ragu Spaghetti Sauce w/meat 15.5 oz.	$1.29	$ .99	$ .91
Starkist Tuna (solid white) 7 oz.	2.19	1.49	1.59
Ranch Style Pinto Beans 15 oz.	.59	.45	.43
Del Monte Sweet Peas 17 oz.	.75	.49	.49
Ocean Spray Jellied Cranbry Sauce 16 oz.	.89	.57	.57
Maxwell House Instant Coffee 6 oz.	4.25	2.95	2.93
Nabisco Oreo cookies 15 oz.	1.99	1.79	1.47
Log Cabin Syrup 12 oz.	1.55	1.19	1.13
Kellogg's Corn Flakes 12 oz.	1.35	.91	.83
Oscar Meyer Bologna 8 oz.	1.39	1.23	1.19
Beer/Wine			
Cella Bianco 750 ml	3.59 (cold)	3.09	2.99
Mateus Rose 750 ml	4.29 (cold)	3.39	3.69
Lite 12 oz., 6 pack	2.75	2.39	2.49
Schlitz 12 oz., 6 pack	2.65	2.39	2.45
Budweiser 12 oz., 6 pack	2.65	2.29	1.89
Candy			
M&M's 7.5 oz.	1.59	1.29	1.25
Tootsie Roll 38 g	.30	.23	.23
Certs	.35	.23	.25
Health/Beauty Aids			
Contac 10 capsules	2.19	1.79	1.79
Pepto Bismol 8 oz.	3.05	2.29	1.89
Flex shampoo 16 oz.	3.39	1.79	1.69
Dry Idea Anti-Persp. 1.5 oz.	2.85	1.89	1.79
Bayer Aspirin 50 tablets	1.89	1.19	1.19
Kleenex 125	.89	.79	.62
Non-Foods			
Tide 49 oz.	2.39	2.05	1.84
Clorox 64 oz.	1.05	.73	.73
SOS 10 pads	.99	.69	.59
Pampers 12 toddler	2.49	2.09	2.19
Hefty Trash Bags 10	2.25	1.79	1.59
Purina Dog Chow 5 lbs.	2.69	2.09	2.13
Kodak Film 35mm-Color Print-36	4.69	2.89	3.29
Baked Goods			
Mrs. Baird's Honey Bun	.49	.41 (Hostess)	.41 (Hostess)
Dolly Madison Variety Donuts 12	1.59	1.39 (Hostess)	1.39 (Hostess)
Mrs. Baird's Xtra Thin White 24 oz.	.99	.89	.89

EXHIBIT 8   (continued)

	7-Eleven	Skaggs	Kroger
Beverage/Soft Drinks			
6 pack, 12 oz. cans	2.39	2.29	2.25
6 pack, 16 oz. non-returnable	2.49	2.39	2.45
2 liter bottle	1.69	1.53	1.55
Hawaiian Punch-Red 46 oz.	1.35	.85	.85
Dairy Products			
Oak Farms Milk ½ gallon	1.33	1.23 (Pure)	1.45 (Borden's)
Oak Farm Half & Half Cream pint	.79	.69 (Quality ✔)	.83 (Borden's)
Minute Maid OJ (carton) 32 oz.	1.19	.99	.89
Farm Field Lowfat Yogurt	.45	.39 (Swss Styl)	.39 (Yubi)
Tobacco Products			
Copenhagen Snuff 1.2 oz.	1.05	.59	.75
Levi Garrett Chwng Tobacco large	.99	.75	.88
Single Pack Cigarettes	.95	.80	.75

Another source of competitive advantage over other convenience stores is the network of the four regional distribution centers located in Florida, Illinois, Texas, and Virginia. These four Food Centers presently supply 4,642 stores in thirty-three states and the District of Columbia with approximately half of their merchandise (other than gasoline). Because of their size, convenience stores depend upon frequent deliveries of small amounts of merchandise to maintain high in-stock positions. For each of the past seven years, the distribution centers have achieved a 98 percent order fill rate. Southland has done this by developing a highly sophisticated merchandise distribution system that enables each store to order pre-priced merchandise in less than case lots. This enables the store to improve inventory turnover, stock fresh merchandise, and realize high levels of sales and profits from the available selling space. In addition, this provides flexibility for the stores to change the product mix in response to customer preferences and seasonal demands.

The order process, which is almost completely controlled by computer, begins at each store. First, a computer-generated order list is completed by the store personnel. The lists, customized for each store's special merchandise needs, are then gathered at the 7-Eleven district offices and transmitted through terminals to the computer center in Dallas. The information is then relayed to the appropriate distribution center, where orders are filled and loaded by delivery sequence into custom-built trucks that have separate compartments for dry, chilled, and frozen merchandise. In addition, the computer schedules and routes each vehicle to achieve maximum time and energy savings.

As for fast foods and ice products, Southland provides these for the stores whenever practical. Products not available from or not supplied by the company are purchased from various independent wholesalers, distributors, and rack jobbers. Inventory is ordered from vendor and merchandise lists which are prepared periodically by the company; this is based on the buying habits of the specific areas.

ADVERTISING

Southland Corporation is the only convenience food store chain that uses national advertising. Television, radio, and newspaper advertising is used extensively to promote fast foods and other products, particularly its most profitable products. In 1981, the company spent almost $20 million on advertising, the third largest amount of any food retailer in the U.S. The company first tried prime-time television advertising in 1978 and found it very successful. In 1980 the company ran five major campaigns, each of which coordinated national television advertising, radio spots, and newspaper advertising. In 1980 the company also began advertising on weekend cartoon shows, promoting the semifrozen carbonated drink, Slurpee.

In the past, all 7-Eleven advertising has been handled by the company's in-house Stanford Agency. In late 1981, however, the company decided it needed additional creative input, particularly with its increasing use of television advertising. It has now turned over all national advertising responsibilities to Young & Rubicam Advertising. Along with this shift, the company is planning to increase the advertising budget considerably over the next few years.

THE CONVENIENCE STORE INDUSTRY

The number of convenience stores in the U.S. has increased considerably over the past few years. As indicated in Exhibit 9, between 1973 and 1980 the number of convenience stores increased 76 percent, from 20,300 to 35,800, while the number of other types of food stores actually decreased. While sales of independent and chain food stores doubled during this period, convenience store sales almost tripled. Although some industry analysts feel that the market for convenience stores might become saturated in the next few years, Southland is not worried about that at all. The feeling of Southland's executives is that industry growth will not slow down any time soon. They believe there are several reasons for this; the major one is the trend for supermarkets to become fewer in number but larger in size. Supermarkets have gone from 7,500 square feet to 30,000 and now 50,000 square feet and have moved from the neighborhoods closer to the shopping centers. This shift has created the market served by 7-Elevens. Another reason for optimism is the fact that 80 percent of 7-Eleven customers live or work within one mile of the store; top executives interpret this as showing that, potentially, there could be a 7-Eleven store every square mile. Even though this is an extreme, they do believe it points out the tremendous room for continuous growth. As shown in Exhibit 10, Southland is by far the largest of the convenience chains, with almost nine times the sales of the nearest competitor.

EXHIBIT 9 Number of food stores and food store sales 1973–1980

| | Number of Stores | | | | Dollar Sales (Billions) | | | |
Year	Inde-pendent	Chain	Conven-ience Stores	Total	Inde-pendent	Chain	Conven-ience Stores	Total
1980	112,600	18,700	35,800	**167,100**	105.285	103.115	12.400	**220.800**
1979	116,050	18,725	34,125	**168,900**	96.025	93.375	10.000	**199.400**
1978	117,650	19,350	32,500	**169,500**	86.610	84.280	8.710	**179.600**
1977	124,890	20,930	30,000	**175,820**	79.160	76.260	7.380	**162.800**
1976	134,750	21,550	27,400	**183,700**	74.340	71.340	6.300	**151.980**
1975	143,730	23,080	25,000	**191,810**	70.300	66.750	5.480	**142.530**
1974	151,240	24,190	22,700	**198,130**	64.275	61.240	5.320	**130.835**
1973	154,235	25,025	20,300	**199,560**	55.805	52.975	4.350	**113.130**

SOURCE: *Progressive Grocer*, April 1981.

EXHIBIT 10 Sales and earnings of convenience chains

Company	Sales (000$)					Earnings (000$)				
	1980	1979	1978	% Change 80/79	79/78	1980	1979	1978	% Change 80/79	79/78
Southland	4,782,605	3,876,059	3,090,094	+23.3	+25.4	77,672	83,141	57,097	−6.6	+45.6
Munford	318,680(e)	292,367	260,032	+9.0	+12.4	NA	2,309	(1,187)	NA	NC
Circle K	533,103	438,559	363,783	+21.6	+20.6	16,825	10,678	7,876	+57.6	+35.6
National Convenience Stores	434,430	320,363	263,705	+35.6	+21.5	8,050	6,005	4,848	+34.1	+23.9
Utotem Group	280,296	247,825	221,423	+13.1	+11.9	NA	10,266	9,291	NA	+10.5
Conna Corp.	303,466	229,644	177,732	+32.1	+29.2	2,517	1,523	1,147	+65.3	+32.8
Sunshine Jr. Stores	151,929	120,072	93,553	+26.5	+28.3	1,461	2,399	1,621	−39.1	+48.0
Shop & Go	111,448	94,570	82,729	+17.8	+14.3	4,476	3,087	2,235	+45.0	+38.1
Hop-in Food Stores	55,148	42,765	31,714	+29.0	+34.8	728	716	658	+ 1.7	+ 8.7
Lil' Champ	30,447	24,956	22,727	+22.0	+ 9.6	1,173	945	766	+24.1	+23.4
Mini Mart Corp.	36,165	29,212	25,254	+23.8	+15.7	1,016	471	496	+116.0	− 5.2
*Paired totals	**6,438,741**	**5,176,200**	**4,151,291**	**+24.4**	**+24.7**	**113,918**	**108,965**	**76,744**	**+ 4.5**	**+42.0**
Grand total	**7,037,717**	**5,716,392**	**4,632,746**	**+23.1**	**+23.4**	**NA**	**121,540**	**84,848**	**NA**	**+43.2**

Note includes sales and earnings from operations other than convenience stores where applicable.
*Based on 9 companies   (e) = Estimated   NA = Not Available   NC = Not Comparable

SOURCE: Progressive Grocer, April 1981.

THE FUTURE

The Southland Corporation has come a long way in a relatively short period of time. The neighborhood 7-Eleven store is fast becoming an American tradition. However, management realizes that the company did not get where it is today by doing things the way they did them yesterday. The company is always evaluating itself, looking at its operations and deciding what it needs to do differently. Presently, S.R. Dole, Vice President, Stores Group, is involved with several strategic decisions, all of which relate to trying to maintain the growth performance of the 7-Eleven stores. The following are a few of the questions Dole is pondering:

☐ What about our store size? One of our competitors, National Convenience Stores, is building some "super stores" with 3,600 square feet. Should we go in that direction?

☐ What about our product mix? Should we expand or reduce? Should we cut out some product lines and add others? Some consumer activists are calling our "hot-to-go" items nothing but junk food, and saying that most of our products are of non-nutritional value. Should we start selling items like fresh meat, fruits and vegetables, or other nutritious items?

☐ Should we change our pricing strategy? Consumer activists and others of the general public complain about our relatively high prices on our products. Should we try to be more price-competitive with the supermarkets?

☐ Where should we try to locate our stores in the future? Should we build more neighborhood stores or more downtown stores?

☐ What about our target market? Should we broaden our scope and try to appeal to more women, or other segments?

☐ Should we make any adjustments to our store layout? Should placement of products, traffic flow, or any other elements be changed?

APPENDIX A   Southland Corporation financial summary by operating group
($,000)

Revenues:			
Stores Group	$4,307,876	$3,463,614	$2,791,035
Dairies Group	534,699	473,367	388,956
Special Operations Group	122,645	113,919	56,161
Corporate	8,864	6,968	4,801
	4,974,084	4,057,868	3,240,953
Intersegment revenues:			
Dairies Group	(175,251)	(158,622)	(135,563)
Special Operations Group	(16,228)	(23,187)	(15,296)
Consolidated revenues	$4,782,605	$3,876,059	$3,090,094
Operating profits:			
Stores Group	$ 176,441	$ 145,831	$ 141,208
Dairies Group	14,457	10,326	6,433
Special Operations Group	(2,791)	7,579	5,668
Consolidated operating profits	188,107	163,736	153,309
Interest expense	(46,337)	(40,236)	(35,129)
Corporate expense — net	(8,258)	(9,942)	(7,641)
Consolidated earnings before income taxes	$ 133,512	$ 113,558	$ 110,539
Identifiable assets (including capital leases) at December 31:			
Stores Group	$1,182,186	$1,045,898	$ 863,228
Dairies Group	116,051	112,854	100,265
Special Operations Group	95,617	108,744	80,206
Corporate	101,531	100,079	90,777
Total identifiable assets	$1,495,385	$1,367,575	$1,134,476
Capital expenditures (excluding capital leases):			
Stores Group	$ 92,112	$ 180,950	$ 110,508
Dairies Group	9,656	11,126	9,710
Special Operations Group	10,712	20,269	23,054
Corporate	2,030	10,659	9,116
	$ 114,510	$ 223,004	$ 152,388
Depreciation and amortization expense:			
Stores Group	$ 75,117	$ 60,822	$ 53,572
Dairies Group	7,474	7,060	5,737
Special Operations Group	4,488	8,571	7,961
Corporate	3,015	2,658	2,864
	$ 90,094	$ 79,111	$ 70,134

SOURCE: Annual Report.

APPENDIX B

CONSOLIDATED STATEMENTS OF EARNINGS

THE SOUTHLAND CORPORATION AND SUBSIDIARIES

	Year ended December 31		
	(Dollars in thousands except per share data)		
	1980	1979	1978
Revenues:			
Net sales	$4,758,656	$3,856,222	$3,076,532
Other income	23,949	19,837	13,562
	4,782,605	3,876,059	3,090,094
Cost of Sales and Expenses:			
Cost of goods sold, including buying and occupancy expenses	3,689,512	2,930,193	2,316,288
Selling, general, and administrative expenses	899,686	778,768	614,255
Interest expense	23,841	18,746	15,804
Imputed interest expense on capital lease obligations	22,496	21,490	19,325
Contributions to Employees' Savings and Profit Sharing Plan (Note 10)	13,558	13,304	11,714
	4,649,093	3,762,501	2,977,386
Earnings Before Income Taxes	133,512	113,558	112,708
Income Taxes (Notes 8 and 12)	55,840	46,082	55,611
Earnings Before Cumulative Effect in 1979 of accounting change for investment tax credits	77,672	67,476	57,097
Cumulative Effect of accounting change for investment tax credits (Note 12)	—	15,665	—
Net Earnings	$ 77,672	$ 83,141	$ 57,097
Earnings Per Share (Note 13):			
Earnings before cumulative effect of accounting change:			
Primary	$3.29	$3.03	$2.67
Fully diluted	$3.19	$2.93	$2.58
Net earnings:			
Primary	$3.29	$3.73	$2.67
Fully diluted	$3.19	$3.61	$2.58
Pro Forma Earnings, with accounting change in 1979 for investment tax credits applied retroactively (Note 12):	$ 77,672	$ 68,273	$ 60,357
Pro Forma Earnings Per Share (Note 13):			
Primary	$3.29	$3.07	$2.82
Fully diluted	$3.19	$2.97	$2.73

SOURCE: Annual Report.

APPENDIX C

CONSOLIDATED BALANCE SHEETS

THE SOUTHLAND CORPORATION AND SUBSIDIARIES

ASSETS	December 31 1980	December 31 (Dollars in thousands) 1979
Current Assets:		
Cash and short-term investments (Note 2)	$ 149,602	$ 79,927
Accounts and notes receivable (Note 3)	99,828	87,954
Inventories (Note 4)	213,445	200,794
Deposits and prepaid expenses (Note 8)	36,121	32,008
Investment in properties	77,900	67,500
Total Current Assets	576,896	468,183
Investments in Affiliates (Note 1)	31,777	28,847
Property, Plant, and Equipment (Note 5)	647,137	630,026
Capital Leases (Note 11)	208,170	208,770
Other Assets	31,405	31,749
	$1,495,385	$1,367,575

LIABILITIES AND SHAREHOLDERS' EQUITY

Current Liabilities:		
Accounts payable and accrued expenses (Note 6)	$ 337,129	$ 275,513
Income taxes	23,178	6,626
Long-term debt due within one year (Note 7)	4,260	4,025
Capital lease obligations due within one year (Note 11)	20,573	20,362
Total Current Liabilities	385,140	306,526
Deferred Credits (Note 8)	18,748	10,294
Long-Term Debt (Note 7)	312,535	326,893
Capital Lease Obligations (Note 11)	224,753	226,257
Commitments for Operating Leases (Note 11)		
Shareholders' Equity (Notes 7 and 9):		
Common stock, $.01 par value, authorized 40,000,000 shares, issued and outstanding 23,643,903 and 22,935,504 shares	236	229
Additional capital	334,311	319,067
Retained earnings	219,662	178,309
	554,209	497,605
	$1,495,385	$1,367,575

SOURCE: Annual Report.

Ozark Saints Hospital (A)

Edward Lofton, hospital administrator of Ozark Saints Hospital, has been a long time proponent of systematic long-range planning and of keeping ahead of the competition. Fifteen years ago he retained the services of a well-known Washington, D.C. health care management consulting firm to develop long-range plans for the hospital. Since that time new pressures and problems have arisen in the health care industry and Mr. Lofton feels that there is now a need to pay greater attention to the marketing aspects of the operation. He feels strongly that a marketing orientation will ensure the successful utilization of expanded facilities and aid other developmental efforts. He has, therefore been taking steps to accomplish more of a marketing orientation for Ozark Saints Hospital.

BACKGROUND

The Hospital

Ozark Saints Hospital is located in a medium-sized city in the southwest region of the United States. In addition to the metropolitan area of the city in which the hospital is located, the hospital's services are included in eight predominantly rural counties. Ozark Saints Hospital is one of the two major hospitals located in the city. The second hospital, Spencer Medical Center, is much larger than Ozark Saints and services the same health care market

The research and written case were presented at the Case Research Symposium (Atlanta, November, 1981) and were evaluated by the Case Research Association's Editorial Board. This case was prepared by C.P. Rao and G.E. Kiser of the University of Arkansas and Stephen W. McDaniel of Texas A&M University as a basis for class discussion.

EXHIBIT 1 Comparative admission data patient origins by county 1967–1977 Ozark Saints Hospital

County	1967	1977
A*	8.0	10.7
B	2.6	5.7
C	4.0	7.2
D	0.4	2.0
E	1.6	2.6
F**	61.4	54.4
G*	6.2	5.5
H*	9.5	5.1
Other Counties	5.8	5.8
Out of State	0.5	1.0
TOTALS	100.0%	100.0%

**The city in which the Ozark Saints Hospital and the Spencer Medical Center are located is in County F.
As noted by the (*) above, the four counties immediately surrounding the city comprise the Regional planning area. These are considered the hospital's primary service area.

area. Both Ozark Saints Hospital (OSH) and Spencer Medical Center (SMC) are actively pursuing facility expansion programs and medical staff development programs. OSH management consider SMC a major competitor in the health care market area.

Based on OSH records, over 93 percent of the patients at the hospital listed as their place of residence one of the eight counties in close proximity to the hospital. A complete breakdown of patient residences in these eight counties is shown in Exhibit 1.

Population Growth

According to population growth projections prepared by the U.S. Bureau of the Census and the Regional Planning Commission, the number of residents within the service market area of Ozark Saints Hospital will increase 35.2 percent between 1970 and 1990. This population growth rate by counties is indicated in Exhibit 2.

The factors responsible for this expected growth are an abundant supply of natural gas energy readily available and proportionately inexpensive, and a stable labor market with a good mix of balanced skills ranging from agrarian and industrially unskilled to well-trained, technologically experienced individuals. The climate is mild and has considerable attraction for those seeking Sunbelt living; several resort-type developments for adults are established or in varying stages of the development process in the area.

Market Characteristics and Health Resources

Together, Ozark Saints Hospital and Spencer Medical Center provide some 873 beds, with an additional 150 beds currently under construction at

EXHIBIT 2   Population projections by county Ozark Saints Hospital service area constituency 1977

County	1970*	1975	1980	1985	1990
A	25,677	30,300	33,300	36,200	39,000
B	11,301	12,000	12,750	13,550	14,400
C	16,789	17,700	18,500	19,300	20,100
D	13,297	14,000	14,900	15,850	16,950
E	8,207	9,000	9,900	10,950	12,000
F	79,239	85,300	91,200	97,000	103,600
G	32,137	35,200	38,000	40,600	42,700
H	23,370	26,300	29,400	32,300	35,200
Totals	210,015	229,800	247,950	265,750	283,950

*Actual 1970 U.S. Census

SMC. However, the five counties surrounding F County only have a total of 269 general care beds in five hospitals varying in size from 26 beds to 99 beds. An additional 22 beds are under construction in County C that will place two community hospitals in C County. Except for the hospitals in F County, presently reported average occupancy in these five hospitals is under 50 percent.

The two hospitals in G County have some 139 general care beds, of which 52 are located at the U.S. Public Health Service Institution. No hospital is reported for H County.

Other market characteristics and health resources are shown in Exhibit 3.

The Market Research Study

As a first step in developing a long-range marketing strategy for the hospital, Mr. Lofton decided that a comprehensive market research study should be carried out as soon as possible. He felt the study should examine the attitudes of local residents toward hospital facilities and services, as well as investigate the behavior of those who would make use of these facilities and services in the local area. To carry out the study, Mr. Lofton procured the services of a local marketing consulting firm. After various and extensive consultations, the marketing consultants submitted a research proposal to Mr. Lofton for his approval. The major parts of this proposal are shown in the Appendix. It includes the consulting firm's statements of the study's objectives and scope, the two questionnaires proposed for the study, and a plan of analysis. The hospital administrator now must sit down, think through the entire situation, and carefully analyze all aspects of the proposal he has just received. He realizes that the cost and time involved in conducting the research makes it imperative that all aspects of the study work to yield the best possible information for making long-term marketing decisions.

EXHIBIT 3   Selected market characteristics and market health resources—1977

Market characteristics	County A	County B	County C	County D	County E	County F
Population density per square mile	49.1	19.9	25.2	16.7	9.9	160.5
Percent urban	32.6	22.9	41.0	34.1	—	82.1
Percent rural	67.4	77.1	59.0	65.9	100.0	17.9
Percent of aged	12.7	16.1	17.0	17.5	15.0	11.2
Aged dependency ratio	23.1	29.2	31.0	32.7	27.1	19.0
Percent aged in poverty	48.2	47.8	48.4	46.4	59.5	34.8
Median per capita family income $	5,226	4,259	4,120	4,515	4,132	6,242
Percent unemployed	8.7	10.1	8.1	10.8	10.5	7.0
Market resources						
Hospitals	1	1	1	1	1	2
Beds	99	40	47	57	26	873
% Occupancy	43.6	88.3	52.0	41.2	47.3	82.9
Public Health Clinics	20	N/A	14	14	N/A	17
Ambulance Services	2	2	1	1	1	2
Professionals						
Doctors	10	1	6	8	2	164
R.N.'s	33	76	20	13	8	378
L.P.N.'s	43	54	25	20	13	334
Other*	31	35	12	16	8	138
Mental Health Services	7	7	9	9	9	11
Detox Facilities	—	—	—	—	—	1
				MH and Detox services based in City (serves regional area)		

*Includes chiropractors, dentists, optometrists, pharmacists, physical therapists.

APPENDIX

A Study Of The Demand For Medical Services Provided By Major Hospitals In The OSH Service Area

Objectives and Scope of the Study

The major purpose of the proposed research study is to delineate the "image" profile of OSH among the general public and physicians in the OSH health care market service area. Concurrently the research study will also identify related patient and physician "choice criteria" when making decisions relative to choosing a medical center in the service area. More specifically the study will be concerned with investigating the following research issues:

1. What factors are considered important to the public and to the physicians when selecting a medical center?

2. Considering the various important factors, how do the public and physicians evaluate OSH and Spencer Medical Center (SMC)? These data will enable the researchers to develop the "image" profile of not only OSH but also the other major medical center in the health care market service area.

3. Develop a comparative analysis between OSH and SMC so that OSH's strengths and weaknesses can be compared and contrasted with those pertaining to SMC.

4. Investigate the various dimensions of patient and physician decision-making processes in relation to their choice of a medical center.

5. The data will be analyzed not only for the groups of households and physicians, but also for sub-groups on the basis of demographics for households and some other appropriate basis, such as medical specialization for physicians.

MEDICAL STAFF QUESTIONNAIRE:

I. *BACKGROUND INFORMATION*

A. AGE (Please circle one)
   30–39   40–49   50–59   60 and over

B. What is your medical specialization?
   _____
   _____

C. CERTIFICATION (Please circle one)
   Board Certified   Board Eligible   Non-Certified

D. How often, on the average, do you admit patients to the hospitals indicated below?

	Spencer Medical Center	*Ozark Saints Hospital*
Several times a day	_____	_____
Several times a week	_____	_____
Infrequently	_____	_____
Other _____		
Please Specify		

II. *CHOICE CRITERIA WHEN SELECTING A HOSPITAL*

A. What is the relative importance of the following factors when you choose a hospital for your patients?

FACTORS	*Important*	*Neutral*	*Unimportant*
Bed availability	_____	_____	_____
Physicians' dining room/lounge	_____	_____	_____
Quality of emergency room	_____	_____	_____
Friendliness of staff	_____	_____	_____
Quality of nursing	_____	_____	_____
Availability of consultants	_____	_____	_____
Quality and type of equipment	_____	_____	_____
Involvement in hospital management	_____	_____	_____
Overall hospital reputation	_____	_____	_____
Patient's choice of hospital	_____	_____	_____
Adequate parking	_____	_____	_____
How well managed the hospital is	_____	_____	_____
Geograhical proximity to patient's home	_____	_____	_____
Quality of medical records	_____	_____	_____
Geographical proximity to your office	_____	_____	_____
Availability of operating room time	_____	_____	_____

B. Please rate the two area hospitals in the following areas:

	Spencer Medical Center			*Ozark Saints Hospital*		
Factors	*Superior*	*Good*	*Inadequate*	*Superior*	*Good*	*Inadequate*
Supplies available	_____	_____	_____	_____	_____	_____
Housekeeping	_____	_____	_____	_____	_____	_____
Nursing staff	_____	_____	_____	_____	_____	_____
Physical therapy	_____	_____	_____	_____	_____	_____
Radiology	_____	_____	_____	_____	_____	_____
Anesthesiology	_____	_____	_____	_____	_____	_____
Operating room facilities	_____	_____	_____	_____	_____	_____
ICU facilities	_____	_____	_____	_____	_____	_____
Emergency room	_____	_____	_____	_____	_____	_____
Medical records	_____	_____	_____	_____	_____	_____
Other _____	_____	_____	_____	_____	_____	_____
(Please specify)						

C. What, in particular, do you *dislike* most about hospital services and facilities in the service area?

_____
_____
_____
_____

   1. Does your dislike relate more to one hospital than another?
      Yes _____   No _____

   2. If yes, which hospital? _____

D. What, in particular, do you *like* most about hospital services and facilities in the service area?

_____
_____
_____

   1. Does your like relate more to one hospital than another?
      Yes _____   No _____

   2. If yes, which hospital? _____

E. Of the two hospitals in the area (Spencer Medical Center and Ozark Saints Hospital), please indicate usage for each hospital.

Hospital	Extensively	Frequently	Infrequently
Spencer Medical Center	_____	_____	_____
Ozark Saints Hospital	_____	_____	_____

F. What sources of information do you find most helpful in forming your opinion of a hospital, in general?

	Importance as a Source				
Source	None	Little	Some	Much	Extensive
Direct, personal contact	___	___	___	___	___
Patients	___	___	___	___	___
Fellow physicians	___	___	___	___	___
Professional staff meetings	___	___	___	___	___
Hospital publications	___	___	___	___	___
Salesmen	___	___	___	___	___
News media	___	___	___	___	___
Other _____	___	___	___	___	___
(Please specify)					

G. What service(s) could logically and realistically be offered on a shared basis with other hospitals? Please indicate the service in Column I (Service) and the hospital at which the service(s) would be located in the second column (Location):

Service	Location
1. _____	_____
2. _____	_____
3. _____	_____
4. _____	_____
5. _____	_____

H. Please circle the group which, in your opinion, generally plays the dominant role in determining to which hospital a patient will be admitted.

Physicians   Patients   Patient's Family   Other _____
                                                                     (Please Specify)

NOTE: Additional surveys of the medical staff will be periodically performed. Please make any comments which you believe would serve to increase the value of this survey instrument. Also list those issues which you believe are important, but not specifically addressed in this questionnaire.

_____

Signature (Optional)

CONSUMER HOSPITAL OPINION SURVEY QUESTIONNAIRE:

The purpose of this consumer survey is to get your opinions about hospitals and their services. You may take your past experience, any information you obtained from others, and your general understanding of hospitals in your area as basis for responding to the various questions below. Your household is selected as a part of a carefully developed sampling plan. Hence, your participation in this survey will greatly help us in achieving the objectives of this research study. Any information you may provide will be treated strictly confidentially, and it will not be used in any other form except as a part of a large sample. Please answer all of the following questions.

1. Did someone in your household use the services of any of the *hospitals* in the service area during the past two years?
   Yes _____   No _____

2. If you answered "yes" to Question 1 above, please indicate the name(s) of the hospital(s) utilized by a member of your household.
   _____
   _____

3. If you answered "yes" to Question 1, please indicate the *number of times* members of your household used the hospital services during the last two years. (Please check one).

   Once   Twice   Three Times   Four Times   More than four times
   _____   _____   _____   _____   _____

4. If members of your household used hospital services during the past two years, please provide the following information about the visit(s).

   Purpose of the hospitalization   Length of the hospitalization (No. of days spent)
   1. _____   _____
   2. _____   _____
   3. _____   _____
   4. _____   _____

5. On the basis of your past experience, discussions with relatives, friends, and neighbors, and your general understanding of the hospitals in the service area, please list your preference among the area hospitals. (Note: If you choose only *one*, please list under first choice).
   First Choice: _____
   Second Choice: _____

6. Please indicate your reasons for choosing.

_____
_____
_____

7. In choosing a hospital for the health care needs of your household members, how important are the advice, suggestions, and influence of the following persons? Please check one alternative for each person(s).

	Advice, Suggestion and Influence are:				
	Very Important	*Important*	*Slightly Important*	*Unimportant*	*Very Unimportant*
Other members of your household	_____	_____	_____	_____	_____
Friends and neighbors	_____	_____	_____	_____	_____
Your physician	_____	_____	_____	_____	_____
Others (Please specify)	_____	_____	_____	_____	_____

8. The following are some characteristics of hospitals in general. In choosing a hospital for health care needs of members of your household how *important* are these characteristics? (Please check one alternative for each aspect).

	Very Important	*Important*	*Not Very Important*	*Not Important At All*
Good doctors	_____	_____	_____	_____
Good nursing care	_____	_____	_____	_____
Good emergency room	_____	_____	_____	_____
Latest medical equipment	_____	_____	_____	_____
Keeps patients informed about their care	_____	_____	_____	_____
Religious affiliation	_____	_____	_____	_____
Comfortable rooms	_____	_____	_____	_____
Good food	_____	_____	_____	_____
Easy to go to	_____	_____	_____	_____
Adequate parking	_____	_____	_____	_____
Flexible visiting hours	_____	_____	_____	_____
Price of service	_____	_____	_____	_____
Good reputation	_____	_____	_____	_____
Provides rehabilitation	_____	_____	_____	_____
Teaches you to stay well	_____	_____	_____	_____
Has health education programs	_____	_____	_____	_____
Overall hospital management	_____	_____	_____	_____
Other _____ (Please specify)	_____	_____	_____	_____

9. On the following scale, please evaluate the hospitals in the area. Mention the name of two hospitals of your choice and evaluate the same hospital on the basis of the various qualities indicated. If your evaluation is very favorable, please circle 7; if your evaluation is very unfavorable, please circle 1. If your evaluation is in between, please circle one of the numbers between 2, 3, 4, 5, or 6, whichever expresses your opinion accurately.

Your First Choice Hospital							*Hospital Aspect*	*Your Second Choice Hospital*						
Name _____								Name _____						
Very Favorable			*Very Unfavorable*					*Very Favorable*			*Very Unfavorable*			
7	6	5	4	3	2	1	Good doctors	7	6	5	4	3	2	1
7	6	5	4	3	2	1	Good nursing care	7	6	5	4	3	2	1
7	6	5	4	3	2	1	Good emergency room	7	6	5	4	3	2	1
7	6	5	4	3	2	1	Latest medical equipment	7	6	5	4	3	2	1

7	6	5	4	3	2	1	Respects your privacy	7	6	5	4	3	2	1
							Keeps patients informed about their							
7	6	5	4	3	2	1	care	7	6	5	4	3	2	1
7	6	5	4	3	2	1	Religious affiliation	7	6	5	4	3	2	1
7	6	5	4	3	2	1	Comfortable rooms	7	6	5	4	3	2	1
7	6	5	4	3	2	1	Good food	7	6	5	4	3	2	1
7	6	5	4	3	2	1	Easy to go to	7	6	5	4	3	2	1
7	6	5	4	3	2	1	Adequate parking	7	6	5	4	3	2	1
7	6	5	4	3	2	1	Flexible visiting hrs.	7	6	5	4	3	2	1
7	6	5	4	3	2	1	Price of service	7	6	5	4	3	2	1
7	6	5	4	3	2	1	Good reputation	7	6	5	4	3	2	1
7	6	5	4	3	2	1	Provides rehabilitation	7	6	5	4	3	2	1
7	6	5	4	3	2	1	Teaches you to stay well	7	6	5	4	3	2	1
7	6	5	4	3	2	1	Has health education programs	7	6	5	4	3	2	1
7	6	5	4	3	2	1	Overall hospital management	7	6	5	4	3	2	1
7	6	5	4	3	2	1	Other _____	7	6	5	4	3	2	1

(Please specify)

10. As measured in driving time how close *should* all area residents be to a hospital? (Please circle one)

    5 minutes   15 minutes   30 minutes   45 minutes   over 45 minutes

11. In your opinion, should additional hospitals be built in the surrounding area?

    Yes _____   No _____

12. If you answered yes to the above question, please indicate where you think a hospital should be built.

    _____
    _____

13. Any other comments you would like to make about hospitals in the area and your household's experience with the hospitals will be greatly appreciated.

    _____
    _____
    _____
    _____
    _____

PLEASE PROVIDE THE FOLLOWING INFORMATION ABOUT YOURSELF AND YOUR HOUSEHOLD:

1. Please check *your* age group on the following:

   _____ Under 20 years   _____ 20-29 years   _____ 30-39 years

   _____ 40-49 years   _____ 50-59 years   _____ Over 60 years.

2. Please check the category that applies to the education of the *HEAD OF YOUR HOUSEHOLD:*

   _____ Grade School   _____ Some High School   _____ High School Graduate

   _____ Some College   _____ College Graduate   _____ Post Graduate Study

3. Which of the following broad categories applies to your *TOTAL FAMILY INCOME:*

   _____ Under $10,000   _____ $10,001-$12,499   _____ $12,500-$14,999

   _____ $15,000-$20,000   _____ $20,001-$24,999   _____ Over $25,000

4. Please indicate: Your Occupation _____

   Your Spouse's Occupation _____

PLEASE NOTE: ANY INFORMATION YOU PROVIDE WILL BE TREATED STRICTLY CONFIDENTIAL AND WILL
NOT BE USED IN ANY OTHER MANNER EXCEPT AS A PART OF A LARGE SAMPLE IN
WRITING A GENERALIZED RESEARCH REPORT.
THANK YOU VERY MUCH FOR YOUR COOPERATION.

PLAN OF ANALYSIS

MEDICAL STAFF QUESTIONNAIRE

The field research data generated with the use of the medical staff questionnaire will be analyzed on the following lines.

1. Frequency distributions and relative proportions for each response will be generated for the entire sample of medical staff. Such data will provide the following information for the entire sample.
   1. Age distribution of the respondents.
   2. Medical specialization of the respondents.
   3. Type of certification of the respondents.
   4. Frequency of admitting patients to the area hospitals.
   5. Relative importance of hospital attributes as perceived by the respondents.
   6. Respondent evaluation of Spencer and Ozark Saints on the basis of hospital attributes.
   7. Respondent preference of one hospital over the others.
   8. Relative extent of the use of Spencer and Ozark Saints by the respondents.
   9. Relative importance of the various sources of information as perceived by the respondents.
   10. Respondent assessment of the "influentials" in hospital selection.

2. Responses to open-ended questions numbers IIC, IID, and IIG will be summarized and reported.

3. A comparative analysis will be performed between Spencer and Ozark Saints. The major purposes of this comparison are:
   1. To identify the strengths and weaknesses of each of the hospitals as evaluated by the respondents.
   2. To identify any significant differences with regard to hospital use related behaviors between those respondents whose preference is for Ozark Saints vis-a-vis those respondents whose preference is for Spencer.

4. On the various aspects under investigation, a segmentation analysis will be performed on the following bases. The major purposes of these segmentation analyses are to see whether there are any significant differences among the various segments with regard to the behaviors investigated. We propose to use the bases for segmentation analyses.

1. Geographic areas.
2. Age of the respondents.
3. Certification.
4. Specialization.

CONSUMER HOSPITAL OPINION SURVEY

After the field research work is completed the following procedure will be utilized to generate the research data which will form the basis for writing the final report.

1. The data generated through field work will be first computerized by utilizing an appropriate coding scheme.
2. The following types of analyses will be performed to generate useful statistical data.

    A. Frequency distributions and relative proportions for each response will be generated for the entire sample. Such data will provide the following types of information for the entire sample.

        1. Area hospitals utilized by respondents.
        2. Number of times hospital services utilized during the last two years.
        3. Purpose of hospitalization.
        4. Length of hospitalization.
        5. Consumer choice pattern of area hospitals.
        6. Relative importance of "influentials" in the choice of hospital.
        7. Relative importance of hospital attributes as perceived by consumers.
        8. Consumer evaluation of area hospitals on a number of attributes.
        9. Consumer preferences as to the driving distance to a hospital measured in terms of time.
        10. Consumer-perceived need for additional hospitals in the surrounding area.

    B. In addition to generating frequencies and relative proportions on the above ten aspects, data generated through open-ended questions numbers 6, 12, and 13 in the questionnaire will be summarized and reported.
    C. A demographic profile will be drawn on the basis of the responses to questions on demographics of the respondents.
    D. For all those questions where scales have been utilized, means and standard deviations will be computed and reported along with frequencies and percentages.

E. A comparative analysis will be performed between Spencer and Ozark Saints. The major purposes of this comparative analyses are:

1. To identify the strengths and weaknesses of each of the hospitals as perceived by consumers.
2. To identify whether there are any significant differences with regard to demographic characteristics of those respondents whose first choice is Ozark Saints vis-a-vis those whose first choice is Spencer.
3. To identify any significant differences with regard to hospital use-related behaviors between those respondents whose first choice is Ozark Saints compared to those whose first choice is Spencer.

F. On the various aspects under investigation, a segmentation analysis will be performed on the following bases. The major purpose of the segmentation analyses is to see whether there are any significant differences among the various segments with regard to the behaviors investigated. We propose to use the following bases for segmentation analyses.

1. Geographic areas.
2. Demographic segments based on:
   a) Age
   b) Income
   c) Education
   d) Occupation.

QUESTIONS

1. If you were the OSH administrator, how would you evaluate the proposed research study?

2. How do you evaluate the research instruments and the analysis plan proposed by the consultants?

3. What modifications, if any, do you suggest before approving the research proposal?

4. Discuss how the information that may be generated from implementing the research study methods proposed would help the OSH management to develop long-term strategies and to impart greater marketing orientation to OSH operations.

Ozark Saints Hospital (B)

Ozark Saints Hospital is one of the two major area hospitals located in a medium-sized city in the southwest region of the United States. Recently, Edward Lofton, hospital administrator, procured the services of a marketing consulting firm in the area for purposes of carrying out customer behavior studies dealing with the area physicians and households. (See Ozark Saints Hospital (A) for details of the health care service market area, research proposal, research instruments and the plan of analysis.) The research findings are expected to be useful for the OSH management to develop an appropriate long-term competitive strategy and generally to impart greater marketing orientation to OSH operations. Eight months after contracting with the local research firm, Mr. Lofton received a copy of the results of the study. The results were presented in tables and divided into two sections: the results of the Physician study and the results of the Consumer study.

PHYSICIAN STUDY

Almost all physicians in the city where OSH was located were sent a questionnaire. Some were screened out initially because they were relatively uninvolved in choosing a hospital for their patients. Out of 159 questionnaires mailed to physicians, 48 were returned. This represents a 30.2 percent response rate of the total and was judged to be above average for these types of surveys. Results from this phase of the study are shown in Exhibits 1-9.

The research and written case were presented at the Case Research Symposium (Atlanta, November, 1981) and were evaluated by the Case Research Association Editorial Board. This case was prepared by C.P. Rao and G.E. Kiser of the University of Arkansas and Stephen W. McDaniel of Texas A&M University as a basis for class discussion.

EXHIBIT 1   Frequency of admission of patients to alternate hospitals in the area

Hospital	Frequency of Admission					
	Several times a day		Several times a week		Infrequently	
	No.	%	No.	%	No.	%
Spencer	21	43.8	16	33.3	7	14.6
Ozark Saints	5	10.6	17	36.2	20	42.6

EXHIBIT 2   Extent of physician usage of the area hospitals

Hospital	Extent of Usage					
	Extensively		Frequently		Infrequently	
	No.	%	No.	%	No.	%
Spencer	18	42.9	11	26.2	13	30.9
Ozark Saints	14	32.6	14	32.6	15	34.8

EXHIBIT 3   Physician choice criteria in selecting a hospital

Factors	Very Important/ Important		Neutral		Unimportant/ Very Unimportant	
	No.	%	No.	%	No.	%
Bed availability	33	74.9	7	15.9	4	9.1
Physician dining room/lounge	5	11.4	12	27.3	27	61.4
Quality of emergency room	34	75.6	9	20.0	2	4.4
Friendliness of staff	32	71.0	11	24.4	2	4.4
Quality of nursing	43	93.4	1	2.1	2	4.3
Availability of consultants	35	76.0	7	15.2	4	8.6
Quality and type of equipment	42	91.2	3	6.5	1	2.2
Involvement in hospital mgmt.	18	39.9	20	44.4	17	15.6
Overall hospital reputation	25	56.8	14	31.8	5	11.4
Patient's choice of hospital	31	65.9	13	27.7	3	6.4
Adequate parking	20	44.4	14	31.1	11	24.4
How well-managed hospital is	36	79.9	6	13.3	3	4.4
Geographical proximity to patient's home	15	33.3	18	40.0	12	22.2
Quality of medical records	28	60.8	11	23.9	7	15.2
Geographical proximity to your office	31	64.6	9	18.8	8	16.7
Availability of operating room time	25	54.3	10	21.7	11	23.9

EXHIBIT 4 Physicians' evaluation of Spencer and Ozark Saints

	Spencer							
	Superior		*Very Good*		*Poor*		*Inadequate*	
	No.	%	No.	%	No.	%	No.	%
Suppliers available	16	44.5	20	55.5	—	—	—	—
Housekeeping	5	13.8	27	75.0	4	11.1	—	—
Nursing staff	11	30.4	25	69.4	—	—	—	—
Physical therapy	9	28.1	23	71.9	—	—	—	—
Radiology	22	59.4	14	37.8	1	2.7	—	—
Laboratory	16	43.2	19	51.4	2	5.4	—	—
Parking for physicians	6	15.1	22	66.7	4	12.1	1	3.0
Office space in close proximity to hospital	11	40.7	12	44.4	4	14.8	—	—
Anesthesiology	19	63.3	9	30.0	2	6.8	—	—
Operating room facilities	18	59.9	12	40.0	—	—	—	—
ICU facilities	23	63.8	13	36.1	—	—	—	—
Emergency room	18	50.0	18	50.0				
Medical records	8	24.2	24	72.7	1	3.0	—	—

	Ozark Saints							
	Superior		*Very Good*		*Poor*		*Inadequate*	
	No.	%	No.	%	No.	%	No.	%
Suppliers available	6	16.6	23	63.9	6	16.6	1	2.8
Housekeeping	10	28.5	23	65.7	2	5.7	—	—
Nursing staff	8	22.2	23	63.9	3	8.3	2	5.6
Physical therapy	—	—	24	77.4	5	16.1	1	—
Radiology	5	13.9	21	58.3	9	25.4	1	6.4
Laboratory	6	16.2	24	64.9	6	16.2	1	2.8
Parking for physicians	5	13.5	24	64.9	6	16.2	2	2.7
Office space in close proximity to hospital	3	13.0	13	56.5	6	26.1	1	4.3
Anesthesiology	13	41.9	17	54.8	—	—	1	3.2
Operating room facilities	7	23.3	20	66.7	2	6.7	1	3.3
ICU facilities	11	33.3	21	63.7	1	3.3	—	—
Emergency room	6	16.2	25	67.6	5	13.5	1	2.7
Medical records	4	11.4	24	68.6	6	17.1	1	2.8

EXHIBIT 5 Physician dislike for the area hospitals

	Yes		*No*	
	No.	%	No.	%
Is the dislike more for one hospital than another?	19	54.3	16	45.7

	Ozark Saints		*Spencer*	
	No.	%	No.	%
Which hospital?	11	57.9	7	36.8

EXHIBIT 6 Physician liking for the area hospitals

	Yes		No	
	No.	%	No.	%
Is the liking more for one hospital than another?	18	50.0	18	50.0

	Ozark Saints		Spencer		Other	
	No.	%	No.	%	No.	%
Which hospital?	8	40	10	50	2	10

EXHIBIT 7 Relative importance of the physician sources of information in forming opinions of a hospital

	Relative Importance of Sources of Information									
Source	Extensive		Much		Some		Little		None	
	No.	%	No.	%	No.	%	No.	%	No.	%
Direct, personal contact	30	66.7	12	26.7	2	4.4	1	2.2	—	—
Patients	10	21.7	20	43.5	13	28.3	3	6.5	—	—
Fellow physicians	13	28.9	14	31.1	12	26.7	5	11.1	1	2.2
Professional staff meetings	4	8.9	7	15.6	16	35.6	12	26.6	6	13.3
Hospital publications	—	—	—	—	6	13.6	12	27.3	26	59.1
Salesmen	—	—	—	—	—	—	10	22.7	34	77.3
News media	—	—	—	—	3	6.9	10	23.3	30	69.8

EXHIBIT 8 Physician perception of the dominant role played by various groups in determining patient's admittance to a hospital

Group	No.	%
Physicians	28	65.1
Patients	14	32.6
Patient's family	1	2.3

EXHIBIT 9   Physicians' demographic profile

		No.	%
Age:	30–39	20	42.5
	40–49	14	29.8
	50–59	5	10.6
	60 and over	8	17.1
Medical Specialization:		No.	%
	Surgery	14	29.8
	Urology	4	8.5
	Psychiatry	2	4.3
	Ophthalmology	2	4.3
	Internal Medicine	6	12.8
	Ob-Gyn	3	6.4
	Hematology/Oncology	2	4.3
	General Practice	7	14.9
	Pediatrics	2	4.3
	Other (Allergy, Pulmonary Disorders, Cardiology, Otolaryngology, Gastro)	5	10.6
Certification:		No.	%
	Board Certified	35	79.6
	Board Eligible	7	15.9
	Non-Certified	2	4.5

CONSUMER STUDY

The consumer hospital opinion survey questionnaires were mailed to about 1000 randomly selected households in the Ozark Saints service market area. (An additional 200 questionnaires were mailed to the past patients of the hospital.) Through the consumer mail questionnaire survey, 308 responses were generated. After adjusting for undelivered questionnaires, the 308 responses accounted for approximately 33 percent of the mailings. This response rate in a consumer mail questionnaire survey was judged to be highly satisfactory. Results from this phase of the study are shown in Exhibits 10-18.

EXHIBIT 10   Consumer use of area hospitals

		Yes		No	
		No.	%	No.	%
1.	Did the household use any hospital in the past two years?	225	73.1	83	26.9

2.	Name of area hospital utilized	Ozark Saints		Spencer		Other	
		No.	%	No.	%	No.	%
		143	48.5	115	39.0	37	12.5

3. Frequency of use in the last two years.	No.	%
Once	96	42.7
Twice	60	26.7
Three Times	37	16.4
Four Times	13	5.8
More Than Four Times	19	8.4

EXHIBIT 11   Consumer choice pattern of area hospitals

Hospital	1st Choice		2nd Choice	
	No.	%	No.	%
Ozark Saints Hospital	179	60.9	64	33.0
Spencer Medical Center	99	33.7	106	54.6
Other	16	5.4	21	12.4

EXHIBIT 12   Influences of consumer hospital choice behavior

	Importance of Influences					
	Very Important/ Important		Slightly Important		Unimportant/ Very Unimportant	
Influences	No.	%	No.	%	No.	%
Other members of household	229	84.9	26	9.6	15	5.5
Friends and neighbors	121	46.1	84	31.9	58	22.0
Your doctor	271	92.8	13	4.5	8	2.7

EXHIBIT 13   Consumer "choice criteria" in selecting a hospital

| | Relative Importance of the Aspect | | | | | | | |
| | Very Important | | Important | | Not Very Important | | Not Important At All | |
Hospital Aspect	No.	%	No.	%	No.	%	No.	%
Good doctors	286	95.7	13	4.3	—	—	—	—
Good nursing care	262	88.2	35	11.8	—	—	—	—
Good emergency room	256	86.5	38	12.8	2	.7	—	—
Latest medical equipment	239	81.3	49	16.7	6	2.0	—	—
Keeps patients informed about their care	207	71.4	75	25.8	6	2.1	2	.7
Religious affiliation	75	26.9	71	25.4	72	25.8	61	21.9
Comfortable rooms	162	55.1	123	41.8	6	2.0	3	1.0
Good food	137	47.0	135	46.2	20	6.8	—	—
Easy to go to	141	48.3	113	38.7	32	11.0	6	2.1
Adequate parking	120	41.5	125	43.3	35	12.1	9	3.1
Flexible visiting hours	110	38.3	124	43.2	45	15.7	8	2.8
Price of service	166	59.1	92	32.7	18	6.4	5	1.8
Good reputation	200	68.7	85	29.2	6	2.1	—	—
Provides rehabilitation	112	40.7	132	48.0	24	8.7	7	2.5
Teaches you to stay well	107	38.8	124	44.9	35	12.7	10	3.6
Has health education programs	85	31.8	115	43.0	49	18.3	18	6.7
Overall hospital management	152	56.3	109	40.4	5	1.8	4	1.5

EXHIBIT 14 Consumer evaluation of their first choice hospital

	Ozark Saints (164 Total)						Spencer (96 Total)					
	Very Favorable/ Favorable		Somewhat Favorable		Unfavorable/ Very Unfavorable		Very Favorable/ Favorable		Somewhat Favorable		Unfavorable/ Very Unfavorable	
Hospital Feature	No.	%	No.	%	No.	%	No.	%	No.	%	No.	%
Good doctors	153	96.8	2	1.2	3	1.8	85	92.4	3	3.3	4	4.3
Good nursing care	145	94.8	7	4.6	1	.6	77	89.5	7	8.1	2	2.3
Good emergency room	132	89.2	14	9.4	2	1.4	66	82.5	8	10.0	6	7.5
Latest medical equipment	140	95.4	8	5.3	2	1.3	75	92.5	4	5.0	1	2.5
Respects your privacy	143	94.7	6	4.0	2	4.3	69	82.1	11	13.1	4	4.7
Keeps patients informed about their care	126	86.9	16	11.0	3	2.1	64	79.0	11	13.6	6	7.4
Religious affiliation	106	74.1	26	18.2	11	7.6	44	59.5	18	24.3	12	16.2
Comfortable rooms	148	96.7	4	2.6	1	.6	67	78.8	12	14.1	6	7.1
Good food	117	78.5	26	17.4	6	4.0	60	72.3	16	19.3	7	8.4
Easy to go to	141	92.8	6	3.9	5	3.3	64	75.3	14	16.5	7	8.2
Adequate parking	127	91.4	10	6.6	3	2.0	54	62.8	22	25.6	10	11.6
Flexible visiting hours	133	89.9	13	8.8	2	1.4	72	85.7	9	10.7	3	3.6
Price of service	114	77.6	25	17.0	8	5.4	51	62.2	20	24.4	11	13.4
Good reputation	141	96.0	3	2.0	3	2.0	74	91.4	4	4.9	3	3.7
Provides rehabilitation	105	84.7	14	11.3	5	4.0	52	81.1	9	14.1	3	4.7
Teaches you to stay well	88	72.1	25	20.4	9	7.4	43	65.2	21	31.8	2	3.0
Has health education programs	75	70.8	25	23.6	6	5.7	40	60.6	20	30.3	6	9.1
Overall hospital management	115	90.4	8	6.4	4	3.2	57	81.4	10	14.3	3	4.3

EXHIBIT 15 Consumer evaluation of their second choice hospital

Hospital Feature	Ozark Saints						Spencer					
	Very Favorable/Favorable		Somewhat Favorable		Unfavorable/Very Unfavorable		Very Favorable/Favorable		Somewhat Favorable		Unfavorable/Very Unfavorable	
	No.	%	No.	%	No.	%	No.	%	No.	%	No.	%
Good doctors	61	89.7	4	5.9	3	4.4	122	91.5	8	6.0	3	2.5
Good nursing care	49	76.6	10	16.6	5	3.1	98	75.4	19	14.6	13	10.0
Good emergency room	49	93.1	4	6.8	6	10.1	92	70.2	25	19.1	14	10.7
Latest medical equipment	45	80.4	7	12.5	4	7.1	124	96.1	5	3.9	—	—
Respects your privacy	47	83.9	3	5.4	6	10.7	86	68.8	28	22.4	11	8.8
Keeps patients informed about their care	39	69.6	12	21.4	5	8.7	78	64.2	32	26.0	12	9.8
Religious affiliation	41	74.5	6	10.9	8	14.5	54	46.5	40	34.5	22	19.0
Comfortable rooms	55	87.4	4	6.3	4	6.3	81	63.3	36	28.1	11	8.6
Good food	44	74.6	13	22.0	2	3.4	73	58.9	38	30.6	13	10.5
Easy to go to	53	81.5	9	13.8	3	4.6	86	65.2	28	21.2	18	13.6
Adequate parking	54	83.0	7	10.8	4	6.2	61	45.5	42	31.3	31	23.1
Flexible visiting hours	57	89.1	2	3.1	5	7.8	89	73.5	26	21.5	6	5.0
Price of service	41	69.5	12	20.3	6	10.2	63	51.2	38	30.9	22	17.9
Good reputation	53	88.4	5	8.3	2	3.3	95	75.4	23	18.3	8	6.3
Provides rehabilitation	32	68.1	11	23.4	4	8.5	82	79.6	16	15.5	5	4.9
Teaches you to stay well	27	56.3	17	35.4	4	8.3	63	61.7	32	31.4	7	6.9
Has health education programs	24	48.0	20	40.0	6	12.0	63	69.2	24	26.4	4	4.4
Overall hospital management	41	80.4	8	15.7	2	3.9	76	73.8	22	21.4	5	4.9

EXHIBIT 16 Consumer preference for the distance to a hospital as measured in driving time

Distance in driving time	No.	%
5 minutes	15	5.3
15 minutes	120	42.1
30 minutes	119	41.8
45 minutes	25	8.8
over 45 minutes	6	2.1

EXHIBIT 17 Consumer opinion as to the need for additional hospitals in the area

	Yes		No	
	No	%	No	%
Should additional hospitals be built?	87	31.2	192	68.8

EXHIBIT 18 Demographic profile of the respondents

Age:	No.	%
Under 20 years	4	1.3
20–29 years	47	15.4
30–39 years	49	16.1
40–49 years	33	10.8
50–59 years	50	16.4
60 and over	122	40.0

Education:	No.	%
Grade school	34	11.4
Some high school	37	12.4
High school graduate	73	24.4
Some college	91	30.4
College graduate	37	12.4
Post graduate study	27	9.0

Total family income:	No.	%
Under $10,000	78	27.5
$10,000 to $12,499	44	15.5
$12,500 to $14,499	35	12.3
$15,000 to $20,000	35	12.3
$20,001 to $24,999	38	13.4
Over $25,000	54	19.0

Respondent's occupations:	No.	%
Professional	48	16.1
White-collar	49	16.5
Self-employed	24	8.1
Blue-collar	61	20.5
Other (retired, student, etc)	115	38.8

QUESTIONS

1. What general conclusions can you draw from the results of both phases of this study?

2. How do the physicians' choice criteria for hospital selection compare with their evaluations of Ozark Saints and Spencer?

3. How do the consumers' choice criteria for hospital selection compare with their evaluations of Ozark Saints and Spencer?

4. What are the strengths and weaknesses of both hospitals?

5. If you were Mr. Lofton, what would be your long-term marketing strategies for Ozark Saints Hospital?

LTV Corporation

During the 1960s, one of the glamour companies in the United States was Ling-Temco-Vought, and one of the glamour executives was Jimmy Ling, the firm's founder and chief executive officer. Ling started as a small electrical contractor and became head of the nation's fourteenth largest firm. At the end of an acquisition binge in the mid-1960s, the company's common stock soared to $169 a share and sales reached the $3 billion level. Jimmy Ling was known as a Texas wheeler-dealer (Ling-Temco-Vought is in Dallas), his company as a conglomerate's conglomerate. Ling-Temco-Vought had acquired such diverse and major operations as Braniff Airlines, Jones & Laughlin Steel Corp., and Wilson & Co., the country's third largest meat packer.

This case was developed by Richard T. Hise, Professor of Marketing at Texas A&M University, as a basis for class discussion rather than to illustrate effective or ineffective marketing management.

Ling built Ling-Temco-Vought with a controversial business strategy, the heart of which he described as "operation redeployment." He viewed Ling-Temco-Vought as a financial endeavor; debt and equity financing were the firm's major sources of working capital, along with the sale of various assets. Through operation redeployment, the company's subsidiaries were spun off into separately listed public companies so that their stock multiples would help fatten Ling-Temco-Vought coffers. The inflated values for the firm's stock were used for acquiring additional loans.

The late 1960s and early 1970s brought trouble to Ling and his company, however. The debt-heavy company found itself plagued by high fixed payments on its loans. Profits, never robust, turned into losses, reaching $71 million in 1970 and $58 million in 1971. During 1970, Ling-Temco-Vought's board of directors succeeded in ousting Ling and replaced him with Paul Thayer, who had headed up the company's aerospace division.

TOP MANAGEMENT

LTV's corporate organization chart as of mid-1981 is shown in Exhibit 1. W. Paul Thayer is LTV's chairman of the board and chief executive officer. Thayer was a decorated naval pilot during World War II who, ironically, flew aircraft manufactured by the Vought Corporation. After a stint as a pilot for TWA, during which he married a stewardess under the wings of an airplane, he was employed by Vought as one of its test pilots. During his eight months on the job, three test pilots were killed and three resigned; Thayer survived six wrecked planes and bailed out of one into Maryland's Patuxent Bay. Even as LTV's head man, Thayer insisted on flying Vought's new planes. One of his favorite maneuvers is to put subsonic planes into supersonic dives using a technique he developed twenty years ago to keep the plane from disintegrating. As a World War II naval pilot leading his squadron into San Francisco, Mr. Thayer once flew his plane under the Golden Gate Bridge. Mr. Thayer also enjoys barrel rolling LTV's executive planes so fast that the centrifugal force keeps passengers' coffee from spilling. Jimmy Ling once grounded him for barrel rolling when Mrs. Ling was aboard.

At Vought, Thayer became chief test pilot, national sales manager, general manager, and president, replacing Jimmy Ling as LTV's chairman and CEO in the middle of 1970. One of the major reasons he was selected was that the company's board of directors wanted someone who had a good reputation at the Pentagon and on Capitol Hill. Thayer is regarded as hardworking and highly competitive; he has been on big game hunts, has been part owner of a stable of race horses, and is an inveterate poker player and crapshooter. He does not always win, however; he once had to sell $24,000 of LTV stock to settle a gambling debt. Once as a test pilot for Vought, he broke his coccyx bone. He now likes to tell people that he is the only chief executive officer he knows who has literally "broken his tail" for his company.[1]

---

[1]"Can LTV Fly Again?" *Dun's,* April, 1973, pp. 45–48 ff., and Rush Loving Jr. "LTV's Flight From Bankruptcy." *Fortune,* June, 1973, pp. 135–138 ff.

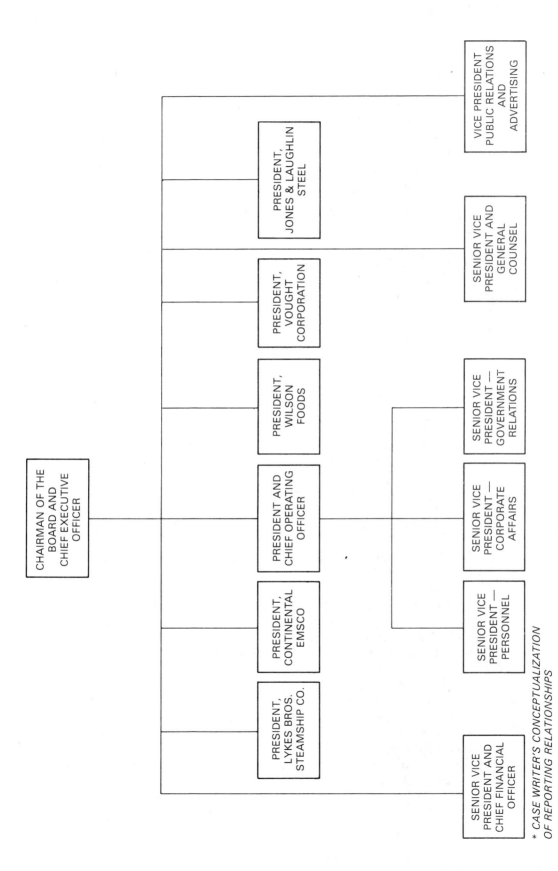

* CASE WRITER'S CONCEPTUALIZATION
OF REPORTING RELATIONSHIPS

EXHIBIT 1 Corporate organization

The president and chief operating officer of LTV is Raymond A. Hay, named to the post early in 1975. He was formerly the president of U.S. Operations for Xerox and Executive Vice President.

Thomas C. Graham is president of Jones & Laughlin. A graduate of the University of Louisville with a degree in civil engineering, Graham's entire business career has been spent with Jones & Laughlin, with tours of duty in the construction, purchasing, and specialty steels divisions.

The president and chief executive officer of Wilson Foods is Kenneth J. Griggy, who has held the position since July, 1975. Prior to joining Wilson, Griggy served as president of the Domestic Operations of Riviana Foods, Inc. and as vice president and director of the Consumer Products Group of the Ralston Purina Company.

Robert L. Kirk has been president and chief executive officer of Vought since April 12, 1977. Before joining LTV, Kirk held various executive positions with International Telephone and Telegraph, the most recent of which was vice president and product line manager.

Joseph T. Lykes, Jr. is president of Lykes, a position which he has held since June, 1977. Lee A. Drake is president of Continental Emsco.

STRATEGIC DECISIONS FOR LTV

Mr. Thayer put together a strategic plan for the salvation of Ling-Temco-Vought. He changed the name to LTV. Vought Aeronautics and Vought Missiles & Space Co. were combined into the Vought Corporation. One level of management at LTV was eliminated. Various subsidiaries were sold off by 1973, including Okonite, Ling Altec, LTV Electrosystems, and Braniff, leaving three major divisions at that time: the Vought Corporation, Jones and Laughlin Steel, and Wilson and Co. A 6,400 acre west Texas ranch, a hotel in Acapulco, and a land development company in Colorado were also sold off. Instead of over emphasizing common stock ownership by outsiders, Thayer began to purchase LTV's common stock so that ownership and the corporation could better determine its own destiny. For example, Thayer was able to transfer $35 million from Wilson to help pay off $93 million in debentures, a move that would have been more difficult with many minority stockholders to contend with.

Probably the most significant of Thayer's changes was to reorient LTV as an operating company, not as a finance company. Trimming the firm to three major divisions gave the strategy a better chance of succeeding and allowed Thayer to be much more involved with the day-to-day activities of LTV than Ling had been.

In 1976, president and chief operating officer of LTV, Raymond A. Hay, developed one major objective for LTV's divisional presidents: they were required to devise a long-term strategy for their companies. To help them implement this requirement, Hay provided the divisional presidents with specific sales and profit targets, and contingency plans. Divisional presidents were also required to develop both short-run and long-run plans. These plans are coordinated with LTV's headquarters and monthly executive committee meetings check progress. For example, Wilson had done little or no planning previously; its executives did not even establish an operating budget.

Exhibits 2 and 3 contain LTV's balance sheets from 1977 to 1980. Exhibits 4 and 5 are the corporation's income statements for 1976 through 1980. Exhibit 6 contains a five-year summary for LTV's five major business segments.

Strategic Decisions for Wilson Foods

Wilson made various strategic changes. Its Brazilian beef operations were closed down when the Brazilian government decided to subsidize domestic beef production. Wilson's management, which had been located in four different cities, was centralized in Oklahoma City. Marketing activities were also centralized, a $5 million promotion campaign highlighting the Wilson brand name was inaugurated, and a new advertising agency was hired. The division's name was changed to Wilson Foods, which reflected a decision to lessen its dependence on commodities (particularly beef and its volatile prices, which frequently caused razor-thin profit margins or losses), and emphasize its consumer marketing orientation. Most of Wilson's executives were released, leaving only one longtime employee in a top position. By 1976, Wilson's top management included Sara Lee's former chairman of the board, the ex-president of Hygrade, and a top marketing executive from Consolidated Foods. Kenneth J. Griggy, previously director of Ralston Purina's Consumer Products Group, was named to head up Wilson Foods.

In the fall of 1975, Griggy decided to close two large meat packaging plants in Omaha and Kansas City, and a smaller operation in England. Although 1,000 jobs were involved, Griggy believed the closings were justified because the operations involved were unprofitable. For the fall quarter of 1975, Wilson's profit was $5 million, while for the whole of 1975, a pretax operating profit of close to $19 million was achieved, compared to a break-even situation in 1974. Other strategic moves made by Griggy included reducing the number of profit centers and selling off an unprofitable pet food line. He also instituted major analyses of Wilson's data processing and distribution systems to improve them. Mr. Griggy stated in 1975 that he would like Wilson's return on sales to hit 2 percent, but indicated that this objective could probably not be attained for three to five years.

Although in 1975 Wilson was the nation's third largest meat packer, and ranked first in pork and lamb, the company lacked brand identity; not one of its products was sold nationwide under the Wilson label. In addition, the company's three major markets, supermarkets, restaurants, and meat markets, were highly competitive. In 1975, Wilson brought out a new pork sausage called Country Man, and had begun a number of marketing research projects.

EXHIBIT 2 Balance sheet, 1977 and 1978 (millions of dollars)

	1978	1977
Current Assets:		
Cash and temporary investments	$ 113,223	$ 52,101
Receivables	690,020	348,105
Inventories	959,863	417,174
Prepaid expenses	49,314	26,201
Total Current Assets	1,812,420	843,581
Current Liabilities:		
Notes payable to banks	140,735	73,874
Accounts payable and accrued liabilities	906,272	511,615
Income taxes	22,302	1,890
Current maturities of long-term debt		
and capitalized lease obligations	36,381	15,665
Total Current Liabilities	1,105,690	603,044
Working capital	706,730	240,537
Investments and other assets	247,427	132,963
Property, plant and equipment	1,628,861	1,100,271
Excess of cost over net assets of purchased businesses	22,327	22,418
Unamortized debt expense	9,226	7,580
Total Assets Less Current Liabilities	2,614,571	1,503,769
Less Non-Current Liabilities:		
Long-term debt	1,520,094	1,033,171
Capitalized lease obligations	81,179	71,615
Deferred income taxes	14,374	15,187
Estimated liability for plant closing costs	196,099	—
Employee compensation and benefits	208,267	16,063
Other	41,419	19,612
Total Non-Current Liabilities	2,061,432	1,155,648
Shareholders' Equity	$ 553,139	$ 348,121

STATEMENT OF SHAREHOLDERS' EQUITY

	1978	1977
$5 Series A preferred stock	$ 1,739	$ 2,524
Excess of redemption value over par value	33,332	48,381
	35,071	50,905
$2.60 Series B preferred stock	4,155	—
Class AA special stock	451	459
Series 1 participating preference stock	691	—
Common stock	11,879	6,655
Capital surplus	494,131	332,550
Retained earnings	40,093	5,933
Less excess of redemption value over par value of		
$5 Series A preferred stock	(33,332)	(48,381)
Total Shareholders' Equity	$ 553,139	$ 348,121

See summary of accounting policies and notes to financial statements.

EXHIBIT 3 Balance sheet, 1979 and 1980 (millions of dollars)

	1980	1979 (1)
Current Assets		
Cash and short-term securities	$ 78,230	$ 90,481
Receivables	853,955	807,947
Inventories	1,047,105	983,451
Prepaid expenses	50,413	52,344
Total Current Assets	2,029,703	1,934,223
Current Liabilities		
Notes payable to banks	50,630	75,500
Accounts payable	536,621	499,130
Accrued liabilities	618,018	537,898
Current portion of long-term debt and capitalized lease obligations	21,708	20,131
Total Current Liabilities	1,226,977	1,132,659
Working capital	802,726	801,564
Investments and other assets	258,667	208,031
Property, plant and equipment	1,741,299	1,702,945
Total Assets Less Current Liabilities	2,802,692	2,712,540
Less Noncurrent Liabilities and Other Items		
Long-term debt	1,418,996	1,476,644
Capitalized lease obligations	70,157	74,564
Employee compensation and benefits	363,053	372,468
Deferred income taxes	27,252	8,324
Other noncurrent liabilities	83,520	62,774
Preferred stock with mandatory redemption	20,768	20,768
Total Noncurrent Liabilities and Other Items	1,983,746	2,015,542
Other Preferred Stock, Common Stock and Other Shareholders' Equity	$ 818,946	$ 696,998
Other Preferred Stock, Common Stock and Other Shareholders' Equity		
$2.60 Series B preferred stock	$ —	$ 4,438
Series 1 participating preference stock	1,000	513
Special stock, class AA	352	432
Common stock	17,896	12,322
Additional capital	501,038	498,300
Retained earnings	318,398	200,731
Less excess of redemption value over par value of $5 Series A preferred stock	(19,738)	(19,738)
Total Other Preferred Stock, Common Stock and Other Shareholders' Equity	$ 818,946	$ 696,998

(1) Reclassified to conform with 1980 presentation.
See summary of significant accounting policies and notes to consolidated financial statements.

EXHIBIT 4   Income statement, 1976 and 1977 (millions of dollars)

	1977	1976(a)
Sales	$4,703,296	$4,448,285
Other operating income	16,136	20,406
Total Sales and Other Income	4,719,432	4,468,691
Operating costs and expenses:		
Cost of products sold	4,413,732	4,103,742
Depreciation	65,057	61,306
Selling, administrative and general expenses	190,602	182,290
Unusual items	(3,129)	–
Interest and debt discount	94,108	89,598
Minority interest in subsidiaries	572	583
Total Costs and Expenses	4,760,942	4,437,519
Income (loss) from continuing operations before income taxes	(41,510)	31,172
Federal, state and foreign income taxes—credit	18,600	4,000
Income (loss) from continuing operations	(22,910)	35,172
Loss from discontinued operations (less applicable income tax credits of $1,800 and $5,076, respectively)	(36,470)	(4,472)
Income (loss) before extraordinary items	(59,380)	30,700
Extraordinary items	20,674	–
Net Income (loss)	(38,706)	30,700

EXHIBIT 5   Income statement, 1978 to 1980 (millions of dollars)

Earnings per share:			
Fully diluted:			
Continuing operations	$ 2.96	$ 3.62	$ 1.09
Discontinued operations	—	0.13	0.33
Before extraordinary credit and accounting change	2.96	3.75	1.42
Extraordinary credit	—	0.17	—
Accounting change	—	0.35	0.67
Net Income	$ 2.96	$ 4.27	$2.09
Primary:			
Continuing operations	$ 3.95	$ 5.02	$ 1.07
Discontinued operations	—	0.21	0.42
Before extraordinary credit and accounting change	3.95	5.23	1.49
Extraordinary credit	—	0.26	—
Accounting change	—	0.54	0.84
Net income	$ 3.95	$ 6.03	$ 2.33
Pro Forma Data:			
Pro forma amounts, assuming retroactive application of 1979 and 1978 cumulative effect of accounting change:			
Net Income		$ 159,204	$ 35,537
Earnings per share:			
Fully diluted		3.92	1.88
Primary		5.49	2.07

See summary of significant accounting policies and notes to consolidated financial statements.

EXHIBIT 6   Five-year summary by major business segment (millions of dollars)

	1980	1979	1978	1977	1976
Sales and revenues:					
Steel......................................	$3,800.2	$4,174.7	$2,410.6	$2,152.2	$1,943.0
Energy products and services................	1,218.0	801.2	261.4	231.5	171.0
Aerospace..................................	652.0	554.8	491.3	462.6	502.5
Meat and food products	2,267.0	2,338.8	2,194.2	1,941.7	1,919.4
Ocean shipping.............................	412.8	334.1	—	—	—
Sales between segments	(340.0)	(206.8)	(97.0)	(84.7)	(87.6)
Total................................	$8,010.0	$7,996.8	$5,260.5	$4,703.3	$4,448.3
Operating income (loss):					
Steel......................................	$ 69.4	$ 170.7	$ 48.7	$ 7.7	$ 42.1
Energy products and services................	114.2	68.8	18.6	12.9	11.7
Aerospace..................................	57.5	51.5	47.5	38.8	39.3
Meat and food products	(4.7)	23.7	(1.8)	.7	17.1
Ocean shipping.............................	35.6	19.8	—	—	—
Adjustments and eliminations	—	(7.3)	—	—	—
Operating income	272.0	327.2	113.0	60.1	110.2
Interest and corporate office expense	(121.1)	(156.0)	(105.6)	(102.8)	(102.2)
Unusual credits.............................	—	—	16.7	3.1	—
Income tax (charge) credit.....................	(23.0)	(24.6)	(4.1)	4.0	13.7
Income (loss) from continuing operations...............	$ 127.9	$ 146.6	$ 20.0	$ (35.6)	$ 21.7

In 1977 Wilson introduced the Thomas E. Wilson Masterpiece one-and-one-quarter-pound ham, the first in the company's line of premium-quality products carrying that label. A three-pound Masterpiece ham and Masterpiece ham steaks followed. Other consumer products added in 1977 included Jumbo meat and all beef franks; Western style brand franks, featuring coarsely ground, deeply smoked and specially seasoned beef; and four cooked meat specialties: corned beef, pastrami, pepper beef, and roast beef, all under the Bavarian trademark.

Higher costs for pork in 1977, caused by the inadequacy and inconsistency of hog supplies, squeezed profit margins. In the same year, the company began to aggressively market branded fresh pork. (In general, fresh pork is marketed without brand names.) Fresh pork chops, ribs, picnic hams, and shoulder blades were brought out under the "Butcher's Trim" label. In Wilson's unique pork evaluation system, only one of seven hogs meets the company's standards for the Butcher's Trim line.

Concept 1999 was developed in 1977 for sale of Wilson's poultry products to institutional markets.

It features larger broilers and additional packaging variations, allowing purchasers to buy the poultry blends they need; the program was handled by 125 food service distributors throughout the country.

During 1977, Wilson's management inaugurated a cost control system and made major changes in its product costing and pricing systems. Many of these new operations were computerized. Throughout 1978, Wilson emphasized more strongly its food service and delicatessen operations, two segments of the market the company had identified as among the fastest growing. Wilson sold its gelatin operation in Calumet City, Illinois, as well as four integrated broiler plants in Arkansas, Georgia, and North Carolina. Facilities in Boston and City of Industry, California were shut down to concentrate production in more efficient units. Wilson increasingly emphasized marketing fresh meats during 1978; it developed a special packaging technique that doubled the storage life of fresh pork, reduced shrinkage, and allowed for more efficient scheduling of shipments. A "100% Lamb" vacuum packed product was introduced.

A new line of delicatessen meats, "Continental Deli," featuring thirty-eight items from fourteen countries, was introduced in 1978. The "Western Style" line was expanded to include bacon, smoked and pork sausage, a boneless ham, and a frank that was a blend of beef and pork.

To spur penetration of its food service business into hotels, restaurants, fast food chains, airlines, and schools, Wilson appointed the food service division of Kraft, Inc. as distributor of its products. Wilson's food service representatives assisted Kraft to make customer presentations, coordinate sales and deliveries, and keep inventory control. New food service products were sausage crumbles and pre-sliced pepperoni for pizza toppings, fully cooked pork ribs, Italian sausage patties, and fully cooked ham patties. Pre-cooked pork sausage was supplied to McDonald's for its breakfast menu. Several new processed poultry products were introduced by Wilson's Plum Brook Farms food service center in 1978, including boneless chicken breasts, breaded chicken breast strips, and chicken foods.

By the end of 1978, Wilson had over 800 different products. The next year, it discontinued its beef slaughtering operations, but continued to sell boxed beef and fabricated cuts, as well as beef products, to the food service industry. In 1980, Wilson introduced its Recipe Ready Pork Program; "case ready" pork products are trimmed, cut, and packaged at the plant and ready for immediate display. "Butcher ready" products are further processed and packaged to meet specific customer needs.

During 1980, Wilson remained the nation's largest processor of lamb, with increases in total volume and boxed lamb sales, but profitability was lowered by higher animal and feeding costs. Wilson also improved its position as the nation's largest packer of pork; cooked ham sales increased 75 percent over 1979, and boneless hams and smoked meats volumes were up 40 percent. Sausage volume increased, but profit margins were down. Although total bacon sales dropped, due to low supplies and private label sales, the sales of higher-margin, branded bacon were up. Packages and labels were redesigned for the company's two major brands, "Wilson" and "Corn King," in 1980, and the new Wilson ribbon and seal were incorporated into all product lines.

Although industry sales of meats to food services and institutional markets in 1980 showed little improvement over 1979, Wilson's jumped 30 percent. Delicatessen sales nearly doubled, as Wilson's superior quality and service enabled it to become the preferred supplier to many deli operators. Many of the fast food chains added breakfast menus in 1980, and Wilson took a good share of this business.

EXHIBIT 7   Percentage of total sales for major product lines for meat and food segment 1973–1978

Product Line	Approximate Percentage of Consolidated Sales Year Ended December 31,					Six months ended June 30,
	1973	*1974*	*1975*	*1976*	*1977*	*1978*
Fresh and frozen meats	67%	66%	66%	66%	67%	68%
Processed meat and food products ..	21	22	23	23	21	21
Shortening, animal fats and vegetable oils	6	5	6	6	6	5
Poultry and dairy products	2	3	2	2	2	2
Other products	4	4	3	3	4	4
	100%	100%	100%	100%	100%	100%

SOURCE: Company Annual Reports.

Because of costly operations, Wilson closed its Oklahoma City hog slaughtering operations in February, 1981, but planned to expand its production of processed and branded meats.

Exhibit 7 shows the percentage of total sales of Wilson's major product lines from 1973 to 1978, and the company's total sales and profits from 1976 to 1980 are included in Exhibit 6.[2]

Strategic Decisions at Jones & Laughlin

Paul Thayer realigned the top management at Jones & Laughlin, bringing in only one executive from the outside—the financial vice president. William R. Roesch, J&L's vice president for steel production, was elected to the top job. Roesch had started as a mechanic at one of the company's coal mines and worked at all of the firm's operating units. While Roesch did not officially become J&L's chief executive officer for eighteen months, the firm's outgoing CEO, William J. Stephens, gave him autonomy from the start. Thayer dispatched Roscoe Haynie, Wilson's former chairman, to Pittsburgh, where he took an apartment across the street from J&L's headquarters, so he could counsel Roesch and give him headquarter's support. Roesch cut the company's salaried payroll by 20 percent, and the hourly work force was slashed by 25 percent at the company's Pittsburgh operation. LTV funded a sorely needed capital improvement program. Six open-hearth furnaces were modernized, while the largest blast furnace was rebuilt. Five open-hearth furnaces in Pittsburgh were eliminated and a costly taconite mine was sold.

A $500 million modernization program was begun by Roesch's successor, Thomas C. Graham, who took over on September 1, 1975. Some $200

[2]Company Annual Reports, and "LTV: Weak Growth In Mature Industries." *Business Week,* April 5, 1976, pp. 50–54.

million was allocated to modernize J&L's obsolete Pittsburgh operations, and $300 million was earmarked for expansion of the company's modern operations in Aliquippa, Pennsylvania.

Graham began to increase productivity. Some fine tuning in a nineteen-year old furnace at a Jones & Laughlin plant in Cleveland increased output from 25,000 to 70,000 tons a month. Plant managers at other locations were encouraged to do the same.

Perhaps the most significant strategic decision made by LTV regarding its steel operations was the acquisition of another steel company, Youngstown Sheet & Tube, in 1978. The annexation made Jones & Laughlin the country's third largest producer, behind U.S. Steel and Bethlehem; it was seventh before the merger. The Jones & Laughlin name was retained for the entire steel operations.

Youngstown Sheet and Tube had been a subsidiary of the Lykes Corp. Lykes' management had acquired YS&T in 1968 for $600 million, much of which was borrowed from banks. Lykes' executives viewed the Youngstown operation primarily as an investment. As a result, none of the Lykes executives could be persuaded to take an active part in the company's management and, furthermore, little capital was provided to modernize YS&T's outmoded facilities. (Between 1970 and 1973, Lykes allocated only $30 million a year to the plants, hardly enough to provide minimum maintenance, let alone make them competitive.) Lykes management belatedly decided to upgrade its facilities (YS&T had a good year in 1974, with sales of about $1.5 billion and net profit of close to $100 million), but an industry-wide downtown in subsequent years curtailed this intention.

Several factors suggested that acquiring Youngstown was ill-advised. (1) Its plants contained old, inefficient facilities. (2) $659 million of Lykes' debt would be added to LTV's debt, which already exceeded $1 billion. (3) The high level of debt meant that LTV would incur fixed annual interest expense of more than $110 million. (4) Both companies historically had profit problems: Jones & Laughlin had been able to generate only marginal profits, and Youngstown had had only one profitable year (1974) in the last ten. (5) LTV could have been better off by purchasing a growth industry, such as high-technology electronics, information processing, or energy. (6) Both companies are high cost producers. (7) Over 50 percent of the new company's production would be in flat rolled steel. While demand, chiefly from the automobile and appliance industries, had remained strong, these items carry the lowest profit margin of any steel product line.

LTV's management, however, believed that there were reasons the YS&T acquisition would be beneficial. These included:

1. Jones & Laughlin and Youngstown Steel and Tube possessed a unique market fit. Youngstown's strongest markets were Chicago, while J&L's were in the East; J&L had long coveted YS&T's strong position in Chicago. According to Mr. Graham, "If you are in the steel business, you had better be in Chicago."

2. J&L'S Aliquippa plant would be able to provide the processed steel (rounds) required by Youngstown's seamless-tube operations. Youngstown formerly made its own processed steel, but was paying a $50 a ton premium because it used antiquated open-hearth furnaces instead of the new modern basic-oxygen furnaces. LTV executives estimated they would save $25 million a year.

3. Combining the companies' faculties was expected to reduce freight costs for both firms.

4. Jones & Laughlin would gain increased production facilities that it needed in the Midwest, particularly, YS&T's fairly modern Indiana Harbor plant in East Chicago. This plant was underused and would provide needed capacity for J&L's Cleveland operation, which was working three shifts.

5. The company expected annual savings on raw materials of around $25 million. Jones & Laughlin produced its own iron ore, but ran an annual short fall of 2.2 million tons. Since Youngstown closed its Campbell Works at Youngstown, Ohio, it freed up exactly that amount of iron ore.

6. Both companies specialize in steel for three basic industries: auto, chemical, and oil and gas.

7. Jointly, J&L and YS&T combine for 12 percent of all domestic shipments of flat-rolled steel.

8. The merged company would be the major supplier of fasteners and machine parts in the United States.

Once the merger between J&L and YS&T was effected, LTV executives split the resulting company into three geographical divisions. The *Eastern Division* includes the Aliquippa Works, the Pittsburgh Works and three cold-finished bar operations in Hammond, Indiana, Willimantic, Connecticut and Youngstown, Ohio. The president of the Eastern Division is responsible for the hot rolled bars, cold finished bars, rod, wire, shaped products, and industrial steel departments. The *Central Division* contains the Cleveland Works and the tubular production facility in Youngstown. The Central Division's president is also responsible for the company's expanded line of tubular products. The *Western Division* has operations in East Chicago's Indiana Harbor Works, and the Hennepin Works in Hennepin, Illinois; this division's president heads up the company's tinplate products.

Two other divisions, specialty steels and raw materials, were formed after the merger. Stainless, carbon and alloy steels, along with specialty tubing, are produced and marketed by the former division. The latter division manages the raw materials operations of the new company, including coal and iron ore mines.

President Graham instituted a new decentralized management structure in the new company, similar to that which he inaugurated at Jones & Laugh-

EXHIBIT 8 Evaluation of LTV's steel operations vs. major competitors, 1980

Factor	Max. Plus or Minus Rating	U.S. Steel	Bethl. Steel	LTV	Nat'l	Republic	Armco	Inland	British Steel	Nippon Steel	Thyssen (Germany)	Pohang (Korea)	Usiminas (Brazil)
1. Coal position/costs	5	+3	+2	+2	+2	+2	+2	+4	−5	0	+1	−3	−5
2. Iron ore position/costs	5	+2	+1	+1	+1	0	0	+3	−2	+3	−2	0	+5
3. Raw materials logistics	5	+1	0	0	0	0	0	+3	−4	0	−2	−3	−4
4. Product & market mix	5	+1	+1	0	−1	+1	+1	0	0	0	0	−5	0
5. Location near customers	5	+2	+1	+2	+2	+2	+2	+5	+1	−3	0	−4	+2
6. Energy availability below market price	5	+2	+2	+2	+2	+2	+2	+2	+2	−2	+2	−2	+2
7. Labor relationships and situation	5	+2	+2	+2	+2	+2	+2	+3	−5	+5	+3	+5	−5
8. Efficiency of equipment	10	0	+5	+3	+5	+4	+4	+7	−5	+10	+5	+5	−5
9. Economics of expansion	5	+1	+2	−1	+1	−1	−1	+3	+3	+5	0	+5	0
10. Financial strength	10	+5	+5	−5	+5	+6	+5	+5	0	+7	+3	+3	−5
11. Nonsteel earnings (relative to size)	20	+10	0	+5	+2	0	+20	+2	0	0	+15	0	0
12. Pollution control costs	5	−2	−2	−2	−2	−2	−2	−2	0	−3	−2	+2	+5
13. Relationship with government	20	−5	−5	−3	−5	−5	−5	−5	−5	+10	+5	+20	+15
14. Management													
15. Other (such as R&D)	5	+2	+2	+1	+1	+1	+1	+1	0	+3	+2	−5	−5
16. Total all factors	100	+24	+16	+7	+15	+12	+31	+31	−20	+35	+27	+18	−5
17. Total, less raw materials	90	+19	+13	+4	+12	+10	+29	+24	−13	+32	+28	+21	−4
18. Total, less nonsteel	80	+14	+16	+2	+13	+12	+11	+29	−20	+35	+12	+18	−4
19. Total, less raw materials and nonsteel	70	+4	+13	−1	+10	+10	+9	+22	−13	+32	+13	+21	−4
20. Total, less raw materials, nonsteel and government	50	+9	+18	+2	+15	+15	+14	+27	−8	+22	+9	+1	−19

SOURCE: *Financial and Stock Market Analysis of Major USA Steel Companies.* Paine, Webber, Mitchell, Hutchins, Inc., 1980, p. 9.

lin before the merger. Individual units will have more autonomy in choosing their markets. In addition, Graham wants closer ties between marketing and production, with both functions as close to the customer as possible.

Exhibit 8 compares LTV to other domestic and international steel makers; the evaluation was prepared by a stock analyst. Exhibit 9 shows the product mix for Jones & Laughlin before the acquisition of Youngstown (1973–1978), and Exhibit 10 indicates the product mix for Youngstown Sheet & Tube before the merger (1973–1978). Exhibit 11 shows the product mix for the two companies combined after the merger (1979–1980). Exhibit 12 shows the major markets for Jones & Laughlin products before the merger (1973–1978), while Exhibit 13 reveals Youngstown Sheet & Tube's major markets before the merger (1973–1978). The major markets for LTV's combined steel operations after the merger (1979–1980) are indicated in Exhibit 14. (Sales and profits for LTV's steel segment are contained in Exhibit 6. The data for 1976–1978 represent J&L's pre-merger performance, while the 1979 and 1980 data show this segment's performance after YS&T was acquired.)

EXHIBIT 9   Product mix for Jones & Laughlin, 1973–1978

	1973	*1974*	*1975*	*1976*	*1977*	*1978*
Hot and cold rolled sheet and strip ..	46%	40%	38%	48%	47%	47%
Bar, rod and wire products	16	14	15	14	15	15
Tubular products	11	14	17	10	11	13
Tin mill products	9	9	10	10	9	7
Galvanized sheets	7	8	7	9	10	9
Light plates	3	7	6	3	4	3
All other	8	8	7	6	4	6
Total	100%	100%	100%	100%	100%	100%

SOURCE: Company Annual Reports.

EXHIBIT 10   Product mix for Youngstown Sheet & Tube, 1973–1978

	1973	*1974*	*1975*	*1976*	*1977*	*1978*
Hot and cold rolled sheet and strip ..	50.7%	48.7%	50.9%	60.0%	58.3%	52.0%
Tubular products	16.4	17.1	20.6	11.5	14.2	17.0
Tin mill products	10.3	10.5	11.3	10.7	10.4	12.0
Galvanized sheets	6.3	5.9	5.4	7.7	9.4	12.0
Light plates	4.9	5.2	5.9	3.9	3.4	3.0
Hot rolled and cold finished bars ...	8.3	8.3	4.1	3.7	3.2	1.0
All other	3.1	4.3	1.8	2.5	1.1	3.0
Total	100%	100%	100%	100%	100%	100%

SOURCE: Company Annual Reports.

EXHIBIT 11 Product mix for LTV's steel segment, 1979 and 1980

	1980	1979
Hot and cold rolled sheet and strip	47%	52%
Tubular products	18	13
Bar, rod and wire products	8	10
Tin mill products	12	10
Galvanized sheets	9	9
Light plates	3	3
All other	3	3

SOURCE: Company Annual Reports.

EXHIBIT 12 Major markets for Jones & Laughlin's products (1973–1978)

	1973	1974	1975	1976	1977	1978
Automotive	28%	21%	21%	25%	24%	25%
Steel service centers and pipe jobbers	21	24	22	21	19	18
Converters and resale	11	10	12	14	16	16
Containers and packaging	9	10	11	10	9	7
Construction	11	11	10	10	10	11
Agricultural, electrical and other machinery	8	9	9	8	9	10
Household appliances and office equipment	6	5	4	5	6	6
Oil and gas	3	4	7	4	4	5
All other	3	6	4	3	3	2
Total	100%	100%	100%	100%	100%	100%

SOURCE: Company Annual Reports.

EXHIBIT 13 Major markets for Youngstown sheet & tube, 1973–1978

	1973	1974	1975	1976	1977	1978
Steel service centers and pipe jobbers	25%	23%	24%	26%	31%	26%
Automotive	16	13	13	17	17	18
Agricultural, electrical and other machinery	9	10	8	9	8	11
Containers and packaging	9	10	10	10	8	11
Oil and gas	4	5	8	4	6	9
Household appliances and office equipment	7	8	7	8	8	8
Construction	8	9	8	9	8	7
Converters and resale	14	13	14	10	10	6
All other	8	9	8	7	4	4
Total	100%	100%	100%	100%	100%	100%

SOURCE: Company Annual Reports.

EXHIBIT 14   Major markets for LTV's steel segment, 1979 and 1980

	1980	1979
Automotive	15%	21%
Steel service centers and pipe jobbers	23	21
Construction	11	11
Converters and resale	8	10
Electrical, agricultural and other machinery	10	9
Containers and packaging	9	9
Household appliances and office equipment	7	7
Oil and gas	11	5
Miscellaneous	6	7

SOURCE: Company Annual Reports.

When YS&T became part of LTV in 1978, LTV also secured two other companies of the Lykes Corporation. These were the Lykes Brothers Steamship Co. and Continental Emsco, which had been a subsidiary of Youngstown. LTV organized these two companies as separate operating divisions: Lykes Brothers Steamship Company becoming the Ocean Shipping Group and Continental Emsco becoming the Energy Products and Services Group.[3]

Strategic Decisions at Lykes Brothers Steamship Co.

Lykes Brothers Steamship Co., one of the nation's largest and oldest ocean carriers, is headquartered in New Orleans. Chartered as a flag common carrier, it moves dry bulk, general cargo, bulk liquids, containerized cargo, heavy lifts, oversized shipments, and refrigerated cargoes. Its ports are located in three major areas—the Gulf of Mexico, the South Atlantic, and the Great Lakes—and these ports serve trade routes to Europe, Africa, South America, Asia and the Far East. The most important commodities carried are industrial machinery, vehicles, iron and steel products, cotton, wood, paper products, food stuffs, and construction materials.

LTV believes that one of the major competitive strengths of the Lykes Division is the versatility of its five classes of ships, allowing the best match of vessel of cargo, schedule, and route. The pride of Lykes' fleet are its three SEABEE barge/container ships, which are 875 feet long and have three decks. Cargo to the SEABEES is transported by rail and truck container units and from inland river ports by commercial barges and Lykes' own fleet of 249 97-foot hopper barges, three special 112-foot heavy lift flat deck barges, and refrigerated barges. Each SEABEE can transport up to 958 twenty-foot container equivalents or 38 barges, or a combination of the two. The unique features of the SEABEES enable them to minimize time in port and costs.

Although world shipping declined in 1978, Lykes had slight improvements in revenues and cargo tonnage (see Exhibit 15). In January, 1979, the

---

[3]Company Annual Reports; "Melding Lykes and LTV Steel." *Business Week,* December 18, 1978, pp. 76–77; "LTV: Weak Growth In Mature Industries." *op. cit.;* "Can LTV Fly Again?" *op. cit.;* and "LTV Also Is Shaking Up Its Steelmaker." *Business Week,* October 3, 1977, p. 86.

company was given authority by the U.S. Maritime Administration to open a new trade route from the West Coast to various ports in the Far East. Lykes expanded its staffs in Long Beach and San Francisco and opened a new office in Seattle. Lykes had traded in the Far East since 1925 through various Gulf ports. To accommodate the expanded Far East business, Lykes' fleet was expanded to forty-four ships, with the addition of three roll-on/roll-off vessels.

Lykes had not provided service to mainland China since 1949. In March, under a new agreement with the Peoples' Republic of China, a Lykes ship arrived in Shanghai. Lykes' intermodal transportation services continued to grow in 1978; this service involves shipments requiring both water and land transportation. Lykes trucks and railroad lines are used for the land portion, while its ships and barges are used for the sea and inland waterway segments. The company considers this complete, integrated service a valuable marketing tool.

The company was granted new authority to serve the west coast of Central America for domestic ports along the Gulf of Mexico. In addition, Lykes was allowed to interchange the type of vessel it operates on its various trade routes. Lykes viewed both authorizations as providing it with greater worldwide service capabilities. In mid-1979, the company shifted one of its three SEABEE vessels from the Continental to the Mediterranean line, improving operations in both areas.

Severe competition lowered rates charged on the Pacific routes from West Coast ports; Lykes revised schedules and refitted two of the three roll-on/roll-off vessels assigned to these routes to improve the company's competitive position. The other roll-on/roll-off vessel and four conventional freighters were chartered to the Military Sealift Command for periods of two to five years. This strategy helped reduce the number of idle status days to 44 in 1980, down from 813 in 1979. In January of 1981, the company completed purchase of two additional roll-on/roll-off ships from the Hansa Line of Bremen, Germany. These ships were to be used to fulfill a $141 million five-year contract with the U.S. Navy's Military Sealift Command.[4]

Exhibits 15 and 16 show the various routes for Lykes, along with the number of voyages and revenue tonnage, 1977 to 1980. Exhibit 6 contains the sales and operating income for LTV's shipping segment.

Strategic Decisions at Continental Emsco

The Continental Emsco Division, with headquarters in Dallas, was formed in 1912. The company produces a wide range of products for drilling contractors and oil and gas producers. Major manufacturing plants are in Houston and Garland, Texas and licensees exist in West Germany, Italy, Japan, and France. Major product lines include machinery and equipment, seamless pipe, and supplies. Specific machinery and equipment are derricks, draw-

---

[4]"What LTV Sees In Lykes." *Fortune,* July 17, 1978, pp. 15–16 and "There's More Than Ships and Steel In The Lykes' Family Vault." *Fortune,* July 17, 1978, pp. 50–54.

EXHIBIT 15   Voyages completed and revenue tonnage according to Lykes trade routes, 1977–1978

Lykes Lines Trade Routes	Voyages Completed		Revenue Tonnage	
	1978	*1977*	*1978*	*1977*
UK/Continent	23	26	1,069,315	1,098,118
Mediterranean	48	50	740,823	665,160
South & East Africa	20	19	233,720	266,681
Far East	31	27	674,562	598,122
West Coast, South America	25	25	317,809	275,208
Great Lakes/Mediterranean	9	9	126,775	131,517
Great Lakes/South America	2	—	15,023	—
Totals	158	156	3,178,027	3,034,806

SOURCE: Company Annual Reports.

works, mud pumps, swivels, blocks, rotary machines, and similar equipment. Continental Emsco is one of the largest producers of marine transfer systems used to load and unload petroleum products to and from small tankers or supertankers.

The company distributes oil country tubular steel products produced by the Jones & Laughlin Division of LTV; it also has similar agreements with other steel companies, such as Lone Star Steel, CF&I, and Liberty. These products are sold and distributed through 100 stores and offices in the United States and Canada, foreign offices in London, Singapore, Mexico, and Maracaibo, and by a network of sales agents throughout the world.

One of the companies in the Continental Emsco group is the Fibercast Company of Sand Springs, Oklahoma, which manufactures glass reinforced

EXHIBIT 16   Voyages completed and revenue tonnage according to Lykes trade routes, 1979–1980

Lykes Lines Trade Routes	Voyages Completed		Revenue Tonnage	
	1980	*1979*	*1980*	*1979*
United Kingdom, Continent	20	20	972,654	931,832
Mediterranean	41	49	644,394	752,486
South & East Africa	32	28	402,614	312,961
Far East	32	34	570,354	674,499
West Coast, South America	26	30	310,014	325,611
Great Lakes/Mediterranean	6	7	89,396	108,741
West Coast/North Pacific	19	18	544,403	476,186
West Coast/South Pacific	15	8	262,632	121,989
Time Charter	20	—	—	—
Totals	211	194	3,796,461	3,704,305

SOURCE: Company Annual Reports.

plastic pipe and fittings for in-plant piping systems used by the chemical processing industry. It manufactures and distributes other piping systems to water treatment plants, sewage disposal plants, waste disposal plants, and waste disposal systems in atomic energy plants.

Continental Emsco had an excellent year in 1979, resulting mostly from increased oil and gas exploration and development around the globe. Expanding markets for corrosion resistant piping systems manufactured by CE's Fibercast Company also contributed to the division's successful year. Ten days after the merger between LTV and Lykes, which brought Continental Emsco under the LTV umbrella, CE announced that it had agreed to furnish the People's Republic of China with seven drilling rig units worth over $40 million.

Continental Emsco's Houston Division builds drilling equipment for both land-based and off-shore drilling. In 1978, domestic and international demand were both strong, but the company believed that domestic demand was leveling off. During 1978, the Garland Division developed and marketed for oilfield use a swivel joint that can contain extra high pressure, above 15,000 pounds per square inch.

The Fibercast Division expanded its marketing effort in 1978 to applications like power plant, environmental scrubbers, and waste water disposal tubing. New markets in pipe coupling and technical services were entered. Several new applications were introduced in chemicals, and Fibercast pipe, used in the process of recovering uranium from phosphoric acid, was operating in the plants of six Fibercast customers. Also, the company began producing a new Easy Disconnect Coupler (EDC) for piping installations that are temporary or that require periodic cleaning or rotation. Fibercast emphasized its technical service capabilities through both a computer-assisted piping system design for customer use and general engineering services.

Several factors explain Continental Emsco's successful year in 1980. Sales of tubular products increased 73 percent over 1979, due to increased demand created by record drilling activity in the nation's oil and gas fields. Because of the merger with LTV, Continental Emsco gained a larger, more dependable, diverse, and efficient source for tubular products—Jones & Laughlin; Continental Emsco takes 50 percent of J&L's tubular products' production. The company also worked aggressively to expand its role as a distributor for other suppliers of tubular products, and the tubular services unit, which threads and tests oil country tubular goods, expanded its operations through a strong tubular market, improved operating efficiency, and new equipment. Drilling equipment sales rose 53 percent in 1980, requiring capacity expansion of the Houston plant. Much of 1980's sales gains were attributed to the replacement parts market, as drilling contractors sought to keep older drilling units in good working order. Continental Emsco opened four new oil field supply stores in 1980 and expanded a number of existing store facilities, for a total of 133 such operations.

Continental Emsco acquired three companies in 1980. The United Meter Company of Andrews, Texas expanded the firm's capability in the market for specialized oil and gas production equipment. The Skagit Corporation, of

Sedro-Woolley, Washington, offered two major advantages to Continental Emsco. Skagit's line of anchor winches, mooring equipment, and pedestal cranes for offshore drilling complemented its line of offshore products. Also, Skagit had underused manufacturing capacity which Continental Emsco used to increase drilling equipment production. The Wilson Oil Rig Manufacturing Co. of Wichita Falls, Texas was acquired because Continental Emsco believed that increased emphasis on secondary and tertiary recovery would expand the demand for wheel-mounted mobile workover and service rigs used in oil and gas well remedial and service work—Wilson's main product line.[5]

Strategic Decisions at the Aerospace/Defense Division

Vought is the second oldest continuous producer of military aircraft in the United States. The company's first airplane, the single engine VE-7, was designed and produced by aerospace pioneer Chance Milton Vought in 1917. Vought has produced over 15,000 military aircraft, with such famous names as Corsair, Kingfisher and Crusader. The Company's A-7 attack fighter has been the backbone of the Navy's carrier-based strike force since 1967. Vought developed the Lance battlefield missile system for the U.S. Army and six other nations; it can deliver a nuclear or non-nuclear warhead. Vought is developing the General Support Rocket System for the Army. The company has contributed substantially to the space program. It was the builder and program manager for the Scout, NASA's space launch vehicle, and supplied components for the Orbiter space shuttle.

Much of Vought's business is subcontracting work, including components for the Boeing 747, McDonnell Douglas DC-10, the Lockheed C-130, SH-60-B Lamps Helicopter, and Bell 222 twin commercial helicopter. In 1974, Vought became involved with ground transportation when its Airtrans transit system went into operation at the Dallas/Fort Worth airport. Kentron International, a Vought subsidiary, employs more than 2000 managers, engineers, and technicians who install, maintain, and operate communication systems, radar systems, missile and satellite tracking systems, telemetry systems, data processing systems and optical instrumentation.

Vought obtained various contracts between 1977 and 1981. The most important of these included:

☐ A contract worth $24 million to provide Greece with five two-seat TA-7H planes.

☐ A contract of $22 million to provide 25 F-8H Crusader fighters for the Philippine Air Force.

☐ A contract for $35 million to produce an additional 360 non-nuclear Lance missiles.

☐ A contract of $59 million to develop and test hardware in support of space defense technology.

---

[5]Company Annual Reports.

☐ A contract estimated to be eventually worth over $4 billion by 1995 to build the Multiple Launch Rocket System (MLRS) for the U.S. Army.

☐ A contract of $268 million from the U.S. Air Force to develop an air-launched anti-satellite weapon.

☐ A contract of $50 million to provide the Pakistan Ministry of Railways with a modern microwave communication and signalling system.

Vought's executives believe that the future outlook for this LTV division is good. Most of the world's airlines are expected to replace major portions of their old and fuel-inefficient fleets. Vought believes that it can obtain contracts to provide various parts of replacement planes, and it is counting on increases in defense spending to help improve its revenues and profits.

Between 1977 and 1981, Vought engaged in a number of research and development projects, some with near-term potential payoffs, others with anticipated longer-run benefits. Some of these more significant projects include computer-aided design and manufacturing, neutron radiography, optical data recording, high-energy laser protection, advanced laminar flow wing concepts, metal laminate materials, high-capacity computer memories, commercial high-speed data printout systems, intelligence analysis, and robot technologies.[6]

Exhibit 17 shows Vought's sales by major product line and sales by major customer. (Vought's sales and profits are indicated in Exhibit 6.)

EXHIBIT 17   Sales by product line and by customer for aerospace/defense segment, 1977–1980

Sales by Product Line	*1980*	*1979*	*1978*	*1977*
Aircraft/aircraft subcontracting	**55%**	51%	60%	70%
Missiles and space	**25%**	27%	24%	23%
Administrative and technical	**20%**	22%	16%	7%
Sales by Customer				
Navy	**30%**	30%	42%	58%
Commercial	**26%**	26%	18%	10%
Army	**17%**	17%	15%	14%
Air Force	**16%**	15%	15%	7%
NASA	**9%**	8%	9%	9%
All Other	**2%**	4%	1%	2%

SOURCE: Company Annual Reports.

[6]Company Annual Reports.

EPILOG

In July, 1981, LTV completed the spin-off of its Wilson Foods division which had been under consideration for several years. Wilson stock was distributed to LTV shareholders. The divestiture of Wilson, according to LTV's top management, was

> predicated on the recognition that LTV's long-term future must be built on a manufacturing and technology base. Wilson, as a consumer products company, did not fit that pattern. . . . This refocusing enables LTV to more effectively concentrate its management and financial resources on the high-growth areas of energy products and aerospace/defense, while maintaining its position of leadership in the steel and ocean shipping industries.

Management was delighted with the Company's 1981 financial results. Net sales and revenues of $7.5 billion resulted in record net income of $386 million. Results for the four remaining operating divisions were:

	Sales and Revenues	Operating Income
Steel	$4.79 billion	$336 million
Energy Products and Services	2.08 billion	220 million
Aerospace/Defense	797 million	39 million
Ocean Shipping	457 million	27 million

Because of record earnings, LTV was able to reinstate dividends on its common stock and participating preference stock; this was the first time since 1970 that the company had paid dividends.[7]

---

[7]Company's 1981 Annual Report

Newell Furniture Company

Robert Bending, sales vice president of Newell Furniture Company, slowly removed the conference materials from his attaché case, sorted them out, carefully placed them on his desk, and then sat down deep in thought. He had just returned from a two-day seminar called "Strategic Marketing Strategy." While in many ways he had felt he could ill afford the time away from the office and the pressing problems facing him there, he had hoped the seminar might spark some ideas for new approaches to these problems.

Heaven knows, new approaches were needed; things had not been going well with the company for some time, and he was well aware of the growing dissatisfaction of the company president, Mr. Steven Clayton, with recent sales performance. This, of course, was Bending's direct responsibility.

Bending had come to Newell a little more than a year and a half ago from the Holden Company, one of Newell's many competitors in the furniture business, where he had been director of marketing. The sales vice president position at Newell was open at that time due to a resignation. It was general knowledge that the resignation of the former vice president was submitted under pressure. The company conducted a search for a successor with a strong background in furniture marketing. Mr. Clayton, having learned through his acquaintances of Bending's performance record with Holden, had contacted him personally to discuss the position at Newell. Negotiations proceeded to mutually satisfactory arrangements on salary and other benefits, and Bending decided to join Newell.

The research and written case information were presented at a Case Research Symposium and were evaluated by the Case Research Association's Editorial Board. This case was prepared by Earl R. Sage and Thomas H. Stevenson of the University of North Carolina at Charlotte as a basis for class discussion.

At that time Mr. Clayton himself had only been with the company approximately one year. Prior to his arrival the company had been managed by members of the Newell family. Due to company problems and increasing frictions it had been decided by family members that outside professional management was needed. When Clayton joined the company as president, he knew he faced a number of challenges but was confident he would be able to show positive results.

Bending glanced over the seminar materials. The seminar had stressed the development of a consistent marketing program: definition of the business, determination of the mission of the total business, the formulation of functional strategies, delineation of target segments, and the development of products, communications, channels, and pricing policies for reaching those segments. These were familiar themes to him, of course, since his undergraduate major had been in marketing, and he had made a conscientious effort to keep up with the significant writings in the area, but he was becoming increasingly concerned with whether he had moved Newell's marketing program in the right direction. Sales and profit figures had been disappointing during the first year he had been with Newell (see Exhibits 1 and 2), but he was not then seriously concerned, because he knew time would be required to make the necessary changes to bring about an improvement. And too, a decision had been made by Mr. Clayton to bring the company's scope of operations to a lower level of sales as a new base for growth, starting the first year Bending was with the company. He was now well into his second year and results continued to be disappointing. Sales for the first two quarters of 1980 were up only 8 percent over the previous year. Actual sales for the six-month period were $24 million, versus a target of $28 million. Due to increases in cost of goods sold, there had been a decrease in gross margin and a resulting net loss for the half which was three times greater than that of the previous year. This was naturally a matter of great concern to Mr. Clayton and all of company management.

Bending sat back, considering his situation. For the first time in his working life he wondered if he was in a job he could not handle. He was disturbed by statements made privately by a former family member of management who acknowledged, "We made a lot of mistakes. We drifted and acted on impulse rather than on the basis of orderly planning. With the rise of the mass merchandisers—Levitz, Wickes, Penney's, Sears—we succumbed to the lure of volume, just as many manufacturers in other lines did. To reduce our prices to them, among other things we reduced our advertising, since they argued, reasonably enough, that sales to them did not require advertising. We gave less attention to our traditional customers, and reduced our quality under the constant pressure to reduce prices. We were forced to carry more inventory to provide quick delivery, and this cost more money than we had. We neglected to realize that we had neither the size nor the strength to be a large-volume producer, yet we tried to act like one. Clayton, of course, recognizes this and is taking steps to correct it, but the adjustment will be painful, because this is a rough time for our industry."

INDUSTRY

The broad category of home furnishings includes consumer purchases of furniture, mattresses, kitchen and household appliances, tableware, carpeting and various other durable and semi-durable products. Consumer expenditures for home furnishings were $77.6 billion in 1978, $85.7 billion in 1979, and were projected, in Standard Poors' *Industry Surveys* to increase 14 percent to an estimated $98 billion (in current dollars) in 1980. In recent years these expenditures have accounted for approximately 5.5 percent of disposable income.

The household furniture industry is a part of this overall industry. Three of the major segments are: wood household furniture (1980 shipments estimated by Predicasts at $5.2 billion), upholstered furniture ($3.9 billion), and metal furniture ($1.5 billion).[1] It is a highly competitive industry made up of small and medium-sized businesses, many of which are still family-controlled. In 1977, according to the Bureau of the Census, there were 2982 wood furniture manufacturing establishments, and over 70 percent of these establishments had fewer than 20 employees.[2]

The industry was originally located in the New England/Middle Atlantic states but then spread to the Middle West as the population moved in that direction. In the 1930s, the Carolinas and Virginia became the center of the industry, because of the abundance of lumber, cheap labor, and a large national market for low-priced furniture. This area of the South continued to be the center, with the majority of the top manufacturers located in a 150-mile belt running from Lenoir, North Carolina to Bassett, Virginia.

The demand for household furniture has historically been related to disposable personal income, residential construction, existing home sales, and interest rates. Housing starts declined 40 percent in 1980, compared to the previous year, and existing home sales were down 20 percent. Higher interest rates influence not only home purchases, but home furnishings as well, since approximately two-thirds of all retail furniture purchases are made through credit. Other factors include demographic changes, such as the maturing population in the U.S., increase in the number of two-income families, and changing life styles. The demand for furniture has declined to an annual "growth" rate of -3 percent over the past three years as a result of these influences, and the long-range forecast indicates at best, a return to modest annual growth rates in the coming decade.

Furniture demand has, over the years, been style- and price-sensitive. Therefore, furniture manufacturers must cope with low margins while at the same time they must commit substantial funds to product development. As competitive pressures increase during periods of reduced consumer buying, manufacturers are forced to generate new styling and distribution to stimulate sales.

---

[1] *Predicast Forecasts.* Cleveland, Ohio: *Predicasts,* Inc., 1980. S.I.C. 250, pp. B166–7.

[2] U.S. Department of Commerce, Bureau of the Census, *1977 Census of Manufacturers,* "Household Furniture." Washington, D.C.: Government Printing Office, 1977. S.I.C. 2511, 12, 14, 15, 17, 19. Industry Series MC 77–1–25A.

Product lines for the coming season are shown several times during the year at wholesale trade exhibits. The major markets are in High Point, North Carolina, Chicago, Dallas, and San Francisco. These shows are attended by buyers from major retailers ranging from furniture specialists to mass merchandisers. It is not unusual for a regional buyer to shop many of the trade shows across the country since design and styling are very dynamic.

Also important to buyers is quick delivery. Consequently, the ability to carry an inventory for quick response to orders is a hardship, particularly for the smaller producers.

COMPANY HISTORY

The Newell Company was founded by Mr. Harold Newell in 1935 in Seymour, North Carolina. Mr. Newell had been a salesman for a small furniture manufacturer in nearby Wayland, North Carolina. From a small beginning, the company developed into a successful concern with a reputation for quality and craftsmanship in both case goods (wood furniture) and upholstered furniture. During World War II, the majority of the company's output was taken up by sales to the government. After the war, the company expanded to meet the pent-up post-war demand for furniture. They continued to emphasize quality products at the middle to upper end of the price line. The company prospered and enjoyed steady growth until Mr. Newell's death in 1969, at which time management was taken over by other members of the Newell family.

Mr. Newell's death marked the turning point in the company's fortunes. Early in the 1970s, the company decided to switch emphasis away from its traditional dealers, full-line furniture stores, toward mass merchandisers (such as Wickes and Sears.) Newell's management reasoned that the big retailers seemed likely to capture a huge share of the furniture market.

By 1976 mass merchandisers accounted for more than 52 percent of Newell's net sales (see Exhibit 1), but these volume sales did not produce profits (see Exhibit 2). Newell offered these biggest customers exclusive lines of furniture, in addition to the regular product lines at lower prices than its other dealers. As a result the traditional dealer base, which had peaked at approximately 5200 dealers in the early 1960s, dropped to 2180 dealers in 1976. With this dramatic decline, Newell found itself heavily dependent on its new

EXHIBIT 1 Percent distribution of sales

	1979	*1978*	*1977*	*1976*	*1975*
Retail Establishments:					
Retail Stores	78.8	69.4	61.2	48.0	48.0
Mass Merchandisers	21.2	29.0	37.0	52.0	50.0
Government	—	1.6	1.8	—	2.0
	100.0	100.0	100.0	100.0	100.0

EXHIBIT 2   Income statement summary (dollar amounts in thousands)

| | Year ending December 31 | | | | |
	1979	1978	1977	1976	1975
Net sales	43,300	40,128	50,134	65,180	68,750
Cost of goods sold:					
Materials	18,058	16,808	21,455	27,073	28,792
Direct labor	11,606	9,747	12,336	17,417	16,830
Overhead	9,121	10,082	11,229	15,120	16,140
Total	38,785	36,637	45,020	59,610	61,762
Gross profit	4,515	3,491	5,114	5,570	6,988
Interest expense	675	623	681	720	630
Total S & GA expense	3,891	4,030	5,020	6,046	8,062
Net profit before taxes	(51)	(1,162)	(588)	(1,196)	(1,704)
Income taxes	—	—	—	—	—
Net profit after taxes	(51)	(1,162)	(588)	(1,196)	(1,704)
Units sold (000)	358.4	359.1	455.8	620.8	667.5

low-margin customers. Sales to traditional outlets had permitted a gross profit of approximately 20 percent in the past, but sales to mass merchandisers produced somewhat less than half that, with continuing pressure to reduce margins even further. They had also begun exerting increasing influence on product design and inventory plans.

NEWELL'S MARKETING PROGRAM

Starting in 1976 and in the ensuing years, Newell changed approaches a number of times, both in styling and distribution. In 1977 Newell entered the so-called designer market, engaging a well-known designer to develop a distinctive line of upper middle price furniture meant to respond to what the company believed was a promising trend. This line was sold primarily to department stores and style stores. Although the line was received well by the press and by exclusive retailers and interior designers, its life was short, due to production inefficiencies and the lack of final consumer acceptance.

During this time they followed a major program to reduce reliance on mass merchandisers as outlets.

In 1977 the company decided to emphasize case goods and other wooden furniture designed for the mass market at the medium retail price point. Each product line was reviewed and as much as 50 percent of each was restyled with the aim of providing a broader appeal to the 25–44 age group, which represents the prime furniture purchasing group. At the same time the company broadened its offering of casual styling for the rapidly-growing family room market. Altogether, forty-eight new pieces were introduced at the fall show that year.

In 1978 a company spokesman announced that Newell's marketing approach would change considerably in the coming year in terms of styling, price points, and distribution of its products. There would be reduced emphasis on "trendy" merchandising programs and more concentration on basic styles considered to have broad appeal to both the retailer and the consumer. This would enable the company to "... achieve an efficient volume, by merchandising basic products for the mass market and important middle retail points."

At the beginning of 1978, the company sold its upholstered furniture line to one of the Newell family members (see Exhibit 3). Arrangements were made for him to continue to produce the line under the Newell name. This action was taken because the line had long been considered unprofitable, and the sale provided badly needed cash. At the 1978 shows the company introduced only twenty-two new offerings.

In recent months suggestions had been made that the company might profitably respond to a new trend, the marketing of unfinished, highly crafted furniture kits for the do-it-yourselfer. This had appeal, for it would utilize production capacity which was idle and available due to the decrease in volume occasioned by the move away from the mass merchandisers.

Development of an appropriate pricing strategy had been a continuing problem. Shortly after he joined the company, Bending had requested historical cost and profitability information by product line (there were approximately 480 different items of furniture being produced in 1978), but Frank Powers, financial officer of the company said he was unable to provide information at that level of detail. Powers himself had only been with the company since 1977. He acknowledged the desirability of such information, but the cost system in existence only provided summary information, primarily by manufacturing operation, and it would require some time (perhaps two years) to develop a new system. No specific action had been taken as yet. Bending felt strongly that Sears and other buyers were buying selectively on the basis of price and Newell was then left with inventories which were difficult to sell. Partly as a result of this, the company opened an outlet store in Gaffney, S.C. in 1979, to dispose of these inventories at discount prices to the public. Gaffney is a well-known consumer outlet center.

Mr. Clayton, in 1979, established an overall gross margin objective of 15 percent. Although 15 percent was below the industry average of 25 percent, it

EXHIBIT 3 Approximate percentage of net sales by product

	1979	1978	1977	1976	1975
Wood living room, bedroom & dining room furniture	98	97	89	79	78
Upholstered furniture	—	—*	8	18	20
Other	2	3	3	3	2
	100	100	100	100	100

*discontinued

EXHIBIT 4   Newell company balance sheet (dollar amounts in thousands)

	1979	1978	1977	1976	1975
Assets					
Current:					
Cash	2,100	3,100	785	2,850	2,000
Marketable securities	1,750	2,005	—	—	—
Accounts receivable	7,200	4,759	7,546	9,980	10,010
Inventories	6,767	4,700	9,500	9,204	9,725
Prepaid expenses	721	520	830	650	200
Total current assets	18,538	15,084	18,661	22,684	21,935
Property and equipment					
(Net of depreciation)	9,200	12,100	13,005	12,300	11,520
Total assets	27,738	27,184	31,666	34,984	33,455
Liabilities and					
stockholders equity					
Current liabilities:					
Notes payable	6,750	6,200	7,510	9,000	7,875
Accounts payable	2,180	2,150	2,630	3,180	3,250
Accruals	2,005	1,980	2,510	3,200	2,530
Total current liabilities	10,935	10,330	12,650	15,380	13,655
Long term debt	3,000	3,000	4,000	4,000	3,000
Stockholders equity:					
Common stock	10,600	10,600	10,600	10,600	10,600
Retained earnings	3,203	3,254	4,416	5,004	6,200
	13,803	13,854	15,016	15,604	16,800
Total liabilities and stockholders equity	27,738	27,184	31,666	34,984	33,455

was considered to be a realistic interim target. Clayton also urged that accounts be required to buy complete product lines, to avoid the selective
buying which damaged profitability, but this was met with resistance by the
company sales representatives.

Promotion is a key marketing element in the industry. Trade shows are
the primary means by which product awareness is built at the retail level.
Newell has always followed the industry in this respect and has maintained
relatively large exhibit spaces. Because of declining volume, in recent years
three of the spaces have been vacated in regional exhibits; however, Newell
continues to attend all major home furnishings shows.

Newel has increased its advertising expenditures in line with its strategy
of expanding its traditional dealer base (see Exhibit 5).

EXHIBIT 5 Advertising expenditures/net sales

	1979	1978	1977	1976	1975
Advertising Dollars (000)	$ 2,122	$ 1,765	$ 1,554	$ 1,304	$ 825
% of Sales	4.9	4.4	3.1	2.0	1.2
Net Sales	$43,300	$40,128	$50,134	$65,180	$68,750

Brand loyalty is fairly strong in the furniture industry, so Newell has attempted to strengthen brand identification through dealer cooperative advertising. Dealer participation has been somewhat unenthusiastic, however. A Newell company salesman said "retailers have the impression that Newell is a name from the past." He remarked that this was undoubtedly due to reduced advertising which occurred during the mass-volume days of the company.

Bending, after considerable deliberation about where the advertising dollars should go, decided upon 50 percent for trade shows, 25 percent print media and 25 percent on miscellaneous promotional and display materials. This had been the historical pattern for the company and Bending concluded he had no good reason to change it.

Direct selling to retail establishments is important in the industry. Newell's sales force is organized on a regional basis, with assigned territories in each region. Although sales dropped nearly 40 percent from 1976 to 1978, the sales force was only reduced from forty-nine to forty-two people. However, they are paid on a straight commission basis, so this does not represent a cash drain for the firm. Bending had hoped to institute a formal sales performance evaluation system, but thus far he has been unable to do so.

In a year-end meeting with company management, December, 1979, Mr. Clayton had stated that several key elements of Newell's competitive strategy would receive increasing attention: product development, quality, and speed of delivery. Although Bending was aware of these statements, his two-day marketing seminar made him wonder whether these were *the* critical considerations.

Poppin Fresh
Pie Shops

Founded in 1869, the Pillsbury Company has grown from a small flour milling operation into a highly diversified, multi-faceted company. The key to
Pillsbury's success has been the ability of the company's top management to foresee the future needs of both the company, the industry, and the
consumer.

Originally production of flour was the most important function at Pillsbury. This stage of the company's history was best described by R.T. Keith, a
top executive, as the "We Make Flour" stage. When competition became
more intense in the 1930s, the company had to aggressively seek new customers and entered the sales era, or the "We Sell Flour" stage. Finally the
marketing era dawned in the 1950s when the management of Pillsbury began
to focus on its customers and asked, "What does the customer want that has
flour in it?"[1] One of the ways Pillsbury responded to that question was the
development of Poppin Fresh Pie Shops.

Pillsbury, unlike its competition, is committed to staying in the food
business. The company operates in three major business segments: (1) agri-
products—flour and rice milling, bakery mixes, grain and feed ingredients;
(2) consumer branded foods—dry grocery, refrigerated, frozen and canned
products sold primarily through supermarkets; and (3) restaurants—Burger
King, Steak and Ale, Poppin Fresh Pie Shops, Le Chateau, and Hoffman
House.

Burger King was purchased in 1967 as Pillsbury's initial involvement in
the foodservice industry. As part of its planned program of expansion, Pillsbury's management also wanted an informal, sit-down, table service restau-

The research and written case information were presented at a Case Research Symposium and
were evaluated by the Case Research Association's Editorial Board. This case was prepared by
Linda Swayne of the College of St. Thomas as a basis for class discussion.

[1]Robert J. Keith. "The Marketing Revolution." *The Journal of Marketing,* January 1960, pp.
35-38.

rant and a formal dinner restaurant. Poppin Fresh was conceived for the informal segment and Steak and Ale was purchased in 1975 to provide a white tablecloth, formal dinner restaurant.

The research and development department was studying a pie shop chain in California, as a sit-down, family style restaurant alternative, when Pillsbury learned that a restauranteur in Des Moines, Iowa, was constructing a similar store. Pillsbury purchased the store and the first Poppin Fresh Pie Shop was opened in 1969. One year later, December of 1970, Poppin Fresh expanded into the Minneapolis-St. Paul area with the opening of a store in suburban Hopkins. The pie shop concept was a success and Pillsbury has continued to add additional units. Today, sixty-nine stores are in operation in seven metropolitan areas in the Midwest (see Exhibit 1). Further expansion has been planned.

In starting Poppin Fresh Pies, Pillsbury wanted to develop a restaurant chain that was a quality leader in the informal market segment. Quality is important throughout the organization as expressed by the company in its motto, "A Cut Above".

Poppin Fresh has defined its strategic goals as:

1. To be, unquestionably, a unique quality leader in the informal, moderate price, waitress service, restaurant segment in every market where we compete.

2. To consistently produce profits that are considered excellent when compared to other full service restaurant chains and Pillsbury criteria.

3. To grow, in profitability, at levels above the industry norm.

To accomplish these goals, Poppin Fresh has defined the target market in the following manner:

☐ adults 25–54 years of age

☐ high school graduate (minimum)

☐ household income of $15,000+

EXHIBIT 1 Restaurant opening history

	70	71	72	73	74	75	76	77	78	79	80
Des Moines (3)	1					1		1			
Twin Cities (12)		1	4			2		2		3	
Chicago (32)						2	5	8	7	6	4
Milwaukee (5)								4	1		
Cleveland (10)										4	6
Indianapolis (3)										3	
Detroit (4)											4
Total: (69)	1	1	4	0	0	5	5	15	8	16	14
Total Stores:	1	2	6	6	6	11	16	31	39	55	69

☐ household size 1 to 4
☐ loves pie

THE POPPIN FRESH PIE STORE

Poppin Fresh is unique in that it is a combination of three businesses:

☐ An informal restaurant that serves meals and pie for dessert.
☐ A pie snack place.
☐ A retail pie bakery (take-out pies).

The fresh, high quality pie of Poppin Fresh is its comparative advantage. Everything on the luncheon/dinner menu attempts to complement pie. There are twenty-five different kinds of pie available and a specialty pie of the month to add variety (see Exhibit 2).

On the average each restaurant in the chain sells 250 pies a day. Carry-out pies account for slightly over 25 percent of total sales, with the average whole pie price of $3.92.

Take-out pie usage is broadly distributed across demographic characteristics. In general, however, *take-out pie* buyers tend to be between 24 and 44 years of age, with large households and upper incomes. Medium and heavy users of Poppin Fresh *restaurants* tend to be upscale in income and are over-represented among those with high school or college degrees and larger households.

Sales vary by day part, week part, and season. Piece pie sales per 100 customers are shown in Exhibit 3. Saturday has the greatest concentration of sales with Monday, Tuesday, and Wednesday all being considerably weaker. December, January and February are relatively poor months for sales, with March, May, and July being the best sales months.

Apple pies are the best whole pie seller while French Silk is the best selling pie by the piece. Exhibit 4 summarizes the top five best sellers for whole pies and piece pies. Strawberry pies sell well but are seasonal. Currently five of the menu pies contain strawberries.

Pie is a very high cost product. The ingredients are expensive and labor costs are high. As an example, French Silk, a rich chocolate filled pie topped with whipped cream, costs Poppin Fresh $2.80 (1979) in ingredients, labor, and overhead to make one pie. Take out retail price is $4.75 for the whole pie. Pies that are sold in-store are cut into six pieces and each piece sells for $1.40.

After market tests in two stores, breakfast has been introduced throughout the chain. Traditional egg, pancake, and french toast breakfasts are offered, as well as quiche, omelettes, fruit pies, and coffee cake. The objective is to increase restaurant sales and profitability through greater use of existing facilities.

Meals you'll remember...

For food that matches our incomparable pies, we apply the same exacting standards; the finest ingredients, clean kitchens, superbly trained bakers and cooks, and, above all, no shortcuts that detract from the quality of your food.

Attention to details like this separate "okay" restaurants from "superb dining" establishments. You'll taste the difference in every dish on this menu.

FRESH & HOT OFF THE GRILL

HAMBURGER & FRIES

CHEESEBURGER & FRIES

BIG CALIFORNIA & FRIES
A big 100% pure ground beef patty, topped with lettuce, tomato slices, melted cheese and our own relish dressing.

PATTY MELT & FRIES
Our big ground beef burger between two slices of melted cheese, topped with sauteed onions and served on grilled rye bread.

BACON BURGER ON ENGLISH & FRIES
Take a crisp toasted English muffin, add our big all beef burger, cheese and bacon, and you have an internationally delightful dish.

MUSHROOM AND BLUE CHEESE BURGER & FRIES
Pour mushroom sauce over a big beef burger, then pour chunky blue cheese dressing over that and put it all on grilled rye bread.

GRILLED CHEESE AND HAM WITH TOMATO Served with fries

GRILLED CHEESE & FRIES

For lighter fare tostitos may be substituted for french fries at no extra charge.

A CUP AND SANDWICH

CHILI AND HAMBURGER

SOUP AND GRILLED CHEESE & HAM WITH TOMATO

SOUP AND HAMBURGER

THE SANDWICH BOARD

FISH SANDWICH & FRIES
A large tasty lightly breaded fillet on grilled bread with cheese and our special Louie dressing.

TURKEY SANDWICH
Sliced roast turkey breast, crisp lettuce leaves and sliced tomatoes. Served with our freshly made five-bean salad.

TURKEY CLUBHOUSE
Sliced roast turkey breast, bacon, crisp lettuce, tomato slices on toast. Served with our own freshly made five-bean salad, a taste-tempter for bean salad fans.

STACKED HAM
Thin-sliced ham and crisp lettuce on rye. Served with our freshly made five-bean salad and hot brown mustard on the side.

TUNA SALAD SANDWICH
A blend of superior water-packed white albacore chunk tuna, chopped celery, relishes and salad dressing. Served with our freshly made five-bean salad.

BOWL AND BREAD

SOUP BOWL & BREAD
A meal-sized bowl of simmering vegetable beef soup, rich with a strong beef broth, hearty beef chunks and six different vegetables. Served with a thick slice of buttered French-style bread.

CHILI BOWL & BREAD
A meal-in-itself bowl of chili . . . our own special recipe, with coarse ground beef, red beans and a wide variety of spices. Served in a crockery casserole accompanied by a thick slice of buttered French-style bread .

FROM THE SALAD CHEF

Each salad is a meal in itself, with chilled, freshly chopped lettuce custom tossed with one of our six delicious dressings, and then garnished with other freshly sliced ingredients — prepared for you specially, after you place your order. There is no fresher salad in town — anywhere, at any price.

DOUGHBOY SALAD
Freshly chopped lettuce and small pieces of melba toast are tossed with our own famous Parmesan dressing. Then we add sliced tomato wedges, hard-cooked egg slices and carrot sticks .

TACO SALAD
A thick bed of chilled lettuce is topped with Poppin Fresh's unique and flavorful chili, sprinkled with natural cheddar cheese and garnished with tomatoes, olives and a ring of crisp tostito chips.

CHEF'S SALAD DELUXE
A classic chef's salad that our chef happens to love to eat. Served with julienned ham, roast turkey breast and cheese over crisp lettuce. Garnished with hard-cooked egg slices and tomato wedges.

TUNA SALAD
A delicate mixture of water-packed white albacore tuna chunks, salad dressing, seasonings and relishes is served up on a bed of lettuce, surrounded by tomato wedges, hard-cooked egg slices and carrot sticks.

SHRIMP SALAD
A mound of bite-sized shrimp, mixed with just enough of our Louie dressing to create excitement among true shrimp lovers. Served on a bed of lettuce and garnished with asparagus, tomato wedges and hard-cooked egg slices .

HOUSE SPECIALTIES

QUICHE LORRAINE
We make this French delicacy right here in our own oven daily. An egg custard filling, natural Swiss & Jack cheeses smoked bacon, in our light flaky crust. Served with a salad.

HAMBURGER STEAK WITH MUSHROOM SAUCE
An oversized hamburger steak topped by our flavorful mushroom sauce, with its hint of garlic and green onions. Served with a salad and a thick slice of buttered French-style bread.

CHILI PATTY MELT
For lumberjack-sized appetites. Our big burger with melted cheese over it. . . surrounded by lots of steaming chili and served with a slice of French style bread and salad.

FOR THE LIGHT TOUCH

SOUP AND SALAD
A light combination that goes great with pie.

SALAD & SLICE
A slice of French style bread and a dinner salad with your choice of dressing .

ON THE SIDE

Cup of Vegetable	French Fries
Beef Soup	Dinner Salad
Cup of Chili	French Bread

BEVERAGES

Hot Tea	Sanka®
Brewed Iced Tea	Coffee with real
Grade A Milk	half & half
Soft Drinks	Hot Chocolate

No Substitutes, please

...and pies you'll never forget.

At Poppin Fresh we permit no shortcut in baking the finest pies we know of. In our bakeries, whipped cream is made by beating fresh cream in a mixer until it stands in peaks. The highest grade fruit we can buy is packed into light, flaky crusts, using an absolute minimum of filler to hold it together.

Pies are baked seven days a week to ensure you the most flavor possible in this most American of desserts.

Perfect pie-making may not be possible in this world, but we honestly believe that right now you are sitting as close to it as you will ever get.

WHIPPED CREAM
Banana Cream
Chocolate Cream
Coconut Cream

FRUIT
Country Apple	French Apple
Blueberry	Peach
Boysenberry	Raspberry
Cherry	Strawberry-Rhubarb

Warmed, with Country Cream or ala Mode; forty five cents extra.

CLASSIC SPECIALTIES
French Silk	Pecan
German Chocolate	Sour Cream Raisin

Carryout pies available whole or by the slice.

FRUIT SPECIALTIES
French Apple Cream Cheese
Fresh Strawberry Cream Cheese
French Strawberry
Sour Cream Strawberry
Fresh Strawberry

EXTRA TREATS
Vanilla ala Mode	Vanilla Ice Cream
Whipped Cream	Country Cream

MERINGUE
Lemon Meringue

OVEN FILLED
Custard	Pumpkin

Warmed, with whipped cream; forty five cents extra.

EXHIBIT 2

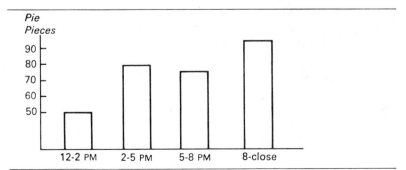

EXHIBIT 3 In-store piece pie sales/100 customers by day part

EXHIBIT 4 Best seller whole
pies/piece pies

Whole Pie	Piece Pie
1. Country Apple	1. French Silk
2. Banana Cream	2. Feature Pie
3. French Silk	3. Banana Cream
4. Lemon Meringue	4. Country Apple
5. Cherry	5. Lemon Merinque

Each store has a pie display case, a counter to seat ten customers, and a sit-down eating area for approximately 138 people. Layout is similar to most coffee shops, although the fixtures have a more upscale appearance. The tables and chairs are substantial, oversized, and constructed of wood and naugahide. The booths are overstuffed naugahide. Everything is kept scrupulously clean. The high ceilings with heavy beam architecture provide stores with an abundance of light, making them open and airy.

The pie display case is not a storage case, but it attractively displays ten to twelve pies with an identifying card. Above the display case is a flexible board used to indicate the take-out pies that are available. Some pies may be sold out and others, particularly strawberry, may be out of season. Above the counter is another similar board indicating the pieces of pie available.

When Poppin Fresh enters a new market, the first store built must include a bakery for the production of pies. The bakery can then service up to six stores by baking as many as 1800 pies and delivering them to each Poppin Fresh store in their own semi-trailer trucks. The trucks have specially built storage racks so that the pies are not damaged in transit. Cream pies and specialty pies are handled in this manner. Fruit and oven pies are baked in-store and are always fresh and available.

Stores are located where there is a 40,000 plus population within a two mile radius, median family income in excess of $15,000, heavy concentration of retail outlets, and minimum 20,000 vehicles passing the site daily.

POSITIONING

Poppin Fresh Pies is positioned as an informal, mid-priced, specialty restaurant/bakery. Specialty through premium pies provides Poppin Fresh with a uniqueness factor which is a definite comparative advantage in the highly competitive mid-range segment of the foodservice industry.

According to Donald Ryan, President of Poppin Fresh Division of Pillsbury, "Premium pie in our presentation is synonymous with quality. The high quality image created through our pies serves as a bridge to gap other critical areas of performance such as menu, overall facilities and personnel. Consistency of quality across all these areas must be maintained in order to continue to effectively position ourselves as above the competitive norm."

This quality positioning is under continued pressure from aggressive competitors in the mid-priced segment who seek to upgrade their menus, service, and facilities. In addition, internal pressures of bigness, growth and profitability make it challenging to maintain a quality position. "Our quality positioning is a moving target which must be protected and enhanced," according to Mr. Ryan.

In tracking studies done for Poppin Fresh in May and November, 1979, 75 percent of respondents interviewed mentioned Poppin Fresh as a pie source on an unaided basis. However, approximately 8 to 12 percent of consumers mentioned Poppin Fresh as a family restaurant on an unaided basis. This does not compare favorably with competition and strongly suggests that Poppin Fresh is perceived as a pie source rather than a family restaurant.

Poppin Fresh Pies is judged as an excellent source for quality pie. Pie source awareness numbers definitely reinforce this finding.

As a restaurant, the following points from the studies converge to create the current perception of Poppin Fresh Pies in the eyes of the consumer:

- ☐ More suitable for women and families
- ☐ Less suitable for men and teens
- ☐ A luncheon restaurant
- ☐ A neat attractive restaurant
- ☐ A friendly, efficient staff
- ☐ Relatively high quality food
- ☐ Limited menu variety
- ☐ Relatively high prices

COMPETITION

The Poppin Fresh Pie Shop concept is designed to compete in the vast, complex, mid-range of the restaurant industry. This broad segment of the foodservice industry is positioned between the dinner house, tablecloth type restaurant and the fast food segment. Typically the mid-range segment includes medium-priced family restaurants, budget steakers, cafeterias, coffee shops and sit-down, table service "specialty" restaurants. Poppin Fresh would be considered one of the latter.

Specific restaurants that are Poppin Fresh's major competition are different in each market. Generally, Sambo's, Denny's, Perkins' Cake and Steak and cafeterias compete with Poppin Fresh for the mid-range target market.

Another more definitive method used by the foodservice industry for determining the size of the mid-range market is to use price positioning. Price positioning is based on typical evening meal costs, including entree, beverage, and dessert (excludes alcoholic beverages). The size of the various segments are shown in Exhibit 5.

Poppin Fresh is in the mid-range, but at the high end. Several menu selections with dessert and beverage are priced higher than $5.00. Poppin

EXHIBIT 5   Top 100 separate eating place chains segmentation by price positioning

Price Positioning	Sales ($ millions)
Under $2.50	$15,529
$2.50–$5.00	6,826
Over $5.00	1,913
	$24,268

SOURCE: Technomic Consultants
IFMA Chain Dynamics—1979.

Fresh sales of approximately $64.5 million represent about a 1 percent share of the mid-range market.

POPPIN FRESH SALES

Sales by market are summarized in Exhibit 6. Cleveland, Indianapolis and Detroit represent new markets where stores have been open for less than two years.

While stores in most markets are reaching the financial objective, real sales have been sliding for the past three years (see Exhibit 7).

EXHIBIT 6   Poppin Fresh Pies 1979 sales by market*

	Des Moines	Twin Cities	Chicago	Milwaukee	Cleveland	Indianapolis	Detroit	Total
Total Sales	$3570	$14109	$30073	$4581	$6437	$2082	$2548	$63400
Av. sales per store	1190	1175	986	916	757	694	1019	983
Avg. number of stores	3	12	30.5	5	8.5	3	2.5	64.5

*in thousands.

EXHIBIT 7   Poppin Fresh Pies, Inc. volume analysis by market* (avg. restaurant deflated sales)**

Market	77	78	79	Latest 12 Mos.
Iowa	871	874	870	835
Minnesota	928	948	956	851
Illinois	859	863	773	702
Wisconsin	748	739	707	656
Indiana	—	—	—	—
Ohio	—	—	—	—
Michigan	—	—	—	—
All Stores	876	870	814	740

*Deflated sales in year of market opening not shown on chart but included in store average.
**Prices adjusted for inflation based on F77 prices. In thousands.

EXHIBIT 8   Price increases 1977–80

	Pricing			
	77	78	79	80
Increases taken during current year	6.4%	10.4%	18.1%	10.2%
Effect of current year increase on current year	2.2	4.2	9.0	4.4
Carry over from prior year	3.5	4.2	6.2	9.1
Price level vs. prior year	5.7	8.4	15.2	13.5

Several economic developments affecting consumers may be responsible for the real sales decline, according to President Ryan: "While family incomes are rising, they never seem to keep pace with rising life style expectations, causing customers to eat out less often and to trade down to less expensive restaurants. Real disposable income is falling and the economic recession causes consumers to be more critical of the value received at each dining situation."

In addition, cost increases for ingredients, equipment, etc., have been steep in recent years, causing substantial price increases. Exhibit 8 summarizes price increases. However, projections for the foodservice industry continue to indicate growth for the next three years.

FOODSERVICE GROWTH

Out-of-home eating has been on the increase as dining patterns are changing. Food served away from home accounted for 35–36 percent of personal consumption expenditures for food in 1978 versus 33 percent in 1971. Expectations are that this proportion will rise to 38 percent by 1983. U.S. per capita food consumption is likely to remain relatively constant, as will population growth (projected to be below 1 percent per year over this period), but consumers are expected to respond to life events and chain store promotions to trade more money for the time savings and other advantages of away-from-home eating.[2]

Foodservice involvement in the three basic meal occasions is uneven. Lunch is the meal most frequently consumed away from home (see Exhibit 9).

Arthur D. Little's estimate is that 32 percent of lunches are consumed away from home. Penetration into dinner and breakfast away from home consumption has been more difficult, but will be sought by foodservice during the period to 1983. The attempt will be made to overcome the relative unpopularity of breakfast by attempting to convince people of the convenience of eating breakfast away from home and by attempting to educate them concerning the nutritional input of the meal.

[2]Arthur D. Little, Incorporated, *Outlook for the Foodservice Industry to 1983,* 1979.

EXHIBIT 9   Meals consumed, by point of consumption, 1978 (% of total)

Meal	At Home	Away From Home
Breakfast	94%	6%
Lunch (includes snacks)	68%	32%
Dinner	82%	18%
Total	81%	19%

SOURCE: Arthur D. Little Inc., estimates.

Various demographic and life style changes will also have an impact on the foodservice industry. There will be a smaller under-21 age group, with the likely effect that fast food will cater to an older customer (who used to be its younger customer) by changes in decor, additional meal occasions, and menu variety. The 25–44 age group will become larger and more important, as will the over-60 age group. The dinner house as well as fast food are vying for the mid-priced segment of the 25–44 age group.

EXHIBIT 10   Average number of meals eaten out per week

SEX: Men	- 3.7	RACE: White	- 2.6
Women	- 2.0	Black	- 2.2

AGE:		INCOME:	
18–24 - 3.7		$35,000 +	- 4.2
25–34 - 3.2		20,000–34,999	- 3.7
35–44 - 2.9		12,000–19,999	- 2.9
45–54 - 2.8		7,500–11,999	- 2.8
55–64 - 2.3		Under 7,500	- 1.9

RESTAURANT

1. 37% of all men eat out on an average day—likewise 24% of women.
2. a. 30% of all breakfasts eaten out are in informal, family style restaurants.
   b. 29% of all lunches eaten out are in family style restaurants.
   c. Surveys show suggestions to eat out were made by:

Male head of household	41%
Female head of household	50%
Children	9%

FAST FOODS

1. Fast foods account for 34% of all eating out expenditures.
2. 44% of all adults eat out at least once a week in fast food outlets.
3. a. 24% of all breakfasts eaten out are in fast food outlets.
   b. 35% of all lunches eaten out are in fast food oulets.
   c. 18% of all dinners eaten out are in fast food outlets.

SOURCE: Radio Advertising Bureau, 1979.

According to the U.S. Bureau of the Census Series II (mid-range) projections, the population segments with the highest growth rates for the period 1977–1985 will be the 25–44 year old age bracket (over 3 percent per year) and the 65 and over segment (2.6 percent per year). Research by various groups has indicated that the 25–44 age group has the stronger disposition toward away-from-home eating, as well as the higher income necessary to pursue this option.

The number of working wives is continuing to increase. As a result of their expanded income and increased demands on their time, they are delegating food preparation, menu planning, food procurement, serving, and clean-up to the foodservice industry.

The Radio Advertising Bureau has completed a general study on Bakeries, Restaurants and Fast Food Outlets for the 1975–78 period. Exhibit 10 summarizes key findings.

The following restaurant frequency indices are derived from Simmons Marketing Research Bureau (Exhibit 11).

Away-from-home eating is occurring with greater frequency and is expected to continue. Since Poppin Fresh Pie Shop's uniqueness is specialty pies, consumer attitudes toward pie affects attitudes toward Poppin Fresh.

EXHIBIT 11 Fast food/family restaurant frequency index

	Fast Food Users Last 30 Days		Family Rest. Users Last 30 Days	
	%	Index	%	Index
SEX				
Males	47.9	100	48.6	101
Females	51.2	100	51.4	99
AGE				
18–24	20.1	110	19.1	105
25–34	24.5	110	24.5	110
35–44	17.3	108	17.3	108
45–54	15.1	100	15.4	102
55–64	12.5	92	13.0	96
65+	10.5	71	10.7	73
HOUSEHOLD INCOME				
$25,000+	28.1	106	30.5	115
$20,000–24,999	13.9	107	15.2	116
$15,000–19,999	15.9	107	16.6	112
$10,000–14,999	21.4	99	20.7	96
$5,000–9,999	13.1	91	11.5	80
Under $5,000	7.6	78	5.6	57

SOURCE: 1979 Simmons Marketing Research Bureau.

ATTITUDES TOWARD DESSERTS

In a 1979 study of the dessert market, Poppin Fresh found that seven out of ten consumers viewed desserts positively. Sixty percent of the study participants agreed with the statement, "Desserts and sweet snacks are okay as long as everyone has a well-balanced meal." Only 21 percent agreed with the statement, "I try to avoid serving desserts and sweet snacks as much as possible."

While served at least once a month by two-thirds of the households, pies represent only five percent of the total dessert volume. Quick desserts and baked, hand-held snacks represent 64 percent and cakes represent 15 percent of the volume.

Pies are served with the highest frequency at a complete weekday family dinner and at special occasion meals. They have low incidence for daytime or evening snacks. (See Exhibit 12).

In general pies have strong appeal to husbands. (See Exhibit 13).

Another independent study commissioned by Poppin Fresh in the Chicago and Twin Cities markets corroborated the results of the general dessert market study. Pies are served infrequently in the home compared to cakes and other desserts, although pie is clearly considered to be the personal all-time favorite dessert. Overall conclusions indicate:

☐ Pies represent a small portion of the total dessert category.

☐ They are perceived as a "specialty" item.

☐ They complement traditional sit down meals such as dinner.

☐ While snacks represent the highest volume of total dessert consumption, this segment is lowest for pies.

☐ Despite low usage, pies rank very high on overall satisfaction, a possible extension of the "specialness."

☐ Husbands generate the most enthusiasm for pies.

EXHIBIT 12   Share of desserts/sweet snacks at each occasion

	Total	A meal that is quick and easy	A complete weekday family dinner	A special occasion meal	A daytime or evening snack	Any other time
Total volume per occasion equals:	100%	100%	100%	100%	100%	100%
Quick desserts (net)	42	52	55	36	40	39
Baked, hand held snacks/desserts (net)	22	25	12	12	26	29
Cakes (net)	15	12	21	34	9	8
Pies (net)	5	4	9	13	3	2
Miscellaneous items (net)	16	7	3	5	22	22

EXHIBIT 13 Who likes specific dessert/sweet snack items—pies

		House-holds with husbands	Housholds with children				
	Respondent/ homemaker		*18 & Over*	*14-17*	*9-13*	*5-8*	*Under 5*
Base: total respondents	(1241)	(989)	(201)	(281)	(318)	(285)	(312)
	%	%	%	%	%	%	%
Pies (net)	27	45	21	30	19	13	6

☐ Pies are served less often than other dessert items.

☐ Nevertheless, they are highly mentioned as favorite dessert.

☐ Homemade pie constitutes the largest sector of pie consumption.

POPPIN FRESH PROMOTION

Spot and network television is used extensively by fast food and family restaurant chains—150–200 GRP's/week in local spot TV, and more in network TV (see Exhibit 14).

External promotion used by Poppin Fresh consists of spot television, spot radio, outdoor and R.O.P. newspaper. All the above media are not used in every market. Media usage is summarized in Exhibit 15.

When used, Poppin Fresh spot television ads are run Sunday through Thursday during prime access, late news, prime and late fringe day parts. The objective is to reach women twenty-five to fifty-four years of age. Exhibit 16 is a storyboard from a 1979 advertising campaign "Poppin Fresh. . . . Where great pies are just the beginning."

A comparison of Poppin Fresh and six major competitors for spot TV (with a summary figure for network TV when it is used) is shown in Exhibit 17.

Internal promotion is used continuously by Poppin Fresh Pie Shops. Window banners, table tents and placemats promote the featured pie or cur-

EXHIBIT 14 Competitive restaurant advertising

Market	# Restaurant advertisers	# Local spots/week	# Local & net. spots/week	GRP/wk. range	Rest. exp. 1978 ($M)
Chicago	23	360	420	2–600	$12,959.6
Cleveland	22	295	355	10–650	6,138.8
Des Moines	21	120	180	10–450	921.3
Indianapolis	26	405	465	10–600	5,748.1
Milwaukee	23	300	360	10–600	2,755.3
Minneapolis	25	290	350	20–650	4,697.3

SOURCE: BAR - Local Retail and Network 1978.

EXHIBIT 15 Poppin Fresh Pie Shops fiscal 1980 adjusted media plan budget recap by medium by market

	June	July	Aug.	Sept.	Oct.	Nov.	Dec.	Jan.	Feb.	March	Apr.	May	Total year
Spot television (6 markets)	90.3	53.0	30.5	195.4	39.1	9.5	—	—	—	212.7	96.7	—	727.2
Spot radio (3 markets)	49.3	53.7	37.2	47.3	10.4	10.9	10.9	—	—	—	—	—	219.7
Outdoor (3 markets)	—	9.0	9.0	5.9	5.9	5.9	5.9	—	—	—	—	—	41.6
R.O.P. newspaper (4 markets)	—	2.7	1.1	—	—	1.5	—	—	—	—	—	—	5.3
Total media	139.6	118.4	77.8	248.6	55.4	27.8	16.8	—	—	212.7	96.7	—	993.8

POPPIN FRESH "Where Great Pies Are Just the Beginning"

ANNCR: Early every morning,

we start baking at Poppin Fresh.

MUSIC: "Where Great Pies are Just the Beginning"

ANNCR: We use only

selected fruits and

a world of sweet tastes

MUSIC: Where great pies are . . .

And when we're through baking,

we really start cooking . . .

MUSIC:

where great Pies are . . .

. . . just the beginning.

SONG: Poppin Fresh,

where great Pies are

. . . just the beginning.

ANNCR: And when we're through baking,

EXHIBIT 16 Storyboard

355

EXHIBIT 17 Poppin Fresh Pie competitive expenditure report 1979 national summary sheet—spot television[1]

(units 1978)

Competitor	Jan.	Feb.	Mar.	Apr.	May	June	July	Aug.	Sept.	Oct.	Nov.	Dec.	Total	Network
Sambo's (1,100)	$ 4.6	$ 2.3	—	$ 31.7	$ 45.1	$ 121.4	—	$ 114.1	—	$ 233.6	292.1	$ 21.6	$ 866.5	$ 7058.3
Denny's (735)	9.8	48.8	—	—	—	590.0	763.1	302.1	.6	888.9	932.7	492.4	4027.3	—
Perkins Cake & Steak (352)	52.2	61.7	118.9	55.8	122.6	239.1	152.1	136.4	193.4	213.6	98.5	—	1444.3	—
Red Lobster	670.0	430.0	990.7	1034.2	36.7	1312.7	1380.4	1757.3	1252.8	1363.2	1416.7	1235.4	12880.1	117.8
McDonald's Drive-In	5247.7	4763.7	6161.8	5898.1	7004.8	6551.6	5525.8	5821.7	7491.3	6427.0	6624.2	7814.7	75332.4	62456.3
Burger King	1673.1	1407.9	1044.2	988.2	960.2	2116.1	2471.4	2340.1	2283.1	2739.0	2922.1	1256.4	22201.8	21403.2
Ky Fried Chicken	929.4	830.3	863.1	1092.0	1265.4	1345.3	1324.0	1224.4	1256.2	1297.6	1338.9	1535.5	14322.1	17233.7
TOTAL	9911.3	8983.4	10292.7	9927.8	10829.7	13578.9	12831.4	12675.6	13546.9	14101.3	14622.4	13335.5	144637.2	108269.3
Poppin Fresh	—	126.2	106.4	83.7	7.6	199.1	162.6	—	347.7	70.5	2.0	—	1105.8	—

In thousands of dollars

rent promotion. In addition, buttons are worn by employee service personnel. Buttons may indicate the feature pie, current promotion, or new menu items.

Internal promotion costs from as little as $650 for window banners and table tents to over $90,000 for a major promotion with giveaways.

As an example, a 1979 promotion, "Swiss Apple Pie Sweepstakes" cost $66,000. During the month of February, patrons could register to win an all expense paid trip for two to Switzerland, free feature pies for a year, and pies of their choice. Free Poppin Fresh refrigerator magnets were given with each whole Swiss Apple pie purchased and prizes for employees in top stores were awarded. A total of 14,000 incremental whole pies were sold.

"We don't want to play the same game as our competitors," commented Don Ryan. "The majority of our competition is promoting price. We don't think that's a good thing for Poppin Fresh because of our quality positioning. Our competition is using discounts and coupons in an attempt to induce customers to eat out more in this uncertain economy. Even using discounts and coupons, our competitors' sales are off and they're losing money. While our sales are off, Poppin Fresh is still profitable and we've maintained our quality image."

IMPLEMENTING MARKETING STRATEGIES *IV*

Implementing Product Strategies

4

A product is "the needs-satisfying offering of a firm,"[1] or, more specifically, it is "anything that can be offered to a market for attention, acquisition, use, or consumption that might satisfy a need; it includes physical objects, services, personalities, places, organization, and ideas."[2] Marketers generally feel that no other area is more critical to the profitability of the firm than decisions regarding the product. No other strategy area is more basic, more profound in its impact, and more difficult to change later than the product strategy. Because of this importance, product strategies are usually given first attention by, not only the marketing managers, but also the top executives in a corporation.

PRODUCT PORTFOLIO DECISIONS

Typically, a company offers more than one type of product or product line. For example, Campbell Soup Company sells soup, but it also sells fruit juice, pastries, TV dinners, candy, and other food products like canned pasta. It also sells nonfood items such as children's toys, and even has a chain of restaurants. Firms like Campbell must continually make decisions concerning the *width, depth,* and *consistency* of the *product portfolio* or the complete set of all products it sells. Width decisions must be made about the number of different types of products or product lines: should Kellogg, for example, add a breakfast bar line to its existing product portfolio of cereal, soup, desserts,

---

[1]E. Jerome McCarthy. *Basic Marketing: A Managerial Approach,* seventh edition. Homewood, Ill.: Richard D. Irwin, Inc., 1981, p. 266.

[2]Philip Kotler. *Marketing Management: Analysis, Planning, and Control,* fourth edition. Englewood Cliffs, New Jersey: Prentice-Hall, 1980, p. 351.

frozen vegetables, frozen waffles, nondairy toppings, and coffee whiteners, among others? Depth concerns the number of individual items within each product line: should Kellogg market another brand of cereal, a sugar-free version of an existing brand, or change any existing product line? Consistency decisions cover the relationship between products, markets, marketing channels, production processes, etc.: Kellogg must decide whether to market nonfood items, or products directed for the industrial market.

To make such product portfolio decisions, a company uses many techniques. Perhaps the most popular is the growth-share matrix of the Boston Consulting Group (BCG).[3] The BCG approach allows a company to evaluate each current or proposed product line along two dimensions: the *annual growth rate* of the industry and the *relative market share* held by the company's product line. This approach helps the firm achieve a balanced mix of products, classified as either *dogs, question marks, stars,* or *cash cows,* in its product portfolio.

Regardless of whether the company uses the BCG approach, one of the other existing approaches, or develops its own method, some periodic, formal analysis is necessary. Also, whenever a significant product decision is made, this analysis should insure that the company's product portfolio harmonized with the company's objectives.

PRODUCT LINE DECISIONS

The product portfolio consists of different product lines, similar products with similar uses and similar characteristics. Decisions about the product line (e.g., cereal) and specific brands within a product line (e.g., Frosted Flakes, Corn Flakes, Raisin Bran) constitute most of a firm's marketing decisions.

Stage in Product Life Cycle

One determinant of appropriate marketing strategy is the stage in the product life cycle. As indicated in Exhibit 1, the four stages in the product's theoretical life are accompanied by appropriate marketing responses. For example, most products are in the *maturity stage* of the product life cycle; this stage is characterized by slow growth, declining profitability, high cash flow, and a highly competitive industry selling to many different customers. As a result, the strategic focus for the product line would be to defend its market share, but do so with a declining level of marketing expenditures (as a percent of sales). The marketing emphasis would be to create brand loyalty among customers with an intensive distribution strategy for a relatively low-priced, differentiated product. In examining this chart, keep in mind that

---

[3]For a detailed treatment of the application of this approach to marketing planning, as well as some limitations in its usefulness, see, Day, George S. "Diagnosing the Product Portfolio." *Journal of Marketing,* April 1977. pp. 29–38.

these characteristics and responses are generalized approximations and should, by no means, be followed religiously. The chart, however, does provide some guideposts for marketing planning and indicates the necessity of changing marketing plans as a product goes through the various phases of its life cycle.

Branding

One of the first product line decisions the marketing manager makes is whether to brand the products. It may be desirable not to brand and either sell a "generic" good through the marketing channel, or allow one of the channel members to put a *private* or *dealer* brand on the product. Del Monte, for example, does both. The company sells canned fruits and vegetables with generic labels on the cans, and canned fruits and vegetables to certain retail grocery chains that put their own private branded labels on for resale. Both strategies permit the company to reduce the marketing costs on those items, but the lower selling price means lower revenue.

Del Monte and other well-known manufacturers also adopt the more costly, but also more lucrative, strategy of branding its products.

EXHIBIT 1   Characteristics and responses of product life cycle stages

	Introduction	*Growth*	*Maturity*	*Decline*
Characteristics				
Sales	Low	Fast growth	Slow growth	Decline
Profits	Negligible	Peak levels	Declining	Low or zero
Cash flow	Negative	Moderate	High	Low
Customers	Innovative	Mass market	Mass market	Laggards
Competitors	Few	Growing	Many rivals	Declining number
Responses				
Strategic focus	Expand market	Market penetration	Defend share	Productivity
Mktg. expenditures	High	High (declining %)	Falling	Low
Mktg. emphasis	Product awareness	Brand preference	Brand loyalty	Selective
Distribution	Patchy	Intensive	Intensive	Selective
Price	High	Lower	Lowest	Rising
Product	Basic	Improved	Differentiated	Rationalized

SOURCE: Peter Doyle, "The Realities of the Product Life Cycle," *Quarterly Review of Marketing,* summer 1976, pp. 1-6.

This, in return, requires the additional branding decision of whether to use a *family brand* (i.e. branding all products with the same brand, as Del Monte does), or *individual brands* (i.e. separate brands for different products, as done by Procter & Gamble with Tide, Cheer, Bold, Dash, etc.) The family branding decision has the advantage of facilitating brand awareness, preference, and loyalty for its products, particularly new ones. But individual branding permits the company to come up with new, and perhaps better, brand names for its new products, and allows the company to establish individual identity for each of its brands.

Product Positioning

A key decision that will directly affect all other marketing decisions is how the company will position its product. *Product positioning* consists of determining how the company wants its product perceived by the customer, relative to the competitors' products. Marketing research determines key product attributes and furnishes the company with an accurate picture of the marketplace; it is critical to discover how customers perceive both the company's product and the competition's. The company makes adjustments, through product modifications, or changes in promotion, channel, or pricing strategies to bring the product in line with the desired product position.

There are a variety of techniques a firm may use to analyze the positioning of its various products and plan for the desired positioning. One workable technique is a *product map*.[4] By constructing this geometric representation of the various brands in a product category, the marketing manager can analyze how a specific product compares, in various ways, with the competitors' products. For example, Levi Strauss wants to compare its jeans with other brands on the basis of "perceived durability" and "stylishness." The closer the brands appear on this product map, the more likely they are perceived to be similar. Results of market research studies on consumer preferences for jeans can be added to this product map to identify the various market segments and the relationship of these segments to the present product positions.

Product Modification

Marketing executives must continually keep an eye on customer perceptions of the product, as well as what possibilities exist for product improvement or other changes. As the company attempts to achieve the desired product positioning, many options are available through product modification. The quality might be improved, new features might be added, or a different version of the product might be developed. Additionally, other components of the "total product" might be altered. For example, the company could offer a better warranty, initiate new services, or develop a different package.

New Product Planning

In many cases product modification may not be adequate to achieve the desired position on the hypothetical product positioning map; the company may decide to introduce a new product. Such a decision should be made only after a logical and thorough investigation of the market and the product, since new product failure is not only expensive, but very common. Estimates of the frequency of new product failure range from 20 percent[5] to over 90

---

[4]For a detailed discussion of product mapping, see: Pessemier, E.A. *Product Management, Strategy and Organization.* New York: John Wiley & Sons, 1977, pp. 215-254.

[5]Hopkins, D.S., and E.L. Bailey. "New Product Pressures." *The Conference Board Research,* June 1971, pp. 16-24.

percent[6]; 80 percent is the most often cited figure. Consumer goods typically have somewhat higher new product failure rates than industrial products.[7] This is a considerable risk when you consider that it usually takes several years and between 2 and 6 million dollars to introduce a major new product.[8] In fact, some recent product failures such as General Motors' Wankel Rotary engine, DuPont's CORFAM leather substitute, and Gillette's "Happy Face" facial cleaning lotion have cost companies over 100 million dollars.

Here are five major reasons for new product failures:[9]

1. *The product lacked meaningful uniqueness.* Most studies indicate that the predominant reason for new product failure is that potential buyers do not perceive the product as having a differential advantage over the existing products.

2. *Poor planning.* This consists of such planning failures as poor positioning, poor segmentation, underbudgeting, poor overall themes, and overpricing.

3. *Wrong timing.* Sometimes a new product fails simply because it hits the market at the wrong time. For example, one of the major reasons for the Ford Edsel's failure was that consumers began losing interest in middle-sized cars just before the car was introduced.

4. *Enthusiasm crowded on facts.* It is always a temptation for certain executives in the company to be so enthusiastic about a new product that they push the product onto the market in spite of the lack of supporting market data.

5. *Product failed.* Many times a product holds up well in laboratory tests, but once it is subjected to actual use, problems develop.

To overcome these problems and improve the success rate for new products, we recommend that you take a logical approach toward developing new products. Such a new product development process might consist of the following eight-step process:[10]

1. Idea generation. A company may get ideas for new products from many different sources: customers, competitors, channel members, or from some element within the organization. Companies should encourage new product ideas from all possible sources.

---

[6]Shaw, S.J. "Behavioral Session Offers Fresh Insights Into New Product Acceptance." *Journal of Marketing,* January 1965, pp. 9-13.

[7]Urban, G.L., and U.R. Hauser. *Design and Marketing of New Products.* Englewood Cliffs, N.J.: Prentice-Hall, Inc., 1980, p. 3.

[8]op. cit., p. 53.

[9]Adapted from Crawford, C.M. "Marketing Research and the New Product Failure Rate." *Journal of Marketing,* April 1977, pp. 51-61.

[10]Adapted from Philip Kotler, *Marketing Management: Analysis, Planning and Control,* fourth edition. Englewood Cliffs, New Jersey: Prentice-Hall, Inc., 1980, pp. 315-342.

2. Idea screening. A firm should have some process for rating all new product ideas. A quantitative evaluation system, such as the G.E. Product Planning Grid, is desirable. Such a system would evaluate each idea according to company strengths and industry attractiveness to screen out those that are not likely to be successful.

3. Concept Development and Testing. Those product ideas that still seem worthy are then further analyzed and refined into a thorough description of the product. This formalized description is known as the *product concept.* It is at this point that marketing research is typically called on to conduct a market research of this concept— the *concept test.* Concept testing involves questioning prospective customers about the product concept to determine their likelihood of buying such a product, as well as soliciting any recommendations for improving the proposed product.

4. Preliminary Marketing Strategy Development. Taking into account information collected from the concept test, marketing should draw up some preliminary ideas for the key elements of the marketing plan. It should identify the most likely target market and determine strategies for each element of the marketing mix—the *total product* to be marketed, as well as the type of promotion, channel, and pricing strategy.

5. Business Analysis. No matter how great a product concept might seem, there is no use considering it if the company will not be able to earn its desired level of profit. The business analysis process seeks to quantify the market demand, project the company revenue from sale of the product, and estimate the costs involved in producing and marketing the product. A company usually has a required level of expected profitability for a new product, for example, a 25 percent R.O.I. after two years. The business analysis step allows the company to investigate whether the product concept is financially sound.

6. Product Development. Those product concepts passing the business analysis stage will be sent to R & D/engineering/production for development of the actual product. Preliminary contacts with these departments should begin with step 2 to gain insight into the production processes. In fact, in step 3, the R & D/engineering/production departments may have been asked to make a prototype, to test the concept. However, these contacts were strictly preliminary since marketing still had primary responsibility for the product idea/concept. In the product development stage, however, the burden is on the technical personnel; they must determine if the product can be mass-produced at the cost determined in the business analysis.

7. Test Market. The next step followed by most companies is the formal test market. Here the product is actually introduced to the market, backed by all of the necessary marketing strategies. However, the introduction is on a small scale. The sales performance in this test market is then evaluated to decide if the product is likely to succeed on a large scale.

8. Commercialization. Of the sixty or so ideas generated in the first stage of the new product development process, perhaps only two are left at this point. These ideas/concepts/products now become new products, launched with a full marketing effort. By the end of the first year, only one of these will probably be profitable and considered a successful new product introduction.

PRODUCT ELIMINATION

Products are not only added to a company's product portfolio—they must also be dropped. Too many times, this process is slighted; the result is an unbalanced product portfolio with less than maximum efficiency.

There are many different reasons why a firm might want to eliminate a product or product line.[11]

1. Low profitability
2. Stagnant or declining sales volume or market share which would be too costly to build up
3. Risks of technological obsolescence
4. Entry into a mature or declining phase of the product life cycle
5. Poor fit with the company's strengths or declared mission

A product elimination may take place gradually or immediately. A *harvesting* strategy allows the company to cut marketing costs but still sell the product for a period of time. A company may decide that, while a product may not be in its long-range plans, it may be too profitable or desirable in some way to abandon. However, if the company feels the product is presently a liability, it should stop producing it immediately.

SUMMARY

In this chapter we have provided an overview of the major factors to consider when implementing product strategies. Not only is it necessary to develop and implement viable strategies for existing products, but it is just as important to systematically identify and develop possible new products. A marketing manager should also continually monitor all elements of the product mix to identify and eliminate products that are no longer viable. Product decisions are probably a marketing manager's most critical decision; the results impact on virtually every other aspect of the business. The next three chapters will explore how promotion, distribution, and pricing affect marketing decisions. Each of these is directly related to the product decisions described in this chapter.

---

[11]Subhash C. Jain. *Marketing Planning and Strategy.* Cincinnati, Ohio: South-Western Publishing Company, 1981, p. 276.

QUESTIONS

1. What decisions are important in determining the company's product portfolio?
2. Fully discuss the characteristics of each stage of the product life cycle, along with the appropriate marketing response for each stage.
3. Name and explain at least three product line decisions facing a marketing manager.
4. What are the main reasons for new product failure?
5. Describe the steps in the New Product Development Process.

SUGGESTED READINGS

Alford, C.L., and J.B. Mason. "Generating New Product Ideas." *Journal of Advertising Research,* December 1975, pp. 27-32.

Blettberg, R.C., T. Buesing, and S. Sew. "Segmentation Strategies for New National Brands." *Journal of Marketing,* Fall 1980, pp. 59-67.

Cadbury, N.D. "When, Where and How to Test Market." *Harvard Business Review,* May-June 1975, pp. 96-105.

Doyle, P. "The Realities of the Product Life Cycle." *Quarterly Review of Marketing,* Summer 1976, pp. 1-6.

Harper, P.C. Jr. "New Product Management: The Cutting Edge of Corporate Policy." *Journal of Marketing,* April 1976, pp. 76-79.

Hise, R.T. *Product/Service Strategy.* New York: Petrocelli/Charter, 1977.

Hise, R.T., and M.A. McGinnis. "Product Elimination: Practices, Policies, and Ethics." *Business Horizons,* June 1975, pp. 25-32.

Holmes, J. "Profitable Product Positioning." *MSU Business Topics,* Spring 1973, pp. 26-32.

Kerin, R.A., M.G. Harvey, and J.T. Rothe. "Cannibalism and New Product Development." *Business Horizons,* October 1978, pp. 25-31.

Kotler, P., *Marketing Management Analysis, Planning, and Control.* 4th edition. Englewood Cliffs, N.J.: Prentice-Hall, Inc., 1980, pp. 289-380.

Kotler, P. "Phasing Out Weak Products." *Harvard Business Review,* March-April 1965, pp. 107-118.

Kotler, P., and G. Zaltman. "Targeting Prospects for a New Product." *Journal of Advertising Research,* February 1976, pp. 7-20.

Klompmaker, J.E., G.D. Hughes, and R.I. Haley. "Test Marketing in New Product Development." *Harvard Business Review,* May-June 1976, pp. 128-138.

Levitt, T. "Exploit the Product Life Cycle." *Harvard Business Review,* November-December 1965, pp. 81-94.

Pessemier, E.A. *Product Management, Strategy and Organization,* New York: John Wiley & Sons, 1977.

Pessemier, E.A., and R.H. Paul. "The Dimensions of New Product Planning." *Journal of Marketing,* January 1973, pp. 10-18.

Polli, R., and V. Cook. "Validity of the Product Life Cycle." *Journal of Business,* October 1969, pp. 385-400.

Shapiro, B.P. *Industrial Product Policy: Managing the Existing Product Line.* Cambridge, Mass.: Marketing Science Institute, September 1977.

Silk, A.J., and G.L. Urban. "Pre-Test Market Evaluation of New Packaged Goods: A Model and Measurement Methodology." *Journal of Marketing Research,* May 1978, pp. 171-191.

Smallwood, J.E. "The Product Life Cycle: A Key to Strategic Marketing Planning." *MSU Business Topics,* Winter 1973, pp. 29-35.

Tauber, E.M. "Reduce New Product Failures: Measure Needs as Well as Purchase Intention." *Journal of Marketing,* July 1973, pp. 61-64.

Urban, G.L., and J.R. Hauser. *Design and Marketing of New Products.* Englewood Cliffs, N.J.: Prentice-Hall, Inc., 1980.

von Hippel, E. "Successful Industrial Products from Customer Ideas." *Journal of Marketing,* January 1978, pp. 39-49.

Wind, Y., and H.J. Claycamp. "Planning Product Line Strategy: A Matrix Approach." *Journal of Marketing,* January 1976, pp. 2-9.

Implementing Promotion Strategies

5

P romotion encompasses all the ways a firm communicates its message to the market. Generally speaking, a company can adopt either a *mass communication* approach (advertising, sales promotion, and publicity) or a *personal communication* approach (personal selling). Although consumer product companies usually emphasize mass communication, and industrial product companies personal selling, a company's promotional message can usually be communicated more effectively through a combination. We now examine some of the strategic concerns of both approaches. However, since the marketing manager cannot always control publicity, we will limit our discussion of mass communication to advertising and sales promotion.

ADVERTISING DECISIONS

Advertising is "controlled, identifiable information and persuasion by means of mass communication."[1] Advertising can be used for several purposes: (1) to sell or help sell a product; (2) to reassure and retain customers; (3) to improve channel member or employee relations; and (4) to project a useful image to one or more of the company publics.[2] To carry out these purposes, the marketing manager has several decisions to make about *the appropriate target market, advertising objectives, size of the advertising budget, advertising message, media selection, media scheduling,* and *evaluation.*

Target Market. The first advertising planning decision requires the manager

---

[1]Wright, J.S., W.L. Winter, Jr., and S.K. Zeigler. *Advertising,* fifth edition. New York: McGraw-Hill, 1982, p. 10.

[2]S.R. Bernstein. "What Is Advertising?" *Advertising Age,* April 30, 1980, pp. 28, 32, 34.

to identify the appropriate target market for the advertising message. Whom does the company want to reach with its message? Although the target market for the product will remain fairly constant, the focus of specific advertising campaigns may change. Some campaigns may attempt to reach several different target markets simultaneously through different media approaches, while others may be directed at only one target market at a time.

Advertising Objectives. Just as the overall marketing plan should have specific objectives, every advertising campaign and, in fact, every advertisement should have stated objectives. A few of the objectives, or purposes, for advertising in general were stated earlier in this section. Some specific objectives for one advertising campaign might be: improve market share from 30 to 32 percent; increase sales by 12 percent; achieve a brand recognition level of 85 percent of the target market; increase retail store traffic flow by 15 percent; stimulate 250 requests for more information; assist the salesforce in obtaining fifty new customers; or improve the favorable public opinion rating to 75 percent of the general public.

Advertising Budget. Determining the amount to spend on advertising is not easy. Here are some common approaches:

1. *The percentage of sales method:* This uses a rule of thumb percentage of forecasted sales (e.g., 2 percent of next year's sales) as a simple formula for determining advertising dollars. Although perhaps the most commonly used method, it is illogical because it implies that sales results in advertising, rather than vice versa.

2. The *affordable method:* Many companies simply set the advertising budget based on what it can afford to spend. Not only does this method imply that advertising is not important, a haphazard approach makes planning for more than one year at a time difficult.

3. The *competitive parity method:* This matches the advertising expenditures of the competition. The firm will spend whatever the leading competitors are spending, or whatever the industry average is (either in dollars or percentage of sales). Although the competitive parity method does consider the competition in planning, it assumes that competitors have the same objectives as your company, and that they spend the correct amount on advertising.

4. The *objective-task method:* The most logical approach is to take the objective or task previously determined for the campaign, and then calculate the level of advertising expenditures necessary to accomplish it. The major limitation of the objective-task method is the difficulty of estimating that level.

Advertising Message. Although the amount of money spent on advertising is important, an equally, or perhaps even more, critical factor is the message.

There are no simple rules on how to develop good advertising. Effective advertisements come in many different creative forms: factual or emotional, positive or negative, sad or funny, commonplace or unusual, short or long, plain or colorful, etc. The only requirements are that it be appropriate for the target market, in line with the advertising objectives, and within the budget limitations. Within those parameters, it is up to the creative experts to develop the most appealing, persuasive, or informative advertisement possible.

Media Selection. The company must deliver its advertising message to the greatest number of potential customers at the lowest possible cost. This is the goal of the media selection process; it decides what types of media to use, as well as which specific media to use within those types. Exhibit 1 lists the major media types and their strengths and weaknesses. Following the media type decision, the firm or advertising agency selects the specific advertising vehicle, deciding, for example, which television program or which specific magazine is most appropriate. These decisions are based on the target market the company is attempting to reach, the advertising objectives, budget, and the type of message it wishes to communicate.

EXHIBIT 1   Strengths and weaknesses of types of advertising media

Media Type	Strengths	Weaknesses
Broadcast		
Television	Wide coverage (97% of homes have TVs)	Most expensive medium
		Less selective of audience
	Excellent production quality (i.e., sight, sound, motion)	"Clutter" of other ads
		Message not permanent
	More attentive audience	
Radio	Wide coverage (98% of homes have radios)	Less attentive audience (listeners usually doing something else)
	Selective audience	Only communicates audibly
	Lower cost than TV	Message not permanent
	Flexible and timely	Reach usually small
Print		
Newspaper	Flexible and timely	"Clutter" of other ads
	Good local market coverage	Short life
	Good opportunity for cooperative advertising with local dealers	Read rapidly
		Low production quality
		Higher rates for national advertisers
Magazines	Highly selective audience	Not as flexible
	High production quality	Not as timely
	Long life, "pass along" readership	Premium price for good position
	High reader interest	

EXHIBIT 1 (continued)

Media Type	Strengths	Weaknesses
Outdoor	Flexible Less expensive Repetitive viewership Good coverage	Creative limitations Less selective audience "Clutter" of surroundings
Direct Mail	Most personal and selective No "clutter" from other ads No creative limitations Relatively high readership	Relatively high cost Bad reputation of "junk mail" Problem in getting and maintaining good mailing lists

Media Scheduling. Proper timing or scheduling of the advertisements is also important. A company can choose a continuous schedule of equal advertising throughout the year, but it is more common to vary the scheduling according to some pattern. For example, a new product might be accompanied by heavy advertising during the month of introduction, and a much lower level of expenditures after. A seasonal product may be advertised most heavily immediately preceding and during its high sales period. There are many possible scheduling patterns, from concentrating the advertising during one time of the year, month, or day, to intermittent scheduling for short periods many times a year, month, or day. Or, it could be consistent, increasing, decreasing, or even alternating at various levels during the period.

Evaluation. It is essential that the effectiveness of the advertising campaign be evaluated. This evaluation should determine whether the advertising objectives set forth earlier have been achieved. Did sales increase as planned? Did brand recognition among target customers increase as planned? If any of the objectives were not achieved, a more thorough evaluation should determine what went wrong. Perhaps some post-testing of customers could be done to obtain their feedback on the advertising campaign; such an investigation would be beneficial for future campaigns. In fact, it may be found that the advertising campaign was good but some extraneous variable, e.g., poor salesperson performance, unusually intense marketing effort by competition, slowdown in the economy, may have undermined it.

SALES PROMOTION DECISIONS

The marketing manager also makes decisions about the sales promotion program. Sales promotion activities are usually coordinated with advertising, since the success of the sales promotion program often depends on advertising's ability to communicate the features of the sales promotion program.

Sales promotion encompasses many promotional activities that are directed at either the final purchaser of the product (consumer or industrial user), an intermediary (dealer or industrial distributor), or even the firm's own sales force. Sales promotion activities are generally those that just do not fall under the categories of advertising or personal selling. Common items are *catalogs, contests, conventions, coupons, discounts, displays, films, gifts, premiums, rebates, sales aids, sales seminars, samples, specials, specialty items, trading stamps,* and *trade exhibits.* Although there are no accurate figures on the amount companies spend on sales promotion, it is safe to say that most companies spend at least as much on sales promotion as on advertising.

There are several different reasons why a marketing manager would want to use some form of sales promotion:

1. *Obtain product trial:* Many times the best way to communicate the benefits of a product is to get people to try it. Giving away samples to prospective customers may be the most effective way to convince people of the product's taste, smell, feel, etc., and it may encourage them to purchase the product.

2. *Achieve competitive advantage:* By using such techniques as a price discount, two-for-one special, rebates, trading stamps, a premium with purchase, or gifts, a firm may gain a differential advantage over the competition. Consumers and industrial or intermediate buyers are always looking for the best deal or something extra; sales promotion may provide an effective means of differentiating the product or the company.

3. *Attract customer's attention:* Contests create excitement. At the same time, the customer may receive a company's advertising or personal selling message, when he or she may otherwise have ignored it. Such sales promotion tools as catalogs, in-store displays, films, specialty items, sales aids, and trade exhibits also attract attention to the company's message.

4. *Stimulate selling effort:* Sales promotion techniques such as sales seminars, conventions, sales contests, and gifts may be directed at the intermediary or the salesforce. A more qualified and motivated salesforce and dealer network can increase sales.

The systematic approach used for advertising planning should also be used for sales promotion planning. The target market should be defined, the sales promotion objectives set, the budget determined, the appropriate technique selected, and the process evaluated to determine the sales promotion program's effectiveness.

PERSONAL SELLING DECISIONS

The other major type of promotion is the personal communication approach with salespeople. Although much more expensive per contact, personal selling may be the best way to sell certain products in certain situations. For example, if the product is new, high-priced, infrequently purchased, or technically complex, the face-to-face relationship of a personal sales call may be the best way to convince a prospect to buy the product. If prospects are geographically dispersed, a personal salesperson may be less expensive than many types of advertising.

Just as the marketing manager must decide on the *appropriate target market, objectives,* and *budget* for the advertising plan, he or she must also make decisions about the personal selling plan. The marketing manager must also determine *the design of the sales organization, the type of motivation and compensation system,* and *the appropriate method of evaluating the sales force.*

Design of the Sales Organization. There are three basic alternatives for the design of the sales organization. The simplest is the *geographic-structured* organization. This divides the market into sales territories with one salesperson responsible for selling all of the company's products within that territory. This organization's primary advantage is that it makes one person solely responsible for sales in an area; it cuts down on travel costs and also encourages much effort, since the salesperson is evaluated on the results in that territory. The major drawback is that the salesperson must sell many different types of products to various types of customers. Since a salesperson must be thoroughly familiar with both products and customers, it may be difficult for him or her to sell many different products.

To overcome this problem, a firm may choose a *product-structured* sales organization. This organizational arrangement is particularly effective when the firm has a large number of technically complex products, each bought by different types of customers. Because of the specialization by product line, products are sold by salespeople who are highly knowledgeable about the product line they sell. Disadvantages of this system include higher travel costs, inefficiency, and strained customer relations. Customer relations can be strained when a customer must deal with a different salesperson for each product line.

A third option for sales organization design is the *customer-structured* sales organization. This involves segmenting the market by type of customer and assigning the sales force based on customer type. Although travel costs may be higher, customer relations tend to be better since salespeople know more about customer needs.

After the best organizational design is chosen, a company must train the appropriate number and type of personnel. You can estimate the size of the sales force by dividing the total sales desired for each product by the number of units each salesperson should be able to sell. The type of salesperson needed depends on the selling job. For example, a pharmaceutical company that wants to sell personally to doctors will probably train its sales force not only in selling techniques, but also in chemistry and related scientific areas.

Motivation and Compensation System One key to a successful personal selling strategy is a highly motivated sales force. Salespeople must feel they are highly regarded by the company and believe that sales managers and other relevant company personnel are working with them to maximize sales and profitability; the entire organizational climate must be one of cooperation and encouragement.

There are many specific methods for motivating a sales force. *Periodic sales meetings* provide an opportunity for social interaction between sales personnel and management, as well as between the salespersons themselves. Meetings can combat the sense of isolation from the company that many salespeople can feel. *Sales contests* are effective ways to encourage higher productivity and provide positive reinforcement for those who excel. *Good communication* between management and the sales force also serves as a powerful motivator. Encouragement in difficulty or appreciation for a job well done will help create a supportive climate for the salesperson and keep communication lines open. A key element in developing a motivated sales force is the compensation system. There are three methods of compensating sales personnel:

1. *Straight salary:* Here the salesperson is paid a flat rate, for example, $2,000 a month. This method is particularly useful when the company wants the salesperson to do things other than sell— provide assistance for channel members, train new sales personnel, or collect market research information. It also provides security for the salesperson. The main disadvantage is that it provides no incentive for the salesperson to do a better-than-average job of selling. In addition, it can be difficult determining the appropriate salary level.

2. *Straight commission:* This method of compensation pays the salesperson a percentage commission on sales, of say, 3 percent. Because this compensation is based solely on sales performance, it provides the maximum incentive for the salesperson. In addition, it facilitates and simplifies marketing cost analysis since sales expenses are directly proportional to sales revenue. The major drawback is the resistance of salespeople to performing duties not directly related to generating sales. Since their compensation depends on sales, people working under a straight commission system will want to do little else for the company; another disadvantage is the lack of security it provides for salespeople. This may lower morale when uncontrollable factors reduce sales.

3. *Combination method:* Most firms use some combination of salary and commission to compensate their sales forces. A plan might pay the salesperson $500 a month plus 2 percent of sales. The combination method is effective since it combines the best of both worlds, providing both security and incentive. Also, it still allows the company some control over the salesperson's activities.

In addition to one of these compensation methods, a firm might also use a *bonus system* or *profit-sharing plan* to encourage better performance.

Under the bonus system, a salesperson is compensated for performance above the stated goals. These goals may be in terms of sales, new customers, new ideas, number of sales calls, or many other areas. With the profit-sharing plan, the salesperson is rewarded for company or territory profitability; this encourages high performance and sales efficiency.

Evaluation. The sales force and each individual salesperson must be periodically evaluated. Personal selling evaluations are vitally important both in making future sales strategy decisions and determining the pay, promotion, and continued employment of each salesperson.

Personal selling evaluations should analyze whether the objectives for the sales force as a whole, as well as for each salesperson, have been achieved. The primary personal selling objective is usually a level of sales; if the salesperson has not met this or any other objective, management should find out why.

Most personal selling evaluation efforts are directed at the individual salesperson. Since the total company sales effort is a sum of its parts, you should give considerable attention to identifying the strong and weak parts of the sales organization and then taking appropriate action. Use the same dimensions for evaluating the sales force as you used for setting objectives: sales volume, profitability, order quantity, number of sales calls, number of new accounts, etc. Then, compare each salesperson to how the other sales personnel performed, to how he or she did during the previous period, and to how well he or she met previously defined goals. The evaluation system may also take into account qualitative factors such as personality, work habits, knowledge of the company, products, customers or competitors, and general contributions to the company.

SUMMARY

This chapter has discussed some of the things a marketing manager must know about promotion. Each element of the promotional mix—advertising, sales promotion, and personal selling—requires a systematic approach. Also, each of these elements requires careful planning so the marketing manager can select the appropriate market for the promotion, set forth the promotional objective, determine the budget, choose the most appropriate tool, and evaluate the promotional effort. These decisions are affected by and influence the strategies the firm uses to distribute the product. Chapter 6 will discuss distribution strategies.

QUESTIONS

1. Explain four commonly used methods for setting the advertising budget.
2. Why is evaluation an important step in each of the promotional tools?

3. For what reasons might a marketing manager use sales promotions?

4. What are the three types of sales organization designs? Explain each.

5. Explain the three methods of compensating sales personnel. What are the advantages and disadvantages of each.

SUGGESTED READINGS

Banks, S. "Trends Affecting the Implementation of Advertising and Promotion." *Journal of Marketing,* January 1973, pp. 19-28.

Bettinghaus, E.P. *Persuasive Communication.* New York: Holt, Rinehart and Winston, Inc., 1973.

Boyd, H.W., Jr., M.L. Ray, and E.C. Strong. "An Attitudinal Framework for Advertising Strategy." *Journal of Marketing,* April 1972, pp. 27-33.

Churchill, G.A. Jr., N.M. Ford, and O.C. Walker, Jr. *Sales Force Management.* Homewood, Ill.: Richard D. Irwin, 1981.

Coogle, J.M., Jr. "Media Advertising, and Public Relations." in *Review of Marketing 1978,* ed., G. Zaltman and T.V. Bonoma, Chicago: American Marketing Association, pp. 481-84.

Delozier, M.W. *The Marketing Communication Process.* New York: McGraw-Hill, 1976.

Fogg, C.D. and S.W. Rokus. "A Quantitative Method for Structuring A Profitable Sales Force." *Journal of Marketing,* July 1973, pp. 8-17.

Gensch, D.H. "Media Factors: A Review Article." *Journal of Advertising Research,* May 1970, pp. 218-221.

Hise, R.T. *Effective Salesmanship.* Hinsdale, Ill.: The Dryden Press, 1980.

Kotler, P. "Toward An Explicit Model for Media Selection." *Journal of Advertising Research,* March 1974, pp. 34-41.

Nickels, W.G. *Marketing Communication and Promotion,* second edition. Columbus, Ohio: Grid Publishing, Inc., 1980.

Porter, H. "Managing Your Sales Force as a System." *Harvard Business Review,* March-April 1975.

Ray, M.L. "A Decision Sequence Analysis of Developments in Marketing Communication." *Journal of Marketing,* January 1973, pp. 29-38.

Shapiro, B.P. "Manage the Customer, Not Just the Sales Force." *Harvard Business Review,* September-October 1974.

"The New Supersalesman: Wired for Success." *Business Week,* June 6, 1975.

Webster, F.E., Jr. "The Role of the Industrial Distributor in Marketing Strategy." *Journal of Marketing,* July 1976, pp. 10-16.

Wright, J.S., D.S. Warner, W.L. Winter, Jr. and S.K. Zeigler. *Advertising,* fifth edition. New York: McGraw-Hill, 1982.

Implementing Distribution Strategies

6

O f critical importance to the success of a marketing plan is getting the product to the customer when and where he or she wants it. The best product and promotion planning is wasted if the customer cannot buy the product; adequate distribution strategies are critical to the marketing plan. The two primary elements in distribution planning are the design of the marketing channel and the design of the physical distribution (logistics) system. All distribution decisions should also take into account the customer service requirements for the product.

CHANNEL DECISIONS

The marketing channel consists of all institutions or intermediaries used to move a product from the producer to the consumer or user. Just as a firm attempts to gain a competitive advantage through product and promotional planning, it should also try to gain a competitive advantage through its channel design. This is best accomplished through systematic decision process for channel design. The steps in this process are:[1]

1. Recognize the need for channel design decisions
2. Set and coordinate distribution objectives
3. Specify the distribution functions
4. Develop possible alternative channel structures

[1]Adapted from: Rosenbloom, Bert. *Marketing Channels: A Management View.* Hinsdale, Ill.: The Dryden Press, 1978, pp. 108-139.

5. Choose the "best" channel

6. Select the appropriate channel members

Recognize the Need for Channel Design Decisions. There is a tendency for marketing managers to accept the present channel structure as a given and base marketing strategies on the status quo in channel design. Actually, conditions often arise that should cause the marketing manager to question and, if necessary, modify the present channel design. A few of these conditions are:

1. *Changes in company direction:* As the firm changes its corporate strategies, adjustments may be required in the channel design, e.g., when acquisitions or mergers take place, the firm starts a new line of business, or other significant corporate changes occur.

2. *Changes in marketing strategies:* Channel design decisions may be necessary when new products or product lines are added, a major product modification takes place, a different geographic or demographic market segment is targeted, a major change in promotion strategy takes place, a new pricing policy goes into effect, or any other major change takes place in the marketing mix.

3. *Changes in marketing channel:* Adjustments may be necessary if problems occur among channel members, as the availability of certain types of intermediaries changes, or as policies of channel intermediaries change.

4. *Changes in the environment:* When economic, technological, competitive, legal/political, or socio-cultural environments change, it may be desirable to modify channel design.

In addition, periodic marketing strategy evaluations may uncover inefficiencies in the channel design, that must be corrected.

Set and Coordinate Distribution Objectives. The distribution objectives are derived from the overall marketing objectives. Typically, the distribution objectives are specific goals set for either an *intensive, selective,* or *exclusive* strategy. Intensive distribution implies an objective of making the product available through every possible intermediary. Selective distribution requires certain criteria for intermediary selection. The objective for an exclusive distribution strategy is to find the one intermediary that would do the best selling job in a particular market area. Based on these general objectives, the marketing manager should set specific goals. For example, a manufacturer of canned vegetables with a general objective of intensive distribution may desire a market coverage of 95 percent of the chain food stores and 90 percent of the independent food stores.

Specify the Distribution Functions. Channel members perform many functions, including transportation, storage, advertising, personal selling, packaging, extending credit, customer service, market information, special handling, grading, processing, assembly, and any other activities necessary between the point of production and point of sale. The specific functions of channel intermediaries should be noted.

Develop Possible Alternative Channel Structures. Channel structures can be either *direct* or *indirect.* A direct channel contains no intermediaries, with the product sold directly from the manufacturer to the final consumer/user. An indirect channel contains any number of intermediaries. Typical alternative channel structures are depicted in Exhibit 1.

There are several decision factors to consider in determining the most appropriate channel structure. Some of the more significant factors, along with characteristics leading to either a direct or indirect channel structure, are shown in Exhibit 2. Remember these decision factor characteristics are only mere generalizations.

Choose the Best Channel. There are many possible methods to analyze alternative channel structures and determine the best one for the company. Base any such analysis on those decision factors your company considers most

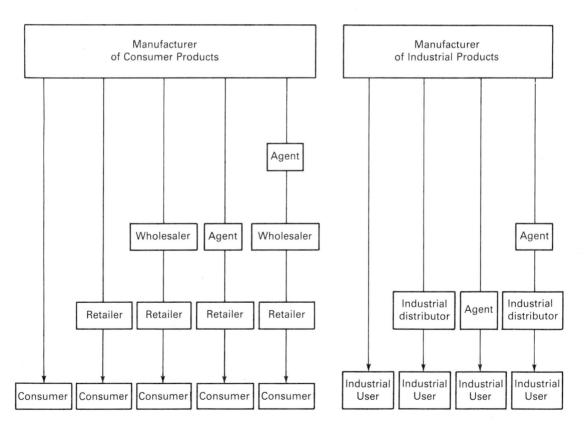

EXHIBIT 1 Alternative channel structures

EXHIBIT 2   Decision factors for direct or indirect channel structures

Factor	Direct	Indirect
Market	Industrial	Consumer
	Few potential buyers	Many potential buyers
	Geographically concentrated	Geographically disposed
	Identified customers	Customers not easily identified
Customer Buying Behavior	Large purchase quantities	Small purchase quantities
	Regular buying	Irregular (seasonal) buying
	Buy at home	Buy outside of home
Product	Heavy, bulky	Lightweight, easy to handle
	Perishable	Durable
	High unit value	Low unit value
	Customized	Standardized
	Technical	Nontechnical
	New products	Established products
	Shopping/Specialty goods	Convenience goods
	Fashion items	Staples
	Extensive product portfolio	Limited product portfolio
Company	Marketing expertise	Less marketing expertise
	Desires control over product	Does not desire control over product
	Strong financial condition	Less strong financial position
	Marketing-oriented	Less marketing-oriented
	Emphasizes personal selling	Emphasizes advertising

important. For example, *short and long run costs* and *short and long run profit potential* will almost certainly be key decision factors for most firms. In addition, a firm may wish to consider such factors as *amount of control, growth potential, amount of initial investment required,* or *effectiveness in reaching customers.* If a firm has more than one decision factor, a weighted factor score approach[2] is desirable. Each decision factor is ranked, the channel structure alternatives are rated from .0 to 1.0 on the basis of each factor, and the overall score for each alternative is then calculated. This technique quantifies the channel selection decision.

Select the Appropriate Channel Members. After you have determined the channel structure, select the channel members. There are three basic categories of intermediaries: (1) merchant wholesalers, (2) agents and brokers, and (3) retailers.

   Merchant wholesalers are institutions that sell to retailers, industrial users, or other channel intermediaries, but do not sell in significant amounts

[2]Kotler, Philip. *Marketing Decision Making: A Model Building Approach.* Holt, Rinehart and Winston, 1971, p. 292.

to consumers. There are three types of merchant wholesalers. *Full-function wholesalers* include industrial distributors, rack jobbers, general merchandise wholesalers, single-line or general wholesalers and specialty wholesalers. Although the wholesale markup taken by such firms is higher than other wholesalers, they also carry out more functions, such as transportation, selling, warehousing, market information, and risk taking.

The second type of merchant wholesaler is the *limited-function wholesaler*. This includes drop shippers, cash-and-carry wholesalers, truck wholesalers, mail-order wholesalers, and producers' cooperatives. These firms operate with a lower markup, but also provide fewer services than merchant wholesalers.

A third type of merchant wholesaler is the *manufacturer's sales branch*. This is a separate institution set up by a manufacturer to sell its products. A manufacturer seeking more control over its marketing channel may find this variation of wholesaling an effective alternative.

Agents and *brokers* are similar to merchant wholesalers in that they also sell to retailers, industrial users, or other channel members. However, unlike merchant wholesalers, agents and brokers do not take title to the products they sell; they are usually compensated by a commission, based on sales volume. A manufacturer choosing not to employ its own sales force may find one of these alternatives desirable. There are several types of agents: manufacturers' agents, selling agents, commission merchants, agricultural assemblers, and auction companies. Brokers, such as food brokers, provide the useful service of bringing buyers and sellers together.

The final category of channel intermediary is the *retailer*. A retailer sells primarily to the ultimate consumer. The major types of retail stores are department stores, discount stores, specialty stores, mail order firms, franchises, variety stores, supermarkets, convenience stores, and vending machines.

Channel Management

Once the best channel and the appropriate channel members are selected, the resulting channel system must be managed. This may be a problem at times because of *channel conflict* between the members. This conflict may be defined as "any adversary-directed action designed to thwart, injure, destroy, or manipulate the actions of some other channel member" and may originate from any of three major sources:[3]

1. Disagreement over the allocation of scarce resources

2. Divergence over the goals sought by separate channel members

3. Rivalry over who is responsible for marketing activities that each firm claims as its own or expects the other to perform

[3]Sims, J.T., J.R. Foster, and A.G. Woodside. *Marketing Channels, Systems and Strategic.* New York: Harper & Row, 1977, pp. 205, 208.

Since channel conflict may jeopardize channel efficiency, it should be resolved or, at least, minimized. Several methods for managing conflict are bargaining with the channel members, developing different goals for the channel, and making organizational changes in the channel system. Perhaps the best way to handle channel conflict is to anticipate potential problem areas and circumvent them.

PHYSICAL DISTRIBUTION (LOGISTICS) DECISIONS

Channel design considers the institutions or intermediaries necessary for the appropriate marketing channels. Physical distribution or logistical decisions focus on the *physical movement* of products between and within the various channel members. There are essentially six major physical distribution decisions areas: transportation, warehousing, materials handling, inventory, order processing, and protective packaging.[4]

Transportation. One of the most important physical distribution decisions concerns transporting the finished goods to customers. First of all, select the proper mode of transportation. Exhibit 3 describes the five major modes of transportation. Next, decide whether to own or lease the carrier or simply use the services of a common carrier. In addition, routing decisions must be made, and the size and scheduling of the shipment must be determined.

EXHIBIT 3   Major modes of transportation ranged by decision criteria
(1 = Highest Rank)

	Cost (per ton mile)	Speed (point-to-point)	Frequency (scheduled shipments)	Dependability (meeting schedules)	Capability (handling variety)	Availability (number of points served)
Air	5	1	3	5	4	3
Pipeline	2	5	1	1	5	5
Rail	3	3	4	3	2	2
Truck	4	2	2	2	3	1
Water	1	4	5	4	1	4

SOURCE: Adapted from Heskett, James L., Robert J. Ivie, and Nicholas A. Glaskowsky. *Business Logistics.* New York: Ronald Press, 1973, p. 71.

Warehousing. A firm must first decide whether it needs warehouses and, if so, whether it will build its own private warehouses or rent space in public warehouses. The company must also decide whether a single-story or multiple-story warehouse would best serve its needs.

[4]Adapted from Hise, Richard T., Peter L. Gillet, and John K. Ryans, Jr. *Basic Marketing: Concepts and Decisions.* Cambridge, Mass.: Winthrop Publishers, Inc., 1979, pp. 385-386, 393-406.

Decide where to locate the warehouses based on such factors as the costs of transportation to and from the warehouse, as well as the service requirements of the customers. A firm must also determine how many warehouses it needs; theoretically, the more warehouses a firm has, the better customer service it can provide. However, more efficiency in the other physical distribution areas (e.g., more rapid transportation or faster order processing) may allow a firm to provide adequate customer service with fewer warehouses.

Materials Handling. Between the time it is produced and sold to the final customer/user, the typical product is lifted, moved, and stored many times, particularly in the warehouse. The major decision in this area is to find the most efficient system of materials handling. Options are forklift trucks, freight elevators, cranes, conveyor systems, as well as manpower. Other decisions involve finding the most efficient materials handling processes, such as palletization, containerization, and computerization of tasks.

Inventory. From a marketing management perspective, the ideal situation is to have enough products in inventory at all times at all locations, so that customer orders could always be filled promptly. But, in most cases, the cost of carrying such high levels of inventory is prohibitive. Inventory costs, including costs for warehouse space, taxes, insurance, and materials handling, increase at an increasing rate as the customer service level approaches 100 percent. As a result, the firm must achieve a fine balance between customer service and inventory levels.

Order Processing. A company must fill orders quickly and accurately, and marketing managers must insure that the fastest and most efficient order processing methods are used. The entire distribution system breaks down if customers are kept waiting longer than necessary, or the incorrect color, style, size, or quantity of product is shipped. The increased availability of computerized order processing systems can help companies improve service.

Protective Packaging. The final major decision area of physical distribution involves protective packaging. A better package can lower costs by reducing breakage and spoilage. Also, tailoring the protective package to better meet customer needs can increase sales.

CUSTOMER SERVICE

There is a tendency to make distribution decisions on the basis of efficiency or cost-savings. However, applying the marketing concept to this important functional area implies a more customer-oriented approach to distribution strategies. It is important for the firm to determine which customer needs are important and then build its distribution system to satisfy them.

The primary customer need in this area is *product availability*—having a needed product at the right time and the right place.[5] The product must be available when and where it is needed so the manufacturer can produce and sell it, the intermediary can resell it, and the industrial buyer or ultimate consumer can use it. Specifically, customer service may comprise any number of different elements. Among the most common elements of customer service are:[6]

1. The elapsed time between receipt of an order at the supplier's warehouse and the shipment

2. The minimum size of order, or limits on the assortment of items in an order which a supplier will accept from customers

3. The percentage of items in a supplier's warehouse which are out-of-stock at any time

4. The percentage of orders filled accurately

5. The percentage of orders filled within a certain period of time from receipt of order

6. The percentage of orders that can be filled completely upon receipt at a supplier's warehouse

7. The percentage of ordered products that arrive at a customer's place of business in good condition

8. The order cycle time, or elapsed time between order placement by the customer and delivery of goods

9. The ease and flexibility with which a customer can place an order

A firm must determine which elements are most important to the customer and then organize and control the distribution system so that these customer service requirements are met.

SUMMARY

In this chapter we have pointed out the major distribution decision areas of importance to the marketing manager. Distribution decisions should take into account the design of both the marketing channel and the physical distribution (logistical) system. All of this will be based on the level of customer service required for the product. Chapter 7 will consider various strategies for pricing a product, once the distribution system has made it available to the customer.

---

[5]Perreault, W.D., Jr., and F.A. Russ. "Physical Distribution Service: A Neglected Aspect of Marketing Management." *MSU Business Topics,* Summer 1974, p. 39.

[6]Heskett, J.L., N.A. Glaskowsky, and R.M. Ivie. *Business Logistics.* New York: Ronald Press, 1973, pp. 250-251.

QUESTIONS

1. What conditions may indicate a need for change in channel design?
2. What are the three types of distribution strategies?
3. What is a channel member?
4. Why might a firm choose to have fewer warehouses than a competitor?
5. What are some considerations in determining inventory levels?

SUGGESTED READINGS

Bucklin, L.P. "A Theory of Channel Control." *Journal of Marketing,* January 1973, pp. 39-47.

El-Ansary, A.I. and R.A. Robicheaux. "A Theory of Channel Control: Revisited." *Journal of Marketing,* January 1974, pp. 2-7.

El-Ansary, A.I. and L.W. Stern. "Power Measurement in the Distribution Channel." *Journal of Marketing Research,* February 1972, pp. 47-52.

Etgar, M. "Channel Environment and Channel Leadership." *Journal of Marketing Research,* February 1977, pp. 69-76.

Etgar, M. "Selection of an Effective Channel Control Mix." *Journal of Marketing,* July 1978, pp. 53-58.

Fair, M.L. and E.W. Williams, Jr. *Transportation and Logistics.* Plano, Texas: Business Publications, Inc., 1981.

Guiltinan, J.P. "Planned and Evolutionary Changes in Distribution Channels." *Journal of Retailing,* Summer 1974, pp. 79-91.

Lambert, D.M. and J.R. Stock, *Strategic Physical Distribution Management,* Homewood, Ill.: Richard D. Irwin, Inc., 1982.

Lusch, R.F. "Sources of Power: Their Impact on Interchannel Conflict." *Journal of Marketing Research,* November 1976, pp. 382-390.

Michman, R.D. and S.D. Sibley. *Marketing Channels and Strategies.* Columbus, Ohio: Grid Publishing Co., 1980.

Perreault, W.D., Jr. and F.A. Russ. "Physical Distribution Service: A Neglected Aspect of Marketing Management." *MSU Business Topics,* Summer 1974, pp. 37-45.

Rosenbloom, B. *Marketing Channels.* Hinsdale, Ill.: The Dryden Press, 1978.

Sims, J.T., J.R. Foster, and A.G. Woodside. *Marketing Channels, Systems and Strategies.* New York: Harper & Row, 1977.

Webster, F.E. "The Role of the Industrial Distributor in Marketing." *Journal of Marketing,* July 1976, pp. 10-16.

7

Implementing Pricing Strategies

*P*erhaps the most critical decision area of the marketing mix involves price. No other decision area involves every product and every buyer-seller situation; no other decision area has such a direct impact on sales revenue. At the same time, though, pricing strategies are generally determined in a very unsophisticated manner, sometimes almost arbitrarily. Since the price is such a critical element of the marketing mix, it is vitally important to take a systematic approach. This approach should contain at least these steps: *select the pricing objective, analyze the pricing situation,* and *select the appropriate pricing strategy.*

SELECT THE PRICING OBJECTIVE

A firm's pricing objective is derived from the overall marketing objective. What it aims to accomplish with a product will determine what it aims to do with its price. Some of the more common objectives are:

1. *Profit maximization:* From a financial standpoint, this is the most desirable pricing objective. This results in pricing at the level where marginal cost is equal to marginal revenue, maximizing the profitability of the product.

2. *Target return pricing:* This is a variation of profit maximation pricing and one that is somewhat more operational. Here the firm determines a desired level of profit as a percentage of sales, say 12 percent, or a percentage of investment (assets), say, 8 percent, and sets the price at the level necessary to achieve this.

3. *Market share:* A firm may set as its pricing objective the attainment of a certain share of the market. It then determines the price necessary to produce the sales volume required for that share. There are many reasons a firm might be particularly concerned with market share. High market share is generally associated with high profitability, prestige, and industry leadership, but too high a market share might subject the firm to government, competitive, or consumer attacks.

4. *Cash flow:* Because of an undesirable liquidity position or uncertainty of a product's future, a firm may be primarily interested in generating a high level of cash flow immediately. Such a situation means setting the price level to yield the maximum sales revenue.

5. *Competition:* A firm may adopt an external rather than internal objective for its pricing strategy. In this case, the pricing objective is established solely on the basis of the competition's pricing strategy. The firm may price to either meet or beat the price set by a competitor.

6. *Status quo:* In some cases, a firm may be satisfied with its financial and/or competitive position and have no desire to change the situation. It may adopt a pricing objective of not wanting to rock the boat, but instead achieve price stability in the industry.

ANALYZE THE PRICING SITUATION

Significant factors that affect any pricing decision are the *product,* the *market demand,* and the *environment.*

The Product. One of the basic determinants of a product's price is the product itself. Such product factors as cost, stage in the product life cycle, and product characteristics all affect the price.

Cost is, of course, a key element in pricing strategy. A firm is normally not going to price its products below cost, so the cost-per-unit of the product will set a "minimum price" for the product. There are other cost considerations, however. A firm can always lower costs by realizing economies of scale through higher sales volume and higher production levels. It may adjust price as this is realized, or it may even set a lower initial price, based on long-run average cost, in anticipation of future lower costs. The relationship between fixed and variable cost elements will also impact on the pricing decision. If fixed costs are high, a firm will want to spread this out over as many units as possible; if variable costs are high, a firm may want to increase its per-unit markup as much as possible.

The *stage in the product life cycle* will affect the pricing decisions. Prices tend to be high in the introduction stage, but this will vary as firms adopt different new product pricing strategies. As the product enters the growth stage, prices tend to stabilize at a lower average price. The maturity stage generally leads to lower prices as economies of scale are realized, competition increases, and inefficient firms leave the market. The product decline stage may see prices drop even more if several competitors remain in the industry. Or, prices may even increase, due to the specialty nature of the product, if only one or two firms remain.

Product characteristics will also affect pricing strategy. Distinctive or high quality products tend to be priced higher, perishable products must be priced to expedite sale, and standardized products are priced lower.

Market Demand. From a marketing viewpoint one of the most important factors a marketing manager should consider in setting a price is what the customer is willing to pay. A company should derive the *demand curve* for its products (i.e., the quantity demanded at different price levels). Two different demand curves are depicted in Exhibit 1. Next, the company should analyze the *price elasticity* or elasticity of demand between certain price levels. The elasticity of demand is calculated like this:

$$e = \frac{\% \Delta Q}{\% \Delta P}$$

If $e > 1$, demand is elastic
If $e = 1$, demand is unitary
If $e < 1$, demand is inelastic

This equation tells us that the coefficient of price elasticity (e) is equal to the percentage change in quantity demanded divided by the percentage change in price. Price elasticity measures how sensitive the quantity demanded is to a price change. For example, in Exhibit 1 the coefficient of price elasticity between points A and B in demand curve I (assuming a price decrease) can be calculated like this:

$$e = \frac{\frac{150,000-40,000}{40,000}}{\frac{\$50 - \$25}{\$50}} = \frac{2.75}{.5} = 5.5$$

This tells us that a 50 percent decrease in price (from $50 to $25) would result in a 275 percent increase in quantity demanded. In this case, the quantity demanded is very sensitive to a change in price, and an *elastic* demand curve results.

In demand curve II of Exhibit 1, the coefficient of price elasticity between points A and B (again assuming a price decrease) can be calculated like this:

$$e = \frac{\frac{40,000-35,000}{35,000}}{\frac{\$75 - \$50}{\$75}} = \frac{.14}{.33} = .42$$

This tells us that a 33 percent decrease in price (from $75 to $50) would only result in a 14 percent increase in quantity demanded. In this case, the quantity demanded is *not* very sensitive to a change in price, and an *inelastic* demand curve results.

The bottom line for pricing decisions is that, in an elastic demand situation, a price decrease would be desirable since total revenue (P × Q) increases as the price decreases. In an inelastic demand situation, the firm should increase the price, since demand is not very sensitive to a price change. The result would be higher revenue as the price increases.

Even though such calculations can be beneficial to the marketing manager, you should realize that customers do not always buy less of a product simply because the price is high, and vice versa. At times, buying decisions are made on an emotional rather than a purely economic basis, so a demand curve might not always be downsloping. It is also difficult to separate price from other marketing mix variables; price is not the sole determinant of quantity demanded. In any event, it is worthwhile to estimate the demand curve for a product, at different price levels, realizing the additional impact of other marketing elements and of the customer's psychological responses.

The Environment. Three major environmental variables have a direct impact on pricing strategies: the political/legal environment, the economic environment, and the competitive environment.

The *political/legal environment* constrains pricing decisions. The firm must examine which way the political winds are blowing and insure that a particular pricing strategy will not be out of line. For example, a firm in an industry that may have temporarily fallen into disfavor with the public should be careful about raising prices immediately after announcing record profits in its annual report. Another major constraint is legal; firms must not violate

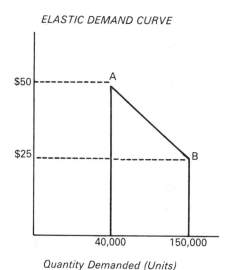

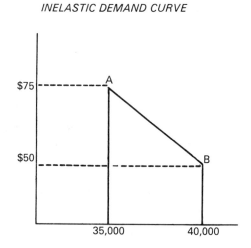

EXHIBIT 1   Two demand curves

laws. Such pricing actions as price fixing and deceptive pricing are illegal, and other pricing actions, such as price discrimination, basing—point pricing, and below-cost pricing may be illegal under the Sherman, Clayton, or Robinson-Patman Acts, or other federal or state regulation.

The *economic environment* will also be a factor in pricing decisions. During inflationary times, price increases are generally needed to keep up with costs and maintain profit margins. In a deflationary economy, prices may have to be decreased since prices for competitive products are also decreasing. During times of price stability or concerted effort to control inflation, firms should exercise great caution in raising prices, due to public pressure against such a move.

The *competitive environment* should also be considered. Many times a pricing decision by a competitor might actually be the impetus for another firm's decision. Also, when a firm sets a price or is considering a price change, it should anticipate what the competitive response will be. The type of competitive response depends on such factors as the size of the competition, its financial condition, and the structure of the industry.

SELECT THE APPROPRIATE PRICING STRATEGY

A firm has many pricing strategy alternatives; there are at least four major categories: cost-plus pricing, new product pricing, psychological pricing, and promotional pricing.

Cost-Plus Pricing. Perhaps the simplest pricing strategy is calculating the average cost of a product (average fixed cost plus average variable cost), and then adding a fixed dollar amount or percentage dollar amount of markup to arrive at the selling price. Such techniques as break-even analysis and marginal cost analysis may be used to examine cost data to arrive at the desired selling price.

New Product Pricing. A firm can adopt either a skimming or a penetration strategy to price a new product (see Exhibit 2).

A *skimming strategy* involves setting a high price on a new product so that high initial profits can be generated and new product development costs recovered quickly. As competitive products enter the market, the price can be lowered. The high initial price may create an image of prestige and quality so that when the price is lowered, consumers may feel they are getting a bargain. A skimming strategy is good when a new product is substantially different from similar products on the market, or when market demand is high, the demand curve inelastic, and the product difficult to duplicate (such as when it is protected by a patent). However, it also has some potential disadvantages. Its high price and high profit margin tend to attract competition, the price may be set too high and destroy demand, and it is not suited as a long-range strategy.

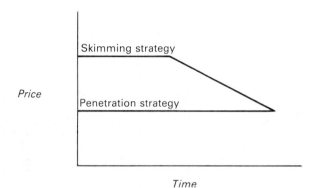

EXHIBIT 2   Skimming–penetration pricing strategies

A *penetration strategy* uses a low price to obtain instant acceptance in the marketplace. Profits may not be very attractive at first, but the low price tends to keep out competition, giving the firm a less competitive marketplace for a longer period of time. A penetration strategy is good when a product is not significantly different from other products on the market, when market demand is low, has an elastic curve, or when the product is relatively easy to duplicate by competition. Its primary disadvantage is the low profit margin that accompanies the low price.

Psychological Pricing. Some pricing strategies are based on the understanding that products are sometimes purchased for emotional rather than economic reasons and that the price can encourage this emotional response. Two of the most common psychological pricing strategies are odd-even pricing and prestige pricing.

Odd-even pricing is setting prices that end in numbers thought to be more attractive to customers. For example, gasoline is priced at $1.39[9], rather than $1.40; a shirt is priced at $9.99 rather than $10. These prices are set because they tend to connote a lower price, or possibly a price reduction from the higher price.

Prestige pricing breaks the law of diminishing demand in economic theory (i.e., the lower the price, the greater the quantity demanded). Prestige pricing takes into account that, with some products, a high price may suggest high quality; a price increase can actually lead to an increase in quantity demanded. Items such as medicines, furs, jewelry, perfume, and fashion items are often priced in this manner.

Promotional Pricing. In some cases, the price itself may be used as a promotional item. Such pricing strategies as leader pricing, special-event pricing, and discount pricing may be used to attract customer attention and encourage the customer to buy the "specially priced" item.

Leader pricing is pricing a few items lower than normal (in some cases below cost) to increase store traffic or increase sales of regularly priced items. A good leader-priced product is one for which consumers have good knowledge of the regular price, and a product that consumers do not stock-pile (if it is, a limit might be placed on the number allowed per customer). You should recognize that leader pricing is different from illegal bait pricing, where a low price is promoted but the product is not actually made available for sale.

Special-event pricing is another form of promotional pricing that uses a special event (a holiday, special day for the company, etc.) as a reason to lower the price on a product, call attention to it, and increase sales. This strategy creates interest and excitement in customers, and is often very successful, if not used too often.

Discount pricing is a pricing strategy that calls attention to the fact that the product is being sold for a "discount price." This promotes the discount with "reduced 50%" or "Was $99, Now $79" in its promotion or on the price tag on the product.

SUMMARY

This chapter has set forth the three basic steps in implementing pricing strategies. Six different pricing objectives, the significant factors in the pricing situation, and different pricing strategies were presented. Chapter 8 will discuss evaluation and control, emphasizing that even the best marketing mix strategies must be continuously monitored and periodically evaluated to insure the success of the product.

QUESTIONS

1. Name and explain five of the most common pricing objectives.
2. What product factors impact on pricing strategy?
3. If a firm determined that the elasticity of demand was equal to 1, what pricing policy changes should be implemented?
4. How do the environmental variables affect pricing strategies?
5. How can pricing be used as a promotional tool?

SUGGESTED READINGS

Bettman, J.R. "Perceived Price, and Product Perceptual Variables." *Journal of Marketing Research,* February 1973, pp. 100–102.

Brooks, D.G. "Cost-Oriented Pricing: A Realistic Solution to a Complicated Problem." *Journal of Marketing,* April 1975, pp. 72–74.

Dean, J. "Pricing Policies for New Products." *Harvard Business Review,* November-December 1976, pp. 141–153.

Fogg, C.D. and K.H. Kohnken. "Price-Cost Planning." *Journal of Marketing,* April 1978, pp. 97–106.

Guiltinan, J.P. "Risk-Aversive Pricing Policies: Problems and Alternatives." *Journal of Marketing,* January 1976, pp. 10–15.

Kotler, P. *Marketing Management, Analysis, Planning and Control,* fourth edition. Englewood Cliffs, N.J.: Prentice-Hall, Inc., 1980, pp. 381–410.

Lambert, Z.V. "Price and Choice Behavior." *Journal of Marketing Research,* February 1972.

McConnell, J.D. "The Price-Quality Relationship in an Experimental Setting." *Journal of Marketing Research,* August 1968, pp. 300–303.

Monroe, K.B. "Buyers' Subjective Perceptions of Price." *Journal of Marketing Research,* February 1973, pp. 70–80.

Monroe, K.B. *Pricing: Making Profitable Decisions.* New York: McGraw-Hill Book Co., 1979.

Monroe, K.B. and A.J. Della Bitta. "Models for Pricing Decisions." *Journal of Marketing Research,* August 1978, pp. 413–428.

Oxenfeldt, A.R. "A Decision-Making Structure for Price Decisions." *Journal of Marketing,* January 1973, pp. 48–53.

Palda, K.S. *Pricing Decisions and Marketing Policies.* Englewood Cliffs, N.J.: Prentice-Hall, Inc., 1971.

Russo, J.E. "The Value of Unit Price Information." *Journal of Marketing Research,* May 1977, pp. 193–201.

Shapiro, B.P. "The Psychology of Pricing." *Harvard Business Review,* July-August 1968, pp. 14–25, 160.

Udell, J.G. "How Important Is Pricing in Competitive Strategy?" *Journal of Marketing,* January 1964, pp. 44–48.

Levi Strauss

Robert Grohman, fifty-six years old and currently the executive vice president and chief operating officer of Levi Strauss & Co., has just been informed that he will be the company's next president and chief executive officer. For the first time in its history, the 130-year old company will be headed by someone other than a descendant of its founder, Levi Strauss. During the past decade, Walter and Peter Haas, great-grandnephews of Levi Strauss, have run the company and turned it into not only the largest, but also one of the fastest growing and most rapidly diversifying, companies in the world. However, next year, Chairman Walter Haas, sixty-five, will move into semiretirement and head the company's executive committee, and Peter Haas, sixty-three, the company's president, will become chairman of the board. Many had speculated that Robert D. Haas, thirty-eight, president of the company's operating groups, and son of the retiring chairman, would take over the top executive post. But when the final decision was made, most industry analysts felt that the board of directors' decision to expand from a family operation and gain outside perspective at the top was a smart move and that Grohman was the best man for the job.

Robert Grohman is no stranger to the apparel industry or to the company. He spent more than fifteen years in top executive positions with the B.V.D. Company and at International Playtex. When Levi Strauss & Co. was having problems in 1974, the Haas brothers hired Grohman to turn things around. During the past seven years, his influence on the company has been dramatic. In fact, his foresight and initiative have helped the company grow from simply a jeans manufacturer to a full-fledged apparel company.

As Grohman considers current operations and ponders all elements of the company he will be running next year, several significant questions come to mind. Can Levi Strauss continue the kind of growth it has realized in recent years? How should future growth come about? Should this growth be from inside the company or should additional acquisitions of smaller complementary companies be considered? Should emphasis be placed on domestic or

This case was prepared by Stephen W. McDaniel, Assistant Professor of Marketing, Texas A&M University, as a basis for class discussion rather than to illustrate either effective or ineffective marketing management.

international sales, or both? Is the present organizational structure in the company appropriate for its growing scope of operations? What should the scope of operations be?

HISTORY OF LEVI STRAUSS

Beginning

No one would have thought that a pair of pants fashioned from a tent would one day be an exhibit in the Smithsonian Institute. It is amazing that a style of pants with such austere beginnings would reach one billion dollars in sales over the next century. But that is exactly what resulted from the novel idea young Levi Strauss had in 1850. An impoverished Bavarian immigrant who came to New York in 1847 to work in his brother's dry goods store, Levi soon headed for the gold rush country of California. Selling dry goods supplied by his brother, he soon realized that the hard-working prospectors needed sturdy, long-lasting pants more than they needed the canvas for tents and wagon covers he was selling. He took some of his canvas to a tailor, who fashioned a pair of pants for him. Word soon spread about "those pants of Levi's," and the rising entrepreneur set up shop in San Francisco to meet the needs of the rapidly growing population in the area.

Following a change in material from canvas to blue-dyed Serge de Nimes (cloth imported from Nimes, France, later shortened to denim), Strauss became partners with Jacob W. Davis, a tailor who began riveting the pocket corners on miners' pants for added strength. In 1873, the two men applied jointly for a patent on the riveting of stress points on pants with copper rivets. This patent helped create a unique long-lasting product identified by these rivets and an orange double arc stitched on the back pockets. Levi Strauss & Co. has kept this same basic design for over a hundred years.

The 1900s

Levi's® blue jeans became standard for cowboys, lumberjacks, farmers, and miners in the West. In the 1930s Levi's blue jeans were introduced east of the Mississippi. Thanks to flourishing dude ranches in the West, many wealthy Eastern vacationers were exposed to Western-style dress and enjoyed taking their new clothes home with them. Soon Levi's blue jeans were sold nationally. Demand became so great that, during World War II, Levi's blue jeans were declared an essential commodity and sold only to people engaged in defense work. By 1946, sales had grown to $8.4 million.

In the early 1950s, the company put new impetus into its growth by adding an additional product line—a new line of denim trousers called "Levi's Lighter Blues." This was followed by the introduction of "White Levi's®," a line of cotton-twill pants styled along the lines of the original blue jeans.

American teenagers swarmed to the stores to buy these white jeans, making it one of the most popular styles of pants ever made.

The 1960s saw the rapidly growing company expand its markets by exporting jeans to Europe, where they were as big a hit as they were in the U.S. Also in the 1960s, a revolution occurred in the apparel industry with the development of sta-prest, which served as the catalyst for myriad fabrics, styles, and colors. A line of Levi's for Gals was soon introduced, and a whole new market for the company's products was opened.

Thanks to the post-war baby boom and the resulting match between the market's desires and Levi's products, the company developed worldwide recognition between 1946 and 1970 and became one of the top brands in awareness in virtually every country of the world. Extremely strong customer support was developed, and Levi's attained a major share of the market in most of the areas the products were sold.

The 1970s and 80s

Levi Strauss & Co. made several significant strategic decisions in the 1970s. The major decision involved the company's business domain: was it simply a jeans manufacturer or more than that? In spite of sales growth from $137 million in 1965 to $350 million by 1970, top management began questioning the wisdom of not having a diverse product mix. Even though the future looked good for continued growth in the demand for jeans, the executive committee of Levi Strauss realized there was no certainty to this. Also, they realized that by expanding the product line into complementary products, the well-known Levi brand could be placed on other products as well, and company sales could multiply. When temporary shortages of denim forced the company to allocate supplies to retail stores carrying its jeans, the need for product line extension was magnified. Soon the decision to expand was made.

Until 1971 Levi Strauss & Co. was a family-owned enterprise. However, to raise funds needed for expansion, the company made its first public stock offering. With capital generated from this, the company formed its sportswear division, with the introduction of slacks, blazers, vests, and sweaters, all coordinated into distinct wardrobes. Soon Levi's for Gals, the Women's Wear Division and the Youthwear Division were also established. In 1972 the company continued its transition into other apparel lines by acquiring Miller Belts, Ltd. of Cincinnati. Shortly afterwards, the company signed licensing agreements with Brown Shoe Company (to make Levi's shoes and boots) and Burlington Industries (to make Levi's® socks).

The company also expanded its overseas operations in the early '70s. Foreign sales quickly grew from $4 million in 1965 to $200 million by 1973.

Marketing Reassessment

As might be expected, the rapid expansion of Levi Strauss' product offerings and the rapid overseas growth brought problems. In 1974 the executive committee took a hard look at the company's marketing program and realized that it needed a proven marketing expert from outside the company to set the foundation for future company growth. The man they brought in was Robert Grohman. As the new chief operating officer, he first implemented an extensive marketing research program that focused on analyses of market segments for the various products. He then made new product development decisions and implemented a new advertising program, unusually strong, not only for Levi Strauss, but the whole apparel industry. Grohman decided that the major emphasis in marketing programs should be placed on women's wear, which represented a $40 billion annual U.S. market, twice that of men's wear. At that time, 90 percent of Levi's business was coming from men's wear. In addition, Grohman provided the initiative as the company introduced new casual clothing for men, youthwear offerings in toddler sizes, and other product lines, such as a line of men's and women's ski apparel called Ski Levi's®. Explained Grohman, "We made a decision that consumers would be ours from cradle to grave, regardless of whatever they may be interested in."

Levi executives agreed that the strongest asset the firm had was its brand name. Therefore, the decision was made to market all products under the Levi's name. The Levi's logo was used for every product in the company and all secondary brand names were eliminated. This was designed to give the consumer "a single vision for any Levi's product, and to reinforce the Levi's brand name through print and TV ads, regardless of the product being advertised."

Although at this time there were four general product categories established in the company (Jeanswear, Youthwear, Menswear, and Womenswear), the segmentation research studies identified another thirty-eight potential product categories. At that point the company began creating separate marketing divisions within each operating division. Each marketing division included all necessary elements, designing, merchandising, and marketing, to handle each particular product segment. The Womenswear division, for example, with sales in 1976 of $38 million in U.S. sales, was divided into five divisions. In 1980 the total of these five divisions was $300 million. The same type of reorganization took place within the other three divisions. Today Levi Strauss has twenty-four separate marketing divisions in twenty-four sales organizations, selling products in the U.S. and many parts of the world. Over the next five years, the current president would like to add at least sixteen new divisions.

ORGANIZATION

By 1981 the company had more than 2,000 different styles, colors, and fabrics worldwide. Manufacturing facilities rose to 155 and the company ranked 90th in the U.S. in net income and 167th in sales. As a result of the rapid growth, several changes were made in the company's organizational structure. Ex-

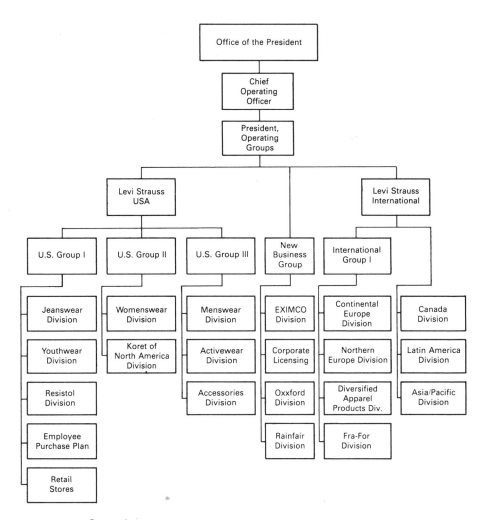

EXHIBIT 1   Operating structure

SOURCE: *1981 Executive Data Book,* Levi Strauss & Co.

hibit 1 depicts the operating structure of the most recent organization concept; it is designed to decentralize operations and allow managers who are in touch with the action to make the day-to-day decisions. This structure was designed also to allow centralization at a higher level, so that all decisions will flow from a common strategy. The first step of the recent reorganization was to divide the company into three business units: Levi Strauss U.S.A., Levi Strauss International and the New Business Group.

Levi Strauss U.S.A.

This operating unit is organized along product lines to serve the entire United States. The largest of the three units, it is comprised of three operating groups, with each subdivided.

U.S. Group I Jeanswear Division. The traditional bread-and-butter element of the company, this division sells not only regular Levi jeans, but also western-wear lines of pants, vests, blazers, shirts, as well as fashion jeans. A separate sales force was established in 1979 to concentrate on the adult male market segment, reached primarily in the Levi's for men line of products.

Youthwear Division. This division markets jeanswear and western product to youth, and is also responsible for girlswear products, Activewear, and attire for toddlers. In 1979 this operating division was separated into two marketing divisions, each with its own merchandising and sales capabilities: Student & Junior Boys®, and Little Levi's® and Girlswear®.

Resistol Hats Division. This division, part of the 1979 Koracorp Industries acquisition, is the world's largest source of brand-name western and dress hats.

U.S. Group II Womenswear Division. The Womenswear Division, the company's most rapidly growing operating division, markets a line of sportswear including pants, shirts, sweaters, skirts, and shorts, styled for juniors, young misses and large women.

Koret of North American Division. Koret of North America, a portion of the Koracorp Industries acquisition, markets moderately priced coordinates including skirts, pants, blouses, sweaters, and jackets. A separate sales force for large sizes was established in 1980.

U.S. Group III Menswear Division. The Menswear Division markets men's and young men's casual and dress slacks, jackets, shirts, vests, sweaters, and outerwear. It is one of the largest manufacturers of men's and young men's slacks in the United States.

Activewear Division. The Activewear Division markets ski wear, warm-up suits, shorts, and tops for a variety of participant sports, styled for both men and women. This division was in a start-up phase in 1980, and cancellation of the Summer Olympics hindered much of its promotional activity.

Accessories Division. The Accessories Division markets primarily belts, casual hats, and wallets for men and women.

Levi Strauss International

This unit is organized along geographic, rather than product, lines; Canada, Latin America, and Asia/Pacific form three of the four geographic groups. The fourth, called International Group I, is made up of four operating divisions: Continental Europe, Northern Europe, and separate divisions specializing in children's apparel (Fra-For) and new European products (Diversified Apparel Products). These divisions are further broken down into areas, headed by an area General Manager, and the areas are then broken into countries, headed by a Country Manager. Each country is considered a separate market and, with few exceptions, is staffed with its own merchandising, sales, and finance personnel. LSI is independent of the other operating units in manufacturing and distribution. LSI's sales consist of basic lines of pants, shirts, and jackets which are moderately diversified by the selective introduction of new products in certain markets including women's-fit jeans, youthwear, menswear and related tops. In addition, the Fra-For Division, another portion of the Koracorp Industries acquisition, manufactures childrenswear.

The New Business Group

This group is composed of three divisions not aligned with either Levi Strauss U.S.A. or Levi Strauss International. It includes Levi Strauss and Eximco, an export/import company which has two major responsibilities: (1) market development and joint ventures in Eastern Europe, China and the Soviet Union, and (2) direct international contract production for all Levi Strauss divisions. The New Business Group also includes Oxford Clothes, a manufacturer of high quality men's apparel, and Rainfair, which makes special protective clothing for industry. Both of these were part of the 1979 Koracorp acquisition.

   Sales figures for each operating unit are shown in Exhibit 2.

   Levi Strauss & Co. does not have a corporate marketing department as such. Instead, it has a "marketing council" composed of senior operating executives from the various operating groups and headed by Grohman. This marketing council provides direction, policy, philosophy, and other perspec-

EXHIBIT 2   Levi Strauss & Co. sales by operating unit (in millions)

Division	1980	1979	1978	1977	1976
Levi Strauss USA					
Jeanswear	$921.0	$743.1	$658.7	$695.5	$569.1
Youthwear	280.0	217.8	184.2	171.6	126.8
Resistol	76.0	—	—	—	—
Sportswear	—	118.0	118.5	108.8	94.1
Womenswear	290.0	197.4	99.2	62.8	47.4
Koret	131.0	—	—	—	—
Menswear	164.0	—	—	—	—
Activewear	8.0	2.7	—	—	—
Accessories	18.0	15.6	14.3	—	—
Diversified products	—	45.0	—	33.6	26.5
TOTAL	$1,888.0	$1,339.0	$1,074.9	$1,072.3	$864.0
Levi Strauss International					
Europe	$487.0	$389.7	$305.7	$237.4	$146.1
Canada	159.0	139.6	114.8	122.7	111.4
Latin America	157.0	134.7	103.5	79.3	51.7
Asia/Pacific	94.0	74.1	61.0	47.6	46.7
TOTAL	$953.0	$737.1	$594.2	$487.0	$356.0

SOURCE: Annual Reports.

tives that help the operating divisions and groups make the best market-oriented decisions.

This effort is also aided by the Corporate Marketing Research Organization, which reports directly to the vice president of corporate planning and policy, who is responsible for strategic long-term planning as well as short-term plans. This corporate marketing research organization provides all operating groups and divisions with important demographic, environmental, and other useful information. The company tries to base its strategies on these market research findings. Grohman is dedicated to marketing planning and has encouraged a marketing orientation in the company, feeling that the company must always respond to changes in the marketplace. He commented, "Marketing permeates every facet of our decision-making process and every facet of our planning process."

CURRENT OPERATIONS

Distribution

The company sells to approximately 25,000 separate retail accounts and 70,000 individual retail stores in the United States. It has had a long-standing policy of not selling through mass merchandisers or major department store chains. Instead, it distributes to traditional department and specialty stores, including some specialty store chains. The reason for this selective distribution policy is to maintain as much control as possible over the final sale of the product, particularly the retail sales price, the product assortment carried by the retailer, and whether or not retailers resell the product to other resellers who undersell Levi's. However, this attempt to control the resale of its products brought Levi Strauss & Co. into conflict with the Federal Trade Commission, as well as with several other parties who filed suit against the company. The controversies centered around whether company practices constituted restraint of trade, especially price fixing and the use of tying contracts. The FTC issued a cease and desist order forbidding the company to continue using "threats, coercion, intimidation, harrassment" or any other measures to enforce retailer compliance with these resale policies. As a result, the company is now very cautious about its resale practices and does not have the control it once did over retailers carrying its products. For example, Levi Strauss may set a "suggested retail price" for its products, but cannot terminate a retailer or even threaten to take any kind of action against a retailer who cuts the price of Levi products. The company can also recommend a retailer's product mix, but cannot require that the retailer carry one Levi product to sell another. Nor is the company able to directly regulate the type of customer to whom a retailer sells a Levi product.

Each retail store carrying Levi products is served by one or all of the company's seven distribution centers. Jeanswear centers are located in Florence, Kentucky; Henderson, Nevada; and Canton, Mississippi. The menswear center is in Little Rock, Arkansas. Womenswear centers are in Amarillo and Waco, Texas. The youthwear center is in Amarillo, Texas. The Diversified Products Division is served from Knoxville, Tennessee. These seven main distribution centers receive goods from eighty-five manufacturing facilities. Distribution managers of each apparel division coordinate the receipt of these goods at their respective distribution center to insure the timely allotment and shipment of goods. The Corporate Traffic and Transportation Department coordinates the shipments of all domestic goods, negotiates freight rates, and deals with regulatory agencies. This department also operates the company's trucking fleet, composed of 90 drivers, 35 tractors and 200 trailers. In 1980 Levi trucks traveled a total of 8.5 million miles and hauled 125,000 tons of Levi products.

The distribution process at Levi Strauss is very complex. The company fleet is constantly crisscrossing the country, picking up finished goods from one plant and transporting them to another, stopping for new materials at a mill or picking up sundries from a supplier. There are three regional transportation centers, located in the same cities as three of the distribution centers. These regional centers serve as home base for the truckers, a place where they get their assignments, where the trucks are maintained, and also a stationary spot where the drivers can rest between runs. Dispatchers coordinate destinations, times, truckloads, and drivers.

A summary of operations data regarding employees and facilities is provided in Exhibit 3.

EXHIBIT 3 1981 operations data Levi Strauss & Co.

	Number of Employees	Number of Employees	Facilities[1] No./Sq. Ft. (in 000s)	
	Total	*Selling Personnel*	*Owned*	*Leased*
LEVI STRAUSS USA				
Jeanswear	13,338	428	17/2,047	13/696
Youthwear	5,224	225	9/1,086	5/166
Resistol	1,502	59	3/230	1/200
Administration	7	—	—	—
US group I	20,071	712	29/3,363	19/1,062
Womenswear	5,754	281	9/1,953	7/532
Koret of North America	1,630	103	4/531	8/418
US group II	7,384	384	13/2,474	15/950
Menswear	3,652	155	7/791	4/180
Activewear	220	28	1/30	—
Accessories	248	47	—	1/105
Administration	3	—	—	—

EXHIBIT 3   (continued)

	Number of Employees	Number of Employees	Facilities[1] No./Sq. Ft. (in 000s)	
	Total	Selling Personnel	Owned	Leased
US group III	4,123	230	8/821	5/285
Administration & other	1,328	207[2]	—	2/61
Total LS USA	32,906	1,533	50/6,658	41/2,358
LEVI STRAUSS INTERNATIONAL				
Northern & Continental Europe	4,706	263	12/645	13/764
Fra-For	739	54	5/373	—
International group I	5,445	317	17/1,018	13/764
Canada	2,919	163	6/515	3/435
Latin America	3,186	180	7/793	3/51
Asia/Pacific	2,001	101	2/140	7/325
Administration	133	—	—	—
Total LS international	13,684	761	32/2,466	29/1,575
Total other operations	739	77[2]	3/394	—
Corporate	644	—	—	—
CONSOLIDATED	47,973	2 371	85/9,518	70/3,933

[1]Manufacturing, permanent press curing and distribution facilities.
[2]Retail sales.

SOURCE: *1981 Executive Data Book,* Levi Straus & Co.

Merchandising

Merchandisers. Each of the twenty-four marketing divisions has its own general merchandise manager who supervises a team of merchandisers. One merchandiser is assigned to each product line and is completely responsible for that product. Each merchandiser compiles and coordinates all market studies, develops new styles, and creates all advertising and selling techniques for the product line. Guidelines for profit and marketing objectives are handed down from the corporate level to the managers and merchandisers.

New Product Process. Merchandisers consider several factors in creating new styles. Each idea is based on seasonal and current fashion trends, success of past styles and items, feedback from salespersons and retailers, and the merchandisers' perception of high fashion abroad. Merchandisers consult with mill representatives for fabric trends, monitor the influence of competitive products, and consult all relevant trade journals.

When an idea is deemed worthy, merchandisers develop a prototype of the product. A model is cut and studies are made for initial fit and appearance. Production estimates are established by costing each component of the proposed garment—fabric, sundries, tooling, labor, and the production costs. The final cost of the raw materials and garment production must be in line with the style, image, and price range set by the division manager for that type of product. These prototypes are shown to sales representatives who, in turn, show them to key retailers for any modifications or suggestions. From this research data, initial sales estimates are made and the final pattern is given to the divisional marketing and general merchandising heads for their approval.

One or more of Levi's eighty-five domestic manufacturing facilities is chosen to produce the new style, and prototypes are made available for the engineering department of that plant. A production schedule is established and a test run made. During this test run stage, the Product Evaluation Department tests the fabric and style for quality and overall wearability. If approved, a sample run is made and the new product is introduced into key market areas via the seven company distribution centers. If successful, the product is put into full production; the average time from idea to market introduction is nine months.

Since merchandisers are responsible for producing a line, they are constantly monitoring, adjusting, and refining the product to conform to all requirements, including the time schedule. It is also their responsibility to end production and close out a line when demand seems to be waning. Timely decisions in this area are very important.

Research and Development

Until the early '70s, there was not much need for a formal R&D department at Levi Strauss. But as the need for new product ideas arose, so did the need for a corporate R&D department. Since its establishment in 1981, over forty patents have been granted nationally and well over 1,000 have been granted internationally.

The department is divided into two groups—Product R&D and Machine R&D. Product R&D investigates new fibers, materials, and finishes to create more durable and less expensive fabrics to give Levi Strauss a marketing advantage as well as easy care products for the consumer. Located in Greensboro, N.C., Product R&D has developed such products as Durawal Plus™, a much improved corduroy jeans fabric blended with polyester for increased durability, fabric smoothness, and minimal shrinkage. Divia Plus™, a high quality denim was also developed by Product R&D and is used exclusively in the boyswear lines of the Youthwear Division. This 64 percent cotton/36 percent polyester blend fabric has been accepted by retailers and welcomed by consumers, since it retains all the qualities of 100 percent cotton denim, but also has the easy care qualities of polyester.

Machine R&D, located in Richardson, Texas, employs engineers and machine designers to plan, build, test, and install new apparel manufacturing equipment. The accurate machine which automatically stitches the famous Levi Strauss & Co. back pocket design was developed here.

Promotion

As the company has grown, so has its expenditures on promotion. Exhibit 4 shows company advertising expenditures for 1980, and Exhibit 5 provides comparative advertising expenditures on sports apparel by the major sportswear advertisers. No single advertising agency is used, as each division of the company handles its own advertising, coordinated in San Francisco.

EXHIBIT 4   Levi Strauss & Co. advertising expenditures—1980

Item	$(,000)	Media
Men's jeans	4,284.6	M,N,S,R,O
Family sportswear	4,014.0	N,S
Children's jeans	3,948.6	M,N,S
Men's sportswear	3,034.1	N,S
Women's sportswear	2,235.9	M,N,S,
Men's slacks	1,771.6	N,S
Women's jeans	1,344.6	M,N,S
Sweepstakes	638.5	M
Mens suits	599.2	N,S
Family multi-products	412.5	M
Men's boots & shoes	237.8	S,O
Women's jeans & coordinates	196.7	M
Womenswear contest	124.7	M
Men & women's sportswear	94.6	M
Children's sportswear	83.4	M,S
Dealer sportswear promotion	10.3	O
Family shoes	9.9	O
	$23,972.1	

By media	
Magazines (M)	3,954.3
Newspaper supplements (P)	—
Network television (N)	14,962.4
Spot television (S)	4,698.7
Network radio (R)	354.8
Outdoor (O)	1.9
TOTAL	$23,972.1

SOURCE: *Ad $ Summary,* Leading National Advertisers, Inc., 1980.

EXHIBIT 5 Yearly advertising expenditures on sports apparel (millions of dollars)

	1980	1979	1978	1977	1976
Levi's	21.5	25.6	13.9	12.0	4.6
Jordache jeans	9.0	3.7	—	—	—
Penneys	8.8	9.7	13.7	6.8	3.7
Gloria Vanderbilt	8.5	4.7	—	—	—
Wrangler	7.4	4.4	3.7	2.5	2.9
Sears	6.2	4.4	4.3	5.7	6.0
Bonjour jeans	5.0	1.3	—	—	—
Lee	3.5	2.6	2.4	.8	1.1

SOURCE: *Ad $ Summary,* Leading National Advertisers, Inc., 1976–1980.

As shown in Exhibit 4, the company's major advertising vehicle is television, both network and spot. Levi's has had most success with animated spots: "Stranger" (1970), "Threads" (1975), and "Roundup" (1979). "Threads" introduced an animation technique called rotoscope, live film with superimposed animation. Its target market was the young, skeptical viewer, and the combination of sight, sound, motion, and color was very effective in presenting fashion ideas. A recent youthwear advertisement, less animated, used talking dogs and cats along with a barking boy and a meowing girl—a reverse which was both humorous and successful. Most network television advertising is scheduled during the peak selling seasons of spring, fall and Christmas.

Magazine advertising is also considered important, primarily to reach specific market segments. For example, ads intended to reach working ranchers and cowboys are placed in *Western Horseman.* Sports magazines such as *Sports Illustrated* are used to promote Activewear, and women's magazines such as *Good Housekeeping* are used for Womenswear ads. In addition, trade publications such as *Daily News Record, Women's Wear Daily* and *Retail Week* are used to announce new merchandise to retailers. The company joins raw material suppliers in combined promotional efforts for trade publications. It uses some co-op advertising to partially reimburse retailers who advertise Levi's products in selected local media. Display advertising is used to provide a broad range of advertising materials for retailers; stores simply insert their names on ad slicks or posters prepared by Levi's ad agencies.

In 1980 Levi Strauss used somewhat more radio advertising than normal. The primary target market with this vehicle was teenagers, so contemporary music stations in major metropolitan areas were used.

Not only does Levi Strauss promote itself and its products with advertising, top management also believes in achieving good public relations. Corporate Communications supports the various operating divisions by performing various p.r. duties: assisting the media, providing information to the public, developing special promotions, and handling product publicity. This last area tends to be most effective. The company targets over 300 newspaper fashion editors in key metropolitan areas throughout the country. Each season these editors receive press kits which contain fashions copy, professional photographs, useful fabric information, garment care qualities, and technical information on new fabrics. By providing fashion editors the necessary information, products receive credible exposure in the media. Products are also publicized in less direct ways, such as outfitting major movie, television, and stage productions, or serving as an information resource for editors and reporters.

Credits and Accounts Receivable

The Elesco Factors Division handles all matters of credit and receivables management, including claims and adjustments arising from domestic transactions. An extensive computer system insures that each dollar of merchandise sold is actually paid for. This means keeping up with 25,000 separate retail accounts, which can be divided into 70,000 individual retail stores, and 300,000 departments within those retail stores. The division is divided into three separate departments: Credit Administration which governs the credit criteria for a customer; Operations which maintains the vast computer files and back-up records; and Customer Claims which handles nonroutine items such as credit disputes.

The firm checks out each prospective retailer and selects only those that pass a credit inspection; it extends credit to retailers and rewards those who pay early. All merchandise, except Womenswear, is sold on a net 10/eom basis. Any merchandise sold to the retailer from the 24th of one month to the 24th of the following month is due on the 10th of the next month. With Womenswear, an 8 percent discount is allowed if payment is made promptly according to terms.

Trademark Protection

The Levi's trademark is one of the best known and most widespread in the world. Other important design trademarks include the Pocket Tab, the Levi's Saddleman, The ARCUATE Design, the Two Horse Brand Ticket, and the Button Design. The company even has a "housemark," which is used to identify the products of each division (see Figure 6).

The company is very concerned about frequent attempts to counterfeit Levi Strauss products. This became a big problem after World War II, because of the new demand created by the thousands of U.S. military personnel who were issued Levis for work clothing. Local manufacturers soon found it easier and cheaper to supply this new demand with facsimiles rather than actual Levis. Levi's sales representatives, local managers, trademark attorneys, and corporate security personnel are constantly on the lookout for counterfeit cases. The company has successfully located and policed infringements and counterfeiting operations throughout the world.

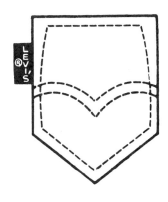

EXHIBIT 6 Levi Strauss trademarks and housemarks

KORACORP ACQUISITION

For almost 130 years, Levi Strauss & Co. achieved its incredible growth without any major acquisitions. In 1979 the executive committee decided that the company's favorable financial position could indeed support a large-scale acquisition, and that this strategy could provide more short-term as well as long-term benefits than any internal strategies could achieve. Therefore, the executive committee began looking for a company that met two major criteria: (1) a large apparel company financially sound enough and large enough for Levi Strauss and Company to build a whole new business, and (2) a company that could provide Levi Strauss with expertise either in the marketplace or in technology.

Koracorp, a $180 million company which ranked twentieth in the U.S. in apparel sales, was the answer to Levi's problem. Founded in 1939, Koracorp was a leader in women's apparel and also sold men's and children's apparel. The following is a summary of Koracorp's operations from the company's 10K report the year it was acquired by Levi Strauss.

Women's Apparel Group (55 percent of sales)

The Women's Group is the senior member of the Koracorp family of companies. Koret of California, Inc. and Koret of California (Canada), Ltd. design, manufacture, and sell five or six lines annually of separates and coordinated misses' and women's large size sportswear, including skirts, pants, blouses, shorts, sweaters, shirts, and jackets. Each line consists of a number of styles made from a diversified fabric selection. These are sold by Koret's sales force to approximately 3,000 accounts throughout the U.S. and approximately 500 accounts in Canada. Koret has eight regional sales offices in principal cities in the U.S. and Canada.

Men's Apparel Group (35 percent of sales)

The Men's Apparel Group conducts operations through various subsidiaries and divisions acquired by Koracorp since 1967. Byer-Rolnick Corporation, a company which has been engaged in the design, manufacture and sale of men's hats since 1927, was acquired by Koracorp in 1967 and later became the Byer-Rolnick Division. This division produces felt, straw and fabric hats, with felt hats providing the bulk of its production and sales volume. Byer-Rolnick's hat products are sold by approximately 35 salesmen servicing approximately 6,000 accounts, chiefly men's stores and department stores throughout the U.S.

KCB Division products include a wide variety of color-related shirts, sweaters, pants and outerwear in denim and other fabrics under the recognized "Koret City Blues" label. Himalaya designs and markets men's sweaters and knit shirts, under the "Himalaya" label. Rainfair Inc. manufactures and sells all-weather dress topcoats, slacks, shorts and weatherproof fabrics and garments. It also sells rubber-coated fabrics to other manufacturers. Oxxford Clothes Inc. produces and sells premium quality ready-to-wear men's suits, sport coats, slacks and overcoats bearing the "Oxxford" trademark. They also have a small collection of women's tailored clothing. Distribution is confined to 100 selected accounts throughout the country.

Children's Apparel Group (10 percent of sales)

The company's children's apparel activities are conducted in Western Europe. Fra-For, headquartered in Troyes, France, is engaged in the manufacture and sale at wholesale of quality infant's and children's apparel, primarily knits, for ages ranging up to 12. It is an integrated operation comprised of knitting, piece-dying, cutting and sewing, and garment finishing facilities. The finished products are sold by its own sales force to approximately 3,000 accounts in France and other European countries.

Final purchase price for the company was $71 million in cash and stock. None of the brand names of Koracorp's products were changed, in hopes that customer loyalty would remain. In the area of women's apparel, the company now had expertise where it previously had none. Management also believed that many of Koracorp's products would complement Levi's lines. Fra-For, for example makes infant's apparel, while Levi's had concentrated on older children. Oxxford clothes, Byer-Rolnick, and the Himalaya divisions put Levi Strauss into higher-priced men's suits, hats, and sportswear for the first time. Koracorp also has valuable merchandising skills that should be beneficial to Levi Strauss.

APPENDIX A Levi Strauss & Co. five year financial summary

(Dollars in Millions Except Per Share Amounts)	1980	1979	1978	1977	1976
Net sales	$2,840.8	$2,103.1	$1,682.0	$1,559.3	$1,219.7
Gross profit	$1,040.2	$ 793.8	$ 623.6	$ 562.6	$ 439.9
Interest expense	25.0	12.4	11.2	20.0	12.2
Income before taxes	401.9	345.6	280.4	270.0	206.8
Provision for taxes on income	178.2	154.1	135.4	140.2	102.1
Net income	$ 223.7	$ 191.5	$ 145.0	$ 129.8	$ 104.7
Earnings retained in the business	$ 170.2	$ 151.1	$ 110.0	$ 108.0	$ 94.8
Cash flow retained in the business[1]	213.3	176.9	125.5	128.7	110.6
Income before taxes as % of sales	14.1%	16.4%	16.7%	17.3%	17.0%
Net income as % of sales	7.9	9.1	8.6	8.3	8.6
Net income as % of beginning stockholders' equity	32.8	33.3	31.3	35.8	39.5
Current assets	$1,122.5	$1,047.1	$ 824.2	$ 694.2	$ 570.1
Current liabilities	452.4	489.7	302.4	263.5	226.6
Working capital	670.1	557.4	521.8	430.7	343.5
Ratio of current assets to current liabilities	2.5/1	2.1/1	2.7/1	2.6/1	2.5/1
Total assets	1,455.4	1,291.1	973.9	824.2	678.0
Long-term debt—less current maturities	$ 138.8	$ 99.1	$ 83.3	$ 80.6	$ 79.2
Stockholders' equity	831.6	681.2	575.3	463.9	362.4
Capital expenditures	$ 119.8	$ 51.3	$ 42.9	$ 31.4	$ 19.5
Depreciation	25.4	18.2	16.1	13.7	11.6
Property, plant & equipment—net	280.8	188.5	141.3	119.3	102.4

415

APPENDIX A (continued)

(Dollars in Millions Except Per Share Amounts)	1980	1979	1978	1977	1976
Number of employees	48,000	44,700	35,100	37,200	32,500
Per share data:					
Net income	$ 5.36	$ 4.58	$ 3.28	$ 2.93	$ 2.35
Cash dividends declared	1.30	1.00	.80	.50	.23
Book value (on shares outstanding at year end)	20.34	16.50	13.14	10.66	8.25
Market price range	44–30	34½–17	19⅜–13⅝	15⅞–12⅛	13⅜–9
Average common and common equivalent shares outstanding	41,763,108	41,784,058	44,229,872	44,257,346	44,476,748

¹Working capital provided by operations minus dividends declared.

APPENDIX B Levi Strauss & Co. income statement

(Dollars in Thousands Except Per Share Amounts)	1980	1979	1978	1977	1976
Net sales	$ 2,840,844	$ 2,103,109	$ 1,682,019	$1,559,341,000	$1,219,741,000
Cost of goods sold	1,800,665	1,309,263	1,058,439	996,767,000	779,850,000
Gross profit	$ 1,040,179	$ 793,846	$ 623,580	$ 562,574,000	$ 439,891,000
Marketing, general and administrative expenses	635,870	464,086	344,536	286,473,000	231,162,000
Operating income	$ 404,309	$ 329,760	$ 279,044	$ 276,101,000	$ 208,729,000
Interest expense	25,018	12,449	11,178	20,048,000	12,156,000
Interest and other income, net	(22,606)	(28,232)	(12,503)	(13,913,000)	(10,252,000)
Income before taxes	$ 401,897	$ 345,549	$ 280,369	$ 269,966,000	$ 206,825,000
Provision for taxes on income	178,208	154,095	135,400	140,173,000	102,137,000
Net income	$ 223,689	$ 191,454	$ 144,969	$ 129,793,000	$ 104,688,000
Net income per share	$ 5.36	$ 4.58	$ 3.28	$ 5.87	$ 4.71
Average common and common equivalent shares outstanding	$41,763,108	$41,784,058	$44,229,872	22,128,673	22,238,374

416

APPENDIX C Levi Strauss & Co. balance sheet

(Dollars in Thousands)	1980	1979	1978	1977	1976
Assets					
Current assets:					
Cash	$ 36,192	$ 27,454	$ 34,866	$ 31,063,000	$ 28,881,000
Temporary investments of cash	51,693	195,297	219,955	129,878,000	108,053,000
Trade receivables (less allowance for doubt-ful accounts: 1980 - $9,368; 1979 - $8,340)	446,461	340,131	241,125	203,239,000	172,980,000
Inventories:					
Raw materials and work-in-process	252,538	216,820	135,146	294,103,000	236,010,000
Finished goods	275,017	225,001	163,348	35,975,000	24,201,000
Other current assets	60,606	42,411	29,787	35,975,000	24,201,000
Total current assets	$1,122,507	$1,047,114	$824,227	$694,258,000	$570,125,000
Property, plant and equipment (less accumu-lated depreciation: 1980 - $113,301; 1979 - $101,989)	280,783	188,495	141,319	119,255,000	102,383,000
Other Assets	52,070	55,510	8,328	10,640,000	5,526,000
	$1,455,360	$1,291,119	$973,874	$824,153,000	$678,034,000
Liabilities and stockholders equity					
Current liabilities:					
Current maturities of long-term debt	14,963	$ 15,832	$ 9,741	$ 6,310,000	$ 5,745,000
Short-term borrowings	48,642	53,535	11,623	35,344,000	43,256,000
Accounts payable	135,006	154,929	89,102	103,081,000	78,193,000
Accrued liabilities	93,875	83,802	65,962	51,089,000	39,303,000
Compensation and payroll taxes	55,313	57,636	57,558	51,089,000	57,325,000
Pension and profit sharing	20,982	27,545	—	—	—
Taxes based on income	68,309	85,069	59,662	61,173,000	57,325,000
Dividend payable	15,335	11,357	8,757	6,529,000	2,745,000
Total current liabilities	$ 452,425	$ 489,705	$302,405	$263,526,000	$226,567,000
Long-term debt-less current maturities	$ 138,754	$ 99,126	$ 83,292	$ 80,647,000	$ 79,231,000
Deferred liabilities	$ 32,552	$ 21,098	$ 12,859	$ 16,125,000	$ 9,851,000

APPENDIX C (continued)

(Dollars in Thousands)

	1980	1979	1978	1977	1976
Stockholders' equity:					
Common stock - $1.00 per value authorized 100,000,000 shares; shares issued - 1980 - 43,998,808, 1979 - 21,999,404	$ 43,999	$ 21,999	$ 21,999	$ 21,999,000	$ 21,957,000
Additional paid-in capital	59,837	82,424	71,895	73,178,000	73,480,000
Retained earnings	806,257	636,010	484,947	374,950,000	266,948,000
Less treasury stock, at cost,: 1980 - 3,105,482 shares; 1979 - 1,354,949 shares	$ 78,464	$ 59,243	$ 3,523	$ 6,272,000	—
Total stockholders' equity	$ 831,629	$ 681,190	$575,318	$463,855,000	$362,385,000
	$1,455,360	$1,291,119	$973,874	$824,153,000	$678,034,000

APPENDIX D Levi Strauss & Co. financial data by geographic areas

	1980	1979	1978	1977	1976
Total sales:					
United States	$1,890,289	$1,339,603	$1,087,837	$1,073,122	$ 867,297
Europe	526,410	412,860	314,968	237,414	146,066
Other international	446,917	374,009	307,851	280,849	220,106
Eliminations	(22,772)	(23,363)	(28,637)	(32,044)	(13,728)
	$2,840,844	$2,103,109	$1,682,019	$1,559,341	$1,219,741
Profit contribution before corporate expenses and interest expense:					
United States	$ 314,294	$ 245,993	$ 200,518	$ 235,589	$ 190,014
Europe	92,197	95,058	77,200	54,966	24,791
Other international	61,991	49,518	36,074	14,068	13,951
Assets:					
United States	$ 882,028	$ 675,142	$ 455,687	$ 413,522	$ 343,454
Europe	240,331	205,582	124,435	107,082	67,401
Other international	253,012	194,382	151,818	138,819	133,510
Corporate	79,989	216,013	241,934	164,730	133,669
	$1,455,360	$1,291,119	$ 973,874	$ 824,153	$ 678,034

APPENDIX E Financial data on major domestic competitors

	Blue Bell		Vanity Fair	
(in $ million)	1980	1979	1980	1979
Sales	$1398	$1029	$603	$544
Net income	68	67	42	39
Gross profit margin %	29.7%	31.0%	N/A	30.4%
Net profit margin %	4.9%	6.5%	7.0%	7.1%
Total assets	$ 869	$ 679	$345	$325
Current ratio	1.8x	2.1x	2.9x	3.6x
Turnover (days)				
Accounts receivable	62	61	60	59
Inventory	156	152	97	103
% Return on avg. assets	8.8%	11.2%	12.2%	12.1%
% Return on beg. equity	22.7%	26.7%	19.0%	18.5%

SOURCE: *1981 Executive Data Book,* Levi Strauss & Co.

APPENDIX F Major international competitors

Northern Europe	Continental Europe	Canada	Asia/ Pacific	Latin America
Wrangler	Wrangler	Lee	Big John	U.S. Top
Lee	Lois	Wrangler	Bobson	R. Lewis
Lee Cooper	Lee		Edwin	Topeka
Marks & Spencer	Lee Cooper		AMCO	Lee
Brutus			Wrangler	Gledson

SOURCE: *1981 Executive Data Book,* Levi Strauss & Co.

Texas Instruments

Few companies in history can match the record of technological break-throughs achieved by Texas Instruments. Called by some the "model U.S. corporation," the Dallas-based company has fifty manufacturing plants in nineteen countries (see Exhibit 1) and employs more than 85,000 workers. An aggressive and fast-growing company which emphasizes technological innovation, Texas Instruments had sales of over $3 billion in 1979, with approximately one-third originating outside the United States. (See Income Statements for 1970-79 and Balance Sheets for 1973-79).

Recently, however, the company has experienced some problems. In early 1980, Texas Instruments introduced a new product, the 99/4 personal computer. In spite of a sales forecast of 50,000 units and $35 million revenue, the company sold only half that. TI has also started losing market share in both digital watches and hand-held calculators. In fact, the company is seriously considering dropping its entire line of digital watches, in spite of the fact that it was, until recently, one of the leaders in the field.

COMPANY HISTORY

Beginning

In 1930 two young scientists, Clarence ("Doc") Karcher and Eugene McDermott, formed Geophysical Service (later to be Geophysical Service, Inc.). A few years before, Karcher had invented the reflection seismograph, an instrument that could be used in oil exploration to calculate the depth of the subsurface reflecting formation. Although at this time oil was virtually worthless, the two men were determined to take their meager resources and Karcher's invention and organize a company to search for oil.

Early in the first year of operations, the fledgling company added two

---

This case was prepared by Stephen W. McDaniel, Assistant Professor of Marketing, Texas A&M University, as a basis for class discussion rather than to illustrate either effective or ineffective marketing management.

TI WORLDWIDE PLANT LOCATIONS

RICHMOND HILL   PLYMOUTH   ALMELO
ATTLEBORO   BEDFORD
CENTRAL LAKE   FREISING
VERSAILLES   NICE
JOHNSON CITY
COLORADO SPRINGS   RIETI
SHERMAN   AVERSA
RIDGECREST
LUBBOCK   TOKYO
ABILENE   OYAMA
MIDLAND-ODESSA   HIJI
LEWISVILLE
DALLAS   TAIPEI
TEMPLE   BAGUIO
AUSTIN   KUALA LUMPUR
COLLEGE STATION   SINGAPORE
HOUSTON   ELIZABETH
MEXICO CITY
BUENOS AIRES   OPORTO
SAN SALVADOR   CAMPINAS   MADRID

EXHIBIT 1   TI worldwide plant locations
SOURCE: TI Publication.

men whose names would later become synonymous with the company: Cecil H. Green, who served as supervisor on seismograph field operations, and J. Erik Jonsson, who was hired as superintendent of GSI's laboratory, which developed and assembled the seismology equipment. Green would later become president and Jonsson, chairman of the board of Texas Instruments.

Early Years

During the 1930s, GSI scored a string of exploration successes and could list all the major oil companies as clients. Although based in Texas, the company soon expanded its operations and, by the end of the decade, had business operations in several other states and nine foreign countries. It was during this period that the company set forth two basic philosophies: its market was the world, and the key to business success was innovation.

A major change occurred in the company in 1939, when GSI's oil business was separated from the exploration activities. Two years later, the oil division was sold to a major oil producer. The exploration division, still known as GSI, was bought by the key executives, Eugene McDermott, Cecil Green, Erik Jonsson, and Dr. H.B. Peacock. This emphasis on exploration with sophisticated electronic equipment led to several defense contracts during World War II, especially in naval submarine surveillance. However, the most significant occurrence during this time was the contact with and eventual hiring of a naval officer, Patrick Eugene Haggerty. He became the principal innovator and architect of a new growth phase, as the post-war company began emphasizing electronic equipment manufacturing. By 1949, it had grown to 792 employees and $5.7 million sales.

Major Technological Breakthroughs

The company's name was changed in 1951 to Texas Instruments, with Erik Jonsson serving as the first president. A year later the entire electronics industry was revolutionized by the introduction of the transistor. Engineers at TI quickly followed up with further development of the new product, and the company soon became the leader in transistor production. The first transistor radio, the Regency radio, was designed by TI engineers. To a large extent, the transistor radio craze of the mid-fifties was created by the success of TI's strategic plan to open up a mass market for its new products through development of high-frequency germanium transistors, of techniques to mass produce them, of circuits to use them, and of a buyer to manufacture and market the end product.

TI quickly adapted the transistor to other products, including oil exploration equipment, which could now be lighter, smaller, and more efficient, and computers. Until the invention of the transistor, computers had been cumbersome, power-consuming, and temperamental; it was the basis for building a massive market for computer components. Shortly afterwards, the commercial introduction of silicon transistors by TI further strengthened its position as a leader in electronic equipment production for both military and industrial applications.

Perhaps the most important invention in the history of electronic equipment occurred in 1958, when a TI researcher, Jack St. Clair Kilby, invented the integrated circuit. This component eliminated the need for many mechanical connections in an electronics system. It earned for him the highest honor for technical achievement, the National Medal of Science. The resulting semiconductor devices and components pushed the worldwide electronics industry, and TI in particular, into dramatic expansion. By 1960, Texas Instruments had sales of $233 million and almost 17,000 employees.

The '60s and '70s

The 1960s and '70s found Texas Instruments regularly introducing innovative products and growing at a rapid pace. Among the new products of the early 1960s were many military electronic components. Although oil exploration was only 20 percent of the total company business at the beginning of the 1960s, this part of the firm grew as a result of the digital seismic technology TI announced in 1963. With TI leading the way, the digital concept of gathering and processing data accounted for about three-fourths of the free world's seismic exploration in search of petroleum reserves by 1972.

By the start of the 1970s, TI's activities included the development, manufacture, and marketing of chemical materials, metallurgical materials, semiconductor materials and products, electrical controls, electronic equipment, and systems for consumer, industrial, and military use. In services, there were also nine digital seismic data processing centers, worldwide geophysical operations, and an international network of TI Supply Company (TISCO) distribution outlets.

In 1971, another technological breakthrough occurred at TI, with the invention of the calculator-on-a-chip, or microcomputer. This single chip of silicon, less than one-fifth of an inch square, contained more than 20,000 transistors or other electronic components that comprised all the necessary elements of a computer; the number of applications was as varied as the number of programs which could be written for each chip. This not only made possible the handheld calculator, but also was widely used in such products as microwave ovens, dishwashers, telephones, vending machines, electronic games, and many industrial products. In fact, by the late 1970s, over half the world's demand for single-chip microcomputers was met by TI's TMS 1000 microcomputer.

Texas Instruments continued to grow throughout the 70s, introducing such products as the first integrated injection logic bipolar microprocessor, the first portable, battery-powered, printing calculator, advanced scientific calculators, electronic digital watches, magnetic bubble memories, the "Speak & Spell" learning aid, and the talking Language Tutor. As indicated by Exhibit 2, the decade of the '70s was even more productive for TI than the previous three successful decades.

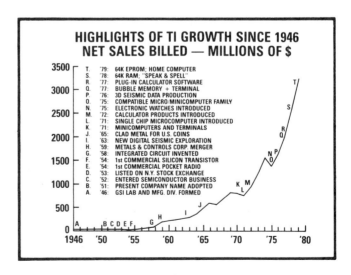

EXHIBIT 2

SOURCE: TI Publication.

CORPORATE PHILOSOPHY AND OBJECTIVES

Since World War II, "the pursuit of innovation to realize long-term company goals" has been Texas Instruments' basic strategy. The following statement, contained in the preamble of the TI Corporate Objective, stresses the fundamental role of innovation in developing TI's business and internal growth:

> Texas Instruments exists to create, make and market useful products and services to satisfy the needs of our customers throughout the world. . . . We believe our effectiveness in serving our customers and contributing to the economic wealth of society will be determined by our *innovative* skills.

The company believes there are four keys to successful business strategy:

1. *Price and cost reductions resulting in market share:* This is accomplished by the "learning" or "experience" curve theory, which states that real unit cost of a product will decline as production volume increases.

2. *Keeping capacity ahead of demand:* This requires a farsighted approach, anticipating demand and constantly replacing old equipment with newer, more productive equipment.

3. *Market growth:* It is much more profitable and easier to gain market share in high-growth markets.

4. *Proper choice of priorities and appropriate allocation of resources:* It is better to divert resources from low-market-growth businesses to foster high-market-growth businesses.

To carry out its business strategies, TI has a well-defined planning system known as "OST" (objectives, strategies, tactics):

Objectives: Long-range goals of the company are broken down into corporate objectives, which deal with policy and overall goals, and business objectives, which describe long-range opportunities for each division of TI.

Strategies: Intermediate goals are set and courses of action are defined to attain these goals. This strategy, for example, might be a market strategy aimed at a specific market segment. Strategies deal with opportunities facing the company, and pinpoint the technology, manufacturing, and marketing innovation needed to take advantage of business opportunities.

Tactics: These are action programs funded annually for carrying out the strategies. Tactics list each person involved in the program and specify completion dates for each program.

According to Patrick E. Haggerty, former president of TI, the OST system "is a system to state in writing succinctly, yet completely, the strategies we intend to follow for further growth and development of TI and the tactics we intend to pursue to implement the strategies."

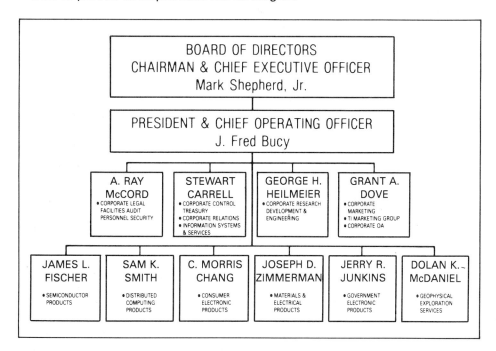

EXHIBIT 3 Organization Chart

SOURCE: TI Publication.

ORGANIZATION

The organization chart for Texas Instruments is shown in Exhibit 3. The two top executives are both thirty-year company veterans who rose to the top through the production and technology side of the business—TI's key avenue of upward mobility. Mark Shepherd, Jr., the chairman of the board and chief executive officer, started with the company in 1948 when he was twenty-five. An engineering honor student, Shepherd was primarily responsible for TI's successful commercial development of the transistor. The president and chief operating officer is J. Fred Bucy, also an engineer. In the early 1950s, he pioneered the development of TI's Digital Field Systems (DFS) to record seismic data for the first time in digital format. He also led TI's development of the all-transistorized Texas Instruments Automatic Computer (TIAC).

Reporting to Bucy are ten senior managers, including Grant Dove, who is in charge of all corporate marketing functions, but not the marketing functions for individual products. These marketing responsibilities are of the managers' in each Product-Consumer Center (PCC).

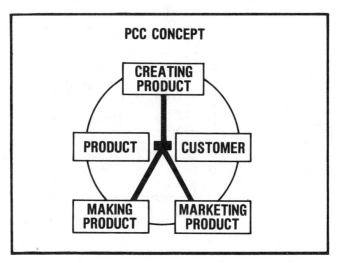

EXHIBIT 4   The product–customer concept (PCC)
SOURCE: TI Publication.

TI's organizational approach is decentralized and pushes responsibility for strategic planning as far down in the organization as possible. There are thirty-two divisions ranging in size from $50 million to $150 million in sales. The basic structural unit is the Product-Customer Center (PCC), a complete business organization with its own management team, which serves a family of products or services. This concept is depicted in Exhibit 4. There are more than eighty PCCs in TI, many having their own engineering, manufacturing, and marketing units. TI pulls together a tactics program from whatever PCCs are required. Although there is some duplication of effort and failure to make use of centralized expertise in such areas as marketing, TI feels that this PCC concept provides the flexibility required in a highly technical and fast-changing business. Each PCC can be expanded or contracted quickly as markets change, without changing the entire organization.

PRESENT OPERATIONS

Product

As you would expect, TI's approach to new product development is very much oriented to technology; the company encourages its engineers to come up with new product ideas. When an idea is judged worthy, the engineer it given the funds necessary to develop it further. This approach has contributed to much of TI's past success. There have been some problems, however; the company has poured large amounts of money into products for which, as it found out later, no market existed. For example, TI recently poured millions of dollars into a giant advanced scientific computer, but canceled the project after producing only seven units when no real market was found for the product. Also, millions were spent developing a word processor that never made it to market; TI discovered, too late, that the market did not really want that type of word processor.

TI has a formal review process for existing products. Meetings are generally held at least quarterly to review the financial and technical performance of products on the market. Included in these meetings are representatives of the marketing department, production department, and top management. After reviewing the effectiveness of the product, they decide to either continue present efforts, develop a new strategy, or discontinue production.

Consumer products. Only in the past few years has TI begun emphasizing consumer products. At a strategy meeting in December, 1971, top management decided, "We should either get into the consumer market or forget about it." TI began putting most of its development money for the next few years into consumer products, rather than computer memories and microprocessors, as its competitors did. Emphasizing consumer products clearly gave TI a new dimension that it continues to develop. In fact, a major market study in 1978 concluded that TI "is the most feared competition in the consumer electronics business." Here are TI's major products, along with the percentage of sales figures for each group.

Semiconductors (46 percent of sales) TI is the world's leading supplier of semiconductor components and materials, including:

- ☐ The industry's broadest line of *solidstate memories,* including the first 64K-bit dynamic RAM, first 16K-bit static FAM, first 32K-bit EPROM, and the largest (16-megabit) bubble memory system ever built

- ☐ The biggest seller in *microcomputers* (the TMS 1000 family)

- ☐ The leading *16-bit microprocessor* family (the 9900)

- ☐ The facility for *VLSI processing,* the Advanced Front-end Prototyping Center (incorporating dry-plasma processing, ion implantation, electron-beam direct slice writing, and multiple air-track handling system)

Consumer Electronics Products (25 percent of sales) This relatively new area includes:

- ☐ *calculators* (TI is the world's leading producer, and the TI 59 programmable calculator is considered the most advanced of all the handheld calculators)

- ☐ *electronic learning aids,* like Little Professor, DataMan, First Watch, Spelling B, and Speak & Spell, designed to help children learn math, spelling and how to tell time

- ☐ *watches.* The TI line numbers more than 80 styles and models. It includes super-thin models, alarm watches for men and women, and sports watches. The Starburst™ watch is completely electronic, using liquid crystals to produce electronic hands

- ☐ *Home computers.* Introduced in late 1979, the TI-99/4 was designed to be the first true home computer. The system features built-in Basic, up to 72K total memory, 26K ROM, 16-color graphics, music and sound effects, built-in equation calculator and 13" color monitor

Government Electronics Products (17 percent of sales) TI's major lines in this area are:

☐ *Air Traffic Control* and other radars. TI is the leading producer of ATC radars. The ASR-8 is considered the most advanced system in the world. The new Discrete Address Beacon System (DABS) is expected to provide even more advanced control capabilities for the 1980s and beyond. TI is also the leading supplier of Forward-Looking Radars for military aircraft.

☐ *Electro-optical systems.* TI is the No. 1 developer/producer of infrared and infrared/laser systems. Inventor of the Forward-Looking Infrared System (FLIR), TI is also the No. 1 producer of Infrared Line Scanners (IRLS), a product in high demand for detection of phenomena ranging from geothermal energy sources to water pollution and crop diseases.

☐ *Defense and guidance systems.* TI has produced more than 60,000 weapons for the U.S. Navy and Air Force.

Engineered Materials Systems (5 percent of sales) TI is the world leader in metallurgical materials technology and production.

☐ TI's electric choke controls are used by about two-thirds of all cars manufactured in the United States.

☐ Stainless-clad aluminum auto trim is being used by General Motors in more than 160 applications on 20 GM models.

☐ Early Fuel Evaporation System made its debut on the 1980 Chevrolet Chevette and is being evaluated for other cars.

Geophysical Services (4 percent of sales) TI is the world's leading independent geophysical contractor.

☐ TI's exclusive 3D surveys are increasing in popularity as the cost of drilling increases. (3D provides a clearer resolution of subsurface features than conventional methods of data gathering and processing.)

☐ TI's 11 seismic data processing centers around the world and fleet of geophysical exploration ships are linked by satellite.

Distributed Computing (3 percent of sales) This is the technology of putting computerization at the point of need. It is opening new markets not accessible to large, centralized computers and a major growth thrust at TI. This area includes:

☐ Development of a broad family of TI modular systems ranging from small stand-alones to a large mini-computer system with 100 megabytes of mass storage;

☐ Selection by the 1980 Olympic Winter Games of the TI-SCORE Computer Results System;

☐ Incorporation of TI distributed computing equipment in some of the largest information and control systems, including the General Electric Information Services Company's MARKLINK* System and Ford Motor Company's automatic transmission testing operation.

Solar Energy Development TI is developing a new approach to solar energy storage and conversion under a cooperative agreement with the Department of Energy.

EXHIBIT 5   TI's Speak & Spell
SOURCE: Photograph provided courtesy of Texas Instruments, Inc.

Promotion

Promotion for individual products is handled by the appropriate Product-Consumer Center on a project by project basis. The major promotion emphasis in the past has been on personal selling; publicity appears in various journals and magazines when new products are introduced. Little sales promotion is done, except in the form of quantity discounts to retailers. Because the promotion tasks are handled on a project by project basis by the PCCs, TI presently uses twenty-six different advertising agencies around the world. Exhibits 7 and 8 show how this advertising is broken down by product lines as well as media.

Distribution

Most industrial products sold by TI are distributed through the Texas Instruments Supply Company. This division handles the distribution of industrial supplies, electrical parts, safety items, power transmission equipment, geophysical supplies and electronic supplies. The supply organization distributes not just TI electronic components, but it also markets more than 50,000 items from some 400 other manufacturers. TI Supply maintains inventories in Dallas, Chicago, Houston, Tulsa, New York, Los Angeles, Kansas City, Boston, Montreal, London, Copenhagen, Paris, and Amsterdam. One of the unique features of TI Supply is its new computer-controlled inventory system; American offices are linked directly to the principal warehouse in Dallas. This facilitates the distribution process by enabling the various offices to place their orders quickly through the central warehouse in Dallas. TI uses a different channel of distribution for semiconductor products. Because these products are not sold to final users, they are distributed through the channels of distribution of the OEMs (Original Equipment Manufacturers), who use the component in their own products.

Recently, TI has had to alter its traditional channels of distribution as it has emphasized consumer markets. To get closer to the market and reduce its intermediary costs, it is shortening its distribution channels and dealing directly with more customers. Within the last year, TI has begun selling calculators by direct mail (a technique perfected by Hewlett-Packard) and through retail outlets. The company envisions a worldwide network of "Western Auto-type" stores, with many different electronic products. By producing many of these products itself, TI forsees the possibility that this will be its primary distribution method in the future.

Pricing

Much of TI's success can be attributed to its pricing strategies. The company looks at its markets over the very long term and is willing to tolerate small margins to acquire large market shares. TI is a leading proponent of "learning curve pricing," which correlates a steady increase in sales and manufacturing with a decrease in product rejection rates and costs. According to this concept, every doubling of production enables the company to chop prices 25 to 30 percent, building a larger market share and allowing it to lower prices even further. TI, therefore, prices very close to initial cost to build up volume and experience, which eventually enables it to drive costs well below prices.

This pricing strategy has worked brilliantly. In 1977, TI was able to capture a major share of the market by launching a digital watch that sold for just $9.95. The SR-51, a popular scientific calculator, was introduced in 1975 at a list price of $225; six years later, a comparable model is priced below $40. As a result, while U.S. consumer prices were dramatically increasing during the 1970s, TI's prices were actually declining. The biggest problem with this pricing strategy, however, is that early buyers of a new product tend to feel cheated when, a short time later, the same product is selling for only a fraction of what they paid for it.

THE 99/4 HOME COMPUTER

The general feeling in electronics circles is that the personal computer industry will be one of the true growth industries of the 1980s. Experts believe that, by the mid-1980s, the personal computer business could top $3.5 billion—more than the combined value of all the digital watches, stereos, and video recorders sold in the U.S. in 1979.

TI, however, got a late start into the personal computer market. Already two to three years behind the competition, and after experiencing additional delays in setting up the distribution of the product, TI introduced the 99/4 with a list price of $1,150 in late 1979. The TI 99/4 has a full-color TV screen, ten programs that simply snap into the keyboard controls, and a speech-synthesis chip that enables it to "talk." The machine is designed to educate children, manage household finances, and play games. In two years, the price had dropped to $650.

The personal computer market can be broken down into (1) home computers for the consumer market ($1,500 and less), and (2) personal computers for the hobbyist/small business/professional market ($1,500-$10,000). As of 1981, the latter is dominated by Tandy Corp. and Apple Computer, Inc.; industry experts predict that IBM and Xerox are probably on the way. TI has focused on the consumer market and has practically excluded itself from the other segment with its approach to software for the 99/4 programs. TI has gone to extraordinary lengths to protect software sales, locking the programs to run the computer into semiconductor memory and building the computer so that outside software suppliers need a $50,000 TI minicomputer to write programs for it. Ironically, these suppliers have helped others in the industry grow by providing software and peripheral equipment to serve specialized small business and professional markets, such as doctors and dentists.

EXHIBIT 6   TI's 99/4 home computer
SOURCE: Photographs produced courtesy of Texas Instruments, Inc.

A recent study by an independent market research firm estimates that the consumer market is only one-eighth the size of the hobbyist/small business/professional segment, and will grow less than half as fast for the next few years. TI, however, disregards such negative information. It claims that it will again educate the consumer to the benefits of TI's technology and create a market that does not yet exist.

Already, TI has spent $20 million trying to crack the home computer market; it will cost a great deal more to gain a share of the market large enough to satisfy its market share requirements. The field should be full of competitors (Atari and Mattel presently), price pressures will be intense, marketing costs high, and effective marketing strategies crucial. Also, the home computer is likely to require better service than a calculator or watch; these are small enough to send back and, often, cheap enough to throw away.

First year sales of the 99/4 were somewhat disappointing. Although its sales revenue totaled almost $20 million, TI had expected more than twice that. One of the top personal computer distributors in the U.S. even quit carrying the product. TI is trying to help its dealers by shifting the 99/4s from the many stores where they are gathering dust to a few stores that might be able to move them.

OTHER CONSUMER MARKET PROBLEMS

Sales of TI's digital watches have been declining over the past four years. This is largely because the company was slow to recognize consumer preferences for watches with fashionable styling and liquid crystal display (LCD). TI gained the leadership in the U.S. market with its revolutionary push-to-see LED model, but only recently started selling the newer LCD model. Particularly among the higher-priced watches, TI has been hurt by the more fashionable watches of competitors such as Seiko and Citizen Watch.

TI has also been slow to recognize consumer preferences for calculators that offer added attractions like alarm clocks, radios, and stylish appearances. For example, at the 1979 consumer electronics show in Chicago, Casio, Sharp, and Canon each showed fifteen new models with various functions. TI showed two fairly traditional models.

Having spread its resources very thin in attempting to compete in both the consumer and industrial markets, TI has recently had difficulty matching supply with demand, as well as with accurately forecasting demand. In 1980, for example, TI received almost three times as many orders for the Speak & Spell as it predicted. Similar problems occurred with calculators because the demand for metal-oxide semiconductors (which are used in calculators) far exceeded the supply. One dealer who received a delayed shipment complained, "This year has been a disaster. We lost the whole back-to-school business for some TI calculators because the product just isn't there." For large retailers, who are used to promoting consumer electronics heavily and must schedule campaigns months in advance, the shortages have been especially costly. At least two chains dropped popular TI models from their Christmas catalogs. Some retailers have recently complained about questionable quality of some TI consumer products, unreliable shipments, and the lack of service given to dealers.

Texas Instruments, with a truly enviable history, plans to continue its growth through the 1980s. Management has set goals of $15 billion in sales and a 12 percent return on assets for the late 1980s. But unless some problem areas are resolved, TI might fall short of its long-term goals for the first time in its history.

NOTE

The following sources are gratefully acknowledged for providing information contained in this case:

"50 Years of Innovation - The History of Texas Instruments." TI publication.

Helms, E.W., Manager Corporate Engineering Center for TI. "Texas Instruments' Objectives, Strategies, and Tactics System." Remarks to the Institute Panamericano de Alta, Mexico; May, 1980.

"Personal Computers: TI's Jazzed Up Pitch." *Business Week,* December 8, 1980, pp. 28–29.

Rice, L.M., Jr., Group Vice-President for TI. "Texas Instruments Management Philosophies and Growth Experience." Remarks to the Institute Panamericano de Alta, Mexico; May 1980.

"Texas Instruments: Pushing Hard into the Consumer Markets." *Business Week,* August 24, 1974, pp. 38–42.

"Texas Instruments Shows U.S. Business How to Survive in the 1980's." *Business Week,* September 18, 1978, pp. 66–92.

Uttal, Bro. "Texas Instruments Wrestles the Consumer Market." *Fortune,* December 3, 1979, pp. 50–57.

Uttal, Bro. "TI's Home Computer Can't Get in the Door." *Fortune,* June 16, 1980, pp. 139–40.

Other TI promotional publications

EXHIBIT 7   Texas Instruments advertising expenditures by product line 1976–1980

TI	1980	1979	1978	1977	1976
Personal computer system	311,600[M.S]	—	—	—	—
Electronic calculators	17,100[N.S]	1,808,400[M.N]	1,432,700[M.N.S.O]	2,138,100[M.N.S]	2,420,500[M.N.S]
Electronic printing calculators	99,900[M]	35,600[M]	136,700[M]	56,100[M]	—
Electronic watches	58,700[S]	2,390,700[N.S]	849,400[N.S]	1,685,500[N.S]	871,800[S]
Systems and components	114,300[M]	616,800[M]	413,400[M]	112,600[M]	—
Software calculators	200,900[M]	45,600[M]	120,600[M]	21,000[M]	—
Terminals and printers	6,900[S]	41,900[M]	—	—	—
Toys and games	2,470,000[M.N.S]	—	67,000	—	546,600[N]
Other	185,400	50,600	60,500	17,800	33,600
Total	3,729,000	4,989,600	3,080,300	4,031,100	3,873,300

M - Magazines
N - Network TV
S - Spot TV
O - Outdoor

SOURCE: "AD $ Summary," Leading National Advertisers, Inc., 1976–1980.

EXHIBIT 8   Texas Instruments advertising expenditures by media 1976–1980

	1980	1979	1978	1977	1976
Magazines	1,299,100	871,000	820,800	350,400	304,400
Newspaper	—	—	—	—	—
Network TV	1,931,300	3,771,300	2,244,500	3,675,800	1,941,000
Spot TV	498,600	347,300	6,700	4,900	1,627,900
Network radio	—	—	—	—	—
Outdoor	—	—	8,300	—	300
Total	3,729,000	4,989,600	3,080,300	4,031,100	3,873,600

SOURCE: "AD $ Summary," Leading National Advertisers, Inc., 1976–1980.

EXHIBIT 9 Texas Instruments, Inc. income statement (in millions of dollars)

	1979	1978	1977	1976	1975	1974	1973	1972	1971	1970
Net sales	$3,224.1	$2,549.9	$2,046.5	$1,658.6	$1,367.6	$1,572.5	$1,287.3	$943.7	$764.3	$827.6
Operating costs and expenses .	2,904.8	2,296.4	1,835.7	1,496.0	1,252.8	1,403.1	1,141.8	860.6	705.1	773.1
Profit from operations	319.3	253.5	210.8	162.6	114.8	169.4	145.5	83.1	59.2	54.5
Other income (net)	8.9	12.3	9.3	23.8	11.9	4.1	6.7	7.2	6.8	4.5
Interests on loans	(19.5)	(8.4)	(9.2)	(8.3)	(10.8)	(10.7)	(6.7)	(5.7)	(6.5)	(7.0)
Income before provision for income taxes	308.7	257.4	210.9	178.1	115.9	162.8	145.5	84.6	59.5	52.0
Provision for income taxes	135.8	117.1	94.3	80.7	53.8	73.2	62.3	36.6	25.8	22.1
Net income	172.9	140.3	116.6	97.4	62.1	89.6	83.2	48.0	33.7	29.9
Employees at year-end	85,779	78,571	68,521	66,162	56,682	65,524	74,422	55,934	47,259	44,752

SOURCE: Annual Reports.

EXHIBIT 10 Texas Instruments, Inc. balance sheet (in thousands of dollars)

ASSETS	1979	1978	1977	1976	1975	1974
Current assets						
Cash and short-term investments .	$116,636	$115,374	$257,131	$293,755	$266,578	$154,782
Accounts receivable	547,978	443,672	334,152	282,251	245,785	293,911
Inventories (net of progress billings)	340,251	300,499	214,278	197,647	142,880	198,183
Prepaid taxes and expenses	78,274	55,952	9,337	9,520	7,322	9,070
Total current assets	1,083,139	915,497	814,898	783,173	662,565	655,946
Property, plant and equipment at cost	1,275,607	927,008	713,787	606,380	538,946	515,311
Less accumulated depreciation . . .	463,137	354,356	319,694	303,507	285,237	234,862
Property, plant and equipment (net)	812,470	572,652	394,093	302,873	253,709	280,449
Other assets and deferred charges . .	12,566	5,932	46,053	41,657	25,203	28,857
Total assets	$1,908,175	$1,494,081	$1,255,044	$1,127,703	$941,477	$965,252

SOURCE: Annual Reports.

Shaklee Corporation

Shaklee Corporation is the leading U.S. seller of vitamins and nutritional products, having achieved this position primarily because of its two-million member direct sales organization. Members of this "Shaklee Family" do not only sell Shaklee products: they live and breathe the whole Shaklee philosophy of good nutrition and health. The importance of the field sales force is recognized by Shaklee president, Gary Shansby, who boasts, "Many people from industry don't understand direct selling. Someone else could copy our products and our sales plan, but they couldn't copy our salespeople."

The company's only advertising is product ads in its monthly publication, *Shaklee Survey.* These ads are directed at its salespeople, who are continually reminded that they must use the products before they can sell them, since they cannot sell any products in which they do not believe. This emphasis on the sales force, making sure morale is high and the salespeople motivated, claims Shansby, has gotten Shaklee Corporation where it is today and will take it where it plans to be tomorrow: "What IBM is to computers, what General Motors is to cars, what Procter and Gamble is to soap, Shaklee will be to nutrition."

HISTORY OF SHAKLEE

As a boy, Forrest Shaklee was fascinated by carnivals and touring shows. Intrigued by the audience appeal and the message of the touring sideshow artists, Shaklee took to heart the showmanship techniques he saw demonstrated, as well as the occasional wisdom he heard expounded. He soon became an assistant for some of these traveling showmen. There was "Professor" Santinelli, a well-known hypnotist, who frequently lectured Shaklee on the power of positive thinking: "What you think, you look; what you think, you do, what you think, you are." There was also the physical fitness and nu-

This case was prepared by Stephen W. McDaniel, Assistant Professor of Marketing, Texas A&M University, as a basis for class discussion rather than to illustrate either effective or ineffective marketing management.

tritionist "expert", Bernarr MacFadden, who toured the country entertaining audiences with awesome weightlifting feats and promoting his health magazine. Shaklee assisted in the feats of strength show by hoisting a hollow ball purportedly weighing 500 pounds.

Shaklee's philosophy of life, good mental and physical health, gradually crystallized, and he became convinced of the effectiveness of salesmanship and showmanship. Besides carnivals, Shaklee tried several other careers. He was a film distributor, an inventor, a chiropractor (who once had a Davenport, Iowa, parade in his honor featuring a fifty-foot replica of a human spine), and a lecturer (whose favorite topic was "Thoughtmanship"—"The trouble with most people is that they emulate the humble sheep . . . blah, blah").

During this time, Shaklee continued to develop his interest in nutrition; it grew as he noticed improvement in his own health by taking food supplements. Shaklee even claims to have cured himself of tuberculosis and terminal cancer by proper nutrition. As a chiropractor, he not only recommended food supplements to his patients, but also developed his own supplements. He soon discovered that he was spending more of his time developing his food supplements and emphasizing this part of his chiropractic business. In 1956, the sixty-two-year-old Shaklee, with his two sons, Forrest, Jr. and Raleigh, decided to form the Shaklee Corporation.

From the beginning, Shaklee planned to develop products that were designed to work "in cooperation with nature." This theme is carried through in Shaklee products today: household cleaning products that are biodegradable and nonpolluting, cosmetics and toiletries that are intended to promote healthy, attractive skin and hair, rather than follow fashion fads, and the vitamins and food supplements that use natural ingredients that are low in potency, as they are found in nature.

Another underlying principle of the Shaklee Corp. is "Dr." Shaklee's belief that a business should be based on the Golden Rule; the company still stresses integrity and fairness in the code of ethics which salespeople are expected to follow (see Exhibit 1). Company literature is sprinkled with sayings like, "An unselfish desire to help others is more effective than just a sales pitch."

THE COMPANY

Shaklee Corporation has a long history of growth. In 1981 the company achieved sales of over $454 million, a 10 percent increase over 1980. Although domestic sales were up only 4 percent, international sales, primarily from Japan, were up 51 percent to $83.3 million. Income Statements and Balance Sheets are shown in Exhibits 2 and 3.

The president and chief operating officer of Shaklee is forty-four-year-old J. Gary Shansby. Before coming to Shaklee in 1976, Shansby was a senior officer and marketing consultant with Booz, Allen, and Hamilton, a consulting firm, and before that, he had been with Colgate-Palmolive, Clorox,

---

CODE OF ETHICS

As a Shaklee Distributor,

(1) I will operate by, and fully support, Shaklee's philosophy of doing business by the Golden Rule.

(2) I pledge not to misrepresent Shaklee products or the Shaklee Corporation. I will present products, information about the Sales Plan and the Shaklee Corporation in an honest, truthful and straightforward manner to my customers and to potential Shaklee Distributors.

(3) I will stand behind the Shaklee Corporation Unconditional Guarantee of product quality and performance and customer satisfaction. I will provide my customers with service reflecting the highest intent of the Golden Rule and Shaklee philosophy.

(4) I will strive to reflect the highest standards of integrity, honesty and responsibility in dealing with my customers and with other Shaklee Distributors.

(5) I will accept and carry out all responsibilities that come with my advancement to various levels of earned honorary rank.

(6) I recognize and support the efforts of the Direct Selling Association of America to establish, implement and maintain the highest standards and practices of truth in selling for all companies in the Personal Selling profession. Shaklee Corporation has been recognized as an active and supportive member of the national organization since 1964, helping to set the standards for the entire industry.

EXHIBIT 1

and American Home Products. When he came to Shaklee, he was faced with declining profitability of the company, due primarily to the company's unsuccessful entry into the European market. He immediately consolidated European operations and took a foreign loss of $3 million for that year. Concentrating on the U.S. market, Shaklee's sales and profits rose in 1977, thanks to the huge demand for Shaklee's Instant Protein®, a meal replacement product that benefitted from widespread consumer interest in liquid protein diets.

About this time, some pricing problems developed. Shaklee had always sold its products for a premium price, claiming that its "natural" vitamins were better than "synthetic" vitamins. In keeping with this pricing strategy, Shaklee's prices increased 35 percent between 1974 and 1977, with an increment of 10 percent posted in November, 1977 (unfortunately just as the company reported record profits). Discount health food stores, such as General Nutrition, were growing rapidly, and Shaklee distributors and customers began complaining about excessive prices. Morale of the sales force was dampened not only by the consumer price resistance, but also by Shaklee's voluntary move to post all ingredients on its labels; this change divulged that

EXHIBIT 2   Shaklee Corp. income statement

In thousands, except per share amounts

Year ended September 30	*1979*	*1980*	*1981*
Sales revenues	$314,149	$411,331	$454,522
Costs and expenses:			
Cost of goods sold	84,874	115,587	116,200
Volume incentives	131,410	171,540	189,569
Selling, general and administrative expenses	62,970	83,719	100,883
	279,254	370,846	406,652
Operating income	34,895	40,485	47,870
Other income (expense):			
Interest income	3,034	3,530	3,895
Interest expense	(545)	(3,218)	(2,208)
Provision for plant closings and discontinued products	—	(16,000)	(1,000)
Foreign exchange gains (losses)	(16)	163	(635)
Miscellaneous, net	(14)	(208)	(1,191)
	2,459	(15,733)	(1,139)
Income before income taxes	37,354	24,752	46,731
Provision for income taxes	16,066	12,681	22,188
Net income	21,288	12,071	24,543
Retained earnings, beginning of year	54,850	71,605	78,723
Cash dividends ($1.00, $.80 and $.74 per share)	(4,533)	(4,953)	(6,228)
Retained earnings, end of year	$ 71,605	$ 78,723	$ 97,038
Net income per share	$ 3.43	$ 1.92	$ 3.85

SOURCE: Annual Reports.

certain formulations were not as completely natural as distributors and customers thought. While Shaklee remained a premium-priced, largely natural product, the concept of natural vitamins was being questioned. For example, the chairman of the American Institute of Nutrition's Committee on Public Information was quoted as saying that Shaklee's claims of superiority for its natural vitamins, as opposed to synthetic vitamins, were "pure drivel and utter nonsense." A further blow to field morale came in 1977, when the FDA issued an advisory opinion warning of the dangers of a liquid protein diet. In the wake of adverse publicity, Shaklee's sales of Instant Protein®, its largest seller, dropped 40 percent. After the initial panic, sales did improve over the next few years.

Shansby made several strategic decisions to correct some problems. He instituted a price freeze to be in effect for several years, even at the sacrifice of gross margins, so that the company could reestablish the price/value rela-

EXHIBIT 3 Shaklee Corp. balance sheet

	1977	1978	1979	1980	1981
Cash	$ 1.4	$ 4.8	$ 2.1	$ 7.0	$ 4.7
Short-term investments	53.4	9.2	24.2	19.4	21.6
Receivables	2.3	1.8	2.8	5.9	8.0
Inventories	25.7	42.6	32.6	42.9	51.3
Other	1.9	3.1	8.9	10.0	12.7
Total current assets	$ 84.8	$ 61.5	$ 70.6	$ 85.3	$ 98.3
Automobiles	$ 18.8	$ 26.5	$ 30.8	$ 27.9	$ 14.6
Machinery improvements and building	16.8	33.6	74.6	69.8	91.3
Gross plant	$ 35.6	$ 60.1	$105.3	$ 97.8	$108.0
Less depreciation	(8.9)	(12.6)	(17.6)	(15.5)	(19.5)
Net property, plant and equipment	$ 27.1	$ 47.5	$ 87.7	$ 82.3	$ 88.5
Land	0.4	0.4	1.9	1.6	2.0
Other	3.3	3.7	4.5	4.0	4.8
Total assets	$115.3	$113.0	$164.7	$173.2	$191.7
Debt currently due	$ 5.6	$ 0.9	$ 8.8	—	—
Payables	7.3	5.2	10.9	12.4	10.6
Advance sales deposits	7.6	0.2	5.5	2.3	0.7
Accrued volume incentives	7.6	7.1	6.4	10.0	11.1
Accrued liabilities and taxes	21.1	16.3	17.5	28.2	28.9
Total current liabilities	$ 49.2	$ 29.6	$ 49.2	$ 52.9	$ 51.3
Long-term debt	$ 16.3	$ 14.9	$ 28.0	$ 22.6	$ 20.2
Deferred taxes	4.6	6.8	8.7	10.7	14.5
Common equity	45.2	61.7	78.9	87.0	105.6
Total liabilities and equity	$115.3	$113.0	$164.7	$173.4	$191.7

SOURCE: Annual Reports.

tionship for its products. He decided the company should have more modern, more centrally located manufacturing facilities; so, in 1980, it built a $50 million plant in Norman, Oklahoma. The 250,000 square foot facility enabled the company to produce its products at a much lower cost than it was able to do in its older and less efficient facilities in California. Also in April, 1981, Shaklee purchased a manufacturing plant in Fort Worth, Texas. With these two facilities, it can now manufacture over 90 percent of its own nutritional products and distribute all its products through the five field service centers located in various parts of the U.S. (see Exhibit 4).

Beginning in early 1978, Shansby brought several key executives into the company to strengthen the company's research, marketing, finance, budgeting, and forecasting.

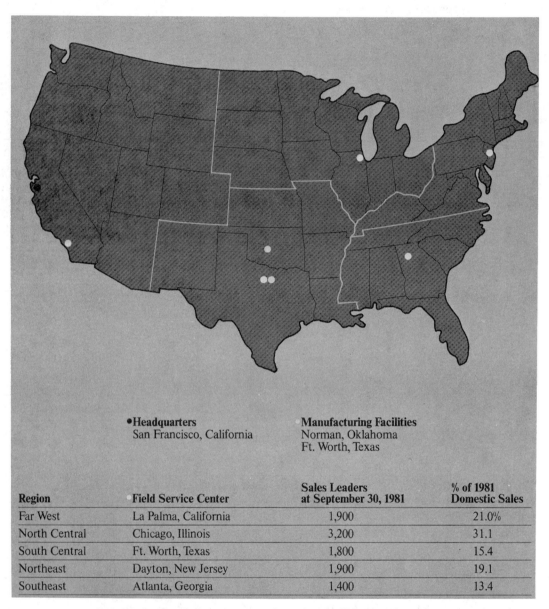

•**Headquarters**	**Manufacturing Facilities**
San Francisco, California	Norman, Oklahoma
	Ft. Worth, Texas

Region	Field Service Center	Sales Leaders at September 30, 1981	% of 1981 Domestic Sales
Far West	La Palma, California	1,900	21.0%
North Central	Chicago, Illinois	3,200	31.1
South Central	Ft. Worth, Texas	1,800	15.4
Northeast	Dayton, New Jersey	1,900	19.1
Southeast	Atlanta, Georgia	1,400	13.4

EXHIBIT 4   Headquarters, manufacturing facilities, and service center locations
SOURCE: Shaklee Corporation 1981 Annual Report.

James Scala, Vice President of Science and Technology, was previously a nutritionist with General Foods. He joined Shaklee in early 1978 to strengthen Shaklee's research effort, which at the time was primarily a quality control program. With a research budget now totaling $7 million, clinical testing was begun in an effort to better document product claims.

Robert Walter, Vice President of Operations had been with Heinz. He is in charge of operations for manufacturing and distribution and orchestrated the start-up of the Norman plant. He is now examining the five regional distribution centers to economize on shipping costs.

Allan Nagle, Senior Vice President, International, joined Shaklee from Brown & Williamson, and has been instrumental in developing the sales literature and marketing aids for each product. This was part of a concerted change in the nature of the selling message delivered by Shaklee distributors and leaders. No longer is the message an individualistic, emotional, and often personal product endorsement, but a more unified, scientifically-based message, with a well documented product benefit story.

Barry Roach, Chief Financial Officer, joined the company from McKinsey. He is improving the reporting of financial information from the field.

Jack Wilder, Vice President, Sales, had previous experience at Mary Kay Cosmetics. He has restructured the sales organization to consist of five regional managers who interact with sales leaders and coordinators. Additionally, thirty to forty counselors handle service requests from distributors and sales leaders. He installed a computerized phone-ordering system in 1980 to expedite shipments to sales leaders, so that the order turnaround is now only one week. Sales promotion, conventions, and promotional planning are handled by about fifty people under his direction.

THE SHAKLEE CUSTOMER

Shaklee Corp. has a unique situation in that its prime customer base consists of its more than 2 million distributors, or salespeople. Generally, these distributors buy for their family and one or two friends, finding that buying direct to eliminate the retail markup is desirable. It is estimated that 90 percent of all Shaklee sales are made in this manner.

According to company research, Shaklee customers, as well as distributors, tend to be highly educated, family-oriented, somewhat religious, and usually suburban. Their alcohol consumption is low and they watch a minimal amount of television. The company has also found that use of Shaklee products is frequently accompanied by a change in life style that includes greater emphasis on proper nutrition and increased exercise.

Current research studies by outside organizations indicate widespread interest in the U.S. in physical fitness and nutrition. For example, a Lou Harris public opinion poll conducted in 1978 revealed that 67 percent of Americans thought they would be healthier if they were more active physically. In that year, 90 million Americans (or 59 percent of those 18 years of age or older) participated in some form of regular exercise. Also, 93 percent of parents wanted their children to develop a deep concern about physical fitness.

As pointed out by a recent stock analysis of Shaklee Corporation, there are several other factors at work in society at this time that should encourage future consumer demand for nutritional products:

☐ As the U.S. population gets older, the demand for vitamins should increase. Children of the post-war baby boom are now in their early- to mid-thirties, and concerned about preserving their youth and active life styles.

☐ It is estimated that one of three Americans is overweight. Since weight control is a constant preoccupation for a large segment of the population, products such as Shaklee's Instant Protein® (a "meal replacement" product) should continue to be in great demand.

☐ It is estimated that one of three meals is consumed away from home. Because of this, and of the fact that snack foods often displace meals, there is concern about a possible lack of nutrition.

☐ There is a significant segment of the population that believes that vitamins generally promote health. Specifically, vitamins B, C, and E are desired by many who believe they can enhance their resistance to colds, promote their ability to withstand stress, and even aid their sexual function. Additional clinical research on the effectiveness of vitamins, as well as the circulation growth of such nutrition-related periodicals as *Prevention,* is expected to encourage this health-conscious trend.

COMPETITION

Shaklee's major competitor is General Nutrition, a retailer of vitamins and health foods, with 800 stores across the U.S. In 1980, General Nutrition had total sales of $242 million, of which approximately $140 million were vitamins and other nutrients (compared with Shaklee nutrition sales that year of $220 million). Typically, General Nutrition's strategy has been to discount vitamins, promote those discounts widely, and then improve its gross margin with higher margin impulse items such as health foods or personal care items. Shaklee executives feel that vitamins/food supplement sales of the company have been hurt somewhat by General Nutrition's discount pricing strategy. There are also approximately 5,000 independent health food stores in the U.S. These have not been as threatening to Shaklee since their focus is on personal service rather than price.

Exhibit 4 lists the leading vitamin producers in the U.S. It is expected that future manufacturing competition will come from smaller manufacturers such as Hudson and Richard Vicks; future competition may also come from such proprietary companies as Bristol Myers. Each of these companies have both substantial marketing skills and resources, and product experience in the food supplements or meal replacement market (e.g., Metrecal). Experts do not expect the major ethical drug companies to enter the vitamin market very heavily, since the profit margins on mainstream vitamins are not very high. However, there may be tougher competition for some of the higher-margin food supplement/vitamin lines like Shaklee's Sustained Release Vita-C.

EXHIBIT 5   Major vitamin producers in the United States

	Approximate 1980 Vitamin Sales
Shaklee	$230 million
General Nutrition	140 million
Miles Labs: "One a Day"	35 million
Ledoile: "Stress Tabs" and "Centrum"	30 million
Squibb's: "Theragram"	30 million

PRODUCTS

Shaklee sells three different product lines: nutritional products (twenty-four items), household products (nine items), and personal care products (twenty-two items). All Shaklee products are premium-priced. A list of these Shaklee products, along with prices for two of the lines, is shown in Exhibit 6.

In May, 1980 the company decided to reduce the number of household and personal care items to concentrate more heavily on nutritional products. The household line was cut from 13 products to 9, while reducing the number of stockkeeping units from 37 to 14. In personal care, the line was cut from 56 products to 22, while the number of stockkeeping units was reduced from 141 to 28. According to President Shansby, this change occurred to:

> refocus the company on nutritional products—the area we feel offers our Sales Leaders the greatest potential for growth. We planned this strategic direction in response to our Sales Leaders' desire to emphasize nutritional products in their individual businesses. Shaklee nutritional products are both door openers and business builders for our own independent distributors. Moreover, the higher turnover of the line helps Sales Leaders better manage their cash flows, thus further strengthening their businesses. The product line rationalization was, therefore, an important strategic advance for them—and, as a result, for us.

Relative breakdowns of sales for the different product lines over the past four years are shown in Exhibit 7.

Shaklee's nutritional products are primarily natural, packaged in glass or polystyrene, with all ingredients listed on the bottle. The present line of nutritional products is shown in Exhibit 8. Among consumers, Shaklee has a reputation for product quality because of its use of natural ingredients, and the amount, variety, and balance of nutrients included in its products. Among many nutrition enthusiasts, Shaklee vitamins have a certain mystique because of their ingredient formulations. This has led to some belief that Shaklee products can even cure gout, cancer, diabetes, and many other diseases. With Shaklee's transition from an entrepreneurial company to a professionally managed company, and due to pressure from the Food & Drug Administration, the company has tried to tone down these claims by salespeople. In fact, company literature directed to its salespeople now warns: "For your own protection and for the integrity of the Shaklee name, NEVER make any claims for a product or recommend any product uses other than those speci-

EXHIBIT 6 Shaklee products

		Distributor Net Price
Nutritional products	Vita-Lea Tablets, 240 or 480 tablets	$7.75–$14.40
	Vita-Lea Chewables, 125 or 250 tablets	5.95 – 11.30
	Liquid-Lea, 8 fluid oz.	5.20
	Instant Protein Drink Mix, regular & cocoa	7.95– 15.00
	Instant Protein Convenience Pack, regular & cocoa	8.50
	Sustained Release Vita-C 500mg. 70 or 180 tablets	3.95– 9.40
	Chewable Vita-C 100mg. 100 or 500 tablets	3.60– 15.40
	400 I.U. Vita-E Plus Selenium Tablets, 100 tablets	10.60
	400 I.U. Vita-E Capsules, 100 or 250 tablets	10.90– 25.75
	Chewable 100 I.U. Vita-E Plus Selenium Tablets, 100 or 500 tablets	6.30– 28.45
	100 I.U. Vita-E Capsules, 180 or 480 capsules	9.70– 24.50
	B-Complex, 120 or 320 tablets	6.45– 16.50
	Calcium Magnesium, 260 tablets	4.00
	Chewable Vita-Cal, 200 & 425 tablets	5.95– 11.90
	Vita-Cal Plus Iron, 100 tablets	4.50
	Zinc, 130 tablets	3.10
	Alfalfa Tabs, 330 or 700 tablets	5.90– 11.50
	Bran 'N Oats Bar	0.75
	Pro-Lecin Nibblers, 200 or 390	7.80– 14.95
	Fiber Wafers, 120 wafers	5.00
	Energy Bar, cocoa & peanut	0.65
	Herb-Lax, 120 tablets	2.95
	Lecithin, 190 capsules	6.80
	Baking Enricher, 28 oz.	12.20
Personal care products	Meadow Blend Soap-Free Cleansing Bar	$2.50
	New Concept Organic Dentifrice	1.85
	Desert Wind Deodorant	2.05
	Foot Cream	3.85
	Deodorant Cream	5.30
	Apricot Hand & Body Lotion	3.90
	Bath Essence	5.55
	Tioga Men's Skin Conditioner	6.45
	Deuvies Body Creme	6.45
	Proteinized Shampoo	3.10
	Arrange Hair Spray	3.50
	Rainsilk Shampoo, 8 fluid oz. or 1 gallon	3.10– 30.20
	Rainsilk Clear Conditioning Rinse, 8 fluid oz. or 1 gallon	3.10– 30.20
	Ester Droplets Replenishing Oil	7.80
	Under-Makeup Moisturizer	4.20

EXHIBIT 6 (continued)

		Distributor Net Price
	Beauty Masque	4.75
	Cream Cleanser	4.05
	Lotion Cleanser	3.60
	Proteinized Cleanser	3.60
	Proteinized Velva Dew Moisturizer	5.55
	Fluid Foundation	3.25
	Gel Blush	3.25
Household products	Basic H. quart, gallon or 5 gallons or 30 gallons	
	Basic L Laundry Concentrate, 10 or 21 lbs.	
	Liquid L Laundry Concentrate, gallon	
	Softer Than Soft Fabric Conditioner, gallon	
	Basic-I Heavy Duty Cleaner, quart or gallon	
	Basic-G Germicidal Cleaner	
	At-Ease Scouring Cleaner	
	Basic-D Automatic Dishwashing Concentrate	
	Satin Sheen Dishwashing Liquid	

SOURCE: Salomon Brothers, Company analysis, May 26, 1981.

EXHIBIT 7 Shaklee Corporation breakdown of product mix

	(% of sales revenues)			
Product Line	*1978*	*1979*	*1980*	*1981*
Nutritional products	70%	68%	69%	76%
Household products	16%	17%	18%	16%
Personal care products	14%	15%	13%	8%

SOURCE: Salomon Brothers, Company analysis, May 26, 1981.

fied in official Shaklee Corporation publications and literature." In spite of these warnings the mystique remains.

The company introduced eight new products in 1980 and five in 1981. A few of these are Sustained Release Vita-C™, Vita-E™ Tablets Plus selenium, Fiber Wafers, Instant Protein® Convenience Packs, Brown 'N Oats™ bar, and Fruit Bar.

PUBLIC RELATIONS

Large corporations are traditionally prone to public relations problems and Shaklee is no exception. For example, the company recently was accused of using improper sterilization techniques on one of its products. In 1973 the company began treating its alfalfa tablets, which were prone to infection with

EXHIBIT 8

salmonella bacteria, with ethylene oxide (ETO), a suspected carcinogen. Shaklee continued the treatments until 1977, when the company discontinued the ETO process and substituted an innovative technique that did not require ETO. In 1982 an investigative report in the *Wall Street Journal* made this information public, leading critics to charge "cover-up," since the company never notified anyone that the sterilization procedures involved the use of a suspected cancer-causing chemical. Shaklee responded, "ETO was a major process used in the mid-70s to sterilize products and is still being used in sterilization of medical devices and certain foods, particularly seasonings and botanicals." The company also claimed that it should be praised for its pioneering efforts in developing a safer sterilization procedure. Because of the importance of good relations with distributors and customers, Shaklee must successfully resolve similar problems that may occur.

SELLING ORGANIZATION

The backbone of Shaklee Corporation is its selling organization. With an incentive-oriented compensation structure that is one of the most attractive in the direct selling industry, Shaklee's selling organization is critical to the company's success. Exhibit 9 summarizes each level in Shaklee's six-step pyramidal selling organization.

At the bottom of Shaklee's selling organization are the more than two million Shaklee distributors who pay a fee of $12.50 to purchase a New Distributor Kit, and which entitles them to buy Shaklee products for "distributor net," basically a wholesale price of approximately 25 to 30 percent less than suggested retail. When a distributor has achieved and maintained $1,000 in monthly sales (i.e., $735 distributor's net), he or she may be appointed assistant supervisor. This person still buys products from a member of the selling organization, rather than directly from the company.

The first significant jump in the organization comes when the distributor or assistant supervisor has attained a monthly sales volume of $3,000 (or $2,200 on distributor net sales). This person is then classified as a "sales leader," a term used for any of the top four levels in the organization. There are presently about 13,000 sales leaders in the organization. Each sales leader is able to purchase products directly from Shaklee, and also receives cash bonuses each month from the Company. Sales leaders who maintain monthly purchase volume of $5,000 ($3,700 distribution net) for six months qualify for free use of a rental car. At the end of fiscal 1981, over 6,000 sales leaders were driving bonus cars, accounting for one of the largest corporate auto fleets in the country. There are twelve different car models available.

A beginning sales leader earns more than $10,000 a year; the typical sales leader, who may have one or more other sales leaders under him or her, earns about $14,000. To encourage development of new management, a sales leader receives 5 percent of the purchase volume of the sales leaders he or she develops, 2 percent of second-generation sales leaders' business, and 1 percent of third-generation sales leaders' business.

When a supervisor has developed four first-level supervisors, he or she may qualify for promotion to coordinator; there are approximately 1,000 coordinators, each earning approximately $50,000 annually. At the top of the selling organization are the key coordinators and master coordinators. These

DISTRIBUTOR	ASSISTANT SUPERVISOR	SUPERVISOR	COORDINATOR	KEY COORDINATOR	MASTER COORDINATOR
		11,700*	1,000*	150*	75*

All who join the Shaklee Family begin as Distributors, sponsored by someone who is already a Distributor or Sales Leader. Distributors buy Shaklee products from the Sales Leader in their sponsorship group for resale to retail customers and for personal and family consumption. Although the Company suggests retail prices for its products, Distributors may sell at any price they wish. There are no territories or franchises; Shaklee Distributors in each country may sell anywhere in their country. In 1981, the Company received an average of over 2,000 Distributor applications every business day.

DISTRIBUTOR

Each new Distributor purchases a New Distributor Kit for $12.50. Distributors have no minimum purchase requirements, and generally do not maintain significant amounts of inventory, relying on their Assistant Supervisor or Sales Leader to supply them with the products their customers order. Distributors may receive monthly cash bonuses from their Sales Leaders, based on the volume of products they purchase.

ASSISTANT SUPERVISOR

Distributors whose purchase volume reaches $1,000 per month may be appointed by their Sales Leaders as Assistant Supervisors. Although they do not buy directly from the Company, they often maintain some inventory to supply the Distributors in their groups, and assist their Sales Leader in training and motivating Distributors.

SUPERVISOR

Distributors who demonstrate leadership abilities, and whose purchase volume reaches $3,000 per month, may be appointed by the Company as Supervisors, the first rank of Sales Leader. Supervisors buy directly from the Company, receive Shaklee cash bonuses, and may qualify for bonus cars and convention attendance. In addition, by sponsoring and training other Distributors who become Sales Leaders, they can earn special leadership bonuses.

COORDINATOR

Supervisors who in turn develop and maintain four Supervisors from Distributors in their own Sales Group may be designated as Coordinators, making them eligible for additional conventions, a Coordinator Bonus, and other recognition.

KEY COORDINATOR

Key Coordinators are Coordinators who have developed, trained and maintained a minimum of nine Sales Leaders from Distributors in their Sales Group, making them eligible for more prestigious bonus cars and recognition from the company.

MASTER COORDINATOR

The highest sales rank in Shaklee is attained by developing a minimum of fifteen Sales Leaders. Master Coordinators receive top-of-the-line bonus cars and additional rewards, and recognition as guest speakers at conventions and as featured success stories in company publications.

*approximate figures

EXHIBIT 9 Shaklee Corporation selling organization

SOURCE: Shaklee Corporation 1981 Annual Report.

individuals earn over $100,000 annually; a handful are presently making over $400,000.

The potential for top earnings, accumulated primarily from bonuses or commissions, is a powerful motivating factor for people rising in the Shaklee selling organization. Additional motivational devices include the international and regional conferences and conventions, which were attended by over 60,000 people last year (at a cost to the company of over $10 million). Shaklee is convinced that company success depends on this selling organization. As stated in the company's *1981 Annual Report:*

> The distributors and Sales Leaders who are the Shaklee family share a common bond of interest in nutrition and health. It is an appreciation of the importance of high-quality nutritional products as a part of an all-around self improvement program that motivates a person to become a Shaklee distributor.
>
> Because members of the Shaklee sales force are consumers first, it is easy for them to share their enthusiasm for the products they trust. Shaklee distributors are not just out plugging some company's line of merchandise—they are telling people about products that have a place in their homes and in their lives. They share their personal commitment to health, and their appreciation for good nutrition. This sharing of products and information with relatives, friends and neighbors leads many distributors to develop their own individual business enterprises by participating in the Shaklee sales plan.
>
> Of the hundreds of thousands of Shaklee distributors, 12,900 have been appointed by the Company as Sales Leaders. These are individuals who have displayed leadership abilities and whose businesses have reached such a size that they are qualified to buy their products directly from the Company. Sales Leaders build their businesses by making Shaklee products available to a wider audience and by encouraging other consumers to become distributors. As enthusiasm about the products and the business opportunity spreads to more and more people, additional consumers become distributors and the sponsoring Sales Leaders' business sales volume expands.
>
> The Shaklee Sales Plan is truly democratic, allowing an individual to go as far as he or she wishes and is able. The Plan provides business-building incentives and benefits-cash bonuses, bonus cars, travel to conventions, and participation in insurance programs.
>
> But every successful Sales Leader from Supervisor to Master Coordinator must take the same steps. And each begins a Shaklee business the same way—as a consumer and distributor.
>
> As Sales Leaders build their businesses, our business will grow. We depend on the motivation, direction and hard work of our sales force to maintain our position as one of the world's leading nutritional products companies. While corporate staff and resources, R&D, and manufacturing and distribution efficiencies are important for our business, ultimately it is the individual in the field —the independent entrepreneur who is building a business—that is the foundation of the Shaklee Corporation.

A comparison of the Shaklee selling organization with that of three other leading direct selling companies is given in Exhibits 10 and 11.

EXHIBIT 10 Four direct selling companies—a comparison of U.S. operations

	Avon	Tupperware	Mary Kay	Shaklee
Sales				
Retail (mils)	$1,950.0	$800	$303.0	$509
Factory (mils)	$1,170.0	$360	$151.5	$356
Factory as pct. of retail	60%	45%	50%	70%
Sales force				
Number of salespeople	425,000 representatives	85,000 dealers	105,000 consultants	2 million distributors who are primarily consumers
Retail sales per salesperson	$4,600	$9,400	$2,900	$255
Factory sales per salesperson	2,900	4,200	1,450	178
Earnings per salesperson	$1,800	$3,300	$1,450	$77 in product savings
Commission	40% of retail sales	35% of retail sales	50% of retail sales	30% of retail sales

SOURCE: Salomon Brothers, Company analysis, May 26, 1981.

EXHIBIT 11 Comparison of sales force management

	Avon	Tupperware	Mary Kay	Shaklee
First level				
Number of managers	2,800 district managers	8,000 managers	2,100 directors	10,100
Salespeople per manager	150	11	50	198
Retail sales per manager	$695,000	$100,000	$144,000	$50,400
Compensation	$15,000 salary + 3% of sales increase + leased car	3%–5% of retail sales or $4,000 + rental car worth $7,000 every 2 years.	12% of retail sales or $17,300 + avg. bonus of 3% of sales ($4,300) rental car worth $8,000 every 2 years.	22% of purchases volume + 5% of sales leaders he develops + 2% of second generation sales + 1% of third generation + rental car program $14,000 average
Second level				
Number of managers	159 division managers	365 distributors	21 national sales managers	1,000 coordinators with five sales leaders
Retail sales per manager	$12.2 million	$2.2 million	$14.4 million	$509,000
Compensation	$35,000	$80,000–$100,000 + net or 20% of retail sales less expenses	12%–15% of 1st-generation retail sales. Smaller percent of 2nd-generation retail sales. $14,000 avg.	$50,000
Duties	Supervise district managers	Purchase inventory and ship product to unit managers		

452

EXHIBIT 11   (continued)

	Avon	Tupperware	Mary Kay	Shaklee
Third level				
Number of managers	7 national sales managers	12 regional vice presidents		200 coordinators
Compensation	$50,000 salary	$40,000–$60,000 salary + incentive		$100,000 plus

SOURCE: Salomon Brothers, Company analysis, May 26, 1981.

THE FUTURE

Shaklee's long-term objective is to be "the world's leading nutritional products company." To accomplish this, the company wants to increase its international thrust, as well as continue to improve its domestic marketing efforts. Internationally, the company has been very cautious since its disastrous international results of the mid-1970s. It appears that some countries such as Japan and Canada are enthusiastic about nutritional products. However, in countries where confectionery consumption is high (such as England), concern about vitamins is lower. Less developed countries, such as Brazil, may be promising markets in the future since other direct-sale companies (such as Avon and Mary Kay) have been very successful here.

The primary concern at the moment for Shaklee executives is to improve the company's marketing efforts in the United States. They are particularly aware of the fact that growth for any direct selling company is largely a function of growth in the sales force—both the number of salespersons as well as the revenue per salesperson. It is this area of company operations that Shaklee executives feel can be most dramatically improved in the near future.

Taylor Farm Implement Equipment Company

BACKGROUND

Lloyd Taylor, age sixty-seven, could be considered a true American entrepreneur. His closely held business, Taylor Farm Equipment Company, had grown over the past eight years from producing farm implements in the back of his retail farming equipment store into a five million dollar per year manufacturing company. Mr. Taylor purchased half interest in a Brisco farm equipment retail store in 1955 and in 1962 acquired sole interest after his partner died.

Having a flair for inventing things, Mr. Taylor, in the summer of 1968, developed a simple reliable method for planting agricultural seeds. He incorporated this technique into a planter and shortly, thereafter obtained a patent. In 1969 production of Taylor's planters began in the service area of his retail store. The planters were built utilizing the spare time of his service store employees. The Taylor planter proved to be successful and sales grew from $85,000 in 1971-72 to approximately $5,175,000 in 1976-77. The retail store was sold in 1972 to devote full time to planter manufacturing. At this time the name of the company was changed to the Taylor Farm Equipment Manufacturing Company. The future indeed appeared bright for the man who had risen from a middle income background into a respected and moderately successful independent businessman.

Taylor Farm Equipment Manufacturing Company was located in Exter, Arkansas, a town of approximately 25,000 people. It was the largest city in an eighty mile radius. Exter, until 1970, had been a predominately agricultural community with cotton, soybeans, rice, and corn being the principal crops. Over the past eight years several major industrial companies had located in Exter with others seriously considering such a move. A plentiful work force,

The research and written case information were presented at a Case Research Symposium and were evaluated by the Case Research Association's Editorial Board. This case was prepared by Dr. James Harbin and Miss June Freund of Missouri Southern State College as a basis for class discussion.

lower wage expectations, local tax incentives, a university, a clean city with a low crime rate, and a good family environment were Exter's drawing points. Arkansas's being a right-to-work state also added to Exter's attraction as an industrial location.

PRODUCT

Planters were Taylor's major product, and the planter industry was under intense pressure to keep up with recent and potential future innovations. The 1970s brought enormous advances in planter design. Recent engineering revolutions in seed metering and depth control had opened the door for extremely versatile planters capable of providing accurate seed placement even under adverse field and management conditions. It was expected that planters in the future: (1) would be built for versatility; (2) would be built increasingly for no-till planting (particularly due to increased fuel costs); (3) that depth control would sharpen (one major farm implement producer had recently made the first major breakthrough in this concept); (4) would be wider in terms of rows; (5) would be able to plant faster and longer; and (6) would utilize more automatic monitors and controls.

Most planters had the same basic design. They were built for two, four, six, eight, ten, and even twelve rows of planting. With only minor parts substitution, such as switching seed plates at the bottom of the planter hopper, a farmer could change from planting corn to cotton, cotton to soybeans, etc.

Taylor expanded production into other farm-related products as manufacturing sales increased. This broader line of products resulted first from the similarity and ease of shifting production between planters and other farm-related items, and second, to provide a greater depth to the Taylor product line. These other products consisted of such items as discs, harrows, plows, and cultivators. The majority of Taylor's products were rather simple to build and to assemble.

Steel, castings, plastic, and fiberglass were the main components of Taylor's products. Quality control was the responsibility of the respective supervisors. Inspections were handled in an unsophisticated "eyeball" manner. If it looked good and fit into the other parts, it passed inspection. However, on the whole the company had few customer complaints and those received were expeditiously and courteously handled.

The nature of the product and sales made the work at Taylor highly seasonal. Attempts to even out this seasonality were made, but the cost of carrying inventories, little storage space, and volatility of orders limited the success. Preliminary sales orders (usually about 20 percent of the annual volume) could be expected starting in October-November. Customers were encouraged to order early, but there was little incentive to bring this into reality. The majority of the year's orders (approximately 50 percent) were received in January-February with the remainder tapering off from April to July. The bulk of planter shipments were made during March-April.

Work slowed to a snail's pace during the summer months of June through August, and only a skeleton crew of hourly employees was retained. Design changes, clean-up, maintenance work, and minimum production took place during these slow months. During this period, all supervisors could take several weeks off (without pay) for vacations and were encouraged to do so. With a few exceptions for extremely valued employees, only those hourly workers whose skills and talents deemed them to be indispensable to year-round operations were retained during these months.

SALES

Planters represented approximately 80 percent of Taylor's yearly sales over the past six years. It was Mr. Taylor's opinion that nonplanter sales, however, provided the company with a slightly higher profit margin.

Sales in the early years of Taylor's existence were generated by Lloyd Taylor and Harry Johnson. Harry was the sales and service manager for the retail business. By loading up the store truck with planters and selling to increasingly larger areas, Lloyd and Harry were gradually able to expand sales utilizing the contacts they had made in the retail store.

In 1972, through its local sales representative, the Brisco Tractor Company learned of the Taylor planter. At this time Brisco had 6 percent of the tractor market and ranked seventh in the farm equipment business. Prior to 1972 Brisco had not offered a full array of farm implements to complement its tractors. Shortly thereafter, Taylor entered into an informal agreement to supply Brisco with planters for its retail outlets. Most of the other major tractor manufacturers produced their own planters and farm implements. These planters were to be marketed under the Brisco label. The only difference between a Taylor planter and a Brisco planter was the color and brand labels. Orders for Taylor's products were placed by Brisco's retailers through Brisco's home office, who in turn passed them on to Taylor. Payment for shipments was made by the Brisco Tractor Company. This association with a major manufacturer and retailer provided Taylor with the volume, outlets, and stability deemed necessary for the growth of the company.

Brisco sales averaged roughly 70-80 percent of Taylor's total sales. Sales expanded so rapidly that Taylor was unable to supply all of Brisco's orders in 1975-76. Brisco then turned to Seon Company to supply those orders that

EXHIBIT 1 Taylor Farm Equipment Company sales (1971-77)

Year	Sales
1971-72	$ 85,000.00
1972-73	107,000.00
1973-74	425,000.00
1974-75	1,110,000.00
1975-76	2,748,000.00
1976-77	5,175,000.00

Taylor could not. Seon was a multi-faceted company with about thirty million a year in sales. It was believed, however, that Brisco preferred Taylor to Seon because of lower prices and a better bargaining position.

The farming implement industry is highly competitive with the top seven companies dominating the market. The planting industry consisted of fifty to seventy producers with about twenty-five of them specializing in a particular product. Customers attributed their purchases of farm products to brand loyalty (his father had always bought brand X), compatability of equipment to brand of tractor (although all the implements were basically interchangeable), price, and loyalty to dealership. Many customers preferred the major brands because of warranties, parts, and service. The importance of these attributes, however, tended to be a highly personal matter.

Retail prices of planters tended to fluctuate widely. Depending upon the versatility and sophistication of the planter, prices in 1976 could range from $400 to $1000/foot. Bargaining with the retail dealers on price was a tradition much like that in the automobile business.

PERSONNEL

Harry Johnson, sixty-four, was Lloyd's right-hand man and a personal friend. He had been with Lloyd since the start of the retail business and was regarded as a knowledgeable and loyal employee whom everyone naturally liked. Anyone wanting to know Mr. Taylor's thinking or having new ideas or suggestions would usually speak with Harry first. Harry would either give his opinion concerning how Lloyd would react, or, if one were lucky, he would introduce the idea to Mr. Taylor, thereby, increasing the chance for its acceptance.

Harry thought very highly of Lloyd as a boss first and a friend second. He knew just how far Mr. Taylor could be pushed or persuaded, when to suggest or to back off, and was usually an insider to privileged information or the thoughts of Mr. Taylor. Lloyd trusted Harry and valued him as an employee. Mr. Taylor had the final say-so and Harry accepted that, yet Harry was not a typical yes-man.

The marketing efforts of the company centered around Harry. It was still common for Harry to load up the company truck and promote their products during the off-season. Harry would promote only the Taylor label. Promotion of the Brisco planter was handled through Brisco's sales representatives. Since the Brisco arrangement, Harry's marketing efforts were curtailed to a few times a year. An elderly manufacturing representative for the Brisco Tractor Company provided the Taylor Company with the only other internal marketing efforts. Taylor sales generated by this representative, to date, consisted of only a relatively minor amount of Taylor's total sales. His primary responsibility was to Brisco Tractor Company, but because of his long association with Lloyd, he promoted Taylor's products as a favor and as a second source of income.

Harry's daily activities presently centered around accepting, logging, and coordinating orders with the production schedule. He made sure orders were shipped at the proper times. In addition, Harry handled all service-related questions or problems. Travel was sometimes necessary to handle problems experienced with Taylor products. Lloyd would often ask Harry to handle the miscellaneous tasks that so often occurred.

In 1974, Lloyd's son-in-law, Leroy Howard was encouraged to enter the business as the general plant manager. Leroy had a mechanical engineering degree with six years experience in an unrelated type of business. However, Leroy had no managerial experience. Leroy possessed an energetic personality with a direct manner. He seemed to enjoy the position of plant manager. Yet, in some cases, there appeared an uncertainty on his part concerning the extent of his authority and responsibility. Mr. Taylor, on his many frequent trips through the plant, would often change an operation or production schedule without notifying Leroy or his subordinates.

Leroy's activities involved overseeing the day-to-day operations of the plant, a task Lloyd did not particularly enjoy. Lloyd retained authority for the financial function of the business. Approximately 30 to 40 percent of Leroy's time was spent handling personnel matters. This was particularly true during the company's peak work season. Interviewing seemed to be a necessary but neverending task due to the large amount of employee turnover. Leroy seemed to enjoy this role in particular and interviewed almost anyone who walked in off the street. If there was an opening the applicants applying that day would invariably get the job. In fact, on several occasions prospective employees would walk in for a job application and go to work the next day, often without any real concept of the type work they were expected to perform.

Jay Mueher joined the Taylor Company in the summer of 1975. His initial duties were truck driver and general errand man. Jay, twenty-four, was not a typical hourly employee of this company and quickly moved into the front office. He gradually assumed the production and inventory control duties of the business. Later Jay also started placing some of the material orders under the close supervision of Leroy. Jay's personality was unpretentious, but he had an innate ability for grasping figures and planning.

Sally Kreps had been with Taylor Company for the last six years. Her responsibilities were to perform all the in-house bookkeeping. Decisions of any scope were referred to Lloyd. The payroll cards and verification of hours worked were Sally's responsibility. The actual computation and issuance of checks was performed through the services of a local computer company on a time-sharing basis. Sally was a rather likeable, introverted, conscientious person. In 1976, Sally enrolled in a night Principles of Accounting class at the local university and was experiencing some difficulties comprehending the mechanics of the course. However, this did represent her first attempt at college classes.

The receptionist, June Simmon, handled the telephone switchboard and performed the necessary typing. Lloyd, Harry, Leroy, Jay, Sally, and June comprised the Taylor team until the fall of 1976. At this time it was the consensus decision of Lloyd, Harry, and Leroy that there was a need to expand the management staff so as to relieve their increasing workload demands.

Tim Berry, thirty, was employed in the fall of 1976 to help provide expertise in the materials planning and scheduling functions of the business. Tim had five years experience in the production and planning departments of two manufacturing companies, and was completing his MBA degree at night. Initially, Tim and Jay worked together in formally organizing the production control function. Gradually Tim took over and expanded the purchasing function leaving Jay with the production and control function. Tim had worked closely with the purchasing departments in his two previous positions.

Richard Youst, thirty-five, was employed as a part-time person to assist in the accounting function. He possessed fourteen years experience in the military as helicopter pilot and was presently in the process of earning his MBA degree. Richard had developed an interest in accounting while working on his degree and hoped to pass his CPA examination in the near future. The primary responsibilities of Richard, as a part-time employee, were to work with Sally in trying to improve the organization's bookkeeping function. Richard also subbed in a variety of other tasks, one of which was a timestudy man. Recognizing that standards were essential to costing, pricing, and planning decisions, Richard convinced Lloyd and Leroy of the standards necessity. A large percentage of Richard's time was devoted to performing time studies. In the spring of 1977, and coinciding with his graduation, Richard was offered and accepted a full-time position with Taylor as Controller. He was promised at that time that he would have the authority in his new position to carry out necessary reforms in the accounting department.

A plant superintendent was also sought in the spring of 1977. Bill Adams, an engineer with eight years of varied experience, was employed by Taylor for this position. Bill, thirty-nine, recently divorced, was an individualist, easy to relate to. He proved to be very popular with the majority of the plant supervisors, who reported to him. Several enjoyed off-duty activities with Bill. He impressed one on the surface, at least, as one capable of performing the tasks assigned to him.

A search for a personnel manager took place in the summer of 1977. Ron Temple, thirty-eight, possessing four years experience in personnel was chosen. Prior to his leaving his present job, Ron was injured in a car accident that prevented his starting to work with Taylor for the next nine months.

In the spring of 1977, Dave Bartlett, thirty-three, a talented mechanical engineer was added to the Taylor team. Dave had previously been employed by MCC, a major producer of a variety of agricultural and military products, which was also located in Exter. The justification for hiring Dave was Lloyd's inability to perfect a new method for planting. Lloyd had devoted much of his time in the past fourteen months to this project. Lloyd felt this new concept in planting could have a revolutionary effect in the industry.

Many of Dave's activities centered around the development of this new planter. Several other projects cut into his time, such as the construction of a new conveyor for the painting of Taylor's parts. This system (which was built in-house) was completed during 1977 and much of its success was attributed to Dave. The new system replaced a very inefficient one.

The hourly workforce consisted of predominately young first-time workers, unskilled workers, and temporarily unemployed workers. Because of the harsh working conditions, few women tended to stay with the company. During the busy season of 1977, the number of employees reached 210, an all-time high for the Taylor Company. Turnover ran at approximately 175 percent for 1977 which was slightly higher than in previous years.

While there was no organization chart *per se* in the company, Exhibit 2 represents a fairly accurate picture of the management team as of 1977.

COMPENSATION AND BENEFITS

Pay and benefits at Taylor Company were established at below average scale for the local geographical area. This was also true for the recently hired new

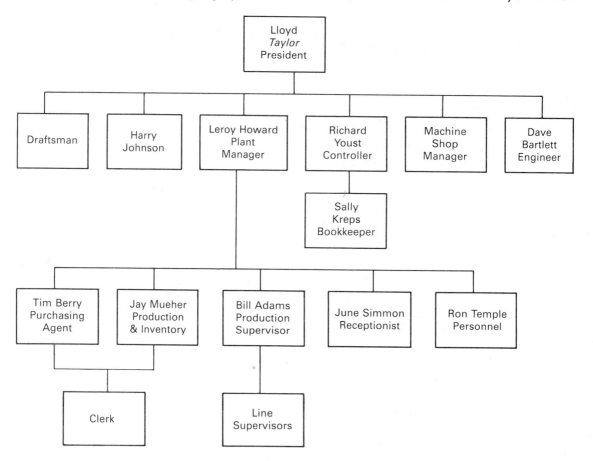

EXHIBIT 2   Organization

managers. The only exception to this policy was Dave, the new engineer. Dave's salary was slightly above the going salary in the area. Lloyd felt this to be justified because of the need to develop the new planter. The possibility of getting in on the ground floor of a fast growing industrial concern appeared to be a prime attraction for the new managers and seemed to balance the inequities of lower salaries.

Compensation for the hourly ranks was established slightly above minimum wage. Certain key positions paid more, such as welders, skilled machinists, etc.; but, again, these were still below average scale for the area. This was partly attributed to Mr. Taylor's cost-conscious philosophy and partly to an assumed conclusion that there was no need to pay more. The logic for this assumed conclusion was: (1) the simplicity of the operations; (2) an adequate labor supply; (3) a short training time for new employees; and (4) little loss of productivity due to labor turnover.

Injuries were a common occurrence within the plant, ranging from minor cuts to lost fingers. Medical insurance was provided, however, lost work-time was not compensated for. There was a rather unhumorous remark once made that "we should start an injury-of-the-week club."

STANDARDS

Standards for production did not exist until the fall of 1976. Pricing of the products was accomplished through the "gut" feelings of Mr. Taylor, Leroy, and Harry. It was Mr. Taylor's philosophy that pricing be comparable to other producers, and he usually attempted to price below the major producers. There was room for price flexibility depending on the need for sales and the bargaining position of his customers.

The lack of a basis for realistic pricing procedures was brought to the surface largely through the efforts of Richard while he was still a part-time employee. With his clipboard and stop watch, Richard developed a record of "averages" for time spent in production for as many parts as time permitted. Production time of less expensive parts was estimated until Richard could observe them.

The standards and efficiency hours generated by Richard resulted in some pricing revisions of Taylor products. Several products in the Taylor line were either over-priced or under-priced.

FINANCES

The financial condition of Taylor Farm Equipment Company was considered to be a private matter. A local CPA firm generated the income statements, balance sheets, capital statements, and tax returns. A line of credit assumed to be sufficient was established with a local bank and had not been increased in the last two years. On several occasions, when financial statements were requested by potential suppliers, Mr. Taylor refused to supply such information and insisted that his line of credit with the local bank should provide sufficient information.

Checks for payments to suppliers required Mr. Taylor's signature. His philosophy on accounts payable was unusual, to say the least. Payments were delayed as long as possible. Notices of payments past due were ignored, and calls from credit managers were diverted by Sally, if possible. Payments occurred only when final credit threats were made. Mr. Taylor viewed this delaying tactic as a form of leverage.

In the past eight months, several of Taylor's suppliers would ship only on a COD basis. Among those demanding a COD policy were all existing steel suppliers. (Steel was the primary raw material cost of Taylor's products.)

In November of 1976, Leroy called a meeting with Jay, Tim, and Harry to discuss purchases and production schedules. At this meeting, Leroy stated that, while there was no danger of inability to meet payroll expenses, other expenses should be kept to a minimum for the next three months. This meant that all possible purchases and receipts of goods should be postponed. Production should center around only those items necessary for immediate shipment or absolutely necessary to generate work for existing personnel. Leroy attributed the money crunch to an excessive amount of in-house inventory.

EL SALVADOR

In the spring of 1977, Mr. Taylor and Leroy flew to El Salvador to participate in an international showing and demonstration of agricultural products. An assortment of the Taylor line was displayed at this exhibit. International marketing agents and sales representatives, as well as agricultural officials from over forty countries, were present to inspect and purchase farming implements.

At this showing an informal agreement was established between the Sanger Marketing Corporation and Taylor Farm Equipment Company. The Sanger Company was to market the Taylor line of products in foreign countries. This company was acknowledged as a leader in international marketing circles.

As a result of this showing and association with Sanger, orders slowly began being received from overseas countries: $35,000.00 from Jordan; $47,000.00 from Israel; and $52,000.00 from Spain. Sanger further informed Mr. Taylor that several other foreign officials were impressed with the planter, and that overseas sales could quite shortly accelerate.

PLANS FOR THE FUTURE

In early summer of 1977, Leroy rented a motel conference room for what was to be the company's first formal planning session. Harry, Jay, Tim, Dave, and

Leroy spent a day mapping out future needs and projections. Anticipated sales and production projections were discussed at length. It was the consensus of those attending that sales could be expected to increase considerably in the future, although perhaps not at the rate they had in the past four years. Some of the more important recommendations were:

1. an additional 50 percent more production space to include warehouse capacity should be rented within the next six months;
2. an additional 50 percent minimum increase in hourly workers would be necessary by next year;
3. a greater emphasis should be placed on cost-efficiency.

THE BLOW

In late summer of 1977 Lloyd and Leroy made their annual trip to Brisco's headquarters to meet with the marketing department to get an estimate of projected sales to Brisco's retailers for the next year. Lloyd and Leroy returned to Exter a very surprised and disappointed pair. Brisco had decided to drop Taylor Farm Equipment Company in the coming year as their prime supplier of planters in favor of Seon Company. The reasons given for discontinuing the Taylor-Brisco arrangement were rather nebulous, although pricing was mentioned by the Brisco executives. As an act of conciliation, Brisco did say that Taylor could expect to receive orders for discs, plows, harrows, etc., and even a few planters. Brisco implied that the arrangement with Seon might not be a permanent one and that things could change in the future.

EXHIBIT 3   Selected farm machines and equipment-shipments: 1960 to 1976 (in millions of dollars. Excludes tractors and irrigation systems.)

Product	1960	1965	1970	1972	1974	1975	1976
Total	$1,001	1,432	1,553	1,981	3,637	4,179	4,481
Farm machines and equip. (complete units)	798	1,169	1,271	1,616	3,042	3,485	3,726
Attachments and parts	203	263	282	365	595	693	755
Complete units, attachments, and parts: Plows	61	96	76	99	182	250	267
Harrows, rollers, pulverizers, stalk cutters	86	133	153	189	395	476	478
Planting, seeding, and fertilizing equip.	98	140	161	197	354	480	517
Cultivators, weeders, sprayers, dusters	96	122	115	138	302	383	383
Harvesting and haying machinery	464	651	631	834	1,501	1,735	1,944
Machinery for preparing crops for market	38	59	85	111	255	262	234

EXHIBIT 3 (continued)

Product	1960	1965	1970	1972	1974	1975	1976
Farm poultry equip.	29	45	73	63	76	70	100
Farm dairy machines and equip.	20	31	42	61	80	68	77
Hog and other barn equip.	44	67	114	135	213	175	220
Farm elevators and blowers	28	37	35	52	92	100	88
Farm wagons and other transport equip.	37	51	69	104	186	179	173

SOURCE: U.S. Bureau of the Census, Current Industrial Reports, series MA-35A.

EXHIBIT 4 General farm machinery and equipment statistics by employment size, 1972

	Establish-ments	Capital expenditures (millions)	End of year inventories (millions)
Total establishments	1,547	$115.8	$640.1
Establishments with an average of:			
1 to 4 employees	551	1.1	.6
5 to 9 employees	216	1.4	.9
10 to 19 employees	217	7.1	.9
20 to 49 employees	266	6.1	4.1
50 to 99 employees	141	7.5	13.0
100 to 249 employees	101	11.7	31.9
250 to 499 employees	21	5.4	38.6
500 to 999 employees	12	13.1	116.1
1,000 to 2,499 employees	15	10.7	207.3
2,500 employees or more	7	51.5	226.6

SOURCE: Census of Manufacturing, 1972.

EXHIBIT 5 General statistics of planting, seeding, and fertilizing machinery, 1972.

	Establish-ments (number)	Value added by manufacturer (millions)	Cost of materials (millions)	Value of shipments (millions)	Capital expenditures (millions)
Planting, seeding, and fertilizing machinery establishments	50	$149.7	$107.0	$209.9	$3.3
Establishments with 75% or more specialization	28	20.1	22.8	42.4	.8

SOURCE: Census of Manufacturing, 1972.

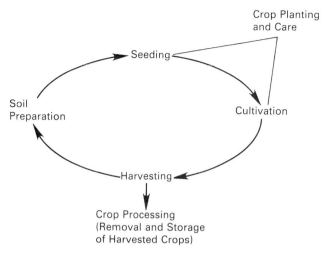

EXHIBIT 6 Agricultural crop cycle

EXHIBIT 7 Soil preparation equipment

Equipment type	Purpose/function	Advantages
Land leveler	Fills low spots; planes off humps	Uniform irrigation
Rod weeder	Kills weeds and mulches soil surface	Conserves soil moisture
Self-loading scrapper	Terraces hilly fields	Conserves topsoil
Subsoiler	Breaks up soil to depths of 3 feet or more	Permits roots/water to penetrate dense soils
Moldboard plow	Inverts slices of soil up to 10 inches thick	
Chisel plow	Loosens soil to greater depth	Treats soils prone to wind/water erosion
Tandem disk harrow	Further breaks up soil processed by moldboard plow	
Rotary tiller	Breaks up soil; shreds and mixes crop residue	Combines in one operation plow and harrow functions
Middlebuster	Prepares alternating trenches and ridges	Plant in low rainfall—crops in trenches; high rainfall—crops in ridges
Spike tooth harrow, spring tooth harrow	Breaks up soil into fine pieces	Final step before planting
Soil pulverizer	Same as above	Same as above

EXHIBIT 8 Seeding and planting equipment

Equipment type	Crop/material/function
Fertilizer spreader	Dry bullk, liquid manure, ammonia gas, combination solid and liquid spreaders
Grain drill planter	Wheat, barley, rye, oats
Row crop planter	Soybeans, edible beans, sorghum
Lister planter	Cotton, corn in low-rainfall areas
Vegetable seed planter	Vegetable crops
Rotary hoe	Soil cultivation
Sprinklers, stationary or traveling	Irrigation
Insecticide sprayer	Insecticide application

EXHIBIT 9 Crop-harvesting equipment

Equipment type	Crop	Function/ application
Cotton picker	Cotton	
Self-propelled grain combine	Soybeans, wheat, oats, barley, rye, or seed crops	Cuts crop; threshes and separates grain from straw
Self-propelled combine (with corn head attachment)	Corn	Husks and shells corn
Windrower	Seed crops; hay	Cuts and gathers crop into windrow* before being processed by combine
Baler	Hay	Makes rectangular or round bales
Stack maker	Hay	Picks up loose hay; compresses into 6-ton stacks
Harvester	Sugar beets, sugar cane	
Combine	Peanuts	
Picker	Sweet corn (human consumption)	

*A windrow is a long, fluffy horizontal column of hay.

EXHIBIT 10   Crop-processing equipment

Equipment type	Crop function	Advantage/ function
Forage harvester	Finely chops already cut hay and corn	Initial preparation for conversion into silage (animal feed)
Forage blower	Moves chopped forage into 100-foot high silos	
Crop dryer	Heats air forced through grain	Inhibits growth of mold
Tub grinder	Coarsely grinds loose hay	Livestock will eat more and waste less
Chain-and-flight elevator	Baled hay and ear corn	Places these into storage units
Grinder-mixer	Grinds and mixes hay and grain	Farmer can custom mix blends of hay and grain
Cooker	Cooks soybeans	Grinds and heats soybeans for conversion into animal feed
Roller mill	Mills feed grains	Cracks and reduces grain to small particles
Stalk shredder	Converts bulky leftover stalks and stems to small pieces	Leftovers plowed under and mixed with soil as natural fertilizer

EXHIBIT 11   Equipment on U.S. farms (thousands of units)

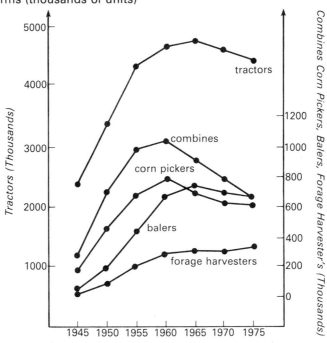

Year

SOURCE: U.S. Department of Agriculture, Bureau of Census (Census of Manufactures).

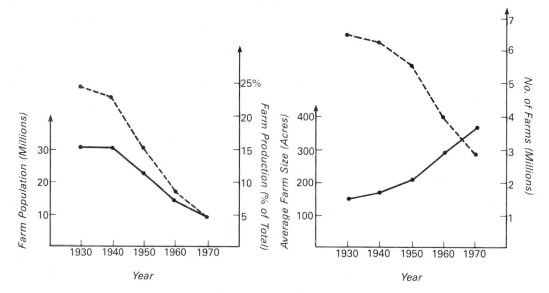

EXHIBIT 12   Farm population demographics (United States)

SOURCE: Department of Agriculture; Department of Commerce.

EXHIBIT 13   Farm income/farm
equipment expenditures*

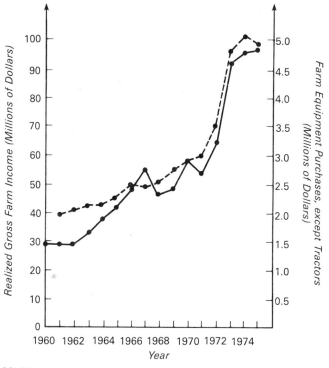

SOURCE: Department of Agriculture; Department of Commerce.

*The dotted curve, farm equipment expenditures, approximates an in-
dustry product life cycle. The decrease in 1975 is not conclusive;
these figures are revised after initial publication.

EXHIBIT 14 World tractor markets

Area	1975 000 Units	%	1980 (est.) 000 Units	%	1985 (est.) 000 Units	%
North America	189	26	170	22	165	19
Latin America	100	14	160	20	235	27
Europe	287	39	250	32	230	26
Rest of world*	152	21	200	26	250	28
Total	728	100	780	100	880	100

*Excludes Japan, under 30 HP, and Eastern Bloc countries.

SOURCE: *Annual Report, 1975*, Massey-Ferguson.

EXHIBIT 15 U.S. tractor unit sales (nearest thousand)

1970	136,000
1971	132,000
1972	157,000
1973	197,000
1974	174,000
1975	161,000

SOURCE: *Iron Age*, May 9, 1977.

Morton Salt

George Tate strolled down Michigan Avenue on a warm spring afternoon in Chicago. He had spent the entire morning with Morton Salt's advertising agency, reviewing the company's past promotions and discussing possible plans for the upcoming fiscal year, which would begin on July first. As he walked, he pondered the problems facing the company, particularly with regard to table salt, traditionally Morton Salt's major product.

WHEN IT RAINS, IT POURS

In the early part of the 20th Century, consumers bought salt in brown paper bags, which had been put up by a grocer from bulk salt he had purchased in barrels. The salt business was keenly competitive, and no firm had been able to gain significant consumer demand or a price advantage. Morton's product was exactly like that of its competition.

If Morton Salt could be differentiated in some way, however, it could improve consumer demand, and thus improve profit margins. By 1920, it developed an innovative way to keep salt from caking or hardening from moisture, and introduced a moisture-proof, two pound cylindrical package with an aluminum spout for easier pouring. With these improvements, Morton embarked upon a modest advertising program, utilizing primarily women's

---

This case was made possible by the cooperation of the Morton Salt Company and the author of the original Morton Salt case, Dr. Nugent Wedding. It was prepared by Nancy Stephens and Richard F. Beltramini, Assistant Professors of Marketing at Arizona State University, as a basis for class discussion rather than to illustrate either effective or ineffective handling of an administrative situation. Comments, views or conclusions stated herein are not to be construed as those of the Morton Salt Company, and the case authors are solely responsible for content.

Morton, the Umbrella Girl design, When it rains it pours, Morton Lite Salt, Sugar Cure, Tender Quick, Nature's Seasons and Dough-It-Yourself are registered trademarks of Morton-Norwich Products, Inc.

Distributed by the Intercollegiate Case Clearing House, Soldiers Field, Boston, Mass. 02163. All rights reserved to the contributors. Printed in the U.S.A.

magazines. "When It Rains, It Pours" was adopted as a slogan for the advertisement, and was also printed on the package.

The idea of branding and advertising was a new one in the salt market, but it seemed to work, as Morton's sales and market share grew. With this increased degree of control over consumer demand, Morton began to gradually increase prices until its packaged salt sold for double that of any competitor (10¢ per package, compared to 5¢ for unbranded bags).

NO SALT SALTS LIKE MORTON SALT SALTS

Since Morton's product and package improvements were unprotected by patents, competitors were quick to imitate. As a result, some consumer resistance to the price differential began to affect Morton Salt sales. At this point, therefore, Morton needed another innovation.

Because of its leadership in the salt industry, Morton was approached by health authorities and medical organizations who had discovered that an insufficient amount of iodine in the body was a cause of goiter (an enlargement of the thyroid gland, often visible as a swelling in the lower part of the front of the neck). Since salt was a universally used food product, these authorities suggested that Morton take the lead in adding iodine to their salt, in a ratio of 1 part iodine to 5,000 parts salt, for goiter prevention.

Iodized salt was introduced in the early 1920s with advertising support, and by 1926 Morton's iodized salt was outselling plain salt. It was able to continue its market leadership and brand preference for many years, maintaining a premium price.

However, in the early 1960s Morton saw its sales and market share slipping again as competitors had matched product innovations, and had engaged in price-cutting tactics. In addition, consumer lifestyles had changed to produce a declining demand for salt. More people were eating away from home, and more prepared, presalted foods were being consumed at home.

Morton expanded its advertising to focus on the 30–40 age group (then found to consume 75 percent of all salt sold), and reemphasized the company's early innovations in the salt market. Magazines, television, and radio carried the message "No Salt Salts Like Morton Salt Salts" to this target audience. In 1968 Morton was able to enjoy the largest market share of any year in the decade.

THE NEXT BEST THING TO THE REAL THING

By the late 1960s, Morton had also expanded its product offerings beyond table salt. Company divisions had been established to produce prepared foods, chemicals, and agricultural goods, partially as a result of the 1969 merger with Norwich Pharmacal Company.

Further growth depended upon properly defining the firm's business position. As consumers had changed, Morton was no longer just in the "salt business;" it was in the "seasonings business."

In 1970, after extensive product and market research, Morton introduced a new consumer product, Salt Substitute. Morton Salt Substitute was initially available in two varieties, regular and seasoned. It was composed of potassium chloride, and had already been in limited use by people on medically supervised, low sodium diets.

The introduction of Salt Substitute as a consumer product was supported by a $242,000 advertising campaign which emphasized taste rather than the product's medical uses. "The Next Best Thing to the Real Thing" was chosen as the slogan, and appeared in magazine and newspaper advertisements. Further, a 10¢-off coupon was featured to stimulate trial purchase of the innovative product. By the end of the decade, Morton's sales achieved higher levels than all other salt brands combined.

MORTON, THE SALT YOU'VE BEEN PASSING FOR GENERATIONS

The decade of the 1970s brought increasing attention and concern among Americans about the potential relationship between the use of salt and certain diseases. Medical researchers observed that when certain patients suffering from hypertension or high blood pressure were fed a diet severely restricted in sodium, their blood pressure decreased. Few researchers were willing to state categorically that sodium *caused* hypertension, but some troubling questions were posed.

Several years later, the U.S. Senate Select Committee on Nutrition and Human Needs responded to concerns about salt usage by including it in a set of Dietary Goals for the United States. One of the stated goals was that salt consumption be reduced to approximately five grams per day from the average of ten or twelve grams normally ingested. Such a goal might be achieved, some suggested, by eliminating most highly salted processed foods and condiments, and by eliminating salt added at the table.

Health concerns about salt intake did not escape Morton management, and in 1973 (well ahead of the U.S. Senate Committee recommendations) Morton Lite Salt was introduced to consumers. Lite Salt was the first iodized salt mixture with the taste of regular salt, but with only half the sodium. Unlike Salt Substitute which was not positioned directly against regular salt, Lite Salt was expected to cannibalize Morton's regular salt to some extent. This was not a major concern to Morton management, however, since Lite was seen as "the salt of the future."[1] A $1 million advertising campaign, largely in television, accompanied the roll-out of Lite Salt.

During the 1970s Morton tested several other new seasoning products including Butter Buds, Sugar Cure, Tender Quick, and Nature's Seasons.

---

[1]"Morton Lite ties into 'RD' special insert." *Advertising Age,* October 29, 1973.

Some of these products were reasonably successful and remained on the market, while others were withdrawn due to insufficient sales.

To supplement Morton's fluctuating advertising budgets during this period (see Exhibits 1, 2, and 3), several sales promotion programs were employed. The first attempt was a set of four porcelain mugs offered for $2 plus a spout seal from a 26-ounce table salt package. Each mug featured a different Morton girl from the four periods of the company's history.

In 1975, another sales promotion program was developed to provide additional uses for salt. Morton introduced salt sculpture (a mixture of flour, water, and salt) for holiday decorations. Film strips were offered to elementary schools, and a ten minute film was sent to television stations, explaining salt sculpture. Print advertising in women's magazines offered Morton's "Dough It Yourself" Handbook for $1.

The promotions for salt sculpture ran during the Christmas season, and were continued during Easter and July Fourth for two years. By 1977, company executives estimated that 700,000 "Dough It Yourself" Handbooks had been sold, and distribution was expanded to craft stores as well.

Despite a series of successful consumer and trade promotions, 26-ounce table salt could not sustain the company. "It's a strong cash producer," commented Morton's president in 1977, "but not a growth market."[2] At the same time, management recognized that table salt could not be abandoned completely, for, although it represented only 5 percent of tonnage sales, it produced at least 35 percent of dollar sales.

Therefore, it was decided in 1977 to continue the sales promotion for Morton 26-ounce table salt. To capitalize on Americans' increased interest in geneology, Morton sponsored a "Visit the Land of Your Ancestors" Sweepstakes. Also featured were mailed kits which contained recipes from the homelands of Americans of current and past generations. The sweepstakes was tied in with the advertising theme, "Morton, the salt you've been passing for generations." Morton table salt maintained its number one position among table salts in 1977 with an all-time high market share.

A third promotion (in addition to the salt sculpture and sweepstakes promotions) was begun in 1978. Special salt packages with labels from four past container designs (1914, 1921, 1933, and 1941) were featured in retail stores. Consumers were urged through media advertising to collect the entire "Keepsake Collection." These innovations in sales promotion were another solution to the perennial problem of maintaining brand preference for a parity product.

SUMMARY

As George Tate opened his office door, marked Director of Communications, he realized that some important decisions now faced Morton Salt. Salt Substitute and Lite Salt were leading the market in their respective product cate-

---

[2]"Morton pours more ad dollars into image-building bid." *Advertising Age,* August 8, 1977.

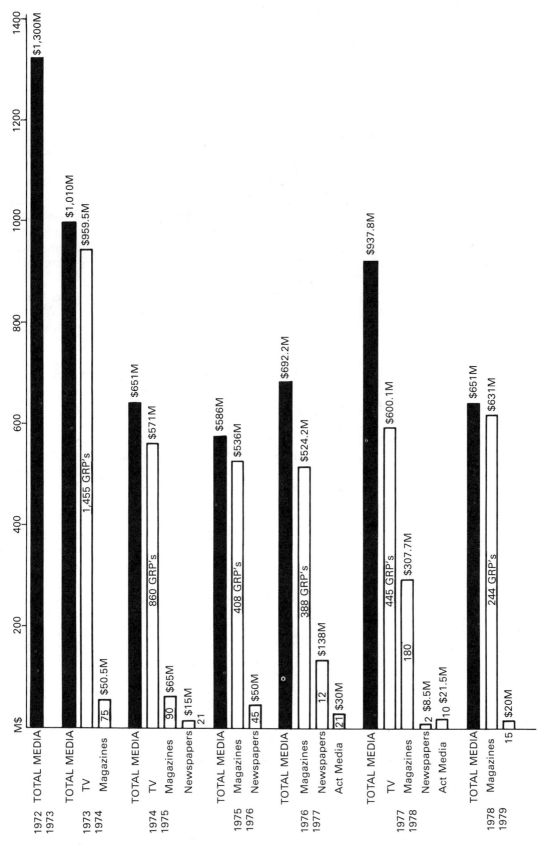

EXHIBIT 1 Blue package media history

474

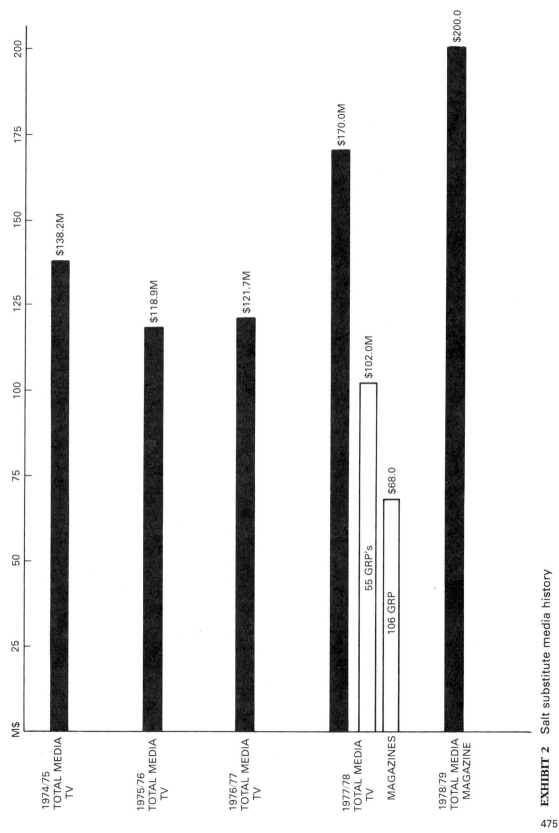

M$

200 — $200.0

175 — $170.0M

150 —

125 — $138.2M $121.7M

100 — $118.9M $102.0M

75 —

68.0

50 —

25 —

1974/75	1975/76	1976/77	1977/78	1978/79
TOTAL MEDIA	TOTAL MEDIA	TOTAL MEDIA	TOTAL MEDIA	TOTAL MEDIA
TV	TV	TV	TV	MAGAZINE
			MAGAZINES	
			55 GRP's	
			106 GRP	

EXHIBIT 2 Salt substitute media history

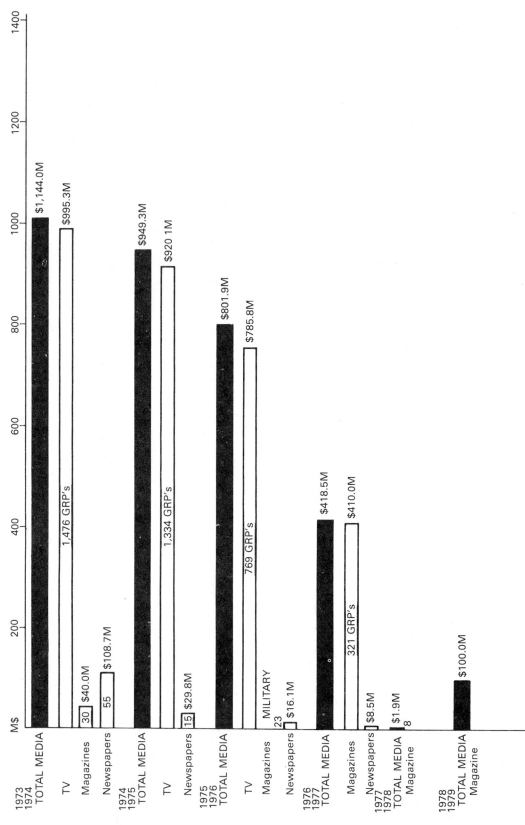

EXHIBIT 3 Lite Salt media history

gories, and Nature's Seasons was growing in sales as well. Regular table salt seemed to be doing well as a result of the sales promotions, although the medical concerns of the 1970s were not expected to fade.

It seemed to Tate that innovations in product development, in packaging, and in sales promotion had always solved past problems. However, he was now concerned with an advertising innovation as a remedy.

QUESTIONS

1. What was the future of Morton's regular table salt—the product upon which the company was founded, and to which it owed much of its success?
2. Could consumer sales be sustained through advertising, and if so, how much should be budgeted in which media?
3. Was it wise to continue special offers, sweepstakes, and similar sales promotions?

Peter Piper Pizza

"Thanks for coming over," waves the familiar, rotund pizza cook on Phoenix late-night television, "to Peter Piper Pizza." That same jocular pizza cook is in reality Anthony Cavolo, the company's chairman, who in just four years has expanded his pizza empire from one to five locations in the Phoenix metropolitan area, and is in the process of franchising several others.

This case was prepared by Richard F. Beltramini and Nancy J. Stephens, Assistant Professors of Marketing at Arizona State University, as a basis for class discussion rather than to illustrate either effective or ineffective handling of an administrative situation.

Cavolo began in the restaurant business in New York, where he operated a delicatessen for several years. He later added tables and chairs, and a take-out service selling buckets of spaghetti, until the business grew to an Italian steak and pasta restaurant. Upon retirement, Cavolo moved to the Phoenix area, but eventually became bored and decided to open his own pizza restaurant after sampling the pizza there.

"I was fifty years old when I got here, and I had no intention of starting a whole brand new career, but that's the way it worked out," reminisced Cavolo. "We looked around and did some research, nothing formal of course, and we saw the opportunity in the fast-food business." Apparently he was right, as the first location alone sold over 200,000 pizzas last year, and Steve Herrgesell, Peter Piper Pizza's president and Cavolo's son-in-law, forecasts, "This year's sales are expected to top $3 million."

MARKETING BACKGROUND INFORMATION

In recent years, Americans have spent about 30 percent of their food dollars in restaurants, and about 70 percent in grocery stores. Fast-food restaurants account for about 25 percent of the restaurant sales, according to a recent survey, and the estimated total dollar amount of sales for this category was $20.4 billion in 1978.

Among the top fast-food restaurants in the United States, only one is a pizza chain (see Exhibit 1). The broader product category of Italian food commanded approximately a 4 percent share of market in 1976 (see Exhibit 2). In total, there are an estimated 15,000 pizza outlets across the country (7,500 chain-related and 7,500 independents).

According to industry experts, fast food will continue to be a rapidly growing sector of the economy. It is pointed out, however, that large, better-financed companies will continue to gain market share to the detriment of smaller, regional companies.

Why do people eat out? The reason given most often by respondents in this survey was "for a change of routine," closely followed by "it's easier than cooking." These two explanations were given by nine out of ten people in the survey.

Consumers in the survey also had some opinions about fast-food restaurants. For example, when asked to compare the cost of eating in a fast food restaurant to the cost of eating at home, a third believed it costs more, a third believed it costs less, and a third believed it costs about the same. Respondents were also asked to compare the nutritional value of food eaten in a fast-food restaurant to food eaten at home. Almost 70 percent believed that food eaten in a fast-food restaurant is less nutritious, while 21 percent believed that fast food and home food are about the same. Only 3 percent felt that fast food is more nutritious. Other attitudes found in the survey are shown in Exhibit 3.

EXHIBIT 1 Top 25 fast-food restaurants, sales and market share by company

Rank	Company	Sales 1976 (000)	Sales 1975 (000)	Market '76	Share '75
1	McDonald's	$2,730,000	$2,256,000	19.6	18.4
2	Kentucky Fried Chicken	1,165,000	999,000	8.4	8.1
3	Burger King	741,600	614,200	5.3	5.0
4	Internat'l Dairy Queen	620,000	620,000	4.5	5.1
5	Pizza Hut	374,200	270,700	2.7	2.2
6	Howard Johnson's	358,000	355,000	2.6	2.9
7	Sambo's Restaurants	348,443	263,170	2.5	2.1
8	Hardee's	324,304	297,900	2.3	2.4
9	Jack-In-The-Box	323,400	274,550	2.3	2.2
10	Burger Chef	305,000	285,000	2.2	2.3
11	Denny's	303,520	243,375	2.2	2.0
12	A & W International	289,000	271,000	2.1	2.2
13	Bonanza International	275,224*	222,600*	2.0	1.8
14	Ponderosa	242,859*	128,693*	1.7	1.0
15	Arby's International	208,900	153,560	1.5	1.3
16	Dunkin' Donuts	205,350	187,714	1.5	1.5
17	Church's Fried Chicken Inc.	194,445	156,075	1.4	1.3
18	Wendy's	187,000	74,463	1.3	0.6
19	Red Lobster	181,000	114,000	1.3	0.9
20	Internat'l House of Pancakes	180,000	139,402	1.3	1.1
21	Long John Silver	156,300	81,700	1.1	0.7
22	Friendly Ice Cream	154,000	122,000	1.1	1.0
23	Shoney's Big Boy	141,279	121,301	1.0	1.0
24	Morrison's Cafeterias	129,000	96,000	0.9	0.8
25	Sizzler	120,800	96,200	0.9	0.8
TOTAL		$10,258,624	$8,443,603	78.2	77.5

*Includes international sales

SOURCE: Maxwell Associates, 1977.

EXHIBIT 2 Sales by product group

Product Group	Number of Firms	Sales 1976	Sales 1975	Percent Total Industry '76	'75
1. Hamburger	17	$5,239,058	$4,385,337	37.7	35.7
2. Full menu	46	2,721,058	2,318,365	19.6	18.8
3. Chicken	5	1,469,150	1,254,004	10.6	10.2
4. Ice cream	3	794,000	760,000	5.7	6.2
5. Steak	12	984,715	741,226	7.1	6.0
6. Italian	4	532,615	402,900	3.8	3.3
7. Donuts	3	289,966	261,138	2.1	2.1
8. Mexican	6	200,270	153,320	1.4	1.2
9. Seafood	5	459,000	284,500	3.3	2.3
10. Other types	8	434,106	341,020	3.1	2.8
TOTAL	109	$13,123,938	$10,901,810	94.4	88.6

SOURCE: Maxwell Associates, 1977.

EXHIBIT 3   Attitudes toward fast-food restaurants

1. Children would rather eat at a fast-food restaurant than eat a meal cooked at home.	agree	79%
	disagree	11%
2. Children often decide which fast-food restaurant the family will go to.	agree	78%
	disagree	12%
3. People eat at fast-food restaurants like McDonald's so they don't have to bother planning and cooking a meal.	agree	77%
	disagree	13%
4. When we decide to go to a fast-food restaurant, it's usually a spur-of-the-moment decision.	agree	77%
	disagree	13%

SOURCE: A.C. Nielson Company, 1979.

Another study by the Newspaper Advertising Bureau indicated that 93 percent of the population over the age of twelve has patronized a fast-food restaurant within the past six months. During this period, they have visited an average of 3.4 different chains.

THE PHOENIX PIZZA MARKET

Competition. Cavolo looks at his business as "a real David and Goliath situation" in reference to the large number of chain pizza restaurants in Phoenix. Village Inn (25 outlets), Pizza Hut (31 outlets), Pizza Inn (10 outlets), Godfather's Pizza (6 outlets), Round Table Pizza (5 outlets), Straw Hat Pizza (6 outlets), Mr. Gatti's (2 outlets), and Noble Roman Pizza (4 outlets) each have restaurants in the Phoenix market. In addition, there are a number of "ma and pa stores" which Cavolo regards as less threatening competitively. "We're more concerned with our unique image being imitated," he stated, adding that his pizza ingredients were of better quality than those used in chains.

Promotion. The Phoenix market is gimmick-oriented. Almost all restaurants utilize coupons and "deals" offering less expensive second pizzas, beer, and plastic pitchers. Cavolo, too, tested half-price deals, but quickly learned that half of his business began coming from coupon sales. He quit "trying to be all things to all people," and today Peter Piper Pizza uses no such promotions as those outlined in Exhibit 4.

Cavolo explains, "Those other places all show the cheese and they say look at all the stuff we put on it. They all have the same message—ours is the best, ours is the best. We don't say ours is the best. We say you come in. You tell us if you like it."

EXHIBIT 4 Competitors' promotions

Competitor	Promotion
Restaurant "A"	$2.00 off any large pizza or $1.00 off any medium pizza
Restaurant "B"	Buy one pizza at regular price, and get the next smaller size for $.99.
Restaurant "C"	Buy any size pizza at regular price, and get another pizza of the same size and value free.
Restaurant "D"	$3.00 off any large pizza, $2.00 off any medium pizza, and $1.00 off any small pizza.
Restaurant "E"	Buy any large pizza and pitcher of soft drinks, and receive a plastic pitcher free which will be refilled free for the next year.
Restaurant "F"	Buy any pizza at regular price and receive a free pitcher of soft drinks.
Restaurant "G"	$1.00 off any large pizza

Price. According to Cavolo, it is difficult to compete with the advertising of chains, who often do over $240,000 a year in business in just one location. His no-frills product is priced about 40 percent lower than the competition, with the most expensive item at $4.50. Only pizza is served, along with beer, wine, and soda in an effort to reduce expenses. He explains, "We don't have sandwiches, we don't have spaghetti—which adds to the cost of doing business because you have to add more help."

ADVERTISING APPROACH

Budget. Peter Piper Pizza started spending approximately $7,000 in advertising during its first year in operation in Phoenix. This amount grew rapidly to $75,000 in 1979, and is anticipated to top $150,000 in 1980 (see Exhibit 5). Cavolo's "spend as much as you can afford on advertising" budgeting approach has usually run at about 5 percent of sales, but at one point approached nearly 10 percent. This is substantially more than the average fast-food restaurant, which normally budgets approximately 2 percent of sales for advertising.

Media. After experimenting with several advertising agencies, Cavolo decided to move all work in-house, "Agencies write copy that's just not me." No radio is currently being utilized, some newspaper, but the largest portion of his advertising budget is devoted to television, written and produced in-house. This approach seems consistent with some of the nationally successful pizza chains (see Exhibit 6).

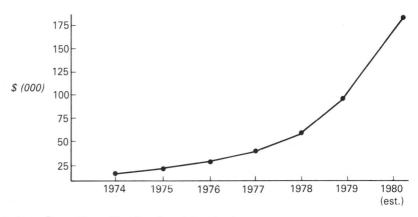

EXHIBIT 5   Peter Piper Pizza's advertising budget

EXHIBIT 6   Pizza leaders' advertising budgets (000)

Media	Pizza Hut	Shakey's
Network television	$6,504.6	$ —
Spot television	2,534.3	2,126.1
Network radio	—	—
Spot radio	580.3	7.7
Magazines	—	—
National newspapers	—	—
Outdoor	21.1	9.0
TOTAL	$9,640.3	$2,142.8

SOURCE: *Media Decisions;* December, 1978.

Production. "Television commercials are expensive. Even a cheap one could cost you $5,000 to produce. We make ours for an average of $150," notes Cavolo. An hour of studio time often yields Peter Piper Pizza as many as three commercials, in contrast to the approximate $50,000 needed per spot by national chain restaurants.

Creative. Cutting expenses is the primary objective of Cavolo, a man who arrives at work at 7:00 A.M. to call New York "before the rates go up." Cavolo spends up to a day on each 30-second spot, writing and editing them. This pizza cook approach is simple and straightforward—quality pizza at economy prices (see Exhibit 7).

Media. Peter Piper Pizza's advertising is placed by the in-house group, and the 15 percent discount obtained from the television stations (newspapers locally will not discount their rates) goes toward stretching the budget even further. The television spots are run in flights—heavy advertising for a three to four week period, then reduced to almost nothing, and back again every third

EXHIBIT 7   Sample Peter Piper Pizza television spot

Advertisement #1

Did you know that at Peter Piper Pizza you can buy a large cheese pizza for $2.75, a large sausage, mushroom, pepperoni or any single item pizza for $3.50 and that $4.25 is the most expensive pizza on our menu. That's about half of what you'd pay elsewhere. These are our regular prices—no coupons, no gimmicks, no Tuesday night specials, just good pizza at low, low prices every day of the week, so come on over to Peter Piper Pizza.

Advertisement #2

You tell me you missed the Tuesday night special at your local pizza parlor, you tell me you don't have a pizza coupon and funds are low, well cheer up friend, come on over to Peter Piper Pizza. A large cheese pizza is only $2.75, a large sausage, mushroom, pepperoni or any large single item pizza is $3.50. A large Peter Piper Special with the works is $4.25 and that's the most expensive pizza on our menu. Remember, no coupons, no gimmicks, just good pizza at low, low prices, so come on over to Peter Piper Pizza.

month. Cavolo explains, "We feel it's better to buy advertising in bunches because you get more notice that way." His perception of the seasonal pattern of his business closely parallels that of national fast-food restaurants (see Exhibit 8).

Effectiveness. The believability of his advertising is a mystery to Cavolo who admits, "We don't know what makes it work. Is it me? Am I that much of a personality?" Although never formally trained in advertising, he appreciates its role, and is receptive to innovative techniques for communicating his unique recipe for combining quality ingredients, a matter-of-fact personality, and a limited line of inexpensive products.

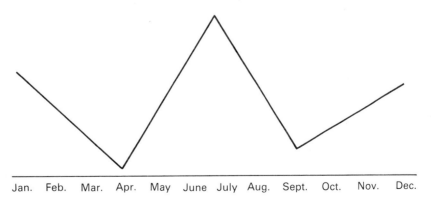

Jan.   Feb.   Mar.   Apr.   May   June   July   Aug.   Sept.   Oct.   Nov.   Dec.

EXHIBIT 8   Seasonality of pizza business

SUMMARY

Cavolo summarizes his approach, "We don't play it up because a lot of people think they're not going to get much for $2.95. A lot of people think cheap is cheap. People see it on TV and they think what are you going to get for $3.00? People tell us we ought to charge more for it, but please don't.

The 10 percent annual inflation of ingredients has caused Peter Piper Pizza to raise prices from $1.70 to $2.95, in the case of a large cheese pizza, in the last four years. Cavolo's decision to maintain high quality ingredients remains, however, despite the current $1.50 per pound price of mozzarella cheese—the biggest and most expensive single ingredient.

Cavolo's "get something good and sell it for less" philosophy has been reasonably successful thus far, but he is concerned about what the future holds. The escalating costs of products and media have shrunk his profit margins. The cost of capital has limited expansion, although franchising seems to be a potential growth avenue. Competition continues to grow, and Cavolo's unique personal approach may begin losing its believability.

Cavolo and Herrgesell have decided to review their plans for the upcoming year's marketing communications program. In particular they are concerned about the appropriateness of their budget size, their media mix, and especially Cavolo's creative approach.

QUESTIONS

1. Develop a creative strategy for Peter Piper Pizza.
2. What changes, if any, would you recommend in its current market communications program?

Anderson Distributors, Inc.

Anderson Distributors Inc. was a Phoenix Corporation which wholesaled a full line of dry groceries. The line included 12,000 items and was sold primarily to independent food retailers in Arizona and parts of Southern California. Stocks were held in three warehouses scattered throughout the territory. The company had prospered since it was formed thirty years earlier by three brothers who had earlier managed a successful small chain of three retail stores. Sales were made by forty-five salespeople who operated out of eight district offices. In brief, the sales organization consisted of the following:

45 Salespeople

8 District Managers

2 Regional Managers

Sales Vice President

Salesperson compensation ranged from $280 to $370 a week, district managers from $380 to $450. Anderson operated as a voluntary cooperative. That is, the member retailers agreed to concentrate the bulk of their purchases with Anderson in return for quantity discounts, a standard, simplified ordering system, special merchandising and promotional programs, and a convenient delivery system by Anderson trucks. All retailers in the system were allowed to use the co-op logo "Best Stores." In 1980, Anderson had over 3000 affiliated retailers, most of whom did concentrate their dry grocery purchases.

As was true with any extensive field sales organization, Anderson experienced most of the routine field management problems concerning salesperson evaluation, compensation, and supervision. A handful of these problems has been summarized in the following pages.

Reprinted from *Stanford Business Cases 1980* with permission of the publishers, Stanford University Graduate School of Business, © 1980 by the Board of Trustees of the Leland Stanford Junior University.

EVALUATING SALESMEN

District managers were required to make quarterly and annual evaluations of their salespeople. Clark Philbin had been a district manager for one month when he received a memo from Dan Pace, his regional manager, stating that all current quarterly evaluations were due in three weeks. The memo concerned Clark because he felt that he could not honestly evaluate his sales force after such a short time in his new position. He had had no management training or experience in evaluating people except for the infrequent occasions when his previous boss had asked him to take over a sales meeting.

Clark knew that he could accept the recommendations of the former district manager in writing his first quarterly evaluations, but there were several which he considered questionable. He could not easily identify specific reasons for his disagreement, but felt strongly nonetheless. Not wanting to make any serious mistakes, he decided to talk with his regional manager about evaluation techniques and standards before making any recommendations:

Pace: Well, Clark, what's on your mind?

Philbin: Dan, I'm worried about this rating business. I've never evaluated anyone for anything before, and rather than make some real blunder, I wanted to ask you if you could offer me any guides or ground rules to follow?

Pace: Well, you've really picked a good question. What's bothering you now has been, and still is, a problem for most managers. As far as I know, there is no effective form or rating chart for evaluating people. This is something you just have to pick up from experience.

Philbin: Yes, Dan, but this is quite a responsibility and I'm afraid of making some big mistakes during the learning process.

Pace: True, Clark, but it's hard for me to be specific. It's something all managers go through. You learn by doing, and basically have to develop your own standards. What I find acceptable performance, you might question. There's a lot of "feel" to it.

Philbin: O.K., Dan. I'll do the best I can. I have one question, though— this business of looking for people with management potential rather than sales potential. I don't understand why there should be so much emphasis on management. Aren't good salespersons just as important to the company as potential managers? After all, the business is becoming so competitive that we have to have top caliber salespeople. Today most of the buyers are pretty sophisticated and the old-fashioned drummer has no place anymore. We need people who can read income statements and talk in terms of profits and other customer benefits.

Pace: I agree with you on the last part, Clark, and I guess the argument can be made that the best salespeople under these new conditions have to be more like managers. And if we continue to grow there will always be room for the best young managers. Good luck with your evaluations!

After returning to his office, Clark began to think over the interview. He realized that experience was undoubtedly a good, if not the best, teacher but he still felt that some effective evaluation technique would be helpful. He decided to try one other approach. He called an old boss, Kelly O'Brien, and asked him for his opinion on the problem. Kelly indicated that he would be glad to help. He said that the same problem had bothered him when he first became a district manager. Consequently, he had attempted to quantify some of the criteria commonly used in determining a person's management and sales potential. He had drawn up a rough chart which was divided into two separate areas of recognition: one for people with management potential and one for those with sales potential. The chart had proven useful to him and he offered it to Clark to use in making his evaluations (see Exhibit 1). Clark, of course, wasn't sure if he could separate the requirements for selling and management, nor was he even sure if an "attribute" approach was reasonable.

EXHIBIT 1 Evaluation of sales & management potential

Management	Points	Sales	Points
1. Judgment	25–35	1. Aggressiveness	20–25
2. Maturity	15–25	2. Enthusiasm	25–30
3. Aggressiveness	15–20	3. Adaptability	25–35
4. Enthusiasm	20–30	4. Planning (sales calls)	30–40
5. Adaptability	20–30	5. Initiative	20–25
6. Planning		6. Dependability	25–30
(organizing ability)	20–25	7. Promptness	15–18
7. Creativity	15–25		160–203
8. Dependability	10–15		
9. Report Writing	10–15	1. Making quota	48–62
10. Motivating	10–15	2. Reports (clean, concise and factual)	8–12
11. Controlling	10–15	3. Servicing accounts	14–18
	170–250	4. New account generation	15–25
		5. Calls/day (quarter beds)	6–10
		6. Appearance	12–14
		7. Care of company property	10–12
			113–153

Rating Scale:	70	80	90	100
	poor	fair	good	excellent

RECOMMENDING SALARY INCREASES

After Clark had finished making his evaluations, he reviewed the salary levels of the salespeople in his territory. He noticed that one man, Larry Gilbert, had been recommended for an increase six weeks earlier by the former manager. Since Clark had just completed his own evaluation of this man, he was interested in seeing how Gilbert had been rated over the years. Gilbert's file showed that he had been with Anderson as a salesman for 12 years but had only progressed to the middle of the current salary range. He had not been granted a salary increase for 22 months, although most salesmen received increases every ten to twelve months. The recommendation written by the former district manager stated, "Larry is continually trying to improve, and some progress is noted every so often. He hasn't had an increase for over a year and a half and should be considered for one soon."

In his own evaluation Clark had ranked Gilbert as one of his poorest salespersons—one who had little or no probability of improving and who should possibly be terminated. Clark realized that he had only worked with Larry for a short time, and felt he should take a second look at Gilbert. However, he felt strongly about his own evaluation in this case and was absolutely against recommending a raise. Although the increase had already been submitted by the former district manager, Clark did not know whether it had been reviewed by the regional manager yet. Clark thought to himself how difficult it would be to give someone an increase and then fire him/her a month later.

AWARDING SALARY INCREASES

The regional manager approved the salary increases that Clark had recommended for his sales staff. Awarding an increase was generally considered fairly routine, but Clark could remember well how, as a young salesman, he had reacted to the way his supervisors had awarded increases to him. Once, his local manager called him long distance and said, "Next week your pay check will be $10 larger. . . ." Before Clark had a chance to say a word his manager had hung up. On another occasion with a different manager, both he and his wife were taken out to dinner by the district manager on the day he had received his raise.

Clark felt that the way in which increases were awarded could make a significant difference in a person's future performance. Moreover, he believed that one should be told why he/she was receiving the raise. However, he was undecided about two things: whether it was a good idea to involve the family in company business by including the spouse; and whether one would be motivated to a greater degree if salary increases were constantly promised.

COMPENSATION POLICY

Anderson's policy was to give fairly quick salary increases (perhaps six to nine months apart) up to the median of the salary range. It was more difficult to earn a salary increase over the median; generally, a person did not receive a raise for ten months or more, depending on his/her efficiency and potential for promotion.

In April, Clark Philbin recommended a salary increase for one of his salesmen, Al Peters. Peters was making $325 per week and had not had a raise in three years. He had been a salesman with the company for about fourteen years. Clark wrote the following as a basis for the salary increase: "Peters has demonstrated consistent up-grading of accounts and increased sales to key accounts and has shown marked improvement in establishing better relations with his customers." Philbin indicated that, after working closely with Peters, he was convinced an increase was warranted. He believed that salary administration was a serious responsibility and that increases should be recommended only when merited by performance.

The regional manager, Dan Pace, thought that Peters was about average. Due to the lapse of time since the last salary increase, however, he approved recommendation and passed it along to the sales vice president for final approval.

The vice president knew that Al Peters had not had an increase for over 18 months, but from past experience he had also considered Peters an average performer. He believed, however, that Clark Philbin was very conscientious about awarding salary increases solely on a merit basis rather than time elapsed since the last raise.

The incident brought a matter to the vice president's mind which he had been pondering for some time. He wondered whether senior salespeople should be given automatic salary increases (other than cost of living increases) or whether (in line with company policy) increases should be awarded strictly on a merit basis. In the case of Philbin's recommendation on behalf of Al Peters, the vice president was not convinced that Peters deserved a merit increase. Possibly this was a case in which a salesperson should be considered for an automatic annual increase. In either event Ken was reluctant to turn down the application since it had been passed by the regional manager and district manager, both of whom he considered very capable. Moreover, these people knew Peters and his capabilities far better than he did because of their closer association with him.

BONUS INCENTIVE PLAN

Clark Philbin was concerned about unrest exhibited by his sales force. He attributed it to the company's newly-instituted bonus incentive plan.

Formerly, Anderson had an individual incentive plan based on each man or woman's sales volume over and above his or her quota. Each person was directly responsible for attaining the individual quota assigned. The percentage by which a salesperson surpassed that quota was applied to his or her base salary for that period, as a bonus.

The new bonus incentive plan was based on the performance of the group rather than the individual. Each district was a team which consisted of the district manager and the salespeople. At the end of a quarter, the district bonus was computed on the basis of combined sales over quotas, and the quota was set so that it would be almost impossible to meet the total requirements unless each team member contributed his/her share. Consequently, if one territory fell short due to a weak salesperson, the whole district could lose its chance for a bonus. It was expected that any staff member would be willing to help out those who were falling behind.

Each individual's share under the new system was based on a "stated percentage" of his/her salary for the preceding quarter (see Exhibit 2). This percentage was determined by the amount by which the district exceeded its budget.

Philbin questioned whether the new plan was better or worse than the old one, and in order to evaluate the two plans he wondered how he could get honest opinions from the sales force. Clark decided that a good way to find out what was troubling everyone was to have a post-sales meeting "gripe" session. He had tried this once before and it had yielded favorable results. The salespeople were asked to participate by writing down any complaints they might have and by bringing them to the "gripe" session. At a previous session Clark had assured them that anything they said would be confidential, and that the point of the meeting was to improve understanding between management and the sales force. Because confidences had been maintained in the past, Clark hoped that the meeting might be beneficial.

At the meeting the following opinions were expressed:

Salesperson 1: Clark, this new incentive plan has killed individual effort. Not only is the weakest person boosted up in each territory, but also one weak territory is helped by stronger or harder working ones. . . .

EXHIBIT 2   Computation table—quarterly incentive

Quarterly Invoiced Sales vs. Total Budget	% Gross Salary* at End of Quarter
I. 100.0 to 105	7%
II. 106 to 110	8%
III. 110 to 115	9%
IV. 115 to beyond	10%

*Weekly Salary Rate x 13.

Salesperson 2:   Yes, and that brings up something else. I don't mean to offend you (turning to a new man), but under this system you guys get the same share of the bonus as we old timers do. I know that we all had to start from scratch and I'm not objecting to that. But, and I think everyone will agree, a new man just isn't worth as much to the company as an older man in terms of actual sales volume. Under the old system a guy really got paid for what he was worth. Any extra effort was rewarded by extra pay.

Salesperson 3:   You bet. This place is becoming a loafer's paradise!

Salesperson 4:   You guys have a point on this "individual effort business," but I still think the team effort idea is good. Everyone works together for the benefit of all. We're all interested in how we do as a district.

Salesperson 2:   Sure, that's fine if everyone works together but how do we know that some guy can't improve his performance?

Salesperson 4:   Well, I'm sure we all want the extra cash flow, as much as we did before under the old system, so I think everyone will work just as hard if not harder.

Clark Philbin began to wonder if the new system really was better than the old one. Just as the meeting was breaking up one of the men approached Clark.

Salesperson 5:   Clark, one of our men puts in about a four day week but still makes quota. There's something strange about this system if things like that can go on.

Philbin: Well, I think we all know that these things can happen in any territory—even in this one—but they happened under the old incentive plan, too. Suppose we have two salesmen. One is a plugger, putting in a ten- to twelve-hour day and barely making quota each time. The other is a whiz-kid. Works six to seven hours a day, four days a week, but is way over quota each time. Now under these conditions is the second person getting away with anything if the quotas are fairly set? Under the new system that person is really helping the other.

Salesperson 5:   Well, I just can't see a guy or gal working only four days a week when everyone else is working five. Somehow it's different when someone overworks—sort of makes a healthy competitive environment.

Philbin: Yes, but don't you resent someone who is *always* putting in extra time trying to get ahead, especially if he or she is barely making quota?

Salesperson 5:   No, as I said, I think it makes a healthier working environment.

Clark Philbin was very interested in this discussion because he felt that the issues were causing the unrest in the sales force. There was not much he could do about the new incentive plan, but he felt he should do something to correct the situation concerning the short work week.

COMPENSATING MANAGERS

The Sales Training department of Anderson was reviewing its current hiring policy for college graduates and MBA's. In the past few years the company had been hiring more and more well-educated people. There was, however, a problem which involved paying these people the salary required to attract them to Anderson. For example, those hired for the product management group were first sent to the field as sales trainees, and in order to get top caliber people, it was necessary to pay them more than the salesperson scale.

One MBA, for example, was hired recently by the Product and Research department and was assigned to the field as a salesman for five months as the first phase of his training. His initial salary was well above the maximum that could be earned by a salesperson. Thus, he had been told by the head office not to discuss his salary with anyone, not even his district manager. All went well for about three weeks until, through the grapevine, the others found out that the new hire was earning more than any of them.

The Sales Training department was stumped as far as future hiring and salary ranges were concerned. They realized that they had to continue to pay high salaries in order to get top caliber people, but on the other hand, it was risky to continue to antagonize the sales force.

INTERNAL CORPORATE POLITICS

The sales vice president was due to visit Clark Philbin after spending a few days with Dan Pace at the regional office. Clark was uneasy about the forthcoming visit because he had heard a number of unpleasant rumors about the vice president from his regional manager. Clark thought highly of Dan, but he felt that it had been poor practice on Dan's part to have passed the rumors down. Clark believed that no matter how well deserved, remarks such as these should not be transmitted to lower levels in the organization.

The vice president's visit went smoothly except for two incidents. The first concerned Andy Smith, a salesman, whom Clark considered an "average to good" performer. The salesman had recently grown a long handlebar mustache and the vice president commented to Philbin, "Clark, why don't you tell Andy to shave off that damn thing, or at least bring it back to normal size. It's so out of keeping with what our customers are used to."

The second incident concerned a saleswoman, Lee Beckwith. The vice president had previously met Lee at a sales meeting shortly after Lee was hired and had been very impressed with her after this brief contact. Now, after spending a few more hours with Lee, he commented to Clark, "That certainly is an outstanding girl; if she receives the proper training she'll make a good manager."

After the vice president had left, Clark pondered what had been said. In recalling the mustache situation he remembered that his regional manager once had expressed a concern about the vice president interfering in the evaluation of his staff. The promotion record showed that, over the years, many of the vice president's favorites had followed him up the corporate ladder.

With these points in mind, Clark wondered what he should do about Andy and Lee. In the recent evaluations he had recommended Andy both for a salary increase and for a possible promotion. On the other hand, he had characterized Lee as an opportunist with not too much potential for sales or management. Clark felt that Pace was a "fair-shooter" and would back him up, but the fact that the vice president had the final say in approving all recommendations could negate Dan's influence.

CHARACTERISTICS OF A GOOD SALES MANAGER

After attending a management training seminar at a nearby university, Dan Pace returned to his office with several ideas in mind for improving the performance of his districts. First, he decided to examine the characteristics of his managers in order to determine what qualities were important.

He summarized his conclusions as follows:

Clark Philbin: Clark is very systematic in his approach to evaluating his staff. He carefully weighs all the important factors which contribute to a person's potential and actual sales ability. So far Clark's recommendations for promotions and increases have been granted exactly as requested. He is neither consistently high nor low in his raise pattern: rather he awards increases as he feels they are due. If someone is worth $40/week raise, then it is requested. Similarly for a $10/week raise. Clark keeps running files on all of his people, so there are few, if any, last minute or "impulse" decisions on a man or woman's value. Clark once commented, "After a framework is outlined, a manager should be permitted to operate autonomously within it." He motivates his staff largely through recognition of jobs well done. On a person's anniversary with the company or on a birthday, he always sends out a card. Also, if someone makes a single outstanding contribution, such as getting a large new account, then in addition to counting it toward a raise or promotion, Clark may take that person out to dinner, give a "pat on the back," or send a letter of commendation.

Jack Steelman: It seems that Jack is always sending in a raise request for one of his staff. He seldom changes the amount; it is always a minimum amount. A number of Jack's raise requests have been turned down because they seem like automatic increases. In many cases the people haven't actually earned them. Jack, however, is a very aggressive guy and an excellent salesman, as well as a good manager. He was once asked whether there was much variance in the quality of his sales force and he commented: "No, they are all great guys and gals who work hard and deserve to be paid well." Jack is sometimes referred to as the "Little King." He tries to maintain self respect and to motivate salespeople by always doing things for them such as recommending raises. On the other hand, he usually keeps all but the most general information quite private. This makes his position appear to have a little more prestige.

Ozzie Davidson: Ozzie is sort of impulsive in the way he awards increases and promotions. On several occasions good salespeople have gone without raises for over a year even though their quality evaluation forms showed excellent progress. In each case, however, when Ozzie worked with someone just before an evaluation, something happened which, in Ozzie's eyes, ruined the person's chances for an increase. He apparently is fairly well liked by his staff and is always promising one of them a raise or promotion. This was often done before the increase was sent in for approval. In several instances this method of motivation caused difficulty when raises were not sanctioned by senior supervisors.

Jerry Hatch: Jerry does not believe in using pats on the back for jobs well done or any other type of non-financial recognition. He thinks that the dollar reward is sufficient, and if his people produce, they get paid for it; or if they don't, they get fired. Jerry has always worked hard himself and is very fond of a dollar. He also feels that actual performance is the best measure of whether or not a person deserves an increase or promotion.

In reviewing his findings, Dan Pace found it difficult to decide which techniques or characteristics peculiar to each manager contributed the most to success in the job. He was not thinking solely in terms of an Anderson manager but more of a sales manager in general.

The Goldman Chemical Company

"A substantial growth in sales and a shift in market strength from the Northeast to the South and Southwest have knocked our sales territories completely out of line," said Bill King, sales manager of the Goldman Chemical Company. "The morale of the sales force is low," he continued, "because some of the salespeople feel that the present territories don't afford an equal opportunity to earn commissions."

THE COMPANY

Goldman Chemical was a wholesale chemical house supplying specialized chemicals to paper processors throughout the country. The several thousand potential users of the company's products ranged in size from small operators to giants such as International Paper and Crown Zellerbach. Competition was intense, with sales going to the firms offering the best combination of quality, service, and price.

The company's sales increased significantly between the years 1976 and 1979. A continuation of this trend was expected in 1980, although there was some concern about general economic conditions. The company started in the East and extended operations westward after 1960. Twenty-four states were serviced in 1979.

THE SALE

The typical Goldman customer purchased $17,000 in chemicals yearly, although the range was from $50 to over $120,000. Some sales were contracted but most were solicited directly by the company's ten-man sales force. About 70 percent of the Goldman line consisted of standard items for which purchasing agents made the final buying decision. The remaining

Reprinted from *Stanford Business Cases 1980* with permission of the publishers, Stanford University Graduate School of Business, © 1980 by the Board of Trustees of the Leland Stanford Junior University.

items were specialized "brand" products and required the approval of production personnel. The chemical companies, in 1979, faced a buyers' market; thus the demands for service were heavy. A purchasing agent from one of the larger paper firms recently said to a Goldman salesman, "We might as well get one thing straight. You know as well as I do that your competitors can meet you in price and quality, so if you want our business we had better see some real service."

Salespeople, during their calls, checked the performance of products sold previously, followed up delivery promises, and sought to introduce the customer to new uses for existing products as well as to new products. Goldman salespeople were expected to have a chemical engineering background because of the technical orientation of their customers.

Salesmen/women averaged five calls daily in metropolitan centers and four in non-metropolitan areas. Typically they spent four days in each week on metropolitan calls. Accounts were classified by purchases as A, B, or C: the limits for A accounts being "over $50,000;" for B accounts, "between $10,000 and $50,000;" and for C accounts, "below $10,000." A accounts were called on weekly, B accounts monthly, and C accounts quarterly. About 10 percent of a salesperson's time was devoted to "service call-backs."

THE SALESMEN

The Goldman Company employed ten salesmen/women ranging in experience from six months to twenty-five years. Mr. King was generally satisfied with his sales force and thought them technically qualified to sell the full line.

Each salesperson had a monthly drawing account of between $1,000 and $1,200. "This," said Mr. King, "is justification for the missionary work that they are required to do." Above the draw, compensation was by straight commission. Commission rates varied with the profitability of products and, according to the sales manager, there was no apparent tendency for salespeople to overlook the full-line in favor of higher-margin items. "The nature of our selling is such," said Mr. King, "that the salesperson first has to establish him/herself with the account. Once this is done, full-line selling is no problem."

Mr. King was convinced that differences in compensation (see Exhibit 1) arose from the distribution of territories rather than the individual abilities of the salespeople. Of this he said, "I would expect some variations in commissions earned, but not to the extent we've experienced. I don't see that much difference among the members of our sales force."

Mr. King gave the following appraisal of his ten salespeople:

Phil Haney is our "old timer," having been with us since 1955. He is one year from our mandatory retirement age of 65 and he likes to remind people of his twenty-odd years of seniority. He hasn't been particularly easy for me to work with. Phil has strong personal ideas about selling, many of which are "academically" outdated but are apparently accepted by his customers. He

EXHIBIT 1 Performance of salespeople, 1978–1979[1]

Salesman	Territory	Terr. #	Sales Record[2] 1978	Sales Record[2] 1979[1]	No. of Accounts Metro	Non-Metro	Total	Compensation	Cost % to Sales 1979[1]	Planned Sales 1980[2]	Planned Accounts 1970	Est. Share of Market 1969[1]	1970	Selling Cost % to Planned Sales
Ives	Me., N.H., Ver.	1	not covered under present territory arrangement							$ 82	7	—	26.0%	
	Mass.		$ 972	$ 816	54	13	67			648	54	24.0%	18.6	
	R.I.		240	160	13	—	13			82	7	39.7	49.6	
	Conn.		240	240	13	7	20			160	13	21.2	19.9	
	Total terr.		$ 1,452	$ 1,216	80	20	100	$ 25,200	2.1%	$ 972	81	23.2	19.9	2.6%
Gordon	N.Y. State	2	488	408	27	7	34	13,200	3.2	324	27	50.2	50.3	4.1
Haney	Manhattan	3	4,054	3,888	162	—	162	37,200	0.96	3,408	142	18.7	18.6	1.1
Richards	Other N.Y. City & L.I.	4	1,452	1,608	61	7	68	28,800	1.8	1,784	74	25.3	25.2	1.6
Whalen	New Jersey	5	324	406	27	7	34			488	40	10.6	16.5	
	Pennsylvania		2,592	2,424	88	13	101			2,112	88	18.2	17.0	
	Total terr.		$ 2,916	$ 2,830	115	20	135	$ 30,000	1.1	$ 2,600	128	16.9	17.0	1.2
Ericson	Del., Md., Wash., D.C.	6	not covered under present territory arrangement							160	13	—	20.0	
	Va., W.Va.		240	324	13	13	26			324	27	19.9	16.2	
	N. Carolina		240	324	20	7	27			408	34	16.5	16.3	
	S. Carolina		82	160	7	7	14			324	27	11.0	16.5	
	Georgia		240	240	7	13	20			240	20	18.5	14.9	
	Florida		160	324	27	0	27			408	34	20.2	16.1	
	Total terr.		$ 962	$ 1,372	74	40	114	$ 20,400	1.5	$ 1,864	155	16.3	16.4	1.1
Davey	Mississippi	7	82	160	7	7	14			160	13	16.7	16.6	
	Alabama		240	324	13	13	26			324	27	18.3	18.3	
	Kty. & Tenn.		—	82	7	—	7			82	7	16.5	16.5	
	Total terr.		$ 322	$ 566	27	20	47	$ 16,800	3.0	$ 566	47	17.4	17.4	3.0
Owens	Ohio & Ind.	8	not covered under present territory arrangement							160	13	—	14.1	
	Illinois		$ 1,534	$ 1,370	51	7	58			1,214	51	16.2	16.2	
	Michigan		564	564	40	7	47			480	40	15.1	15.1	
	Wisconsin		not covered under present territory arrangement							82	7	—	16.6	

EXHIBIT 1 (continued)

		Total terr.												
		Total terr.	$ 2,098	$ 1,934	91	14	105	$ 27,600	1.4	$ 1,936	111	15.1	15.7	1.4
Billings	9	Minn., Iowa, N.Dak, S.Dak, Nebraska	not covered under present territory arrangement							240	20	—	18.6	
		Missouri	160	564	40	7	47			730	61	11.4	15.1	
		Kansas	—	82	7	—	7			160	13	8.3	16.6	
		Ark., La., Okla.	not covered under present territory arrangement							160	13	—	16.7	
		Texas	160	324	20	7	27			816	67	6.6	14.6	
		Total terr.	$ 320	$ 970	67	14	81	$ 18,000	1.9	$ 2,106	174	7.9	15.5	.85
Sharp	10	Mont., Wyo., Idaho	not covered under present territory arrangement							240	20	—	18.7	
		Utah, Col., Az., N.M.	not covered under present territory arrangement								20	—	18.7	
		Wash., Ore.	$ 160	$ 240	7	13	20			324	27	18.9	16.6	
		California	564	648	38	7	45			816	67	11.3	14.3	
		Nevada	not covered under present territory arrangement									—	—	
		Total terr.	$ 724	$ 888	45	20	65	$ 18,000	2.0	$ 1,380	114	15.2	15.4	1.3
		GRAND TOTAL - United States	$14,788	$15,680	749	162	911	$235,200	1.5	$16,940	1,053	16.6	17.8	1.4

[1]Projected
[2]000's omitted

498

has what you might call an old-time personality and has been tremendously successful over the years. I often wonder what kind of volume could be generated by combining Phil's personality with some of our new merchandising techniques. Phil has always worked Manhattan, although initially he sold to all of New York City.

Mary Whalen is in her sixth year with the company and sells to accounts in the New Jersey-Pennsylvania area. Whalen is an excellent saleswoman who is obviously aware of the "smoothness" of her sales approach. She carries this self-assurance to the extent that she often becomes very indifferent whenever I offer a few suggestions for improvement in her sales techniques.

Norman Ives is probably the most ambitious, aggressive, and argumentative salesman we have. He has been with the company since 1966 following his discharge from the Army. He reached the rank of Lt. Colonel at the age of 30 but had no interest in a military career. Norman really stormed into his present territory in 1969 and, in the first year, doubled its volume. He's extremely independent but will work hard to implement any sales program that he agrees with. If he doesn't agree, though, I get absolutely no cooperation. In 1976, Norman's territory began to slip—primarily, I think, because of a shift in market strength. Moreover, his compensation fell from $30,000 in 1976 to $25,000 in 1979.

Bob Ericson has been with the company three years now and I still get the feeling that he is unsure of himself. He seems somewhat confused and over-worked, probably because he's trying to serve too many accounts in too large an area. Surprisingly enough, though, the general growth in the territory has given Bob a significant increase in sales in 1979.

Dick Richards is the "mystery man" of the sales force. Neither the other salespeople nor I know very much about Dick's personal life. He's quiet and unassuming and knows the Goldman line amazingly well. I've often wondered why Dick chose sales over research work. Sales in his territory have continued to grow, which is unusual considering an opposite trend in neighboring territories.

Warren Sharp is the guy on the sales force who keeps the rest of us going. Warren is slightly rotund and always good-natured. His accounts seem genuinely happy to see him when he makes a call. He worked the New York State territory for his first two years and then moved into the West Coast when we took on Joe Gordon. At first I worried about Warren's ability to get serious long enough to make a sale. However, this has not proved to be a problem.

Gus Billings joined the company in 1973 after four years with a competitor. Gus is easygoing, eventempered, and very popular with his customers. Despite his even temperament, Gus was somewhat upset the last time I saw him. We plan to activate five more states in his territory during 1980. This would make Gus responsible for a geographic area covering roughly one fourth of the United States. He is already calling on eighty-one accounts in six states, and this keeps him away from home much of the time.

Barbara Owens joined us in 1975 after receiving an M.S. degree in Chemistry from the University of Pennsylvania. After the normal three-month training program, during which time Barbara travelled with Mary Whalen, she stepped into her territory and was immediately successful. Barbara is earnest and conscientious, and has increased her sales volume each year. She's not what you would call the "sales type" but she is always exceedingly successful in using the merchandising techniques that I try to implement.

Joe Gordon is the youngster of our sales force at twenty-three. Joe went into New York State in the spring of 1978. The territory is relatively inactive and we usually try to assign it to new salespeople. Sales have dropped from the time that Joe took over and he is very apologetic about the situation. I've told him that he would have to expect some tough moments and I think his determination to "make a go of it" will be realized because of his conscientiousness. He's always receptive to any help that is offered and tries hard to put suggestions to use. That territory has always been a "dog."

Jim Davey is in his third year and I'd say he's good at selling. Jim always dresses impeccably in ivy league fashion and he has good bearing. He responds well to any suggestion that I make to him. It's a funny thing, but whenever I travel with Jim the sales in the territory increase for the next several months. After that, right back to the previous level. Accounts within the territory are scattered, which keeps Jim on the road most of the time.

Aside from the morale problem, Bill King had other reasons for wanting to change the territories. "We expect continued growth," he said, "and at least for the time being I plan to add no new people. I'm positive that by redistributing the sales territories we can get more sales effort from the sales force as a group and thus handle our growth."

EXHIBIT 2 Number of customers by $ volume for the year 1979

Salesperson	0 to 1,999	2,000 to 4,499	4,500 to 9,999	10,000 to 19,999	20,000 to 29,999	30,000 to 49,999	50,000 to 99,999	100,000 to 199,999	TOTAL
Ives	32	30	15	10	5	5	2	1	100
Gordon	10	5	4	12	1	2	—	—	34
Haney	26	30	20	31	22	20	10	3	162
Richards	9	3	13	15	15	8	4	—	67
Whalen	16	40	30	10	10	21	6	2	135
Ericson	34	32	21	8	8	7	4	—	114
Davey	14	10	6	7	9	—	1	—	47
Owens	33	11	19	13	15	9	3	2	105
Billings	30	6	13	14	16	2	—	—	81
Sharp	10	12	24	8	10	—	—	1	65
Total	214	179	165	128	111	74	30	9	910
$ Volume totals (000)	256	730	1,488	2,304	3,328	3,552	2,700	1,620	15,978
Cumulative $ total (000)		986	2,474	4,778	8,106	11,658	14,358	15,978	
cumulative % $ volume	1.6	6.2	15.5	29.9	50.7	73.0	89.8	100	
Cumulative % accounts	23.5	43.2	61.3	75.4	87.6	95.7	99.0	100	

Golden Bear Distributors

John Gray, president of Golden Bear Distributors (GBD), had been pleased with his company's performance, but felt that the lack of an extensive training program for his salesmen might be a limiting factor in the company's growth plans. Thus, in November 1979, Gray hired a San Francisco consulting firm to study the GBD salesforce and to outline a sales training program. Specifically, he wanted the consultants to define the training that would be best for his salesmen, to indicate the material which should be covered, and to recommend how it should be presented.

BACKGROUND

Golden Bear distributed several nationally advertised brands of electrical home appliances as well as a line of home entertainment equipment through more than 200 dealers in California. The product lines included stereos, automatic washers and dryers, vacuum cleaners, air conditioners, television sets, radios, ranges, refrigerators, garbage disposals, dishwashers, mixers, toasters, and complete kitchen installations.

GBD's sales organization included four product sales managers who reported to a general sales manager. (See Exhibit 1.) Each product sales manager was assigned to three or four of the company's lines and was held responsible for sales and profits.

The sales force consisted of twenty-five salesmen supervised collectively by the product sales managers. Each salesman was assigned a specific geographic territory made up of approximately 4 percent of the total Retail Distribution Index of GBD's trading area.[1] Each time a new man was hired, he was assigned a territory equal in potential to the other twenty-four salesmen.

This case was prepared by Professor Robert T. Davis, Stanford University, Graduate School of Business.

Reprinted from *Stanford Business Cases 1980* with permission of the publishers, Stanford University Graduate School of Business, © 1980 by the Board of Trustees of the Leland Stanford Junior University.

[1]Taken from *The Survey of Buying Power*

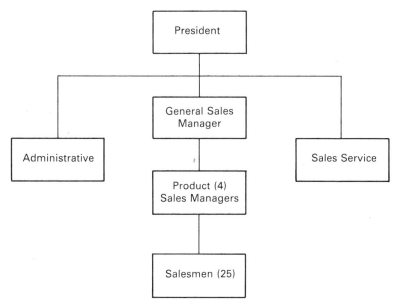

EXHIBIT 1 Organizational chart

There was little *formal* sales training. Whenever a new man was hired, the product sales managers took turns "going the rounds" with him to acquaint him with his territory and to introduce him to his customers. Each salesman sold all of the products in the company's line; if his sales fell off in one product area, that product sales manager usually discussed at regular biweekly meetings any problems the salesman had encountered.

Each salesman could draw a salary of $250 a week against commissions. Since the average commission rate was 2½ percent, each salesman had to sell $520,000 of merchandise per year in order to cover his draw. Net annual commissions for the different salesmen varied between $15,000 and $25,000. All selling expenses were paid out of the salesmen's gross, although several salesmen received a mileage allowance when extensive travel was required.

The salesmen filled out detailed weekly route sheets describing all planned activities for the following week. In addition, they made out a daily call report which they mailed in to the home office at the end of each work day.

GBD's 200 outlets consisted primarily of small, independent merchants who accounted for perhaps one-third of the area's total volume. The other two-thirds was represented by discounters and mass merchandising chains who typically dealt directly with the suppliers, or bought through large buying groups. Although the discounters continued to grow, their increased share of the market was beginning to slow. The independents were presumably starting to offer a service alternative, as well as more aggressive pricing, which appealed to certain segments of the population. Price cutting, nonetheless, remained a serious problem for the independents.

MR. MURPHY'S INTERVIEWS

The consulting firm assigned the GBD account to one of its top young men, Kelvin Murphy. Murphy had received an MBA from a leading western business school in 1975 and upon graduation had taken a job with a large industrial equipment manufacturer. He left his sales management job there four years later to join the consultant.

Shortly after John Gray's initial discussion with the consultants, Murphy contacted GBD's general sales manager, Lynn Philips, at the home office in Oakland. After getting some background data on the sales organization, Murphy asked Lynn for his views on sales training at GBD. He responded:

> As far as I'm concerned, the training job has to be two-fold; retail salesmen need training just as much as distributor salesmen. Right now we have a policy whereby we invite dealer personnel to our home office in small groups for meetings to demonstrate and discuss all of the appliances that we carry. On the other hand, as I mentioned earlier, our salesmen's only on-the-job training is by the product sales managers. Such limited training probably isn't sufficient, but I'm not sure what kind of training they do need. That's what I expect *you* to tell *me* after you spend some time with them.

Lynn Philips then arranged for Murphy to "make the rounds" with several of the GBD's salesmen. Murphy first met Bob Boatwright who serviced part of Monterey County, south of San Francisco. Bob was thirty-one years old and had been with GBD over four years. His initial reaction to Murphy was, "I never hear from the office unless my sales are down"; but when Murphy explained that he was merely interested in learning how he sold as part of a general study on sales training, Bob talked more freely:

> You gotta learn to sell like a retailer sells. New salesmen oughta be given all kinds of product information, and the company should demonstrate the operation of our products to the new men.
>
> Next, you gotta follow up on the new men, so they tell their story to the retailer *every* time they go into a store. The idea is to get 'em to give the story to the retailer and his salesmen so many times that when a customer walks in the store and asks about a dishwasher, the retailer goes into the pitch on our machines automatically.
>
> According to the home office we're supposed to be "sales consultants" to the dealers, but I don't go for that much. I tried to help out a couple of small retailers once by showing 'em how I'd sell our product line, but they both thought I was tryin' to run their business. I think the best way is to bring the retail salesmen into the home office every once in a while and show 'em how to operate our equipment and explain it thoroughly—just like we do now. That's how to train 'em to sell.

Bob's first stop Friday afternoon was at Harry's TV and Radio Shop. Before he and Murphy went in, Bob explained his sales approach.

> I go in and say hello to the salesmen first because if there's any service problem with any of our stuff, they're sure to know about it. That way, the boss won't surprise me if something's gone wrong. Next, if I have a chance, I slip back into the stock room to see how many TV's they have left. This guy, Harry, sells TV's and

that's about all. Incidentally, most of my sales are on TV—I can't sell much white goods down in this area.

Well, after that, I usually check with the service manager to make certain that anything I've promised him in the last week or so has been taken care of. Then, of course, I tip my hat to the secretary, and ask to see the boss.

When Bob entered the store, he greeted the two retail salesmen, walked over to a quiet corner of the store, and conversed with one of the salesmen in low tones. Shortly thereafter, he went downstairs for about ten minutes. When he came back upstairs, he headed for a desk at the back and motioned for Murphy to follow. He greeted the service manager and introduced Murphy as his helper. The service manager was apparently mad at GBD and Bob in particular because Bob had promised him a replacement transmission for an automatic washing machine which had not yet been delivered. After Bob stated that he had relayed the information to GBD's service department a week or so ago, he phoned the GBD service manager and a short, heated argument ensued. When Bob finished the call, he informed Harry's service manager that he would have to "check further." Although Harry's service manager was not satisfied, Bob explained that he wanted to see Harry first and that he would talk with him later.

Bob then knocked on a door marked "Private" and motioned Murphy to follow. As they entered, a man on the telephone looked up and waved them to a seat. After he hung up, Bob introduced Murphy and proceeded to ask Harry if there was anything he wanted in the line of TV sets. Harry answered by questioning Bob about the automatic transmission. When Bob assured him that he was following it up, Harry stated, "That's O.K. for me, Bob."

Bob then began to explain a new window display GBD had designed for its dealers for the Christmas holidays. Harry turned down the display because "Panasonic pays me 100 bucks a year to put their line in the window during the first three weeks of December, so you can forget about that for me."

Bob glanced at his note pad and informed Harry that he needed to stock up on several models. Harry replied, "I'm O.K. for now, but I'll give you an order next week." After leaving Harry's office, Bob stopped by the service manager's desk and reviewed the transmission problem. Bob concluded by stating that he would check on the unit the following morning when he reported to the home office. He promised to call the service manager with a report.

As they left the store, Bob remarked, "Harry evidently wasn't in a buying mood today, but I'll definitely get an order from him next week." Since it was then nearly 4:30 P.M., Bob wanted to call it a day, but he offered to take Murphy to visit other stores on Monday if he wished.

The following week Murphy spent most of one day with Walt Warren. Walt was about forty years old and had sold for GBD about one-and-one-half years. He had left a comfortable job as a feed and seed wholesaler because a back injury prevented him from carrying and stacking the heavy bags of seed and grain. Walt had a large territory north of San Francisco, which covered a number of small towns. Murphy met Walt about 9:00 A.M. and they chatted over a cup of coffee before beginning their calls.

When Murphy explained that he was helping to do a study for GBD on methods of training salesmen, Walt evidently interpreted this to mean that he should talk about his job, for he started explaining his daily call routine. His suggested approach to the retailer was much the same as that voiced by Bob Boatwright.

Walt and Murphy first visited Anderson's Gas and Appliance Company, which sold butane and propane gases as well as a large line of home appliances. Walt quickly introduced Murphy to Mrs. Anderson, listened to a complaint about a scratched cabinet on a television set, and checked the company's inventory. After discussing with Mrs. Anderson the aggressive price cutting initiated by a local discounter, Walt took an order for four mixers. The call lasted about twenty minutes.

As they walked toward the second stop several blocks away, Walt stated, "I always try to get on a first-name basis with my retailers as soon as I can because it helps me establish rapport with them. Another thing about calling on a territory that you haven't visited in a week or so is to walk along the main street and window shop and see who's got what bargains displayed. That helps you get a 'feel' for the town. I also buy a local paper most every time I come into these little towns to see who's advertising what. I think that helps me get a feel for my competition, too."

The second call, which lasted about forty-five minutes, was at a large home service center. As soon as they entered the store, Walt introduced Murphy to Joe, the owner. The following conversation took place:

Walt: I see you're leasing a couple of our video recording systems, Joe. Great—that should help to boost your sales.

Joe: Yeah, that's true. But the reason I'm renting 'em is that I can't sell 'em. As long as the payments keep coming in, though, I should care.

Walt: Joe, portable radios and hi-fi's should be picking up pretty soon now—Christmas, you know. Over half of these sales should come in November and December.

Joe: What's good?

Walt: Everything, Joe.

Joe: (Looking at display) I've got some G.E.'s here, got 'em at a special price. But the last I sold was about three months ago.

(Walt began to talk about a new warranty program on the food mixer. Joe explained he was aware of it.)

Walt: Well, we do have a nice gift promotion on the mixers.

Joe: I don't need all that stuff. I've got plenty now.

Walt: We can send it to you prepaid you know, Joe, plus a 10 percent dating. These mixers will really go well. . .

Joe: I just don't need any.

Walt: Well, anything else? How about taking an ad in your local paper on the automatic washer. I've never seen your newspaper feature any of our products. What's the cost over there anyway?

Joe: $1.60 a line.

Walt: Well, of course, we'd split the cost fifty-fifty with you, Joe, on any ads you'd like to run.

Joe: Fifty-fifty?

Walt: Yep, on all the lines you run with our mats.

Joe: On everything?

Walt: That's right. Just send us the tear sheets.

Joe: Why don't you mail me some mats then? I can use 'em.

Walt: O.K. Now, how about those radios, Joe?

Joe: Send me a couple of those new brown FM sets—you know the ones I mean.

Walt: The FM-36B? Yeah, that's the popular one, Joe.

Joe: O.K. I'll see you next week.

Walt: Fine, Joe, see you.

As they left the store, Walt remarked, "Gee, sure looks like a good day. You know, the personal approach means everything in this business. I'm trying to build goodwill so that when I leave a store, those retailers will want to sell GBD because I'm a good guy. Now Joe there thinks that I'm a nice guy, so he tries to sell my line. Incidentally, the reaaon I pushed some advertising is that he's got to advertise if he wants to sell. These dealers often look upon advertising as a cost instead of an investment. Or they think the manufacturer should do it all.

The next stop was a new TV dealer. Walt had taken an order from the dealer for a new combination stereo TV and home recording system on the promise that it would be delivered in two days. Three days after taking the order, Walt had received a phone call from the dealer who stated that unless the set were delivered that very day, Walt was to cancel the order. Walt commented to Murphy, "I checked with our delivery people yesterday after I got the call, and they weren't sure the set would go out. If it isn't there now, I'll be in trouble with him. Seeing as how he's a new dealer, I don't want to rock the boat."

In the TV dealer's window was the system distributed by GBD. "Well," remarked Walt, "I guess it's safe to go in." As soon as they entered the store, a thin man greeted Walt with, "The set arrived just as I was closing last night." Walt explained some of the features of the set to the dealer, and gave him some literature on several other models. Then Walt inquired about what other sets the dealer was planning to install. The dealer replied that he wouldn't carry any others until he had sold this one. After a few more words, Walt and Murphy left the store. Several minutes later Walt remarked, "You know, bringing people around with you hurts your sales. . . but he's a tough dealer to sell, anyway."

Murphy and Walt then drove twenty miles to another town further north. During the trip, Walt talked about why he had left his wholesaling business and why he liked selling. When they arrived at the next stop, Walt explained, "I have to try to collect a check from the dealer, and report my results back to the home office by telephone." Since the man he wishes to see was not in, he made arrangements to call back later that afternoon.

During lunch at a small diner, Walt talked more about the seed and grain business. He also expressed a desire to obtain a territory closer to the city. After lunch, as they began walking toward the next call, they passed a newly-renovated hardware store. Walt paused, "This is a new store. I haven't got them for an account. It's just possible they haven't got a kitchen line. I think I'll go in cold and see what I can do." They entered the store and looked around for a clerk. A woman came out and Walt explained the purpose of his call, stating that his company had just started up with a new line of complete kitchen installations. When he mentioned the brand name, the woman remarked that the store carried that line, and added that she could show it to him. In a corner of the store, a complete kitchen was installed in a little room off the main part of the building. The woman explained that she and her husband had recently purchased the store, and were in the process of renovating it. Walt noted the fixtures that she had, and explained that on his next call he would supply her with some promotional material on the line. He also added that the distributor who formerly handled the line had gone out of business and that GBD would gladly provide them with the components from now on. The woman thanked him, and they left the store.

* * * *

After similar experiences traveling with three other salesmen, Kelvin Murphy felt that he had a good feeling for the GBD selling job and its requirements. Since two men were retiring soon from GBD's salesforce, John Gray was very anxious that Murphy complete his recommendations for a sales training program before new men had to be hired to take over the territories. Thus, Murphy began outlining a training program for GBD which would include recommendations for training dealer sales personnel as well as the firm's own salesmen.

QUESTIONS

1. What is the basic role of the distributors' salesmen in this situation?
2. What skills do these salesmen need?
3. What specific training program (coverage, subjects) do you recommend?
4. Elaborate upon one particular training subject in your program that you consider important: points to be covered, specific training technique to be used, measurement objectives, etc.

Exxon Company U.S.A.—Retail Automotive Stores

To 100 million American motorists, probably nothing is more familiar than the myriad red, white, and blue Exxon signs scattered across the country. Exxon Company, U.S.A., with over 23,000 service stations, sells more gasoline than any other company in the United States (See Exhibit 1). A superb marketer of its products, the company is continually analyzing the business environments and adapting to new situations in the retail marketplace. One example is the company's 1980 decision to eliminate its well-established Exxon Extra brand of gasoline from all of its service stations. It was replaced by a new brand, Exxon Extra Unleaded, more appropriate for newer model cars. Today the company is trying to maintain its competitive edge in the marketplace and build on the image it has created.

Exxon Company, U.S.A. is one of the four major divisions of Exxon Corporation; the other three are Exxon Middle East, Exxon International, and Exxon Chemical Company.

HISTORY OF EXXON CORPORATION

In gross revenue, Exxon Corporation is the number one oil company in the U.S., the number one American business, and larger than most countries in the world. With operations in over 100 countries, the mammoth corporation is the epitome of vertical integration: exploring for oil and gas on every continent and every ocean; leading the world in oil production with a yearly output of over 2 billion barrels of oil and natural gas liquids, and over 3 trillion cubic feet of natural gas; managing or having an interest in sixty-two refineries in thirty-three countries; owning or having a share in over 40,000 miles of crude and product pipeline; running the world's largest fleet with over 25 million tons of tankers and other ships owned or under long-term charter; and serving over 6 million customers every day at one of over 23,000 retail service stations. From the drilling rig to the service station pump, Exxon is involved in every phase of the oil business.

This case was prepared by Stephen W. McDaniel, Assistant Professor of Marketing, Texas A&M University, as a basis for class discussion rather than to illustrate either effective or ineffective marketing management.

EXHIBIT 1   Motor gasoline sales by major U.S. companies (January–November 1980)

	Sales Mil. Gals.	% Total U.S. Market	% Sales Change 1979–1980
Exxon	7,198	7.54	(7.7)
Shell	7,178	7.51	(3.3)
Amoco	7,008	7.34	(8.3)
Mobil	5,736	6.01	(2.0)
Texaco	5,682	5.95	(7.4)
Chevron	5,502	5.76	2.5
Gulf	5,138	5.38	(20.6)
Arco	3,737	3.91	(5.7)
Total top 8	47,179	49.40	(6.8)
Other integrated majors[1]	15,082	15.78	(8.8)
All others	33,256	34.82	(2.7)
Total U.S.	95,517	100.00	(5.8)

[1]DOE definition includes: Citgo, Conoco, Getty, Marathon, Phillips, Sun, Union

SOURCE: Exxon Company, U.S.A., *Pocket Data on Exxon and the Energy Industries,* May 1981, p. 31.

Exxon Corporation was founded in 1882 as Standard Oil Company of New Jersey. Headed by the illustrious John D. Rockefeller, the company quickly made its mark, although by some controversial means, as the premier oil company in the world. In 1911 the Supreme Court ruled that the company constituted a monopoly and was in violation of the Sherman Anti-Trust Law. As a result, the Rockefeller empire was broken up into thirty-three new and separate companies. Since the Standard name was so well known, eight of the resulting companies kept this in their corporate names: Standard Oil Company (California), Standard Oil Company (Indiana), Standard Oil Company (Kentucky), Standard Oil Company (Nebraska), Standard Oil Company (New York), Standard Oil Company (Ohio), Standard Oil Company (Kansas), and Standard Oil Company (New Jersey). For a while this was no problem, since informal relationships still existed between the companies and each company marketed its products only in its particular market area. In fact, the several Standard names probably helped the image held by individual consumers, who perceived all the companies as being part of the same large company.

The harmonious relationships between the newly created oil companies did not last forever. Soon the companies began expanding into market areas of other companies and competing for the same resources and the same customers. In particular, Standard Oil Company of New Jersey began rapid expansion in the 1930s and 1940s, and the Standard Oil Company name soon created problems as a corporate name, as well as with product identification. The courts ruled, for example, that the ESSO name, derived from the pronunciation of "S.O.", could not be used by the company in states that had their own Standard Oil Company. Therefore, in these states the company began using the trademark ENCO (for *En*ergy *Co*mpany). In Ohio the trademark Humble was used (from the company's merger with Humble Oil Company, which became the company's major domestic component, Humble Oil and Refining Company). The trademark ENJAY was used for chemical and other products sold by Standard Oil Company of New Jersey.

By the 1970s the name situation had evolved into a marketer's nightmare. The lack of a nationally recognizable corporate name and brand name caused unlimited problems with national advertising as well as people's image of the company. National ads had to mention all of the relevant brands. Many consumers thought that Standard Oil Company of New Jersey was just a regional firm. All of this no doubt contributed to the fact that, even though the firm was the world's largest oil company, Texaco and Shell were each selling more gasoline in the United States. International operations were hindered by not having a uniform brand name, and by the double meaning of some of the existing brand names in other languages (Enco is part of a phrase that means "stalled car" in Japanese, and Enjay is an obscene word in Chinese).

In 1970, the company launched a sophisticated, market-oriented approach to come up with a corporate and brand name that would remedy these problems. The result was a $100 million changeover in 1972, as the company selected the name Exxon as its product and corporate name. At the same time, Humble Oil and Refining Company became Exxon Company, U.S.A.

Over the past few years, Exxon has been diversifying into such areas as office products, as well as increasing its search for and development of alternative energy sources such as coal and nuclear energy. In 1979, it acquired Reliance Electric Company, a billion dollar company that develops, manufactures, markets, and services a broad line of industrial equipment, including electric motors. Exxon hopes this company will provide them with the means for developing a new power system for the automobile. The company presently has a prototype, a hybrid car powered by both a battery-driven motor and a small gasoline engine. The Federal Trade Commission has challenged this acquisition and is investigating whether Exxon's newly acquired ability to enter the automobile business with an electric car will violate antitrust laws.

Organization

The largest division of Exxon Corporation is Exxon Company, U.S.A., accounting for more than one third of corporate net income. Exxon Company, U.S.A., is responsible for refining and marketing all gasoline and other petroleum products in the United States. It is also responsible for the exploration, production, and distribution of crude oil, natural gas, and other petroleum products in the U.S. Formerly Humble Oil and Refining Company, Exxon U.S.A. is headquartered in Houston, Texas. Randall Meyer serves as President and Chief Operating Officer.

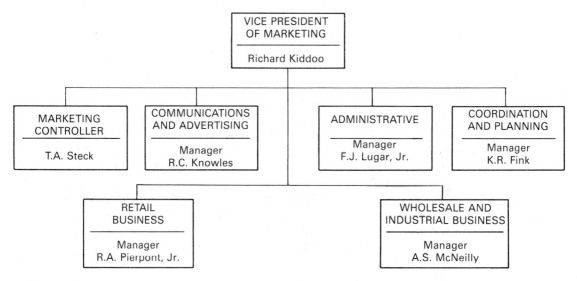

EXHIBIT 2   Organizational chart, Exxon U.S.A. marketing department

Retail products

Exxon Company, U.S.A. sells a wide range of products including aviation, railroad, marine, pleasure boats, and industrial products, solvents, fuels, asphalts, and waxes. Most of its sales come from the line of automotive products it sells in retail service stations across the country.

EXXON AUTOMOTIVE STORE

The meeting point between Exxon Co. U.S.A. and the customer is the service station. Presently, Exxon has 23,672 branded retail outlets, classified according to one of the following types of service station facilities:

1. *Conventional Stations* (33 percent of the stations) provide a well-rounded mix of services for the customer: gasoline, automotive products (oil, tires, batteries, accessories), and basic automotive repair and servicing. These stations usually have two to four service bays.

2. *Gasoline Only Stations* (43 percent of the stations) provide no auto repairs and servicing, and sell no TBA (tires, batteries, accessories) items. The only products these stations sell are gasoline and oil.

3. *Car Care Centers* (12 percent of the stations) are similar to conventional stations in services and products provided. But Car Care Centers are considered the "ultimate" in service, with eight to twelve service bays, and offer complete automotive diagnostic services for customers, along with gasoline and oil sales.

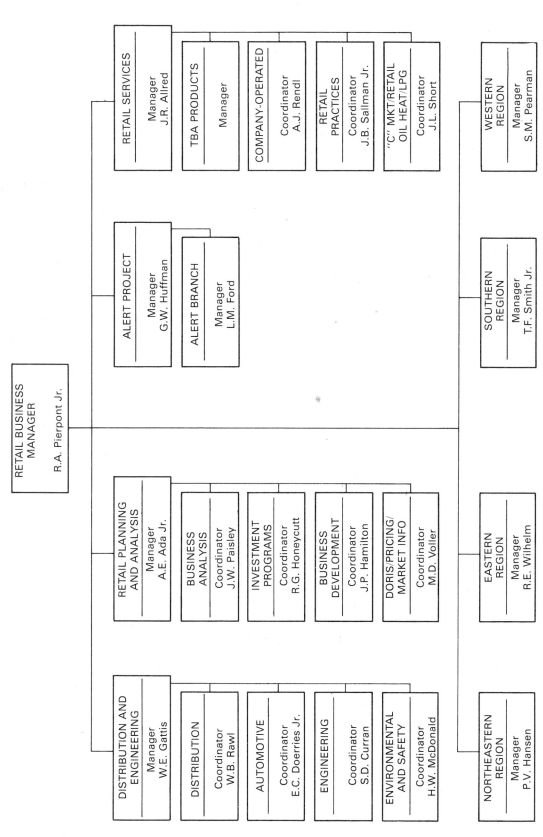

EXHIBIT 3 Organizational chart, Exxon retail business operations

513

EXHIBIT 4

4. *Car Washes* (8 percent of the stations) emphasize the car wash facility which is provided as an extra service for customers, along with gasoline and oil sales.

5. *Turnpike Stations* (4 percent of the stations) are located on turnpikes or toll highways, primarily in New Jersey and Pennsylvania. These stations provide the same full line of products and services as conventional stations.

There are a variety of ways major oil companies handle product distribution and ownership of the intermediaries, particularly the retail service stations (see Exhibit 5). Exxon also uses different types of arrangements with its dealers.

Direct-serviced stations. Exxon has 12,261 stations supplied directly by Exxon U.S.A. These stations fall into one of three categories:

1. *Company-owned stations* 970 stations are a part of Exxon's Company-Operated Store Program (COSP). These service stations are run di-

EXHIBIT 5 Product distribution by major oil companies, 1980.

Major oil companies	Total branded retail outlets	Total number of states where gasoline brand is marketed	Total branded service stations	Supplied directly	Supplied through jobbers and commission agents	BRANDED SERVICE STATIONS Lessee dealer operated	Salary operated	Commission operated	100% full service	100% self service	Service and self service	Total
Amoco Oil Co. (A)	21,251	43	20,985	7,389	13,596	20,830	155	0	NA	NA	NA	2,332
Atlantic Richfield Co. (C)	8,312	34	8,312	5,301	3,011 (D)	NA	NA	NA	NA	NA	NA	1,070
Chevron U.S.A., Inc.	13,965 (R)	40	8,653	7,573	1,080	8,550	103	0	5,022	168	3,463	518(L)
Exxon Co. U.S.A. (E)	23,672	44	23,672 (F)	12,261	11,411	22,702	970	—	10,572	600	12,500	1,251
Gulf Oil Co. U.S.	17,003	40	17,003	15,721	1,282	16,060	943	—	9,012	5,084	2,907	422
Mobil Oil Corp. (G)	17,749	48	(H)	NA	NA	NA	NA	NA	NA	NA	NA	1,972
Shell Oil Co.	7,137	39	16,559 (N)	7,137	9,422	7,079 (O)	58 (O)	0	1,917 (O)	1,101 (O)	4,119 (O)	769
Texaco Inc.	25,631	51	25,631	7,121	18,510	25,597	8	26	—	—	—	1,403

SOURCE: 1980 National Petroleum News Factbook Issue.

Major oil companies	BRANDED JOBBERS NUMBER SELLING Gasoline only	Fuel oil only	Gasoline & fuel oil	Total	COMMISSION AGENTS NUMBER SELLING Gasoline only	Fuel oil only	Gasoline & fuel oil	Total	BULK PLANTS COMPANY OPERATED Salary operated	Commission operated	Jobber-operated bulk plants	TERMINALS COMPANY OPERATED Total	Salary operated	Commission operated	Jobber-operated terminals
Amoco Oil Co. (A)	0	0	2,332	7	NA	NA	(B)	22	22	0	2,635	100	100	0	3
Atlantic Richfield Co. (C)	16	755	299	2	1	0	1	1	0	1	NA	61	61	0	NA
Chevron U.S.A., Inc.	41	135 (M)	141	476	0	0	476	537	26	511	173	135	115	20	19
Exxon Co. U.S.A. (E)	31	218	1,002	203	0	0	203	203	0	203	—	84	84	0	—
Gulf Oil Co. U.S.	0	183	181	620	0	0	620	642	22	620	422	128	128	0	43
Mobil Oil Corp. (G)	72	786	1,114	82 (I)	—	—	—	673(J)	87	—	1,768	115	115	—	0
Shell Oil Co.	0	43	726	0	—	—	—	87	101	0	1,076	40	40	—	(P)
Texaco Inc.	NA	NA	NA	342	NA	NA	NA	325	101	224	1,154	NA	NA	NA	NA

SOURCE: 1980 National Petroleum News Factbook Issue.

(A) Includes Omega Oil Co.
(B) "Almost all"
(C) Includes Prestige Stations Inc.
(D) Estimate
(E) Includes Alert
(F) Figures are for total retail outlets
(G) Includes Sello, Reelo, Hi-Val and Big-Bi
(H) Mobil maintains records on total branded retail outlets only
(I) Excludes 476 commission consignees

(J) Total wholesale distributing plants including terminals
(K) Includes 8 in American Samoa
(L) 201 and branded lube oil and grease jobbers
(M) 27 sell fuel oil on an unbranded basis
(N) Includes those supplied through jobbers and commission agents
(O) Direct supplied stations only. Data not available for jobber supplied stations
(P) Unknown
(Q) Includes 26 sub-agents
(R) 257 are "management fee" operated

rectly by the company; Exxon hires employees, trains its managers in the COSP managers' school at a Houston Car Care Center, sets prices, and establishes operating procedures. There are some of each type of service station facility owned by the company. Most Car Care Centers and Car Washes fall in this category because the specialized nature of these type of facilities and the large capital investment involved.

Exxon's involvement in company-owned stations has fluctuated in recent years. During the 1960s, Exxon expanded its geographical marketing areas into the South, Midwest, and West Coast. As it did, the company found it difficult, because of lack of brand acceptance, to attract high quality dealers. So, most new stations were opened as company operations. As a result Exxon began the 1970s with 3,649 company-operated service stations. As the brand recognition increased in these areas, Exxon was able to attract high quality dealers, and began converting many of these company operations to dealer-operated stations. Also in the mature market areas, many company operations were converted to dealer operations because rising accounting, inventory control, and administrative costs made company stations less profitable. By 1973 Exxon had reduced to 968 the number of company-operated service stations; that figure has remained about the same since then.

Exxon has had good success with the COSP. These company-owned stations provide a means for experimenting with new marketing techniques, service concepts and products. If experiments are successful in the company-owned stations, Exxon can implement these ideas at the dealer stations as well. One new program, used at Car Care Centers, involves a consumer complaint arbitration policy. If a customer has a problem with automobile repair or servicing, Exxon submits to arbitration by a Better Business Bureau mediator. The company will then abide by the mediator's decision, even though the customer does not have to.

Exxon is having some problems with its COSP program, however. Some dealers and other parties fear that it is a threat to the independent dealer concept. They feel that the company, with its vast financial resources is, in effect, competing with the independent Exxon dealer. Maryland has passed a law forbidding any COSP operations, and Georgia and Louisiana are considering similar legislation.

2. *Company-leased station*   Exxon leased almost 6,000 stations. In this case, the dealer signs a retail service station lease agreement and a supplier agreement with Exxon. The company's relationship with such a "leasee dealer" is similar to that of a landlord with a tenant, in addition to that of a supplier with a customer.

3. *Dealer-owned stations*   Approximately 5,000 stations directly served by Exxon are owned by the dealer or by a third party. In these situations, the dealer signs only a supply agreement with Exxon; the company's relationship with such an "open contract" dealer is that of a supplier with a customer.

Distributor served station. Exxon presently has 11,411 stations that are not served directly by Exxon, but instead are supplied by jobbers and commission agents. Exxon has no formal dealer contract with these stations, but they are still Exxon stations carrying Exxon products.

Dealer Lease Agreements

Exxon offers its dealers lease agreements with three-year terms, except that dealers new to Exxon are offered one-year contracts. Although Exxon encourages each station to operate at hours that best meet the needs of the particular market it serves, the majority of the dealer contracts do not require specific minimum hours of operation. There are some, located on interstates or other key locations, that are required to be open twenty-four hours, or keep certain minimum hours. Exxon dealers pay the company rent which may vary from $300 to $3,000 per month, depending on such factors as local property value and the retail service station economy. All rentals are negotiated individually with each dealer, and are usually reviewed annually.

Some dealer organizations in the petroleum industry today are seeking legislation that would permit dealers to assign, sell, or transfer the franchise right to another individual or to transfer such rights to their heirs or to their estates in case of death. Exxon is opposed to any such legislation for the following reasons:[1]

☐ *Basic nature of the franchise.* The petroleum franchise relationship is intended to be a personal one between the supplier and the dealer or distributor. A personal relationship is indicated because the actions of the franchisee can reflect adversely on the franchisor's image and can create exposure to legal liability. A petroleum supplier should have the right, therefore, to enter into a franchise agreement with an individual of its own choice.

☐ *Protection of property rights.* If the right to assign or devise the franchise is given to the franchisee, reversion of the leased premises to the franchisor may be delayed, denying the franchisor a timely opportunity to make a business decision concerning the future use of his property. Moreover, conferring the transfer right to the franchisee denies the franchisor the limited protection to insure the proper use and maintain the business value of the property which is afforded by careful selection of the individual who will occupy the premises.

☐ *Protection of consumer interests.* The installation of operators who may not be qualified candidates for a franchise is not in the best interests of consumers. The franchisor has an obvious interest in selecting a qualified candidate for a franchise opening. On the other hand, the franchisee who has been given the right to transfer his franchise, has an economic incentive to sell to the highest bidder regardless of qualifications. Further, surviving heirs of a deceased franchisee may not possess the qualifications necessary to be a successful operator.

---

[1]Company publication

In the past, all dealers were required to carry certain accessory items such as Atlas tires, batteries, etc. However, legislation now prevents oil companies from requiring dealers to carry these "TBA" (tires, batteries, accessories) items; if Exxon dealers choose to carry such items, they are free to purchase them from any source. Exxon reports that 15 percent of the lessee dealers do not purchase any TBA items from the company, and about 35 percent of the TBA items sold by these dealers have been purchased from outside suppliers. The majority of dealers do purchase the Atlas/Exxon TBA products, since the total package of favorable credit terms, stocking programs and product quality is preferable in most cases to outside purchases. (For information on average Exxon dealer longevity, see Exhibit 6).

Surplus Stations

Over the past few years Exxon has been "surplusing" or shutting down several hundred stations each year from its owned and leased chain. The number has been as high as 1,268 in 1973, but averages about 700 per year. These marginal units are identified from a careful economic screening process and then two basic principles are involved in the decision whether to keep a station in the chain:

1. The station must have a profit potential for an independent dealer commensurate with his opportunities elsewhere, since he has some capital invested.

2. The station must provide an adequate return on the company's investment (presently this is considered to be at least 15 percent). In cases where a decision is made to surplus a station, and yet the dealer is doing an adequate job and wishes to continue in the service station business, Exxon attempts to relocate that dealer to an existing location or a new station.

THE RISE OF SELF-SERVICE

Gasoline

Consumer demand for self-service merchandising of gasoline increased in the 1970s. In an attempt to shave a few cents off the inflated price of gasoline, many consumers patronized those stations that had the self-service option. Exxon has approximately 600 Full Self-Service and 12,500 Partial Self-Service stations and is wondering whether to change full service stations into and/or open new full or partial self-service stations in the future. Exxon consumer research indicates that, given currrent trends, only a minority of retail gasoline customers will want full-service gasoline merchandising in the future. However, the company is concerned about whether more self service stations will present a lower quality image, and whether current trends will continue.

EXHIBIT 6   Exxon dealer longevity rates average over recent years

A. *Turnovers: 1,188/year*	*(17%/year)*
Causes for dealer turnover:	
Illness	73
Retired	177
Death	19
Lost to competition	60
Financial	337
Personal	136
Other (mainly, other employment)	386
	1,188

B. *Number of nonmutual turnovers (not mutual agreements signed by Exxon and the dealer):*	*48/year (7%/year)*
Causes of nonmutual turnovers:	
Death	18
Illness	0
Abandoned stations	12
Financial problems	4
Failure to agree to new lease	2
Retired	2
To other business	7
Lease violation	3
	48

C. *Deactivations:*	*576/year*
Reasons for deactivations:	*(Avg. per year)*
Bought/leased Exxon branded station	252
Relocated to other Exxon outlets	53
Relocated to competitive outlets	19
Relocated to some other type of business	175
Retired	27
Illness or death	8
New employment unknown	17
Other	25
	256

D. *Present length of tenure of Exxon dealers:*	
Less than 1 year	13%
1–5 years	29%
5–10 years	29%
More than 10 years	29%
	100%

SOURCE: "Questions and Answers on Major Marketing Issues," publication of Exxon Company, U.S.A., March 1979.

In the 1960s and '70s, when the self-service approach began, there was opposition to self-service because of concern over fire hazards. Figures provided by the National Fire Protection Association, however, indicate that this is not a problem. Two states, New Jersey and Oregon, still ban self-service gasoline dispensing, and there are many local ordinances that prohibit self-service stations. Exxon initially was opposed to self-service, but now feels that as long as self-service operations conform with generally accepted safeguards, it would be inappropriate to ban or restrict it.

Some local authorities require that partial and full self-service stations have remote read-out equipment; the cost for this equipment runs about $2,000 per island, installed. Exxon carefully reviews the costs and returns from installing remote control self-service equipment and installs it for dealers where it can be justified.

Another obvious problem with the self-service approach is that consumer auto service and repair needs cannot be fully met. When the station is most concerned with low prices with few services, higher margin auto repairs, as well as tires, batteries, and other accessories are not emphasized or unavailable.

Oil

In recent years, more customers have started doing some automobile maintenance tasks, like adding and changing their own oil, themselves. Service stations accounted for 78 percent of all motor oil sales during 1960; in 1981 the figure was less than 40 percent. So, Exxon has begun selling its motor oil through mass merchandisers as well as Exxon service stations to reach this do-it-yourself market. The company has also attempted to attract this segment by offering motor oil to dealers in five quart carry-out containers.

ALERT BRAND

Not only has Exxon responded to price-sensitive consumers with self-service, it has introduced and is experimenting with a second brand, "Alert". Exxon consumer research confirmed that there is a "major brand" segment of the market that considers product quality features, credit cards, and other services an inherent part of the major brand image and are willing to pay a higher price for this "value package." However, this research also identified a rapidly growing segment interested in fast service, convenient hours, and the "no frills" prices offered by the typical private brand markets. Private brand market share has grown by one to two absolute percentage points each year since 1968 and presently stands at about 18 percent. This consumer research indicated that private brand users are not necessarily attracted to a conventional major brand station for price reasons alone. In view of these findings, Exxon decided to investigate appealing to the private brand market segment with products and services comparable to those offered at competitive private brand stations.

Exxon has twenty-nine Alert brand stations, fifteen of which are conversions from Exxon stations. Generally, the gasoline sold at the Alert stations is produced by other refiners and obtained through exchange agreements; it is comparable to the gasoline sold at competitive private brand stations. While Exxon carefully controls the quality of the gasoline sold under the Exxon brand, the company does not have a sophisticated quality control program for the Alert brand. Also, in contrast to Exxon products, the Alert brand has lower quality specifications for warm-up and starting characteristics. The octane rating for unleaded is well below current Exxon branded unleaded.

Alert stations sell only gasoline and motor oil, and provide only windshield and motor oil check services. Self-service facilities for air, water, and vacuuming are available. Exxon or other credit cards are not accepted. The pricing policy at these Alert stations is to post retail gasoline prices at reduced prices, lower than the major companies' prices, but competitive with prevailing private brands. No credit cards are accepted.

Some Exxon dealers have objected to this additional "competition" created by the parent company. There has also been some public criticism about whether Exxon should be allowed to compete with the private brand market. Exxon is undecided on discontinuing or expanding the Alert operations.

POLITICAL ENVIRONMENT

Fueled by rapid price increases of gasoline and high oil company profits, there have been calls over the past decade for divestiture in the oil industry. For the last seven years, a subcommittee of Congress has been considering legislation that would prohibit Exxon and other major oil companies from operating at more than one level in the channel of distribution. These oil companies would be broken up into separately owned and managed companies dealing individually in production, refining, distribution, or retailing of gasoline. Such legislation would also apply to horizontal integration and force the oil companies to dispose of investments already made in non-oil energy sources such as coal, nuclear, and synthetic fuels.

At present, few observers expect this proposed legislation to ever be passed by Congress. However, the fact that such legislation is even being considered serves as a caution to Exxon, as well as other major oil companies, to keep a good public image and communicate to the public that they are serving the public's interest. To help communicate this, the major oil companies have been spending a substantial portion of their advertising budgets on institutional advertising. This advertising has ranged from Shell's free energy-related consumer information booklets, and Mobil's heavy sponsorship of the Public Broadcasting Service, to Exxon's attempts to inform the public of the multi-faceted, people-oriented, workings of the largest oil company. These attempts to quell public scorn of the oil companies have been fairly effective. (See Exhibit 7 for summaries of advertising expenditures for the major oil companies in 1979 and 1980.)

EXHIBIT 7   Expenditures by major oil companies for different types of advertising, 1979–1980 (,000 of $)

	1980			1979		
	Corporate[1]	Products[2]	Dealer[3] Services/ Promotions	Corporate[1]	Products[2]	Dealer[3] Services/ Promotions
Exxon	$11,016.1	$3,739.6	$ 615.0	$ 5,834.0	$3,903.6	$<40.0
Amoco	3,044.8	3,668.7	2,986.4	4,209.8	2,740.8	1,991.2
Shell	10,222.0	3,745.5	2,704.7	14,318.4	5,017.5	2,288.7
Gulf	6,737.7	4,554.9	490.7	4,617.6	<1,000.0	1,195.8
Texaco	10,157.9	6,762.5	<280.0	6,831.2	4,811.9	1,085.3
Mobil	3,431.0	6,104.9	<280.0	4,476.2	5,017.5	<40.0
Chevron	5,921.8	3,000.0	751.0	2,585.4	<1,000.0	1,210.6
Arco	12,715.1	5,370.1	2,986.4	5,925.1	3,903.6	<40.0

[1]Corporate advertising—Institutional advertising emphasizing aspects of the company, itself, rather than individual products or services.
[2]Product advertising—Advertising emphasizing specific brand name products of the company.
[3]Dealer services/promotions—Advertising paid for by the company but centered on specific products, services, and special offers available from dealers.

SOURCE: Leading National Advertisers, Inc., *Ad $ Summary,* 1979, 1980.

MARKETING VS. CONSERVATION

During the 1970s, major changes occurred in the petroleum industry and the world as a result of the 1973 Arab oil embargo, the subsequent cutbacks in the supply of crude oil, and the dramatic price increases by members of OPEC (the primarily Arab "Organization of Petroleum Exporting Countries" that supplies 40 percent of U.S. crude oil). Not only did retail gasoline prices more than triple (see Exhibit 8), but the reduction in supply forced virtually all retail stations to cut back their hours of operation and, in some instances, limit the quantity of gasoline a customer could purchase. The resulting long lines and inconveniences produced a different kind of public relations problem for Exxon and the other oil companies.

EXHIBIT 8   55-City motor gasoline[1] price ¢/gallon (year average)

	Price Excluding Tax	Tax	Pump Price
1950	20.08	6.68	26.76
1960	20.99	10.14	31.13
1970	24.55	11.14	35.69
1975	45.44	11.77	57.21
1977	50.70	12.37	63.07
1978	53.09	12.62	65.71
1979	74.32	13.44	87.76
1980	107.32	14.36	121.68

[1]Regular grade, full service

SOURCE: Exxon Company U.S.A., *Pocket Data on Exxon and the Energy Industries,* May 1981, p. 32.

As public discontent grew over the oil and gasoline situation, U.S. businesses and consumers began calling for a greater emphasis on development of alternative sources of energy, as well as energy conservation. As this need for conservation has now been realized by virtually everyone, some observers feel that a strong marketing program designed to encourage product use is contrary to social benefit. Why should a company selling a product that is in short supply try to persuade people to buy it (or buy more of it)? This is Exxon's response:[2]

> Exxon USA believes that both a reduction in energy consumption and an increase in domestic supplies are vital to the national objective of reducing the nation's dependence on imported petroleum supplies. The Company's position on energy conservation has been consistently supported through legislative testimony and in letters, bulletins, meetings and other forms of communications with Exxon dealers and distributors. Our advertising programs and public statements have emphasized energy conservation.
>
> Exxon further believes that, even in the context of the conservation ethic, the motoring public is entitled to convenience and service in the purchase of their gasoline requirements, and that the petroleum companies and retail dealers are entitled to compete to retain or increase their business and their income by being more responsive to customer needs through good marketing practices, such as providing convenient hours of operation, pricing competitively, maintaining clean and attractive facilities, and performing driveway services. Further, our counseling recommendations to our dealers not only take into consideration the needs of retail customers, but the dealers' economics of service station operations as well. These counseling activities will not discourage conservation, but rather will tend to ensure that Exxon gasoline will be available to customers on a convenient and competitive basis. We cannot require nor have we encouraged Exxon dealers to adopt marketing practices that would result in financial harm to dealer.

In 1980 consumers responded to higher gasoline prices by adopting personal conservation measures and using less oil and gas. As a result, Exxon U.S.A. refinery output of 1.3 million barrels of oil per day was the lowest since 1976 and the five Exxon U.S.A. refineries operated at only 82 percent of their rated capacity.

Although 1980 dollar revenue was up, sales volume in units sold was down almost 10 percent. As Exxon executives look at these figures and analyze the future, they are concerned over what the future holds and what strategic decisions should be made now to continue sales growth. Even though alternative forms of energy are being explored, it appears that oil-related products will still be essential for many years to come. Therefore, Exxon's retail service station network is where the key marketing strategy decisions must be made and implemented. As the company keeps an eye on the political environment, it hopes the crucial decisions it makes about its retail stations will set a solid foundation for the future.

---

[2]Company publication

MARKETING CONTROL

Marketing Control

8

*M*arketing management must constantly evaluate its performance. By instituting a marketing control system that compares results to objectives, marketing managers can tell how effective the marketing area has been. Marketing control will also help managers plan for the future.

STEPS IN MARKETING CONTROL

Marketing control consists of the six basic steps indicated in Exhibit 1. In the first step, *decide the specific aspect of marketing* which you will evaluate. In general, you will want to evaluate all aspects of a company's marketing operations, including personnel, products, customers, activities, etc. For this example, let's assume you want to evaluate the sales force's performance.

In the second step, *establish a specific measurement criterion.* Usually, these criteria will be the major strategic objectives of profit, market share, product protection, sales volume, and growth, or the various tactical objectives developed to achieve your firm's strategic objectives. Number of sales calls will be our performance measurement criterion.

The third step, *establishing a peformance standard,* requires you to attach a quantitative measure to the performance criterion: each salesperson will be required to make 1,000 sales calls a year. In establishing performance standards, marketing management may use internal or external standards. For example, you might discover that the average number of sales calls per salesman the previous year was 1,000. Or, you might have decided on the 1,000 sales calls a year standard from information supplied by a trade association or a marketing periodical. Regardless of whether internal or external standards are used, both superiors and subordinates must work together to establish standards of performance.

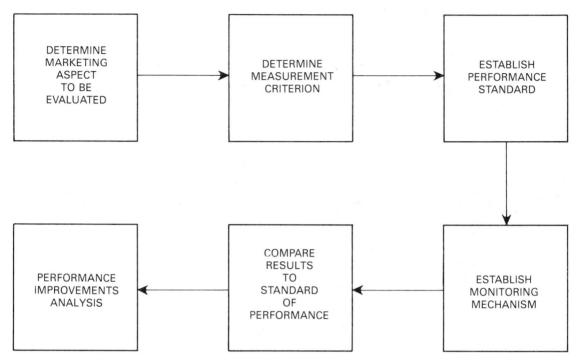

EXHIBIT 1   The marketing control process

Establishing a monitoring mechanism is the fourth control step; you must decide how to record and evaluate performance. A call report, on which sales personnel indicate which customer they called on, as well as other important information, could be an appropriate monitoring mechanism. In many companies, a marketing information system is the major means through which they gather information about performances. Purchase orders, shipping records, accounting records, and direct observations by a superior are other monitoring mechanisms.

Comparing results to the standard of performance is the fifth control step: each salesperson's number of sales calls is compared at the end of the year to the performance standard of 1,000.

If the results are not up to the established standard, *performance improvement analysis* is necessary. In this sixth control step, sales personnel not achieving the 1,000 sales call goal would, in cooperation with superiors, try to decide how to improve their performance. Establishing a better routing plan and telephoning in advance of sales calls for appointments might be ways to achieve the desired results.

MARKETING CONTROL TOOLS

Six important tools to use in a marketing control system are (1) *profitability analysis,* (2) *20/80 analysis,* (3) *productivity measures,* (4) *percentage analysis, (5) budgets,* and (6) *network diagrams.*

Profitability Analysis. Since profit is probably the most important strategic objective, profitability analysis is frequently used to (1) determine the profitability of products, orders, sales personnel, and customers, and (2) compare profitability within these categories. Exhibit 2 shows profitability analysis for three retailing customers of a manufacturer marketing men's clothing. The results indicate that the sales to Store A resulted in a loss of $2,000, the profit ($4,000) made from the sales to Store B amounts to a 5.0 percent return on sales, and a $2,000 net profit from Store C represents a 2.9 percent return on sales.

20/80 Analysis. The 20/80 principle means that a small percentage of a company's products, salespeople, orders, customers, etc. account for a large percentage of its total sales or profits. Conversely, and perhaps even more significantly for control purposes, a large number of products, salespeople, orders, customers, etc. account for a small percentage of total sales or profits.

The 20/80 principle is common:

1. 224 of the largest 1,000 manufacturing companies estimated that 23 percent of their products gave them 80 percent of their sales.[1]

2. Eighty manufacturing companies reported that one-third of their customers accounted for 75 percent of their total profits.[2]

3. Ducommun Metals and Supply Company of Los Angeles estimated that 10 percent of its customers provide 70 percent of its sales and 82 percent of its net profit.[3]

4. One Sears store found that 15 percent of its open-store hours generated 86 percent of its sales volume.[4]

5. Sixty-one machine tool manufacturers estimated that 25 percent of their customers and 20 percent of their orders accounted for 80 percent of their sales volume.[5]

The results of 20/80 analysis are important for control. The small percentage of orders, salespeople, products, customers, etc. that account for most of sales and profits can be designated as *key elements* that you can:

EXHIBIT 2 Example of profitability analysis

	Store A	Store B	Store C
Sales to store	$100,000	$80,000	$70,000
Less cost of goods sold	80,000	48,000	49,000
Gross margin	20,000	32,000	21,000
Less marketing expense	22,000	28,000	19,000
Net profit	−2,000	4,000	2,000
Return on sales	—	5.0%	2.9%

1. examine for characteristics that differentiate them from the large percentage of those that account for small percentages of sales and profits. Perhaps this investigation will indicate what to do to make the rest more valuable to the firm.

2. accord more resources than they may be receiving. For example, 20/80 analysis may indicate that more sales personnel time should be given to those accounts (customers) which generate most sales and profits.

3. regard as especially important to a company's success, and be careful not to lose. For example, the few sales personnel generating much sales and profit may be rewarded with higher-than-average increases in compensation to retain them.

You may designate those aspects of the marketing operation in which a large percentage represents a small percentage of sales and profits as *marginal elements.* You should analyze them to see how to improve their performance. For example, marginal salesmen may need to sharpen their closing skills, or improve their routing plans. You could also pull resources away from marginal entities; your company's sales force may stop making calls on marginal accounts. Another possibility is eliminating the marginal entities, like marginal products.

Exhibit 3 shows the results of a 20/80 analysis of a firm's products; notice the pronounced 20/80 phenomenon (actually 15/75). The most important results for purposes of marketing control are the high average profit of the 300 key products ($25,000), and the low average profit of the 1,700 marginal products ($1,471). Marketing management should do all it can to maintain the competitive position of its 300 key products, and insure that these products are getting their fair share of the firm's resources. On the other hand, marketing management should be concerned that, due to the low average profit for the marginal products, many may actually be unprofitable. Are these 1,700 marginal products receiving too much of the company's resources (e.g., advertising dollars, sales force time, management time, marketing research budgets, and warehousing time and effort)?

John Deere, aware of the disappearance of the family, small-sized farms in the United States, made good use of 20/80 analysis. It knew that the aver-

EXHIBIT 3   Results of 20/80 analysis

---

1. A company has 2,000 different products.
2. The company's annual profit is $10 million.
3. 20/80 analysis reveals that 15% of the company's products generates 75% of its profit and, conversely, 85% of its products account for 25% of its profit.
4. Thus, 300 products account for $7.5 million in profit, with an average profit of $25,000 per product.
5. Thus, 1,700 products account for $2.5 million in profit, with an average profit of $1,471 per product.

---

age acreage of surviving farms was increasing, and that 20 percent of American farms were accounting for about 80 percent of total farm production. So, the company began developing a product line to suit large farms. In 1979, Deere estimated that it had a 45 percent market share of tractors and combines costing from $60,000 to $90,000. According to Charles V. Bromely, an analyst with Duff and Phelps, Inc., "Deere has the biggest share of the biggest machines with the biggest profitability."[6]

Productivity Measures. Productivity measures enable a company to determine how effectively it is using various marketing resources. Productivity measures express some result as a function of one unit of a resource. Some examples of productivity measures in marketing include:

1. Sales volume per sales person
2. Cost per sales call
3. Sales volume per dollar of advertising
4. Number of calls per salesperson
5. Number of inquiries per advertisement

Percentage Analysis. Percentage analysis can be used to determine effectiveness of a number of different marketing areas, and is also helpful in discerning trends over time. Expressing various marketing costs, such as advertising, marketing research, warehousing, transportation, and sale force salaries, commissions and travel expenses, as a percentage of total sales volume over time is one frequently employed application of percentage analysis. This calculation will reveal those marketing expenses which are increasing in relative terms, as well as those which are decreasing. Market shares are another example of percentage analysis, as is calculating the percentage of total sales volume accounted for by individual products or product lines. Mary Kay Cosmetics found that between 1975 and 1979, skincare products for women changed from 52 percent in 1975 to 49 percent in 1979, while makeup items increased from 21 percent to 26 percent. Sales managers frequently determine the percentage of their sales force's time taken up in various selling activities, including presentations to prospects and customers, travel, paperwork, and customer relations.

Budgets. Budgets are funds which are appropriated for various marketing activities, such as marketing research, advertising, and personal selling. You should develop budgets based on the resources needed to accomplish objectives. For example, if your firm wishes its sales force to make 10,000 sales calls during a year, and the average cost of a sales call was believed to be $80, the personal selling budget would be $800,000 (10,000 × $80 = $800,000). Budgets are important control devices because they force management to consider how much money is needed to achieve various objectives—budgets guard against overspending. They also provide a performance standard; they should not be exceeded unless it results in better achievement of objectives.

Network Diagrams. You can better control time and cost by using network diagrams. They will also help you assign specific authority and responsibility and practice management by exception. Network diagrams, such as *Program Evaluation and Review Technique* (P.E.R.T.) and *Critical Path Network* (C.P.M.), involve diagramming the various steps required to complete a project, for example, developing a new product. The marketing executive must emphasize when steps in the diagram should be performed. Once they have constructed the diagram, marketing managers can see how long the entire project will take by tracing the critical path, the one that takes the shortest time to complete the *entire* project. Any activity on this path that takes longer than planned jeopardizes the project's deadline. However, you can transfer resources, such as manpower and money, to the problem activity to keep the project on schedule.

MAKING MARKETING CONTROL MORE EFFECTIVE

There are various approaches to use to help make marketing control systems more effective. The most important of these are:

1. Obtain input from those individuals who will be evaluated. This will mean a better control system, and those providing the input are likely to be more enthusiastic about the control system.

2. Show people how they can benefit from the control system. If, for example, salesmen can see how a performance standard of having 40 percent of their time devoted to selling will increase their compensation by 15 percent, they will be more willing to accept the standard and work harder to achieve it.

3. Insure that performance standards reflect differences. Not all salesmen, for example, should be asked to make the same number of sales calls a year. Consider discrepancies in their territories, like distances between customers.

4. Assign responsibility for marketing control. Generally, top marketing executives and the heads of various departments should be responsible.

5. Review appropriately. The frequency of review depends on how often marketing executives need to evaluate control data. Savings and loans, for example, monitor their savings levels daily; manufacturers prefer quarterly data about their products.

6. Use computers. Computers are necessary in marketing control systems to process the vast quantities of information, and also bring other benefits. Bergen Brunswig Corp., the nation's second largest drug wholesaler, introduced a computerized order system which, over a five year period, decreased operating expenses as a percent-

age of sales by 30 percent; quadrupled pre-tax return on investment, to 36 percent; improved inventory turnover 14 percent; and improved net sales per employee by 50 percent.[7]

7. Practice management by exception. A marketing control system must not inundate marketing decision makers with too much data; marketing control systems need to isolate critical areas where performance is sub-par.

8. Be cost-effective. The cost of a marketing control system must not exceed the dollar value of its benefits. Marketing control systems tend to be costly (computers, employee time, etc.), and their expected benefits must exceed these costs.

SUMMARY

Marketing control is the way to evaluate a marketing department's performance. It is helpful to view marketing control as a process consisting of six basic steps: Determining marketing aspect to be evaluated, determining measurement criterion, establishing performance standards, establishing monitoring mechanism, comparing results to standards of performance, and performing improvement analysis. There are a number of marketing control tools. Some important ones are profitability analysis, 20/80 analysis, productivity measures, percentage analysis, budgets, and network diagrams.

To implement an effective marketing control system, you should assign responsibility for marketing control, practice management by exception, and show individuals how they can benefit from the control procedure.

QUESTIONS

1. Describe the six steps which make up the marketing control process.
2. For what aspects of a company's marketing operations is profitability analysis applicable?
3. Explain how 20/80 analysis can be used as a marketing control tool.
4. Can you think of any additional examples of how percentage analysis can be used?
5. What are the major benefits of using network diagrams as a control device?
6. What is meant by "management by exception" in marketing control systems?

REFERENCES

1. R. Visvanathn. *An Empirical Investigation of the Factors Affecting the Formality, Sophistication and Structure of Product Elimination Programs in Manufacturing Firms.* Ph.D. Dissertation, Texas A&M University, 1982.

2. Harry Deane Wolfe and Gerald Albaum. "Inequality in Products, Orders, Customers, Salesmen, and Sales Territories." *Journal of Business,* July, 1962, p. 300.

3. "Keying Sales Calls to Profits." *Dun's Review and Modern Industry,* November, 1960, p. 42.

4. Richard H. Buskirk. *Principles of Marketing.* New York: Holt, Rinehart & Winston, Inc., 1970, p. 488.

5. Richard T. Hise, Stanley H. Kratchman and Thomas A. Ulrich. "Distribution Cost Analysis and Performance Standards For Industrial Selling." Paper presented to the third annual meeting of the northeast region of the American Institute of Decision Sciences, May, 1974.

6. *Business Week,* November 19, 1979.

7. *Infosystems,* July, 1979.

SUGGESTED READINGS

Beik, L.L., and S.L. Busby. "Profitability Analysis by Market Segments." *Journal of Marketing,* July, 1973, pp. 48–53.

Dhalla, N.K. "How To Set Advertising Budgets." *Journal of Advertising Research,* October, 1977, pp. 11–17.

Dunn, P.M., and H.I. Wolk. "Marketing Cost Analysis: A Modularized Contribution Approach." *Journal of Marketing,* July, 1977, pp. 83–94.

Goodman, S.R. *Techniques of Profitability Analysis.* New York: Wiley-Interscience, 1970.

Hulbert, J.M., and N.E. Toy. "A Strategic Framework For Marketing Control." *Business Horizons,* December, 1978, pp. 65–73.

Kotler, P. "From Sales Obsession to Marketing Effectiveness." *Harvard Business Review,* November-December, 1978, pp. 67–75.

Kotler, P., W. Gregor, and W. Rogers. "The Marketing Audit Comes of Age." *Sloan Management Review,* Winter, 1977, pp. 25–43.

Mossman, F.H., P.M. Fisher, and W.J.E. Crissy. "New Approaches To Analyzing Marketing Profitability." *Journal of Marketing,* April, 1974, pp. 43–48.

Naylor, J., and A. Wood. *Practical Marketing Audits.* New York: Halstead Press/Wiley, 1978.

Sevin, C.H. *Marketing Productivity Analysis.* New York: McGraw-Hill, 1965.

Wooton, L.M., and J.L. Tarter. "The Productivity Audit: A Key Tool For Executives." *Business Topics,* Spring, 1976, pp. 31–41.

Exxon Company, U.S.A.: "Swing Store Program"

Brian Walters[1], Regional Market Development Manager for Exxon Co., U.S.A., has just returned from a trip to Alpha district, the largest district in his region. For the past two weeks he has been evaluating Exxon retail automotive stores in the district. He must sort through the mass of data he has collected and make some recommendations to solve the problem he has been investigating.

The problem came to his attention last month, when the latest report from Exxon's Market Investment Program Group (which keeps close tabs on the profitability of each of Exxon's 23,000 retail stores) indicated that 41 of the 300 stores in Alpha district were consistently yielding an unsatisfactory return on investment—despite favorable market conditions and solid company support of marketing efforts in the district. Walters decided an in-depth evaluation of each of these forty-one stores was needed; he would give the matter his personal attention. The program was known as the "swing store program" because the stores investigated were hovering between success and failure. Exxon hoped it could identify problems and "swing" some of these stores into the successful category rather than shutting them down. Walters described the swing store program and what he hoped to discover from it:

> Here is the problem: We have $15 million invested in these stores. They are not yielding us a satisfactory return on investment. Our current monthly rent collected does not come close to our market value rent. We, of course, have two relationships with our dealers: landlord/tenant and supplier/customer. Our target is to have the current monthly rent at or close to the market value rent, and to sell monthly motor fuels at each store at or close to IMOD projection.[2] Therefore the major questions we are asking are: 1) have we made poor individual investments, and/or is the quality of the dealer at each location such as to retard the store income potential? 2) what can we do about it?

This case was prepared by Stephen W. McDaniel, Assistant Professor of Marketing, Texas A&M University, as a basis for class discussion rather than to illustrate either effective or ineffective marketing management.

[1]All names have been changed.

[2]IMOD Projection: A quantitative estimate of sales based on the computerized "investment model" (IMOD). See further explanation in section on sales performance.

ALPHA DISTRICT RETAIL STORES

Alpha District includes one of the top five metropolitan areas in the United States. Because of its size, the district is divided into three areas. Heading up the retail store operations in each district is a field sales manager; Each field sales manager is responsible for about 100 retail stores.

Alpha District is a relatively new geographic market for Exxon. The company has marketed products in the area for only the past fifteen years. However, due to its rapid population growth, the company has been trying to establish a stronger foothold. Exxon would like to see the present 300 retail stores in Alpha District increased by 50 percent over the next five or ten years.

Virtually all Exxon retail stores in Alpha district are company-leased stations; the company owns the grounds and facilities, but leases all of the property to an independent businessman—the Exxon dealer. The dealer signs a three-year dealer lease agreement and a supply agreement with Exxon. Exxon agrees to supply gasoline and other automotive products, and the dealer agrees to pay a fixed monthly rent to Exxon, purchase the products from Exxon distributors, and maintain certain quality standards set forth by Exxon. These dealer quality standards concern primarily cleanliness and safety. The leadership agreement gives Exxon the right to terminate the rela-

EXHIBIT 1

tionship if the dealer does not maintain the standard. As a rule, Exxon generally waits until the lease period is up before terminating a dealer. But, explained Walters, "Even then it is very difficult to terminate a dealer who has been with you for a while, even three years. We find it better to work with the dealer and help him correct the problems he is having, rather than just get rid of him."

Sales Performance

Walters looked first at the 1981 figures showing monthly sales performance for each of the stores (see Exhibit 2). He then compared these with the IMOD projections he had previously calculated for each store. The IMOD projection is a monthly motor gasoline volume projection of the amount of fuel each store is expected to sell, based on Exxon's investment in that store. Several different variables are included in the computer model used to calculate this figure: traffic count at the corner of the site; the number of automobile registrations within one-and-a-half miles of the site; the number of other competitors nearby; the average market price or competitors' price in the vicinity; the number of regional shopping centers in the area; and whether there are any other traffic generators in the area. Since the IMOD projection indicates sales potential, it is typically higher than the actual sales volume figures. For example, for all 300 stores of Alpha district, the IMOD is approximately 80 (i.e., an average of 80,000 gallons of gasoline per month), while the actual sales volume is closer to 45. Since Alpha District is still a relatively new market for Exxon, this ratio of actual to projected is less than for the U.S. as a whole. Nationwide, actual sales volume averages 80 percent of IMOD projections. Walters is particularly concerned about those retail stores having a smaller-than-average actual to projected sales ratio.

Along with data on monthly motor gasoline volume, Walters also has figures showing the after-market actual sales volume and after-market projected sales volume. After-market sales are store sales of all products and services excluding gasoline: TBA items (tires, batteries, and accessories), as well as automotive repair and service. This information is also provided in Exhibit 2.

Dealer Quality

The second part of the swing store program was more time-consuming. He decided to visit each problem store over two weeks and formally evaluate each one. Before the evaluation, Walters informed each dealer that he would be visiting Alpha district over the next two weeks to talk with the dealer and check on different aspects of the store. Each dealer knew he was coming and had time to prepare.

The evaluation form Walters used was the standard Exxon Retail Store Evaluation Form, which is divided into five sections: store appearance, personnel appearance, product merchandising, selling and service capability,

EXHIBIT 2   Exxon retail automotive stores average monthly sales
performance—1981

	Store #	Gasoline Actual Sales Volume (,000 gallons per month)	IMOD Projected Sales Volume (,000 gallons per month)	After-market After-market Actual Sales Volume ($,000 per month)	After-market Projected Sales Volume ($,000 per month)
AREA 1	1	44	58	4.9	10.8
	2	31	69	2.9	12.6
	3	15	74	1.0	5.8
	4	32	57	5.1	12.0
	5	28	95	15.7	21.7
	6	38	80	0	13.5
	7	41	69	13.2	17.3
	8	31	71	8.0	13.0
	9	16	53	5.1	9.9
	10	36	71	5.7	5.2
	11	39	76	7.2	13.8
AREA 2	12	41	114	4.1	15.1
	13	29	102	4.2	15.3
	14	30	52	1.9	24.6
	15	32	60	18.9	23.3
	16	30	68	4.4	14.2
	17	26	81	6.0	19.1
	18	25	69	5.4	18.2
	19	30	71	9.8	17.7
	20	30	70	8.0	13.7
	21	30	53	8.2	14.5
	22	29	65	12.8	14.4
	23	46	70	6.4	14.4
	24	30	50	2.8	19.7
	25	20	78	4.1	15.6
	26	27	75	7.9	16.1
	27	30	80	8.6	11.3
AREA 3	28	40	74	6.2	5.9
	29	31	36	5.8	13.8
	30	50	83	10.1	19.2
	31	35	69	8.4	12.9
	32	30	60	9.3	19.0
	33	23	102	4.2	19.1
	34	21	117	4.0	19.1
	35	45	69	7.2	19.4
	36	37	81	7.7	30.4
	37	33	77	4.3	36.4
	38	35	115	28.8	51.2
	39	46	88	9.0	19.4
	40	30	74	13.7	33.6
	41	32	88	13.9	20.9

and retailer or dealer evaluation. For each individual item, he gave a score of between *0* and whatever the item's weight factor was. As a general rule, each item was rated either *satisfactory,* in which case the weight factor score was given, or *unsatisfactory,* in which case a score of *0* was given. Walters spent from one to three hours at each retail store talking with the dealer about the operation, observing the activities at the store, and checking all relevant aspects of the business.

EXHIBIT 3   Items included in Exxon retail automotive store evaluation

I. STORE APPEARANCE

Outside

1. Grounds well kept. (No junk cars, motors, etc.)
2. Drive swept clean.
3. Perimeter curbing neat and clean.
4. Islands neat and clean.
5. Pumps and pump glass clean.
6. Pump glass not broken/out.
7. Vending machines/oil cabinet clean/painted.
8. Exterior walls clean and free of dirt.
9. All exterior windows clean.
10. Islands and ramps not closed/blocked.
11. Rear of store is neat, clean, uncluttered.
12. Landscaping neat.
13. Exterior signing ok/lights working.

Inside

14. Floor swept clean. (Bays/sales room)
15. All walls clean.
16. Sales room ceiling clean.
17. Shelf displays clean/neat.
18. Sales room/kiosk neat/orderly/clean.
19. Equipment/tools/inventory neat, orderly.

Restrooms

20. Walkway clean.
21. Floor clean.
22. Walls and ceiling clean.
23. Ventilation fresh.
24. All equipment in working order.
25. Mirror clean.
26. Commode/urinal clean.
27. Wash basin clean.
28. Waste basket available.
29. Lights working.
30. Hand soap available.
31. Towels available.
32. Toilet tissue available.

II. PERSONNEL APPEARANCE/SERVICE

First Impression

1. Prompt attention.
2. "Good Morning" or appropriate greeting.

Sales Service

3. Asked for the order and/or fill up.
4. Cleaned windshield (street island).
5. Cleaned rear window (street island).
6. Under the hood sales inspection (customer permitting) street island.
7. Cashier/customer salesman settled the purchase in a courteous manner.
8. All personnel in approved uniform.
9. All personnel neat and clean.

III. PRODUCT MERCHANDISING

1. Motor fuel price sign prominent and attractive.
2. Enough motor oil displayed.
3. Motor oil displayed prominently and attractively.
4. Enough tires displayed at island (area permitting).
5. Enough tires displayed in front bays.
6. Enough tires displayed in front of sales room (area permitting).
7. Tires displayed attractively.
8. Tires are price merchandised.
9. Batteries displayed prominently and attractively.
10. Enough batteries displayed.
11. Impulse items displayed outside at island or store front.
12. Accessories/coolant well displayed in bay and sales room.
13. Window displays fresh, current and attractive (zoning permitting).
14. Prices indicated on Value Center advertising.
15. Other seasonal Value Center ads current and attractive.

EXHIBIT 3 (continued)

16. Vacuum and vending machines working and attractive.
17. Store merchandised for Self Service sales/express service (if has Self Service/express sales).

IV. SELLING/SERVICE CAPABILITY

Tires

1. Adequate coverage of fast moving sizes.
2. Adequate coverage by line (radial, belted, conventional).
3. Adequate tire selling skills by retailer/employees.
4. Retailer has planned system for selling tires (price cards, codes, etc. that customer salesmen understand and use).
5. Mogas customers solicited for tire sales or service at island.
6. Tires checked while car is being serviced.
7. Tire changer.
8. Spin or bubble balancer.
9. Air wrenches.
10. Wheel alignment.

Batteries

11. Adequate coverage of fast moving sizes.
12. Adequate coverage by line.
13. Adequate battery selling skills by retailer/employees.
14. Retailer has a planned system for selling batteries (price cards, codes, etc. which customer salesmen understand and use).
15. Hydrometer.
16. Battery charger.
17. Battery tester used.
18. Battery tester used while car is being serviced.

Accessories/Impulse Items

19. Adequate accessory/impulse item inventory level.
20. Coverage of fast moving lines and sizes.
21. Customer salesmen/cashier solicit accessory/impulse item/motor oil sales.

Motor Oil

22. Adequate motor oil inventory.
23. Employees trained to sell add oil and oil change at the island.

Services

24. Tune up.
25. Brake service.
26. Air conditioning service.
27. Road service.
28. Pick-up and delivery service.
29. State inspection/license.
30. "Customer Reminder" system in use.
31. Of services performed, has proper equipment to produce work quality of other top notch service centers in the market.

V. RETAILER EVALUATION

1. Spends enough time meeting people on the front.
2. Adequate product knowledge.
3. Work/car wash quality equal to top notch service centers/car washes in the market.
4. Customer complaints within an acceptable level.
5. Employees are punctual and dependable.
6. Discipline evident among employees.
7. Sends qualified employees to special classes teaching automotive repair.
8. Trains driveway salesmen in proper island service procedures.
9. Runs reference checks on prospective employees.
10. Uses a work order system.
11. Does business records on a daily basis (or supervises the completion of them.)
12. Storeroom locked.
13. Full-shelf inventory program.
14. Shift leaders responsible for stock and cash control.
15. Prompt in payment of bills to Exxon.
16. Consistently have higher profit/salary than profit demand.
17. Adequate working cash. (Dealers only-automatic credit for salary stores.)
18. Sets sales and profit objectives.
19. Receives monthly P/L statements (Dealers only).
20. Adequate compensation program.
21. Offers wages and benefits needed to attract qualified technician.
22. Offers wages and benefits needed to attract qualified driveway salesmen.
23. Has motivation and desire to achieve sales potential at the location.

AREA 1 — columns 1–11 AREA 2 — columns 12–27 AREA 3 — columns 28–41

Store Appearance	Weight Factor	1	2	3	4	5	6	7	8	9	10	11	12	13	14	15	16	17	18	19	20	21	22	23	24	25	26	27	28	29	30	31	32	33	34	35	36	37	38	39	40	41
A. Outside																																										
1. Grounds	8	0	8	8	8	8	8	0	0	8	8	0	0	8	0	8	8	8	8	0	0	0	0	0	8	8	0	0	8	0	8	0	0	0	0	8	8	0	0	0	0	8
2. Driveway	3	0	0	0	0	3	3	3	3	3	3	3	0	0	3	3	3	3	3	3	3	0	0	3	3	3	0	3	0	0	3	0	3	3	3	3	3	3	0	3	0	0
3. Curbing	3	3	3	3	3	3	3	3	3	3	3	3	0	0	3	3	3	3	3	3	3	3	3	3	3	3	3	3	3	3	3	3	3	3	3	3	3	3	3	3	3	3
4. Islands clean	8	0	8	8	8	0	8	0	3	8	8	8	8	8	0	8	8	8	8	8	8	8	8	8	8	8	8	8	0	0	0	8	0	8	8	8	8	8	8	0	0	0
5. Pumps	4	0	0	0	0	0	0	0	0	0	4	4	0	4	4	4	4	4	0	0	0	0	0	0	0	0	0	0	0	4	4	4	4	4	0	0	4	4	0	0	0	0
6. Pump glass	3	3	3	3	3	3	3	3	3	3	3	3	3	0	0	3	3	3	3	3	3	3	3	3	3	3	3	3	3	3	3	3	3	3	3	3	3	3	3	3	3	3
7. Vending machine	3	3	0	0	3	3	3	0	0	3	3	3	2	2	0	3	3	3	0	2	2	2	2	0	0	0	0	0	2	2	2	0	2	0	0	3	3	3	0	3	0	0
8. Walls	2	2	2	2	2	0	0	2	0	2	2	2	2	2	2	2	2	3	2	2	2	2	2	2	2	2	2	2	2	2	2	2	3	3	3	3	3	0	2	2	2	0
9. Windows	3	2	2	3	3	3	3	3	3	3	3	3	2	2	3	3	3	3	3	2	3	2	3	3	3	3	3	2	3	3	2	3	3	3	3	3	3	3	2	2	2	2
10. Islands Open	8	8	3	8	3	8	8	8	3	0	3	8	8	8	0	8	8	8	8	8	8	8	8	8	8	8	8	8	8	3	3	8	8	8	8	8	8	8	8	8	8	8
11. Rear	3	0	3	0	3	0	0	0	0	0	0	3	3	0	0	0	0	3	3	0	0	0	7	0	3	0	0	0	3	3	3	3	0	0	0	3	0	0	0	0	0	0
12. Landscaping	7	0	0	0	7	0	0	7	7	0	7	0	0	0	0	0	0	0	7	7	7	7	0	7	0	7	0	0	0	0	7	7	7	7	7	7	7	7	0	3	0	0
13. Signs/lights	7	7	7	7	7	7	7	7	7	7	7	0	7	0	0	0	7	7	7	7	7	7	7	7	7	7	7	0	0	7	7	7	0	7	7	7	7	7	0	0	0	0
B. Inside																																										
14. Floor	2	0	0	0	2	2	2	2	0	2	2	2	0	0	2	2	2	0	2	2	0	0	0	0	0	0	0	0	0	0	0	0	2	2	0	0	0	0	0	0	0	0
15. Walls	2	0	0	0	2	2	2	0	0	2	2	2	0	0	0	0	0	2	2	2	2	2	0	0	0	0	0	0	2	2	2	2	2	2	2	2	2	0	0	0	0	0
16. Ceilings	2	2	2	2	2	2	2	2	0	2	2	2	2	2	2	2	2	2	2	2	2	2	0	0	0	2	0	0	2	2	2	2	0	2	2	2	2	0	0	2	2	2
17. Shelf Display	2	0	0	0	2	2	2	2	0	0	2	2	0	2	0	0	0	2	2	2	0	0	0	0	0	2	0	0	2	2	2	2	0	0	2	2	0	2	0	0	0	0
18. Salesroom	2	2	2	2	2	0	0	0	0	0	2	2	0	0	2	0	0	2	2	2	2	2	0	0	0	2	0	0	2	2	2	2	2	2	2	2	2	2	2	2	2	2
19. Equipment/tools	2	2	2	2	2	2	2	0	0	0	2	2	0	0	0	0	0	2	2	2	2	2	0	0	0	2	0	0	2	2	2	2	0	2	0	0	2	0	0	0	0	0
C. Restrooms																																										
20. Walkways	2	2	2	2	2	2	2	2	2	2	0	2	2	2	2	2	2	2	2	2	2	2	0	0	0	2	0	0	2	0	0	2	2	2	2	2	2	2	0	0	2	2
21. Floor	2	2	0	0	0	0	0	0	0	2	2	2	2	2	0	2	2	2	2	0	2	2	0	0	0	2	0	0	2	0	0	2	0	2	2	2	2	2	0	0	2	2
22. Walls/ceilings	2	2	2	2	2	2	2	2	0	2	2	2	2	2	2	2	2	2	2	2	2	2	0	0	0	2	0	0	2	2	2	2	2	2	2	2	2	2	0	2	2	2
23. Ventilation	2	0	0	2	2	2	2	2	0	2	2	2	0	2	2	2	2	2	2	2	2	0	0	0	0	2	0	0	2	2	2	2	2	2	2	2	2	2	0	2	2	2
24. Equipment	2	2	0	2	2	2	2	2	2	2	2	0	2	2	2	2	2	2	2	2	0	2	0	0	0	2	0	0	2	2	2	2	2	2	2	2	2	2	0	2	2	2
25. Mirror	2	0	0	0	0	0	0	0	0	2	2	2	2	2	2	2	2	2	2	2	2	2	0	0	0	2	0	0	2	2	2	2	2	2	2	2	2	2	0	2	2	2
26. Commode/urinal	2	0	0	0	0	0	0	0	0	2	2	2	2	2	2	2	2	2	2	2	2	2	0	0	0	2	0	0	0	0	0	2	2	2	2	2	2	2	0	2	2	2
27. Wash Basin	2	0	0	0	0	0	0	0	0	2	2	2	2	2	2	2	2	2	2	2	2	2	0	0	0	2	0	0	2	2	2	2	2	2	2	2	2	2	0	2	2	2
28. Waste Basket	2	0	2	0	2	2	2	2	2	2	2	2	2	2	2	2	2	2	2	2	2	2	0	0	0	2	0	0	2	2	2	2	2	2	2	2	2	2	0	2	2	2
29. Lights	2	2	2	2	2	2	2	2	2	2	2	2	2	2	2	2	2	2	2	2	2	2	0	0	0	2	0	0	2	2	2	2	2	2	2	2	2	2	0	2	2	2
30. Soap	2	0	0	0	0	0	0	0	0	2	2	2	2	2	2	2	2	2	2	2	2	2	0	0	0	2	0	0	2	2	2	2	2	2	2	2	2	2	0	2	2	2
31. Towels	2	2	2	2	2	2	2	2	0	2	2	2	2	2	2	2	2	2	2	2	2	2	2	0	2	2	2	2	2	2	2	2	2	2	2	2	2	2	2	2	2	2
32. Toilet Tissue	2	2	2	2	2	2	2	2	0	2	2	2	2	2	2	2	2	2	2	2	2	2	2	0	2	2	2	2	2	2	2	2	2	2	2	2	2	2	2	2	2	2
APPEARANCE SCORE	100	21	58	58	82	75	63	38	75	80	85	82	26	63	44	50	51	76	73	65	66	47	48	13	75	38	41	21	55	33	67	43	54	61	53	59	54	87	43	34	30	36

	Weight Factor	AREA 1											AREA 2																AREA 3													
		1	2	3	4	5	6	7	8	9	10	11	12	13	14	15	16	17	18	19	20	21	22	23	24	25	26	27	28	29	30	31	32	33	34	35	36	37	38	39	40	41
IV. Selling/Serv. Capability	100																																									
A. Tires	50																																									
1. Fast moving sizes	5	0	5	5	0	5	5	5	0	5	5	5	0	5	5	5	0	0	5	5	0	5	5	5	5	0	0	0	5	5	5	5	0	5	0	0	0	0	5	5	5	5
2. Coverage by line	5	5	5	0	5	0	5	5	0	10	5	0	0	0	0	5	0	0	0	5	5	5	0	5	0	0	0	0	0	5	5	0	5	0	5	0	0	0	5	5	5	5
3. Tire selling skills	10	0	0	10	10	5	10	5	10	10	0	0	0	0	0	10	0	10	10	0	0	10	10	0	0	0	0	0	0	0	0	10	10	10	0	10	10	10	0	0	10	0
4. Planned sales sys.	5	0	0	0	5	5	0	5	0	0	5	0	0	0	0	0	0	0	0	0	0	0	0	0	0	0	0	0	0	5	0	0	0	0	0	0	5	0	0	0	0	0
5. Suggestion selling	2	0	0	0	0	0	0	2	0	0	0	0	0	0	0	0	0	0	2	0	0	2	0	0	0	0	2	2	0	0	0	0	0	0	0	0	0	0	0	0	0	0
6. Tires checked	2	2	0	2	2	2	2	2	2	2	2	2	2	2	2	2	2	2	2	2	2	2	2	2	2	2	2	2	2	2	2	2	2	2	2	2	2	2	2	2	2	2
7. Tire changer	2	2	2	2	2	2	2	2	2	2	2	2	2	2	2	2	2	2	2	2	2	2	2	2	2	2	2	2	2	2	2	2	2	2	2	2	2	2	2	2	2	2
8. Balancer	2	2	2	2	2	2	2	2	2	2	2	2	2	2	2	2	2	2	2	2	2	2	2	2	2	2	2	2	2	2	2	2	2	2	2	2	2	2	2	2	2	2
9. Air wrenches	2	0	0	0	0	0	0	0	0	2	2	2	0	2	2	2	0	0	2	0	0	2	2	2	2	2	2	2	2	2	2	2	2	2	2	2	2	2	2	2	2	2
10. Wheel alignment	2	0	0	0	0	0	0	0	0	2	0	0	0	0	0	0	0	2	2	0	0	0	0	2	0	0	2	2	0	0	0	0	0	0	0	0	0	2	0	0	0	0
B. Batteries																																										
11. Fast moving sizes	5	0	5	5	5	5	5	5	0	5	5	0	5	5	5	5	5	0	0	5	5	5	5	5	5	0	0	0	5	5	5	5	5	5	5	0	5	5	5	5	5	5
12. Coverage by line	5	0	5	0	0	5	5	5	0	0	5	0	0	0	0	5	5	0	5	5	5	5	5	5	0	0	0	0	5	5	5	5	5	0	5	5	5	5	5	5	5	5
13. Batt. selling skills	6	0	0	0	6	6	6	6	6	6	6	6	0	6	6	0	0	0	0	6	6	4	0	0	0	0	0	0	0	6	6	0	0	0	6	6	6	6	6	6	6	0
14. Planned sales sys.	4	0	0	0	4	4	4	4	0	4	4	0	0	0	0	0	0	0	0	4	4	4	0	0	0	0	0	0	0	0	0	0	4	4	2	2	4	4	4	4	4	2
15. Hydrometer	2	2	2	2	2	2	2	2	2	2	2	2	2	2	2	2	2	2	2	2	2	2	2	2	2	2	2	2	2	2	2	2	2	2	2	2	2	2	2	2	2	2
16. Battery charger	2	2	2	2	2	2	2	2	2	2	2	2	2	2	2	2	2	2	2	2	2	2	2	2	2	2	2	2	2	2	2	2	2	2	2	2	2	2	2	2	2	2
17. Battery Tester	2	2	2	2	2	2	2	2	2	2	2	2	2	2	2	2	2	2	2	2	2	2	2	2	2	2	2	2	2	2	2	2	2	2	2	2	2	2	2	2	2	2
18. Battery tester used	2	2	2	2	2	2	2	2	0	2	2	2	2	2	2	2	2	2	2	2	2	2	2	2	2	2	2	2	2	2	2	2	2	2	2	2	2	2	2	2	2	2
C. Acc./Impulse Items																																										
19. Adequate supply	2	2	2	0	0	0	2	2	0	2	2	0	0	0	0	2	2	2	2	2	2	2	2	2	2	2	2	2	0	0	2	2	2	2	2	2	2	2	0	2	2	2
20. Fast moving items	4	4	4	4	4	4	4	1	4	4	4	4	2	4	4	4	4	4	2	4	4	4	2	2	4	4	4	4	2	4	4	4	0	0	4	2	4	4	4	4	2	2
21. Suggestion selling	2	0	0	0	0	0	0	2	0	2	2	2	2	0	2	0	0	2	2	0	0	0	0	0	2	2	0	0	0	0	0	0	2	2	2	0	0	2	0	0	0	0
D. Motor Oil																																										
22. Adequate supply	4	4	4	4	4	4	4	4	0	4	4	4	4	4	4	4	4	4	4	2	4	4	4	4	4	4	4	4	4	4	4	4	4	4	4	4	4	4	4	4	4	4
23. Employee competence	4	4	4	4	4	4	4	4	0	4	4	4	4	4	4	4	4	4	4	4	4	4	4	4	4	4	4	4	4	4	4	4	4	4	0	4	4	4	4	4	4	4
E. Services																																										
24. Tune-up	2	2	2	2	2	2	2	2	2	2	2	2	2	2	2	2	2	2	2	2	2	2	2	2	2	2	2	2	2	2	2	2	2	2	2	2	2	2	2	2	2	2
25. Brake service	2	2	2	2	2	2	2	2	2	2	2	2	2	2	2	2	2	2	2	2	2	2	2	2	2	2	2	2	2	0	2	2	2	2	2	2	2	2	2	2	2	2
26. Air Cond. Service	2	2	2	2	2	2	2	2	2	2	2	2	2	2	2	2	2	2	2	2	2	2	2	2	2	2	2	2	2	2	2	2	2	2	2	2	2	2	2	2	2	2
27. Road service	2	2	2	2	2	2	2	2	0	2	2	2	2	2	2	0	0	0	2	0	2	2	2	2	0	0	2	2	0	0	0	0	2	2	2	2	2	2	2	2	2	2
28. Pick-up & delivery	2	2	2	2	2	2	2	2	2	2	2	2	2	2	2	2	2	2	2	2	2	2	2	2	2	2	2	2	2	2	2	2	2	2	2	2	2	2	2	2	2	2
29. State inspect./lic.	2	0	0	0	0	2	0	0	2	0	0	0	0	0	0	0	0	0	2	2	2	0	0	0	0	0	0	0	0	0	0	0	0	0	0	0	0	0	0	0	0	0
30. "Customer reminder"	2	0	0	0	0	0	0	0	0	0	0	0	0	0	0	2	0	0	0	0	0	0	0	0	0	0	0	0	0	0	2	0	0	0	0	0	0	0	0	0	0	0
31. Proper equipment	2	5	5	5	5	5	5	5	5	5	5	0	0	0	0	5	5	5	5	5	5	5	5	5	5	0	0	0	0	5	5	5	5	5	5	5	5	5	5	5	5	5
SERVICE CAPABILITY SCORE	100	50	40	65	48	80	85	91	20	88	88	71	40	46	67	85	42	36	56	90	47	71	70	53	57	34	38	40	47	33	96	53	69	74	50	58	63	81	91	53	90	63

Table: Service Station Evaluation Form — columns 1–41 grouped under AREA 1 (cols 1–11), AREA 2 (cols 12–27), AREA 3 (cols 28–41).

	Weight Factor	1	2	3	4	5	6	7	8	9	10	11	12	13	14	15	16	17	18	19	20	21	22	23	24	25	26	27	28	29	30	31	32	33	34	35	36	37	38	39	40	41
I. Personnel Appearance/Service																																										
A. First Impression																																										
1. Attention	10	10	10	10	10	10	10	10	0	0	10	10	10	0	10	10	10	0	10	10	10	10	0	0	0	0	10	10	10	0	10	10	5	0	10	10	10	10	10	10	0	10
2. Greeting	10	10	10	10	10	0	10	10	0	10	10	10	0	10	10	10	10	10	10	10	10	10	0	10	0	0	10	10	10	10	10	10	10	10	10	10	10	10	10	10	10	10
B. Sales/Service																																										
3. Order/Fill up	10	0	10	10	10	10	10	10	0	10	10	10	0	10	10	10	10	10	10	10	10	10	10	10	0	0	0	10	10	10	0	10	15	10	0	0	10	10	10	10	0	0
4. Windshield	10	0	10	10	10	0	10	10	10	10	10	10	0	0	0	0	10	0	10	10	10	10	10	10	10	10	10	10	10	10	10	10	0	10	10	0	10	10	10	0	10	10
5. Rear Window	10	0	10	10	10	0	0	10	0	0	10	10	0	0	0	0	0	0	0	0	0	0	0	0	0	0	0	0	0	0	0	0	0	0	0	0	0	0	0	0	0	0
6. Hood Inspection	15	15	15	15	15	15	15	15	0	15	15	15	15	0	15	15	15	15	15	15	15	15	15	15	15	0	0	15	15	15	15	15	0	15	15	15	15	15	15	15	15	15
7. Transaction	10	10	10	10	10	10	10	0	0	10	10	10	0	10	10	0	0	10	10	10	10	10	10	10	10	10	0	0	10	10	10	10	10	10	10	10	10	10	10	10	10	0
8. Approved Uniforms	15	0	0	0	15	15	0	0	15	15	15	15	0	15	15	0	0	15	10	0	15	0	0	0	0	15	0	0	0	0	15	0	15	15	0	0	0	0	0	15	0	0
9. Personnel Appear.	10	10	10	10	10	10	10	10	10	10	10	10	10	10	0	0	10	10	10	10	10	0	10	10	0	0	0	0	0	0	0	10	0	10	0	0	10	10	0	0	10	0
PERSONNEL SCORE	100	65	75	85	100	90	75	85	25	100	100	100	25	50	70	85	85	60	95	85	100	75	65	45	55	35	75	65	55	45	75	90	85	100	75	65	85	85	75	80	65	65
II. Product Merchandising																																										
1. Price Sign	15	0	15	0	0	0	0	0	0	15	15	15	0	15	15	15	0	0	15	15	15	15	15	0	0	15	10	15	15	15	15	5	15	0	15	15	10	10	0	0	0	0
2. Oil Display	3	0	0	0	0	0	5	0	0	3	3	3	0	0	0	0	0	0	0	0	0	0	3	3	3	3	0	0	3	3	3	0	0	0	0	0	0	3	3	0	5	2
3. Oil Displ. Attract	3	0	0	0	0	0	5	0	0	3	3	3	0	0	0	0	0	0	0	0	0	0	0	0	5	0	3	0	3	5	5	0	0	0	0	0	3	3	3	3	0	3
4. Tires at Island	6	0	0	0	0	0	0	0	0	0	6	6	0	0	0	0	0	0	0	0	0	0	0	0	0	0	0	0	0	0	0	0	0	0	0	0	0	0	0	0	0	0
5. Tires at Bay	6	0	0	0	0	0	0	0	0	6	6	6	0	0	0	0	0	6	6	0	0	0	0	0	0	0	0	0	0	0	6	6	0	0	0	6	0	0	0	0	0	6
6. Tires in Sales Room	6	0	0	0	0	6	0	0	0	6	6	6	0	0	0	0	0	0	6	0	0	0	0	0	0	6	0	0	0	0	0	0	0	0	6	6	0	0	0	0	0	6
7. Tires Displ Attraction	6	0	0	0	0	10	0	0	0	0	0	0	0	0	0	0	0	10	0	0	0	10	10	0	0	0	0	0	0	0	0	0	0	0	0	0	0	0	0	0	0	0
8. Tires Price Displ.	6	0	0	0	0	0	0	0	0	0	0	0	0	0	0	0	0	0	0	0	0	0	6	0	0	0	0	0	3	3	0	3	0	0	0	0	0	0	0	0	0	0
9. Batteries Dis. Att.	3	0	0	0	0	0	0	0	0	0	0	0	0	3	3	0	0	0	3	3	3	3	0	0	3	3	0	0	0	3	0	3	3	3	0	0	3	3	3	3	0	0
10. Batteries Displ.	3	0	0	0	0	0	0	0	0	0	0	0	0	3	3	0	0	3	3	3	3	3	3	0	3	3	0	0	0	3	0	3	3	3	0	3	3	3	3	3	0	0
11. Impulse Items Displ	6	0	0	0	0	0	0	0	0	6	6	6	0	0	0	0	0	6	0	0	0	6	0	6	0	0	0	0	0	6	0	0	0	0	0	0	6	6	6	6	0	6
12. Accessories Displ	6	0	6	6	0	6	6	6	0	0	6	6	0	6	6	6	6	6	6	6	6	6	6	6	0	6	0	0	6	0	6	6	6	6	6	6	6	6	6	6	6	6
13. Window Displays	6	0	0	0	0	0	0	6	0	6	6	0	0	0	6	6	0	0	0	6	0	6	6	0	6	0	0	0	0	6	6	6	6	6	6	6	6	0	6	0	6	6
14. Value Cent. Adv.	6	0	6	6	3	6	6	6	0	6	6	6	0	0	0	6	0	0	0	6	0	0	0	0	6	6	0	0	0	0	0	6	6	6	6	6	6	0	6	6	6	6
15. V.C. Ads. Current	6	0	0	0	3	6	6	6	6	6	6	6	3	3	3	6	3	3	6	6	3	3	6	3	3	3	0	0	3	3	3	6	6	6	6	6	0	3	3	0	3	6
16. Machines Working	3	3	3	3	3	3	3	3	6	3	3	3	3	3	3	6	3	3	3	3	3	3	3	3	3	3	3	0	3	3	3	3	6	6	6	6	3	3	3	3	3	3
17. Self Service/Expres	6	6	6	6	6	6	6	6	6	6	6	6	6	6	6	6	6	6	6	6	6	6	6	6	6	6	3	6	6	6	6	6	6	6	6	6	6	6	6	6	6	6
MERCHANDISE SCORE	100	6	24	21	9	43	37	21	6	36	92	60	9	42	45	39	9	52	33	36	33	42	61	12	56	30	16	24	39	30	68	23	48	15	30	31	37	31	33	30	17	38

V. Retailer Evaluation

Evaluation matrix — AREA 1 (columns 1–11), AREA 2 (columns 12–27), AREA 3 (columns 28–41).

Retailer Evaluation	Weight Factor	1	2	3	4	5	6	7	8	9	10	11	12	13	14	15	16	17	18	19	20	21	22	23	24	25	26	27	28	29	30	31	32	33	34	35	36	37	38	39	40	41
1. Meets People	5	0	5	5	5	5	5	5	0	5	5	5	0	0	0	0	5	5	5	5	5	5	0	0	0	5	5	5	0	5	0	0	5	5	5	0	5	5	5	0	0	0
2. Product Knowledge	5	0	0	0	5	5	5	5	5	5	5	5	0	0	5	5	5	5	5	5	5	5	5	5	5	0	0	0	5	5	5	5	5	5	5	5	5	5	5	5	5	5
3. Car Wash Quality	5	0	0	5	5	5	5	5	0	5	5	5	0	5	0	5	5	5	5	5	5	5	5	5	5	5	5	5	5	5	5	5	5	5	5	5	5	5	5	5	5	5
4. Customer Complaints	5	5	5	5	0	0	5	5	0	2	2	5	0	0	2	5	2	2	2	5	5	2	5	2	2	5	2	2	2	2	5	5	5	5	5	5	2	2	2	2	2	2
5. Employees Dependable	2	2	0	5	2	2	2	2	2	2	2	2	0	2	2	2	2	2	2	2	2	2	2	2	2	2	0	2	2	2	2	2	2	2	2	2	2	2	2	2	2	2
6. Discipline	2	2	2	2	2	2	2	2	2	2	2	0	0	0	2	2	2	2	5	2	2	2	0	0	0	0	0	0	0	0	5	5	2	2	2	0	2	2	2	2	2	2
7. Auto Repair Class	2	0	0	2	2	2	2	5	0	5	5	5	2	2	5	0	2	5	5	5	5	5	5	5	5	5	5	5	5	5	5	5	2	5	5	0	5	5	2	0	5	5
8. Trains Salesmen	5	2	2	0	5	5	5	5	0	5	5	5	0	5	5	0	0	0	0	0	0	0	0	0	0	0	0	5	0	0	5	0	2	0	2	0	5	5	5	0	5	5
9. Empl. Reference Checks	2	2	2	2	2	2	2	2	2	2	2	2	2	2	0	2	2	2	2	2	2	2	2	2	0	0	2	2	2	2	5	2	2	2	2	2	2	2	2	2	2	2
10. Work Order System	2	2	2	2	2	2	2	2	2	2	2	2	2	0	0	0	2	2	2	2	2	2	2	2	2	0	0	2	2	5	5	5	2	5	2	2	2	2	2	2	2	2
11. Business Records	5	5	5	5	5	5	5	5	0	5	5	5	5	5	5	5	5	5	5	5	5	5	5	5	5	5	5	5	5	5	5	5	5	5	5	5	5	5	5	5	5	5
12. Storeroom Locked	2	0	0	0	0	0	0	0	0	0	0	2	0	2	2	0	0	0	0	0	0	0	0	0	0	0	0	0	0	0	0	0	0	0	0	0	0	0	0	0	0	0
13. Inventory Program	2	0	2	2	2	2	2	0	0	2	2	2	2	2	2	0	0	0	2	0	2	2	2	2	2	2	0	2	2	2	0	0	0	0	0	0	0	0	0	0	0	0
14. Shift Leaders Resp.	2	2	2	2	2	2	2	2	2	2	2	2	2	2	2	2	2	2	2	2	2	2	0	2	2	2	2	2	2	2	5	5	5	5	2	2	5	5	2	2	2	2
15. Payment of Bills	2	2	0	2	0	0	5	5	0	5	0	0	5	0	0	5	5	0	5	5	0	0	0	5	5	5	5	0	0	5	5	5	5	5	5	5	5	5	5	5	5	5
16. Profits/Salary	5	5	5	0	5	5	5	5	0	5	5	5	0	0	0	0	0	0	0	0	0	0	0	0	0	0	5	0	0	5	5	5	5	0	0	5	0	0	0	0	0	0
17. Working Cash	7	0	0	7	0	0	0	0	7	7	0	0	0	0	0	0	0	0	0	0	0	0	7	7	7	0	0	0	0	0	0	0	0	0	0	0	0	0	0	0	0	0
18. Sales and Profit Obj.	7	5	5	5	5	5	5	5	5	5	5	5	5	5	5	5	5	5	5	5	5	5	5	5	0	0	0	5	0	5	5	5	5	5	5	5	5	5	5	5	5	5
19. P/L Statements	5	5	0	0	0	0	0	0	0	0	0	0	0	0	0	0	0	0	0	0	0	0	5	0	0	0	0	0	0	0	0	5	5	0	0	0	0	0	0	0	0	0
20. Compensation Programs	10	10	10	10	10	10	10	10	0	10	10	10	10	10	10	0	0	0	10	10	10	10	10	10	10	0	0	0	0	0	0	10	10	10	10	10	10	10	10	10	10	10
21. Qualified Technician	5	5	0	5	5	5	5	5	0	5	5	5	5	5	5	5	5	0	5	5	5	5	5	5	0	0	0	0	0	5	5	5	5	5	0	0	5	5	5	5	5	5
22. Qualified Salesman	5	5	5	0	0	5	5	5	0	5	5	5	0	0	0	0	0	0	0	0	0	0	5	0	0	0	0	5	0	5	5	0	0	0	0	0	5	5	5	0	0	5
23. Motivation and Desire	10	10	10	10	0	0	10	10	0	10	10	10	0	0	0	0	0	0	5	0	0	0	0	0	0	0	0	0	0	0	10	0	10	0	0	0	0	0	0	0	0	0
RETAILER SCORE		62	52	59	64	89	87	96	12	91	81	71	43	49	48	74	44	42	67	78	79	59	57	39	57	19	38	51	27	41	71	77	59	81	52	55	74	74	74	60	52	69
OVERALL EVALUATION SCORE		204	249	288	303	377	347	331	78	395	446	384	143	250	274	333	323	266	324	354	325	294	301	162	300	156	208	201	223	182	377	286	315	331	260	268	313	358	316	257	254	27

Walters could also make a few additional notes at the end of the form. Here are some examples:

Store 12 - had pay rest rooms which are quite irregular

13 - dealer was drinking beer in his office during the day

14 - watchdog was quite uninviting

13, 31, 39 - dealer has language problem

25 - store still has an Enco sign up

35 - abandoned canopy makes store look like it's partially closed or going out of business

37 - store has a canopy under which there are no pumps

2, 8, 15, 30, 41 - side island closed

Most of the other miscellaneous comments dealt with junk cars on the premises, high weeds, grass, or shrubs that need cutting, and faded signs that need repainting.

With the information he has obtained, Walters feels confident he can identify the problem stores and recommend action in each case.

Boulder Company

J.D. Roberts, the sales manager for the Boulder Company, was concerned in the summer of 1980 with evaluating the adequacy of his company's sales person deployment procedures. His concern was based less on specific evidence of any problem than it was on the realization that population shifts, particularly in the West, had been significant. The last audit of manpower deployment had been done in 1970.

Boulder was headquartered in Sacramento, California, but sold its line of household wax products and insecticides nationally. 60 percent of the sales went through conventional grocery outlets while the rest, labeled as "wholesale," went through hardware wholesalers, department stores, and variety chains. In California, Boulder had 20 percent of the market, although its national market share was much less. Sales were made by 230 salespeople who operated out of thirty district offices and six sales regions.

Roberts knew that any territory analysis would need to look at the work load required and the potential dollar sales volume. Before asking his field managers for an evaluation of their territories, he decided first to establish some broad measurement criteria for his field managers to follow, and to make a test case study of the San Francisco district.

The criteria considered were the following:

1. Don't divide sales responsibility for particular accounts among several salespeople.

2. Limit each sales supervisor to supervision, i.e. no selling!

3. Base territory assignments primarily upon work load requirements modified by sales potential.

4. Establish work load standards that are consistent within each district.

5. Be sure the analyses are impersonal.

Reprinted from *Stanford Business Cases 1980* with permission of the publishers, Stanford University Graduate School of Business, © 1980 by the Board of Trustees of the Leland Stanford Junior University.

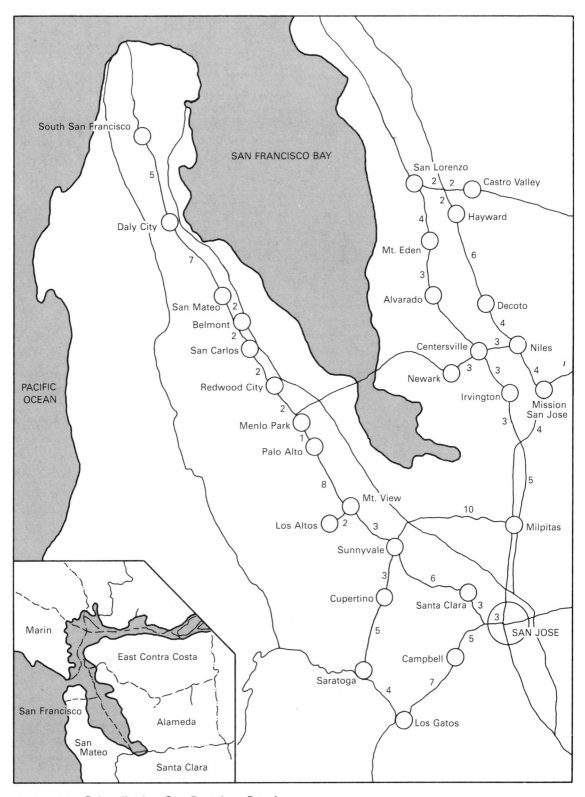

EXHIBIT 1 Sales districts San Francisco Bay Area

San Francisco was selected as the test case because of its proximity to the company headquarters, and because it represented the area of the United States most affected by the population moves of the 1970s.

The California region consisted of five districts, one of which was the Bay Area (see Exhibit 1 for a map of the district). Four teams of salespeople worked the district and their average weekly sales per salesperson are summarized below:

Supervisor	# of salespeople	Average weekly sales	Area
Wigmore	3	$17,949	San Francisco
Balter	2	$15,501	North Peninsula and Marin
Edmonds	3	$12,693	San Jose, Hayward San Leandro and South Peninsula
Brommer	2	$ 7,623	Richmond-East Contra Costa

It was decided to use the Edmonds team as the focal part of the study. A report by the Survey of Buying Power in 1978 illustrates the differences in retail food sales among the cities and are summarized in Exhibit 2.

Roberts took a closer look at the Edmonds team and discovered that the individual weekly averages for the three salesmen were: San Jose $12,051; South Peninsula, $16,239 and Hayward-San Leandro, $10,947. The intriguing question, of course, was whether the differences in yield represented important differences in work load, or whether the work loads were well balanced.

In order to determine territorial work loads, standards had to be set for the various parts of the selling job. Roberts decided on the following:

1. Standards would reflect "the average salesperson" so that the superior performer could exceed them and the weak salesperson would have trouble keeping up.

2. Wholesalers were classified as affiliated[1] (large) or non-affiliated (small). Six large account calls and ten small account calls were to be the daily averages. Large accounts were to be visited every four weeks and small accounts every six weeks.

3. Buying offices of chains, both national and local, were to be called on every four weeks. Six such calls per day were expected.

4. Salesmen could make turnover[2] sales for wholesalers and chains but were restricted to 15 percent of the customer's purchase. The minimum average turnover business was established at $750 per day.

---

[1]Attached to buying groups or voluntaries.

[2]While making missionary calls on the individual stores of a chain, the salesperson might write some orders which were "turned over" to the wholesaler or chain's buying office.

5. Call lengths on other direct buying accounts (department and variety stores) were hard to estimate (they varied considerably). As a compromise, the standard was set at $1,500 sales per day.

6. The salesperson was expected to be able to handle five special promotions (displays) per day.

7. Yearly selling time was estimated at 240 days.

Exhibits 3, 4, and 5 summarize the data for the Edmonds team. Using Roberts' standards, what conclusions do you reach for each salesperson? How would you bring the system into balance?

EXHIBIT 2   1980 population and food sales for selected San Francisco Bay area markets

	Population (Thous.)	Food Sales ($000)
North Peninsula Market Area		
South San Francisco	50.7	61,827
Daly City	76.3	71,871
San Mateo	78.3	91,379
South Peninsula Market Area		
Redwood City	54.9	75,006
Palo Alto	55.7	58,465
Mountain View	56.8	69,581
San Jose Market Area		
Sunnyvale	106.3	89,156
Santa Clara	84.2	99,602
San Jose	603.3	516,223
Hayward-San Leandro Market Area		
Alameda	71.3	63,770
San Leandro	67.7	99,588
Hayward	96.3	114,082

EXHIBIT 3 Sales results—San Jose area

	Number of Accounts								$ Volume (in thousands)							
	2nd Half - 1979				1st Half - 1980				2nd Half - 1979				1st Half - 1980			
Type of Accounts	Act.	Pot.	Act.	Pot.	Act.	Pot.	Act.	Pot.	Act.	Pot.	Act.	Pot.	Act.	Pot.	Act.	Pot.
Wholesale Accounts	*Affiliated*		*Non-Affiliated*		*Affiliated*		*Non-Affiliated*		*Affiliated*		*Non-Affiliated*		*Affiliated*		*Non-Affiliated*	
Wholesale grocers	14	16	16	20	14	16	18	20	22.2	93.0	15.6	79.0	24.2	100.6	17.2	85.6
Wholesale hardware	6	8	8	10	6	10	10	12	8.8	56.6	9.0	42.2	9.6	54.4	9.8	45.6
Wholesale, other	4	6	8	12	4	6	6	10	6.2	44.4	7.0	38.0	6.8	48.0	7.6	41.0
Total wholesale	24	30	32	42	24	32	34	42	37.2	188.0	31.6	159.2	40.6	203.0	34.6	172.2
Chain stores	*National*		*Local*		*National*		*Local*		*National*		*Local*		*National*		*Local*	
Grocery	10	12	16	18	10	12	16	20	32.0	114.2	15.0	75.0	35.0	123.4	16.4	81.0
Department	2	6	4	8	2	8	4	10	7.2	85.6	4.0	34.0	7.8	92.6	4.4	36.8
Variety	2	6	2	6	2	6	4	6	7.0	30.2	3.8	25.8	7.4	32.6	4.2	27.8
Total chains	14	24	22	32	14	26	24	36	46.2	230.0	22.8	134.8	50.2	248.6	25.0	145.6
Other direct	*Class A&B*		*Class C&D*		*Class A&B*		*Class C&D*		*Class A&B*		*Class C&D*		*Class A&B*		*Class C&D*	
Department stores	10	16	40	52	12	20	44	56	2.6	13.6	1.2	6.8	2.8	14.8	1.4	7.4
Indep. variety	32	40	76	98	30	42	82	104	4.4	27.4	2.2	10.0	4.8	29.6	2.4	10.8
Indep. grocery	100	114	278	314	104	120	280	320	17.4	80.2	6.6	33.6	19.0	88.6	7.2	36.4
Total other	142	170	394	464	146	182	406	480	24.4	121.2	10.0	50.4	26.6	133.0	11.0	54.6
Grand total	180	224	448	538	184	240	464	558	107.8	539.2	64.4	344.4	117.4	584.6	70.6	372.4

50 displays per ½ year.

EXHIBIT 4 Sales results—South Peninsula area

Type of Accounts	Number of Accounts 2nd Half - 1979 Affiliated Act.	Pot.	Non-Affiliated Act.	Pot.	1st Half - 1980 Affiliated Act.	Pot.	Non-Affiliated Act.	Pot.	$ Volume (in thousands) 2nd Half - 1979 Affiliated Act.	Pot.	Non-Affiliated Act.	Pot.	1st Half - 1980 Affiliated Act.	Pot.	Non-Affiliated Act.	Pot.
Wholesale Accounts																
Wholesale grocers	4	14	8	20	5	16	8	20	12.9	120.2	7.1	72.6	13.2	124.2	7.6	78.6
Wholesale hardware	2	6	1	4	2	6	2	6	4.8	63.8	3.2	34.4	5.1	69.6	3.5	36.6
Wholesale, other	3	8	5	10	3	8	4	10	3.9	51.4	2.7	30.8	3.8	54.8	3.0	33.0
Total wholesale	9	28	14	34	10	30	14	36	21.6	235.4	13.0	137.8	22.1	248.6	14.1	148.2
Chain stores	*National*		*Local*		*National*		*Local*		*National*		*Local*		*National*		*Local*	
Grocery	6	14	8	22	6	16	8	20	35.1	379.0	16.1	188.2	36.5	402.2	16.6	197.4
Department	2	6	2	8	1	6	3	8	7.9	91.6	4.1	46.8	8.4	101.8	4.5	50.2
Variety	2	6	5	10	2	6	5	10	7.6	91.2	3.7	42.6	8.2	98.4	4.2	46.8
Total chains	10	26	15	40	9	28	16	38	50.6	561.8	23.9	277.6	53.1	602.4	25.3	294.4
Other direct	*Class A&B*		*Class C&D*		*Class A&B*		*Class C&D*		*Class A&B*		*Class C&D*		*Class A&B*		*Class C&D*	
Department stores	8	20	19	50	10	24	18	48	1.1	16.2	0.3	2.2	1.4	18.2	0.4	4.2
Indep. variety	17	48	36	88	18	46	37	92	1.6	18.4	0.5	4.2	1.9	20.6	0.6	5.6
Indep. grocery	59	142	113	252	62	148	115	254	7.2	107.8	1.8	18.4	7.9	112.2	2.1	20.6
Total other	84	210	168	390	90	218	170	394	9.9	142.4	2.6	24.8	11.2	151.0	3.1	30.4
Grand total	103	264	197	464	109	276	200	468	82.1	939.6	39.5	440.2	86.4	1002.0	42.5	473.0

60 displays per ½ year.

EXHIBIT 5 Sales results—San Leandro-Hayward area

Number of Accounts

Type of Accounts	2nd Half - 1979 Affiliated Act.	Pot.	2nd Half - 1979 Non-Affiliated Act.	Pot.	1st Half - 1980 Affiliated Act.	Pot.	1st Half - 1980 Non-Affiliated Act.	Pot.
Wholesale Accounts								
Wholesale grocers	5	14	6	16	6	14	7	18
Wholesale hardware	1	4	2	4	1	4	2	6
Wholesale, other	1	2	2	6	1	2	2	6
Total wholesale	7	20	10	26	8	20	11	30
Chain stores	*National*		*Local*		*National*		*Local*	
Grocery	4	10	7	16	4	10	8	18
Department	2	6	3	6	2	6	3	6
Variety	2	4	2	4	2	4	1	4
Total chains	8	20	12	26	8	20	12	28
Other direct	*Class A&B*		*Class C&D*		*Class A&B*		*Class C&D*	
Department stores	9	26	27	72	10	26	29	70
Indep. variety	12	32	30	80	13	34	31	80
Indep. grocery	44	106	119	258	44	110	120	260
Total other	65	164	176	410	67	176	180	410
Grand total	80	204	198	462	83	216	203	468

$ Volume (in thousands)

Type of Accounts	2nd Half - 1979 Affiliated Act.	Pot.	2nd Half - 1979 Non-Affiliated Act.	Pot.	1st Half - 1980 Affiliated Act.	Pot.	1st Half - 1980 Non-Affiliated Act.	Pot.
Wholesale Accounts								
Wholesale grocers	15.7	133.4	12.9	101.4	15.9	134.6	13.2	105.6
Wholesale hardware	2.6	36.2	3.2	33.8	2.8	39.2	3.5	35.2
Wholesale, other	2.5	18.4	2.9	32.8	2.6	19.8	3.1	33.6
Total wholesale	20.8	188.0	19.0	168.0	21.3	193.6	19.8	174.4
Chain stores	*National*		*Local*		*National*		*Local*	
Grocery	10.3	89.4	13.6	115.6	10.5	91.4	13.8	117.4
Department	4.8	54.4	4.4	35.2	5.1	56.4	5.2	36.8
Variety	5.1	34.4	1.9	31.0	5.5	34.6	1.9	32.4
Total chains	20.2	178.2	19.9	181.8	21.1	182.4	20.9	186.6
Other direct	*Class A&B*		*Class C&D*		*Class A&B*		*Class C&D*	
Department stores	0.6	8.6	0.3	1.4	0.7	8.8	0.3	1.8
Indep. variety	1.3	10.6	0.3	2.2	1.5	11.8	0.3	2.4
Indep. grocery	5.3	50.4	1.5	15.8	5.6	52.0	1.6	16.2
Total other	7.2	69.6	2.1	19.4	7.8	72.6	2.2	20.4
Grand total	48.2	435.8	41.0	369.2	50.2	448.6	42.9	381.4

40 displays per ½ year.

The Ford Motor Co.

On October 1, 1979, Henry Ford II retired as chief executive officer of the Ford Motor Co., a post he had held for thirty-four years. About six months later, he also stepped down as chairman of the board of directors, but chose to remain a member of the board of directors and chairman of the board's finance committee. Replacing Mr. Ford as chairman of the board and CEO was Philip Caldwell, who had recently served as the company's president.

At the end of 1981, Ford's top management team consisted of Caldwell and Donald E. Petersen, president and chief operating officer; Will M. Caldwell, executive vice president and chief financial officer; and William C. Ford, vice chairman of the board. William C. Ford, Henry Ford's younger brother, had formerly served as chairman of the company's executive committee and vice president-product design.

1980 and 1981 were disastrous years for Ford. In 1980, the company lost $1.543 billion, and in 1981, $1.060 billion. In these two years, Ford sold only 4.3 million cars and trucks, compared to 6.4 million as recently as 1977 and 1978. The company's market shares, both domestic and international, dropped steadily during the last half of the 1970s.

OPERATIONS

Ford's major line of business is the manufacture, assembly, and sales of cars and trucks and their related parts and accessories (Automotive Division). Other lines include the manufacture of tractors, the Steel Division, Glass Division, Ford Aerospace, Ford Credit, American Road Insurance Company, Ford Leasing Development Company, and Ford Motor Land Development Corporation. Exhibit 1 shows the company's sales and operating income by the automotive and other sectors for 1978-1981. Exhibit 2 contains a ten-year financial summary, 1972-1981.

This case was developed by Richard T. Hise, Professor of Marketing at Texas A&M University, as a basis for class discussion rather than to illustrate either effective or ineffective marketing management.

EXHIBIT 1 Worldwide sales and operating income by line of business (dollar amounts in millions)

	1981		1980		1979		1978	
	Amount	Percent	Amount	Percent	Amount	Percent	Amount	Percent
Sales								
Automotive	$34,673	91%	$33,303	90%	$39,899	92%	$40,040	94%
All other*	3,574	9	3,783	10	3,615	8	2,744	6%
Total	$38,247	100%	$37,086	100%	$43,514	100%	$42,784	100%
Operating income								
Automotive	$(1,246)	(99)%	$(2,179)	(96)%	$ 736	80%	$ 2,380	101%
All other*	(10)	(1)	(99)	(4)	181	20	(21)	(1)
Total	$(1,256)	(100)%	$(2,278)	(100)%	$ 917	100%	$ 2,359	100%

*All Other category includes Tractor Operations and the nonautomotive products of Steel Division, Glass Division and Ford Aerospace & Communications Corporation.

SOURCE: Company Annual Reports.

Summary of Operations	1981	1980	1979	1978	1977	1976[1]	1975	1974	1973	1972
Sales	$38,247.1	$37,085.5	43,513.7	42,784.1	37,841.5	28,839.6	24,009.1	23,620.6	23,015.1	20,194.4
Total costs	39,502.9	39,363.8	42,596.7	40,425.6	35,095.9	27,252.7	23,572.7	23,015.4	21,446.1	18,568.4
Operating income (loss)	(1,255.8)	(2,278.3)	917.0	2,358.5	2,745.6	1,586.9	436.4	605.2	1,569.0	1,626.0
Interest income	624.6	543.1	693.0	456.0	299.1	232.6	155.8	171.4	189.9	109.3
Interest expense	674.7	432.5	246.8	194.8	192.7	216.6	301.0	281.5	174.7	133.6
Equities in net income of unconsolidated subsidiaries and affiliates	167.8	187.0	146.2	159.0	150.0	136.3	107.0	58.5	48.5	60.9
Income (loss) before income taxes	(1,138.1)	(1,980.7)	1,509.4	2,778.7	3,002.0	1,739.2	398.2	553.6	1,632.7	1,662.6
Provision (credit) for income taxes	(68.3)[2]	(435.4)[2]	330.1[2]	1,175.0	1,325.6	730.6	151.9	201.5	702.1	773.3
Minority interests	(9.7)	(2.0)	10.0	14.8	3.6	25.5	18.8	25.0	24.1	19.3
Income (loss) before cumulative effect of an accounting change	(1,060.1)	(1,543.3)	1,169.3	1,588.9	1,672.8	983.1	227.5	327.1▲	906.5▲	870.0▲
Cumulative effect of an accounting change[3]	—	—	—	—	—	—	95.2	—	—	—
Net income (loss)	(1,060.1)	(1,543.3)	1,169.3	1,588.9	1,672.8	983.1	322.7	327.1	906.5	870.0
Cash dividends	144.4	312.7	467.6	416.6	359.3	263.4	242.6	298.1	317.1	272.9
Retained income (loss)	$(1,204.5)	(1,856.0)	701.7	1,172.3	1,313.5	719.7	80.1	29.0	589.4	597.1
Income before minority interests as percentage of sales	*	*	2.7%	3.7%	4.4%	3.5%	1.4%	1.5%	4.0%	4.4%
Stockholders' equity at year-end	$ 7,362.2	8,567.5	10,420.7	9,686.3	8,456.9	7,107.0	6,376.5	6,267.5	6,405.1	5,961.3
Assets at year-end	$23,021.4	24,347.6	23,524.6	22,101.4	19,241.3	15,768.1	14,020.2	14,173.6	12,954.0	11,634.0
Long-term debt at year-end	$ 2,709.7	2,058.8	1,274.6	1,144.5	1,359.7	1,411.4	1,533.9	1,476.7	977.0	993.9
Average number of shares of capital stock outstanding (in millions)	120.3	120.3	119.9	119.0	118.1	117.6	116.6	116.8	124.1	127.7
A share (in dollars) Income (loss) before cumulative effect of an accounting change	$ (8.81)	(12.83)	9.75	13.35	14.16	8.36	1.95	2.80▲	7.31▲	6.81▲
Cumulative effect of an accounting change[3]	—	—	—	—	—	—	0.82	—	—	—
Net income (loss)[4]	$ (8.81)	(12.83)	9.75	13.35	14.16	8.36	2.77	2.80	7.31	6.81
Net income assuming full dilution[4]	$ —	—	9.15	12.42	13.08	7.74	2.65	2.69▲	6.86▲	6.53▲
Cash dividends	$ 1.20	2.60	3.90	3.50	3.04	2.24	2.08	2.56	2.56	2.14
Stockholders' equity at year-end	$ 61.06	71.05	86.46	80.77	71.15	60.14	54.09	53.58	51.66	46.99
Common Stock price range (NYSE)	$ 26	35¾	45⅜	51⅞	49¼	49½	36¼	43½	65⅞	63⅞
	$ 15¾	18⅛	29⅜	39	41⅜	34⅞	25⅞	23	30⅞	48¾

▲Pro forma amounts assuming the investment tax credits accrued after 1970 flowed through to income in the year the assets were placed in service:

Net income (in millions)	—	—	—	—	—	—	—	$363.9	938.9	886.4
Net income a share	—	—	—	—	—	—	—	3.12	7.57	6.94
Assuming full dilution	—	—	—	—	—	—	—	2.98	7.10	6.66

Facility and Tooling Data										
Capital expenditures for expansion, modernization and replacement of facilities (excluding special tools)	$ 1,257.4	1,583.8	2,152.3	1,571.5	1,089.6	551.0	614.2	832.5	891.7	690.9
Depreciation	$ 1,168.7	1,057.2	895.9	735.5	628.7	589.7	583.8	530.8	485.1	455.0
Expenditures for special tools	$ 970.0	1,184.7	1,288.0	970.2	672.7	503.7	342.2	618.7	594.3	462.8
Amortization of special tools	$ 1,010.7	912.1	708.5	578.2	487.7	431.0	435.3	392.7	463.1	458.3

Employee Data—Worldwide										
Payroll	$ 9,380.1	9,519.0	10,169.1	9,774.9	8,338.3	6,639.2	5,629.2	5,892.6	5,769.2	4,905.5
Total labor costs	$12,238.3	12,417.3	13,227.2	12,494.0	10,839.2	8,653.3	7,165.7	7,317.3	7,108.2	5,996.0
Average number of employees	404,788	426,735	494,579	506,531	479,292	443,917[6]	416,120	464,731	474,318	442,607

Employee Data—U.S. Operations										
Payroll	$ 5,507.5	5,248.5	6,262.6	6,581.2	5,653.4	4,380.4	3,560.5	3,981.9	4,027.0	3,536.1
Average hourly labor costs per hour worked[5] (in dollars)										
Earnings	$ 12.75	11.45	10.35	9.73	8.93	8.03	7.10	6.61	6.12	5.70
Benefits	$ 8.93	8.54	5.59	4.36	3.91	3.98	3.86	2.88	2.31	2.13
Total	$ 21.68	19.99	15.94	14.09	12.84	12.01	10.96	9.49	8.43	7.83
Average number of employees	170,806	179,917	239,475	256,614	239,303	219,698[6]	203,691	235,256	249,513	232,869

Share data have been adjusted to reflect the five-for-four stock split that became effective May 24, 1977.
*1981 and 1980 results were a loss.
[1] Change to LIFO reduced net income by $81 million.
[2] See Note 5 of Notes to Financial Statements.

[3] Cumulative effect of change (as of January 1, 1975) to flow-through method of accounting for investment tax credit.
[4] See Note 6 of Notes to Financial Statements.
[5] Excludes data for subsidiary companies.
[6] Excludes effect of UAW strike.

EXHIBIT 2 Ten-Year financial summary (dollar amounts in millions). Ford Motor Company and consolidated subsidiaries.

Automotive

Before 1978, Ford did not separate the sales of the Automotive Division into car and truck categories. For 1978, 1979, and 1980, car sales accounted for 68, 67, and 66 percent of the Automotive Division's sales, while trucks generated 32, 33, and 34 percent. Trucks under a gross weight of 14,000 pounds (light trucks) represented 90 percent of the company's unit truck sales in 1978 and 1979, and about 88 percent in 1980. Ford executives estimated that light trucks accounted for around 90 percent of its total unit truck sales in 1976 and 1977.

The automotive industry in the United States is highly competitive. Most companies offer many models and introduce new ones annually. The introduction of new models requires costly changes in design, engineering and manufacturing. A company's success is largely determined by its ability to satisfy changing consumer preferences in prices, fuel economy, vehicle size, reliability, utility, and safety. Ford's sales volume depends on unit sales, product mix, option volume, and vehicle price; sales vary according to total industry demand and the shares of this demand that the company secures. The level of demand is a function of the health of the economy, the costs of cars and trucks, the cost and availability of credit, and the cost and availability of gasoline.

Ford's executives believe that their company's profit in the automotive division is determined by many factors: the relative mix of vehicles sold; options purchased; the achievement of cost efficiencies; and the ability to cover increasing costs through higher prices. Because the automotive industry is capital intensive, its fixed costs are relatively high; this means wide fluctuations in earnings because of relatively small changes in unit volume. Ford and other car manufacturers must recognize various governmental standards and regulatory agencies that affect emission, safety, and noise control, and fuel economy. The most important of these are:

1. *The Federal Clean Air Act* established more stringent exhaust emission control standards for 1981 and subsequent years. These standards are expected to increase the price of automobiles and could reduce the number and kind of vehicles available for sale in the United States.

2. *The Federal Environmental Protection Agency* can impose standards more stringent than those existing under the Federal Clean Air Act. The Environmental Protection Agency adopted emission control requirements for the 1982 and 1983 model-year cars and light trucks which require compliance (or the capability of compliance) with high altitude standards. By 1984, the Federal Clean Air Act requires that cars must comply with emission standards regardless of the altitudes at which they are sold. Ford believes that it may have to reduce the kinds of passenger cars it can produce and sell because of this restriction. Under the Federal Clean Air Act, manufacturers can be forced, at

their expense, to remedy any emission standard deficiencies for any line of cars. Costly automobile recalls can be ordered and production halted.

3. *The Energy Policy and Conservation Act* established minimum average fuel economy standards for automobiles for 1978 and later years, and for certain trucks for 1979 and later years. The standard for passenger automobiles for 1981 is 22 miles per gallon, and the standards become progressively more stringent by 1985, when an average of 27.5 miles per gallon is required. Similar increases in the miles-per-gallon requirements for trucks by 1985 are also mandated.

Failure to achieve the established standards will subject Ford to monetary penalties. The average fuel economy for each class of vehicle will be computed and for every one-tenth of a gallon below the specified standard, Ford will be charged $5 for each vehicle produced in that class. The Secretary of Transportation is allowed to increase the penalty to $10 per vehicle. Exhibit 3 shows Ford's weighted average passenger car fuel economy figures for 1975-1982.

Other Divisions

Tractors. Ford, along with its subsidiaries, is one of the world's largest manufacturers of wheel-type tractors, which have both agricultural and industrial uses. Manufacturing plants are located in the United States, Belgium, France, Brazil, and Great Britain, and are sold in these and other countries throughout the world. (Unit sales of tractors from 1972-1981 are part of Exhibit 7.)

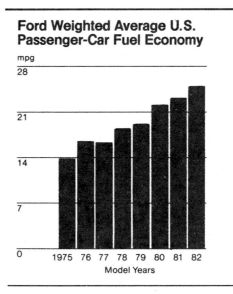

Ford Weighted Average U.S. Passenger-Car Fuel Economy

EXHIBIT 3
SOURCE: Company Annual Reports.

The Steel and Glass Division. Ford manufactures steel, glass and other products, and uses most of these items to manufacture its automobiles and trucks.

Ford Aerospace. Ford Aerospace manufactures communications and electronic systems and equipment for use by government and industry, and also distributes television sets, radios, and other consumer products in Brazil. It conducts research and development activities for other companies and provides them services. It provides communication systems, systems and equipment, satellites and ground stations, central systems for missiles, and defense systems to governments; it also provides radios and other automotive components to Ford's Automotive Division.

Ford Credit. Ford Credit is a wholly owned subsidiary of Ford which provides wholesale financing to its franchise Ford dealers and also purchases retail installment sales contracts from them. The subsidiary also makes loans to vehicle leasing companies and finances commercial, industrial, and real estate projects. Additional loans are made to various affiliates of Ford, and Ford Credit finances certain receivables of the parent company. On January 25, 1980, and January 13, 1981 Ford Credit paid $100 million in cash dividends to Ford; Exhibit 4 shows Ford Credit's income statement for 1978, 1979, and 1980.

American Road Insurance Company. American Road Insurance Company is a wholly owned consolidated subsidiary of Ford Credit. This company issues physical damage insurance covering vehicles and equipment financed at the wholesale level. The company issues credit life and credit disability insurance to the retail purchasers of Ford vehicles.

Ford Leasing Development Company. This wholly owned unconsolidated subsidiary owns and leases real property primarily to franchised Ford vehicle dealers.

Ford Motor Land Development Company. This company is involved with two major projects: Fairlane, a planned commercial and residential community on Ford-owned property in Dearborn, Michigan and Allen Park, Michigan, and the Renaissance Center, a large multi-faceted real estate development in Detroit.

PRODUCT LINE

In 1974, Ford doubled its capacity to produce new cars. The Chicago assembly plant was changed from producing full-size Fords to producing the smaller Torino, Elite, Granada, and Monarch; the smaller cars were also produced at the Wayne, Michigan and Mahwah, New Jersey plants. Granada and Monarch are smaller, lighter, and more economical to operate than the

EXHIBIT 4   Ford Motor Credit Company and consolidated subsidiaries consolidated statement of income and of earnings retained for use in the business (in millions)

	For the Years Ended December 31		
	1980	1979	1978
Financing revenue			
Retail	$1,331.0	$1,062.8	$ 811.1
Wholesale	569.9	642.0	371.7
Commercial, industrial and real estate	107.5	105.7	78.1
Other	164.0	99.8	80.8
Total financing revenue	2,172.4	1,910.3	1,341.7
Insurance premiums earned	122.7	124.4	101.6
Investment and other income	106.8	63.5	37.5
Total revenue	2,401.9	2,098.2	1,480.8
Expenses			
Operating expenses	324.5	290.7	245.3
Provision for credit losses	131.1	85.2	58.7
Insurance losses and loss expenses	65.0	75.5	58.8
Short-term interest expense	1,020.9	853.3	494.2
Long-term interest expense	602.0	539.8	415.6
Total expenses	2,143.5	1,844.5	1,272.6
Income before provision for income taxes	258.4	253.7	208.2
Provision for income taxes (note 12)	99.2	100.5	88.1
Net income	159.2	153.2	120.1
Earnings retained for use in the business			
Beginning of year	751.3	598.1	478.0
Cash dividend	(100.0)	—	—
End of year	$ 810.5	$ 751.3	$ 598.1

SOURCE: Company Annual Reports.

company's intermediate offerings, but they offered a comfortable ride and appointments usually available only in larger, more luxurious models. In March, 1975, Ford's Lincoln-Mercury Division introduced two subcompact cars, the Bobcat and sporty Capri II. Bobcat was available as a three-door runabout and as a Villager station wagon.

The SuperCab, introduced in 1974, expanded Ford's entries in the pickup truck market; SuperCab had the stretch-cab option providing forty-four cubic feet of space behind the front seat. The new F-150 series, which combined the comfort and handling of the F-100 with a load carrying capacity of more than 6,000 pounds, slightly less than the F-250, appeared in September, 1974. In February, 1975 Ford initiated a major effort to secure a higher market share of vans and club wagons by introducing a completely revamped Econoline. An industry first was body-on-frame construction designed to provide a quieter, more comfortable ride and increase its gross vehicle weight rating to 10,000 pounds. Later that spring, Ford increased plant capacities at the Ohio truck plant and the Lorain Assembly plant to produce more Club Wagons and Econolines.

Many of Ford's product line modifications in 1975 were designed to increase the gasoline mileage ratings of its automobiles. In mid-June, the company brought out "MPG" models of the Pinto, Bobcat and Mustang II, which were rated 34 highway, 23 city miles-per-gallon by the E.P.A. In 1975, the newly added Granada was the top selling Ford and the newly-added Monarch was Lincoln-Mercury's top seller. Ford's Pinto was the top selling subcompact car, and its station wagon was the industry's sales leader for station wagons. (In 1975, Ford led all manufacturers in the sales of station wagons for the eleventh consecutive year.)

In 1976, Ford expanded its truck line with the addition of a four-wheel drive F-150 pickup and a "Flareside" short-box half-ton pickup, and a top-of-the-line LTL-9000 extra-heavy truck was introduced; the latter contained a variety of options, such as a factory-installed citizens' band radio.

Ford's 1977 models included new entries in the increasingly popular intermediate segment, which obtained 27.3 percent of retail automobile sales in 1977, the first time the intermediate's market share exceeded the full-sized models'. The new intermediate offerings in 1977 were the LTD II, Cougar, Cougar XR-7, and Thunderbird. Continental Mark V, possessing a more sculptured look, replaced the Mark IV in the luxury class. In April, 1977, the Lincoln Versailles, a trim-size luxury sedan, was brought out. In late summer of 1977, Ford introduced the imported Fiesta, and, in the fall, the new Ford Fairmont and Mercury Zephyr. Ford's executives estimated that the Fairmont and Zephyr represented a $600 million investment, the largest outlay for a new U.S. product offering in the company's history. Fairmont and Zephyr contained competitive interior roominess and luggage space, improved front- and rear-suspension systems, rack-and-pinion steering, and front disc brakes.

Several new trucks were introduced in 1978. A large Bronco was unveiled in October. Based on the F-150 light duty truck chassis, Bronco was expected to strengthen Ford's competitive position in the growing off-road four-wheel drive market. Ford redesigned and reengineered its standard-sized and sports-specialty car lines for 1979. Two standard-size cars—the LTD and Mercury Marquis—were lighter, more fuel efficient and had more head, leg, and shoulder room than the 1978 models. Greater fuel efficiency and more headroom were available in the 1979 Ford Mustang and Mercury Capri. Ford's 1979 truck lineup featured fuel economy improvements and various engineering refinements.

During 1979, Ford conducted thirty-six safety-related recalls using a new computerized recall information system installed in 1978 which enables it to instantaneously determine the repair status of any company vehicle sold in the United States since 1968. The federal government initiated six of the recalls, Ford, thirty. The major recall effort in 1979 involved 1.3 million Pintos and Bobcats, made from 1971 to 1976. Ford modified fuel tanks to increase the resistance of the cars' fuel systems to fuel leakage which might result from rearend crashes.

During the third quarter of 1979, Ford instituted the largest new-model changeover in its history. Ford's Thunderbird was redesigned for 1980, Thunderbird's 25th anniversary year. Compared to the 1979 model, Thunderbird was 800 pounds lighter and gave 45 percent more miles per gallon. The 1980 Ford pickup truck had an increased payload and 14 to 21 percent better fuel economy. The 1981 Ford Granada and Mercury Cougar were smaller by 400 pounds, and were 20 percent more fuel efficient than the 1980 models. Fuel economy increases, to 24 miles per gallon, were effected for the 1981 Lincoln Town Car.

There were significant improvements in the Ford Escort and Mercury Lynx for the 1982. Fuel efficiency was increased to 31 miles-per-gallon (city) and 47 (highway). Both Escort and Lynx had two-seater models introduced in mid-1981. The 1982 Lincoln Continental was the lightest, most technically advanced, most fuel-efficient Lincoln ever. For the first time, the Granada was available in a station wagon, and the Cougar had a station wagon for the first time since 1977. 5.0-liter V-8 engines were added to the 1982 Mustang GT and Mercury Capri RS models to improve performance without sacrificing fuel economy. Improved versions of the LTD, Marquis, Fairmont, and Zephyr were also available for 1982, and in March of that year, Ford introduced the Ranger, a new small pickup truck, with almost the same payload capacity as the larger F-100 pickup truck.

Many of Ford's automobiles and trucks have achieved prominence in the market place. Some of these are:

1. In 1974, Pinto, Mustang II, and Thunderbird were the best-selling cars in their respective market segments.

2. Ford captured the highest market share, 32.8 percent, of any truck manufacturer in 1974.

3. Combined sales in 1975 for Granada and Monarch exceeded combined sales for all five new competitive cars introduced in that year.

4. In 1975, Pinto was the top-selling subcompact and its station wagon was the best selling wagon. In total, Ford's station wagons were the top selling wagons in 1975.

5. Mustang II outsold its competition in 1975.

6. In 1976, Granada was the third best selling car in the United States.

7. The 1977 Ford pickup truck was the top-selling vehicle, car or truck, in the United States.

8. Fairmont became the best selling new car in the history of the automotive industry in 1978, selling 406,000 units.

9. In 1978, Ford trucks had the highest market share, 33 percent, of any automobile manufacturer.

10. The 1979 Mustang was the industry's leader in the small-specialty car market, with sales of 304,000 units.

11. Fairmont had sales of 339,000 in 1979, giving it the top position in its class.

12. Pinto ranked fifth in the industry in the subcompact class, with sales of 188,000 units in 1979.

13. Ford's F-series truck was the best selling vehicle—car or truck—in the United States in 1979.

14. Escort was named 1981 "Car of the Year" by *Road Test* magazine and "Most Significant New Domestic Automobile of 1981" by readers of *Car and Driver*.

15. In 1980 Ford trucks outsold all competitor's trucks.

16. Through February of 1982, Ford's 1982 Escort was the top-selling automobile in the United States, domestic or foreign.

17. The Ford EXP and Mercury LN7 were the top selling two-seater cars for 1981.

Redesigning in 1982 and Beyond

Exhibits 5 and 6 show unit sales for individual Ford and Lincoln-Mercury models from 1977 to 1980. In early 1982, Ford announced it was radically redesigning some of its automobiles. The company is committed to the new designs through 1987, and company executives hope that they will enable Ford to eventually improve its market share to 20 percent.

These new designs will feature aerodynamic styling, stressing low front ends and softly curved fenders. Aerodynamic styling has several advantages. It means less drag, gaining fuel efficiency at a lower cost. According to Ford's chief domestic engineer, Jack Telnack, "To gain a tenth of a mile more in fuel efficiency mechanically can cost $200 million. You can get the same thing for far less just by bending sheet metal differently." Another advantage is that aerodynamically styled cars will look different than the slab-slided, square-cornered automobiles that Ford and its competitors have been producing for the last ten years.

The first aerodynamically styled Ford introduced will be the 1983 LTD, due in showrooms in the fall of 1982. The 1983 Thunderbird, due in January, 1983, is expected to appeal to a relatively small, affluent market. Ford's biggest gamble is bringing out two aerodynamically designed cars in the mid-priced, compact market. The Ford Tempo and Mercury Topaz will contain most of the aerodynamic features incorporated into the Thunderbird, and will be competing in the market in which Ford has had the most trouble. The cars will be small, front-wheel drive models designed as a family sedan.

Ford undertook a number of steps to reduce the risk involved in marketing their aerodynamically designed cars. Full-scale mockups were used with consumers to obtain their reactions, and comments from the market enabled company designers to modify the styling. Ford has used several publicity and promotion techniques, including displaying models at automobile shows, advertising, and showing the new cars to the automotive press. The latter effort appeared to be paying off, as *Motor Trend* featured the new cars in a cover story, and *Car and Driver* was expected to use a photograph of the new Thunderbird on a cover. Ford officials decided to introduce the new aerodynamically designed models sequentially to convince the market that they are

EXHIBIT 5 Unit sales of various models, Ford division, 1977–1980

Make	1977	1978	1979	1980
Ford	380,499	332,930	245,565	142,819
LTD II	203,922	138,947	26,700	3,012
Thunderbird	323,823	304.430	215,698	127,248
Club Wagon	38,761	45,964	38,818	24,783
Granada	355,186	219,026	141,737	88,371
Fairmont	167,841	405,780	338,819	285,272
Pinto	220,775	167,880	187,708	142,467
Mustang	170,659	199,960	304,053	225,290
Fiesta	40,549	76,145	78,109	68,595
Escort	—	—	—	60,196

SOURCE: Company Annual Reports.

EXHIBIT 6 Unit sales of various models, Lincoln-Mercury division, 1977–1980

Make	1977	1978	1979	1980
Mercury	140,610	136,719	94,654	52,645
Cougar	53,207	35,251	3,955	31,710
XR-7	129,779	159,687	121,185	51,857
Monarch	106,821	78,824	55,347	—
Zephyr	42,234	120,781	99,335	87,032
Lynx	—	—	—	18,196
Bobcat	35,481	30,201	44,674	26,821
Lincoln	92,985	97,009	60,797	30,144
Mark V	74,807	75,731	—	—
Mark V/VI	—	—	56,888	—
Mark VI	—	—	—	35,371
Versailles	13,490	15,747	13,586	4,219
Capri	22,458	22,114	90,850	62,592

SOURCE: Company Annual Reports.

not unusual and are aesthetically appealing. Experts predicted that competitors, especially European and Japanese manufacturers, would introduce aerodynamically designed models as well.

The idea for aerodynamic automobiles at Ford came from designer responses to a question posed by the company's new president, Donald E. Petersen, in 1980. Petersen queried company designers if they were satisfied with the projected styling of Ford cars through 1983. When they answered with an emphatic "no," Petersen gave them more latitude in designing the cars they wanted. Ford's European designers were using aerodynamic principles at that time, and these were then adopted by the firm's domestic design staff.[1]

COMPETITION

Ford Motor Company competes in both the domestic and international markets. Exhibit 7 shows the company's ten-year summary of car, truck, and tractor sales in each of these markets.

Domestic Competition

Ford's major U.S. competitors in the domestic market are General Motors, Chrysler, and American Motors. During the 1970s and early 1980s, increasingly tougher competition was provided by foreign automobile manufacturers, chiefly Toyota, Nissan (manufacturer of Datsuns), Volkswagen, Peugeot-Citroen, Renault, Fiat, Mercedes-Benz, Mitsubishi Motors, Volvo, and BMW. Foreign companies have been successful in the U.S. market mainly because of increased buyer interest in the smaller cars they produce. The trend toward purchasing smaller cars is indicated in Exhibit 8, which shows market shares of small, middle, large, and luxury cars in the United States from 1976 to 1980. Exhibit 8 also indicates the percentage of Ford's total automobile sales in these four car classifications between 1976 and 1980. Exhibit 9 contains market shares of the small car market in the United States for domestic and foreign manufacturers from 1976 to 1980. Market shares for all cars sold in the United States from 1976 to 1980 are shown in Exhibit 10 for both domestic and foreign automobile manufacturers; the same information is provided in Exhibit 11 for truck manufacturers.

General Motors has traditionally dominated the domestic market for automobiles and its financial performance has reflected this dominance. However, as General Motors' competitive position has eroded, its financial performance has declined as well. Here is a summary of General Motors' performance from 1977 to 1981:

---

[1]"Ford's Sharp Change In Auto Design Seen As Big Gamble To Raise Sales." *Wall Street Journal,* June 21, 1982.

	1981	1980	1979	1978	1977	1976	1975	1974	1973	1972
U.S. and Canadian Cars and Trucks*										
Cars										
United States	1,385,174	1,397,431	2,044,461	2,632,190	2,625,485	2,197,039	1,867,713	2,336,415	2,685,423	2,617,112
Canada	148,515	162,576	236,437	248,285	247,427	210,049	225,293	258,980	231,598	207,692
Total cars	**1,533,689**	**1,560,007**	**2,280,898**	**2,880,475**	**2,872,912**	**2,407,088**	**2,093,006**	**2,595,395**	**2,917,021**	**2,824,804**
Trucks**										
United States	716,648	753,195	1,183,016	1,458,132	1,345,282	1,017,736	809,360	991,447	1,086,281	946,152
Canada	104,136	109,006	160,160	153,955	149,756	131,186	131,104	143,079	98,326	77,110
Total trucks	**820,784**	**862,201**	**1,343,176**	**1,612,087**	**1,495,038**	**1,148,922**	**940,464**	**1,134,526**	**1,184,607**	**1,023,262**
Total cars and trucks	**2,354,473**	**2,422,208**	**3,624,074**	**4,492,562**	**4,367,950**	**3,556,010**	**3,033,470**	**3,729,921**	**4,101,628**	**3,848,066**
Cars and Trucks Outside the United States and Canada**										
Germany	737,383	657,258	880,325	847,529	891,390	815,279	636,799	496,780	728,514	708,989
Britain	418,629	468,472	555,496	433,191	563,384	515,368	468,255	559,534	615,276	656,387
Spain	254,006	266,522	252,917	247,408	212,855	16,448	—	—	—	—
Australia	127,181	93,490	115,148	107,389	112,376	108,549	124,600	131,393	130,881	131,497
Brazil	125,346	165,703	169,631	158,935	129,466	169,707	172,235	177,698	144,739	120,126
Mexico	107,312	84,668	74,703	68,009	49,216	45,498	55,909	54,649	44,242	43,570
Argentina	78,671	106,463	89,669	52,702	52,466	35,318	39,793	53,810	61,373	47,995
South Africa	66,962	52,671	40,447	46,201	34,156	33,638	36,878	40,155	35,473	33,178
Other countries	43,225	10,995	7,894	8,139	9,042	8,629	9,833	14,993	8,902	3,240
Total outside United States and Canada	**1,958,715**	**1,906,242**	**2,186,230**	**1,969,503**	**2,054,351**	**1,748,434**	**1,544,302**	**1,529,012**	**1,769,400**	**1,744,982**
Total worldwide— cars and trucks	**4,313,188**	**4,328,450**	**5,810,304**	**6,462,065**	**6,422,301**	**5,304,444**	**4,577,772**	**5,258,933**	**5,871,028**	**5,593,048**
Tractors										
United States**	31,517	35,286	51,361	35,789	39,650	34,643	38,342	41,090	40,223	40,980
Overseas	57,757	62,415	82,267	59,448	90,880	83,177	73,981	68,202	61,624	64,226
Total worldwide— tractors	**89,274**	**97,701**	**133,628**	**95,237**	**130,530**	**117,820**	**112,323**	**109,292**	**101,847**	**105,206**
Total worldwide factory sales	**4,402,462**	**4,426,151**	**5,943,932**	**6,557,302**	**6,552,831**	**5,422,264**	**4,690,095**	**5,368,225**	**5,972,875**	**5,698,254**

*Factory sales are by source of manufacture, except that Canadian exports to the United States are included as U.S. vehicle sales and U.S. exports to Canada are included as Canadian vehicle sales. Prior year data have been restated for reclassification of Club Wagons from cars to trucks.
**Includes units manufactured by other companies and sold by Ford.

EXHIBIT 7 10-year summary of Ford's vehicle factory sales in domestic and international markets

Year	Sales	Net Profit	Return on Equity	Net Profit Margin
1977	$55.0 billion	$3.3 billion	21.2%	6.1%
1978	$63.2 billion	$3.5 billion	20.0%	5.5%
1979	$66.3 billion	$2.9 billion	17.0%*	4.4%
1980	$57.7 billion	$763 million (Loss)	—	—
1981	$62.7 billion	$333 million	16.6%	3.8%

Chrysler has had a similar decline, only the figures were even worse than General Motors'. Here are Chrysler's sales, net profits, return on equity, and net profit margins from 1977-1981:

Year	Sales	Net Profit	Return on Equity	Net Profit Margin
1977	$16.7 billion	$163.2 million	5.5%	11.0%
1978	$16.3 billion	$205 million (Loss)	—	—
1979	$12.0 billion	$1.10 billion (Loss)	—	—
1980	$ 9.2 billion	$1.71 billion (Loss)	—	—
1981	$10.8 billion	$476 million (Loss)	—	—

American Motors' performance in 1977, 1978 and 1979 was respectable, but sizable losses plagued the company in 1980 and 1981:

Year	Sales	Net Profit	Return on Equity	Net Profit Margin
1977	$2.3 billion	$ 8.3 million	2.6%	.4%
1978	$2.6 billion	$36.7 million	10.2%	1.4%
1979	$3.1 billion	$68.1 million	24.0%*	2.2%
1980	$2.6 billion	$198 million (Loss)	—	—
1981	$2.6 billion	$137 million (Loss)	—	—

*Approximation

While the results for all three of Ford's domestic competitors between 1977 and 1981 have been discouraging, analysts generally believe that General Motors, because of tremendous size and sound financial position, will be able to ride out the storm. The same may not be true, however, for Chrysler and American Motors.

EXHIBIT 8 Market shares by type of automobile for all U.S. automobile manufacturers and Ford

| | U.S. Industry Car Sales by Segment Years Ended December 31 | | | | |
	1980	1979	1978	1977	1976
Small	42.9%	38.5%	29.4%	27.1%	24.8%
Middle	40.2	39.9	45.5	46.5	50.7
Large	11.2	15.2	18.7	20.3	18.5
Luxury	5.7	6.4	6.4	6.1	6.0
Total U.S. industry car sales	100.0%	100.0%	100.0%	100.0%	100.0%

EXHIBIT 8   (continued)

	Ford Car Sales by Segment in U.S.				
	Years Ended December 31				
	1980	*1979*	*1978*	*1977*	*1976*
Small	39.1%	32.4%	19.0%	19.0%	20.5%
Middle	43.7	46.0	55.9	53.7	51.1
Large	12.7	15.6	17.9	20.2	21.4
Luxury	4.5	6.0	7.2	7.1	7.0
Total Ford U.S. car sales	100.0%	100.0%	100.0%	100.0%	100.0%

SOURCE: Company Annual Reports.

EXHIBIT 9   U.S. market shares of small cars for domestic and foreign manufacturers

	U.S. Market Shares of Small Car Segment				
	Years Ended December 31				
	1980	*1979*	*1978*	*1977*	*1976*
U.S. manufacturers (including imports)					
General Motors	23.5%	26.0%	32.1%	30.2%	34.5%
Ford	15.8	17.5	15.2	16.3	18.8
Chrysler	9.6	10.2	9.5	4.0	3.2
American Motors	1.9	1.4	0.8	1.3	2.1
Total U.S. manufacturers	50.8	55.1	57.6	51.8	58.6
Imports by foreign companies					
Japanese	41.4	35.8	32.9	36.6	30.0
All other	7.8	9.1	9.5	11.6	11.4
Total imports by foreign companies ...	49.2	44.9	42.4	48.2	41.4
Total U.S. small car sales	100.0%	100.0%	100.0%	100.0%	100.0%

SOURCE: Company Annual Reports.

EXHIBIT 10   U.S. car market shares for domestic and foreign car manufacturers

| | U.S. Car Market Shares Years Ended December 31 | | | | |
	1980	1979	1978	1977	1976
U.S. manufacturers (including imports)					
General Motors	46.0%	46.6%	48.3%	46.7%	48.0%
Ford	17.3	20.7	23.6	23.4	22.6
Chrysler	8.8	10.0	10.7	11.7	13.3
American Motors	2.0	1.6	1.5	1.7	2.5
Total U.S. manufacturers	74.1	78.9	84.1	83.5	86.4
Imports by foreign companies					
Japanese	19.7	15.1	10.8	11.1	8.5
All other	6.2	6.0	5.1	5.4	5.1
Total imports by foreign companies ...	25.9	21.1	15.9	16.5	13.6
Total U.S. car retail deliveries	100.0%	100.0%	100.0%	100.0%	100.0%
Memo:					
Total U.S. car retail deliveries (in thousands of units)	8,947	10,510	11,110	11,006	9,959

SOURCE: Company Annual Reports.

EXHIBIT 11   U.S. market shares for truck manufacturers

| | U.S. Truck Market Shares Years Ended December 31 | | | | |
	1980	1979	1978	1977	1976
U.S. manufacturers (including imports)					
General Motors	37.4%	39.2%	40.3%	40.0%	42.4%
Ford	31.6	32.6	32.8	32.6	30.6
Chrysler	9.9	10.7	12.7	13.7	14.6
American Motors	3.1	3.8	3.8	3.0	2.8
International Harvester .	3.2	3.4	2.8	2.9	3.2
All other	2.5	2.3	1.9	1.9	1.4
Total U.S. manufacturers	87.7	92.0	94.3	94.1	95.0
Imports by foreign companies					
Japanese	10.6	7.5	5.1	5.2	4.4
All other	1.7	0.5	0.6	0.7	0.6

EXHIBIT 11   (continued)

	1980	1979	1978	1977	1976
	U.S. Truck Market Shares				
	Years Ended December 31				
Total imports by foreign companies ...	12.3	8.0	5.7	5.9	5.0
Total U.S. truck retail deliveries	100.0%	100.0%	100.0%	100.0%	100.0%
Memo:					
Total U.S. truck retail deliveries (in thousands of units)	2,518	3,636	4,309	3,849	3,330

SOURCE: Company Annual Reports.

Chrysler. As Chrysler's financial troubles worsened, the company's executives tried a number of strategies to keep the firm afloat. Some of Chrysler's work force was either furloughed or released; by December, 1980, Chrysler employed 79,000 workers, down from 141,000 in August, 1979. Chrysler's creditors agreed to make concessions on outstanding loans. The federal government decided on May 10, 1980 to guarantee $1.5 billion in new loans for the company. By December 4, 1980, Chrysler had used $800 million of this amount. It began an $11 billion capital spending program, cut back from $13.6 billion, in 1980, which was to extend through 1985. Chrysler estimated it would accumulate about $600 million in profits between 1981 and 1983. This projection assumed a down year in 1981 (the company lost $476 million in 1981) and improved performances in 1982 and 1983.

Chrysler's cars had long been perceived by the buying public as imitative, lacking prestige and advanced styling. To compete, it had to sell its automobiles at attractive prices, which meant lower profit margins. Chrysler laid off many engineers and designers during the '74-75 recession, and since then, its vehicles have been plagued by missed introductions and quality problems. For example, Chrysler's Volare and Aspen compacts, introduced in 1976, went through eight different recalls, causing many loyal customers to swear that they would never buy another Chrysler product.

Chrysler's subcompact Omnis and Horizons sold well in 1979 but not well enough to prevent the company's first billion dollar loss. In 1980, Chrysler brought out its K-cars, the Dodge Aries and Plymouth Reliant; their performance was expected to be a major factor in the eventual turnaround predicted by Chrysler's management. However, in their first two months, the K-cars sold only 34,000 units, far below the predicted figure 70,000. Although Chrysler's chairman, Lee Iacocca, blamed spiraling interests rates, industry observers offered the following reasons for their poor performance:

☐ Chrysler introduced the K-car 18 months after General Motors' competitive X-car.

☐ Chrysler priced its K-car close to the X-car.

☐ A large percentage of K-cars were loaded down with so many options that the base price of $6,100 ballooned to $8,000.

Compounding the company's 1980 problems was the decrease in sales of Omnis and Horizons. Total sales during the year were 223,000, far below the projected figure of 394,000 units.

Some industry observers believe that Chrysler's long-run solution lies in a merger; two potential prospects are Mitsubishi Motors and Peugeot. Chrysler has a 15 percent equity interest in both firms, but in spring 1981 neither firm had shown any interest in merging with Chrysler. Another plan is for Chrysler to sell its unprofitable businesses and retain only the profitable segments. Chrysler's defense operations have historically been profitable and with its procurement of a contract for the Army's new XM-1 tank, this will probably continue through the 1980s.[2]

American Motors. During 1979, American Motors' executives developed a strategic plan to regenerate the performance of the number-four domestic auto maker. Under the leadership of Chairman of the Board Gerald C. Meyers, the plan consisted of:

☐ Reducing unprofitable operations

☐ Strengthening its highly profitable line of Jeeps

☐ Abandoning a longstanding policy of competing head on with General Motors, Ford, and Chrysler

☐ Distributing Renault cars through its existing dealers

☐ Building a Renault "world car" in its plant for the 1983 model year. Anticipated volume is 200,000 units a year

☐ Emphasizing its broad line of tactical military vehicles, particularly for overseas markets

By the middle of 1980, it became apparent that the new strategic plan was not succeeding; the company was on the way to a $198 million loss for the year. In September, the company announced that Renault had committed $200 million that would make it the owner of 46 percent of American Motors' stock by December 31, 1980, with eventual ownership of 55 percent possible.[3]

---

[2]"Peugeot's Frayed Lifeline To Chrysler." *Business Week,* February 25, 1980, pp. 49–50 and Ross, Irwin. "Chrysler On The Brink." *Fortune,* February 9, 1981, pp. 38–42.

[3]Burck, Charles G. "A Fresh Start—Again For American Motors." *Fortune,* July 16, 1979, pp. 66–80.

International Competition

Ford Motor Co. has historically had extensive operations throughout the world. Its sales in Canada and Europe have long been an important part of its non-U.S. sales, but Latin America and other parts of the world, primarily Asia and the Pacific, have also made significant contributions. In 1981, over half of Ford's sales were in foreign markets.

In 1981, Ford sold more than two million vehicles outside the United States. For the seventeenth consecutive year, it was first in overseas sales by American automobile manufacturers. In Europe, Ford's increase in market share was attibuted to the success of its European Escort, particularly in the United Kingdom and West Germany. The European Escort was named Europe's Car of the Year for 1981 by a panel of automobile writers and its heavy-duty cargo truck was named Truck of the Year.

Escort held a 4.3 percent market share in 1981 in Europe, followed by Fiesta (3.6 percent), Taunus (3.1 percent) and Cortina (3.1 percent). In various European countries, Ford held dominant market share positions in 1981. These included:

- ☐ Great Britain: Cortina, Escort and Fiesta were the top-selling cars in Great Britain.
- ☐ West Germany: Combined car and truck sales gave the company third place in this market.
- ☐ Denmark, Ireland, and Norway: Ford held the top market share in these countries.

Ford held the top market share for cars and trucks in Latin America in 1981, and the top market share in Argentina, Mexico and Venezuela. The new Del Rey achieved 27 percent of the midsize-car market in Brazil. This car contains either two or four doors, alcohol or gasoline engine, and front-wheel drive. The Pampa, a small pickup truck, was introduced in Brazil in 1982.

Improved sales in the Asia-Pacific region in 1982 were largely attributed to an affiliation with Toyo-Kogyo in Japan; Ford assisted Toyo-Kogyo with the design and engineering of the Laser. Sold in more than fifty markets in this region, demand outpaced production. The Laser was available in three- and five-door hatchbacks and four-door notchbacks, with a 1.3- or 1.5-liter engine and a manual or automatic transaxle. Ford planned to expand its presence in the Japanese market through an agreement with Toyo-Kogyo to sell Japanese-built Ford products and U.S. Ford products through a new dealership organization beginning in late 1982.

Ford sales in the Middle East and Africa increased 19 percent in 1981 over 1980 sales. Record levels of cars and trucks were sold in South Africa; Cortina continued to be the best-selling car in its class in South Africa. The company's dealer-assembler in Morocco agreed to assemble Brazilian-based F-series trucks beginning in 1981, and Ford products returned to Zimababwe

Geographic Area	1981	1980	1979	1978	1977
			(in millions)		
Sales to unaffiliated customers					
United States	$19,739	$18,429	$24,408	$27,799	$24,769
Canada	1,830	1,855	2,382	2,030	1,950
Europe	9,882	10,209	11,050	8,433	7,621
Latin America	4,122	4,521	3,723	2,754	2,104
All other (primarily Asia-Pacific)	2,674	2,072	1,951	1,768	1,397
Total	$38,247	$37,086	$43,514	$42,784	$37,841
Intercompany sales among geographic areas					
United States	$ 3,743	$ 3,453	$ 3,783	$ 3,220	$ 2,993
Canada	2,360	2,217	2,581	3,361	2,937
Europe	738	1,204	1,388	1,080	977
Latin America	171	159	203	203	216
All other (primarily Asia-Pacific)	25	15	22	17	15
Total	$ 7,037	$ 7,048	$ 7,977	$ 7,881	$ 7,138
Total revenue					
United States	$23,482	$21,882	$28,191	$31,019	$27,762
Canada	4,190	4,072	4,963	5,391	4,887
Europe	10,620	11,413	12,438	9,513	8,598
Latin America	4,293	4,680	3,926	2,957	2,320
All other (primarily Asia-Pacific)	2,699	2,087	1,973	1,785	1,412
Elimination of intercompany sales	(7,037)	(7,048)	(7,977)	(7,881)	(7,138)
Total	$38,247	$37,086	$43,514	$42,784	$37,841
Net income (loss)					
United States	$ (1,195)	$ (2,018)	$ (199)	$ 809	$ 942
Canada	(252)	(101)	(9)	10	26
Europe	289	323	1,219	581	609
Latin America	(87)	196	132	93	79
All other (primarily Asia-Pacific)	185	57	26	96	17
Total	$ (1,060)	$ (1,543)	$ 1,169	$ 1,589	$ 1,673
Assets					
United States	$11,533	$12,547	$13,354	$12,907	$10,933
Canada	1,669	1,617	1,730	1,699	1,668
Europe	8,003	7,691	7,607	5,949	5,409
Latin America	2,354	2,374	1,755	1,566	1,376
All other (primarily Asia-Pacific)	2,372	2,000	1,722	1,516	1,286
Elimination of intercompany receivables	(2,910)	(1,881)	(2,643)	(1 536)	(1.431)
Total	$23,021	$24,348	$23,525	$22,101	$19,241
Capital expenditures (facilities, machinery and equipment and tooling)					
United States	$ 1,039	$ 1,417	$ 2,347	$ 1,884	$ 1,280
Canada	191	395	182	160	120
Europe	653	718	728	327	239
Latin America	276	175	103	85	78
All other (primarily Asia-Pacific)	68	64	80	86	45
Total	$ 2,227	$ 2,769	$ 3,440	$ 2,542	$ 1,762

EXHIBIT 12 Sales results by geographical areas, 1977-1981

CARS / TRUCKS — 1977, 1976

	CARS				TRUCKS			
	1977		1976		1977		1976	
	Industry Unit Sales	Ford Market Share	Industry Unit Sales	Ford Market Share	Industry Unit Sales	Ford Market Share	Industry Unit Sales	Ford Market Share
United States	11,169,000	23.4%	10,098,000	22.6%	3,686,000	33.0%	3,191,000	30.9%
Canada	993,000	20.7	946,000	19.6	350,000	32.7	342,000	32.0
Germany	2,516,000	14.5	2,270,000	14.9	183,000	7.6	179,000	8.1
United Kingdom	1,324,000	25.7	1,286,000	25.3	225,000	31.2	209,000	31.3
Other European Markets*	6,037,000	8.4	5,805,000	6.6	748,000	9.5	718,000	8.7
Brazil	714,000	13.8	748,000	17.0	137,000	22.7	146,000	29.0
Mexico	195,000	13.1	200,000	11.4	96,000	27.4	105,000	23.2
Argentina	151,000	22.5	130,000	15.2	61,000	28.2	49,000	26.5
Other Latin American Markets*	326,000	16.4	288,000	14.7	223,000	19.4	187,000	19.7
Australia	427,000	23.5	464,000	22.4	133,000	18.7	139,000	19.1
South Africa	167,000	16.6	185,000	15.2	90,000	12.8	115,000	13.5
All Other Markets*	4,146,000	1.6	3,977,000	1.5	2,408,000	1.8	2,252,000	2.0
Worldwide Total	28,165,000	15.8%	26,397,000	14.9%	8,340,000	20.2%	7,632,000	18.9%

*1977 data estimated.

CARS / TRUCKS — 1979, 1978

	CARS				TRUCKS			
	1979		1978		1979		1978	
	Industry Unit Sales	Ford Market Share	Industry Unit Sales	Ford Market Share	Industry Unit Sales	Ford Market Share	Industry Unit Sales	Ford Market Share
United States	10,510,000	20.7%	11,110,000	23.6%	3,636,000	32.6%	4,309,000	32.8%
Canada	1,005,000	20.7	992,000	21.4	392,000	33.2	376,000	32.8
Germany	2,567,000	11.8	2,614,000	13.9	227,000	10.1	206,000	7.4
United Kingdom	1,716,000	28.3	1,592,000	24.6	301,000	30.4	256,000	28.8
Other European Markets*	6,067,000	7.5	5,835,000	8.0	803,000	8.5	746,000	8.1
Brazil	830,000	15.8	800,000	15.6	186,000	19.4	173,000	18.8
Mexico	268,000	13.7	228,000	15.0	159,000	24.8	135,000	27.2
Argentina	196,000	28.7	146,000	24.5	63,000	50.1	47,000	33.2
Other Latin American Markets*	334,000	15.6	334,000	16.4	216,000	18.8	240,000	21.4
Australia	458,000	22.9	446,000	22.4	116,000	18.4	130,000	16.7
South Africa	213,000	15.4	205,000	17.6	101,000	14.0	99,000	16.1
All Other Markets*	4,721,000	1.9	4,555,000	1.7	2,789,000	1.3	2,570,000	1.1
Worldwide Total*	28,885,000	14.3%	28,857,000	15.6%	8,989,000	19.1%	9,287,000	20.3%

*1979 data estimated

CARS / TRUCKS — 1981, 1980

	CARS				TRUCKS			
	1981		1980		1981		1980	
	Industry Unit Sales	Ford Market Share	Industry Unit Sales	Ford Market Share	Industry Unit Sales	Ford Market Share	Industry Unit Sales	Ford Market Share
United States	8,514,956	16.6%	8,946,849	17.3%	2,281,879	31.4%	2,518,308	31.6%
Canada	903,532	15.2	937,006	16.4	287,290	30.2	334,194	30.2
Germany	2,264,634	11.8	2,361,515	10.3	214,261	7.7	240,215	8.7
United Kingdom	1,484,622	30.9	1,513,525	30.7	213,460	30.6	266,509	32.9
Other European Markets*	5,917,915	7.8	6,091,967	6.5	839,679	7.0	844,046	8.4
Brazil	448,256	19.2	794,347	15.2	132,677	17.9	186,428	21.1
Mexico	342,724	15.9	286,735	13.8	230,939	25.6	180,157	27.4
Argentina	172,640	31.7	240,209	28.5	56,965	45.8	81,563	52.6
Other Latin American Markets*	426,210	11.6	429,189	11.0	243,243	14.1	260,399	14.8
Australia	453,808	23.0	450,241	19.9	152,476	13.1	124,940	16.6
South Africa	301,528	16.7	277,058	15.0	152,013	10.7	127,698	13.6
All Other Markets*	4,456,502	1.9	4,435,299	1.4	3,323,413	1.0	3,191,981	1.0
Worldwide Total*	25,687,327	12.6%	26,763,940	12.2%	8,128,295	14.2%	8,356,438	15.8%

*1981 data estimated

EXHIBIT 13 Ford shares of major car and truck markets

EXHIBIT 14 Car and truck market shares outside U.S. and Canada for Ford and other automobile manufacturers[1]

	1980	1979	1978	1977	1976
Toyota	10.9%	10.5%	10.8%	10.3%	10.1%
Nissan	9.4	9.0	8.7	8.6	8.9
Volkswagen	9.3	9.5	9.3	9.5	9.5
Ford	9.0	9.6	9.5	9.6	9.2
Peugeot-Citroen[2]	8.7	10.1	10.8	11.2	11.1
Renault	8.5	7.8	7.5	7.8	7.6
Fiat	7.6	7.2	7.5	8.2	8.3
General Motors	7.5	8.1	8.4	8.1	8.4
All other	29.1%	28.2%	27.5%	26.7%	26.9%
Total car and truck retail sales outside U.S. and Canada	100.0%	100.0%	100.0%	100.0%	100.0%
Memo: Total car and truck retail sales outside U.S. and Canada (in thousands of units)	22,041	22,329	21,335	20,351	19,452

[1]Retail sales are based on publicly available information—compiled by country from manufacturers' associations, industry trade journals, government statistics and other industry-recognized sources.
[2]Adjusted to include retail sales of Talbot (formerly Chrysler's European operations).

EXHIBIT 15 Percentage of total company sales and net income and return on sales within and outside the United States

	Percentage of Total Company				After-Tax Return on Sales		
	Sales		Net Income				
	U.S.	Outside U.S.	U.S.	Outside U.S.	U.S.	Outside U.S.	Total Company
1980	50%	50%	—%[1]	—%[2]	—%[1]	2.5%	—%[2]
1979	56	44	—[1]	117	—[1]	7.2	2.7
1978	65	35	51	49	2.9	5.3	3.7
1977	66	34	56	44	3.8	5.6	4.4
1976	63	37	44	56	2.4	5.4	3.5
1975	60	40	31[3]	69[3]	0.7[3]	2.5	1.4[3]
1974	65	35	50	50	1.1	2.3	1.5
1973	69	31	64	36	3.7	4.9	4.0
1972	69	31	73	27	4.5	4.2	4.4
1971	70	30	86	14	4.9	2.1	4.1

[1]Ford's U.S. operations incurred after-tax losses of $2,018 million and $199 million in 1980 and 1979, respectively.
[2]Ford's operations outside the United States earned $475 million in 1980; the Company's worldwide results in that period were a loss of $1,543 million.
[3]After change to flow-through method of accounting for investment tax credits.

SOURCE: Company Annual Reports

EXHIBIT 16 Sales and profit figures for major foreign automobile manufacturers, 1977–1979.

Company	1977 Sales	1977 Profit	1978 Sales	1978 Profit	1979 Sales	1979 Profit
Fiat	$4.5 billion[1]	$71 million[1]	$5.3 billion[1]	$88 million[1]	$18.3 billion	N.A.
Peugeot-Citroen	$8.5 billion	$239 million	$10.6 billion	$300 million	$17.3 billion	$254 million
Volkswagen	$10.4 billion	$180 million	$13.3 billion	$276 million	$16.8 billion	$372 million
Renault	$10.0 billion	$4 million	$12.7 billion	$2 million	$16.1 billion	$242 million
Daimler-Benz	$8.6 billion	$211 million	$12.1 billion	$295 million	$14.9 billion	$348 million
Toyota Motor	$9.6 billion	$453 million	$12.8 billion	$530 million	$14.0 billion	$510 million
Nissan Motor	$7.7 billion	$293 million	$9.8 billion	$372 million	$12.7 billion	$331 million
British-Leyland	$4.5 billion	$91 million (LOSS)	$5.9 billion	$72 million (LOSS)	$6.3 billion	$307 million (LOSS)
Adam Opel	$4.0 billion[1]	$146 million[1] (LOSS)	$5.3 billion[1]	$245 million[1] (LOSS)	—	—
Volvo	$3.6 billion	$44 million	$4.2 billion	$69 million	$5.5 billion	$97 million
Honda Motor	$2.8 billion	$82 million	$3.7 billion	$106 million	$5.0 billion	$70 million

[1]Parent Company Results only.

EXHIBIT 17 Return on assets, stockholders equity and sales for major foreign automobile manufacturers, 1977–1979.

Company	1977 R.O.A.	1977 R.S.E.	1977 Margin	1978 R.O.A.	1978 R.S.E.	1978 Margin	1979 R.O.A.	1979 R.S.E.	1979 Margin
Fiat	1.5%	6.7%	2.0%	15.4%	5.0%	1.7%	—	—	—
Peugeot-Citroen	3.9%	14.5%	2.8%	3.4%	10.3%	2.8%	2.1%	7.2%	1.5%
Volkswagen	2.4%	9.3%	1.7%	2.8%	9.6%	2.0%	2.9%	11.2%	2.2%
Renault	.05%	.38%	.04%	.02%	.10%	.02%	—	11.2%	1.5%
Daimler-Benz	4.7%	16.4%	2.4%	4.2%	13.0%	2.4%	4.3%	13.4%	2.3%
Toyota Motor	7.3%	17.6%	4.7%	6.0%	13.5%	4.2%	7.7%	13.3%	3.6%
Nissan Motor	4.7%	14.0%	3.8%	4.4%	14.5%	3.8%	3.3%	10.3%	2.6%
British-Leyland	—	—	—	—	—	—	—	—	—
Volvo	1.2%	17.2%	1.2%	1.7%	13.7%	1.6%	1.9%	15.1%	1.8%
Honda Motor	4.0%	16.7%	3.0%	3.9%	14.2%	2.8%	1.9%	7.5%	1.4%
Adam Opel	7.2%	16.9%	3.7%	9.2%	23.1%	4.6%	—	—	—

after a sixteen-year absence, assembling Lasers in a government-owned plant.

Ford has made major investments outside the United States, particularly in Canada, Great Britain, West Germany, and Spain, for a number of reasons. Car and truck sales overseas exceed those in the United States and have grown at a faster pace than in the U.S. Many foreign governments do not allow entry into their markets unless there is local investment. Local sourcing for overseas sales typically has economic advantages over American sourcing. Diversification into many markets makes the company less dependent on economic conditions in a single market.

Outside the United States, many producers exist, but no single producer accounts for significant market shares in all countries. Some producers, however, tend to dominate in several countries, especially in their country of origin. Many manufacturers have joined forces through a variety of means, including acquisitions, joint ventures, co-production agreements, cooperative R&D efforts, and intercompany sourcing of components. An example includes Ford's acquisition of a 25 percent equity interest in Toyo-Kogyo, the Japanese manufacturer of Mazdas.

There are several possible risks in overseas markets that would jeopardize future earnings: potential increase in overseas labor costs; rapid shifts in demand; high inflation; energy shortages; increasingly stringent government relations; increasingly tough competition, particularly from Japanese and European automobile manufacturers.

PRICING

In May, 1982, Ford ran an extensive rebate program. Purchasers were urged to make their best deals and then receive a 5 percent discount from that price. Purchasers could either take the 5 percent rebate in cash, or use it for a down payment. A similar rebate effort was conducted during January and February, 1981. At the conclusion of the 1981 rebate program, Ford executives concluded that "these programs had the effect of inflating the annualized rates of industry deliveries in that period" and that they "are expected to result in a substantial increase in its marketing costs for that period."

Ford has had pricing problems in the last half of the 1970s and the early 1980s; it had difficulty raising the price on its popular Escort in 1981, for example, even though it was selling every one it could make, and made little or no profit on a price of $5,158. Ford's executives believed that low-priced cars could not stand a price increase at that time. On the other hand, they did not consider a price decrease feasible because high interest rates held the demand relatively inelastic. To make up for the lack of profit on Escort, Ford increased the price by about 2 percent on larger cars like Thunderbird and LTD. Americans are apparently reluctant to pay high prices for small cars. In Britain, where the Escort is the top-selling car and solidly profitable for Ford, the car costs $1,600 more than in the U.S. Many of Ford's cars have a reputation for poor quality and safety, and this reputation makes it difficult for the company to charge higher prices.

Cost advantages enable Japanese manufacturers to price substantially lower than Ford on competitive models; since Japanese automobiles competed in 60 percent of the U.S. market in 1982, this is a major problem for Ford. Analysts estimated that a Japanese auto maker could sell a comparable 1982 subcompact for $1,300 to $1,700 less than Ford could. Since shipping and import duties amounted to $400 to $500, Japanese automobiles were produced for about $2,000 less than Ford's. Lower Japanese production costs have resulted from greater productivity; a Japanese compact or subcompact could be assembled in fourteen worker-hours in 1982, compared to thirty-three for a similar American automobile. Lower inventory levels and better production scheduling and planning are also cited to explain higher Japanese productivity in the automobile industry.[4]

ADVERTISING

Ford has consistently been one of the leading advertisers in the United States, measured by total expenditures. Its advertising appropriation in 1978 was $210 million, up 14 percent from 1978, making it the nation's eighth largest advertiser. It was tenth in 1979, with $215 million, and eighth again in 1980 with $280 million. Expenditures in 1981 were $287 million, making Ford the nation's eleventh leading advertiser. Typically, the Ford division accounts for 67 to 69 percent of all automobile advertising, the Lincoln-Mercury division the rest.

Since 1977, Ford has stressed television advertising. In 1977, 59.6 percent of its advertising budget was appropriated for network and spot television advertising. For 1978, 1979, 1980, and 1981 the percentage of Ford's advertising appropriations allocated to network and spot television were 64.4, 66.6, 63.6, and 47.5 percent. Network television has accounted for most of Ford's total television advertising budget, and its share has steadily increased between 1977 and 1981. In 1977, 70.2 percent of the company's television advertising dollars went for network television; by 1981, the percentage was 83.5 percent.[5]

Newspapers, magazines and radio are three additional media Ford uses. Newspaper advertising accounted for the following percentages of Ford's total advertising budget between 1977 and 1981: 17.1, 15.7, 6.2 9.7, and 11.2; magazines: 15.8, 14.0, 20.9, 14.6, and 19.2; radio: 5.7, 4.1, 6.2, 10.1, and 12.8.

In 1978, ads for the compact Pinto stressed its performance against other subcompacts, and Granada's performance was compared to a Mercedes-Benz's. Thunderbird's ads emphasized "style at a surprising

[4]Burck, Charles G. "Can Detroit Catch Up?" *Fortune,* February 8, 1982, pp. 34–39.

[5]*Advertising Age* Special Issues On 100 Leading Advertisers, 1978, 1979, 1980, 1981, and 1982.

price;" Fairmont was billed as the "Ford in your future;" ads for Mustang II were directed to the youth market. In 1979, Mustang ads featured "excitement, fun and pizzazz," and the car was billed as a "New Breed of Mustang." LTD was hailed as the "new American road car," Fiesta, a German import, was called the "Wundercar," Fairmont was billed as "America's success car," and Thunderbird's ads suggested, "Come Fly With Me."

Ford's Lincoln-Mercury division pushed the 1979 Versailles with heavy advertising, and the downsized Marquis was touted as "the most scientifically engineered Marquis in history." Capri's slogan was "The sexy new Capri, a miracle under $4,700." This slogan differed from the 1978 slogan for Capri, "the sexy European," but was necessary because the division began producing Capri in America in 1979. Lincoln Continental and Mark V were referred to as the "last of the breed" in 1979, because both were downsized in 1980. The Lincoln-Mercury division spent over $3 million to push sales of its fuel-efficient Bobcats, Zephyrs, Monarchs, and Capris in 1979.

In spring, 1979, Lincoln-Mercury was informed by its advertising agency, Kenyon and Eckhardt, that it was dropping the division as a client and shifting to Chrysler. The move left the division with little time to ready its advertising campaign for the 1980 introductions.

Some of Ford's ad spending in 1979 and 1980 was dictated by developments which occurred after initial budgets had been determined. In 1979, a $2 million campaign touting Ford's high mileage was launched after favorable mileage figures were released for the company's cars. A 1979 ad program stressed rebates when sales lagged and dealers needed inventory space available for the 1980 models. Announcer Ed McMahon was featured in Ford's "Countdown Clearance" ads; Lincoln-Mercury had a "Smart buyer's sale" campaign. Actress Lauren Bacall and Actor Peter Graves praised models that were selling briskly at mid-year.

In 1980, Wells, Rich, Greene advertising agency took over the Ford corporate account. In one of its first major moves, it replaced long-time spokesman Bill Cosby with a new campaign: "Ford—that's incredible." The campaign stressed Ford's advanced engineering and invited people to take a tour of its River Rouge production facility.

Ads in 1980 touted the Thunderbird as a sporty car for its class, "the high-volume, middle specialty segment," according to executives at J. Walter Thompson ad agency, which held the Ford division account. Ford ads pushed Mustang in the women's market, with horse imagery and young female models; advertisements also told consumers that Mustang had been named its official sports car by the U.S. Auto Club. Pinto was advertised as a trustworthy, inexpensive car, and ads featured families that owned more than one Pinto. In the summer of 1980, Ford developed a new advertising campaign around the theme, "The incredible world of Ford." The 1981 Escort was shown under six flags, and the Lincoln-Mercury cat, a lynx, was placed on top of a globe. The EXP/LN-7, the two-seater spinoff subcompacts from Escort and Lynx, were launched with the advertising theme, "Tomorrow is coming."

Ford aimed its parts and services advertising at the do-it-yourself market. Ford's Motorcraft Oil was introduced to this market; then, the "Motorcraft. . .for sure" campaign widened to include all Ford parts and services products. The Parts and Services Division in the winter of 1980 became Ford's first unit to advertise on cable TV, sponsoring college basketball on Ted Turner's super station, WTBS in Atlanta. Ford Tractor used Rex Allen, a country music star, to advertise its new "Blue Power Special" tractors featuring improved four-cylinder diesel engines. Advertising also introduced the new front-wheel drive option in Ford's 60-2-163 farm tractors.

RESEARCH AND DEVELOPMENT

Figure 18 shows Ford's expenditures for research and development from 1972 through 1981. In addition to these figures, Ford had outlays of $291 million in 1978, $430 million in 1979, and $765 million in 1980 for customer-sponsored research and developmental activities, chiefly in conjunction with governmental contracts.

Ford's R&D activities are directed primarily toward improving the performance (including fuel efficiency), safety, and comfort of its vehicles. A staff of engineers and scientists is also employed in basic research. Principal research facilities are in Dearborn, Michigan; Dunton, England; and Merkenich, Germany. Ford has a car and truck design center in Dearborn for the design and development of exterior surfaces, configuration, ornamentation, colors, interior trim materials, and other styling features. R&D activities are also carried out at Ford Aerospace, primarily involving government contracts.

Exhibit 19 shows Ford's technological firsts in the automobile industry from 1971 to 1980; its R&D efforts in the early 1980s focused on alternative

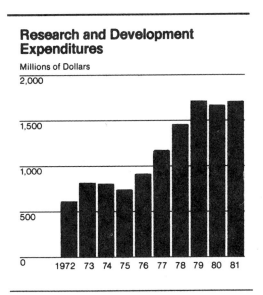

Research and Development Expenditures

Millions of Dollars

EXHIBIT 18
SOURCE: Company Annual Reports.

fuels, aerodynamics, and electronics. Its alternative fuels research program is investigating only those fuels that could substitute for gasoline. One such alternative, methanol, is being tested jointly by Ford and the State of California and Los Angeles County. Ethanol made from sugar cane has been used extensively in Brazil; over 40,000 Fords using ethanol have been in operation with no significant fuel-caused problems.

Ford's involvement with aerodynamic styling design has been estimated to have improved the company's overall fuel economy by 4 percent.

R&D activities also focus on improving manufacturing efficiency and productivity. Lasers make critical measurements on torque-converter surfaces and automatic transaxle components. Computers design components and test and inspect subassemblies and completed vehicles. Robots weld and perform other demanding production line jobs.

DEALER ORGANIZATION

Ford considers its dealer organization one of its primary assets. In 1980, Ford numbered around 13,500 dealers who sold cars, trucks, and tractors in nearly 200 countries and territories around the world, and it believes these dealers increased the effectiveness of their sales staffs and parts and service facilities in 1980-1981. The company has developed several merchandising and financial support programs to assist dealers. Because of the economic recession, aggressive competition, particularly from Japan, and record-high interest rates in 1980, some 895 Ford franchises were given up. About 350 new dealers were attracted, however, leaving the company with about 13,000 dealers in 1981.

WARRANTIES/CUSTOMER SERVICE

In 1976, Ford announced its Extended Service Plan, which offered service contracts for new Fords and used vehicles sold by its dealers. A wide range of various contracts can be purchased—up to 50,000 miles for five years for new cars, 20,000 miles or two years for used cars.

Ford emphasized its Extended Service Plan in its promotion and advertising. A concentrated effort in 1979 increased dollar sales of parts and accessories by 7 percent over the previous year, with the sales of Motorcraft sparkplugs up by 34 percent. About 20 percent of new car customers purchased an Extended Service Plan, and by 1981, more than 1.8 million contracts had been purchased.

TOWARD THE FUTURE

Ford's financial performance in 1982 continued the stream of red ink. For the year, it lost $658 million on sales of $37.1 billion. General Motors generated

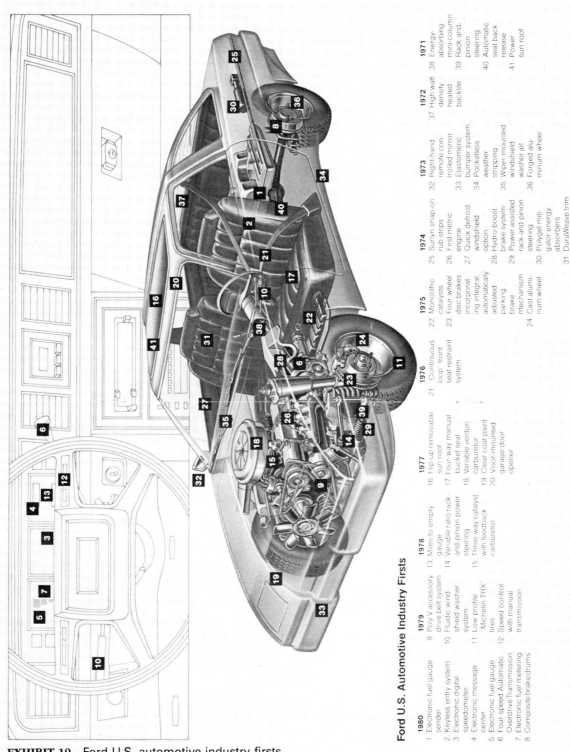

Ford U.S. Automotive Industry Firsts

1980
1 Electronic fuel gauge sender
2 Keyless entry system
3 Electronic digital speedometer
4 Electronic message center
5 Electronic fuel gauge
6 Four-speed Automatic Overdrive Transmission
7 Electronic fuel metering
8 Composite brake drums

1979
9 Poly V accessory drive belt system
10 Fluidic windshield washer system
11 Low profile Michelin TRX tires
12 Speed control with manual transmission

1978
13 Miles-to-empty gauge
14 Variable ratio rack and pinion power steering
15 Three-way catalyst with feedback carburetor

1977
16 Flip-up removable sun roof
17 Four-way manual bucket seat
18 Variable venturi carburetor
19 Clear coat paint
20 Visor mounted garage-door opener

1976
21 Continuous loop front seat restraint system

1975
22 Monolithic catalysts
23 Four-wheel disc brakes incorporating integral, automatically adjusted parking brake mechanism
24 Cast aluminum wheel

1974
25 Surlyn snap-on rub strips
26 First metric engine
27 Quick defrost windshield option
28 Hydro boost brake system
29 Power assisted rack and pinion steering
30 Polygel mitigator energy absorbers
31 DuraWeave trim

1973
32 Right-hand remote controlled mirror
33 Elastomeric bumper system
34 Pocketless weather stripping
35 Wiper-mounted windshield washer jet
36 Forged aluminum wheel

1972
37 High watt density heated backlite

1971
38 Energy-absorbing mini-column
39 Rack and pinion steering
40 Automatic seat back release
41 Power sun roof

EXHIBIT 19 Ford U.S. automotive industry firsts

SOURCE: Company Annual Report, 1979.

profits of $963 million on sales of $60.0 billion. Chrysler ended its streak of losses, obtaining a net profit of $170 million on sales of $10.0 billion. American Motors lost $154 million, with sales of $2.9 billion.

In 1982, Ford's market share was 17.0 percent, General Motors' was 44.3 percent, Chrysler's was 8.7 percent, and American Motors' was 1.0 percent. The percentages for the leading imports were Volkswagen (6.7), Toyota (5.9), Datsun (1.1), and Honda (4.6). For 1981, the market shares for Ford, General Motors, Chrysler, and American Motors were 16.3, 44.8, 8.6, and 1.1; For the imports, 1981: Volkswagen (6.8), Toyota (5.5), Datsun (1.9), and Honda (4.4).

Eastern Air Lines, Inc.

Eastern Air Lines may well be the most visible of the ten trunk air carriers in the United States. In 1979, 1980, and 1981, Eastern flew more passengers than, as their advertisements say, "any airline in the free world." During this time, Eastern averaged about 40 million passengers a year. The man extolling the virtues of flying Eastern on television is former astronaut Frank Borman, the company's chairman of the board, president, and chief executive officer.

Despite this visibility, Eastern has some problems. Although many of the company's performance measures consistently improved during the 1970's, the bottom line, profit, has disappointed the firm's executives and shareholders. Increases in such areas as passengers flown, passenger load factors, and yield-per-revenue-passenger-mile have been encouraging, but

This case was prepared by Richard T. Hise, Professor of Marketing at Texas A&M University, as a basis for class discussion rather than to illustrate either effective or ineffective marketing management.

cumulative profits in the 1970s are among the lowest in the industry, the net losses that have occurred in some years have been sizable, and no dividends have been paid to stockholders since 1965. While many of Eastern's problems are caused by factors indigenous to its industry, company-related difficulties also play a part.

BUSINESS

Eastern Airlines, Inc. was incorporated in 1938. The company is a certified air carrier which provides service predominantly between the major metropolitan areas of the northeast and southeast sections of the United States. However, Eastern has recently established some east-west routes, and it provides service to the Caribbean, Mexico, Bermuda, Canada, and the Bahamas. Its classes of passenger service include first class, leisure class, day coach, and night coach. No reservation, assured space service is available on Eastern's shuttle operations between Boston and New York and New York and Washington, D.C. On some of its routes, the company transports mail, express and air freight.

DEREGULATION

Until October 24, 1978, the airline industry in the United States was regulated by the Civil Aeronautics Board (CAB). On that date, President Carter signed the Airline Deregulation Act, which is designed to free the airlines from CAB control. Decontrol will occur in stages: by 1983, the CAB's authority over airline routes and fares will be eliminated, and the agency itself will be abolished in 1985.

Specifically, the Airline Deregulations Act affects Eastern and its competitors in five important ways:

1. Certification requirements have been liberalized. Thus, it is now easier for new carriers to enter the market.
2. Carriers have expanded freedom to enter new or dormant routes.
3. Airlines are granted new authority to regulate fares. Initial authority allowing increases of up to 5 percent and decreases to 50 percent have been further relaxed.
4. Restrictions on charter flights have been eased.
5. Carriers can drop unprofitable routes.

The purpose of CAB control of airline operations in the United States had many objectives. One was to enable airlines to obtain an adequate return on their investment; the CAB generally believed that a 12 percent return was desirable.

Eastern Airlines has consistently not favored deregulation. Its 1975 annual report stated:

> Hovering also over the entire air transportation industry is the cloud of threatened unbridled deregulation, which has been proffered as a solution to the industry's ills by well-meaning but unknowledgeable critics. One of the key elements of the deregulation proposals is "free entry and exit" whereby anyone could enter into a market or withdraw from it at will. Such a situation would create chaos. An Air Transport Association study showed that 372 of the trunk carriers' 994 nonstop routes are unprofitable. If the profits of the other 622 were to be diluted or wiped out by unnecessary competition, smaller communities and airports would be hurt the most as service on the unprofitable segments was reduced or eliminated. Further, if every airline could drop its smaller cities and concentrate all its surplus aircraft into the highly-desired markets we would immediately be plunged into a situation of ruinous over-capacity.

In March of 1981, Eastern officials were still reluctant to endorse deregulation:

> In the opinion of the Company, the financial resources of some of Eastern's principal competitors are greater than Eastern's, and the greatly increased competition following implementation of the Deregulation Act could be more unfavorable to the Company than to these principal competitors. In particular, liberalized route-entry provisions have already been heavily utilized and the Company has been exposed to intense competition on certain routes. In addition, the Company and its competitors have introduced a variety of reduced or discount fares which could have an adverse impact on the Company's finances if lower fares fail to generate the volume of traffic necessary to offset the fare reduction.[1]

1979 and 1980, the two years immediately following deregulation, were disappointing for the major trunk airlines. In 1978, the trunk airlines accounted for a total net profit of about $1.05 billion. In 1979, this figure had dropped to $250 million. Total 1980 results for the trunk airlines was estimated to have been a *net loss* of about $220 million, causing many airline executives and analysts to call 1980 the worst year in the history of the industry. The disastrous 1980 performance was marked by almost a doubling of fuel prices (from 57¢ to $1 a gallon), a reduction of 5 percent in the number of miles flown by passengers, and increased competition by regional and commuter carriers. Selling off planes, laying off personnel, abandoning numerous short-haul routes, and discounting fares vigorously were the responses of the trunk lines to the events of 1980. Between August, 1978 and August, 1980, the major airlines dropped an estimated 1,200 flights of 200 miles and under, and around 400 flights of between 201 and 500 miles. (About 400 flights of over 500 miles were added.) During the first seven months of 1980, cut-rate travel (fares less than full prices) amounted to 57 percent of coach travel. This compared to 49 percent for 1979, 38 percent for 1978, and 27 percent for 1977.[2]

---

[1]Company Annual Report.

[2]Stuart, Alexander. "The Airlines Are Flying In A Fog." *Fortune,* October 20, 1980, p. 52.

MANAGEMENT

In March 1981, Eastern's top corporate management consisted of eleven positions. These positions are indicated in Exhibit 1, along with the individual holding the position in March of 1981, and their ages at that time.

Before joining the company, **Frank Borman** was an officer in the United States Air Force for more than twenty years. His association with Eastern began in 1969 as a special advisor to the corporation. He was a vice president of Eastern from July 1970 to December 1970; senior vice president - operations group from January 1971 to February 1974; senior vice president - operations from February 1974 to June 1974; executive vice president - general operations manager from July 1974 to May 1975; president and chief operating officer from June 1975 to December 1975; and president and chief executive officer from January 1976 to December 15, 1976. He has been Eastern's chairman of the board, president, and chief executive officer since December 16, 1976, and a director since July 1974. Borman is also a director of Cameron Iron Works, Inc., Southeast Banking Corporation, Hospital Corporation of America, Southern Bell Telephone and Telegraph Co., National Geographic Society, Electronic Data Systems, Inc., and Eastern Air Lines, S.A.

Charles Simons has served the company in various capacities since February 1940. He was Eastern's senior vice president - chief financial officer from April 1969 to July 1971; executive vice president - finance and administration from July 1971 to July 1975; and executive vice president - finance from July 1975 to April 1976. He has been Eastern's vice chairman and executive vice president since May 1976 and a director since April 1970. Simons is also a director of Southeast First National Bank of Miami, Bank of Commerce (New York, N.Y.), Executive Sports, Inc. Wometco Enterprises, Inc., Aero Spacelines Inc., Dorado Beach Development, Inc., Dorado Beach Estates, Inc., Eastern Air Lines, S.A., Eastern Air Lines of Puerto Rico, Inc., EAL Inc., Twin Fair, Inc., and Terminal Sales Company.

Marvin Amos has served the company in various capacities since January 1965. He was Eastern's vice president - personnel from May 1975 to August 1976; vice president - personnel and corporate administration from August 1976 to January 1978; and, since that time, he has been senior vice president - personnel and corporate administration.

William Bell joined the company as staff vice president - legal in May 1967, and served in that capacity until April 1974. He was vice president - legal from April 1974 to December 1976; vice president - legal and assistant secretary from December 1976 to July 1977; vice president - legal affairs from July 1977 to January 1978; senior vice president - legal affairs from January 1978 to January 1980; and senior vice president - legal affairs and secretary since January 1980.

Thomas Buttion joined the company in June 1949 as a pilot and served as a pilot and in various supervisory positions until July 1974. He was vice president - flight standards and training from July 1974 through October 1975; vice president and chief pilot from November 1975 through May 1977;

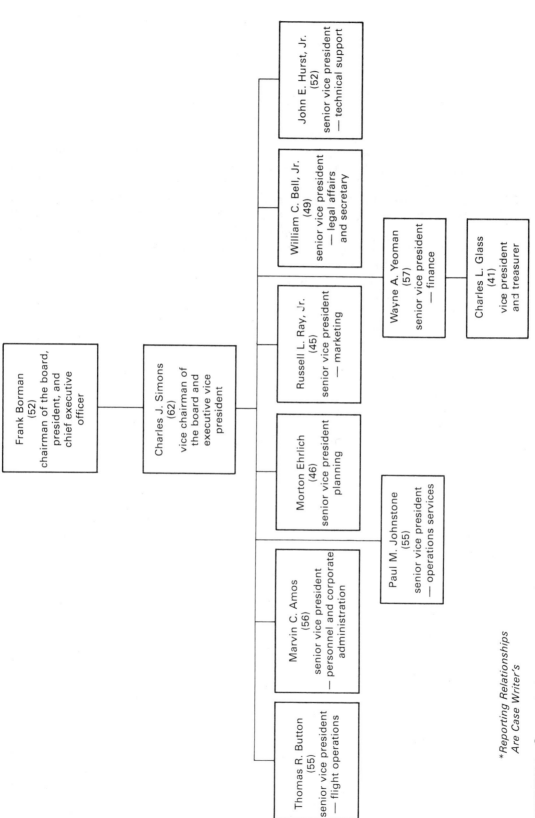

EXHIBIT 1 Corporate top management

SOURCE: Company's Annual Reports and 10-K Report.

*Reporting Relationships
Are Case Writer's

vice president - flight operations from June 1977 to January 1978; and since that time he has been senior vice president - flight operations.

Morton Ehrlich joined the company in 1968 and served in an executive position until August 1970. He was Eastern's division vice president - economics and marketing research and development from August 1970 to November 1972; vice president - marketing research and planning from December 1972 to February 1974; vice president and corporate economist from February 1974 to January 1975; and vice president - planning from January 1975 to June 1976. He has been senior vice president - planning since July 1976 and a director of the company since April 1978. Ehrlich is also a director of IBM World Trade Americas/Far East Corporation, National Bureau of Economic Research, and Eastern Air Lines, S.A.

Russell Ray served in various marketing capacities with Lockheed Aircraft Corporation before joining the company in November 1971. He served as Eastern's vice president - consumer affairs from November 1971 to December 1972; vice president - marketing and operations from December 1972 to March 1974; vice president - sales and services from March 1974 to July 1975; and he has been senior vice president - marketing since that time. Ray has served as a director of the company since October 1977 and is also a director of Ohio Sealy Mattress Company, Patlex Corporation and Eastern Air Lines, S.A.

Wayne Yeoman joined the company in September 1972 as staff vice president - development planning and served in that capacity until April 1974. He served as vice president - development planning from April 1974 to January 1976; as vice president - finance from February 1976 to November 1977, when he became senior vice president - finance. Prior to joining the company, Yeoman was an officer of the United States Air Force for twenty-six years, retiring as brigadier general. He served as a member of the faculty and head of the Department of Economics and Management at the Air Force Academy prior to his association with the company, and he holds a doctorate in Business Administration from Harvard University.

Charles Glass joined the company in 1964 and served as assistant treasurer - financial administration and taxes from September 1970 to August 1972; as vice president - investor relations from August 1972 to February 1976; as assistant treasurer from February 1976 to June 1977; and as vice president and treasurer from June 1977 to the present. Prior to September 1970, Glass served the company in various capacities.[3]

Eastern's management is viewed as one of the leanest in the industry; it was reorganized in 1975. While no operating positions were touched, the company eliminated 195 management slots. Eastern believed its total of forty-seven officers was one of the lowest in the industry. In 1977, 335 additional management and staff positions were lopped off; this reduction saved the company an estimated $8.4 million in wages, salaries, and benefits, and trimmed 4.4 percent of the total management force. This reduction of man-

---

[3]Company's 10-K Report.

agement personnel left Eastern with only thirty-eight vice presidents—the lowest of any airline company in the United States.[4]

COMPETITION

Eastern's competition comes from three major sources: other trunk carriers, regional carriers, and commuter airlines. Before deregulation, most of Eastern's competition came from the other trunk carriers; while this was still true in 1981, there is increased competition from regional and commuter airlines. In 1981, analysts estimated that the ten trunk airlines accounted for about 85 percent of all domestic revenue passenger-miles. The established regional carriers garnered approximately 10 percent of domestic revenue passenger-miles, with the commuter airlines capturing the other five percent. The smaller operations have been growing faster, though. During the 1970s, for example, the trunks averaged about a six percent annual increase in passengers flown, but the commuters averaged 14 percent. In 1980, the number of passengers flown by the trunks declined, but the commuters served 11 percent more passengers than in 1979.[5]

The Trunk Lines

Until January, 1980, there were eleven trunk carriers in the U.S. But Pan American acquired National at that time, and Braniff filed for bankruptcy in 1982, leaving nine. Exhibit 2 shows the cumulative profits between 1971 and 1980 for the 10 trunk carriers still in existence in 1981. Delta generated the largest cumulative profit during this time, outdistancing its closest competitors, Northwest and United.

American. American Airlines is the second largest trunk carrier in the United States, with headquarters in Dallas. The company's 1979 profits were $87.4 million, but it lost $75.8 million in 1980. For the second quarter of 1981, American's revenue passenger miles dropped 15.5 percent, and the load factor slipped to 60.4 percent from 67–68 percent in 1979. Executives attributed the company's poor 1980 showing to a recession economy, higher fuel prices, the fare cutting tactics of competitors, and the "continued use of inefficient 707 passenger aircraft."

American has some excellent market shares on a number of important routes, including 41 percent on New York to Los Angeles, and 35 percent on New York to San Francisco. During 1980 and 1981, American added a number of new routes: Chicago to Seattle; Dallas/Fort Worth to Seattle; Dallas/Fort Worth to Sacramento; Hawaii to Los Angeles, Chicago, New York, and Dallas/Fort Worth; Dallas/Fort Worth to Minneapolis/St. Paul; and eleven new desti-

---

[4]Company's Annual Reports.
[5]Nulty, Peter. "Friendly Skies For Little Airlines." *Fortune,* February 9, 1981, pp. 45–53.

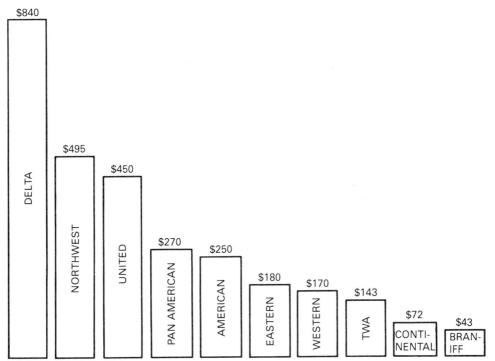

EXHIBIT 2 Approximate ten-year profit for trunk airlines, 1971–1980 (millions of dollars)

SOURCE: Reprinted from the August 31, 1981 issue of *Business Week*, by special permission, © 1981 by McGraw-Hill, Inc., New York, NY 10020. All rights reserved.

nations through Dallas/Fort Worth in Texas, Louisiana, Alabama, Florida, Mississippi, and Oregon. Service to Providence, R.I., Charleston, W.Va., Oakland, Cal., and Islip, N.Y. was discontinued.

Officials announced in 1980 that "fuel inefficient" 707s would be replaced by more fuel efficient 767s, which should be in service by September, 1982. The airline has also bought new 757s and 727-223s.

American implemented several plans to increase revenue and decrease costs in 1980. It expanded seating capacities on its 727-223s, 727-023s, DC-10s, and 747s. The company expects that with an occupancy rate increase of 13 percent, revenues will rise by $26 million annually. To reduce fuel costs, lighter weight seats were added to its Boeing 727-200 planes; this was expected to save $3 million a year.[6]

Braniff. Braniff Airways, Inc., one of the smaller trunk lines, was a leading proponent of deregulation. It viewed deregulation as a way to gain national and international recognition. Within a year, it had added twenty-five new destinations, eighteen domestic and seven international (four in Europe and three in the Far East and Pacific). Domestically, the upsurge in service put the

[6]Loving, Rush Jr. "How the Airlines Will Cope With Deregulation." *Fortune,* November 30, 1978, pp. 38–41 and *Advertising Age,* September 10, 1981.

company in fifty-seven of the nation's top sixty airline markets. Braniff increased its seat-mile capacity by 33 percent in 1979.

This expansion in capacity could not have occurred at a worse time. Braniff was hit with skyrocketing fuel costs, rapidly rising interest rates, and decreased traffic. In the first quarter of 1980, the company lost $24.3 million—$6.9 million on domestic operations, $12.4 million on the North Atlantic routes, and $5.1 million on the new Far East/Pacific routes. The Latin American routes turned a $100,000 profit. Because of the financing crunch caused by the losses, Braniff had to sell some of its fleet to raise the cash to pay off debts. It sold fifteen of its 727-223s to American, and also sold four DC-8-51s, two Boeing 727-100s, and one 727-200.

Despite having filed for bankruptcy, Braniff had some competitive strengths. Harding L. Lawrence, Braniff's former chairman, was considered the industry's premier scheduler. It was in the best position of the trunk carriers to route passengers from South America into its Dallas/Fort Worth, and other, hubs. It also enjoyed a virtual monopoly on nonstop service between several European capitals and the Southwest and was able to fly European travelers to every major U.S. city.[7]

Continental. Continental accounts for only 3 percent of total trunk line revenues. In 1978 and 1979, it was considering a merger with Western. Such a merger, it was argued, would help Continental/Western be more competitive with the main trunk lines. The merger would increase the number of feeder routes into Continental's Los Angeles hub and give the combined airline a giant-sized hub of fourteen spokes in Denver, allowing both carriers to reach such eastern cities as Philadelphia, Cleveland, and Detroit. Continental's fleet in 1979 was relatively new and virtually paid for.[8]

Delta. Delta, the nation's sixth largest trunk airline, has run up thirty-three consecutive profitable years, and is generally regarded as the most profitable and financially secure of all U.S. air carriers. Between 1975 and 1979, the company averaged a 19.3 percent pretax return on its invested capital, far above the other trunk lines. (Northwest had the second-highest return, 12.4 percent).

Delta's success is attributed to two major factors: effective long-range planning and high levels of employee productivity. The airline uses fifteen-year plans; executives follow these plans despite fuel shortages, the air traffic controllers strike, and surging fuel costs. It achieves high employee productivity through such motivational effort as not laying off employees (there have been no layoffs in the last twenty-five years for economic reasons), offering attractive benefit packages, and recognizing outstanding employees. Delta is the least unionized of the trunk carriers; its workers are considered

---

[7]Loving, op. cit.; *Business Week,* December 15, 1981, pp. 80–81; *Business Week,* July 28, 1980, pp. 43–44; and *Business Week,* October 29, 1979, pp. 184–188.

[8]Loving, op. cit.

more flexible. In 1980, Delta enjoyed a 24 percent increase in revenues and earnings over 1979. Its 38.6 million passengers ranked it second to Eastern's 39.1 million.

Delta emphasizes a system of short-haul routes which feed into its hub cities, especially Atlanta, which allows passengers to reach their ultimate destination via Delta. Between January and July, 1980, an estimated 88 percent of the passengers Delta brought into Atlanta continued their trip on Delta; many of Delta's passengers come from cities in the southeast and east who connect in Atlanta for other flights. Delta has the shortest average flight of the main trunk lines, about 700 miles, and believes that a high proportion of its revenues comes from business travelers.

Delta has followed a cautious policy since deregulation to avoid overextending itself. However, it expanded service at its Dallas/Fort Worth and Cincinnati hubs and began nonstop service between Dallas/Fort Worth and New York, bringing it into competition with American and Braniff, who were well entrenched on that route. The company continued to emphasize low-cost night coach flights, it is the industry's leader, and was one of the few carriers to make available a system excursion fare. In 1980, Delta announced it was purchasing $3 billion worth of new aircraft from Boeing; its financial strength allowed it to pay for these planes mostly with internal funds.[9]

Northwest. By several measures, Northwest Airlines, Inc. is the second most profitable airline in the United States. Its cumulative net profit of $495 million between 1971 and 1980 outpaced all trunk lines except Delta, and its 12.4 percent pre-tax return on invested capital was surpassed only by Delta's 19.3 percent. During the first six months of 1980, however, financial woes struck. The company reported a net loss of $16 million, the first time in years that it had suffered losses in two consecutive quarters. Although the company rebounded in the last half, net income was only $7 million, for a return on assets of one half of one percent.

Northwest achieved its success prior to the 1980 downturn despite several competitive disadvantages. The company's routes never fitted the hub and spoke system used so well by Delta and others. Linear routes, from its Minneapolis-St. Paul hub and headquarters to Florida, predominated. Northwest's international routes proved troublesome. The formerly lucrative East Asia routes are now plagued by low yield traffic; the transatlantic routes have incurred huge start-up costs, losing close to $27 million in the fiscal 1979 year. Other problems include a relatively low load factor of 50 percent and the lowest level of fleet use in the industry—about seven hours a day, compared to about nine for the industry.

Northwest's major competitive advantages are its labor cost, cargo operations, and strong balance sheet. Its labor costs are reportedly the lowest in the industry, and its cargo operations make up 25 percent of the company's

---

[9]Loving, op. cit.; Harold Seneker. "Delta Is Ready." *Forbes,* September 15, 1980, pp. 81–85; "Delta: The World's Most Profitable Airline." *Business Week,* August 31, 1981, pp. 68–72; and *Advertising Age,* September 10, 1981.

total revenues, one of the highest percentages in the industry. Northwest is so financially sound that it *could* compete on some of the high density, competitive routes and *could* use fare discounts as a weapon. Other pluses include its low debt costs, plane availability (because of its low fleet use), and spacious seating.

Company executives in late 1980 were considering moving to a hub and spoke system. One problem, however, is that the firm's present fleet is considered inadequate for this route system. Another difficulty is in choosing a hub; most viable hub cities have already been staked out by competitors. For example, Northwest considered St. Louis, but TWA has a stranglehold there.

A merger with Braniff is possible. Braniff international routes would give Northwest an entry into Latin America and would increase traffic for its fleet of 747s during the winter season, when traffic is usually down.[10]

Pan American. Pan American World Airways was the fourth most profitable airline between 1971–1980, with $270 million in profit. But in the first six months of 1980, Pan Am lost $141 million. This figure included results from National, the trunk line it acquired. Pan American is chiefly an international carrier. Major routes include the north Atlantic and north Pacific runs, with some service to South America. During the 1970s, Pan Am cut back its north Atlantic service because of what company officials considered the overly competitive nature. Simultaneously, service to the north Pacific was increased. In the late 1970s, Pan Am's prices on the north Pacific routes were undercut by airlines from South Korea, Taiwan, Thailand, and Singapore.

The acquisition of National was a natural for Pan American; National's routes complemented Pan Am's. Those routes are essentially in the Sunbelt, either from northern cities to Florida, or across the Sun Belt, from Florida to cities like New Orleans, Houston, Los Angeles, and San Francisco. National's routes are expected to provide some feeder traffic into Pan Am's overseas flights.

On July 28, 1980, Pan American announced that it was selling the fifty-nine-story Pan American building in New York for an expected net of $340 million, to help offset its expected 1980 losses. The company was also trying to sell off three planes a month, which it hoped would bring in $79 million.[11]

TWA. Trans World Airlines, a domestic and international carrier, lost $27 million in 1979 and in 1980. The majority of its domestic routes run east/west, and most of its international routes are transatlantic. In 1980, TWA carried 2.4 million passengers on its transatlantic flights, down slightly from the 1979 figure, and its market share of domestic air travel, 13.2 percent in the early 1970s, dropped to 11.4 percent in 1979.

[10]Loving, op. cit. and "Why Northwest Is Caught In a Tailspin." *Business Week,* August 25, 1980, pp. 100–104.

[11]Loving, op. cit.; "Meshing Problems For Pan Am and National." *Business Week,* January 21, 1980, pp. 56–60; "Why Pan Am Sold the Pan Am Building." *Business Week,* August 11, 1980, pp. 25–26; and *Advertising Age,* September 10, 1981.

Both of TWA's major routes are highly competitive; it gets almost 50 percent of its revenue from transcontinental and transatlantic flights. The major reason for TWA's slippage in domestic market share is the population shift from the East and the Midwest to the Sunbelt, an area where it has few routes. The company added service from ten northern cities to Florida in late 1979, and obtained a market share of 5.4 percent on its Florida service. TWA's transatlantic business is hurt by the subsidies foreign governments provide competitive airlines.

TWA's fleet is believed to be one of the oldest and least fuel efficient in the industry. Out of its 194 planes in 1980, 72 were fuel inefficient Boeing 707s and 727s whose profitability has been jeopardized by high fuel costs. In 1978 and 1979, fuel costs increased 55 percent at TWA, probably ten percentage points higher than most competitors. Also, because of its many different planes, TWA has high maintenance costs.[12]

United. United Airlines lost $15 million in 1980 which, while disappointing to the company's executives, was far less than the $100 million net loss in 1979. During 1980, United's load factor dropped 8.29 percent to 57.8 percent; total traffic grew 3 percent. The airline's total capacity increased by 17.5 percent.

During 1980, United completed a program to eliminate most of its routes of 150 miles or less, and add long-haul routes from various medium-size markets. The airline's average route length in 1980 increased 17 percent to around 900 miles. In fall, 1980, the company began to aggressively enter new markets, beginning flights from Chicago to Phoenix, Tuscon, and Houston. By July, 1981, it added the following new service: Chicago to Tulsa, Oklahoma City, Wichita, and Cincinnati; Denver to Phoenix, Tucson, and Houston; and San Francisco to Phoenix and Houston. Overseas service from Chicago and New York to the Mexican resort cities of Cancún, Cozumel, and Mérida was initiated in late 1980.

A significant competitive challenge to United came from American Airlines in 1980; American announced direct service from New York, Dallas/Fort Worth and Chicago to Honolulu. United has about 55 percent of this market, and defended it by increasing advertising expenditures 25 percent. But both American and United suffered because higher air fares and more expensive ground accommodations deterred tourists.

United also suffered fierce competition on its transcontinental routes. Eastern inaugurated service from New York to Los Angeles and San Francisco, and used a $195 one-way fare as an incentive to fly Eastern. Both carriers continued heavy discounting through the first half of 1981, with Eastern eventually reducing its number of flights due to over-capacity.[13]

Western. Western Airlines is based in Los Angeles, and its routes are mainly concentrated in the Western half of the United States, with limited service to

---

[12]Loving, op. cit.; "The Strategy Squeeze on the Airline." *Business Week,* May 19, 1980, pp. 104–115.

[13]Loving, op. cit. and *Advertising Age,* September 10, 1981.

Florida. Major cities served are Minneapolis-St. Paul, Denver, Salt Lake City, Phoenix, San Diego, Los Angeles, San Francisco, and Seattle. In late 1978, Western had sixty-six route segments, but only six of these were estimated to be profitable. Its fleet was relatively old and inefficient. A merger with Continental, which was proposed in 1978–1979 but not consummated, would have provided feeder service into some of Western's destinations. Continental's more modern fleet would have balanced Western's older planes. In 1980, Western generated operating revenues of $1 billion, but lost $30 million.

Western was hurt more than most carriers by fuel increases. Its main fuel supplier, Union Oil Co. of California, buys most of its aviation fuel on the spot market, paying a premium which it passed on to Western. In late 1979, Western was paying about 80¢ a gallon, double what it paid in January. For 1979, Western's fuel bill increased by $170 million, accounting for 27 percent of its total expenses, compared to 20 percent in 1978. In September of 1979, Western had to ground six Boeing 720Bs because they were no longer fuel-efficient.[14]

Regional Carriers

Regional airlines recognized the opportunity of deregulation and began to chip away at the major trunk lines. Based on 1980 performance, the largest of the regional airlines was *U.S. Air,* formerly Allegheny Airlines. Revenues in 1980 were $972 million, not far below those of the tenth largest trunk line (Continental, $992 million). Net profit was $60.4 million, more than any trunk line carrier except Delta. The profits represented a 6.2 percent return on sales and an 8.4 percent return on total assets. U.S. Air's routes are concentrated in the Northeast; its major hub city is Pittsburgh. The company opened service to Houston from Pittsburgh soon after deregulation and, in 1980, began service to Florida from Pittsburgh. U.S. Air has effectively tied into a number of commuter operations. In return for painting "U.S. Air Commuter" on their planes, U.S. Air will assist the commuter lines with ticketing and baggage handling. The arrangement steers passengers to U.S. Air flights.

The second largest regional carrier in 1980 was *Republic Airlines.* This Minneapolis-based airline obtained $917 million in revenues in 1980, but suffered a set loss of $25 million. Republic Airlines was formed by the July, 1979 merger of North Central Airlines, Inc. and Southern Airways, Inc. North Central's routes were concentrated chiefly in the upper Midwest, while Southern's were located primarily in the Southwest.

Two other regional airlines, *Piedmont Aviation* and *Frontier Airlines,* made money in 1980. Piedmont, headquartered in Winston-Salem, North Carolina, earned $16 million on sales of $484 million. Its routes are located primarily in the Southeast, although, after deregulation, it expanded to some cities, like Houston. Frontier Airlines made $23 million in profit in 1980 on

---

[14]Loving, op. cit.

sales of $469 million. With routes mainly in the Rocky Mountain region, its headquarters are in Denver.

Hughes Airwest also has routes predominantly in the Rocky Mountain area. In 1979, the company lost $22 million on sales of $312 million; much of this loss was attributed to a sixty-one-day strike.

A newcomer, *Air Florida,* has experienced tremendous growth. Initially limiting service to destinations within Florida, the company branched out to include service down the Atlantic seaboard to Florida, and across the Sunbelt to such cities as New Orleans and Houston. In 1980, Air Florida's revenues approached $300 million (seventy-five times what they were just four years earlier), and profits were expected to double.

World Airways, headquartered in Oakland, California, traditionally relied on charter business to generate revenues. Military charters at one time accounted for 75 percent of its business, but they have plummeted to 22 percent after the Vietnam War. Shortly after deregulation, the company began transcontinental service, competing with the more established trunk carriers on a price basis. World Airways got off to a good start because it started transcontinental service during a strike at United, but, after the strike, United and TWA quickly undercut World's fares. Since the company relied heavily on DC-10s for its transcontinental service, it was severely hurt when all DC-10s were grounded in 1979 because of the American Airlines DC-10 crash at Chicago's O'Hare airport which killed 275 people.

Commuter Airlines

In 1981, there were about 240 commuter airlines in the United States. For many years, these operations had the reputation of being "white-knuckle, tree-top airlines." They usually operated propeller driven airplanes with a seating capacity of under twenty, although some used planes with up to fifty seats. Commuter operations expanded as the trunk and regional airlines cut back service after deregulation. Within one year, trunk carriers eliminated service to 170 cities. Seventy-nine of these cities were left without air service until commuter airlines began operations, usually with smaller planes and less reliable schedules. Between 1978 and 1980, commuter airlines doubled their revenues to $1.1 billion. Some experts have estimated that, by 1990, 10 percent of all domestic passengers will fly on small commuter lines.

One of the most successful commuters is *Southwest Airlines,* which began providing shuttle service between Dallas and Houston in 1971 and which now blankets the state of Texas. Service in 1981 was extended to Albuquerque and New Orleans. During 1972, its first full year of operation, Southwest carried 300,000 passengers. By 1980, it was carrying 6 million passengers and net income was $21 million, up 67 percent.

Southwest stresses efficiency. Only one type of plane made up its fleet —the small and thrifty Boeing 737, with low fuel and maintenance costs. The company operates its fleet an average of eleven hours a day, well above the industry average of eight hours. Pilots are not unionized and fly an average of seventy-five hours a month, 25 percent more than unionized pilots with competitive lines. No meals are served and cash register receipts are used as tickets. Southwest's economy emphasis has paid off. It cost Southwest $20.38 per passenger on the Houston to Dallas flight, compared to $43.96 for United Airlines. Its labor costs amount to 30 percent of its total costs, compared to an average of about 40 percent for trunk lines. Southwest's cost advantages are used to charge lower ticket prices, which lure passengers away from competitors. For example, its Houston to Dallas fare was $40 in 1981, compared to an average of $71 for competitors.

Another successful commuter carrier has been *Texas International.* After deregulation, TI took on the look of a regional carrier by adding such routes as Houston to Baltimore/Washington. In 1980, TI decided to transplant its success formula to woo Eastern Airlines' shuttle passengers: it formed New York Air to compete directly with Eastern's New York to Boston and New York to Washington commuter routes.

NYA plans to cut costs to undercut Eastern's fares by 18 to 52 percent. No backup planes will be used because New York Air will sell only reserved seats and will not guarantee to carry all potential passengers. It will use non-union pilots, flight attendants, and ticket and reservation agents; all of these jobs, except the pilots', will be interchangeable. NYA's 115-seat, twin engine, two-man cockpit DC-9's are more fuel- and labor-efficient than Eastern's 727s. NYA's facility at LaGuardia Airport is an inexpensive portion of American Airlines' hangar, while Eastern has constructed a new $2 million terminal. Not all of NYA's passengers will be siphoned from Eastern; some analysts believe that they will be people who formerly took the train or bus.[15]

CORPORATE STRATEGIES

In 1975, Eastern's management stipulated a "continuing dedication to running a reliable, quality airline." Eastern's objective was to maintain its share of a stagnant market and attract new passengers when traffic picked up again. Eastern executives believe that this objective would be achieved by "improving service in almost every category of performance that is important to passengers."

In 1976, Eastern reviewed the key objectives of a massive restructuring study which it initiated in 1974. These included:

---

[15]"World Airways: When an Upstart Airline Owns Mostly DC-10s." *Business Week,* June 25, 1979, pp. 110–111; "Texas International's Quiet Pilot." *Business Week,* August 20, 1979, pp. 65–66; "Move Over Boeing." *Forbes,* September 17, 1979, p. 92; "Texas Gets Bigger." *Forbes,* November 12, 1979, pp. 88–93; "Republic Air Takes on a New Merger Problem." *Business Week,* March 24, 1980, pp. 54–55; "A Plucky Challenge To Eastern's Shuttle." *Business Week,* September 22, 1980, pp. 42–44; "A New Airline Flies Against The Odds." *Business Week,* August 18, 1980, pp. 27–28; Stuart, Alexander, op. cit.; "East Coast Dogfight." *Forbes,* November 24, 1980; and Nulty, op. cit.

☐ To deseasonalize the airline

☐ To strengthen business markets

☐ To revise the company's route structures so that (1) routes with sub-marginal profit potential could be eliminated, and (2) new routes could be added which would be profitable and compatible with the existing route structure

In 1977, the company's top management indicated that its "first attention must be the day-to-day provision of reliable, superior airline service." Another priority included attaining "maximum efficiency in production of this service." To obtain this objective, it "must get the most seat miles for every drop of fuel burned and eliminate any waste of either time or materials." A third priority was to "exercise every means at [its] disposal to upgrade [its] fleet in a manner that offsets the continuing rise in operating costs, and gives [it] the capacity to capitalize on the growing demand for air travel."

In 1979, as Eastern turned a profit for the fourth consecutive year, management indicated that the company was continuing to "progress with a proven plan for consistent profitability—a plan which calls for a cost-conscious management, an expanded and well balanced route system, a fleet of efficient aircraft and optimum productivity."[16]

It appears that Eastern's executives have been pursuing a number of major strategies to achieve their objectives: improving operating performance, controlling costs, upgrading fleet, and restructuring routes. Other important strategies include fare modifications, potential mergers, advertising, and sales promotion.

Improving Operating Performance

Airlines gauge their operating performance by many different measures. Various operating results for Eastern are provided in Exhibit 3. The specific operating statistics obtained in this exhibit are determined as follows:

☐ *Revenue plane miles* are the total number of miles flown by Eastern's planes for which revenue was generated.

☐ *Available seat miles* are the total number of seats on a flight multiplied by the number of miles flown. For example, if a 200-seat plane is flown 500 miles, the seat miles are 100,000 (200 x 500 = 100,000).

☐ *Revenue passenger miles* refers to the number of *occupied* seats on a flight multiplied by the number of miles flown. For instance, in the example above, if 120 seats were occupied, a total of 60,000 revenue passenger miles would result (120 x 500 = 60,000).

☐ *Passenger load factor* is the number of revenue passenger miles divided by available seat miles. In the example above, the passenger

---

[16]Company Annual Reports.

EXHIBIT 3   Operating statistics (1976–1980)

	1980	1979	1978	1977	1976
Revenue plane miles*	312.7	303.8	288.9	284.3	277.0
Available seat miles*	46,028.4	43,050.7	39,117.5	36,783.5	34,766.2
Revenue passenger miles*	28,227.0	28,917.7	25,228.2	20,657.3	19,520.5
Passenger load factor	61.33%	67.17%	64.49%	56.16%	56.15%
Break even load factor	62.23%	65.62%	62.45%	55.28%	54.54%
Revenue passengers carried*	39.1	42.2	37.4	31.3	29.3
Available ton miles*	5,640.8	5,171.3	4,740.9	4,499.2	4,323.1
Revenue ton miles*	3,175.6	3,224.4	2,839.7	2,351.4	2,214.5
Weight load factor ..	56.30%	62.35%	59.90%	52.26%	51.23%
Percent performance	98.55%	97.94%	98.07%	98.68%	98.77%
Yield per revenue passenger mile ...	11.15¢	9.08¢	8.53¢	8.87¢	8.42¢
Yield per revenue ton mile	104.40¢	85.80¢	80.22¢	82.35¢	78.44¢
Total operating expenses per available seat mile	7.50¢	6.44¢	5.84¢	5.38¢	4.97¢
Total operating expenses per revenue passenger mile	12.22¢	9.58¢	9.05¢	9.57¢	8.86¢
Total operating expenses per available ton mile	61.17¢	53.57¢	48.15¢	43.96¢	39.99¢
Total operating expenses per revenue ton mile	108.66¢	85.92¢	80.39¢	84.11¢	78.07¢
Aircraft utilization— hours per day	9:33	9:44	9:31	9:14	9:05
Number of personnel employed at year-end	40,000	38,900	37,100	34,300	33,200
Average flight length	563	526	509	520	518

*Millions

SOURCE: Company Annual Reports.

load factor would be 60 percent (60,000 ÷ 100,000) = 60 percent). The passenger load factor measures an airline's use of its passenger carrying capacity.

☐ *Break even load factor* is a company's estimate of the load factor it needs to break even. If the company makes a profit for the year, the break even load factor is less than the passenger load factor. If it loses money, the break even load factor is higher than the passenger load factor.

☐ *Revenue passengers carried* is the total number of fare-paying passengers carried.

☐ *Available ton miles* measures an airline's total cargo-carrying capacity. To calculate available ton miles, the weight (in tons) available for cargo on a flight is multiplied by the number of miles flown. For example, if a cargo hold could accommodate 20 tons and the plane was flown 300 miles, 6,000 available ton miles would result (300 x 20 = 6,000).

☐ *Revenue ton miles* refers to the total number of tons of cargo actually carried multiplied by the miles the cargo was flown. In the example above, assume that 13 tons of cargo were flown 300 miles. This is 3,900 revenue ton miles.

☐ If revenue ton miles is divided by available ton miles, a carrier's *weight load factor* is calculated. In the example above, a weight load factor of 65 percent results (3,900 ÷ 6,000 = 65 percent). The weight load factor for a company's cargo operations is similar to the passenger load factor for its passenger operations; it measures an airline's use of its cargo-carrying capacity.

☐ *Percent performance* for Eastern refers to the percentage of all flights that leave "on time" (within one hour of scheduled departure).

☐ *Yield per revenue passenger mile* is calculated by dividing total revenues from passenger operations by the total number of passenger revenue miles. In 1980, Eastern's total operating revenues from passenger operations was $3,151,798,000 and its total number of passenger revenue miles was 28,227,000,000. Dividing $3,151,789,000 by 28,227,000,000 results in a yield per revenue passenger mile of 11.15¢.

☐ *Yield per revenue ton mile* is calculated by dividing total revenues from passenger and cargo operations by total revenue ton miles. For 1980, Eastern's yield per revenue ton mile was 104.40¢ (total revenues from passenger and cargo operations of $3,315,270,000 divided by 3,175,600,000 revenue ton miles = 104.40¢).

☐ Dividing total operating expenses by available seat miles, revenue passenger miles, available ton miles, and revenue ton miles will result in *total operating expenses* being expressed *per* unit of *seat mile, revenue passenger mile, available ton mile,* and *revenue ton mile.* To illustrate: Eastern's total operating expenses in 1980 were $3,450,685,000 which, when divided by 46,028,400,000 available seat miles, results in total operating expenses per available seat mile of $7.50¢.

☐ The *aircraft utilization* figure indicates the average number of hours a day that each plane is in the air.

☐ *Average flight length* refers to the average number of miles flown per trip.

Exhibits 4 and 5 show productivity figures for Eastern from 1971 to 1980: available seat miles per employee and revenue passenger miles per employee. Exhibits 6, 7, and 8 show Eastern's income statements and balance sheets from 1976 to 1980.

Cost Control

Eastern mounted an aggressive program of cost containment and reduction during the second half of the 1970s. Exhibit 9 shows Eastern's total operating expenses for each year from 1975 through 1980, and the percentage of the total that each type cost accounted for. This exhibit shows that Eastern's two major costs are salaries, wages, and benefits, and fuel; it has devoted most of its cost control efforts to these areas.

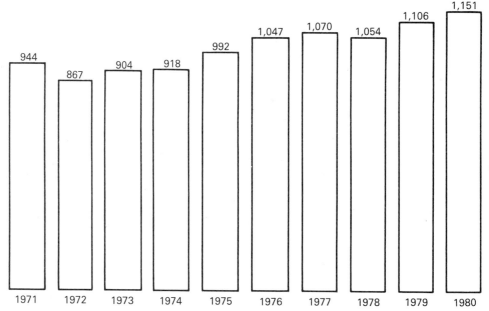

EXHIBIT 4   Available seat miles per employee (1971–1980) (thousands of dollars)
SOURCE: Company Annual Reports.

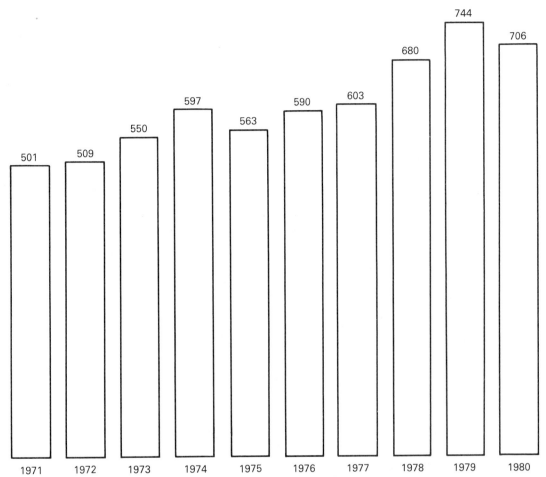

EXHIBIT 5   Revenue passenger miles per employee (1971–1980) (thousands of dollars)

SOURCE: Company Annual Reports.

Salaries, Wages, and Benefits. In 1975 Eastern began to eliminate unnecessary management personnel and these reductions-in-force dropped 530 superfluous positions. The 1977 reduction of 335 management slots saved the company an estimated $8.4 million.

However, the Variable Earnings Program is Eastern's main commitment to controlling personnel costs. VEP was instituted voluntarily by Eastern employees in 1977; all employees participate in the five-year program. VEP's objective is to "provide a foundation for achieving at least a minimum level of profitability," which is pegged at 2 percent of sales. To guarantee the company a profit of 2 percent of its sales, employees are paid 96.5 percent of their base salaries. If the 2 percent figure is not met, Eastern uses the VEP funds to bring profits up to this level. If Eastern's profits exceed 2 percent, employees receive one-third of the amount above 2 percent, up to a maximum of 3.5 per-

EXHIBIT 6   Income statement, 1976 and 1977 (thousands of dollars)

	Year Ended December 31, 1977	Year Ended December 31, 1976
Operating revenues		
Passenger	$1,835,132	$1,648,062
Cargo	101,334	89,123
Incidental and other revenue	92,267	88,290
Retroactive mail settlement	7,160	—
Total operating revenues	2,035,893	1,825,475
Operating expenses		
Flying operations	686,719	561,789
Maintenance	288,914	264,871
Passenger service	187,839	158,930
Aircraft and traffic servicing	354,571	318,731
Marketing and administrative ...	323,937	285,475
Depreciation and amortization ..	107,408	103,144
Cost of incidental revenue	52,085	54,234
Total operating expenses	2,001,473	1,747,174
Operating profit	34,420	78,301
Nonoperating income and (expense)		
Interest income	6,133	5,740
Interest expense (exclusive of $2,545 and $2,128 capitalized)	(39,523)	(43,718)
Profit (loss) on sale of equipment	21,996	(620)
Gain on extinguishment of debt	4,050	—
Other, net (notes A & D)	7,661	5,536
Total	317	(33,062)
Income before income taxes and extraordinary item	34,737	45,239
Provision for income taxes (note E)	—	10,857
Income before extraordinary item	34,737	34,382
Extraordinary credit—utilization of tax loss carryforward	—	10,857
Net income	34,737	45,239

SOURCE: Company Annual Reports.

EXHIBIT 7   Income statement, 1978–1980 (thousands of dollars)

| | Year Ended December 31 | | |
	1980	1979	1978
Operating revenues:			
Passenger	$3,151,798	$2,628,721	$2,156,182
Cargo	163,472	137,791	121,714
Incidental and other revenues	137,272	115,014	101,668
Total operating revenues	3,452,542	2,881,526	2,379,564
Operating expenses:			
Flying operations:			
Aircraft fuel	1,019,546	672,689	425,191
Other	381,357	321,558	297,517
Maintenance	396,174	344,625	304,202
Passenger service	314,639	280,997	232,795
Aircraft and traffic servicing	550,685	481,320	409,511
Marketing and administrative	520,470	438,043	375,922
Depreciation and amortization	200,572	174,769	166,331
Cost of incidental revenues	67,242	56,458	71,313
Total operating expenses	3,450,685	2,770,459	2,282,782
Operating profit	1,857	111,067	96,782
Non-operating income and (expense):			
Interest income	41,118	28,877	13,113
Interest expense (exclusive of $10,276, $6,303 and $2,274 capitalized)	(109,836)	(84,335)	(74,980)
Profit on sale of equipment	17,886	5,723	25,084
Gain on extinguishment of debt ...	—	—	4,368
Other, net	2,708	(922)	2,890
Total	(48,124)	(50,657)	(29,525)
Income (loss) before income taxes and extraordinary item	(46,267)	60,410	67,257
(Reduction in) provision for income taxes	(4,255)	2,779	
Income (loss) before extraordinary item	(42,012)	57,631	67,257
Extraordinary item—net of a provision in lieu of income taxes of $2,498	24,654	—	—
Net income (loss)	(17,358)	57,631	67,257

SOURCE: Company Annual Reports.

EXHIBIT 8   Balance sheet, 1976–1980 (millions of dollars)

	1980	*1979*	*1978*	*1977*	*1976*
Assets:					
Current assets	$ 810.6	$ 732.3	$ 381.0	$ 338.7	$ 371.6
Operating property and equipment, net	1,964.2	1,675.4	1,486.3	1,281.3	1,254.7
Other assets	41.4	45.3	41.2	44.0	37.7
Total assets	$2,816.2	$2,453.0	$1,908.5	$1,664.0	$1,664.0
Liabilities:					
Current liabilities	$ 724.4	$ 624.2	$ 466.2	$ 402.2	$ 420.2
Current obligations—capital leases	56.5	54.6	49.3	41.2	33.3
Long-term debt	754.2	661.2	399.7	435.8	566.0
Long-term obligations— capital leases	688.4	591.6	538.9	444.9	379.6
Deferred credits and other long-term liabilities	17.9	33.3	13.9	8.8	11.9
Total liabilities	2,241.4	1,964.9	1,468.0	1,332.9	1,411.0
Redeemable preferred stock	139.3	47.4	47.4	47.3	—
Common/non-redeemable preferred stock and retained earnings:					
Common stock	24.9	24.9	24.9	19.8	19.8
Non-redeemable preferred stock	—	—	—	—	—
Capital in excess of par value	355.4	341.0	340.8	298.6	295.7
Earnings (deficit) retained for use in the business	56.3	78.3	27.4	(34.6)	(62.5)
Treasury stock as a reduction	(1.1)	(3.5)	—	—	—
Total common/non-redeemable preferred stock and retained earnings	435.5	440.7	393.1	283.8	253.0
Total liabilities, capital stock and retained earnings	$2,816.2	$2,453.0	$1,908.5	$1,664.0	$1,664.0

SOURCE: Company Annual Reports.

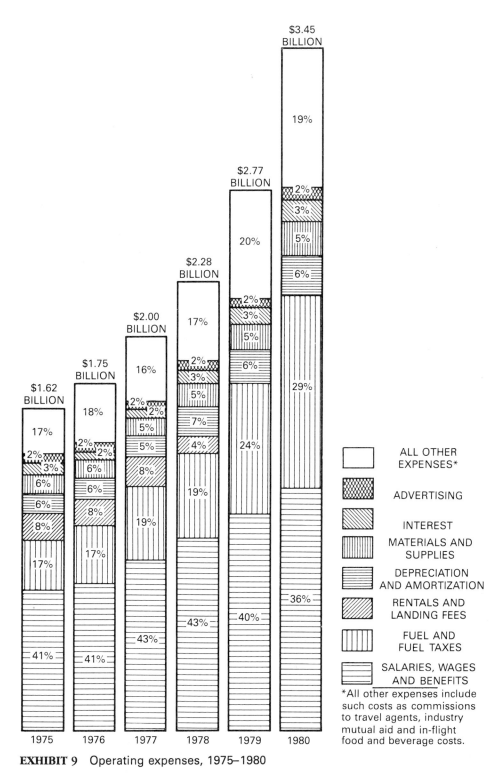

EXHIBIT 9 Operating expenses, 1975–1980

All other expenses include such costs as commissions to travel agents, industry mutual aid and in-flight food and beverage costs.

cent above their base salaries. In 1978, Eastern's net profit exceeded 2 percent of its revenues (2.8 percent), but was right at the 2 percent benchmark figure in 1979.

Fuel Costs. Exhibit 10 shows the tremendous increases in fuel costs from 1971 through 1980. In 1975, the following measures were used to save nine million gallons of fuel: lower cruise speeds, reduced engine operating times while aircraft are on the ground, and slower climb and descent procedures.

Conservation efforts in 1977 included following more optimum flight profiles, shutting down one or two engines during taxi, instituting more precise accountability for fuel supplies, and stripping the white paint off aircraft. (It takes 447 pounds of white paint on an L-1011, equal in weight to two passengers or a quarter ton of revenue cargo.) These fuel cost conservation efforts helped save $3.4 million, well above the planned figure of $2.1 million. While fuel conservation has been helpful, it does not have the long-range impact on reducing costs that acquiring more fuel-efficient aircraft would have.

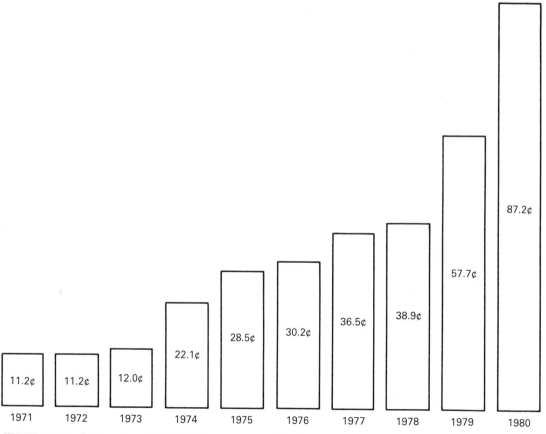

EXHIBIT 10 Fuel costs—1971–1980 (cents per gallon)
SOURCE: Company Annual Reports.

Fleet Upgrading. At the end of 1975, Eastern's fleet consisted of 244 aircraft, primarily Lockheed L-1011s, Boeing 727s, and McDonnell Douglas DC-9s. Fifteen Electras were used as backups for shuttle operations. By the end of 1980, the company's fleet had expanded to 275 aircraft, including 34 L-1011s, 142 Boeing 727s, 75 McDonnell Douglas DC-9s, and 19 A300s. By the beginning of January, 1981, 55 aircraft were on order: 12 Boeing 727s (the 225 series), 15 A300s, 27 B-757s, and four McDonnell Douglas DC-9s (51 series). At that time, future options existed for 50 additional aircraft.

The A300 (Airbus) is a European aircraft manufactured jointly by France, West Germany, and Great Britain. By the mid-1980s, over 100 of these new planes were in service and they were showing the lowest cost-per-seat-mile of any aircraft flying shorter routes. Experts estimate the Airbus can cut fuel consumption by 25 to 30 percent; it uses only two engines instead of three, as do most competitive planes. Eastern considers this airplane perfect to fly its high-density New York to Florida routes.

Eastern was cautious about purchasing the Airbus. It convinced Airbus Industrie to let it use several Airbuses free for six months in 1977 on the New York to Florida routes. Although there were no leasing charges, Eastern had to commit $7 million to new training and associated costs. Eastern found that the Airbus was very reliable, and both pilots and passengers were impressed. Fuel costs were estimated to be one-third lower than for Eastern's 727s and L-1011s. The A300 features the same technology as the American widebody planes (the L-1011, DC-10 and 747), but Eastern will have the A300 outfitted to seat 230 passengers. The Airbus will fit in the middle of Eastern's fleet— between the 140-seat 727 and the 290-seat L-1011. The A300's optimal range is a medium-length 2,500 miles. Boeing's B757 has an optimal range of 2,200 miles and seats about 180 passengers.

Route Restructuring

When deregulation relaxed the CAB's control over airline routes, the trunk carriers moved aggressively to restructure their routes. Like its competitors', Eastern's strategies involved adding new destinations and eliminating old ones. Exhibit 11 shows Eastern's route structure on December 31, 1977, approximately one year before deregulation. Exhibit 12 shows the route structure on December 31, 1980, approximately two years after deregulation.

New service inaugurated in late 1978 included the following: Atlanta-San Francisco, Miami-San Francisco, St. Louis-Salt Lake City, Ft.Myers-New York, Austin-Houston, and Atlanta to Detroit, Cleveland, Savannah, Charleston, S.C. and Columbia, S.C. Service from Miami to Port-au-Prince, Haiti and Mérida and Mexico City (via Tampa) was opened, as was service from New Orleans to Cozumel, Cancún and Mérida in Mexico. Service to Memphis, Macon, Roanoke, Canton-Akron, Chattanooga, Cincinnati, and Huntsville was eliminated.

In 1979, the western expansion of Eastern's routes continued. Service to Rochester, Albuquerque, Tucson, Phoenix, Denver, Reno, and Norfolk was in-

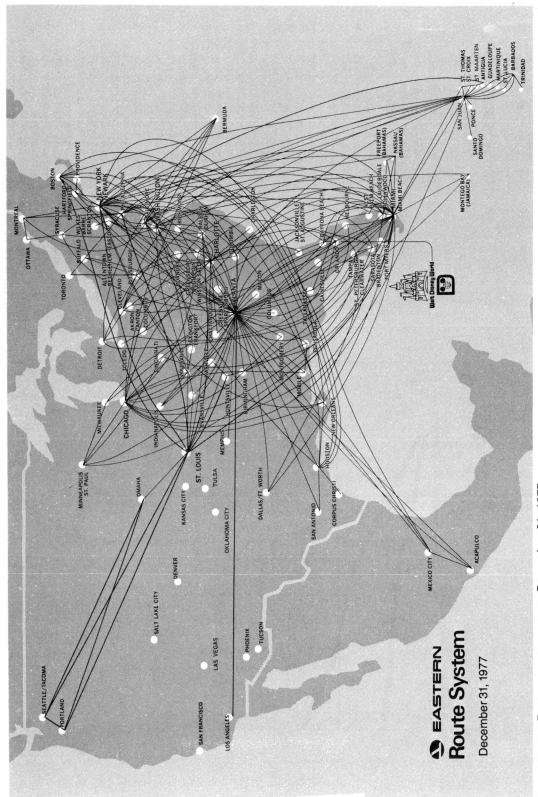

EXHIBIT 11   Eastern route system, December 31, 1977

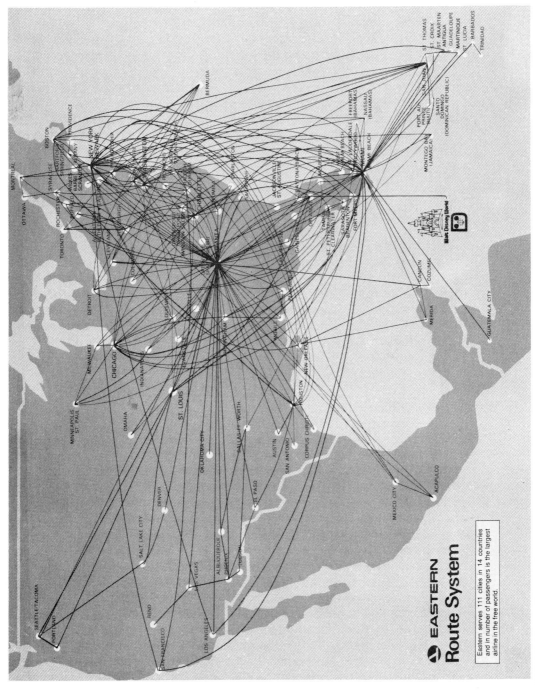

EXHIBIT 12 Eastern's route system, December 31, 1980

609

augurated. All these destinations were served with one-stop or nonstop service through Eastern's Atlanta hub. Internationally, new nonstop service was begun to Santo Domingo and Guatemala through Eastern's Miami hub.

Eastern experienced increased competition on its routes in 1979, especially on its routes from the Northeast to popular Florida winter vacation spots. TWA began service from Boston and New York to Miami and Fort Lauderdale, United initiated service from Chicago, and American, Braniff, and U.S. Air also began flying to Florida. Despite this increased competition, Eastern was able to retain its position as the number one carrier to and from Florida.

In 1980 and 1981, new service was inaugurated from Atlanta to Las Vegas, Reno, Oklahoma City, and El Paso. Service was expanded to Phoenix, Norfolk, Rochester and Albuquerque. Nonstop service was begun to Allentown/Bethlehem/Easton and Omaha, formerly served by one-stop service.

Destinations in the Caribbean were provided additional service in 1980. These included Guadalajara, Mazatlán, Puerto Vallarta, Cancún, and Cozumel in Mexico, Aruba, Curacao, and Barranquilla, Columbia. The Barranquilla route provided the company with its first service to the South American mainland. The major route addition in 1980 was transcontinental service from New York to Los Angeles and San Francisco. Eastern believed that these routes would use the L-1011 efficiently. However, Eastern lost $3 million to $5 million on its transcontinental routes in 1980. Service to Lexington, Montgomery and Toledo was suspended. While the CAB granted Eastern new routes to Guatemala, Honduras, Costa Rica, and Panama, it lost its authority to serve Mexico City.

Eastern's increased service between 1978 and 1981 strengthened Atlanta and Miami as its two most important hubs. Eastern, like the other trunk lines, uses what is referred to as a hub-and-spoke system. A hub is a city where an airline collects, switches, and dispenses passengers in many different directions. Most airlines believe that they should fly into their hubs from as many cities (spokes) as possible in order to feed passengers into their planes leaving for other destinations. Exhibit 13 shows the major hub cities for the trunk carriers. Once a carrier has developed a strong hub city, it becomes difficult and expensive for other trunks to compete effectively. Perhaps the most formidable hub is Delta's in Atlanta; in 1980, Delta averaged about 350 flights a day out of Atlanta. United, trying to make Atlanta a hub city, believed that it would have had to have flown at least 50 flights a day. Rather than increase its service to that level, it withdrew. In 1980, Eastern's management estimated that it needed nine flights a day out of St. Louis to secure an acceptable market share. Because of TWA's entrenched position there, Eastern decided not to make the commitment.

Eastern has more flights each year out of Atlanta than any airline does out of any city. The Atlanta hub handles more than eight million Eastern passengers a year. In 1980, Eastern completed $137 million worth of additions to its Midfield Terminal in Atlanta's Hartsfield International Airport, increasing gate facilities and quadrupling the size of a cargo terminal.

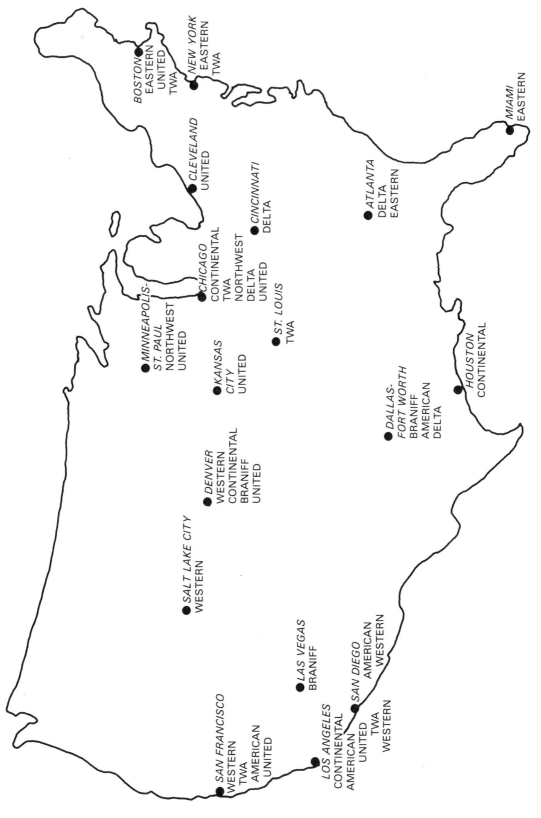

EXHIBIT 13 Some important hub cities for major air carriers

One of Eastern's most important routes is its "shuttle" service. Operating between New York and Boston and New York and Washington, D.C., the Air-Shuttle has carried 51 million passengers in twenty years. In late 1980, Eastern completed a new $25 million terminal for its Air-Shuttle operations at New York's La Guardia Airport. Reservations are not required for the shuttle, nor is advanced ticketing available. However, all passengers are guaranteed a seat; if there is an overflow for one plane, Eastern will run another one to accommodate the passengers.

Eastern's shuttle has captured an estimated 90 percent of Boston-New York-Washington air travel. Company executives claim that its shuttle is "marginally profitable," despite high market share and steadily increasing ticket prices (over $60 in 1981). Eastern officials blame the back-up airplanes and crews required for not obtaining more profit. One solution to the backup problem is to use aircraft with more seats (most planes on the shuttle seat 177, with older backup planes on the Washington run seating 105). Eastern would like to use two 282-passenger widebody A-300s during peak hours, but all widebody aircraft have been banned from Washington National.

Fare Modifications

Eastern discounted fares on a broad front in 1980 and 1981. It used this, along with heavy advertising support, to inaugurate its transcontinental service in June, 1981. By the end of the year, these fares returned to their normal levels. It discounted some fares on its shuttle routes in response to price cutting tactics of the new competitor, New York Air. Eastern matched New York Air's weekend fares and maintained a price differential of $10 on weekday fares. Discount fares also encouraged vacation travel, and were revived during the summer of 1981 on the transcontinental routes.

In 1977, Eastern initiated its innovative unlimited mileage fare. The company has continued to offer this fare, in which two adults traveling together can take a twenty-one-day tour on Eastern's domestic and international airlines.

Potential Mergers

Eastern has considered merging with two airlines, National and Braniff, since 1978. A merger with National would have provided Eastern with transatlantic and Sunbelt routes, where it was relatively weak. In 1978, Eastern and National connected on only eighteen non-stop routes, and, on ten of these routes, other carriers are also competing. Only two of competitive routes were major: New York to Miami and Washington, D.C. to Miami. This merger would have allowed the numerous East Coast cities served by Eastern to feed passengers to National's transatlantic routes. Eastern's management estimated that the merger would have freed seventeen aircraft for other routes. In spite of these potential benefits, National was acquired by Pan American on January 7, 1980 for $394 million.

Preliminary merger discussions between Eastern and Braniff began in December, 1980. Acquiring Braniff would have brought Eastern a strong South American route structure, somthing it had long coveted. Eastern eventually backed off the merger talks because 1,000 to 1,500 Eastern jobs would have been jeopardized. Outside analysts, however, believed that a major reason for the breakdown of talks was the heavy debt carried by both airlines. In September, 1980, the combined long term debt of Eastern and Braniff was close to $2 billion, about four times their stockholders' equity.

Advertising

Exhibit 14 shows Eastern's advertising expenditures from 1975 to 1980. Exhibit 15 shows the organization of its advertising department. Eastern's 1980 allocation ranked it ninety-first among American advertisers. Exhibit 9 shows that Eastern's advertising expenditures were about 2 percent of total expenses from 1975 through 1980. Other major trunk lines are also heavy advertisers. In 1980, TWA allocated $60 million for advertising, United, $60.2 million, American, $46.3 million, and Delta, $38.7 million.

Approximately 44 percent of Eastern's 1980 advertising budget was spent on newspaper advertisements. About 20 percent was allocated to television advertising, 12 percent to magazines, 16 percent to radio, and 7 percent to outdoor. As much as 15 percent of the company's total advertising

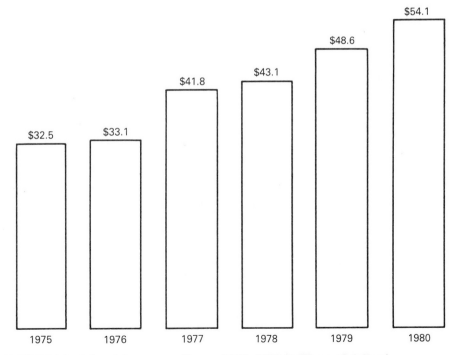

EXHIBIT 14 Advertising expenditures, 1975–1980 (millions of dollars)
SOURCE: Company Annual Reports.

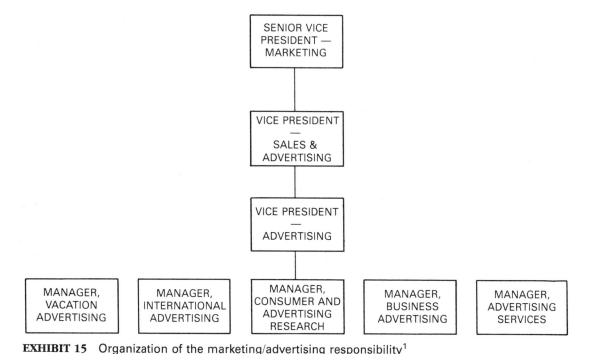

EXHIBIT 15   Organization of the marketing/advertising responsibility[1]

[1]Case writer's perception of reporting relationships.

SOURCE: *Advertising Age,* September 10, 1981.

budget may be international. TWA emphasized television advertisements, followed by magazines, newspaper, and outdoor. American Airlines allocated 42 percent to newspapers, 29 percent to television, 19 percent to radio, 10 percent to magazines, and 2 percent to outdoor. Delta devoted 54 percent of its advertising funds to newspapers, with 16 percent spent on radio, 14 percent on television, 8 percent on outdoor, and 7 percent on magazines.

Eastern's advertising has traditionally used three major themes: business travel, vacations, and corporate image. Corporate ads usually feature Frank Borman, and carry the message that Eastern was interested in improving itself.

Delta's advertising is considered the "no-nonsense" type, and it uses the slogan, "Delta is ready when you are." American Airlines launched an aggressive advertising campaign in magazines in 1980 and 1981, and some ads stressed American's status as the favorite carrier based on a survey conducted by the Airline Passenger Association. TWA's advertising in 1980 and 1981 stressed cost and convenience. United's advertising in 1980 and 1981 emphasized low fares and the company's various destinations.[17]

---

[17]*Advertising Age,* September 10, 1981.

Sales Promotion Efforts

Deregulation and increased competition has created a spate of sales promotion efforts in recent years. For the airline industry, the use of sales promotion was a new approach to generating passengers. Here are some of the promotional campaigns:

☐ Pan American gave away souvenir plates to its international passengers. However, it withdrew the offer when passengers complained about getting duplicate plates.

☐ United ran a thirty-day "Take-off" contest in April, 1980. Passengers received a card with nine spots. After rubbing the spots off with a coin, any passenger having a card with three airline drawings in a row received a free round-trip flight. About 15,000 free trips were awarded and over three million cards distributed.

☐ American Airlines introduced its "A Advantage" program, a bonus plan for frequent fliers, in April, 1981. Depending on the number of miles flown, American passengers could win prizes ranging from an upgrade to a first class ticket to free first class flights.[18]

As of mid-year 1981, Eastern had been reluctant to develop any sales promotion efforts.

EPILOG

Eastern's top management was concerned and disappointed in early 1982 as they reflected on the company's 1981 performance. Although revenues had increased nine percent over 1980's figures to $3.7 billion, Eastern Airlines incurred a net loss of $66 million, well in excess of 1980's $17 million loss. Although Eastern led all carriers in 1981 with 35.5 million passengers flown, this was a decline of about 11 percent from the 1981 level of 39 million.

Several other major airlines revealed their profits at about the same time. American Airlines generated a net profit of $47.4 million, compared to its 1980 loss of $76 million. Delta's 1981 profit of $146 million was $53 million better than its 1980 figure. TWA incurred a pretax loss of $28 million, $1.2 million worse than its performance in the previous year. United's deficit stood at $104 million for 1981.

Frank Borman indicated a number of factors contributing to the firm's 1981 performance. He specifically mentioned the worsening recession, fare cuts, and the strike by air traffic controllers.

---

[18]*Advertising Age,* September 10, 1981 and "Now the Battling Airlines Try Mass Marketing." *Business Week,* April 28, 1980, p. 104.

Southwest Airlines

"It's been a hectic few months," reflected Camille Keith (Southwest Airlines' vice president of public relations), "but we're finally spreading love outside of Texas." While the urge to sit back and relax was very strong, she knew that the job of expanding air service to the three new markets had just begun. Was the introduction successfully launched? What did the new market customers think of Southwest? Was the advertising working?

Ms. Keith knew that marketing research held the answers to many of her questions, and that a thorough review of recent strategy was in order. Some information was already available, but some other would probably need to be collected. "Let's see where we stand," she commented to Tom Volz (Southwest's vice president of marketing and sales).

"Fine!" replied Mr. Volz, "Let's get together first thing tomorrow morning."

"Tomorrow's meeting means a long today," thought Ms. Keith, as she began reviewing the background on the campaign planning. "Hold my calls and see if my other meeting this afternoon can be postponed," she called to her secretary.

THE COMPANY

Southwest Airlines began intrastate service in Texas on June 18, 1971 with three Boeing 737-200 aircraft, and a marketing strategy which highlighted several unique attributes:

1. simplicity of operations (one type of aircraft, Dallas' Love Field headquarters, simplified passenger check-in and fare structure, and no food service)

This case was prepared by Richard F. Beltramini, Assistant Professor of Marketing and Advertising at Arizona State University, as a basis for class discussion rather than to illustrate either effective or ineffective handling of an administrative situation. Some figures contained herein have been disguised.

© Richard F. Beltramini, 1980

2. high productivity (daily aircraft utilization of more than eleven hours, and ten minutes turnaround times between most flights)

3. focus on passenger business (no large air freight and no U.S. mail)

4. serving short-haul, mass transit commuter markets (flight segments under two hours and fare structure competitive with bus and auto travel)

As of March 15, 1980, Southwest had grown to 1,600 employees, 41 aircraft, 1,852 total system-wide weekly flights, and an average load factor of 68.3 percent (based on 1979 figures and a 118 seat capacity). Exhibit 1 illustrates the

SOUTHWEST AIRLINES PASSENGER BOARDINGS

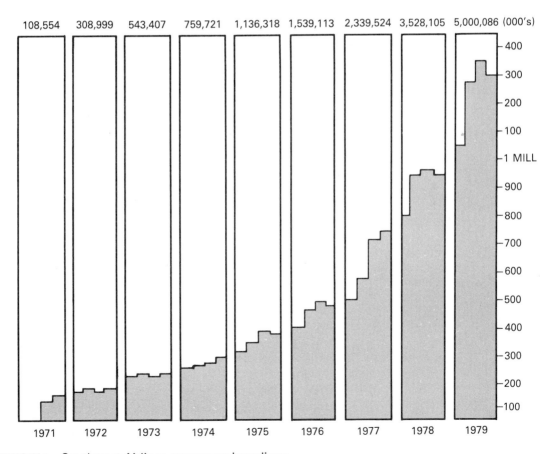

EXHIBIT 1   Southwest Airlines passenger boardings
SOURCE: Southwest Airlines Boarding Reports.

growth in passenger boardings over the years in operation, and Exhibit 2 shows operating statistics in relation to income.

Between 1972 and 1979, passengers carried grew at an annual rate of 48.9 percent. The reason for this growth, according to Southwest's management, was that it offered a good product in a receptive market at a fair price the average person could afford.

In late 1978, Southwest Airlines served eleven major Texas cities as an intrastate carrier subject to the economic regulation of the Texas Aeronautics Commission. However, in December of that year, Southwest received their Certificate of Public Convenience and Necessity from the Civil Aeronautics Board, providing the authority to extend its service beyond Texas. The first route outside Texas was to New Orleans almost immediately, and routes were added to Oklahoma City on April 1, to Tulsa on April 2, and to Albuquerque on April 3, 1980.

THE MARKET

1979 was a year of considerable change within the airline industry. Deregulation had precipitated many fare reduction programs; however by the end of the year, the fuel crisis had seemingly reversed this policy, and fares had increased once again.

Fuel costs in 1978 averaged 37¢ per gallon, while 1979 saw an increase to 80¢ per gallon by the year's end. Southwest Airlines' management projected that fuel costs would exceed $1.00 per gallon in 1980, representing 40 percent of its budget for operating costs.

The deregulation trend, however, afforded Southwest the opportunity to expand service into new markets, and its business philosophy pointed to three cities with apparent growth potential. The Oklahoma City, Tulsa, and Albuquerque markets are described briefly in Exhibit 3. It was felt that expanding air service to these cities from the Dallas headquarters offered a profitable strategy to capitalize on the regulatory changes. Exhibit 4 illustrates the relative location of these new markets.

MARKETING RESEARCH

The potential for expanding service appeared profitable, given the trends evident in executive class boardings (see Exhibit 5), total passenger boardings (see Exhibit 6), the 1979 load factors (see Exhibit 7), and the projected growth (see Exhibit 8). To supplement these data, however, a research project was conducted in the fall of 1979. A random, system-wide survey of 7,900 Southwest Airlines passengers was conducted on board flights to identify the frequency of flying and the attributes deemed important by these passengers.

EXHIBIT 2   Southwest Airlines financial statement

Consolidated Balance Sheet
(in thousands)

	March 31, 1980	1979
Assets		
Current:		
Cash and commercial paper	$ 8,936	$ 8,374
Accounts receivable	11,678	5,447
Other	1,590	1,058
	22,204	14,879
Flight and ground equipment, at cost, less reserves	169,507	112,763
Other non-current assets	877	366
Total assets	$192,588	$128,008
Liabilities and net worth		
Liabilities		
Current:		
Accounts payable and accrued liabilities	$ 10,615	$ 6,287
Current maturities of long-term debt	4,720	1,750
	15,335	8,037
Long-term debt less current maturities	98,487	63,250
Deferred federal income tax	14,186	10,398
Deferred other	942	387
Total liabilities	128,950	82,072
Net worth		
Common stock and paid-in capital	15,828	14,448
Retained earnings	47,810	31,488
Total net worth	63,638	45,936
Total liabilities and net worth	$192,588	$128,008

Share Data:

Common stock issued and outstanding (note A) (000)	4,567	4,500
Book value per share	$ 13.94	$ 10.21

Comparative Operating Statistics

	Three Months Ended March 31, 1980	1979
No. of flights	18,833	15,935
Passengers carried	1,189,745	1,038,657
Passenger miles flown (000)	383,773	317,806
Passenger load factor	63.9%	67.9%
Operating revenues per flight	$ 2,134	$ 1,611
Operating expenses per flight	1,734	1,222
Operating income per flight	$ 400	$ 389

Consolidated Statement of Income
(in thousands)

	Three Months Ended March 31, 1980	1979
Operating revenues:		
Passenger	$38,878	$24,732
Package express	1,116	799
Other	192	146
Total operating revenues	40,186	25,677
Operating expenses:		
Flight operations excluding fuel	3,470	2,453
Fuel and oil	12,631	5,286
Maintenance	2,383	1,521

EXHIBIT 2   (continued)

Consolidated Statement of Income
(in thousands)

	Three Months Ended March 31, 1980	1979			1980	1979
Passenger services	1,654	1,173	Interest expense		2,459	1,813
Terminal opera-					1,439	1,773
tions	4,485	3,126	Income before fed-			
Promotion and			eral income tax		6,093	4,425
sales	1,808	1,479	Provision for federal			
Insurance, taxes			income tax		1,784	1,097
and administra-						
tive	2,662	1,895	Net income		$ 4,309	$ 3,328
Depreciation	2,638	1,858				
Employee profit						
sharing expense	923	688	Weighted average			
Total operating			common and com-			
expense	32,654	19,479	mon equivalent			
			shares outstanding			
Operating income	7,532	6,198	(note A) (000)		4,544	4,500
Non-operating expense			Net income per			
(income):			share	$ .95	$ .74
Interest and other						
income	(1,020)	(40)				

EXHIBIT 3   Southwest Airlines' new markets

Oklahoma City, the capital of Oklahoma, is the largest municipality in the state with a population of 368,164 (1970 census). Located in Central Oklahoma on the North Canadian River, the city represents the state's financial, commercial, and industrial center built on rich oil and gas lands. Its industry includes meat packing, electronic components, production of transportation equipment, and oil field supplies. A frequent convention center, it has also grown into an aeronautical complex, housing Federal Aviation Administration facilities and Tinker Air Force Base. Additionally, a variety of tourist attractions such as the National Cowboy Hall of Fame and the Western Heritage Center are located in Oklahoma City, approximately 181 air miles from Dallas.

Tulsa, Oklahoma, a city of 330,350 (1970 census), has been dubbed "The Oil Capital of the World" and is the western-most inland water port in the United States. Next to oil, aviation and aerospace industries are the next largest employers. A beautiful city of parks and old homes, Tulsa is also the home of the University of Tulsa and Oral Roberts University. Located at the base of the Ozark Mountains, the city is surrounded by lakes, and is a water sports haven. Tulsa is approximately 237 air miles from Dallas.

Albuquerque, New Mexico is the largest city in New Mexico with a population of 243,751 (1970 census). Located in north-central New Mexico on the Upper Rio Grande, it is a fast-growing center of trade, small industry, Federal agencies, and a famous health resort. Following World War II, growth accelerated rapidly due primarily to Sandia Corporation's nuclear weapons laboratory and Kirtland Air Force Base, a nuclear effects research

EXHIBIT 3 (continued)

laboratory and satellite tracking station. Albuquerque's main manufacturing industry includes brick and tile, wood products, Indian jewelry, clothing, and buiness machines. Additionally, several railroad shops, lumber mills, and food processing plants are located there, as well as the University of New Mexico. Albuquerque is approximately 580 air miles from Dallas.

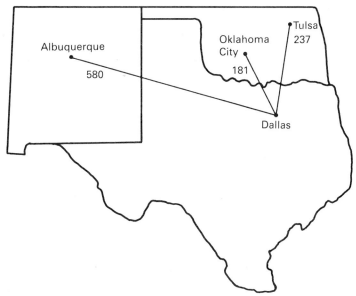

EXHIBIT 4 Air miles between new markets

Each respondent was asked how many round-trip flights he had taken on Southwest during the past year. The results (shown below) indicated that 18.7 percent of the respondents accounted for 55 percent of the total trips.

# of flights	% respondents	% trips
1-2	22.9%	3%
3-6	29.0	11
7-12	16.7	13
13-20	12.7	18
21-40	10.9	28
41 +	7.8	27
	100.0%	100%

Respondents were also asked to evaluate various airline attributes in terms of importance, using a four-point rating scale (4 = very important; 1 = not important at all). As shown below, departing on time of schedule was rated as the most important attribute by the majority of those surveyed.

attribute	rank	% respondents rating important
on-time departure	1	98.61%
frequency of scheduled departures	2	97.86
friendly ground personnel	3	97.12
convenient departure times	4	96.99
courteous hostesses	5	95.51
baggage handling	6	93.01
lower fares	7	91.05

After assessing what passengers generally wanted in air service, respondents were also asked to indicate their particular likes and dislikes concerning Southwest Airlines. Low fares was the highest ranked positive attribute.

Seasonality

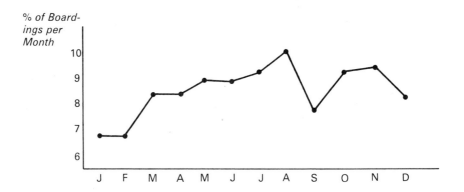

% of Boardings Per Market

EXHIBIT 5   Executive class boardings 1979

Seasonality

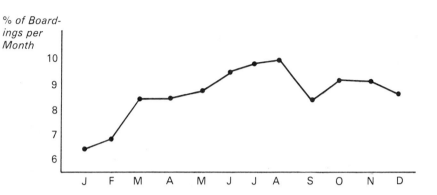

% of Boardings Per Market

EXHIBIT 6 Total passenger boardings 1979

Attribute	Rank
low fares	1
convenient airports	2
pleasant hostesses	3
convenient (in general)	4
on-time departure	5
frequency of scheduled departures	6
prompt and efficient service	7

In another independent survey, *Texas Business* polled their subscribers concerning airline service. The results of this survey coincidentally appeared in their February 1980 issue, just as Southwest Airlines was granted their

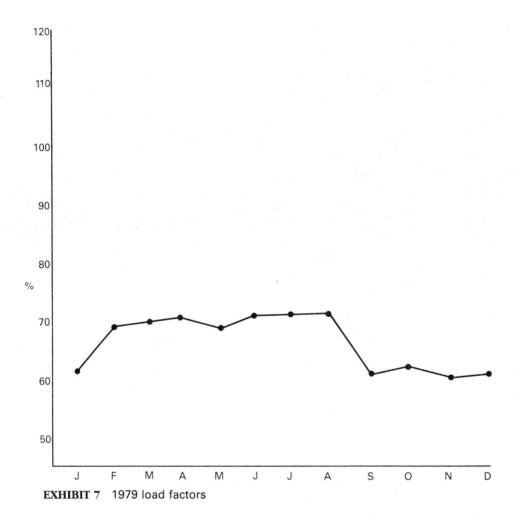

EXHIBIT 7   1979 load factors

EXHIBIT 8   1980 forecast

	1979	1980	Increase Number	%
Total passenger board-ings	5,000,000	7,000,000	2,000,000	40%
Total trips	76,000	105,000	29,000	38%
Available seat miles	2,500,000,000	3,500,000,000	1,000,000,000	40%
Revenue passenger miles	1,500,000,000	2,500,000,000	1,000,000,000	67%

three new interstate routes. The results (shown below) indicated Southwest was rated as "excellent" or "good" by over 90 percent of those 795 respondents.

	meals	ticketing performance	luggage handling	hospitality	overall performance
Southwest	*	1	1	1	1
American	2	2	3	2	3
Delta	3	3	2	3	2
Continental	1	4	4	4	4
Braniff	4	7	7	6	7
Eastern	5	5	5	5	5
Texas Int'l.	6	6	6	7	6

*no meal service

SOURCE: *Texas Business;* February, 1980.

Marketing Strategy

Besides maintaining a consistent growth pattern in previously established routes, Southwest Airlines' management's highest priority in 1980 was the introduction of the new routes to Oklahoma City, Tulsa, and Albuquerque on April 1, 2, and 3 respectively. Service from Dallas' Love Field to these new markets was established as follows.

Market	Schedule
Oklahoma City	7 round-trips daily
Tulsa	7 round-trips daily
Albuquerque	4-5 round-trips daily

Passengers arriving from these cities to Dallas' Love Field could connect with flights to the rest of the Southwest Airlines' system from Love Field. Likewise, passengers from other destinations could travel to these new cities through a connection at Love Field. However, Southwest did not plan to have any direct flights from the new cities to other Southwest Airlines' markets until passenger load factors to Dallas' Love Field were deemed successful.

To assist in the planning and development of these new routes, Southwest obtained a traffic history analysis of the 1978 origins and destinations (O&D) from each of the new markets. Dallas/Ft. Worth was the O&D leader from each of the new cities, with Houston ranking a strong second (particularly from Tulsa and Oklahoma City). The latter was hypothesized to be the result of petroleum-related industry traffic. Albuquerque was marked not only by an increasingly growing business community (particularly in electronics), but also as a pleasure travel market. The New Mexico area was becoming a very popular ski market to Texans. Exhibit 9 illustrates the 1978 O&D's from each new market.

EXHIBIT 9   1978 origins and
destinations report

From Oklahoma City

150,000	Dallas/Ft. Worth
115,000	Houston
30,000	New Orleans
26,000	San Antonio
13,000	Midland/Odessa
12,000	Austin
10,000	El Paso
27,000	N/A
383,000	

From Tulsa

160,000	Dallas/Ft. Worth
150,000	Houston
34,000	New Orleans
15,000	San Antonio
13,000	Midland/Odessa
9,000	Austin
3,000	Rio Grande Valley
29,000	N/A
413,000	

From Albuquerque

108,000	Dallas/Ft. Worth
50,000	El Paso
40,000	Houston
20,000	San Antonio
11,000	New Orleans
11,000	Midland/Odessa
10,000	Lubbock
24,000	N/A
274,000	

ADVERTISING STRATEGY

The introduction of the new routes was supported by a heavy radio and newspaper advertising campaign created by The Bloom Agency, Southwest's advertising agency of record. Two weeks before the inaugural flights, the campaign broke with small "teaser" advertisements in the new market newspapers. The advertisements contained headlines such as "Here Comes Love, Southwest Style," and listed a phone number to make reservations.

That same week also began sixty-second radio spots, running primarily in the morning and late afternoon, designed to reach the businessman during drive time. It was felt by both Southwest's marketing team and the

THANKS TO YOU, WE'RE STILL IN LOVE.

On February 15, 1980, a compromise bill authorizing limited interstate service from Love Field was signed into law. The bill permits Southwest Airlines to use Love Field both for flights within Texas and to states bordering Texas. It also signals the end of a long and heated controversy over Love Field's use as a satellite airport.

We at Southwest have held fast in the belief that Love Field represents a valuable service to our passengers, both for intrastate and interstate travel. And hundreds of thousands of Texans feel the same way. The strength of those convictions was demonstrated when Love Field was threatened by a bill proposing total elimination of all interstate flights from Love.

Last November when the contents of that proposed bill became public, supporters of Southwest and of Love Field made their feelings known in editorials, letters, mailgrams, and over 160,000 signatures on petitions circulated by Southwest. One particularly heartwarming show of support was the response to our "Now is the time to fight for Love" ad asking for endorsement in the form of a mail-in coupon. We ran that ad only one time and received an overwhelming response of over 16,000 coupons.

These massive demonstrations of support by citizens throughout the state helped convince the U.S. Congress that Southwest Airlines and Love Field do indeed provide a valuable service to Texans.

The generous support of our passengers and friends was particularly meaningful to all of us here at Southwest. Not only because it aided in a compromise bill which permits our continued growth, but also because it shows that the service we provide is important to you. And we're reaffirming our service commitment by opening flights to Oklahoma City, Tulsa and Albuquerque in April.

In the meantime, we hope you'll accept a less tangible display of gratitude in the form of one simple statement: thank you.

Herbert D. Kelleher
Chairman of the Board

Howard D. Putnam
President and Chief Executive Officer

SOUTHWEST AIRLINES

EXHIBIT 10   Southwest Airlines print advertisement

agency that businessmen represented the heaviest travellers, and the appropriate target audience for these messages.

The week before the initial flights, the newspaper advertisements were stepped up to twice daily, and the radio schedule was doubled. Nearly every radio station in the new markets was running Southwest Airlines' spots. On Monday, March 31, just days before the inaugural flights, full-page advertisements appeared in addition to the teaser newspaper advertisements in each of the local markets.

Monday also marked the posting of thirty-sheet outdoor posters with messages such as "Tightwads Rejoice" and "Big D, Little $" on the major arterials throughout the new market cities. The full-page advertisements ran once daily through each inaugural flight, and radio stations continued to broadcast "That's Love, Southwest Style." Exhibit 10 illustrates another print advertisement which appeared in *Southwest,* its in-flight publication.

EXHIBIT 11   Southwest Airlines advertising recall study: Oklahoma City service

1. Where do you recall seeing or hearing the Southwest Airlines advertising of the new route service?

Newspaper	145	Billboard	29	Other	14
Radio	92	Magazine	16		
TV	43	Don't Know	24		

2. In which newspaper(s) did you see this advertising?

Ft. Worth Star Telegram	6	Daily Oklahoman	69
Dallas Morning News	53	Oklahoma Journal	11
Dallas Times Herald	40	Other	12

3. On which radio station(s) do you recall hearing this advertising?

KBYE, Oklahoma	0	KXXY, Oklahoma	1	KNTU, Texas	0	Other
KEBC, Oklahoma	21	KZUE, Oklahoma	5	KOAX, Texas	3	
KFNB, Oklahoma	0	WKY, Oklahoma	5	KRLD, Texas	17	
KOCY, Oklahoma	7	KAAM, Texas	1	KVIL, Texas	9	
KOFM, Oklahoma	7	KBOX, Texas	3	WFAA, Texas	5	
KOMA, Oklahoma	7	KFJZ, Texas	2	WRR, Texas	2	
KTOK, Oklahoma	13	KLIF, Texas	8	KNUS, Texas	4	

4. On which television station(s) do you recall seeing this advertising?

KOCO, (Ch. 5) Oklahoma	19	KERA, (Ch. 13) Texas	3
KTVY, (Ch. 4) Oklahoma	15	KTVT, (Ch. 11) Texas	2

EXHIBIT 11   (continued)

KWTV, (Ch. 9) Oklahoma	4	KXAS, (Ch. 5) Texas	6
KDFW, (Ch. 4) Texas	8	WFAA, (Ch. 8) Texas	11

5. Do you recall seeing or hearing NEWS coverage about the new routes? Where?

Newspapers	63	TV	35
Radio	43	Magazine	6

6. Did you hear about the new route service from a travel agency?

Yes	29
No	215

7. What in the advertising attracted you?

Convenience of SWA	132	Friendly Service	59
Low Fares	140	Close in Airports	124
High Frequency	78		

8. What is your occupation?

Professional/Technical	118	Service Workers	2
Managers/Administrators	107	Student	5
Sales Workers	37	Retired	3
Clerical Workers	3	Unemployed	5
Craftsmen/Foremen	1	No Answer	1
Operatives	0		

9. Into which of the following age categories do you fall?

18–24	18	45–54	57
25–34	78	55–64	26
35–44	90	65 over	8

10. Into which of the following categories does your total yearly household income fall?

$10,000 and under	5	$20,000–$24,999	16
$10,000–$14,999	9	$25,000 and over	210
$15,000–$19,999	57	No Answer	26

11. How frequently do you fly?

EXHIBIT 11   (continued)

Once A Week Or More	76
Two Or Three Times A Month	129
Seldom	73

EXHIBIT 12   Southwest Airlines advertising recall study: Tulsa service

1. Where do you recall seeing or hearing the Southwest Airlines advertising of the new route service?

Newspaper	131	Billboard	40	Other	17
Radio	90	Magazine	16		
TV	51	Don't Know	26		

2. In which newspaper(s) did you see this advertising?

Ft. Worth Star Telegram	8	Tulsa Tribune	53
Dallas Morning News	64	Tulsa World	82
Dallas Times Herald	32	Other	21

3. On which radio station(s) do you recall hearing this advertising?

KAKC, Oklahoma	7	KVOO, Oklahoma	13	KOAX, Texas	4
KCFO, Oklahoma	1	KXXO, Oklahoma	2	KRLD Texas	10
KELI, Oklahoma	8	KAAM, Texas	2	KVIL, Texas	8
KFMJ, Oklahoma	0	KBOX, Texas	7	WFAA, Texas	8
KMOD, Oklahoma	17	KFJZ, Texas	4	WRR, Texas	0
KRMG, Oklahoma	33	KLIF, Texas	2	KNUS, Texas	7
KTOW, Oklahoma	2	KNTU, Texas	1	Other	2

4. On which television station(s) do you recall seeing this advertising?

KOTV, (Ch. 6) Oklahoma	17	KERA, (Ch. 13) Texas	4
KTEW, (Ch. 2) Oklahoma	18	KTVT, (Ch. 11) Texas	5
KTUL, (Ch. 8) Oklahoma	21	KXAS, (Ch. 5) Texas	5
KDFW, (Ch. 4) Texas	14	WFAA, (Ch. 8) Texas	16

5. Do you recall seeing or hearing NEWS coverage about the new routes? Where?

Newspapers	106	TV	58
Radio	56	Magazine	9

EXHIBIT 12 (continued)

6. Did you hear about the new route service from a travel agency?

Yes   49

No   242

7. What in the advertising attracted you?

Convenience of SWA	127	Friendly Service	82
Low Fares	206	Close in Airports	141
High Frequency	84		

8. What is your occupation?

Professional/Technical	112	Service Workers	3
Managers/Administrators	105	Student	4
Sales Workers	49	Retired	5
Clerical Workers	8	Unemployed	7
Craftsmen/Foremen	4	No Answer	7
Operatives	2		

9. Into which of the following age categories do you fall?

18–24	25	45–54	60
25–34	96	55–64	37
35–44	97	65 over	9

10. Into which of the following categories does your total yearly household income fall?

$10,000 and under	10	$20,000–$24,999	35
$10,000–$14,999	11	$25,000 and over	239
$15,000–$19,999	13	No Answer	13

11. How frequently do you fly?

Once A Week Or More	96
Two Or Three Times A Month	143
Seldom	94

EXHIBIT 13   Southwest Airlines advertising recall study: Albuquerque service

---

1. Where do you recall seeing or hearing the Southwest Airlines advertising of the new route service?

Newspaper	104	Billboard	24	Other	18
Radio	49	Magazine	13		
TV	29	Don't Know	17		

2. In which newspaper(s) did you see this advertising?

Ft. Worth Star Telegram	7	Albuquerque Journal	36
Dallas Morning News	45	Albuquerque Tribune	9
Dallas Times Herald	36	Other	5

3. On which radio station(s) do you recall hearing this advertising?

KABQ, New Mexico		KRST, New Mexico	1	KNTU, Texas	
KDQQ, New Mexico	6	KZIA, New Mexico		KOAX, Texas	5
KJOY, New Mexico	9	KZZX, New Mexico	1	KRLD, Texas	14
KKIM, New Mexico	1	KAAM, Texas		KVIL, Texas	12
KOB, New Mexico	11	KBOX, Texas	2	WFAA, Texas	4
KPAR, New Mexico		KFJZ, Texas	1	WRR, Texas	
KQED, New Mexico	1	KLIF, Texas	6	KNUS, Texas	4
KRKE, New Mexico	4			Other	4

4. On which television station(s) do you recall seeing this advertising?

KGGM, (Ch. 13) New Mexico	7	KERA, (Ch. 13) Texas	3
KMXN, (Ch. 23) New Mexico		KTVT, (Ch. 11) Texas	1
KOAT, (Ch. 7) New Mexico	10	KXAS, (Ch. 5) Texas	14
KOB, (Ch. 4) New Mexico	6	WFAA, (Ch. 8) Texas	16
KDFW, (Ch. 4) Texas	12		

5. Do you recall seeing or hearing NEWS coverage about the new routes? Where?

Newspapers	44	TV	28
Radio	32	Magazine	5

6. Did you hear about the new route service from a travel agency?

Yes	16
No	130

EXHIBIT 13 (continued)

7. What in the advertising attracted you?

Convenience of SWA	72	Friendly Service	50
Low Fares	116	Close in Airports	60
High Frequency	28		

8. What is your occupation?

Professional/Technical	75	Service Workers	1
Managers/Administrators	58	Student	2
Sales Workers	18	Retired	2
Clerical Workers	3	Unemployed	3
Craftsmen/Foremen	0	No Answer	2
Operatives	3	Other	1

9. Into which of the following age categories do you fall?

18–24	6	45–54	46
25–34	61	55–64	13
35–44	52	65 over	3

10. Into which of the following categories does your total yearly household income fall?

$10,000 and under	3	$20,000–$24,999	13
$10,000–$14,999	9	$25,000 and over	131
$15,000–$19,999	22	No Answer	10

11. How frequently do you fly?

Once A Week Or More	41
Two Or Three Times A Month	87
Seldom	53

Dresser Industries

Dresser Industries, Inc., is one of the world's largest suppliers of technology, products, and services to industries involved in the development of energy resources, particularly petroleum, natural gas, coal, and synfuels. The company was incorporated in Delaware in 1956, as a successor to a corporation in Pennsylvania formed in 1938 by the merger of S.R. Dresser Manufacturing Company and Clark Bros. Company, both started in 1880. In 1977, Dresser acquired Marion Power Shovel Company, of Marion, Ohio, a leading producer of walking draglines and mining shovels, and other products designed to serve the coal and surface mining industries. The company, which employed about 55,000 people in 1981, is headquartered in Dallas. A ten-year financial summary of the company and its various industry segments is provided in Exhibit 1.

Most of Dresser's sales come from sales to energy-oriented industries, such as oil and gas exploration, drilling and production; gas transmission and distribution; petroleum and chemical processing; production of electricity; coal mining, processing, and conveying; and marketing of petroleum products. Other industries served by Dresser include steel, water, sewage, mining, transportation and construction.

MAJOR INDUSTRY SEGMENTS

To effectively serve these markets, Dresser's operations are divided into five major segments: These are petroleum operations segment, energy processing and conversion equipment segment, refractories and minerals operations segment, mining and construction equipment segment, and industrial specialty products segment. Exhibits 2–9 give financial and performance data for these five major segments.

This case was developed by Richard T. Hise, Professor of Marketing at Texas A&M University, as a basis for class discussion rather than to illustrate either effective or ineffective marketing management.

Dollars in Millions Except Per Share Data—Years Ended October 31.		1981	1980	1979	1978	1977	1976	1975	1974	1973	1972
Net sales and service revenues	$	4,614.5	4,016.3	3,457.4	3,054.0	2,538.8	2,232.2	2,011.6	1,398.0	1,025.2	906.9
Cost of sales and services [1]	$	3,047.1	2,704.1	2,329.2	2,032.8	1,658.5	1,475.8	1,355.1	971.3	701.9	619.8
Interest expense	$	52.7	48.4	50.6	52.4	44.9	36.2	33.2	26.4	16.9	14.8
Earnings before taxes	$	528.6	448.2	407.1	378.7	335.6	273.0	224.7	114.3	72.3	65.6
% of sales		11.5	11.2	11.8	12.4	13.2	12.2	11.2	8.2	7.1	7.2
% of avg. shareholders' investment		29.6	29.2	30.7	32.9	33.6	34.8	37.5	23.9	18.4	17.5
Income taxes	$	212.0	187.1	179.1	174.8	150.5	116.2	100.1	50.9	28.3	26.7
Net earnings	$	316.6	261.1	228.0	203.9	185.1	156.8	123.9	63.2	44.2	38.9
% of sales		6.9	6.5	6.6	6.7	7.3	7.0	6.2	4.5	4.3	4.3
% of avg. shareholders' investment		17.7	17.0	17.2	17.7	18.6	20.0	20.7	13.2	11.2	10.4
Total dividends paid	$	51.7	43.9	39.7	35.6	32.0	27.6	27.1	26.3	24.7	24.7
Per Share Data [2]											
Net earnings	$	4.04	3.35	2.94	2.61	2.37	2.09	1.78	0.97	0.74	0.66
Common dividends	$	0.660	0.562	0.512	0.455	0.410	0.375	0.350	0.350	0.350	0.350
Assets Employed											
Current assets		2,064.2	1,880.5	1,681.7	1,620.5	1,450.5	1,191.0	980.0	836.3	508.7	452.3
Current liabilities		910.2	781.5	635.7	663.6	627.9	456.5	449.3	398.8	204.1	160.4
Current ratio		2.3	2.4	2.6	2.4	2.3	2.6	2.2	2.1	2.5	2.8
Working capital		1,154.0	1,099.0	1,046.0	956.9	822.6	734.5	530.7	437.5	304.6	291.9
% of sales		25.0	27.4	30.3	31.3	32.4	32.9	26.4	31.3	29.7	32.2
Property, plant and equipment—net	$	967.2	798.2	666.5	582.2	564.6	411.2	350.4	292.4	227.5	230.5
Total assets	$	3,273.3	2,897.2	2,522.9	2,371.9	2,169.3	1,721.1	1,424.4	1,209.0	806.0	748.8
Total assets less current liabilities	$	2,363.1	2,115.7	1,887.2	1,708.2	1,541.4	1,264.6	975.1	810.2	601.9	588.4
Capitalization											
Long-term debt	$	317.7	344.5	353.7	398.3	414.0	291.4	288.1	221.0	163.0	170.4
% of long-term debt & shareholders' investment		14.2	17.3	19.9	24.5	27.8	24.0	30.8	28.5	28.7	30.8
Shareholders' investment	$	1,924.6	1,648.2	1,422.3	1,227.2	1,074.9	920.8	646.3	553.5	404.6	383.5
Other Data											
Capital expenditures	$	329.9	238.5	191.3	122.8	126.9	128.4	115.7	73.7	36.4	32.1
Depreciation, depletion and amortization (property)	$	151.8	128.7	107.1	95.3	74.6	62.5	52.5	42.3	37.1	35.4
Research and engineering	$	151.1	121.7	101.8	89.2	73.6	62.2	51.1	36.9	30.6	26.8
Number of employees		57,000	52,800	55,200	55,100	53,100	52,600	51,000	50,000	35,100	31,500
Revenues by Industry Segment											
Petroleum operations	$	2,062.5	1,603.9	1,100.6	886.1	743.2	634.9	546.4	402.8	329.9	296.5
Energy processing & conversion		900.9	724.6	750.2	709.2	640.1	546.0	449.3	256.7	180.3	162.5
Refractories & minerals operations		438.9	460.7	425.2	344.2	306.2	283.6	272.2	252.5	184.0	150.3
Mining & construction equipment		578.1	575.0	585.7	566.8	363.8	333.8	301.1	125.8	49.2	35.6
Industrial specialty products		713.1	719.2	658.0	572.4	519.8	480.9	507.4	394.8	302.2	268.0
Less intersegment revenues		79.0	67.1	62.3	24.7	34.3	47.0	64.8	34.6	20.4	6.0
Net sales and service revenues	$	4,614.5	4,016.3	3,457.4	3,054.0	2,538.8	2,232.2	2,011.6	1,398.0	1,025.2	906.9
Operating Profits by Industry Segment											
Petroleum operations	$	393.7	248.1	152.7	146.7	124.2	106.8	87.2	43.4	30.8	29.0
Energy processing & conversion		100.6	100.5	141.2	144.6	143.1	96.3	59.1	22.2	13.7	9.2
Refractories & minerals operations		37.1	53.7	63.7	40.9	43.5	40.1	43.2	37.7	22.7	16.9
Mining & construction equipment		(10.0)	38.9	46.5	56.7	45.9	53.0	49.3	13.6	5.1	2.7
Industrial specialty products		46.2	62.4	60.0	57.3	44.1	41.6	52.2	40.0	37.0	38.4
Less corporate expenses, net		39.0	55.4	57.0	67.5	65.2	64.8	66.3	42.6	37.0	30.6
Earnings before taxes	$	528.6	448.2	407.1	378.7	335.6	273.0	224.7	114.3	72.3	65.6

EXHIBIT 1 Ten year financial summary Dresser Industries, Inc. and subsidiaries

Years Ended October 31,	1981	1980	1979
Sales and service revenues to unaffiliated customers			
Petroleum Operations	$2,044.9	$1,584.7	$1,087.0
Energy Processing & Conversion Equipment	869.4	709.8	734.9
Refractories & Minerals Operations	437.9	460.2	425.0
Mining & Construction Equipment	576.3	564.8	573.6
Industrial Specialty Products	686.0	696.8	636.9
Intersegment sales and service revenues			
Petroleum Operations	17.6	19.2	13.6
Energy Processing & Conversion Equipment	31.5	14.8	15.3
Refractories & Minerals Operations	1.0	.5	.2
Mining & Construction Equipment	1.8	10.2	12.1
Industrial Specialty Products	27.1	22.4	21.1
Eliminations	(79.0)	(67.1)	(62.3)
Total sales and service revenues	$4,614.5	$4,016.3	$3,457.4
Operating profit			
Petroleum Operations	$ 393.7	$ 248.1	$ 152.7
Energy Processing & Conversion Equipment	100.6	100.5	141.2
Refractories & Minerals Operations	37.1	53.7	63.7
Mining & Construction Equipment	(10.0)	38.9	46.5
Industrial Specialty Products	46.2	62.4	60.0
Adjustments and eliminations	2.0	(1.0)	(1.8)
Total operating profit	569.6	502.6	462.3
Equity in earnings of unconsolidated subsidiaries and affiliates	17.9	19.6	7.5
General corporate expenses	(48.8)	(59.9)	(46.3)
Interest expense, net	(10.1)	(14.1)	(16.4)
Earnings before taxes	$ 528.6	$ 448.2	$ 407.1
Identifiable assets			
Petroleum Operations	$1,320.8	$ 931.3	$ 714.2
Energy Processing & Conversion Equipment	427.3	374.0	329.2
Refractories & Minerals Operations	245.3	266.0	255.9
Mining & Construction Equipment	496.3	488.1	476.1
Industrial Specialty Products	396.6	386.6	348.7
Adjustments and eliminations	(63.9)	(43.0)	(15.3)
Total identifiable assets	2,822.4	2,403.0	2,108.8
Equity investments	115.1	76.5	45.3
Corporate assets	335.8	417.7	349.7
Total assets	$3,273.3	$2,897.2	$2,503.8

EXHIBIT 2   Financial data for major product segments

Petroleum Operations Segment

Dresser's petroleum operations segment is a leading worldwide supplier of products and services essential to oil and gas exploration, drilling fluid systems, oilfield products (bits, rigs, and tools), petroleum services (well logging, well completion, acidizing, fracturing, cementing, and remedial work), and gasoline dispensing systems.

Drilling fluids systems.   The company markets a variety of drilling fluids and related services under the Magcobar trademark for drilling oil and gas wells. Drilling fluids, which are usually barite and bentonite combined with other

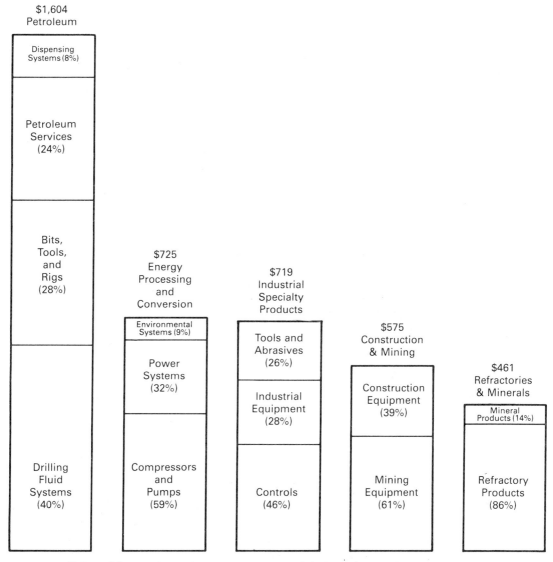

EXHIBIT 3 Sales of five major industry segments and their major product areas, 1980 (millions of dollars and percentages)

SOURCE: Company Annual Reports.

chemicals in a water or oil base, are used to clean the bottom of a hole so that a bit can drill, remove cuttings and transport them to the surface, cool and lubricate the bit and drill string, control formation pressures, and provide information about the formation it is cutting. The amount of drilling fluid depends on footage drilled, average well depth, and conditions encountered. Magcobar engineers provide on-site, around-the-clock analysis and advice on the selection and use of fluids appropriate to the drilling conditions and formations encountered, as well as analysis important in detecting hydrocarbons.

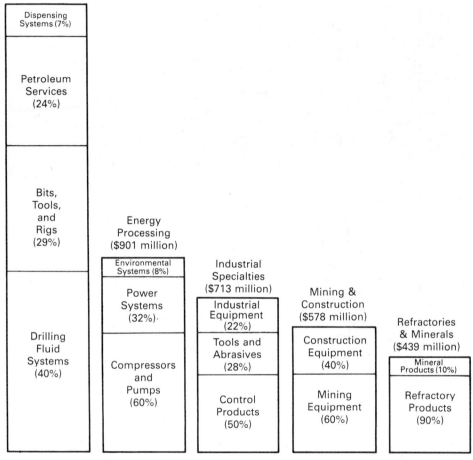

EXHIBIT 4   Five major industry segments and their major product lines, 1981

SOURCE: Company Annual Reports.

Dresser's Swaco Division designs, builds, and markets a broad line of detection and control equipment used during drilling, often with Magcobar fluid systems, and shakers, desilters, and degassers to remove solids and gas before the fluids are re-used. The company also produces and sells production chemicals used in secondary and tertiary oil and gas production, and in reducing corrosion and scale in oil and gas wells. Dresser markets its products and services through its own sales force to major domestic and international oil companies, independent drilling operators and contractors, and foreign government-owned companies.

Oilfield products (bits, rigs, and tools).   Dresser produces a full line of oilfield rock bits under the Security trademark for drilling oil and gas wells. It manufactures Ideco onshore drilling rigs which include a complete line of self-propelled drilling rigs. In addition, Ideco manufactures workover rigs which perform a variety of remedial operations on producing wells to help increase production. The firm's Guiberson Division produces and markets tools which are sold to the completion, production, and workover segments of the oil production industry. Drilling and well servicing contractors are the primary market for bits, rigs, and tools.

Petroleum Services. Wireline services include well logging, a technique used to record information about downhole conditions and the geological formation encountered during or after a well has been drilled; perforating services to initiate or increase the oil and gas flow in a prospective production well; and production logging services, which monitor information on producing wells. The perforation process was developed and introduced by Dresser Atlas. Dresser provides wireline services to oil and gas companies and government agencies throughout the world, and sells wireline equipment to oil and gas companies and government agencies outside the United States in those countries where foreign companies are not allowed to provide wireline services. Dresser Titan furnishes pumping services for oil and gas wells and fracturing acidizing of existing wells to increase production of oil and gas.

Dispensing Systems. Dresser manufactures and sells gasoline dispensing systems and related equipment. Approximately 70 percent of the sales of this equipment and related services are sold either outside of, or for use, outside of the United States.

EXHIBIT 5 Financial data for petroleum industry segment (millions of dollars and percent)

Sales analysis	1980	1979	1978	1977	1976	1975	1974
Domestic $	973	655	548	437	339	303	217
Export $	249	150	97	98	40	82	186
Foreign $	382	296	241	208	256	161	
Total $	1,604	1,101	886	743	635	546	403
% of Dresser	40	32	29	29	28	26	28
By geographical area							
United States $	973	655	548	437	339	303	217
Canada $	89	63	43	42	40	34	32
Latin America $	134	116	82	67	74	53	39
Europe $	235	159	113	85	86	66	43
Mid & Far East, Africa $	173	108	100	112	96	90	72
Total $	1,604	1,101	886	743	635	546	403
By major product area							
Drilling fluid systems $	633	437	368	289	257	226	169
Petroleum services $	381	247	200	189	127	106	86
Bits, tools & rigs $	456	295	191	158	163	135	83
Dispensing systems $	134	122	127	107	88	79	65
Total $	1,604	1,101	886	743	635	546	403

EXHIBIT 5   (continued)

Sales analysis	1980	1979	1978	1977	1976	1975	1974
By type of product							
Capital goods $	260	239	187	169	139	89	66
Expendable goods $	1,344	862	699	574	496	457	337
Total $	1,604	1,101	886	743	635	546	403
By quarter							
First—1/31 $	356	248	190	156	147	126	83
Second—4/30 $	373	254	208	175	163	136	94
Third—7/31 $	427	284	223	213	160	137	106
Fourth—10/31 $	448	315	265	199	165	147	120
Year $	1,604	1,101	886	743	635	546	403
Backlog by quarter							
First—1/31 $	113	111	85	83	121	95	32
Second—4/30 $	168	101	126	84	103	109	38
Third—7/31 $	172	103	140	57	86	116	80
Fourth—10/31 $	193	97	132	64	82	105	89
Operating profits							
Total $	248.1	152.7	146.7	124.2	106.8	87.2	43.4
% of segment sales	15.5	13.9	16.6	16.7	16.8	16.0	10.8
% of Dresser EBT	55	38	39	37	39	39	38
Capital expenditures							
Total $	136.1	96.9	54.5	60.1	56.0	48.4	23.6
% of Dresser	57	51	44	47	43	42	32
Research & eng.							
Total $	43.5	30.5	26.2	21.0	18.0	14.2	11.5
% of Dresser	36	30	29	29	29	28	31
Assets							
Total $	931	714	594	—	—	—	—
% of Dresser	32	29	25	—	—	—	—
Depreciation, etc.							
Total $	65.9	46.0	35.3	—	—	—	—
% of Dresser	49	41	35	—	—	—	—
Employees							
Total	17,300	15,000	15,000	14,100	12,600	—	—
% of Dresser	34	27	27	27	26	—	—

SOURCE: Company Annual Report.

Energy Processing and Conversion Equipment Segment

This segment designs, manufactures, and markets highly engineered products and systems for energy producers, transporters, processors, distributors, and users throughout the world. Products and systems of this segment include compressors and pumps, mechanical power systems, and environmental control systems.

Compressors and Pumps. Dresser Clark, a leader in compressor technology, manufactures reciprocating compressors, centrifugal compressors, axial compressors, axial expanders and gas turbines which are used in gas pipelines, gas reinjection, steel mills, and chemical and petrochemical plants, including plants for the production of synthetic natural gas and liquefaction of natural gas. Reciprocating compressors of up to 16,000 horsepower are used in gas reinjection systems, gas pipelines, and refinery and petrochemical processes involving high pressures, such as the production of polyethylene. Centrifugal compressors of up to 360,000 cubic feet per minute inlet capacity and over 10,000 pounds per square inch discharge pressure are used in processes requiring constant pressures, like gas reinjection and the production of ammonia, liquified natural gas, and ethylene. Axial compressors of up to 542,000 cfm inlet capacity are used in coal gasification, blast furnace blowers, nitric acid plants, and refinery processes. Gas turbines of up to 29,000 hp are used primarily as drivers for the compressors, but also for pump and generator drive applications.

Pacific Pumps designs, develops, manufactures, and markets centrifugal pumps of up to 55,000 gallons per minute which are used for critical applications in energy processing and petrochemical markets, as well as in utility and industrial markets. Roots air blowers and vacuum pumps are used primarily in municipal sewage waste water treatment, foundry, and paper and pulp markets.

Power Systems. Dresser's Waukesha and Power Transmission Divisions produce power systems consisting of heavy-duty reciprocating gas and diesel engines, power transmission equipment, and components for power transmission of power such as engineered and roller class chains, gear reducers and electric motors.

Environmental Systems. Dresser produces Lodge-Cottrell electrostatic precipitators and associated pollution control equipment. Electrostatic precipitators are used to remove fly ash and other impurities from stack emissions; the primary markets for this equipment are coal-burning electric plants, cement plants, and steel plants.

EXHIBIT 6 Financial data for energy processing & conversion industry segment (millions of dollars and percent)

Sales analysis	1980	1979	1978	1977	1976	1975	1974
Domestic $	428	419	378	362	320	298	180
Export $	133	149	134	132	128	103	77
Foreign $	164	182	197	146	98	48	
Total $	725	750	709	640	546	449	257
% of Dresser	18	22	23	25	24	22	18
By geographical area							
United States $	428	419	378	362	320	298	180
Canada $	35	32	25	14	22	26	8
Latin America $	66	51	34	37	42	27	13
Europe $	103	120	122	94	125	71	38
Mid & Far East, Africa $	93	128	150	133	37	27	18
Total $	725	750	709	640	546	449	257

EXHIBIT 6   (continued)

Sales analysis	1980	1979	1978	1977	1976	1975	1974
By major product area							
Compressors & pumps $	428	484	453	445	355	260	170
Power systems $	235	204	182	151	158	151	48
Environmental syst. $	62	62	74	44	33	38	39
Total $	725	750	709	640	546	449	257
By type of product							
Capital goods $	405	466	478	418	330	283	177
Expendable goods $	320	284	231	222	216	166	80
Total $	725	750	709	640	546	449	257
By quarter							
First—1/31 $	163	180	168	139	132	93	41
Second—4/30 $	168	188	182	178	137	101	46
Third—7/31 $	172	176	178	159	143	115	65
Fourth—10/31 $	222	206	181	164	134	140	105
Year $	725	750	709	640	546	449	257
Backlog by quarter							
First—1/31 $	568	536	608	664	696	598	184
Second—4/30 $	607	580	628	641	678	614	235
Third—7/31 $	617	565	620	643	642	647	408
Fourth—10/31 $	650	519	581	623	674	733	523
Operating profits							
Total $	100.5	141.2	144.6	143.1	96.3	59.1	22.2
% of segment sales	13.9	18.8	20.4	22.4	17.6	13.2	8.6
% of Dresser EBT	22	35	38	43	35	26	19
Capital expenditures							
Total $	27.9	17.7	12.4	20.9	20.4	11.2	8.7
% of Dresser	12	9	10	17	16	10	12
Research & eng.							
Total $	27.3	24.3	22.6	21.9	16.2	14.1	10.1
% of Dresser	22	24	25	30	26	28	27
Assets							
Total $	374	329	276	—	—	—	—
% of Dresser	13	13	12	—	—	—	—
Depreciation, etc.							
Total $	12.3	11.9	10.6	—	—	—	—
% of Dresser	9	11	11	—	—	—	—
Employees							
Total	8,200	9,600	9,100	9,200	9,200	—	—
% of Dresser	16	17	16	17	19	—	—

SOURCE: Company Annual Report.

Refractories and Minerals Operations Segment

This segment is a leading supplier of refractory technology and products to a wide range of industries that use high-temperature processes. Dresser also mines and processes metallic and non-metallic ores for internal use and for sale to third parties.

Refractory Products. Dresser, through its Harbison-Walker and Canadian Refractories operations, and refractory producing joint ventures in Australia, Chile, Mexico, Peru, Venezuela, and West Germany, is the free world's leading supplier of refractory products and technology. Dresser mines, processes, and manufactures over 200 refractory and abrasion-resistant, specialty ceramic, and insulation products that cover complete ranges of classes and types in various shapes, sizes, and forms. Refractories, which are made principally from magnesite, chromite, bauxite, quartzite, and fire clays, are used in virtually every industrial process requiring heating or containment of a solid, liquid, or gas at a high temperature. Iron and steel producers use Dresser's products in various types of iron- and steel-making furnaces, in coke ovens, and in iron and steel handling and steel finishing operations. Industrial markets for the firm's refractory products include non-ferrous metals producers, mineral processors (cement, lime and glass), fossil-fueled power plants, chemical and petroleum processing plants, and general industry.

Mineral Products. Dresser operates over 100 mines and processing plants throughout the world; these produce barite, bentonite, and lignite for its drilling fluids business as drilling mud additives. It also produces, for sale to third parties, bentonite for iron ore-pelletizing and civil engineering purposes; silica sand for glass manufacture; and kaolin and calcium carbonate for construction, feed, chemicals, fertilizers, and fillers and extender purposes. The company also has an undivided one-half interest in lead deposits in Missouri.

EXHIBIT 7 Financial data for refractories & minerals industry segment (millions of dollars and percent)

Sales analysis	1980	1979	1978	1977	1976	1975	1974
Domestic $	328	339	285	244	222	209	195
Export $	44	28	15	24	32	16	57
Foreign $	89	58	44	38	30	47	
Total $	461	425	344	306	284	272	252
% of Dresser	11	12	11	12	12	13	17
By geographical area							
United States $	328	339	285	244	222	209	195
Canada $	57	39	33	30	27	31	30
Latin America $	20	9	5	7	11	9	4
Europe $	28	23	12	13	9	9	7
Mid & Far East, Africa $	28	15	9	12	15	14	16
Total $	461	425	344	306	284	272	252
By major product area							
Refractory products $	398	358	298	265	250	242	218
Mineral products $	63	67	46	41	34	30	34
Total $	461	425	344	306	284	272	252
By type of product							
Capital goods $	2	4	1	1	—	—	—
Expendable goods $	459	421	343	305	284	272	252
Total $	461	425	344	306	284	272	252

EXHIBIT 7   (continued)

Sales analysis		1980	1979	1978	1977	1976	1975	1974
By quarter								
	First—1/31 $	112	97	76	73	62	72	56
	Second—4/30 $	124	106	74	77	71	71	61
	Third—7/31 $	107	110	94	79	74	65	64
	Fourth—10/31 $	118	112	100	77	77	64	71
	Year $	461	425	344	306	284	272	252
Backlog by quarter								
	First—1/31 $	137	118	90	68	72	104	69
	Second—4/30 $	148	133	108	73	69	95	71
	Third—7/31 $	112	134	95	79	65	90	86
	Fourth—10/31 $	93	127	92	79	67	76	98
Operating profits								
	Total $	53.7	63.7	40.9	43.5	40.1	43.2	37.7
	% of segment sales	11.6	15.0	11.9	14.2	14.1	15.9	14.9
	% of Dresser EBT	12	16	11	13	15	19	33
Capital expenditures								
	Total $	17.4	29.2	26.0	22.9	16.8	18.0	12.8
	% of Dresser	7	15	21	18	13	16	17
Research & eng.								
	Total $	10.9	10.3	9.2	6.9	5.8	4.7	4.5
	% of Dresser	9	10	10	9	9	9	12
Assets								
	Total $	266	256	222	—	—	—	—
	% of Dresser	9	10	9	—	—	—	—
Depreciation, etc.								
	Total $	14.3	15.7	15.1	—	—	—	—
	% of Dresser	11	14	15	—	—	—	—
Employees								
	Total	5,500	7,100	7,000	6,500	6,400	—	—
	% of Dresser	10	13	13	12	13	—	—

SOURCE: Company Annual Report.

Mining and Construction Equipment Segment

Dresser's construction equipment is Galion motor graders, road rollers, and road planers, which are used in the maintenance of roads and other surfaced areas, and Galion rough terrain hydraulic cranes, which have lift capacities of eight to twenty-two tons and are used in heavy construction and industrial materials-handling applications. Major customers include state and local governmental agencies, private contractors, and fleet rental companies. Le Roi portable and stationary compressors and air tools account for the remainder of the construction equipment sales. Mining equipment includes both underground and surface mining equipment, and repair parts and services are also provided.

The Jeffrey Mining Machinery Division produces underground continuous mining machines and related equipment used in underground bituminous coal mines. This equipment is also sold for use in mining underground deposits of trona, potash, and other materials, both in the United States and abroad. Jeffrey usually sells equipment directly to users through the company's sales engineers and support personnel. Dresser also produces components such as shearers for use in the long wall method of underground coal mining.

The Marion Power Shovel Division is a leading producer of walking draglines and power shovels used in surface mining and quarrying; principal users of Marion surface mining equipment are operators of surface coal mines, both in the United States and abroad. The company also produces drills, drill bits, and cutters which are used in mining, quarrying, and construction activities.

EXHIBIT 8 Financial data for mining and construction industry segment (millions of dollars and percent)

Sales analysis	1980	1979	1978	1977	1976	1975	1974
Domestic $	297	366	334	210	175	167	74
Export $	100	77	98	44	54	63	52
Foreign $	178	143	135	110	105	71	
Total $	575	586	567	364	334	301	126
% of Dresser	14	17	19	14	15	15	9
By geographical area							
United States $	297	366	334	210	175	167	74
Canada $	52	31	41	25	16	17	15
Latin America $	54	50	60	38	41	24	6
Europe $	72	46	42	28	31	26	11
Mid & Far East, Africa $	100	93	90	63	71	67	20
Total $	575	586	567	364	334	301	126
By major product area							
Const. equipment $	222	235	199	169	195	179	73
Mining equipment $	353	351	368	195	139	122	53
Total $	575	586	567	364	334	301	126
By type of product							
Capital goods $	371	392	399	226	228	239	74
Expendable goods $	204	194	168	138	106	62	52
Total $	575	586	567	364	334	301	126
By quarter							
First—1/31 $	120	135	114	63	82	58	11
Second—4/30 $	139	140	133	76	91	80	14
Third—7/31 $	143	145	145	75	75	73	39
Fourth—10/31 $	173	166	175	150	86	90	62
Year $	575	586	567	364	334	301	126
Backlog by quarter							
First—1/31 $	343	374	525	73	137	175	8
Second—4/30 $	322	349	500	76	107	172	11
Third—7/31 $	300	322	463	86	89	184	157
Fourth—10/31 $	286	319	389	493	72	153	168
Operating profits							
Total $	38.9	46.5	56.7	45.9	53.0	49.3	13.6
% of segment sales	6.8	7.9	10.0	12.6	15.9	16.4	10.8
% of Dresser EBT	9	11	15	14	19	22	12

EXHIBIT 8   (continued)

Sales analysis		1980	1979	1978	1977	1976	1975	1974
Capital expenditures								
	Total $	12.8	12.0	12.1	8.1	9.1	11.0	4.3
	% of Dresser	5	6	10	6	7	10	6
Research & eng.								
	Total $	20.9	20.6	17.1	11.0	9.4	6.4	2.8
	% of Dresser	17	20	19	15	15	13	8
Assets								
	Total $	488	476	457	—	—	—	—
	% of Dresser	17	19	19	—	—	—	—
Depreciation, etc.								
	Total $	20.7	18.7	21.5	—	—	—	—
	% of Dresser	15	17	21	—	—	—	—
Employees								
	Total	7,500	8,600	9,500	9,300	6,900	—	—
	% of Dresser	14	16	17	18	14	—	—

SOURCE: Company Annual Report.

Industrial Specialty Products Segment

Dresser's industrial specialty products segment produces several hundred products with a wide variety of industrial uses. Major products and markets are: control products (valves, instruments, and fittings, used by utilities and process plants); industrial products (bulk conveying and process systems, rail car components, and cranes and hoists for specialized use in mining, rail cars, and general industry); and tools and abrasive products (mechanics' hand tools, pneumatic tools, and abrasives used by mechanics and general industry).

Control Products. Control products are measurement and control instruments, gauges, meters, and valves for measuring and controlling pressure, temperature, level, and flow of liquids and gases, and are marketed under the Ashcroft, Consolidated, Dresser, Duragauge, Hancock, and Roots trademark. Dresser sells them to the process, power, and gas distribution industries. The firm also produces pipe fittings and couplings, repair devices, and valves for gas and water utilities; these are marketed under the Dresser and MH trademarks.

Industrial Equipment Products. Industrial equipment products include cranes and hoists, bulk conveying and processing systems, castings, and rail car components. Dresser produces Shaw-Box overhead cranes and electric wire rope hoists, Budgit electric and manual chain hoists, and Tugit level-operated chain hoists for overhead materials-handling in municipal sewage, electric utility, paper and pulp, and general industrial markets. Materials-handling products include Jeffrey bulk materials-handling conveying systems and components, processing equipment (such as crushing and shredding equipment), and engineered conveying systems for the coal mining industry and general manufacturing markets. The company also produces steel castings used as original and replacement components in railroad rolling stock.

Tools and Abrasive Products. Tools include hand and pneumatic tools and various abrasive products, including hand tools, pneumatic tools, grinding wheels and cut-off blades, positive feed drills, cleaners and expanders, torque tools, and aluminum oxide, alumina zirconia, and silicon carbide abrasives.

EXHIBIT 9 Financial data for industrial specialty products industry segment (millions of dollars and percent)

Sales analysis	1980	1979	1978	1977	1976	1975	1974
Domestic $	525	513	444	396	355	367	322
Export $	39	31	31	23	32	41	73
Foreign $	155	114	97	101	94	99	
Total $	719	658	572	520	481	507	395
% of Dresser	18	19	19	20	21	24	28
By geographical area							
United States $	525	513	444	396	355	367	322
Canada $	54	48	39	39	42	47	30
Latin America $	38	24	23	23	19	18	9
Europe $	65	53	44	42	39	42	24
Mid & Far East, Africa $	37	20	22	20	26	33	10
Total $	719	658	572	520	481	507	395
By major product area							
Controls $	333	278	240	237	208	205	167
Tools and abrasives $	186	186	167	135	117	125	129
Industrial equipment $	200	194	165	148	156	177	99
Total $	719	658	572	520	481	507	395
By type of product							
Capital goods $	243	181	174	159	215	224	142
Expendable goods $	476	477	398	361	266	283	253
Total $	719	658	572	520	481	507	395
By quarter							
First—1/31 $	163	139	128	108	108	113	79
Second—4/30 $	185	170	147	131	124	127	90
Third—7/31 $	173	157	150	131	119	125	102
Fourth—10/31 $	198	192	147	150	130	142	124
Year $	719	658	572	520	481	507	395
Backlog by quarter							
First—1/31 $	285	226	168	139	165	248	111
Second—4/30 $	261	241	176	138	152	250	138
Third—7/31 $	236	262	179	158	150	227	238
Fourth—10/31 $	223	284	189	159	140	195	236
Operating profits							
Total $	62.4	60.0	57.3	44.1	41.6	52.2	40.0
% of segment sales	8.7	9.1	10.0	8.5	8.7	10.3	10.1
% of Dresser EBT	14	15	15	13	15	23	35

EXHIBIT 9   (continued)

Sales analysis		1980	1979	1978	1977	1976	1975	1974
Capital expenditures								
	Total $	30.5	23.1	13.5	12.7	18.8	22.7	15.5
	% of Dresser	13	12	11	10	14	20	21
Research & eng.								
	Total $	18.1	15.5	13.1	11.8	11.5	11.0	7.2
	% of Dresser	15	15	15	16	18	22	20
Assets								
	Total $	387	349	313	—	—	—	—
	% of Dresser	13	14	13	—	—	—	—
Depreciation, etc.								
	Total $	15.8	15.5	13.3	—	—	—	—
	% of Dresser	12	14	13	—	—	—	—
Employees								
	Total	13,500	14,000	14,000	13,500	12,400	—	—
	% of Dresser	26	25	25	25	26	—	—

SOURCE: Company Annual Report.

TOP MANAGEMENT

Dresser's top management organization is indicated in Exhibits 10–12. Exhibit 10 shows the company's top level operations organization; Exhibit 11 shows Dresser's top level administration organization; and Exhibit 12 shows the group-reporting relationships. Following is a discussion of the positions most involved with Dresser's marketing operation. The primary responsibilities of the chairman of the board and chief executive officer are to:

1. Provide guidance for the development of and approve corporate policies, under which the company and its operating units would function.

2. Provide long-term direction and emphasis of the company's business.

3. Approve goals, objectives, and specific plans that will carry the company toward profitable growth.

4. Represent the company and maintain appropriate relationships with high-level contacts in government, industry, associations and communities.

As of March, 1981, John V. James was Dresser's chairman and chief executive officer. After graduating from high school, Mr. James obtained an office job in a bakery in his home town of Wilkes-Barre, Pennsylvania. Orphaned when he was twelve, James and a brother were raised by two uncles who operated anthracite coal mines in the Wilkes-Barre area. By 1942, when he was drafted in the army, James had become office manager and controller

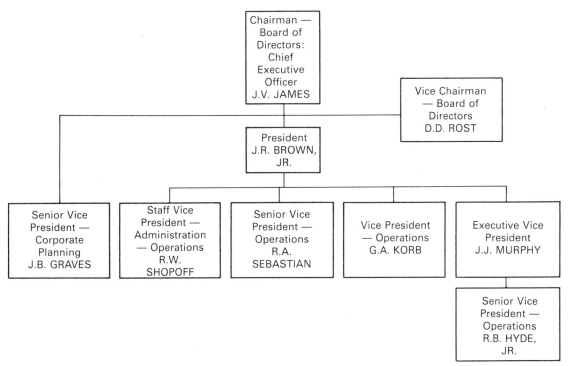

EXHIBIT 10 Executive office operations organization (1981)

of the bakery. Once in the army, he was sent to Fort Lewis, Washington for basic training. Later, he completed officer training school and was assigned to serve as an intelligence officer on General Dwight Eisenhower's staff at Supreme Headquarters, Allied Expeditionary Forces (SHAEF). Returning to the United States as a captain in 1946, James completed his studies at the University of Pennsylvania, earning a bachelor's degree in economics and a master's degree from that university's Wharton School.

His first job after graduation was with the Corning Glass Works in Corning, New York. As a member of the controller's staff, he became an associate of W.C. Taylor, the world-renowned chemist who had invented pyrexglass and other materials. He was involved with the development of mass production techniques for television tubes and optical glass.

Within several years, James had received exposure to all aspects of research and development and manufacturing. One of his major accomplishments was devising techniques that allowed scientists to evaluate their efforts. Additional responsibilities involved him with machinery manufacturing, plant construction, and production.

After ten years with Corning, James was employed by Dresser as the controller of its largest subsidiary, Clark Bros., Inc., in Olean, New York. He was with Clark Bros. for three years, eventually becoming Clark's vice president of finance. In 1960, James was named Dresser's corporate controller. In 1965, he became vice president in charge of the machinery group and was

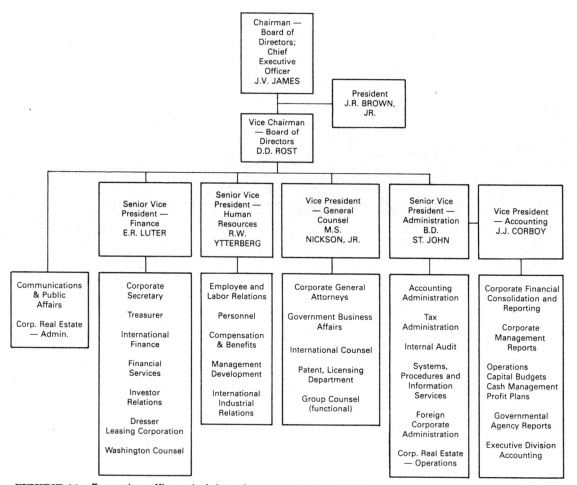

EXHIBIT 11 Executive office administration organization (1981)

named executive vice president for administration and planning in 1968. James was elected Dresser's president and chief executive officer in 1975, and became chairman of the board in 1976.

The vice chairman of the board reports to the chairman and CEO. His primary responsibilities include: (1) conducting the activities of the various financial services functions; (2) providing guidance in the establishment of policies and objectives in the corporate accounting, financial, industrial relations, legal, and communications functions; (3) developing the organizational structure of the functions assigned to his office; (4) directing the acquisition, sale and construction of the company's real estate holdings; and (5) ensuring that other members of the executive office are operating within the law and the company's corporate policies and objectives. Dresser's vice chairman of the board, Duane D. Rost, formerly served as Dresser's executive vice president and as its senior vice president-accounting and administration.

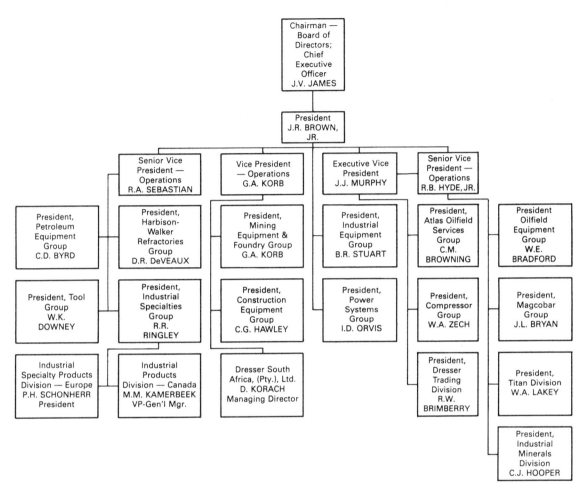

EXHIBIT 12   Group reporting relationships (1981)

The president of Dresser directs the activities of all operating units. He recommends capital budgets and approves appropriation requests for all operating units and insures that each operating group has developed profit plans to which it is committed. Technical planning and services and the Advanced Technology Center are the responsibility of the president, who helps formulate long-range objectives and programs for the Advanced Technology Center. His office has major responsibility for providing long-range direction for the R&D programs in the operating groups, and the president is expected to develop high-level customer contacts. James R. Brown, Jr., the company's president, formerly served as its executive vice president and as its second vice president-operations.

The executive vice president assists the operating executives reporting to him to formulate long-range objectives and programs. He reviews and coordinates the short- and long-term objectives of the operating groups assigned to him so that they are compatible and supportive of corporate policies, goals, and objectives. The executive vice president reviews proposals for major changes in businesses, markets, products, and organization, and makes recommendations to the president. Review of capital expenditure appropriations of the operating units reporting to him is another responsibility, and he is expected to develop high-level customer contacts. Dresser's executive vice president, John J. Murphy, served most recently as the company's senior vice president-operations.

The senior vice president-operations formulates long-range objectives, plans and programs for the markets and business areas served by the groups assigned to him. Along with the group presidents, he develops specific plans and operating performance requirements for each group. The senior vice president-operations continually audits the performance of his groups in key areas such as marketing, manufacturing, product development, and research. He reviews proposals for major changes in business, markets, products, and organization. R.B. Hyde, Jr., Dresser's present senior vice president-operations formerly served as the firm's vice president of operations and president of Dresser's oilfield product group.

The senior vice president-corporate planning assists the chairman of the board in formulating and implementing long-term goals and objectives of the corporation. If directed by the chairman, he assists in the evaluation of candidates for acquisition. He acts as liaison for the chairman or other members of the executive office in coordinating foreign activities and developments between corporate departments and operating units. The vice president for information systems planning, the director of international business planning, and the representative director of Dresser Japan, Ltd. report to the senior vice president-corporate planning. James B. Graves, the incumbent senior vice president-corporate planning, formerly held the position of vice president-corporate planning and staff vice president-planning.

CORPORATE MISSION

John V. James, the company's chairman of the board and CEO has stated

> Defining the purpose and mission of a business is difficult and painful. But it also enables a business to set objectives, to develop strategies, to concentrate its resources and to go to work. It alone enables a business to be managed for performance.
>
> Dresser's long established business charter has been to be a major supplier of technology, products and services to industries involved in the development of energy and natural resources, including air, gas, coal, and nuclear power.
>
> Dresser has positioned itself to be one of the principal participants in helping to find, develop, produce, process and distribute oil and gas. In recent years, Dresser has enhanced its role by providing engineered products and technology for coal mining and processing, coal gasification and liquefaction processes and power generation.

Dresser's other markets primarily relate to the earth's resources. Most of these market opportunities involve the extraction, processing, movement, and conversion of non-energy raw materials. In large part, they represent logical extensions of the company's engineering, manufacturing or marketing expertise.

James added, "We don't try to do everything for everybody." He believes that "the customer defines our business." What Dresser learns from its customers determines the firm's future objectives.

OBJECTIVES

Growth, profits and market share are Dresser's major objectives. Its growth objective is to "provide a maximum return on invested capital over the long term and steady profit growth that results in growing stock market values per share of common stock." Operationally, the growth objective has been defined as average annual earnings growth of 10 to 15 percent. Company executives believe that this objective is attainable and that it represents a real growth rate of one-and-one-half to two-and-one-half times the growth of the U.S. gross national product. Since John James has been chairman and CEO of Dresser, about half of the company's growth has come from acquisitions.

Dresser's profit goal for the corporation as a whole is a minimum pre-tax return of 35 percent on its capital. For individual products and operations, a minimum pre-tax return of 25 percent on its capital is desired. Management immediately scrutinizes any product or operation with a return less than 25 percent. In market share, Dresser wants to be among the top three companies, since it believes this is necessary for it to have influence in pricing.

STRATEGIES

Dresser uses a number of strategies to pursue its various objectives. These can be grouped in these areas: marketing (market identification, pricing, product management, personal selling, distribution, and advertising); research and development; organization; cost control; acquisitions; and international operations. John James has summarized Dresser's strategic effort: "A basic element is to reduce the company's exposure to economic cycles and market fluctuations through a balanced diversification of products and markets related to the energy and natural resources industries."

Marketing

Dresser's management philosophy stresses marketing in the performance of its mission and achievement of its goals:

> Successful marketing is the key to our future. Although every element of the business must be dynamic and strong, we believe we must constantly strive to

be market oriented, since our future depends on serving our customers today and tomorrow better than our competition.

Dresser's management team tries to identify growth market opportunities for its products, delineating new energy markets that will require Dresser products beyond the next ten years. Once it identifies these opportunities, it develops a plan that pinpoints specific customer needs in these markets. There are two types of needs: Short-term customer needs are identified so that the most appropriate products and services to beat competition can be developed. Long-term customer needs are those which offer growth and profit opportunities. When determining the short-range and long-range needs of its customers, Dresser divides design engineering and application engineering. After identifying customer needs, Dresser develops the selling effort required to meet these needs.

Pricing is important; the company feels it must be among the three largest firms in the area so it can influence pricing. Coupled with the firm's strategy of being the lowest cost producer, its pricing flexibility is designed to better achieve its growth and profit objectives.

Much of Dresser's product planning is done each year in February, at company headquarters. At that time, division and group engineering and product managers meet to decide (1) which products are no longer viable and should be eliminated; (2) which products can be improved through further development; and (3) which new products should be developed to serve the markets of the future. These meetings place special emphasis on product and technological constraints and new, emerging markets requiring Dresser products.

In the United States, Dresser uses either sales organizations in a group or division or independent distributors to distribute its products; a division of Dresser's Canadian subsidiary sells in Canada. Distribution in other countries is handled either by a Dresser division or subsidiary, foreign subsidiaries or affiliates, distributors, or independent sales agents. Dresser's logistics system is based on the military system.

Dresser uses many types of sales literature and advertisements appear in trade publications that serve the company's various markets. In recent years, the company has done a lot of corporate advertising; James offered this explanation:

> One of the problems we have is getting people to understand the economic effects of regulations issued from Washington. This concerns us because it affects our business and our employees. We think that there has been a great deal of legislation that's been put into the mill without a lost of careful consideration. For example, we called attention to the current energy problem back in 1977. To me, as an individual, it's appalling that we've had such a morass of misguided effort in Washington regarding energy. There's a lot of energy still to be found in this country and developed, but I must say the government has done nothing to encourage it.

How Dresser serves you in refining and petrochemical processing.

Dresser products used to transport petroleum and natural gas have corollary applications in petroleum refining and petrochemical processing.

Dresser Clark's high-pressure centrifugal compressors have successful application histories in ethylene, methanol and ammonia plants throughout the world. High-pressure reciprocating compressors meet requirements in the polyethylene market. Clark pioneered the use of centrifugals for reforming service, and both reciprocating and centrifugal types have many refining applications.

All Pacific process pumps meet API 610 requirements and are engineered to customer specifications. A wide variety of sizes and configurations results in high efficiencies and the best hydraulic fit for each application. Typically, they operate under pressures up to 5000 psig and deliver liquids ranging from cryogenic ethylene to heavy hydrocarbons at 750°F (400°C).

Dresser Machinery International, with offices in major cities worldwide, provides international sales and service of Dresser Clark and Pacific Pumps products.

Ashcroft gauges and Consolidated valves provide accurate and reliable temperature and pressure measurement and control. Dresser's AL-CLAD coatings for butterfly valves and pipeline accessories provide cost-effective corrosion control in process applications.

Harbison-Walker offers a variety of refractory products for high-temperature processes and corrosion control.

DRESSER CLARK

PACIFIC PUMPS

DRESSER MACHINERY INTERNATIONAL

INDUSTRIAL VALVE & INSTRUMENT

DRESSER MANUFACTURING

HARBISON-WALKER REFRACTORIES

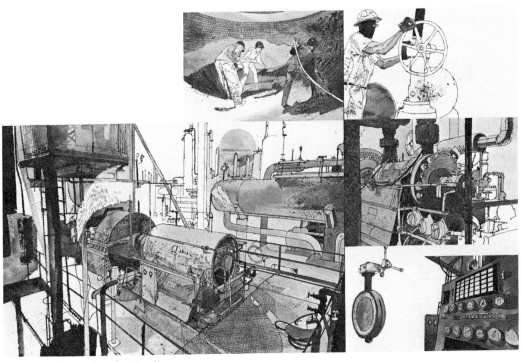

EXHIBIT 13   Example of sales literature

Research and Development

Dresser conducts research and development in over thirty laboratories. As of October 31, 1980, Dresser and its various subsidiaries owned 4,208 patents, with 1,985 patents pending.

James believes that Dresser's technical strength is "equal to that of any competitor and exceeds most." He estimates that the company may spend as much as $1 billion for research and development from 1980 to 1985. Exhibit 14 shows the company's expenditures for research and engineering from 1972 to 1981.

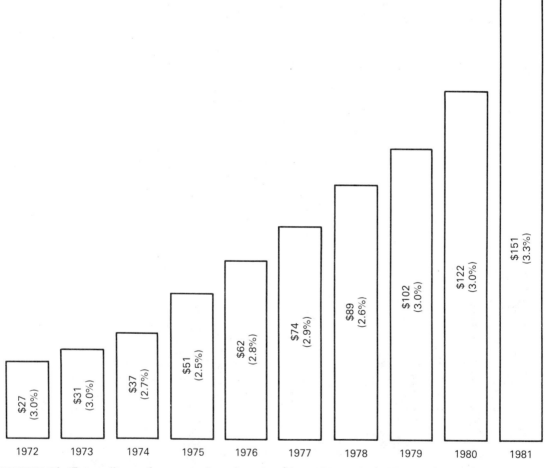

EXHIBIT 14 Expenditures for research and engineering, 1971-1980 (millions of dollars and as percentage of sales)

SOURCE: Company Annual Reports.

ORGANIZATION

James is a believer in good organizational theory; he feels that the most advanced organizational theory exists in the military. Dresser executives have "examined military organizational concepts very carefully and have organized the company into manageable units."

An important part of the company's organization is its system of internal communications. James has stated, "We're quite proud of our internal communications. We say you can get a critical decision from Dresser headquarters within twenty-four hours from any place in the world."

Two of Dresser's organizational policies involve its marketing operations:

1. Separating manufacturing and marketing, when such separation is economically feasible and would generate better results.

2. Combining field or area administrative overhead and functions to serve multi-product marketing organizations.

Line individuals are responsible for getting a job done; staff members are specialists who assist line individuals in performing tasks, but only at the request of the line person.

All managers at Dresser are responsible to someone for results. Subordinates are expected to keep their superiors informed of plans to achieve specific results, progress toward results, and possible roadblocks. They report all significant operating problems to their bosses, as well as plans for solving them.

Dresser's management philosophy is management by objectives (MBO); group and corporate executives are expected to spend sufficient time in conceiving, organizing, delegating, and executing business plans and concepts to achieve objectives. Dresser's MBO system emphasizes the achievement of measurable results. Managers are expected to define jobs and tasks in terms of measurable results, not just the functions to be performed. If possible, Dresser establishes profit centers to judge success or failure. By the fourth business day of the month, corporate headquarters knows the net return for about 300 different profit centers in 100 countries; any return below a 25 percent R.O.A. concerns company executives. Dresser stresses promotion from within, although occasionally it will go outside for "leadership positions." Those who "cannot stand the pace" are expected to "make the necessary adjustments without delay." Management fosters teamwork by good communications, clean interfaces, and clearly understood administrative rules.

Cost Control

Dresser wants to become the lowest-cost producer in competitive markets. Group and division selling, engineering, and manufacturing costs are rigorously controlled to enable Dresser to meet this goal, and Dresser's cost center system is considered among the most sophisticated in the United States.

Acquisitions

During the last half of the 1970s, about 50 percent of Dresser's growth came from acquisitions; James expects, however, that most of the company's future growth will occur internally. He believes that "steady, profitable growth from within demonstrates internal strength and is proof we control our destiny." However, acquisitions will accelerate Dresser's achievement of its long-term goals. In general Dresser considers a company for acquisition when it believes the two companies combined would grow faster than if they remained separate, and the acquisition would provide some synergism in engineering, manufacturing, or marketing.

While various specific criteria are used to evaluate a potential acquisition, probably the most important (and rigorous) is that it yield at least a 35 percent pre-tax return on investment on a discounted cash flow basis. Other factors are:

1. Does the acquisition complement Dresser's existing product lines and markets, with particular emphasis on those companies which have products with multi-market applications?
2. Would the acquisition create antitrust problems? In general, leading firms in a concentrated industry or those with sales or assets above $10 million are not considered for acquisition unless prior approval in writing and a preliminary antitrust screen have been obtained.
3. Does the company have a history of efficient management?
4. Does the company have a history of being a low-cost producer?
5. Does the company have a proprietary position on products?
6. Can the company help penetrate overseas markets?
7. Can the company provide economies of scale?
8. Can Dresser offer an advantage to the potential acquisition in the engineering, marketing, or administrative areas?
9. Does the company have new product lines serving new markets and provide secondary benefits to Dresser's existing product or service lines?
10. Does the company have a reputation for high quality?
11. Does the company sell most of its goods or services to the energy industry?
12. Does the company have a rural-based labor force with a strong work ethic?
13. Is the company available at or below its current book value?

International Operations

Dresser has aggressively pursued international markets. In 1980, about 14 percent of Dresser's sales volume came from export sales and about 24 percent of its sales were from foreign operations. Out of its total of $1.533 billion of sales in international markets, about 19 percent went to Canada, 20 percent to Latin America, 33 percent to Europe, and 28 percent to the Mideast, Far East, and Africa. Dresser's major foreign subsidiaries are indicated in Exhibit 15, and Exhibit 16 shows financial data for various geographical regions of the world.

Dresser's international business operations are considered by its top management to be one of its greatest challenges. The company is committed to searching worldwide for new products, services, markets, joint ventures, and acquisitions that "add to our capabilities to move the corporation forward." It believes that new and expanding markets offer attractive opportunities for global business growth. Worldwide operations are expected to play an increasingly important role in Dresser's future. In pursuing overseas opportunities, Dresser has developed a specific international business philosophy; some dimensions of this international business philosophy are:

1. We will be responsive to the impact our operations have on host countries.

2. We will attempt to promote a long-term relationship with the host country.

3. If Dresser discontinues an overseas operation, any adverse impact on the host country will be minimized if possible.

EXHIBIT 15   Major foreign subsidiaries (as of October 31, 1981)

Country	Number of Subsidiaries	Country	Number of Subsidiaries
Algeria	1	Libya	2
Antilles	1	Liechtenstein	2
Argentina	1	Luxembourg	1
Australia	4	Malaysia	1
Belgium	2	Mexico	10
Bermuda	1	Netherlands	2
Brazil	4	Nigeria	2
Cameroon	1	Norway	1
Canada	2	Panama	1
Chile	2	Peru	1
Congo	1	Saudi Arabia	2
France	1	Scotland	1
Gabon	1	Singapore	1
Greece	1	South Africa	1
Hong Kong	1	Sweden	1
Indonesia	1	Switzerland	2
Ireland	2	Thailand	2
Japan	1	Venezuela	1
Kuwait	1	West Germany	1

Years Ended October 31,	1981	1980	1979
Sales and service revenues to unaffiliated customers			
United States	$3,551.7	$3,061.6	$2,688.7
Canada	221.6	224.6	164.5
Latin America	175.6	158.0	120.2
Europe	381.5	384.5	307.3
Mid East, Far East and Africa	284.1	187.6	176.7
Intergeographic area sales and service revenues			
United States	181.5	138.8	103.5
Canada	28.6	25.6	24.1
Latin America	1.9	1.4	2.1
Europe	73.1	50.8	44.5
Mid East, Far East and Africa	29.8	15.5	3.1
Eliminations	(314.9)	(232.1)	(177.3)
Total sales and service revenues	$4,614.5	$4,016.3	$3,457.4
Operating profit			
United States	$ 531.5	$ 420.6	$ 385.4
Canada	18.6	33.7	21.1
Latin America	8.4	10.3	5.6
Europe	15.5	32.9	42.0
Mid East, Far East and Africa	16.0	18.3	11.3
Adjustments and eliminations	(20.4)	(13.2)	(3.1)
Total operating profit	$ 569.6	$ 502.6	$ 462.3
Years Ended October 31,	1981	1980	1979
Identifiable assets			
United States	$2,303.3	$1,854.0	$1,633.5
Canada	186.4	163.1	141.6
Latin America	111.0	105.2	74.0
Europe	295.5	295.7	236.6
Mid East, Far East and Africa	214.8	165.9	131.6
Adjustments and eliminations	(288.6)	(180.9)	(108.5)
Total identifiable assets	$2,822.4	$2,403.0	$2,108.8
United States export sales			
Canada	$ 29.8	$ 49.1	$ 40.0
Latin America	164.5	128.3	127.6
Europe	78.8	165.2	85.0
Mid East, Far East and Africa	252.5	222.3	182.9
Total United States export sales	$ 525.6	$ 564.9	$ 435.5

EXHIBIT 16 Financial information by geographic area

4. We will respect the sovereign rights, customs, laws, and regulations of host countries.

5. The support and cooperation of host governments is a prerequisite to long-range growth and development.

6. We will endeavor to develop and market products and services which are specifically tailored for host country markets.

7. We will use host country suppliers where their price, quality, delivery, and service meet Dresser's requirements for the low-cost manufacturing of its products.

8. A key element in achieving corporate goals is a steady outflow of innovative, high technology products to worldwide energy and industrial markets.

One of Dresser's international sales drew a storm of protest in 1978—the transfer of a $146 million plant for making oil-drilling bits to the Soviet Union. Part of the sale was a computer-controlled electron beam welder that opponents of the sale claimed could be used to manufacture jet aircraft. Critics of the sale pointed to the vast potential military use of the increased oil produced. Leading critics included President Carter's national security adviser, Zbigniew Brzezinski, Energy Secretary James Schlesinger, and J. Fred Bucy, president of Texas Instruments, who headed up a research team for the Pentagon. In favor of the sale were President Carter, who did not hold up the sale, Secretary of State Cyrus Vance, Secretary of Commerce Juanita Kreps and a number of U.S. businessmen, most of whom believed that attempts to pressure the Soviet Union through trade would not be effective.

Dresser officials, particularly Jack Murphy, executive vice president, defended the sale; he pointed out that Japan had sold $6 million worth of petroleum drilling bits to the Russians in 1978. By May of 1980, virtually all of the plant equipment had been shipped to Russia. Only the machine tool suppliers' shipments were still needed, and these materials were easily obtainable elsewhere.

PLANNING

Like Dresser's cost control system, its planning system is considered one of the most sophisticated among American corporations. Dresser's corporate officers view planning as their most important managerial function, one which precedes all others. Planning is designed to strengthen managers' judgment, leadership, and vision. Dresser believes that four factors are crucial in making strategic planning successful:

☐ Systematic and purposeful work on attaining objectives is necessary.

☐ Planning starts out with sloughing off yesterday and that abandonment be planned as part of the systematic attempt to attain tomorrow.

☐ New and different ways of achieving objectives need to be considered, rather than automatically doing more of the same.

☐ Managers must ask themselves when work must be begun to get the results desired when they are needed.

Even the lowest levels of management are affected; all managers, throughout the planning process, are held accountable for specific, detailed goals. Planning occurs at three major levels. The president's office is concerned with acquisitions outside existing group areas, establishing economic guidelines for forecasting, setting planning requirements, and reviewing plans. The major responsibility for long term planning to meet customer needs and exploit market opportunities rests at the group level. Specific responsibilities include new product development and technology, new market development and increased penetration, acquisitions that fit within the group, and financial analysis. The division level is charged for providing support for the group level efforts.

Dresser's planning cycle is indicated in Exhibit 17. Each group puts together a long-range growth plan, which consists of an introduction (definition of the group's existing business, its long-term business environment, and goals, objectives and strategies), and fourteen sections.

Section 1 contains the following: financial summaries; level of growth of current operations; market share improvement; major new products, markets, or ventures; and planned acquisitions. *Section 2* summarizes the group's competitive position relative to its five major competitors. *Section 3* assesses the impact of various economic and marketing changes on the previous long-term plan. *Section 4* projects the market outlook, sales and profitability objective, and competitive position for all product lines in each market. *Section 5* lists by SIC code each end-user market served. *Section 6* identifies new product and new market voids, and acquisition opportunities. *Section 7* assesses current markets served by divisions with existing products, or markets that could be penetrated by product modifications and additions. *Section 8* lists all components or products supplied by an industry to markets served by Dresser, so that new product opportunities can be identified. *Section 9* delineates growth products. *Section 10* indicates any organizational changes required to achieve long-term growth plans. *Section 11* analyzes the impact of any organizational changes on personnel costs. *Sections 12, 13, and 14* involve several financial summaries, including earnings, cash flow, return on investment, balance sheet projections, and major capital requirements.

1982 RESULTS

In 1982, Dresser's sales were $4.16 billion. Net profits were $172 million. Total assets were $3.3 billion and stockholders' equity was $2.02 billion. The company employed approximately 45,000 persons.

The decrease in sales and net profits for Dresser in 1982 from 1981 figures concerned top management. At a meeting of the company's executives early in 1983, it was decided that, although much of the firm's financial problems could be attributed to a general softening in the economy and energy-

EXHIBIT 17   The Dresser planning cycle

1. November 1	—	Begin new fiscal year
2. November	—	Engineering & technical conference leadership center/Dallas
3. February	—	Product & technical planning meetings. Corporate reviews plans preparatory to long term plans at group or division locations
4. Feburary 20	—	Second quarter forecast (revise 2nd, 3rd and 4th quarter forecast changes from profit plan)
5. April 1	—	Long term plan (5 year forecast)
6. April	—	Corporate review with group management of long term plans
7. May 22	—	Third quarter forecast (revise 3rd and 4th quarter forecast changes from profit plan)
8. June-July	—	Development of field sales forecast, expense projections and departmental budgets for annual profit plan (1 year forecast)
9. July 21	—	Annual cost/price study (1 year forecast)
10. August 23	—	Fourth quarter forecast for current year (revise 4th quarter forecast changes from profit plan; preliminary profit plan for next fiscal year (1 year forecast)
11. September	—	Corporate review with group management of preliminary profit plan
12. October 1	—	Final profit plan (1 year forecast)
13. October	—	Corporate review with group and division management of final profit plan at group or division locations

related segments, it was necessary to evaluate a number of factors about its operations. Specifically, management recommended examining these areas:

1. How successfully is Dresser achieving its basic objectives?

2. Does the corporation's organization need modifying?

3. Are the performances of the firm's various industry segments acceptable?

4. How effectively are Dresser's domestic and international operations performing?

5. How effective is Dresser's planning process? Are any modifications necessary?

6. How viable is Dresser's strategy for achieving growth? Should this strategy be modified?

Crazy Joe's Fashion Stores Inc.

Joe Bryant, co-owner of "Crazy Joe's Fashion Stores Inc.," commented on what he felt was the place of his business in today's economy: "Everything is headed toward buying quality and saving money. From designer cars to designer clothes, we're turning into a country of intelligent, informed consumers. People are looking for a way to beat the money crunch, and Crazy Joe's is here to provide them with fashion at a modest price."

Crazy Joe's is a small group of three factory outlet fashion stores in central and southeast Texas. The three stores are located in Austin, the capital city, Houston, and McAllen. The Austin and Houston stores carry designer and better dresses and separates, along with a limited selection of accessories. The McAllen store, while carrying most of these same lines, also has a limited menswear and shoe department.

Austin Crazy Joe's is one of several outlet fashion stores in the area. Besides being the capital of Texas, Austin is also the home of the University of Texas with an enrollment of 44,000. The store is located across a main street from Highland Mall, the largest shopping mall in central Texas and an important source of traffic to the store.

The McAllen store, originally called "Factory Outlet Fashions", is located in the Rio Grande Valley, a short distance from the border with Mexico. McAllen has an approximate population of 40,000, which increases in the winter with the influx of winter tourists from the north. The Valley is primarily an agriculture economy, the main crops being citrus, cotton, and vegetables. The store is located on the "Miracle Mile" a highway and shopping area connecting the neighboring smaller communities of Mission, Pharr and San Juan.

The Houston store, the newest of the three, opened in September of 1979, and is located in the Galleria West. This small shopping center is across from the new Marshall Fields in the Galleria Mall. It is in the middle of a major

The research and written case information were presented at a Case Research Symposium and were evaluated by the Case Research Association's Editorial Board. This case was prepared by Kenneth Olm of The University of Texas at Austin, with the assistance of M.B. Swofford as a basis for class discussion, and is distributed by the Case Research Association. All rights reserved to the authors and the Case Research Association. Permission to use the case should be obtained from the Case Research Association.

convention center of Houston and derives a lot of its trade from conventions and persons shopping in high traffic Galleria. Houston has been experiencing a rapid growth in its economy and population over the past decade.

Crazy Joe's total sales have risen steadily over the past year to over $1.0 million annually. The Austin store stocks approximately $60,000 in inventory; the Houston store, $70,000; and the McAllen store, $75,000. On an overall basis an inventory turn of approximately three times is realized. The stores are owned by Joe and Ellen Bryant and Hartwell Kennard, Ellen's father. Joe and Ellen manage the Austin store, along with an assistant and visit the Houston store every two weeks. Hart manages the McAllen store and a hired manager, Nancy Lodwig, supervises the Houston operation.

HISTORY AND BACKGROUND

Crazy Joe's is an outgrowth of *Factory Outlet Fashions,* which was started in McAllen in 1974 by Hart Kennard. After his daughter Ellen married Joe Bryant, Hart interested Joe in opening a similar operation in Austin, Texas. Thus, Crazy Joe's was established in Austin in June of 1977.

Joe serves as vice president and merchandise manager and Hart serves as president and financial officer. Hart is also an accountant by profession. Joe was raised in McAllen and attended the University of Texas at Austin before deciding that he could "learn more by doing." He met Ellen while working as a garment wholesaler in Dallas. Ellen graduated from the University of Texas at Austin with a degree in Spanish and had worked as a personnel officer for the university before her marriage. She serves as the bookkeeper for the firm.

In addition to the corporation, a separate distribution company has been formed in the past year to handle the buying and distribution of merchandise to the three stores. The distribution company charges each store the cost of merchandise plus ten percent to cover transportation and costing out of merchandise equitably between the three stores. The distribution operation is headquartered in the Austin store because of space available, low labor costs, good accessibility, and because Joe prefers to live in Austin. There is a distribution manager in charge of checking in, tagging, shipping and billing merchandise to the three retail stores.

MERCHANDISING CONCEPT

The original name Factory Outlet Fashions was changed to Crazy Joe's because it was felt that the name provided easier identification with their theme of "crazy low prices," and because the new name had a higher retention value. The Austin area was chosen for a second store because they felt that trends in Austin were favorable for a fashion outlet of this type. Although there were several factory outlet stores in the Austin area in 1977, Bryant believed that none were targeted strictly to the 18-35 age market to which Crazy Joe's hoped to appeal.

Originally the store opened featuring lower-end goods and the decor of the store could best be described as "early warehouse." By the second year of operation, the store had moved from the McAllen concept to upper-end lines, with more designer labels and higher pricing points. The store was remodeled, and carpeted to provide expanded office space, more comfortable dressing rooms, and a more soothing atmosphere to be in harmony with the higher priced merchandise.

The fashion outlet concept was relatively new to the Southwest in 1977, while firmly established on the East coast. The buyer takes advantage of manufacturers' sales by going to buy when manufacturers are trying to liquidate their seasonal merchandise. By doing this, the buyer can take advantage of off-price buying, and, with lower wholesale prices the outlet operation can offer merchandise similar to a regular retail operation at substantially lower prices. Off-price buying does entail more buying trips. Bryant goes to market for the three stores every six to eight weeks, while Kennard goes several times a year to merchandise the special needs of the McAllen market. All merchandise is billed and shipped to the distribution company in Austin.

As in any retail ready-to-wear operation, there is substantial financial risk concentrated in the merchandising aspect of the business. The buyer must know the target market and be able to predict what trends will be for his target market. In the off-price market, the buyer must also be able to "wheel and deal" with the various manufacturers, who are often reluctant to sell off-price for fear that their regular customers will withdraw their trade. Bryant's personality is suited to operate in the rough and tumble atmosphere of rapidly changing fashion. He is outgoing, friendly and, at the same time, able to drive a hard bargain. He refuses to accept less than the best and will often return merchandise which he feels is unsuitable for Crazy Joe's market image.

The Austin store averages approximately $20,000 a month in sales with square footage of 5000 feet, 2500 of which is used for storage. The Houston store averages $50,000 per month with 5000 square feet. The McAllen store averages $40,000 a month in sales with store space of 6000 square feet. The McAllen store differs from the Austin and Houston stores in that it derives most of its target market from the winter tourist trade and substantial trade from Mexico.

The Houston store opened on Labor Day, 1979. Joe, Hart, and Ellen felt that the growing economy of Houston lent itself to Crazy Joe's concept of fashion and the target market they were aimed at. They searched for almost a year until they found a location in Galleria West. The space had been a fast-food outlet and build-out estimates from architects came to $100,000. Feeling that this cost was prohibitive, Joe and Hart decided to put their handyman talents to work and do the transformation themselves. They obtained free-lance labor from the Texas Employment Commission, started the work in June of 1979, and finished in late August at a direct cost of only $30,000.

The search for a manager for the Houston store ended in McAllen. There, they met Nancy Lodwig, a departmental manager for a national chain department store, who was willing to relocate to Houston. Nancy had graduated from a Midwestern university and had moved to the Valley to work with a relative in a car dealership. She then went with the department store before joining Crazy Joe's in Houston. The new manager handles the Houston operation with its ten employees with little direct supervision from the owners. The Houston operation took off with such sales success that Hart and the Bryants are looking to expand the Houston operation to at least one more outlet.

CRAZY JOE'S MARKETING

Joe Bryant had definite ideas as to how he would promote Crazy Joe's. He says that an ideal is to have a young woman come into his store with one of his ads and say, "I want to look like this girl." He caters to the 18-35 aspiring professional, who knows what she wants, but may not have the salary to afford regular price fashion merchandise.

Joe and Ellen have an excellent grasp of the type of person who shops at Crazy Joe's. The Austin store draws primarily young career women and college girls. The Houston store has the young career woman and also some convention visitor trade. As Ellen says, "Many of the shoppers are from out of town and even though they can get the same thing at home, they want something from Houston." The McAllen store is different from the Houston and Austin stores in that they have an interesting clientele mixture. They have many tourist customers who are retired and want comfortable summer-wear the year round. Another important part of their clientele is from Mexico. They have less of the young aspiring professional trade.

Joe feels that much of his customer satisfaction comes from the ability of the sales staff to relate to the customer. He seeks out for his sales staff someone who first has "clothes sense," personality, and someone who will not overwhelm but show alternatives and, overall, seek to establish a "clean, positive image." Vivacious, young, fashion-conscious, attractive, and still in high school or college were his criteria for his salespersons. Part-time sales people were often preferred over full-time.

Austin has several fashion outlet stores in competition, but Joe is not concerned, because, as he says, "we have established a good image with no junk, and these other stores can't maintain that same image."[1] He feels that their judicious choice of location has increased their edge over regular retail stores. Persons shopping in the malls will often stop in to see what they have. Seeing identical merchandise as some of the department stores had, he be-

---

[1] These included "Kinda Krazy," "Fashion Discovery," "Fashion Conspiracy," and "Rags to Riches," among others.

lieved that many customers will buy from Crazy Joe's at their lower prices.

Despite increasing competition, Joe feels that Crazy Joe's offers what the customer wants: quality at a good price. In his opinion, any future competition can only help increase the positive image which Crazy Joe's has established with its market segment.

Crazy Joe's derives most of its marketing information from observation and questioning. Joe feels that their instinctive feel for customer taste generates a lot more business than an expensive market survey. Joe invariably asks customers how they heard about the store and keeps a running tally of this information in his head.

Crazy Joe's utilizes a regular retail 50 percent margin on most merchandise. If, for some reason, he is unable to buy at off-price and has to buy at regular wholesale prices, a short 40 percent margin is used in order to keep retail prices highly competitive. When a particularly good buy is obtained, a 60 percent margin may be used. If there is no price resistance the price remains as is, and if there is resistance, mark downs will be made and the name of the merchandise will be advertised.

In promoting Crazy Joe's, several types of media are utilized. In McAllen and Austin they use mainly newspaper ads. In the past year they have started running ads in *Texas Monthly,* one of the most widely circulated and read magazines in the state. See Exhibit 1 for example of an ad.

Joe initially used a local Austin ad agency, which he dismissed because of their high costs and steadfast refusal to adapt to the image he wanted. Joe now does all of the ads himself and supervises all photo shooting sessions personally. He utilizes friends who freelance to do copy work, and he and Ellen have final approval on all ads. They feel that their return on promotional investment is very good. An art director with an Austin ad agency commented, "One thing about those people at Crazy Joe's; they aren't afraid to spend money and they get what they pay for—the quality shows."

CRAZY JOE'S FINANCES

Sales and net profits for Crazy Joe's, Inc. have risen steadily over the years. Because the expansion into Houston proved to be a judicious move, that store is operating on a margin comparable to the McAllen store. Costs in the Houston store are much higher because of the premium location, but volume is sufficient to offset any disadvantage.

Sales performance remains fairly steady during the year. There are predictable rises in the fall, in December, and in the spring. Only in the summer of 1980 had the Austin store fallen below expectation. (See Exhibit 2 for a financial statement.)

The newly established fiscal year ends on May 31, at which time a physical inventory is taken in all the stores. Each day, reports are filled out concerning the previous day's business. These are used to make journal entries and post ledger accounts. Ellen does the bookkeeping for Austin and the dis-

EXHIBIT 1

tribution company. Nancy takes care of Houston and Hart takes care of records for McAllen. Financial statements are drawn up formally at the end of the fiscal year for the corporation by Hart, now that a uniform fiscal year has been adopted.

All sales for each store are handled on a cash, check, or bank credit card basis. No credit is given to customers. "Lay-away" is used to a limited degree for those customers desiring that convenience.

Another serious problem which the stores have is shoplifting. In the past year they have installed an electronic screening device which automatically scans a special magnetic ticket attached to the clothing. This device, they estimate, has cut shoplifting 75 percent, mainly because its imposing structure at the entrance of the store scares off many potential shoplifters.

Inventory is purchased on an 8 percent, 10 day, net 30 day basis from most of its vendors. Because it has established a good credit reputation, there are no problems receiving the goods ordered on credit. The addition of the Houston store has increased buying volume substantially. The greater volume has increased its leverage in the market with the larger vendors.

FUTURE PLANS

For the near future, they would like to expand by one more unit. They were considering going into Bryan/College Station (home of Texas A&M University with 36,000 students), but they feel that they already have spread themselves out too much to run the stores in the different cities that they have now. They are also experiencing a shortage of trained persons, which is limiting their ability to look for expansion possibilities in Houston. In regard to their staffing problems, Joe and Ellen see some of their mistakes as poor hiring policies. They rarely check references, preferring to go with a person as an employee about whom they have a "good feeling."

The now-understood danger of this loose policy became quite clear to the owners when a crisis was encountered. After a brief vacation in July of 1980, Joe and Ellen made a startling discovery. While doing the daily reports, Joe noted that the sequential numbering on the cash register was off. He was alerted to a possible discrepancy when an eager young salesclerk had remarked to him how excited she was to have had a $300 cash sale to one customer the previous day just before closing. Joe noticed no such sale on the cash register tape. Upon closer investigation, he discovered that the tapes had been altered to show less than the actual daily sales. There were several other clues as to mishandled funds. After going through records and register tapes, they found that approximately $11,000 had been misappropriated.[2] To their surprise, they learned that it was a trusted store manager to whom they had recently given increased responsibilities and a substantial raise, so that

---

[2]See Exhibit 3 for report prepared by the company for authorities. The company initiated polygraph testing by a recognized authority immediately after the incident was discovered. The "trusted" manager "resigned" before the polygraph test could be given to her.

they could be free to go to Houston to plan for a new location. Joe and Ellen began to seriously rethink their ideas about expansion to new locations. They also began to think about setting up and adhering to some more established policies in regard to hiring, training, and supervising employees. Joe realized that neither he nor Ellen had taken time to check any references on the errant manager when she was hired because she seemed so ideal for the job.

The end result was a determination to slow down expansion until better control systems could be developed and implemented, and qualified managerial prospects could be recruited and trained. Joe was convinced that the polygraph was a necessity, even though he preferred not to have to use the technique to maintain cash control in his branch stores. In addition, both Joe and Ellen questioned whether they wanted to develop a more formal organization with more rigid rules and procedures, as a prerequisite to expanding their company. They had enjoyed very much what they had created in the past, and did not want to lose the good features of their business.

EXHIBIT 2   Crazy Joe's, Inc. combined income statement fiscal year 1979–80

	$Austin^2$ 12 mon.	$Houston^2$ 8 mon.	$Valley^2$ 12 mon.	*Combined
Net sales revenues	249,588	359,992	417,840	1,027,420.
Cost of goods sold				
Beg. inventory	49,582	-0-	58,790	
Purchases & freight	142,875	234,027	259,322	
Goods available	192,457	234,027	318,112	
End. inventory	55,934	66,172	74,399	
Cost of goods sold	136,523	167,855	243,713	548,091.
Gross profit	113,065	192,137	174,127	479,329.
Operating expenses				
Salaries	25,851	32,697	59,061	
Rent	6,900	20,995	7,200	
Advertising	17,857	24,960	13,040	
Amortization	3,075	8,129	4,144	
Credit card discounts	2,251	3,857	2,202	
Taxes	2,189	2,418	4,432	
Utilities	4,015	4,885	2,754	
Supplies	1,887	1,348	3,860	
Repairs	551	1,018	410	
Travel	—	129	5,260	
Insurance	1,112	783	131	
Interest	3,875	9,034	—	
Telephone	832	1,085	2,124	
Misc. services	601	309	1,499	
Uncoll. checks	667	695	—	
Security	1,937	1,938	—	
Misc. other	3,601	2,950	667	

EXHIBIT 2   (continued)

	Austin[2] 12 mon.	Houston[2] 8 mon.	Valley[2] 12 mon.	*Combined
Total oper. exp.	77,452	117,780	106,784	302,016.
Allocated dist. exp.	19,509	31,830	—	51,339.
Total expenses	96,961	149,610	106,784	353,355.
Net before taxes and other corporate expenses and income	16,104	42,527	67,343	125,974.

*Note:
[1]Fiscal year for Valley ended 12–30–79
[2]Fiscal years for A. & H. ended 5–31–80
Houston began operation 9–1–79
After 5–31–80 all locations will have same fiscal year

EXHIBIT 3

CRAZY JOE'S INC.
6019 Dillard Circle
Austin, TX 78752

PRESIDENT: H.J. Kennard   1001 Miracle Mile
McAllen, TX 78501
512-682-7804

VICE PRESIDENT: Joe Bryant   Austin   512-458-3650

RE: Cash and Merchandise Shortage
Discovered 8–1–80

STORE MANAGER:

CASH SHORTAGES:

Cash was taken by the following three methods:

1. Substitution of the cash register "Z" tapes (final daily close-out tapes that give the total sales of the day).

STANDARD PROCEDURE: Z tapes, which give sales total and zero the register, are made after the day's business either at the end of the day or the following morning. Totals from the Z tape are used to prepare the daily report and balance receipts with cash register totals.

Subject would either stay late until all other employees had left or would return after closing store. She would remove and inspect the permanent "journal tape" (which normally stays in the register until roll is full). The "journal tape" is a record of all cash register individual transactions

EXHIBIT 3   (continued)

and Z tapes. Then she would determine the amount that could be absconded by the total amount of customer checks and charge card sales versus cash sales. Then a new day's business would be rung up on the register using the same date. The "fake" new day's business transactions naturally would be less than the actual day's business. She would pocket the difference and balance the daily report with the remaining checks, VISA and American Express sales slips, and cash after taking a "Z tape" of the false transactions which she substituted for the correct tape. At this time she removed and destroyed the part of the permanent journal tape reflecting the actual daily transactions and began a new journal tape with the false transactions. Evidently, she did not realize that there were three safeguards built in the machine.

(A) Each "Z" tape is consecutively numbered. EXAMPLE: "0366Z" indicating that this is the 366th "Z" tape made. The next day's final "Z" tape would be "0367Z." (B) Like the above, there is also a customer transaction number shown at the bottom of the tape. EXAMPLE: "3592" at the end of the day's Z tape indicates that this is the number of that day's last transaction. The following day's first transaction would be "3593." (C) As in the above, the register provides for a running total on each "Z" tape of the cumulative funds received since the register was first put into operation.

EXAMPLE: 7–30–80 total was	$287,026.03
7–29–80 total was	$286,411.81
Difference is total funds received 7–30–80:	614.22

This cumulative total cannot be reset by normal operation means. Therefore, a missing Z reading tape would be readily apparent by comparing these numbers.

To determine the amount of actual daily receipts for a day where tapes were destroyed and fake daily transactions were rung up and a new "Z" tape was made, one would proceed as follows:

Cumulative Total for Preceding Day:	$275,071.38
Cumulative Total on Fake Tape:	$275,872.45
Difference Is:	801.07

This should, but does not, reflect funds received as indicated on the daily sales report and on attached Z tape which are:

	$	315.89
The Difference Is:	$	485.18

This difference represents the actual or legitimate funds received for the day. The difference between the actual day's amount and the fake day's amount is the amount stolen.

EXAMPLE:	Actual Day's Amount:	$	485.18
	Fake Day's Amount:	−$	315.89
	Amount Stolen	$	169.29

2. Illegally taking cash and enabling cash drawer to balance by use of the "return merchandise key." The use of the return merchandise key was expressly forbidden to all employees. The use of this register key provides a negative cash figure and decreases the funds received total on the

EXHIBIT 3   (continued)

register tape. Therefore it is possible to negate any sale and pocket the received funds. The use of the "return merchandise key" is indicated on the "Z" tape.

3. Taking receipts of layaway payments by recording payment on layaway garment tags and not ringing up in register. If payment was by check, she placed a check in cash drawer and extracted the amount in cash. There is a layaway key on the register which is used exclusively for ringing up layaway payments as it does not include sales tax. On days in question, payments have been recorded on layaway garment tag but no corresponding payments have been entered in the cash register as indicated on the day's "Z" tape.

Index